Operations Management

Operations Management

Martin K. Starr
Columbia University

Prentice-Hall, Inc., Englewood Cliffs, New Jersey   07632

Library of Congress Cataloging in Publication Data

STARR, MARTIN KENNETH, (DATE)
  Operations management.

    Bibliography: p.
    Includes index.
    1. Production management. I. Title.
TS155.S75873   658.5   77-22692
ISBN   0-13-637603-7

Printed in the United States of America

10 9 8 7 6 5 4 3 2 1

PRENTICE-HALL INTERNATIONAL, INC., *London*
PRENTICE-HALL OF AUSTRALIA PTY. LIMITED, *Sydney*
PRENTICE-HALL OF CANADA, LTD., *Toronto*
PRENTICE-HALL OF INDIA PRIVATE LIMITED, *New Delhi*
PRENTICE-HALL OF JAPAN, INC., *Tokyo*
PRENTICE-HALL OF SOUTHEAST ASIA PTE. LTD., *Singapore*
WHITEHALL BOOKS LIMITED, *Wellington, New Zealand*

To My Mother
Melanie Starr

This book is organized to reveal
in an operational way
the sequence of reasoning that is needed
to produce and run high-productivity systems.

contents

preface

The intention of this book is to make the benefits of production and operations management (P/OM) knowledge available to students at the beginning of their academic training in business rather than later on. To accomplish this goal, it was essential that the book:

1. Require no complex math or statistics.
2. Be readable so that students can really learn from it—if they want to.
3. Motivate students to want to read it.

Let us consider motivation first. Students will be motivated to study if it is clear to them that there will be opportunity to use what they are reading. So many textbooks turn students off because they cannot figure out how to apply the materials they are learning—to improve a real situation. The improvement must have value. In this text, we repeatedly demonstrate that such opportunity exists.

Question: What important opportunity exists? *Answer:* There is a productivity crisis in the world. It is worse for public systems than private ones;

worse for developing countries than for developed ones; worse for some industries than for others; far from getting better, it is getting worse. Anyone who can improve productivity in a substantial way will gain personally in monetary ways as well as social and organizational status.

Question: How can students be taught to apply the materials they are learning? *Answer:* This book uses focused applications for explanations of techniques. Focusing cuts out nonessentials and, by using applications, addresses without gaps in reasoning all of the steps that one must understand in order to go from problem to solution. The natural bent of an author is to surround a problem with discussion that appears to be relevant for a good grasp of the subject. In the process, the students learn, for example, why a radio works, but not how to build or repair one. Often, the wrong problem is surrounded, epitomized by the details of how to bail the boat rather than plug the hole.

Application writing calls forth a different sequence of reasoning: a stepwise logic that is organized, simple, and gap-free. Further, this book uses designed redundancy to reinforce the essential concepts.

To summarize, students are motivated to read the book because they can apply what they read to improve the productivity of systems of which they are a part.

To the extent of the author's ability, using what is known about learning through reading, this book has been made attractive and well-organized; it has been designed to be readable.

It is an introductory book divided into 24 chapters. These chapters are equivalent to teaching units. Some move faster than others (such as introductory materials) and can be combined with appendixed technical sections. Chapter 24 can be used either as an introduction or conclusion, depending on personal preference (my preference is apparent). Using the optional materials of 23 appendixes, one can obtain the necessary number of modules for various course lengths and different course levels.

Some teachers like to concentrate on a broad spectrum of the fundamentals, whereas others prefer to advance certain topics in depth. The appendixes allow a great deal of choice for those instructors who wish to concentrate on specific topics. Problems are given at the end of each chapter. In all, there are 249 problems, and 20 percent of these problems have their answers furnished. This is meant to provide positive reinforcement of certain ideas and to allow the student practice at applying what has been learned.

The theme of the book is how to choose and use the best possible production configuration, i.e., the flow shop, or the job shop, or the project, or combinations. This covers just about every conceivable way that work can get done. The book emphasizes that most of the time there are options as to how to do something, but it is necessary to recognize the options in order to choose the best one. Choosing what is best can make a big difference.

I want to thank Professor David G. Dannenbring of the University of North Carolina for his thoughtful discussions with me (before I undertook to write this text) concerning the kind of book that would be most useful at the introductory course level of production and operations management. Also, the reviewers of this manuscript worked diligently and influenced my revisions of the manuscript in many ways. I am grateful to them and wish to acknowledge them by name: Professors Douglas A. Elvers, University of North Carolina; Michael P. Hottenstein, Pennsylvania State University; William N. Ledbetter, Auburn University; Will Rayms, University of Wisconsin—Milwaukee; Matthew F. Tuite, Northwestern University; and Robert R. Westerman, California State University—Sacramento.

Martin K. Starr

Operations Management

foundation concepts of production systems

Part 1 is comprised of Chapters 1, 2, and 3, which present the most basic models of production systems. These are the input/output model and the break-even model. The latter relates the costs of inputs and the costs of the process to the revenues derived from the outputs of goods or services.

To understand what is known about production systems and operations management, a number of special words are required. Many of these terms are introduced in Part 1. To do justice to our subject, it is essential to recognize that production and operations management is as broadly applicable to public systems as it is to private industries, manufacturing being but one type of production process.

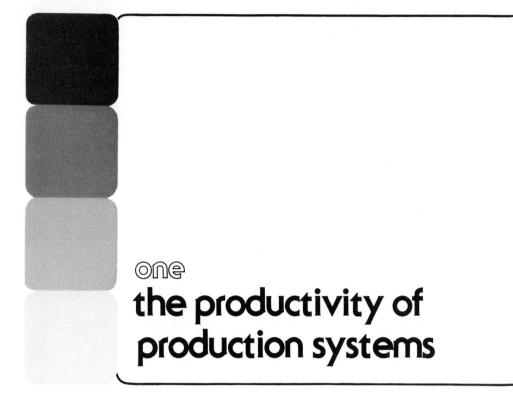

one
the productivity of production systems

To begin with, we must understand what elements make up production systems (see the three questions below). In this chapter, we shall explore a little of the history of production systems to better recognize why productivity is an issue crucial to our studies. The important economic concept of price elasticity relates to productivity, and it is necessary that we comprehend that relationship. When we understand this highly interrelated system of costs and prices, the time will have come to explain how different types of production systems have different productivities and different cost structures. With this chain of reasoning, we introduce Chapter 1.

Question: What are production systems?

Answer: They are working arrangements of people, materials, energy, and machines, whereby agreed upon forms of work are accomplished.

When *materials are transformed* (such as wood being cut, metal being worked, or liquid being mixed), work is accomplished.

When *information is processed* (such as letters being typed or filed and calculators being used to obtain sums), work is accomplished.

When *people are treated* (such as being served food, being X-rayed, having

3

teeth filled, being moved by elevator, or being transported by bus), work is accomplished. Production systems include transportation, distribution, communication, manufacture, assembly, packaging, mining, caring for the sick, and running libraries and schools. The key to understanding specific production systems is the determination of what work must be done and how best to do it.

Question: What are the foundation concepts of production systems?

Answer: First, there is the input-output system, which consists of three factors:

1. What is to be worked on (called *inputs*).
2. How work is accomplished (called the *production process*).
3. What is produced (called *outputs*).

Second, there are the interrelationships between the costs of inputs and process and the revenues obtained from outputs.

There are many forms of inputs and as many kinds of outputs, but there are only *three* basically different ways to get work done, that is, three fundamentally different arrangements of the production process.

These are the project, the flow shop, and the job shop. We shall spend much time in explaining each of these arrangements and examining their special characteristics. But it is essential that we have some idea, to begin with, of the way in which they differ.

A project is done once, like writing a book.

The flow shop has highly repetitive operations. A commonly used term for a flow shop process is mass production.

The job shop produces a variety of outputs in small batches.

Question: What criteria are used for evaluating the production process?

Answer: The efficiency (or productivity) of the production process is measured in terms of the investment in the process, the costs of the inputs, and the value of the outputs. Another criterion is the extent of human satisfaction with the work system and its outputs.

Industrial Systems

The twentieth century is outstanding among all centuries for the massive and pervasive changes in the way of life of a rapidly expanding population. The basis for production of food and clothing and shelter, of sports equipment and entertainment devices, of home furnishings and kitchen equipment, etc., moved from craftsmen to mechanized industrial systems.

There are still parts of the world where the production process remains in the hands of artisans, but that too is rapidly disappearing. At the same time, technology continues to develop in the industrialized portions of the world and is spreading from *goods* to *services*. Transport and communication serve as excellent examples of highly technologized service functions; among the most recent to join this list is the fast foods service industry. Hospital activities, library functions, and even the dissemination of education are undergoing related changes. Consequently, it behooves us to know how to manage production systems of many kinds and to understand that they are all changing, both in the developed and developing countries. To properly manage such important dynamic systems poses a real challenge. Yet much is known about production systems in general and how to manage them.

Productivity

With the knowledge that exists about production systems and operations management (P/OM) it is hard to comprehend why there is a productivity problem in the world—yet there is one. Productivity is a measure of production efficiency.

Productivity refers to a comparison between the quantity of goods or services produced and the quantity of resources employed in turning out these goods or services.[1]

Thus, productivity is a ratio of output to input.

There are different kinds of productivity measures. Output can be compared in ratio to the man-hour inputs required to achieve that level of output. This is called *labor productivity*. Alternatively, output can be compared to the combination of man- and machine-hours required to achieve that level of output. This is called *total productivity*. The latter measure of output per unit of labor *and* capital reflects the overall efficiency of the production system.[2] It is important to know that the type of production system used will affect the amount of output obtained per unit of labor and capital.

Further, it has been widely observed that when productivity increases, the per unit costs of production output go down. When productivity falls, if the payroll stays the same, there is less output to sell or fewer services to distribute, and the cost of each unit of output has increased. Declining productivity can play a major role in creating inflationary pressures. The producer raises prices to cover increased costs. The same goods and services cost more than they did before; demand falls off as prices mount, which further increases costs (see Fig. 1-2). The process can prove relentless, and the seeds of recession are planted. The conditions for high productivity can be known and understood by any student of production and operations management.

---

[1]Soloman Fabricant, *A Primer on Productivity* (New York: Random House, 1969), p. 3.

[2]Total productivity is computed by using a sum of weighted man-hours and weighted machine-hours, where larger weights reflect higher salaries and more expensive equipment. Output is generally measured in terms of its value (corrected for inflation).

Poor productivity cannot be accepted. It is unnecessary. High productivity is available for those who will read and heed what is written on the many pages of this text. This book is organized to reveal in an entirely operational way the sequence of reasoning that is needed to produce and run high-productivity systems.

The economic production of goods and services is always based on the belief that demand exists for the output of the production system. Therefore, it is worth studying the alternative designs of how the job might be done in order to choose the best one. Production is the transformation of a set of inputs that are available (at a cost) to a set of outputs that are wanted (at a price), as shown in Fig. 1-1. The inputs typically consist of some combination of labor and capital as well as expenditures for materials and energy.

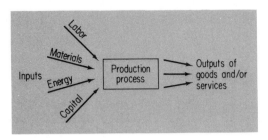

FIGURE 1-1. The production system

The production system requires a process for converting an appropriate set of inputs into the desired set of outputs. Here there is opportunity for creative ideas to prevail. *Good systems reasoning* tells us that the process and its goods and/or service outputs should be *designed together* to produce the best possible production system. "Best possible" means that demand is fully satisfied, output quality is highest, competitive position (if that applies) is advantaged—e.g., market share is maximum—cost of output is lowest, and thus profits or benefits are maximum. Realistically, "best possible" is some combination of these good effects, because seldom can they all be obtained together.

As previously stated, the process is not limited to manufacturing; it can be a data processing system or an airline or a mining process. Further, the goods or services do not have to be sold for profit. They can be production outputs of a public sector. That is why we speak above about maximum benefits.

Price Elasticities

Whether in the public or private sector, production costs money. It is always desirable that the production system be able to produce as inexpensively as possible, given the specifications of required quality and the output volume to be sustained. There are important relations between prices, costs, output volumes, quality levels, and shares of market. The share of market is an indicator of competition that can be affected by various factors, but price is one of the most important of these. In general, we know that as price increases, demand decreases. Figure 1-2 illustrates a situation where demand

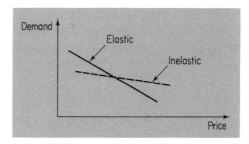

FIGURE 1-2. Demand elasticity with
changes in price

elasticity to a change in price is great (solid line) and another situation where demand is relatively inelastic to price changes (dashed line).[3] The more elastic demand is to price changes, the more critical it is that production costs be kept low so that a low price can be charged. This is especially true when there is a great deal of competition, since share of market decreases much as demand does when the price we charge is higher than that of our competitors. Figure 1-3 shows what such a curve might look like.

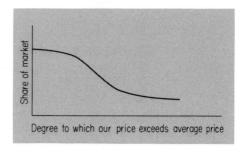

FIGURE 1-3. Share of market elasticity with changes in price

These notions that we have been discussing apply to public as well as private systems. For example, when the cost of public transportation rises, the number of users decreases. Thus, if bus fares go up, the share of market held by buses decreases as compared to all other means of transportation. Public systems often compete with each other as well as with private systems for time, expendable income, etc.

Planning with Price Elasticities

When demand is price elastic, a low price is required to generate enough demand to consume all production output. Figure 1-4 shows why a high

---

[3]Elasticity measures, in this case, the degree to which demand increases or decreases in response to a change in price.

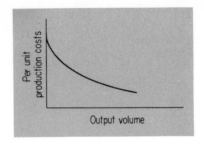

FIGURE 1-4. Per unit production costs decrease
with increasing output volume

volume of output is needed to keep production costs low and productivity high. It is critical to plan output volume and price with these concepts in mind. Consider the sequence:

1. Select output volume.
2. Determine per unit production costs.
3. From production costs determine satisfactory selling price (include estimates of marketing and administrative costs plus required profit).
4. Determine the demand that will be generated by the selling price.
5. If demand is too low to consume production output, determine at what price it would be sufficient.

   If demand is greater than production output, selling price can be raised. Demand would decrease, as would share, but profits would increase.

   Other alternatives exist as well. For example, we could increase production output to match demand. This should also result in higher profits if per unit production costs decrease sufficiently to offset added investments in the production facilities.
6. Going back and forth between output volume, per unit production costs, selling price, and demand, can a satisfactory match be found?

Planning in this fashion is central to the systems approach to operations management. Operations management helps us to get the lowest per unit production costs possible for a given volume of output (see the next section on cost leverage).

Cost Leverage

The price that can be charged for goods or services must equal or exceed the costs of producing the goods or providing the services. Therefore, costs form a base upon which all price structures are built. The design of the total production system has many facets which, if recognized, can be used to maintain minimum costs. By missing a few such opportunities, the organization provides cost leverage to its competitors. In turn, if some competitors have overlooked specific opportunities to design minimum cost systems, then the advantages of cost leverage accrue to those organizations that did not miss these specific items.

The kinds of opportunities that we are discussing include inventory policies, scheduling work, plant layout, purchase quantities, etc., and, in general, all of the production operations that are required to produce the goods and/or services that are in demand. *Operations management* is the term we use to describe our knowledge of how to deal with specific production operations in the best possible way so as to maximize the cost leverage of the organization.

Before we study the different kinds of operations that one encounters in the production of goods and services, we should note that *efficient* operations are a goal to be achieved *after* it is entirely clear that the operations being used are the correct ones. Consequently, it is essential to design an *effective* system of operations that can be made as efficient as possible. The *systems view* of the production process is required to shed light on what constitutes the effective interrelations of operations. We call this combination of considerations to achieve effectiveness and assure efficiency *production and operations management* (P/OM).

The question to be asked is, for a chosen output volume, what kind of production system is to be used? This is a systems question about the configuration of the production facility. The answer regarding the type of production system is not arbitrary; it is based on the character of the output technology and the existing facilities of competitors. The type of system to be used for a given output volume will greatly influence costs (which in turn affect price). But if large, efficient competitive facilities exist, it *may not be possible* to attain a sufficient share of market and thereby sufficient volume to allow any form of low-cost configuration to be used. What if the large competitors were not so efficient? Could we use cost leverage to gain a price advantage and thereby a large enough share of the market to support a high volume? Or might we produce a product of superior quality at a high price? Does new technology exist, allowing us to lower costs by a large enough increment to warrant changing the type of production system? To pose such critical questions, we must understand the three basic types of production systems.

Types of Production Systems

As previously mentioned (see p. 4), the most important distinction that can be drawn between different kinds of production systems is whether they are (a) projects, (b) flow shops, or (c) job shops. However, to understand these production systems, it is desirable to have some knowledge of the marketplace for goods and services. Part 2 is devoted to the interaction between production and marketing forces.

Part 2   Life Cycle Management (new product introduction, established franchise, declining share of market)

Then, we shall examine the special production planning characteristics of these work process configurations in Parts 3, 4, and 5.

Part 3   Project Management
Part 4   Flow Shop Management
Part 5   Job Shop Management

With a clear understanding of how each type of production system functions we shall go on to treat the major management control elements of the operations management field. Thus:

Part 6   Materials Management (purchasing, inventory, etc.)
Part 7   Facilities Management (location, layout, etc.)
Part 8   Human Resource Management (time studies, wage rates, etc.)
Part 9   Quality Management (acceptance sampling, statistical quality control, etc.)

Models of Production Systems

The above brief description presents the structure of this book. Throughout, we shall describe the different kinds of problems that each type of production system encounters and the methods that are useful to resolve them. To do this effectively we shall talk about a variety of *models* of production systems. By models we mean that important elements of a particular kind of situation or problem have been identified and named. Often, the relationships of these problem elements to each other and to the managers' goals and objectives are also identified and are clearly stated in specific terms. Each model is comprised of elements and relationships that have been fully articulated. Let us further develop this concept of models in general and then relate it to one of the fundamental models of production systems, namely, the cost structure of input-output systems.

Flow Shops, Job Shops, and Project Management

The character of production models will differ markedly for the three different kinds of production systems: namely, the flow shop, the job shop, and the project shop. Later, we shall discuss, in detail, the special structure of each type of shop. For the moment, let us go a little further in explaining them. The flow shop exists when the same set of operations is performed in sequence repetitively; the job shop exists where the facilities are capable of producing many different jobs in small batches; the project is a major undertaking that is usually done only once. It consists of many steps that must be sequenced and coordinated.

The flow shop employs special-purpose equipment (*designed* specifically to mass produce a particular item or provide a special service). The job shop contains general-purpose equipment (each unit is capable of doing a variety of jobs). The project shop, like the flow shop, requires a sequence of operations, except that the sequence lacks repetition. Each project operation is unique and seldom repeated. To exemplify: the production line for automobiles is a flow shop; the machine shop that makes hundreds of different gears in batches of 50 at a time is a job shop; building a bridge or sending astronauts to the moon is a project. Many other examples of each kind of production system will be given throughout the text.

Some Background on Models

A model is a representation of reality. It is constructed in such a way as to explain the behavior of some but not all aspects of that reality. The reason that a model is employed is that it is always *less complex* than the actual situation. It is a convenient way of studying the interacting complexities of the real world. That is why planes are flown in wind tunnels or small ships towed through tanks filled with mercury (which fairly well simulates how water would act with the big ship). Flight simulators allow pilots to be trained to handle dangerous situations that in reality could be deadly. In all cases, the model must be a good representation of those dimensions that are related to the systems objectives; otherwise, it will not be useful and, therefore, will not be used.

Without question, the recognition that we can employ models has increased their use and the use of models has completely altered the nature of operations management. Many successful models have been developed in the production management field. Undoubtedly, the production function is represented by the most complete set of problem-solving and decision-making models that exist in any organizational division of industry.

Models can be concrete (such as architectural models of buildings, designer's prototypes of autos, maps, charts, and blueprints) or abstract (such as organization charts and systems of mathematical equations). The total unification of the production management field would be achieved if we could write out the entire system of equations to describe the effect of all relevant factors on the systems objectives. (These equations would certainly have to contain probability or risk statements.) All the relevant variables would interact with each other much as they would in the real world. Given such equations, it would be theoretically possible to solve them and, thereby, to determine the optimal course of action for the organization.

At this time it is impossible to write, let alone solve, such a total system of equations. But, at least in theory, a production department equation, a total enterprise equation, a national equation, or a world equation might be written. The theoretical possibilities are not challenged or altered by the scope of the undertaking, even though the practical limitations become formidable at a level far below that of the production department's system. Because we are unable to produce or solve such equations, it is essential that we structure our thinking to parallel the underlying meaning that is implicit in the total system. Fortunately, we are able to do this to some extent.

PROBLEMS

1. Total productivity between 1889 and 1970 increased in the U.S.A. at an average annual rate of 1.7 percent. During the same period, labor productivity grew at an average annual rate of 2.4 percent. How can this be explained?

   Answer: Capital investment per man-hour worked went up. The increased capital investment includes both tangible capital in the form of machines and the less tangible capital investments in education and general improvement of the work force.

2. What two production principles account for the high level of productivity obtained in the U.S.A. before 1950? What third principle has only recently begun to take effect?

   Answer: See pp. 181–89 and p. 593.

3. Company A, which has priced its service at the competitive average, is about to make a small increase in price. Company B has traditionally considered itself to offer a premium service and accordingly has charged premium prices. Company B now intends to make a large increase in its price. Which statement below generally is correct?

   a. Company A will lose little share of market, while Company B will experience a sharp drop in market share.

   b. Company B will lose little share of market, while Company A will experience a sharp drop in market share.

   c. Neither Company A nor Company B will lose more than a little share of market.

   d. Both Company A and Company B will experience a sharp drop in their respective market shares.

4. There is a sequence of relationships between production volume, costs, prices, demand, etc. Explain this sequence and draw a figure to illustrate the fact that each factor affects every other one.

5. Define operations management. How does operations management relate to the systems view of the production process?

6. Explain what a model is and why it is used in P/OM.

7. It has been stated that P/OM models apply to both goods and services. What differences exist between goods and services? Explain the possible significance of such differences to the operations manager.

8. From Fig. 1-5, curve A, what happens to demand for Product A when price goes from 50¢ to 60¢?

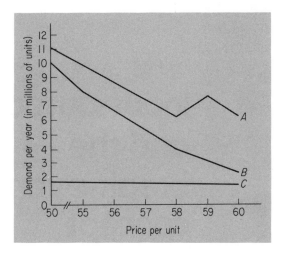

FIGURE 1-5.

Answer: At first demand is highly elastic, decreasing until the price of 58¢ is reached. Then a kink occurs in the demand curve. Between 58¢ and 59¢ demand rises, but begins to fall again above 59¢.

9. Production management is said to be cost conscious. In what way can this attitude lead to poor decisions?

10. Name several input-output systems. Discuss their components and describe the process used to transform inputs.

11. In psychology, stimulus-response experiments are frequently utilized. What kind of a system is this? Why is it used? Does it have any implications with respect to the utilization of men and machines in a production system?

Answer: A stimulus-response system is another commonly encountered form of an input-output system. It is used by physiologists and psychologists to provide an effective model for studying human behavior patterns. In production we encounter it as a basis for the design of systems where men and machines must work together. The literature on human factors will provide many examples of the way in which this approach is utilized.

two
input-output models and the break-even concept

Input-output Models

Production is *any* process or procedure designed to *transform* a set of *input* elements into a specified set of *output* elements. The *system* is the set of all such interconnected input-output elements.

A production system can be broken down into the three component parts of inputs, outputs, and process. The diagram shown in Fig. 1-1 illustrates the way in which various ingredients are brought together and transformed to accomplish the *objectives* for which the system was designed.

The process can be complicated; many kinds of inputs can be required; a variety of outputs can emerge. But the idea of *transforming* a set of inputs so that they yield a set of outputs is not complex.

The design of an actual input-output process for manufacturing, computer processing, transportation, etc., is another matter. It can be expensive and difficult.

Outputs and Revenue

Specification of the desired output or outputs is usually the starting point for production management systems planning. Outputs are moved to the marketplace where they generate revenue. Financial considerations may dictate that a search be made for some activity that will produce a satisfactory return on the invested capital.[1] The possession of extra capital is frequently the prime motivation for a search to discover desirable outputs.

Juxtaposed to this is the case where a potentially valuable output is known but sufficient capital is not at hand and must be raised by the financial officers of the company. The qualifications that earn the title of "valuable output" are that some group of individual consumers, companies, or institutions would be interested in acquiring one or more units of this output under conditions that can be profitable (or somehow beneficial) for the producer.

For example, the sales manager learns that a competitor has introduced a new product or service that is receiving strong consumer acceptance. He then suggests that his own management consider this new product or service possibility. New ideas can also come to the sales manager from sources operating in the marketing field and from users. Frequently a market survey will uncover a consumer need that is not being satisfied. A creative employee in the organization may just "dream up" an output that will achieve an economically satisfying level of demand.

The starting point can also be traced to input factors and to process factors. If a new material or a new energy source is developed, the discovery may suggest an output that was either overlooked or one that was previously technologically or economically unfeasible. Similarly, a technological discovery can lead to the design of a new process that is capable of producing an entirely new output that could satisfy a public need or an unquenched consumer demand. Numerous cases are on record of a byproduct of a process suddenly being recognized as having marketable characteristics. Here, the existence of one output creates the possibility for another. Because of the dynamic character of the marketplace, new public and private output opportunities are continually developing. A previously unwanted product or service can unexpectedly shift into a situation where it is under substantial demand. Of course, the converse is also true. An accepted product or service can begin to lose popularity. This can be traced, sometimes, to the activities of a competitor, but it can also be explained as a shift in consumer wants. Part 2, Life Cycle Management, explores the different phases in the life of a product or service.

The Process and Fixed Costs

The output is expected to have *greater value* than the combined values of the inputs and the investment in the process, when the latter is properly

---

[1]ROI = return on investment; a common abbreviation.

depreciated. This is different from the engineering expectations for physical systems where, at a theoretical best, the output can equal the input. Because of friction and heat losses the usable output in the physical world is less than the sum of the input energies. Thus, the efficiency of a process η in engineering terms is

$$\eta = \frac{\text{useful output}}{\text{input}} \leq 1$$

Such efficiency would produce bankruptcy in the economic world. The efficiency of a production process, from the viewpoint of the physical system, is measurable in the above terms, but operations management is beholden to economic criteria. In economic systems, the efficiency η must be greater than one, indicating that a benefit can be had or a profit can be made. Furthermore, it is only partly true that as the engineering efficiency increases so does economic efficiency. Production and operations managers understand and integrate both the engineering and the economic points of view, in their daily activities.

A process consists of production elements that represent primarily *fixed costs*. These are costs that do not vary as a function of the output rates. What kind of costs are invariant to the operating level of the company? Although there is a convention that applies here, nevertheless, a good deal of interpretation is possible in the assignment of costs to this fixed-charge category. For example, depreciation allowances that result from the aging of machines are invariant to the amount of use that the equipment receives. Consequently, it is appropriate to include such expenses as part of the fixed-cost category. (On the other hand, depreciation that results from use of the machine violates this concept.) Another fixed cost might be municipal taxes that are independent of the company's revenue. Fixed power and light charges and basic insurance charges also belong in this fixed cost category. For the most part, fixed costs arising as a result of investments in plant and facilities are depreciated as a function of time and not as a function of production volume.

Inputs and Variable Costs

Inputs are *variable* cost production elements. Such costs are paid out on a per-unit (of volume) basis. Direct labor and direct material costs are typical. They can be charged directly to each unit of production. Variable costs also create certain anomalies of classification. There are, for example, indirect labor charges that are associated with office work. Such costs are difficult to attribute to a particular unit of output or on a cost-per-piece basis. Therefore, normally they are assigned to the accounting category of (fixed) overhead costs. Similarly, salaries paid to supervisory personnel fall outside the definition of variable costs. In fact, irregularities are generally treated as fixed costs.

Basically, materials, labor, and energy constitute the input. Plant and facilities make up the process. By means of scheduling inputs to the production process, management exercises most of its *day-to-day* control over the outputs.

Fixed- and Variable-Cost Systems

Management exercises *operating control* over the production system in two different ways.

1. By controlling the inputs with respect to input rates, cost, quality, and so on, it controls the *variable costs*.
2. By altering the process (or procedure), that is, by rearranging the process elements, it controls the *fixed systemic costs*.

Managers have found it convenient to model the production system in terms of three parts.

1. Variable-cost systems—considered to be the major P/OM responsibility.
2. Fixed-cost systems—considered to be partly a P/OM responsibility but fundamentally a major responsibility of financial management.
3. Revenue—considered to be a major marketing responsibility, falling outside the production and operations management domain.

Variable-cost systems have generally been touted as being the major concern of production operations managers. Over the years, it has become increasingly apparent that fixed-cost systems are also fundamental to P/OM, requiring real cooperation between the financial managers and the production managers.

Revenue considerations have not been as well integrated. It is no revelation that quality, cost and therefore price, product availability, and variety are completely related to demand. In turn, demand affects production volumes and, thereby, output cost per unit. In spite of these obvious interdependencies, marketing and production divisions seldom achieve the level of cooperation that is necessary for coordinated decision making.

The Break-even Chart[2]

The break-even model is an extension of the fundamental input/output model. It associates costs and revenues with the input/output factors. As

---

[2]An important achievement of the 1930s was the invention by Walter Rautenstrauch, an industrial engineer and professor at Columbia University, of the planning model known as a break-even chart. See W. Rautenstrauch and R. Villers, *The Economics of Industrial Management* (New York: Funk & Wagnalls Co., 1949).

such, it is also a fundamental model of P/OM, providing important insights about production systems.

While it can be expressed in several ways, the break-even concept is easily presented by means of the break-even chart. (Appendix 2-I at the conclusion of this chapter offers optional material describing the mathematical formulation of the break-even model.) The rapid acceptance and application of the break-even chart by the production field illustrates the concern of production and operations management with these three factors. This schematic device is illustrated in Fig. 2-1.

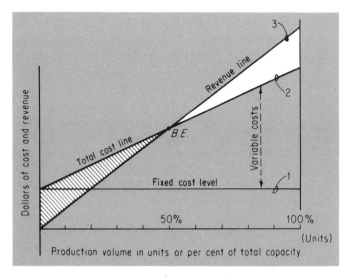

FIGURE 2-1. The break-even chart (*B.E.* is the break-even point.)

The chart consists of an *ordinate* (*y* axis) and an *abscissa* (*x* axis), so it can be represented by conventional Cartesian coordinates. The *ordinate* presents a scale of dollars against which fixed costs, variable costs, and dollars of revenue can be measured.

The *abscissa* can be dimensioned in terms of the production volume, that is the number of units that are made by the company *in a given period of time*. Alternatively, the abscissa can be dimensioned as a percentage of the total production capacity that the company has available. All the aforementioned dimensions will be found in Fig. 2-1.

We observe that three lines have been marked on the chart. Let us consider each of these in turn. Line number 1 is a fixed-cost function. Since the break-even chart applies to a specified period of time, we note that the fixed charges behave in the expected manner; that is, they do not change as a function of increased volume or increased utilization of capacity. We previously defined fixed costs by this particular characteristic.

Line number 2 in Fig. 2-1 is an increasing linear, monotonic function that increases with increasing production volume.[3] In the real world such linearity is neither expected nor obtained. Nevertheless, for our first examination of the break-even chart the assumption of linearity is not a major concession, because linear relationships do adequately describe many situations. In any event, the production field has, in the past, accepted this assumption for a great number of cases. Line 2 reflects the sum of the fixed- plus variable-cost components. The latter by definition increase with additional volume. On our chart, variable costs do not begin at the zero level. They are instead added to the fixed costs, which exist in all cases, even at a zero production level. Consequently, this second line is the total cost line, which results from the summation of fixed and variable costs. Vertical distances measured across the triangular area lying between fixed costs and total costs represent the variable costs that are assigned to specific production volumes.

For example, each unit of a particular item that we make requires a certain given amount of labor, and the necessary materials that must be assembled and utilized to produce that unit are also given. If materials that are used for one unit cost $0.10, then the total material charges for one hundred units would be $10.00, and the total material charges for one thousand units would be $100.00. That is why this variable-cost function increases as we move to greater utilization of capacity. Harking back to our original fixed-cost elements, we now observe why only depreciation that is applicable to machine utilization would be included in the variable-cost section. Taxes that are levied on the basis of units produced or revenue obtained would also be appropriately included in the variable-cost class. Some power and light charges, heating charges, storage charges, and insurance charges are characterized by the definition of variable costs.

We have now defined the total costs that are applicable to a company's operations. The categorization of fixed- and variable-cost charges is completely relevant to the analysis of the production function. It fits conveniently the basic assumptions of an input-output system. The schematic model that we are explaining can be translated into mathematical terms. But for purposes of communication with production people the break-even chart in its graphical form is an extremely useful device. It is accepted and understood by practicing production and operations managers. As such, it constitutes an important bridge between modern production practice and older approaches.

Line 3 shown in Fig. 2-1 is our revenue line. It is also a monotonic function that increases with greater production volume. Here, too, we have a situation in which we are utilizing the assumption of linearity. But at what volume does linearity no longer apply? At some point we know that total revenue will not increase at the same rate, as the company manufactures greater and greater quantities of an item. Its production costs per unit decrease while its marketing unit costs increase because the market for the

---

[3]Either increasing or constant, never decreasing. For this example, the increase is at a constant rate because of the assumption of linearity. Decreasing monotonic functions can be explained in the same way, but in the reverse direction. In Appendix 2-II, the nonlinear break-even chart is introduced and examined, as optional material.

item becomes saturated. It may be necessary for the company to lower its price in order to obtain a greater share of the total market that is available.[4] Traditionally, a linear relationship is utilized to describe revenue. This implies that our company is operating at a low enough share of the total market that free competition can adequately describe its situation. Often that assumption is satisfactory. (For when it is not, see the optional material in Appendix 2-II, pp. 27–32.)

In Fig. 2-1, the cross-hatched area between the total cost line and the revenue line represents loss to the company, that is, the area to the left of the break-even point. The white area between these same lines represents profit to the company and lies to the right of this point. Therein lies the definition of the break-even point—*no profit, no loss:* profit to the right of it, loss to the left of it. The break-even point (B.E.) occurs for a given volume of production or a given utilization of plant capacity. Figure 2-2 shows the relationship of profit and loss to production volume. The y axis measures amount

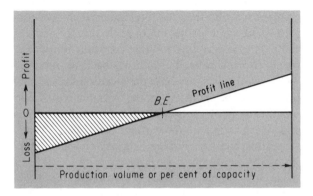

FIGURE 2-2. Profit vs. production volume (*B.E.* is the break-even point.)

of profit or loss. Here we observe the character of the linear system. Profit begins as negative profit (or loss), which decreases until it reaches the break-even point, and then it increases linearly throughout the range of values of positive profits. It is a good enough approximation, in many cases.

Analysis of the Break-even Model

Two factors must be considered in reaching conclusions about any specific break-even situation. The first is the production volume position of the break-even point. The second is the amount of profit on a marginal basis that can be obtained for each additional unit of capacity that can be utilized. This

[4]The elasticity of demand with respect to price can be a mysterious and ill-defined area. Although we have generalized the effect of saturation as being correlated with price, this is not always the case. There are well-known instances where a company achieves a major market or at least increased demand as a result of raising price. Here we are dealing with the psychology of the consumer and the fact that a market may not exist for a low-priced product because it does not carry sufficient prestige value to the consumer.

second point is represented by the slope of the line in Fig. 2-2. If the profit line shown in Fig. 2-2 were rotated clockwise so that it fell almost on top of the x axis, then very little profit would be obtained as a result of increased utilization of plant capacity. If the slope of this line were increased (in terms of the figure this means mechanically rotating it counterclockwise about the break-even point), then greater returns could be obtained *once* demand exceeded the break-even point. At the same time it should be noted that, because of the assumption of linearity, the losses or penalties for operating under the break-even point also become proportionately greater as we move farther away from the break-even point. This is more or less true in most practical situations.

Our first concern mentioned above has to do with the position of the break-even point itself. If it is moved to the right, then the organization must operate at a higher level of capacity before it is worthwhile for it to engage in business. Conversely, by reducing the break-even point volume (moving it to the left) the pressure to secure a larger demand volume is decreased.

Decisions can be complex with respect to these two criteria. Notice that in Fig. 2-3 we have drawn 2 profit lines. Each is meant to be descriptive of a

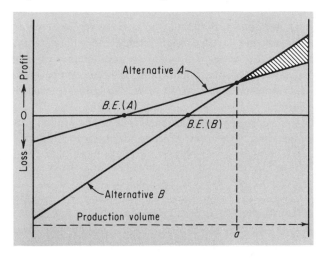

FIGURE 2-3. Profit vs production volume for alternative production configurations A and B. B.E. (A) is the break-even point for A. B.E. (B) is the break-even point for B.

result obtained from different production configurations. Alternative A has a lower break-even point than alternative B. This makes A more desirable than B with respect to this single criterion. But the profit function B has greater marginal returns once the break-even point has been reached. Alternative B is preferred, therefore, with respect to this other criterion. If the organization is able to generate sufficient demand so that it can operate at point a, then both alternatives yield equal profit. If we can operate at a volume in excess of point a, then alternative B is preferred. If we cannot, then our choice would be for alternative A.

The interrelationships of fixed and variable costs, sales volumes, revenues, and profits give rise to situations similar to the one depicted in Fig. 2-3. Thus, one plan may require a smaller investment than another but produce a product or service of poorer quality, resulting in lower sales volume and increased variable costs of production. Of course, we could decrease the selling price to achieve increased sales volume, but this might not compensate as far as revenue is concerned. Often, the lower investment process must operate with higher variable costs. Specifically, we invest in facility improvement to achieve lower variable costs, improve quality, and derive the associated market benefits. Each alternative has its own patterns of interconnected expenditures, costs, and benefits. The whole system is integrated. (For mathematical analysis of the break-even model, see the optional material in Appendix 2-I.)

An Example: Break-even Analysis
for a Small Computer Service Center

This example is given to illustrate how the break-even computations are made.

Going into business entails risks. However, two young computer programmers, having saved enough money, are willing to invest it in a small computer service center *if* they have a good chance of making a profit. The planned capacity of an efficient center is 400 units processed per week. However, it is expected that demand often will fall as low as 250. Other relevant data follow.

The fixed cost per week for rental of a minicomputer is $200. Space rental is $100 per week. The variable processing costs include:

cards and magnetic tape   15 cents per unit of work
labor   35 cents per unit of work

The standard charge (or price) per unit of work is $2.

Question: At what percentage of capacity is the break-even point achieved? We construct the break-even chart (see Fig. 2-4).

Answer: Break-even occurs at 50 percent of capacity, or 200 units. Thus, as far as this kind of analysis goes, the service center should be profitable almost every week.

Break-even Related to Production Configuration

Much necessary perspective about production and operations management (but not all) is available through diligent study of the break-even chart. Additional factors will appear when we consider the production planning potentials of the flow shop, the job shop, and the project.

At the outset, we know that the fixed costs associated with designing and setting up a flow shop are much higher than the fixed costs of a job shop (where general-purpose rather than special-purpose equipment prevails).

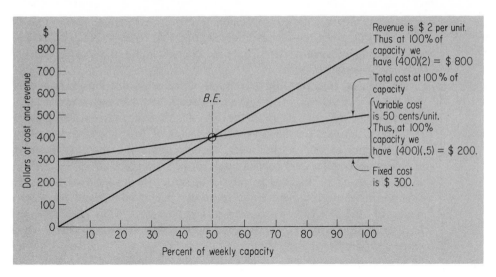

FIGURE 2-4. An example of break-even analysis for a small computer service center

General-purpose equipment is commercially available, whereas special-purpose equipment must be designed to specifications. Also, the movement of materials between equipment is mechanized for the flow shop, whereas it is done mostly by hand in the job shop.

For the higher fixed costs of the flow shop, the manager expects to obtain lower variable costs. The job shop manager must do everything possible to keep the high variable costs under control. If there is sufficient stable demand to warrant investment in flow shop design and if technology exists to deliver low variable costs at the required quality level, then the manager will invest in flow shop design.

The decision to employ flow shop design requires careful analysis of all relevant factors. For example, assume that expensive materials are required per part and that these are the same for either the flow shop or the job shop. Then, unless the decrease in labor costs per part (as a result of using the flow shop) more than compensates for the larger fixed costs required, the decision will be in favor of the job shop.

As another example, say that demand is very elastic with respect to price, and that flow shop design cuts total costs per unit dramatically for relatively high volumes of output. Then if it can be shown that sufficient demand can be realized and sustained (in the face of both existing and potential competition), the flow shop will be chosen.

Break-even analysis is of critical importance to the reaching of such decisions; so is an understanding of demand elasticity.[5] Japanese industry in the 1970s specialized in flow shops, allowing it the cost advantages of great productivity. By reducing prices and spending more than competitors for

---

[5]Demand except by contract is not certain. It must be forecast. We shall discuss forecasting applied to the break-even model in Chapter 3, where the break-even *decision model* is explained. Then a more detailed discussion of forecasting will be given, pp. 40–43.

marketing, Japanese industry was able to capture very large shares of world markets. Yet, when petroleum prices skyrocketed (circa 1974), the variable-cost advantage began to deteriorate the overwhelming fixed-cost benefits of flow shop specialization.

As a general rule, the flow shop is the preferred production configuration, but special constraints on its use must always be taken into consideration. When the decision is made to use the job shop, then the most efficient possible job shop is desired. We shall discuss the design of flow shops and job shops, spending more time on the latter, because the skills and knowledge of engineering specialists are needed (and can be justified) in designing the flow shop. However, we shall not ignore the design of the flow shop, because the situation often arises where a flow shop design can be put into place for a period of time. We call this an *intermittent flow shop*. Although it does not have the productivity of a permanent flow shop, it still provides cost leverage when compared to the job shop.[6]

The considerations that we have been discussing will affect and be affected by parallel decisions concerning materials, labor, facilities, and quality—as well as the life cycle planning for the introduction and deletion of goods and services into and from the established product line of the organization. Life cycle planning recalls to our attention the need to forecast demand (at given price, promotion, and advertising levels) as well as the relevance of R&D (research and development) to bring about innovations in both process and outputs.[7] For the flow shop, long-range forecasts are required; for the job shop, shorter-range forecasts are in order. Most projects[8] are based on contracts, yet forecasting is needed to specify completion dates and costs.

To make break-even analysis even more valuable as well as to obtain further insights concerning the cost and profit structure of production systems, let us now recognize that the demand levels of production volume (the x axis of the break-even chart) must be forecast.[9]

APPENDIX 2-I
Mathematical Form of the Break-even Model
(Optional Material)

It is quite straightforward to translate the graphical break-even chart into its algebraic equivalent. Some individuals prefer the graphical form, whereas others prefer the mathematical statement. The choice ultimately depends upon the use that is to be made of such analyses. When communication with production personnel is required, the graph approach is generally more effec-

---

[6]See p. 180.

[7]With respect to R&D, see Appendix II of Chapter 4, pp. 80–82.

[8]Break-even analysis is appropriate for the project to the extent that job shop activities are used to furnish goods and services for various phases of the project.

[9]This topic is a fundamental consideration of Chapter 3.

tive. Both methods provide the same solutions to any specific problem, namely, the production volume or percentage of capacity utilized at the break-even point. The capacity measure is frequently used with the flow shop, which is always designed with a maximum capacity. Capital-intensive industries (such as iron and steel production) relate their performance to the percentage of capacity that is utilized. On the other hand, labor-intensive industries (such as the production of garments) are more likely to use measures of production volume than capacity.

To construct the mathematical model, let us assign symbol equivalents to the relevant factors.

Rev = gross revenue-per-time-period T.

Price = price per unit with the assumption that the market will absorb everything that can be made at the same price.

Vol = number of units made in time period T and, therefore, sales volume in time period T.

FC = fixed costs-per-period T.

VC = variable costs-per-unit of production.

TC = total costs-per-period T.

Profit = total profit-per-period T.

The revenue line for period T is given by:

$$Rev = Price \times Vol$$

The total cost line for period T is equal to

$$TC = [FC + (VC)Vol]$$

Total profit for the interval T is (*in terms of volume*) then

$$Profit = (Rev - TC)$$
$$= [Price \times Vol - FC - (VC)Vol]$$
$$= [(Price - VC)Vol - FC]$$

EXAMPLE 1. *Question:* Should we install a conveyor belt?

Method: We will use break-even analysis, where the time period $T = 1$ year.

	Alternative 1 No Conveyer	Alternative 2 Install Conveyer
Vol	18,000 units per year	18,000 units per year
FC	$10,000 per year	$12,000 per year
VC	$0.50 per unit	$0.45 per unit
Price	$2.00 per unit	$2.00 per unit

For Alternative 1: (at 100 per cent of Vol)

$$\text{Profit} = (2 - 0.50)(18{,}000) - 10{,}000 = \$17{,}000 \text{ per year}$$

For Alternative 2: (at 100 per cent of Vol)

$$\text{Profit} = (2 - 0.45)(18{,}000) - 12{,}000 = \$15{,}900 \text{ per year}$$

The break-even point is easily calculated by setting Profit = 0; then[10]

$$\text{Vol (Break-even point)} = \frac{\text{FC}}{\text{Price} - \text{VC}}$$

For Alternative 1:

$$\text{Vol (Break-even point)} = 10{,}000/(1.5) = 6667 \text{ units}$$

For Alternative 2:

$$\text{Vol (Break-even point)} = 12{,}000/(1.55) = 7742 \text{ units}$$

It is a simple matter to convert from units of volume to percentage or fraction of capacity. For example, the break-even point as a fraction of total capacity for Alternative 1 is $6667/18{,}000 = 0.37$; for Alternative 2, it is $7742/18{,}000 = 0.43$. We note that the profit at full capacity utilization for Alternative 1 promises \$1100 more profit than Alternative 2. Also, in terms of the break-even point we prefer Alternative 1 because it has a lower value.

Answer: In this example, there is no doubt that we should select Alternative 1.

EXAMPLE 2. *Question:* Should we buy machine *A* or machine *B*?

Method: We employ break-even analysis where the time period $T = 3$ months or 1 quarter.

	Alternative 1 Machine A	Alternative 2 Machine B
Vol	5000 units per quarter	5000 units per quarter
FC	$2500.00 per quarter	$3500.00 per quarter
VC	$0.50 per unit	$0.10 per unit
Price	$2.00 per unit	$2.00 per unit

---

[10] This relationship is valid only when $\text{Price} - \text{VC} \geq 0$, i.e., when $\text{Price} \geq \text{VC}$. Ordinarily, it is assumed that pricing follows an analysis of costs and, therefore, no competent manager would accept a price that does not cover the variable costs *with room to spare*. Consider, however, the plight of regulated industries, e.g., airlines, where operating costs could grow faster than changes in rate structure. The worst possible break-even value would be infinite, arising when $\text{price} = \text{VC}$. Negative break-even volumes have no meaning.

First, let us test the profit for each alternative at an estimated 3000 units per quarter, which is 60 percent utilization of capacity.

For Alternative 1:

$$\text{Profit} = (2 - 0.50)(3000) - 2500 = \$2000 \text{ per quarter}$$

and for Alternative 2:

$$\text{Profit} = (2 - 0.10)(3000) - 3500 = \$2200 \text{ per quarter}$$

Next, for full-capacity utilization, for Alternative 1:

$$\text{Profit} = (2 - 0.50)(5000) - 2500 = \$5000 \text{ per quarter}$$

and for Alternative 2:

$$\text{Profit} = (2 - 0.10)(5000) - 3500 = \$6000 \text{ per quarter}$$

Thus, Alternative 2's profit is preferred both at the point of estimated plant utilization and at full utilization. The break-even points are:

for Alternative 1:

$$\text{Vol (Break-even point)} = \frac{2500}{1.5} = 1667 \text{ units or } \frac{1667}{5000} = 0.333$$

for Alternative 2:

$$\text{Vol (Break-even point)} = \frac{3500}{1.9} = 1842 \text{ units or } \frac{1842}{5000} = 0.370$$

Answer: Alternative 1 has a superior break-even point, but it does not have better profit, even at 60 percent utilization. The conflict between expected profit and break-even point advantage must be resolved by the decision model approach, discussed in Chapter 3.

APPENDIX 2-II
The Nonlinear Break-even Chart (Optional Material)

The anticipated volume of operations is a critical factor in the determination of a production system's design. If the market is such that at a certain price *unlimited* demand exists, then for these linear systems we would always operate as far to the right as our plant capacity permits. Of course, in reality at some point linearity ceases to be a reasonable description of the market's responses. Increased volume can be obtained only by a decrease in price or by an increase in promotional and selling costs. These two situations are shown in Figs. 2-5 and 2-6. The combination of these effects is illustrated in Fig. 2-7.

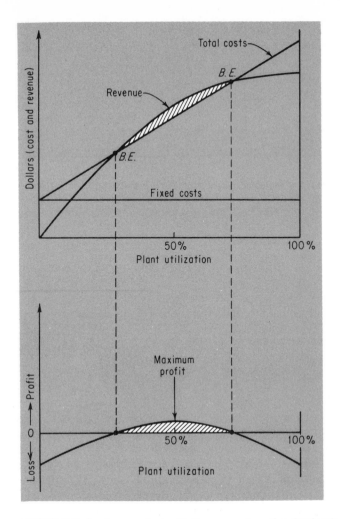

FIGURE 2-5. Break-even chart with the assumption of a decelerating revenue as product price is lowered to achieve full plant utilization.

There is another effect that might have to be taken into account, namely, the decreasing per unit costs of production which The Boston Consulting Group has found with increasing output experience.[11] Part of the cost advantage is derived from economies of scale. Another part is derived from the learning phenomenon, where productivity increases with experience. But there is an over-all systems effect as well, such that marketing, distribution, and production efficiencies benefit each other.[12] The result reported by The

---

[11]See pp. 7–9 for a discussion of the decrease in per unit costs of production as the output volume increases.

[12]To justify a flow shop, high output volume is needed. Given that volume, productivity improves. There are various levels of flow shop mechanization which can be related to the successive decreases in per unit costs that occur with increasing output volume.

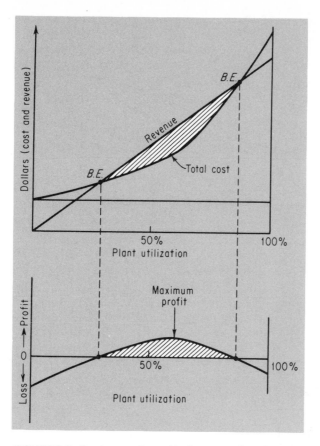

FIGURE 2-6. Break-even chart with the assumption of accelerating promotional costs required to achieve full plant utilization. Note that the maximum profit point has shifted from 50 percent utilization (Fig. 2-5) to a higher value of plant utilization.

Boston Consulting Group is approximately a 25 percent decrease in unit costs for each doubling of production output. If such an effect is present, the shape of the total cost curve in Fig. 2-7 will be altered, perhaps enough to look like the revenue curve. As shown in Fig. 2-8, it is quite possible that such a situation could produce the same break-even consequences as strictly linear functions, namely, produce as much as you can, since there is only one break-even point.

Each of these diagrams is accompanied by a graph of the profit that can be obtained at different percentages of productive capacity. We may note there is a "best possible" point, that is, a point at which the total profit is maximized.[13] To achieve this level of production requires cooperative effort on the part of all the major management divisions. Financial management must

---

[13]With the exception of Fig. 2-8.

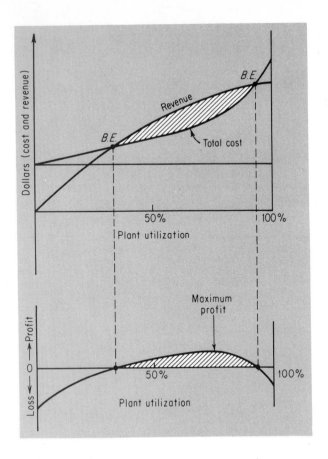

FIGURE 2-7. Break-even chart with both assumptions, that is, decelerating revenue and accelerating costs

provide enough funds so that adequate capital exists to create the facilities necessary for the specified volume of production. The marketing department must be able to deliver the estimated number of customers and their sales at the price that is incorporated in the revenue line. And, of course, production must be able to deliver on time the goods in the required volume at the expected cost and quality.

We see that production management must help to determine a *configuration of production elements* that will yield a maximum profit—if that is the company's objective. However, the problem of succeeding in doing this is complicated far beyond anything that a break-even chart can show. A danger of abstractions is that all kinds of difficulties are represented in a simple fashion that belies the truth of the situation. Accordingly, one must be very careful in applying such tools as the break-even chart.

Let us examine this warning with respect to the break-even model. First of all the break-even chart, even when couched in nonlinear form, represents

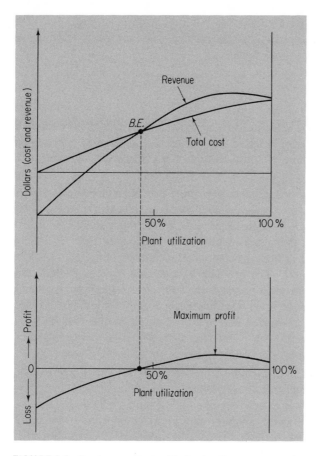

FIGURE 2-8. Break-even chart with decelerating revenue and costs

only one product. For most companies, decisions must include the fact that a product-mix is involved. The line consists of a number of different items or services. These must share resources, including capital and management time. The break-even chart is difficult to utilize when such additional complications are encountered. In addition, a specific period of time is embodied in each break-even chart. If we assume that the company can sell 5 million units over a 5-year period, but only 10,000 in the first year, then the result of a 5-year analysis may be quite appealing; whereas on the basis of a 1-year analysis, the product would be rejected. But cost estimates applied to a 5-year period might not be sufficiently believable to allow management to act on them. Further, unexpected costs can arise. For example, if the company overproduces, then overstock units could be sold only by reducing the price. If the unsold units are held in inventory, they will create additional costs such as storage, insurance, and carrying costs.

For each situation some maximum profit (optimal) situation exists. Whether it can be found or not is another matter. But *only* with the nonlinear break-even chart does this fundamental optimization objective of management appear. The traditional break-even approach overlooks this particular aspect of the problem.

1. With reference to Fig. 1-5, a break-even chart cannot be constructed for product B based on a price of 58¢ per unit and a maximum production volume of 8 million units. Describe what is feasible.

2. Discuss the following observation: The break-even chart can represent only one product at a time. For most companies, decisions must include the fact that a product-mix is involved. The line consists of a number of different items or services. These must share resources, including capital and management time. The break-even chart is difficult to utilize when such additional complications are encountered.

Answer: The problem of assigning fixed costs between different items in the product line is at the root of this difficulty. Accounting for fixed costs must be done whether or not break-even analysis is used. The application of break-even for one product at a time will provide results that are partially consistent with management's view of fixed-cost allocations; it violates the system's view.

3. Discuss the following observation: A specific period of time is embodied in each break-even chart. If we assume that a company can sell 5 million units over a 5-year period, but only 10,000 in the first year, then the result of a 5-year analysis may be quite appealing; whereas on the basis of a 1-year analysis, the product would be rejected. But cost estimates applied to a 5-year period might not be sufficiently believable to allow management to act on them. Further, unexpected costs can arise. For example, if the company overproduces, then overstock units could be sold only by reducing the price. If the unsold units are held in inventory, they will create additional costs such as storage, insurance, and carrying costs.

4. Detail some situations in which nonlinear analysis might be required for the breakeven chart.

Answer: It is rare that the per unit profit of an item can be held constant over a wide range in demand. If it is considered desirable to increase sales beyond a certain point, it becomes necessary to incur some additional expenses. This creates nonlinearity in the variable-cost sector. Sometimes it is more advantageous to achieve the same effect by lowering prices, thus creating a nonlinear revenue line. Demand-stimulating devices such as quantity discounts or advertising allowances are some other frequent causes of nonlinearity in the system.

A less obvious cause of nonlinear relations in the break-even chart arises as a result of a change in the fixed costs of the process. As an example, assume that the demand for the product increases sharply. At first it is necessary only to increase total expenditures for labor and raw materials, while holding per unit expenditures constant; i.e., the variable costs associated with increased production are unchanged. However, as full plant capacity is approached, a decrease in efficiency occurs. Such factors as overtime premiums and overutilization of machinery create an increase in per unit variable costs. Then, if still more production is required, a new machine may be purchased or a new plant must be constructed. This will alter the fixed-cost component, producing nonlinear discontinuities.

It should be noted that for a system without nonlinearities, rational management would attempt to increase production without limit, since increased production would always mean increased profit.

See pp. 27–32 for further discussion of the nonlinear break-even model.

5. The Gamma Company has engaged a management consultant to analyze and improve its operations. Her major recommendation is to totally conveyorize the production floor. This would, of course, represent a sizeable investment to the Gamma Company. In order to determine whether or not the idea is feasible, a break-even analysis will be utilized. The situation is as follows: The cost of the conveyor will be $200,000, to be depreciated on a straight-line basis over a 10-year period, that is, $20,000 per year. The reduction in operating cost is estimated at $0.25 per unit. Each unit sells for $2.00. The sales manager estimates that, on the basis of previous year, the Gamma Company can expect to obtain a sales volume of 100,000 units—this represents 100 percent of their capacity. Present yearly contribution to fixed costs is $100,000. Present variable-cost rate is $0.50. Should the company install this conveyor?

6. The Omega Corporation is considering the advantages of automating a part of their production line. The company's financial statement is shown below:

Omega Corporation

TOTAL SALES		$40,000,000
Direct Labor	$12,000,000	
Indirect Labor	2,000,000	
Direct Materials	8,000,000	
Depreciation	1,000,000	
Taxes	500,000	
Insurance	400,000	
Sales Costs	1,500,000	
Total Expenses		$25,400,000
Net Profit		$14,600,000

The report is based on the production and sale of 100,000 units. The production manager believes that with an additional investment of $5,000,000 he can reduce variable costs by 30 percent. The same production volume would be maintained. Using a 5-year, straight-line depreciation (that is, $1,000,000 per year), construct a break-even chart. If the company insists on a 20 percent return on its investment, should they automate? (Discuss briefly your treatment of all costs.)

7. **a.** List as many variable costs as you can.
   b. List as many fixed costs as you can.
   c. To what extent are accounting data available in various organizations with respect to such items?
   d. What is overhead cost or burden? How should it be treated in a break-even analysis?

three
the break-even decision model

We know what break-even analysis is about, but what is a decision model? It is a basic model applicable to all managerial decision problems. It is the product of the intensely studied field of decision theory.

Decision Theory

Every decision situation is composed of five basic elements. These are:

1. *Strategies or plans constructed of controllable variables.*[1]
2. *State of nature* composed of noncontrollable variables.

---

[1] Variables are *factors* that can appear in a problem with different values. Some variables have only two states, as, for example, a switch which is either on or off. This is called a *binary variable*. Other variables exist within a closed range, such as time of day, which runs from 00:01 to 24:00. Some variables cannot take on negative values, for example, age or hardness. Profit and loss, where loss is treated as negative profit, can, unfortunately, assume large minus values. Finally, certain variables are limited to discrete scales (only integer values can occur), for example, the number of students in a class. Others, such as temperature and weight, are continuous.

3. *Outcomes* which are observations of results that occur when a specific strategy is employed and a particular state of nature exists.

4. *Forecasts* of the likelihood that each state of nature will occur.

5. *The decision criterion* that dictates the way in which the information above will be used to select a single plan to follow.

Decision theory applies to all types of decision situations, but we are concerned only with P/OM decisions. We must discuss all the elements of the decision process *as they particularly relate to the production function*. It has been recognized by those conversant with the field of P/OM education that the traditional treatment of this area tended to overlook some of the vital aspects of the problem.[2] Further, lacking a comprehensive framework for the consolidation and organization of information, the tendency was to pile fact upon fact, logical analysis upon logical analysis, and method upon method. The result was fragmentation (analysis) and not integration (synthesis). Present-day practitioners, however, have recognized the role that decision theory can play in relating the parts to each other. P/OM education need no longer be treated in terms of an amorphous collection of facts, principles, and methods. This advance is attributable in large part to decision theory.

Analysis and Synthesis

The key word is *synthesis*. Over the course of many years, the multitude of decision problems that comprise P/OM have been identified and their special characteristics have been analyzed. Analysis is the process of breaking down a system into parts that can be more easily examined. Synthesis is the reverse procedure—where the parts are integrated to form the whole. Both are essential if the solution to a problem is to be obtained, understood, and implemented.

We know a lot about analysis; little about synthesis. The decision model brings all of the decision elements (the five listed above) together and provides synthesis.

Strategies

By *strategies* we mean alternative courses of action. They are different plans for achieving the agreed-upon *objective*, such as more profit, higher output, lower cost, etc. Strategies are often called actions because they are composed of the steps that can be taken by management, for example, *install* a conveyor belt or *maintain* the present materials-handling system. From the above discussion, we see why strategies are constructed of controllable variables.

---

[2]See the following reports concerning methods of business education: Robert A. Gordon and James E. Howell, *Higher Education for Business* (New York: Columbia University Press, 1959); Frank C. Pierson, *The Education of American Businessmen* (New York: McGraw-Hill Book Company, Inc., 1959), pp. 475–503.

States of Nature

States of nature describe those factors in a situation that affect the expected results of a plan of action but which are fundamentally not under the manager's control. Weather, political events, and the state of the economy are three examples. Appropriate to the P/OM area are such states of nature as failure rates of equipment, price changes by vendors, invention of new materials, process technology innovations, consumer demand levels, labor turnover rates, and absenteeism. Under some circumstances, a degree of control can be exercised over such states of nature. For example, by selecting different kinds of equipment, or by utilizing preventive maintenance—both of which are strategic functions—some control over failure rates is available. Similarly, salary level—a strategic variable—can alter turnover and absenteeism, but the control is both indirect and incomplete.

A probability distribution is the only possible basis for attempting to forecast which state of nature will prevail in a given situation. In other words there is an observed or estimated *likehood* that each state will occur, say x times in one hundred trials, That likelihood is measured as the probability of occurence of the state of nature. There is a 0.50 probability that the state of nature "heads" will occur with each toss of a true coin. [We can represent this as p (heads) $= 0.50$.] The meteorologist just announced a 30 percent probability of precipitation tomorrow, i.e., p (rain) $= 0.30$. Figure 3-1 illustrates a five-state probability distribution where the state of nature, A, has

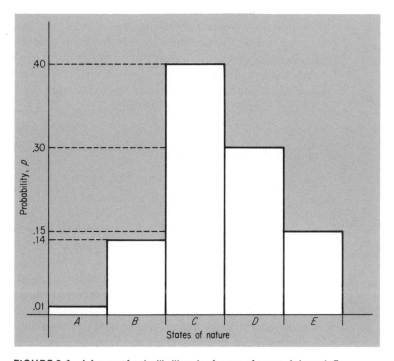

FIGURE 3-1. A *forecast* for the likelihoods of states of nature A through E

only one chance in a hundred trials of appearing, i.e., $p_A = 0.01$, whereas state of nature C has the highest probability $p_C = 0.40$. The sum of these probabilities will be 1.00, indicating that one of these states of nature must occur, thus: $p_A + p_B + p_C + p_D + p_E = 1$.

When we are able to ignore states of nature, we call this class of decision problem "decision making under certainty," (DMUC). Some typical examples of production systems models that are based on the assumption of certainty are

1. Machine loading models, that is, assigning various jobs to different machine centers; sequencing these jobs through specific facilities.
2. Determining an optimal product mix.
3. Optimal assignment of people to jobs.
4. Deriving an optimal traffic plan for shipping goods from factories to warehouses.
5. Determining optimal production runs; that is, how many units to produce at one time.

Exceptions exist for each of the five situations listed above, but the majority of cases are solved without considering uncontrollable variables and, therefore, states of nature. Even though many problems seem to fall into the DMUC category, the assumption of certainty must never be taken for granted. There are cases when management must be prepared to enumerate explicitly the relevant states of nature. Such cataloging of the uncontrollable features of the problem may be vital to the success of the decision maker.

For problems where risk or uncertainty exist, the planner must surely have some states of nature in mind. Too frequently, these are only the most probable states of nature. Unless some kind of objective, formal procedure is used, there is no opportunity for group participation in this endeavor. Oversights cannot be remedied. The decision function cannot be logical until all *relevant* states of nature are recognized.

Setting Up the Decision Matrix

Let us symbolically represent strategies by S_i, where i can take on any value 1 through n. Thus, if $n = 2$, we have only two strategies; if $n = 5$, we have five strategies.

We shall represent states of nature as N_j, where j can take on any values 1 through m. When $m = 1$, then each company strategy produces a unique result, i.e., DMUC. It is equivalent to say that no matter what happens in the environment the same outcome will result from using a specific strategy. When the noncontrollable variables can combine in two different ways, then $m = 2$.

A particular strategy and a specific state of nature produce a unique set of results called an outcome, O_{ij}. This is the outcome for the ith strategy and the *j*th state of nature. We observe, measure, and record only those results that are of interest. P/OM objectives determine what is of interest. For example, a product design S_1 operating under a given set of environmental conditions N_1 will fail after a stated number of hours. If we wish to select the design that has the longest life, then "time to failure" is our outcome of interest. Other possible outcomes include quality of performance, amount of maintenance, number of returns, plant capacity used, amount of materials, labor, and energy consumed, and contribution to profit.

Below, we present an example of an *outcome matrix* where 4 designs are being evaluated under 5 different environmental or use conditions.

The generality of the matrix is apparent. In the form that it is written, the strategies might equally well describe such diverse situations as the best way to lay out the plant, the choice of an optimal numbering system for a catalogue, or where to go on a vacation. Accordingly, the states of nature would describe relevant noncontrollable factors applicable to each case. For each intersection an outcome measure must be obtained that would adequately describe the realization of objectives of the planning operation.

	N_1	N_2	N_3	N_4	N_5
S_1	3	5	4	2	8
S_2	5	3	2	4	6
S_3	4	4	4	4	4
S_4	4	5	4	2	8

For this example, let us presume that the objective is to choose that design which promises the longest expected lifetime of use. The (4 × 5) matrix produces 20 cells or intersections. At each intersection an entry can be made that describes the average lifetime of the particular design, operating under the specific conditions.

Outcomes are obtained in at least three basically different ways:

1. By means of estimates and guesses.
2. By observation, laboratory experimentation, engineering data, etc.
3. By a knowledge of relationships that have previously been hypothesized (a theory).

All three of these methods are commonly used. In many cases combinations can be employed. It is worthwhile to point out that we are not discussing the means by which a choice is to be made between strategies. Outcomes relate only to what will happen when a particular strategy is used and a specific state of nature has occurred.

The controllable variables of a strategy may be representable in numerical terms. The same applies to the noncontrollable variables. A mathematical function is used to relate these 2 kinds of variables and to derive the outcomes that they will produce. In mathematical terminology, outcomes are called *dependent variables*. The controllable and noncontrollable variables are called *independent variables*. As before, the outcomes are represented by O_{ij}, where i is the particular strategy used and j is one of the states of nature that can occur. Let us write this symbolically.

$$O_{ij} = f(S_i, N_j)$$

We read this as follows: The dependent variable O_{ij} is a function of the independent variables S_i and N_j. Now, of course, the critical question concerns the nature of the actual function. We require a specific model. For example, a hypothetical relationship might be

$$O_{ij} = S_i N_j$$

(If S_i were a variable length and N_j a variable width, then O_{ij} is quickly recognized as a measure of area.)

Alternative product or service plans do not lend themselves easily to such kind of expression. Neither do plant location plans, process design plans, or most of the other long-term production management problems. Engineering problems, inventory problems, and scheduling problems, on the other hand, do fit this pattern. A great number of situations can be resolved within a mathematical framework. For example, it is possible to use a mathematical description of the break-even decision model.[3]

Adding Forecasts to the Decision Matrix

The manager must determine how likely it is that each state of nature will occur before an optimal strategy can be selected. To begin, we must be able to identify *all* of the relevant states of nature. Then, we *forecast* the likelihood of occurrence for each of the states of nature. The existence of a forecast completes the decision matrix.

For example, assume that the manager is concerned with the costs of 4 possible ways of scheduling production (strategies 1, 2, 3, and 4). The costs relate to how a number of different items are sequenced through machine centers and how the size of the production runs that are used affect the efficiency of these operations. States of nature N_1 through N_5 are 5 different patterns of demand for the various items that include all demand patterns that could possibly arise. The forecast $\{p_j\}$ for each demand pattern has also been supplied. The decision matrix might be as shown in Table 3-1.

It appears that a complex relationship describes the way in which the controllable variables interact with the noncontrollable variables to produce outcomes. In fact, this would be true; costs of overstock, carrying stock,

---

[3]This is illustrated in the optional materials of Appendix 3-I, pp. 51–52.

**TABLE 3-1 DECISION MATRIX OF WEEKLY COSTS
(IN THOUSANDS OF DOLLARS) FOR ALTERNATIVE
SCHEDULING STRATEGIES**

State of Nature: N_j	N_1	N_2	N_3	N_4	N_5
Forecast: p_j	0.1	0.2	0.1	0.4	0.2
Strategy 1	10	12	14	12	8
Strategy 2	8	12	16	14	10
Strategy 3	16	14	12	14	15
Strategy 4	14	14	14	14	14

understock, setting up equipment, and of idle facilities would be interacting with each other in a variety of ways.[4]

Twenty different computations were required to produce this matrix. In addition, the forecast for the 5 states of nature had to be derived. The first forecasting step would be to identify the states of nature by specifying the range of demand levels that might occur for each item.

Then, several questions must be answered: What is the probability of each demand level? Reference is often made to what has happened in the past. Even so, should observations be taken over the total year, a particular season, or a particular month? Such questions, having been answered, a set of observations based upon forecasting skills would be made and grouped into a frequency distribution (see p. 37). Assume that 50 weeks of observations are available. When they were sorted into their appropriate classes it might have been found that:

Demand Pattern	Observed Frequency	Probability
N_1	5	0.1
N_2	10	0.2
N_3	5	0.1
N_4	20	0.4
N_5	10	0.2
	50	1.0

How believable are these probabilities? We can have a high degree of confidence in our forecast if we know that the system that *underlies* the appearance of the states of nature is unchanging, and that our sample provides a good description of the relative frequencies with which the states of nature occur. Both of these conditions are required. We could have a very accurate

---

[4]We shall be dealing with all of these issues in later chapters of this text.

description of what happened in the past, but the past may not be indicative of the future. Assuming that the fundamental conditions from whence the states of nature are derived remain unchanged, then we say that the system is stable. Stability is a vital concept for all management decision making that uses a forecast. Stability is much more likely to exist for a short rather than a long time interval. Statistical quality control (pp. 557–62) is one of the most powerful tools that the manager possesses because, when properly used, it can inform him of the fact that a once stable system is no longer so.

Let us now review what we know about states of nature and their associated predictions. The vital considerations are

1. How many states of nature are relevant?
2. Are we able to identify all the relevant states of nature?
3. Can we determine the "true" frequencies of occurrence of these states of nature?
4. Are these frequencies fixed; that is, is the state of nature (causal) system stable?

We have gathered enough information to proceed to the final step of the decision process. Strategies, states of nature, outcomes, and forecast are assembled in a decision matrix. Now what do we do?

Decision Making under Risk (DMUR)

If two or more states of nature are relevant, if all the relevant states of nature can be identified, and if a high degree of believability can be placed on the forecast with respect to the probability of occurrence of these states of nature, then decision making under risk (DMUR) exists. Let us say that each state N_j has a probability p_j of occurring. Then the sum of all p_j's, taking into account every possible value for j, must be one. Mathematically we write

$$p_1 + p_2 + p_3 + p_4 + p_5 + \ldots + p_j + \ldots + p_m = 1.00$$

If there are five relevant states of nature, then $m = 5$.

We know that when a problem conforms to the specifications of DMUR it must be resolved by using *averages* or *expected value*. This satisfies the fact that over a period of time the ups and downs of the system will average out to produce the result given by the expected value. Let us now use the information presented in the decision matrix on p. 000 to reach a decision. We proceed to obtain the expected value EV_i for each strategy, i. Because the probabilities sum to one, the expected value will be given by the formula

$$EV_i = p_1 O_{i1} + p_2 O_{i2} + \ldots + p_j O_{ij} + \ldots + p_m O_{im}.$$

For example, $p_1 O_{11} + p_2 O_{12} + p_3 O_{13} + p_4 O_{14} + p_5 O_{15}$ equals the expected value for the first strategy. Thus, we are saying that the average value of the *i*th strategy will be equal to the sum of the products of each row entry multiplied by its appropriate p_j. In this way we derive

$$EV_1 = 1.0 + 2.4 + 1.4 + 4.8 + 1.6 = 11.2$$
$$EV_2 = 0.8 + 2.4 + 1.6 + 5.6 + 2.0 = 12.4$$
$$EV_3 = 1.6 + 2.8 + 1.2 + 5.6 + 3.0 = 14.2$$
$$EV_4 = 1.4 + 2.8 + 1.4 + 5.6 + 2.8 = 14.0$$

The scheduling strategy S_4 is invariant (insensitive) to demand patterns.[5] By studying the abstract decision matrix, we do not find out why this is so. We need an explanation of what constitutes S_4. Perhaps it is as simple as letting the foreman and his dispatchers determine schedule—subject to a budget limit of $14,000. If we assume that our objective is to utilize that plan which affords the lowest total weekly cost, then S_1 is the indicated choice.

Some examples of problems that properly belong to systems of DMUR would be machine breakdowns and process failures, frequency of rejects, distribution of delivery intervals (lead times), measures of worker productivity, and the analysis of relatively stable consumer demand systems. These same methods are not likely to be useful when an attempt is made to forecast events that will occur in a vaguely seen future, such as long-term consumer demand for a new service, new product consumer demand (where the new product represents a substantial innovation and there is nothing comparable to utilize as a guide), speculative real estate ventures, developments in architectural style and available building materials, technological changes, stock market indices, wage rate demands and union attitudes, and the state of the economy.

Decision Matrix and the Break-even Chart

Let us consider an example of break-even analysis where the volume of demand is not known with certainty. We shall use a service industry for this illustration, viz., airline transport. This is a legitimate P/OM problem, and one in which forecasting has tended to be neglected. Airlines have made equipment decisions based on the supposed competitive advantage of being first with new technology. In other words, it was assumed that with faster, newer, and bigger equipment, demand would always rise to exceed the break-even point.[6] By the middle 1970s, it was recognized that this assumption was incorrect. With such perspective, this example takes on added significance.

---

[5] There is the same outcome for all the states of nature.

[6] The newer and bigger equipment has greater capacity than the older planes, i.e., more passenger seats. Consequently, even a lower B.E.P. applied to greater capacity could represent a requirement to fly more passengers.

Various equipment strategies exist for the airlines. Suppose that a company called Alpha Airlines wants to determine whether it should convert from regular jets to jumbo jets. The company draws up break-even charts for the alternatives it is considering. Assume that it is determined that Fig. 3-2 holds for regular jet planes and that with the conversion to jumbo jet aircraft Fig. 3-3 applies.

Table 3-2 presents hypothetical data used to construct Figs. 3-2 and 3-3. The time period is assumed to be 1 year.

TABLE 3-2

	Regular Jet Fleet	Jumbo Jet Fleet
Fixed costs*	$100,000,000	$120,000,000
Variable costs†	500,000	250,000
Unit Revenue† (or price)	2,000,000	2,000,000

*Fixed costs include ground installations and are depreciated on an annual basis.

†Based on 1 percent (a unit) of capacity utilization, where capacity is measured in terms of passenger miles flown in a year. Note: we are assuming that both jet fleet configurations have the same total capacity and unit revenues.

From Fig. 3-2, we observe that the break-even point for regular jets is 66.7 percent of full-capacity usage. Figure 3-3 reveals that the break-even point for jumbo jets is 68.6 percent of full-capacity utilization. We emphasize that these are hypothetical constructs. The airlines claim much lower break-even percentages ranging from 45 to 55 percent. (See Problem 10 at the end of this chapter.)

Figure 3-2 and the tabled data show that Alpha Airlines requires a smaller investment in regular aircraft and related ground facilities than for jumbo jets, but its variable costs of operating flights are higher with regular jet equipment. By converting to a jumbo fleet (Fig. 3-3) Alpha Airlines will increase its fixed costs, but it will also reduce its variable costs. We are assuming that no surcharges exist for jumbo aircraft and, therefore, that the same revenue line can be used for both situations.[7] As an additional point, we are not considering mixtures of regular and jumbo jets, although such combinations make sense and should ordinarily be analyzed.

We now have demonstrated that the present regular jet fleet achieves a lower break-even point than the proposed jumbo equipment. This means that the "load factor" will be higher if the conversion is approved—a result that would disturb most executives in the airline industry.[8]

At the same time we note that as compensation for this poorer break-even point, the jumbo jet aircraft produce higher marginal returns on profit. This

---

[7]If we had increased the unit revenue of the jumbo jets by a surcharge of $250,000, the B.E.P. would have dropped to 60 percent.

[8]Load factor is the airline industry term for break-even.

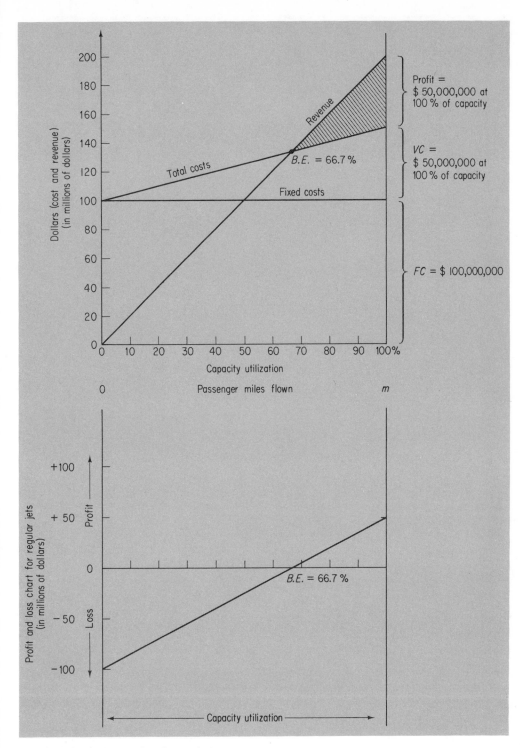

FIGURE 3-2. Break-even chart for regular jets

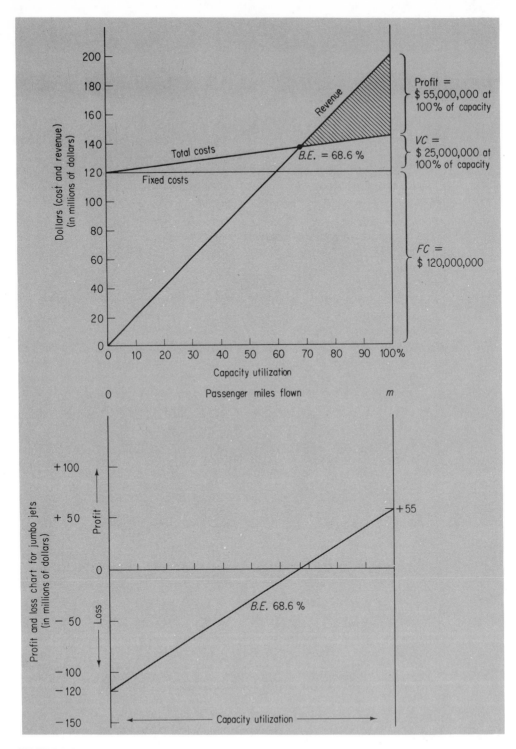

FIGURE 3-3. Break-even chart for jumbo jets

means that if Alpha Airlines is able to operate at higher passenger (and cargo) loads than the break-even point, then a substantially greater profit can be obtained by converting the fleet to jumbo equipment.

Something, however, is missing from this analysis. Namely, a forecast is required for the various levels of demand for seats and for aircraft miles to be flown. Forecasts can be used for many purposes, e.g., to provide estimates of public demand for a service or to estimate sales volume in the private sector. Both cases are related to decisions about optimal production capacities and the kinds of production configurations to be used.

Flow Shop Air Travel

What constitutes a flow shop in the airline situation? One requirement is large planes so that the number of takeoffs and landings can be minimized. Another requirement is essentially totally booked aircraft—i.e., planes do not depart until all seats are filled. This might mean that customers must either wait for service until a plane is filled or else commit themselves to the kinds of regulations that apply to charter flights. Probably, planes would not fly on fixed schedules. Competition for seats among airlines would be eliminated. Thus present government regulations concerning flight schedules would have to be changed significantly. These conditions for flow shop airline activities may be politically unacceptable. They may be rejected by the public. They would, however, *substantially* reduce airline fares for the public.

Assume that you have been summoned as an expert (P/OM) witness by a Congressional committee. What questions should they ask? What answers will you give?

After careful analysis, we determine that the probability of annual consumer demand is as shown in Table 3-3.

TABLE 3-3

Demand Level D	Probability of Demand Level D
40% of capacity	0.05
50% of capacity	0.10
60% of capacity	0.15
70% of capacity	0.20
80% of capacity	0.25
90% of capacity	0.20
100% of capacity	0.05
	1.00

It should be noted: We assume that demand probabilities are independent of the type of plane that is flown. We shall apply the same probability distribution to both jumbo and regular aircraft. This assumption might not stand up to reality.[9] As is the case for all probability distributions, the sum of the probabilities equals one. A distribution such as this one can be derived in a variety of ways, including (when necessary) the use of experienced judgment and intuition.

A different amount of profit is associated with each level of demand. This amount of profit can be read from the break-even charts (revenue minus total costs) or directly from the accompanying profit and loss charts. Thus, from Fig. 3-2 at 0 percent demand, there is a *loss* of $100,000,000 and at 100 percent capacity there is a profit of $50,000,000. We apply our probability distribution to the profit at each demand level D by multiplying profit at D times the probability of D. When we add up these products for all demand levels, we obtain the average (or expected) profit for the given strategy. As derived in Table 3-4, the expected profit for a fleet of regular jets is $9,500,000.

TABLE 3-4 COMPUTATION OF EXPECTED PROFIT FOR REGULAR JETS*

(1) Demand D	(2) Profit at Level D (*in millions of dollars*)	(3) Probability of D	(2) × (3) (*Profit*)(*Probability*)
0%	−100	0	0
10	−85	0	0
20	−70	0	0
30	−55	0	0
40	−40	0.05	−2
50	−25	0.10	−2.5
60	−10	0.15	−1.5
70	+5	0.20	+1.0
80	+20	0.25	+5.0
90	+35	0.20	+7.0
100	+50	0.05	+2.5
		1.00	+9.5

Expected profit = $9,500,000

*Note: This is the calculation for one of the two strategies in the decision matrix.

We know that the break-even point for regular jets is 66.7 percent. By multiplying columns (1) and (3) we can determine the expected (or average) demand that our probability distribution implies. Ignoring the values of demand associated with 0 probability, we calculate the expected value of this irregular distribution to be equal to a load factor of about 73 percent, i.e.,

---

[9]See Problem 11 at the end of this chapter.

$0.05(40\%) + 0.10(50\%) + 0.15(60\%) + 0.20(70\%) + 0.25(80\%) + 0.20(90\%)$
$+ 0.05(100\%) = 73$ percent. Consulting the break-even chart for regular jets (Fig. 3-2), we can measure the profit at 73 percent capacity utilization and determine that it is $9,500,000.

Turning to jumbo jets, we perform the same kind of calculations. Consulting the break-even chart for jumbo jets (Fig. 3-3), we measure the profit at 73 percent capacity utilization and determine that it is $7,750,000.

On the basis of this analysis, we recommend that Alpha Airlines retain its fleet of regular jets. This is because *the expected profit with regular jets is greater than the expected profit with jumbo jets.* Management should, however, be on the lookout for changes in conditions that might alter this decision. For example, the probabilities might shift to be more favorable for the jumbo-size planes. Alternatively, new technology could lower fixed costs, which could change our recommendation.

A comparative break-even chart such as the one drawn in Fig. 3-4 might provide useful insights concerning the interaction of factors that lead to the selection of one strategy over another.

TABLE 3-5 COMPUTATION OF EXPECTED PROFIT FOR JUMBO JETS

(1) Demand (D)	(2) Profit at Level D (in millions of dollars)	(3) Probability of D	(2) × (3) (Profit) × (Probability)	(1) × (3) (Demand) × (Probability)
0%	−120	0	0	0
10	−102.5	0	0	0
20	−85	0	0	0
30	−67.5	0	0	0
40	−50	0.05	−2.50	2
50	−32.5	0.10	−3.25	5
60	−15	0.15	−2.25	9
70	+2.5	0.20	+0.50	14
80	+20	0.25	+5.00	20
90	+37.5	0.20	+7.50	18
100	+55	0.05	+2.75	5
		1.00	+7.75	73

Expected Profit = $7,750,000
Expected Demand = 73 percent

With the addition of forecasting, the break-even model has become a *decision model*, which recommends a particular solution. Using this approach has enabled us to override the problem of what to do when one strategy has a better break-even point than another but a poorer marginal rate of return.

The fact that we can choose between strategies means that we can test flow shop conditions against job shop conditions to determine which configura-

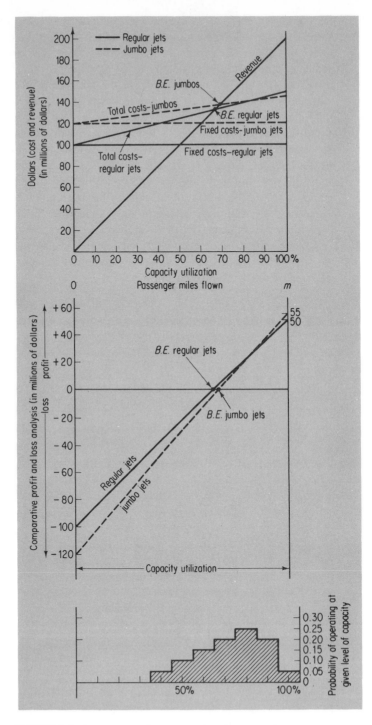

FIGURE 3-4. A comparative break-even chart for regular jets versus jumbo jets

tion should be used. If the flow shop is indicated, we may have to reexamine the question, including the costs of changing over from a job to flow shop.

By using a forecast, we have removed the need for traditional break-even analysis, which considers only the position of the break-even point. This is true because it is fundamental to the entire concept of the break-even point that all decision makers have in mind an estimate of the likelihood that the company will operate below or above that point. Without this estimate in mind, the break-even point is meaningless. By using a statistical decision model approach, we have succeeded in relating the two factors that previously were treated as separate components: namely, the position of the break-even point and the marginal rates of return. Our method has merged them into a single problem. (The mathematical form of the decision model is presented as optional material in Appendix 3-I.)

APPENDIX 3-I
Mathematical Form of the Break-even Decision Model
(Optional Material)

In Appendix 2-I (pp. 24–27) we developed profit for different levels of sales volume. This was

$$\text{Profit} = [(\text{Price} - \text{VC})\text{Vol} - \text{FC}]$$

Now, let us make this profit function more specific by requiring that the strategy and state of nature be identified. We shall write the equation for the profit of the ith strategy as a function of the jth level of demand (as a percentage of total capacity). For example, the profit obtained by using regular jets ($i = 1$) at 0 percent of capacity ($j = 0$); or the profit obtained by using jumbo jets ($i = 2$) at 10 percent of capacity ($j = 10$), at 20 percent of capacity ($j = 20$), etc. This equation is:

$$\text{Profit}_j\,(i) = \{[\text{Price}(i) - \text{VC}(i)]\,\text{Cap}_j\,(\text{MV}) - \text{FC}(i)\}.$$

All terms of this equation have been defined in Appendix 2-I, except Cap_j, which represents demand as a percentage of total capacity. Also new is MV which stands for the maximum volume, in units, at 100 percent capacity. (Note $\text{Cap}_j \times \text{MV} = \text{Vol}_j$.)

Then, let $p_j =$ the probability of the jth level of demand (as a percentage of total capacity). The sum of these probabilities equals 1; that is,

$$\sum_{j=0}^{j=100} p_j = 1.00$$

where $j = 0, 10, 20, 30, \ldots, 80, 90, 100$.

The average or expected profit[10] of the ith strategy [Eprofit (i)] can be expressed as

$$\text{Eprofit}(i) = \sum_{j=0}^{j=100} (p_j)\text{Profit}_j(i)$$

$$= \sum_{j=0}^{j=100} p_j\{[\text{Price}(i) - \text{VC}(i)]\text{Cap}_j\,(\text{MV}) - \text{FC}(i)\}$$

As an example, let us reexamine the question of regular jets ($i = 1$) versus jumbo jets ($i = 2$). Here, the data are organized in a table (Table 3-6), which is called a *decision matrix*.

TABLE 3-6

p_j % of capacity (j)	0 0	0 10	0 20	0 30	.05 40	.10 50	.15 60	.20 70	.25 80	.20 90	.05 100	*Eprofit* (i)
Profits (or losses) $i = 1$ in millions	−100	−85	−70	−55	−40	−25	−10	+5	+20	+35	+50	+9.50
of dollars $i = 2$	−120	−102.5	−85	−67.5	−50	−32.5	−15	+2.5	+20	+37.5	+55	+7.75

Our objective is Max Eprofit.
We have for $i = 1$ (regular jets):

$$(0)(-100) + (0)(-85) + (0)(-70) + (0)(-55) + (0.05)(-40)$$
$$+ (0.10)(-25) + (0.15)(-10) + (0.20)(+5)$$
$$+ (0.25)(+20) + (0.20)(+35) + (0.05)(+50) = +9.50$$

and for $i = 2$ (jumbo jets):

$$(0)(-120) + (0)(-102.5) + (0)(-85) + (0)(-67.5) + (0.05)(-50)$$
$$+ (0.10)(-32.5) + (0.15)(-15) + (0.20)(+2.5)$$
$$+ (0.25)(+20) + (0.20)(+37.5) + (0.05)(+55) = +7.75$$

We select regular jets ($i = 1$), because this strategy has the largest expected profit.

PROBLEMS   1. Why is it particularly useful for P/OM to differentiate between decision making under certainty and under risk?

---

[10]See pp. 42–43 and 48–49 for discussion and an example of the calculation of the expected value (or average).

2. What is the significance of a break-even strategy as compared to other kinds of strategies?

3. With respect to strategy invention, it has been suggested that a methodological discovery can have as marked an effect as a technological breakthrough. Discuss this idea from the point of view of determining whether there is any precedent for the statement.

   Answer: Methodological advances can bring about great changes in the production system. They may not seem as spectacular, on the whole, as some kinds of technological breakthroughs. Nevertheless, the development of modern inventory control techniques has created important new methods for mail-order retail companies, manufacturing companies, and department stores that have clearly had a major impact. Blending by linear programming methods and scheduling work using network algorithms are two other examples of methods that have revolutionized the production system. In years to come, this effect should be accentuated as computers and the methods they model become more sophisticated. Looking at this question in a somewhat different light, we see that such methodological developments as writing and arithmetic have revolutionized our world to the extent that we cannot conceive of having been without them. Even the changeover from Roman to Arabic numbers, which was strongly resisted in its time, has become so much a fabric of our way of life that it is impossible to imagine what things were like before this change. Perhaps, in as fundamental a sense, inventory theory is affecting and modifying business cycles and altering the swings between recessions, depressions, and inflationary periods. This last notion has been seriously suggested as a result of empirical observations of the United States economy in the 1960s.

4. Why is it important to differentiate between analysis and synthesis?

5. Solve the decision problem posed on p. 39 (where the objective is to choose that design which promises to maximize the expected life of the product), under the following four probability conditions:

	\multicolumn{5}{c}{Values of p_j}
	N_1	N_2	N_3	N_4	N_5
Condition 1	0	1.00	0	0	0
Condition 2	0.20	0.30	0.50	0	0
Condition 3	0	0	0.30	0.30	0.40
Condition 4	0.20	0.20	0.20	0.20	0.20

Comment on the character of these various conditions and their effects on the results.

6. How do catastrophic events, such as earthquakes and floods, relate to states of nature?

7. Explain to a group of ecologists how states of nature apply to their area of concern.

8. Develop an appropriate decision matrix for each of the problems below. This requires describing specific strategies and relevant states of nature. Load the cells of the matrix with reasonable estimates for the outcomes. Assign appropriate probabilities. Solve the problem that you have designed. The generality of the decision matrix approach for resolving problems should be evident from the ubiquitousness of these situations.

I	Strategies:	A number of different equipment selection plans for a fire company
	States of nature:	Equipment failure rates
	Outcomes:	Measures of downtime
	Objective:	Minimize downtime
II	Strategies:	Various hospital layout arrangements
	States of nature:	Varying demand levels for different treatments in the hospital's service mix
	Outcomes:	Measures of bottlenecks and delay
	Objective:	Minimize delay
III	Strategies:	Different production materials, for example, various metals versus various plastics
	States of nature:	Varying costs for these materials and different levels of consumer demand
	Outcomes:	Profit measures
	Objective:	Maximize profit
IV	Strategies:	Varying number of repairmen
	States of nature:	Probabilities of machine breakdowns
	Outcomes:	Measures of the cost of downtime
	Objective:	Minimize cost
V	Strategies:	Different computer systems
	States of nature:	Varying data loads on the department
	Outcomes:	Measures of the age of information
	Objective:	Minimize age of information in the system
VI	Strategies:	Different numbers of toll booths
	States of nature:	Varying numbers of arrivals
	Outcomes:	Measures of customer waiting time
	Objective:	Minimize customer waiting time
VII	Strategies:	Various arrangements of supermarket checkout counters

	States of nature:	Number of customers with small and large orders that come into the store
	Outcomes:	Measures of idle time of checkout clerks and customer waiting time
	Objective:	Minimize total cost of checkout clerks' idle time and waiting time of customers

VIII	Strategies:	Different catalog numbering systems
	States of nature:	Various users of the catalog
	Outcomes:	Measure of errors in ordering
	Objective:	Minimize ordering errors

Answer: This problem is intended to encourage discussion and to permit consideration of a great variety of operations management situations. Many other problems can be set up in addition to the eight that have been suggested.

Choosing Case V as an example, let us examine four different hypothetical computer systems. The data load may be light, medium, or heavy. Some corresponding estimates have been developed and are shown in the decision matrix of Table 3-7.

TABLE 3-7 MATRIX OF THE AGE OF INFORMATION (IN HOURS)

Strategies		Light	Medium	Heavy	EV_i
	p_j	0.2	0.7	0.1	
System 1		1.0	2.1	4.0	2.07
System 2		0.7	2.5	4.3	2.32
System 3		1.2	2.8	2.7	2.47
System 4		1.1	2.0	3.7	1.99

The minimum expected age of information occurs with computer system 4. Perhaps, however, the fourth system is too costly, as compared to system 1, with respect to the expected differences in performance.

If properly used with fully amplified discussion, such examples can show the general applicability of the decision matrix to operations management problems.

In this sense let us carry the example one step further, bearing in mind the concept of sensitivity of the solution to changes in the data. In Table 3-8, we shall change the values of the p_j's, but only slightly.

**TABLE 3-8 MATRIX OF THE AGE OF
INFORMATION (IN HOURS)**

		State of Nature		
Strategies	Light	Medium	Heavy	EV_i
p_j	0.2	0.6	0.2	
System 1	1.0	2.1	4.0	2.26
System 2	0.7	2.5	4.3	2.50
System 3	1.2	2.8	2.7	2.46
System 4	1.1	2.0	3.7	2.16

The result is unchanged in that the fourth system will provide the minimum expected age of information. However, we observe that the change in the p_j values has raised the expected age for all but one of the systems. This is shown in Table 3-9.

TABLE 3-9

System	1	2	3	4
After change	2.26	2.50	2.46	2.16
Before change	2.07	2.32	2.47	1.99
Difference	+0.19	+0.18	−0.01	+0.17

Relatively speaking, systems 1, 2, and 4 are invariant to the type of change that is suggested, whereas system 3 appears to be highly sensitive.

9. Explain the statement: The problem of achieving synthesis is too complex to permit the exclusive use of judgment. It is too large for a purely methodological treatment. Properly used, the combination of objective and subjective treatments can be synergistic. (Synergistic means that the total effect of the system is greater than the sum of the individual effects of the parts of the system operating independently.)

Answer: The exclusive use of (subjective) judgment, as a means of selecting an optimal strategy for a complex P/OM system, is virtually impossible, because the relevant problem detail is too great for individual perception, human memory, and cerebral calculation. Similarly, (objective) methodology cannot reflect the scope of interacting subsystems. A combination of the two approaches is essential.

Thus, design of alternatives accepts intuition. Evaluation depends heavily on objective, analytic methods. By combining subjective and objective methods, the total benefits usually will exceed the sum of the benefits derived from each method's being used alone. Therefore, an appropriate combination is said to be synergistic. To achieve such advantages, the combination must be coordinated by management.

10. For the break-even analysis discussed in the text, assume that 100 percent capacity utilization for the jumbo jets is twice the number of passenger miles flown as compared to 100 percent capacity utilization for the regular jets. Does this affect the analysis? Explain.

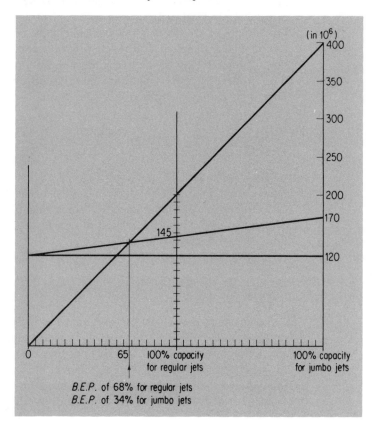

FIGURE 3-5.

Answer: As can be seen from Fig. 3-5, with the above assumption, the B.E.P. drops to 34 percent from 68 percent. The probability distribution used in the text should no longer apply, but if it does, that means that Alpha Airlines has invested in a lot of useless capacity. If there are significant probabilities for flying at capacities that are more than 100 percent of regular jet capacity, then the jumbos look very attractive.

11. If the demand probabilities are dependent on the type of plane that is flown, what different steps would you take in analyzing Alpha Airline's choice situation?

Chapter 1

The spread of industrial systems to developing countries and from goods to services reveals the potential breadth of application of production and operations management knowledge. There is a worldwide productivity problem, which can be relieved if production management approaches are implemented.

All production is based on demand that is more or less elastic to changes in price. The dependence of price (and thereby demand) on cost is explained in Chapter 1. Cost analysis and cost control differ markedly for the three major types of production systems, namely, the flow shop, the job shop, and project management. The flow shop is the most productive configuration, but it cannot always be used. The most appropriate configuration (whatever it turns out to be) can be made as efficient as possible by means of the various operations management models treated throughout the text.

Chapter 2

The nature of fixed and variable costs is first explained in terms of the input-output model of production systems. These cost concepts are then extended to the break-even model. Some examples are presented, and the break-even methodology is related to type of production configuration, i.e., flow shop, job shop, and project.

Chapter 3

To conclude Part 1, the decision matrix and then the break-even decision model are developed. A forecast of demand is required to use this model, which has the advantage of enabling one to select the best possible alternative in such diverse choice situations as different blood bank procedures, competing conveyor-belt systems, alternative office copy equipment, manual versus machine systems, and flow versus job shop production configurations.

REFERENCES
PART 1

ACKOFF, R. A. (ed.), *Progress in Operations Research*, Vol. I. New York: John Wiley & Sons, Inc., 1961.

ARONOFSKY, J. (ed.), *Progress in Operations Research*, Vol. III. New York: John Wiley & Sons, Inc., 1968.

BAUMOL, WILLIAM J., *Economic Theory and Operations Analysis*, 2nd ed. Englewood Cliffs, N.J.: Prentice-Hall, Inc., 1965.

BECKETT, JOHN A., *Management Dynamics: The New Synthesis*. New York: McGraw-Hill Inc., 1971.

BIERMAN, H., JR., C. P. BONINI, and W. H. HAUSMAN, *Quantitative Analysis for Business Decisions,* 5th ed. Homewood, Ill.: Richard D. Irwin, Inc., 1977.

BUDNICK, F. S., R. MOJENA, and T. E. VOLLMAN, *Principles of Operations Research for Management,* Homewood, Ill.: Richard D. Irwin, Inc., 1977.

CARZO, R., JR. and J. N. YANOUZAS, *Formal Organization: A Systems Approach.* Homewood, III.: Richard D. Irwin, Inc., 1967.

CHURCHMAN, C. W., R. A. ACKOFF, and E. L. ARNOFF, *Introduction to Operations Research.* New York: John Wiley & Sons, Inc., 1957.

CHURCHMAN, C. WEST, *Prediction and Optimal Decision.* Englewood Cliffs, N.J.: Prentice-Hall, Inc., 1961.

——, *Theory of Experimental Inference.* New York: The Macmillan Company, 1948.

DEAN, JOEL, *Managerial Economics.* Englewood Cliffs, N.J.: Prentice-Hall, Inc., 1951.

DOOLEY, A. ET AL., *Basic Problems, Concepts, and Techniques,* Casebooks in Production Management. New York: John Wiley & Sons, Inc., 1968.

ECKMAN, D. P. (ed.), *Systems Research and Design.* New York: John Wiley & Sons Inc., 1961.

ELLIS, D. O. and F. J. LUDWIG, *Systems Philosophy: An Introduction.* Englewood Cliffs, N.J.: Prentice-Hall, Inc., 1962.

FABRICANT, SOLOMAN, *A Primer on Productivity.* New York: Random House, 1969.

FORRESTER, J. W., *Industrial Dynamics.* New York: John Wiley & Sons, Inc., 1961.

GARRETT, LEONARD and MILTON SILVER, *Production Management Analysis.* New York: Harcourt Brace Jovanovich, Inc., 1966.

GOLD, BELA, *Foundations of Productivity Analysis.* Pittsburgh, Pa.: University of Pittsburgh Press, 1955.

GREENLAW, P. S., L. W. HERRON, and R. H. RAWDON, *Business Simulation in Industrial and University Education.* Englewood Cliffs, N.J.: Prentice-Hall, Inc., 1962.

HALL, ARTHUR D., *A Methodology for Systems Engineering.* Princeton, N.J.: D. Van Nostrand Co., Inc., 1962.

HARE, VAN COURT, JR., *Systems Analysis: A Diagnostic Approach.* New York: Harcourt Brace Jovanovich, Inc., 1967.

HERTZ, D. B. and R. T. EDDISON (eds.), *Progress in Operations Research,* Vol. II. New York: John Wiley & Sons, Inc., 1964.

HOUGH, LOUIS, *Modern Research for Administrative Decisions.* Englewood Cliffs, N.J.: Prentice-Hall, Inc., 1970.

HOWELL, JAMES E. and DANIEL TEICHROEW, *Mathematical Analysis for Business Decisions,* 2nd ed. Homewood, III.: Richard D. Irwin, Inc., 1971.

KASNER, EDWARD and JAMES NEWMAN, *Mathematics and the Imagination.* New York: Simon and Schuster, Inc., 1963.

KAUFMANN, A., *The Science of Decision-Making.* New York: McGraw-Hill Book Company, 1968.

LUCE, R. DUNCAN and HOWARD RAIFFA, *Games and Decision.* New York: John Wiley & Sons, Inc., 1958.

MARSHALL, P. W. ET AL., *Operations Management (Text and Cases).* Homewood, Ill.: Richard D. Irwin, 1975.

MCKEAN, R. N., *Efficiency in Government through Systems Analysis.* New York: John Wiley & Sons, Inc., 1958.

McMILLAN, CLAUDE, JR. and RICHARD F. GONZALEZ, *Systems Analysis: A Computer Approach to Decision Models*, (rev. ed.) Homewood, Ill.: Richard D. Irwin, Inc., 1968.

MILLER, D. W. and M. K. STARR, *Executive Decisions and Operations Research*, 2nd ed. Englewood Cliffs, N.J.: Prentice-Hall, Inc., 1969.

M. I. T. Notes on Operations Research, 1959. Cambridge, Mass.: M. I. T. Press, 1959.

OPTNER, S. L., *Systems Analysis for Business Management* 2nd ed. Englewood Cliffs, N.J.: Prentice-Hall, Inc., 1968.

POSTLEY, JOHN A., *Computers and People*. New York McGraw-Hill, Inc., 1960.

RIGGS, J. L., *Economic Decision Models*. New York: McGraw-Hill Book Co., 1968.

SASIENI, M., A. YASPAN, and L. FRIEDMAN, *Operations Research Methods, and Problems*. New York: John Wiley & Sons, Inc., 1959.

SCHLAIFER, R. ROBERT, *Analysis of Decisions under Uncertainty*. New York: McGraw-Hill Book Company, 1967.

SCHODERBEK, PETER P. (ed.), *Management Systems*. New York: John Wiley & Sons Inc., 1967.

SHULL, F. A., JR., A. L. DELBECQ, and L. L. CUMMINGS, *Organizational Decision Making*. New York: McGraw-Hill Book Company, 1967.

SIMON, H. A., *The New Science of Management Decision*. New York: Harper & Row, Publishers, 1960.

SPENCER, M. H. and L. SPIEGELMAN, *Managerial Economics*. Homewood, Ill.: Richard D. Irwin, Inc., 1959.

STARR, MARTIN K., *Systems Management of Operations*. Englewood Cliffs, N.J.: Prentice-Hall, Inc., 1971.

WAGNER, H. M., *Principles of Management Science*, Englewood Cliffs, N.J.: Prentice-Hall, Inc., 1970.

WALD, A., *Statistical Decision Functions*. New York: John Wiley & Sons, Inc., 1950.

ZIMMERMANN, H. J. and M. G. SOVEREIGN, *Quantitative Models for Production Management*. Englewood Cliffs, N.J.: Prentice-Hall, Inc., 1974.

2

life cycle management

All products and services go through life cycle stages.

They are introduced to their market, where they must be accepted by a sufficient number of users to justify their continued existence. Some new goods or services require such costly investment that it is essential to pretest them carefully. For example, before a new subway line is built, much data should be collected and analyzed to estimate the probable number of riders that will choose this method of transport. On the other hand, a new bus route can be instituted directly on an experimental basis. Many P/OM decisions are specifically related to the introductory life cycle phase of goods or services.

Established goods or services provoke a different set of P/OM decision problems. It is essential to maintain the high level of demand which resulted from growth over time. Vulnerability to new competition, which can afford to offer consumers (or the electorate) a change, poses real problems, since the established goods or services are more certain of the success of the status quo than they are of modifications to the proven product or service mix. By means of continual improvements, price can be lowered and quality improved, and such changes can act as deterrents to the entry of new competitors (or the election of a different set of officials).

P/OM must deal with all of these stages, and care must be taken to make the right moves at the right *time*. This is what is meant by life cycle management. Coordination is required to link production and marketing efforts with those of the research department, personnel, accounting, and finance. Coordination is a general management requirement that is possible *only* if one is aware of the need.

Part 2 consists of Chapters 4, 5, and 6. The relationship of these chapters to life cycle phenomena and to each other is indicated below.

Chapter 4 examines product and service Marketing Stages. These are ① new product or service introduction, ② established franchise, ③ declining franchise bolstered with innovations, ④ withdrawal of marketing support, and ⑤ termination of distribution. Then, the management of the inflows and outflows of cash over the different life cycle intervals is treated.

Chapter 5 examines the activities necessary to move from premarket production planning to an operating production system that can deliver the required goods or services at an acceptable cost. The feasibility of this entire process must be established before major investments are committed to specific decisions.

Premarket Production Stages (I)

I-A. Designing the Production Output (Products and Services)

I-B. Designing the Production Process

I-C. Implementing the Systems Design

In-market Production Stages (II)

II-A. Operating the Production Process

II-B. Changing the Production System (in response to marketing requirements, changes in technology and of input resources)

Chapter 6 relates life cycle planning to the variety level (of the product line or service mix) that should be obtained, for maximum profits or benefits, from a chosen production configuration. In addition to the marketing consequences of variety, there are economic issues stemming from the pattern of utilization of equipment and other resources. The organizing model is linear programming (called LP).

four
life cycle stages and present value

Marketing and production decisions are tightly interrelated. It is not reasonable to specify that the production process should be a flow shop, job shop, or project configuration without knowing about the marketplace and its elasticities of demand with respect to quality, price, advertising, promotion, distribution, etc.

The design of the production process affects quality and price. The efficiency of the production process will determine how much gross profit is available to support lower prices and higher qualities as well as advertising, promotion, and distribution. Consequently, it is essential to understand the production-marketing interaction before we proceed to examine in detail the three basic kinds of production process configurations that we have stated are the fundamental work-design classifications of P/OM.

The marketplace concept of supply and demand applies equally to both public and private sectors. At present, almost 100 percent of all public systems are either project- or job-shop-oriented. With respect to projects, the service is offered or required only once (e.g., a national vaccination program or building a new rapid transit system). As for job shops, the service is regularly available in individual units or in small batches (e.g., city bus service, selection of a trial jury, putting out a fire, or obtaining license plates when you buy your car).

The costs of supplying almost all public services on a project or job shop basis are exorbitant. This applies to the delivery of mail, intercity transport, police and fire protection, public health, etc. With increasing population size, it has become imperative to design public system flow shops that can achieve high-level productivity (efficiency) with no decrease in the quality of the outputs demanded by society. The computer capability offers the prospect of regularizing public activities so that they come closer to a flow shop than a job shop.

The public sector is especially weak with respect to productivity, but the private sector is also vulnerable. This means that in the marketplace, costs are higher, service poorer, etc. and the consumer is dissatisfied. *The marketplace is where the production system is judged.* That is why the material in Part 2 is presented so early in this text. Therefore, before we begin to examine the characteristics of different production system configurations, we shall examine the marketing (life cycle) properties of the goods and services that are produced.

Product and Service Marketing Stages

A *new* product or service must build consumer awareness, so it must spend a lot on advertising and promotion if it is to build a sufficient market to achieve a stable franchise. An *established product* or *service* must maintain its market. It must hold on to its existing customers. Even small downturns can affect its profitability, because, lacking growth, it is vulnerable to economic changes and competitive actions. A sales volume curve (shown in Fig. 4-1) illustrates the market situations of growth, maturity, and decay. Mature products will be found on the portion of the curve that is close to the saturation level for that particular product or service. New products and services must grow fast enough to achieve their share potential (i.e., saturation level). Obsolete products are represented by the dashed portion of the curve, which depicts the declining sales of the decay region of the growth curve. Often, before this occurs, the product or service is restaged, which means an effort is made to present an improved version to reverse an expected (or actual) decline in demand.

New products and services have experienced increasingly higher failure rates. Many reasons can be given for this fact. Competitive pricing may be decisively detrimental. Changes in the economy can produce chaotic conditions. Trouble with the production process can lead to erratic delivery or inconsistent quality, and if such troubles are not remedied fast enough, the required growth can never be achieved. The share of market is permanently damaged; the share potential is unachievable. Still, it may be the case that in spite of high failure rates, the optimal strategy for a company is to introduce many new products. Although each new product has a relatively high likeli-

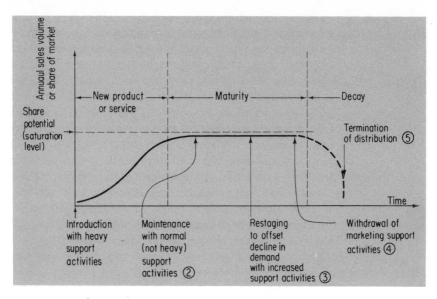

FIGURE 4-1. The marketing evolution of goods and services

hood of failure, the one product that is a success provides sufficient payback to profitably (beneficially) support the whole program. This kind of approach requires a life cycle management capability to cope with the great number of new products that are consistently being introduced.

Some companies follow this pattern. Others take quite a different view. They utilize careful analysis and deliberation before the introduction of a single product—or very few products—all of which have been shown through tests to have relatively high probabilities of success. The question of which approach or combination of approaches is better is a problem to be resolved by life cycle management.

It should be recognized that the problem is a tough one under the best of circumstances. A major stumbling block lies in the inability to develop good forecasts for marketplace responses.[1] The production costs for alternative configurations can be derived, under the assumption that believable predictions of production volume are available. Circular reasoning is at work, since sales volume is a function of price, cost is a function of production volume, and price is a function of cost. Circular reasoning can be used to converge on a solution, or to show that no solution exists. Thus, life cycle management must be based on a sequence of analytic steps that consider all relevant factors as a system.

Change of Pace

Before 1950, time spent in the Marketing Stage ② (established franchise with loyal customers) was generally ample and unhurried. Stage ② is the

---

[1] Test marketing can supply useful forecasts, but at the real cost of delaying introduction while the test market is set up and run.

most profitable (or beneficial) one; development costs are completed, capital investments have been made, and heavy introductory advertising, promotion, and sales effort of Stage ① have been substantially reduced. Because of inherent market stability, improvements could be brought about slowly.

There was no need to rush into new product or service introduction, forcing completion of the Production Stages I-A, B, and C (see pp. 87–91). Since 1950, however, the effects of accelerated competition, changing social values, greater consumer affluence, larger volume of sales, new technologies, resource shortages, consumerism, and governmental regulation have increased the rapidity of transition from marketing stage ② to ③, ④ and ⑤ (see p. 65).

As a result, the premarket production stages which are the responsibility of the P/OM department are often completed under great time pressure or are called into play hastily and even unexpectedly (as in II-B, changing the production system, to support market restaging ③).

How Responsive Should the Production System Be to Changes in What the Market Wants?

An auto manufacturer had a successful marketing policy of selling only compact cars. Then the marketplace, which had been demanding mostly small cars, suddenly shifted to larger ones.

It would be costly to convert its flow shop production. Even partial redesign of the product line would take time. And the move would be risky. It had been expected that the high cost of fuel would be a boon to the compact car market. The company's marketing strategy had seemed right on target. There was a possibility that the shift to large cars might be temporary.

Careful coordination between marketing and production planning is essential. Are there any strategies that have been overlooked, such as luxury fittings for compacts or importing larger cars from abroad? If not, the best conversion plan must be found; it must be acceptable to production (budget) and successful for marketing (sales volume, share, and profit).

As another example, if a particular raw material becomes scarce on the world market, then a substitute must be found. The product or service that uses the substitute material must be test marketed[2] and, if it is satisfactory, the production system has to be altered accordingly. Similarly, governmental regulation (such as the removal of saccharin from diet soft drinks, or the

---

[2]A test marketing stage usually precedes ①. Production is required to make up enough units of product or to provide enough service capacity for consumption by the test markets. This output is necessarily produced by job shop-type production operations.

ban of detergent phosphates by municipalities, or the control of noise levels for aircraft, or the requirement for seat belts and pollution deterrents for automobiles, etc.) can lead to relatively rapid shifts in product and service designs. Often these require substantial and costly changes in the production process. Speed is generally of the utmost importance so that distribution can be maintained.

Further, new products and services must be brought to the marketplace more rapidly than ever for a number of reasons, among which we include getting the jump on competition. Being first into the market has a big advantage. Also, it has been increasingly difficult to secure broad enough patent production to allow for more leisurely deliberation before beginning the introductory stage. Partly, this is due to the advances in technology that have already been made, and the consequent cost of coming up with something that meets the increasingly more stringent requirements resulting from stricter interpretations of the patent law.[3] Further, market instability can appear with little warning, creating a need to alter or replace quite hastily a faltering product or service line.

Cash Flow

Because of the increased change of pace, it is even more important than previously that the *cash flow* of an organization be well-managed. That is, over time the cash requirements of the company to meet debts (i.e. payroll, purchase obligations, rentals, interest payments, telephone, etc.) must be balanced by cash receipts. Bringing a new product or service into being often involves significant outlays of funds against which the return on investment (ROI) will be delayed by months or years. Thus, cash flow management hinges on adequate life cycle planning. Figure 4-2 captures some of the elements of this critical requirement, couched in product terms, but the example applies equally well to services.

Accounting for Present Value

We have talked about balancing cash flows over time so that within any specific period the cash receipts (plus funds from the bank and by other borrowing) match the debts of the organization (which include payroll, purchases, rents, and interest owed). For balancing cash flows, it is convenient to work in cash terms without discounting the value of money. That is because a dollar that must be spent a year from now is correctly offset by a dollar that will be earned a year from now. However, we should note that a dollar spent or earned today is worth more than a dollar spent or earned a year from now.

---

[3]For further discussion of patents, see Appendix 4-I, pp. 74–80. Appendix 4-II presents some aspects of research and development (R&D).

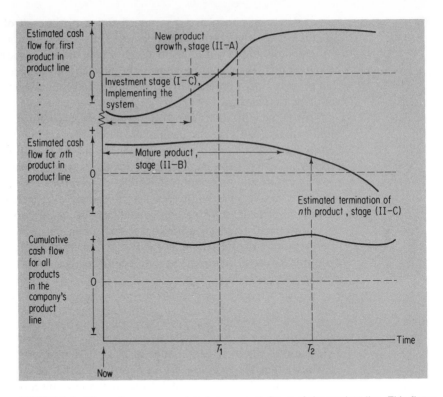

FIGURE 4-2. Life cycle management to balance cash flows of the product line. This figure shows that the first product in the product line is producing a larger outflow of cash than an inflow. At time T_1, it is expected to break-even. Thereafter, it should produce profit. There are n products in the product line. Each has its own cash flow pattern. Thus, the nth product is mature and profitable at a stable level until some time after T_1, when its profit is expected to begin to falter. A small restaging effort will be made with the expectation that it will halt only temporarily the decline in demand. Estimated termination of this nth product is time T_2. At the bottom is the cumulative cash flow curve representing the sum of all positive and negative flows from the n products.

To explain, let us compare 2 plans. In the first we shall build a plant. In the second we shall rent it. These 2 kinds of costs are not incurred in the same way. Some method is required to compare costs that are immediate or within a short period with those that represent a *stream* of costs over a period of time. Immediate costs result from buying; a stream of smaller costs results from renting. Similarly, we require a way of comparing the income that will be obtained over a period of time from alternative product designs, where one product has an expected life of 5 years and another promises a smaller income stream, but taken over a 10-year life. Consider the value of improvements, such as a process design or an inventory system change. Each requires a given expenditure now and will produce different streams of savings over various periods of time. We must calculate the present value of the savings and then compare it against the expenditure to see whether either or both of the proposed improvements is worthwhile.

A method of *discounting* is required to resolve the issue that has been raised. The premise upon which discounting is based is that a sum of money to be received at some future time has less value than the same sum of money owned at the present time. Essentially, this method provides for a comparison between an investment made in the present and a stream of smaller payments made over a period of time. We can either derive the *present value* (or worth) of the stream of payments and compare it to the investment, or we can determine what stream of payments (perhaps borrowed from the bank) would be equivalent to the investment. In both cases, an interest rate and an interval of time must be specified. The length of time over which the monetary stream is reckoned will affect the conclusions.

To illustrate, assume that it is possible to buy a plant for $1,000,000. An alternative is also offered, namely, to rent at $80,000 per year. The question that we wish to answer is: How do these plans compare? It is our purpose to measure the stream factors (annuities) in the same terms as the investment.

First, we must obtain an estimate for the interest value of money. For example, 6 percent per year would be the amount that could be obtained by investing a given sum of money in savings bank certificates. The estimate of this interest rate will vary depending upon the size of the company, its growth potential, and capital requirements. Some companies can earn much higher returns, simply by ploughing back all available cash into their production output. We shall employ the 6 percent rate, recognizing that it is not easy but absolutely necessary to determine the appropriate rate of interest.

We ask the question: What is the present value of an $80,000-per-year rental payment stream as a function of the length of the time period that is employed? The formula for present value that we utilize is

$$PV = N \sum_{n=1}^{n} \left(\frac{1}{1+r} \right)^n$$

where

PV = present value

N = $80,000, the yearly rental value

r = interest rate, 6 percent per year

n = the planning horizon of n years, ($n = 0, 1, 2, \ldots, n$).

Expanding the summation, which must still be multiplied by N, we obtain

$$\sum_{n=1}^{n} \left(\frac{1}{1+r} \right)^n = \text{the sum of terms:} \left(\frac{1}{1+r} \right)^1 + \left(\frac{1}{1+r} \right)^2 + \ldots + \left(\frac{1}{1+r} \right)^n$$

The equation for PV assumes that the first rental payment is made at the *end* of the period. Consequently, each dollar paid out at the end of the first year costs us less than a full dollar, viz., $0.94. If we had that dollar at the beginning of the period, we could have invested it at 6 percent per year. At the end of the year we would have $1.06, but we would be required to pay out only

$1.00. The actual cost would be $1.00 − 0.06 = $0.94. Thus, by deferring payment we decrease the cost of such payments to us.[4]

Table 4-1 shows the way in which present value changes as a function of the time period.[5]

TABLE 4-1 PRESENT VALUES
(where $r = 0.06$ and $N = 80,000$)

n (years)	Column 1 $\left(\dfrac{1}{1 + 0.06}\right)^n$	The Sum of Column 1 $\sum\limits_{n=1}^{n}\left(\dfrac{1}{1 + 0.06}\right)^n$	$N \times$ the Sum of Column 1 $(80,000)\sum\limits_{n=1}^{n}\left(\dfrac{1}{1 + 0.06}\right)^n$
1	0.943	0.943	75,440
2	0.890	1.833	146,640
3	0.840	2.673	213,840
4	0.792	3.465	277,200
5	0.747	4.212	336,960
6	0.705	4.917	393,360
7	0.665	5.582	446,560
8	0.627	6.209	496,720
9	0.592	6.801	544,080
10	0.558	7.359	588,720
11	0.527	7.886	630,880
12	0.497	8.383	760,640
13	0.469	8.852	708,160
14	0.442	9.294	743,520
15	0.417	9.711	776,880
16	0.394	10.105	808,400
17	0.371	10.476	838,080
18	0.350	10.826	866,080
19	0.331	11.157	892,560
20	0.312	11.469	917,520
21	0.294	11.763	941,040
22	0.278	12.041	963,280
23	0.262	12.303	984,240
24	0.247	12.550	1,004,000
25	0.233	12.783	1,022,640

To Buy or Rent

We see that in the twenty-fourth year the rental stream of $80,000 per year is equivalent to the purchase price of $1,000,000. Thus, it takes about

---

[4]If the payments start at the beginning of the period, the first payment would be one dollar (N times), and we would add this to the series of numbers that are summed.

[5]Tabled values are available for different interest rates and time periods. See, for example, R. S. Burington, *Handbook of Mathematical Tables and Formulas*, 5th ed. (New York: McGraw-Hill Book Company, 1973). Such tables make present value analysis very easy.

24 years to balance the investment proposal. It is likely that the decision would be to rent, because a planning period of 24 years is quite long, and up to that time it is less expensive to rent the facility. A computing formula for the present value of a stream of payments at the end of the nth year is also available:

$$PV = N\left[\frac{(1 + r)^n - 1}{r(1 + r)^n}\right]$$

It is easy to use with pocket calculators, some of which are designed specifically to yield PV. This saves computing and adding each one of the stream of numbers. Let us carry our thinking one step further: if an infinite period of time is utilized ($n = \infty$), then the series of payments converges, so that the sum can be well approximated by N/r. Thus, for our example, the value of the payment stream over an infinite time period is

$$PV = \frac{N}{r} = \frac{\$80,000}{0.06} = \$1,333,333$$

If an infinite planning horizon had applied to the prior analysis, then it would have been better to invest $1 million.

If we acknowledge that a variety of possibilities exists for choosing the span of the discount period, what factors underlie an appropriate choice? In the case of the buy versus rent decision, one fundamental question is, How long will the purchased facility be utilized? A second important question is, When does the sum of the rental stream equal the purchase price? A third factor must also be considered, namely, What is the resale value of the purchased facility at the time that it will no longer be used?

> When the cost of the purchased facility less the discounted resale (at the nth year) is greater than the sum of the rental stream (for n years), we would prefer to rent.[6]

When they are equal, we might prefer to rent because uncertainties have not been taken into account, and renting allows us greater flexibility to change what we are doing. On the other hand, if an increase in rent might occur, our preference could switch to buying (or building).

An important corollary is that only products or services that *are very likely* to have a long mature stage in the market can justify large immediate expenditures for special-purpose equipment which has poor (if any) resale value. Further, because flow shop planning generally involves much longer term investment commitments than does job shop planning, the effects of discounting will be far more pronounced on flow shop decisions. With reference to our example, without discounting it would take only 12.5 years for the rental payments of $80,000 to equal the purchase price of $1,000,000 (i.e.,

---

[6]See pp. 414–16 for some numerical examples of discounting procedures.

1,000,000 ÷ 80,000 = 12.5). With discounting, it takes 24 years. Clearly, discounting works to the disadvantage of immediate purchase decisions except where a relatively long period of commitment to a facility can be made. And, as we have previously said, long-term commitments characterize the flow shop and not the job shop (nor the project). Discounting presents the truer picture for cash flow management.

Although life cycle management is concerned with the marketing stages of the company's products and services, we see that these marketing dimensions directly interact with financial planning for process decisions. Cash flow management balances the discounted income streams derived at the various stages of product and service life against the discounted purchase investments and streams of expenses that are incurred to support production, distribution, and sales.

The Payoff Period

Some organizations do not even use discounting when determining how long it will take to recover an investment, i.e. the payoff period. This is the length of time required before an investment pays for itself, that is, before it begins to produce additional capital for the company. If the computation of the payoff period is performed *without discounting*, we have

$$\text{Payoff period} = \text{investment/income per time period}$$

This straight computation, which ignores the discounting effect, will indicate a shorter period than would be obtained if discounting were used. Thus, for example, if the investment required for a new product or service is $630,000, and it is expected to produce an *income* stream of $80,000 per year, the payoff period (without discounting) would be

$$\frac{630,000}{80,000} = 7.9 \text{ years}$$

However, when discounting is taken into consideration, we can see (from Table 4-1) that a period of 11 years would be required for the investment to pay for itself. Generally speaking, it is advisable to utilize discounting for such computations. However, it must be pointed out that the payoff period will be critically affected by the choice of interest rate that is used. If a 5 percent rate per year is used, then less than 11 years would be required to pay off the investment. If the rate is 3 percent per year, then the result would be less than 10 years. If 10 percent per year is used, then about 16 years is required. (See Table 4-3.)

There is a variety of criteria that can be employed for investment decisions. The choice depends upon the life cycle character of the production output, and the process configuration. Thus, for example, we can describe 3 criteria for accepting an investment.

$$\frac{\text{Annual income stream}}{\text{Investment}} \geq r \qquad (4\text{-}1)$$

$$\frac{\text{Required income stream at present value for } n \text{ years}}{\text{Investment}} \geq 1 \qquad (4\text{-}2)$$

$$\frac{\text{Required income stream at present value for lifetime}}{\text{Investment}} \geq f \qquad (4\text{-}3)$$

where $f > 1$.

The first formulation is the inverse of the payoff period computation. It expresses the fact that the annual return on our investment must be equal to or greater than the interest rate that could be obtained by using an alternative investment. The planning period, in this case, is just one year. This criterion at best might be acceptable for short-term investments in batch production of the job shop.

The second formulation is based upon the selection of a period of time n. We require that the break-even point occur in the nth year. This criterion is appropriate for both job shops with standard items in inventory (not custom production) and for low-investment flow shops.

The third formulation represents the number of times that we would like the income stream to pay for a given investment over its lifetime. Here, the planning period is infinite. This criterion is appropriate for high-investment flow shops where mature products and services have long lifetimes.

Each criterion can result in different decisions. Production and operations management should be aware of the significance of the planning period and the investment criterion that is used. A consistent policy that is generally understood and agreed to by the participants of the company is a necessary requirement for successful operations.

The Difference between Products and Services

The differences between products and services is less than one might suppose. True, in general, products like food and toothpaste can be stored, whereas services like hotel rooms and the work of a carpenter can not be put in the cupboard. Nevertheless, all products have services built into them; this includes durable goods, such as typewriters and refrigerators, and consumables, such as shoes and cornflakes.

The production of goods does not necessarily require larger investments than the production of services. On the one hand, there is a class of service functions that is labor-intensive. Thus, an employment agency or a travel agency can have minimum investments and almost no fixed assets. On the other hand, many capital-intensive service organizations exist. For example, telephone companies, electric power utilities, airlines, hotels, railroads, and hospitals require sizable investments.

Upon careful consideration, it turns out that although there are differences between products and services, the differences are often unimportant for production and operations management planning. The differences within each category leading to alternative production configurations (project, flow shop, and job shop) will have greater influence on decision making, planning, and controlling. The difference between providing goods and services will have greater importance for marketing and distribution, and may even have an impact on the organizational characteristics and managerial style.

However, for production and operations management, the generality of the P/OM function emerges, and the paramount issue is how to configure the system and how to run it.

APPENDIX 4-I
Concerning Patents (Optional Material)

Monopolistic advantage is granted by the patent laws to those who qualify for patent protection. Not unexpectedly, the rules for qualification have changed over time in many ways, especially as a result of court interpretations. Patents, when granted, drastically change the life cycle character of a new product or service. Patents do this by completely altering the competitive environment.

The award of a patent raises the question of whether it might not be suitable to finance flow shop operations. If this competition-free situation provides a basis for realizing a large enough demand, then the patent holder can attract sufficient financing to insure a stable, profitable operation. However, there are many examples of patents that never achieve sufficient demand. This raises a question of whether the patent laws address the right questions. We shall not try to answer that here, but we shall take a look at some facts concerning patents.

The patent law (established in 1836) acts in two directions: (1) as a *reward* for research efforts and (2) as a *penalty* for imitating someone else's patented work even if that fact is unknown to the imitator.

The intention of the patent law[7] is to encourage the development of new ideas and the bringing of these ideas to fruition. The patent law is not arbitrary in its definition of fruition, but various court decisions over time have indicated that a degree of ambiguity exists in the interpretation of what this means. Nevertheless, it has always been intended that an individual or a company should be encouraged to develop new products and processes, and that

---

[7]This law was passed pursuant to the Congress' power under Article 1, Section 8, Clause 8, of the Constitution of the United States of America.

a degree of protection for a reasonable period of time should be given inventors so that their ideas and their work cannot be imitated by competitors.

Without the patent law there would be little incentive to spend large sums of money for the development of entirely new products and services. Usually, large expenditures of time and money are required to research and develop a new product. If a company, having had no expenditure of research funds, could copy someone else's idea and begin to produce it, then, in effect, the first company would be *subsidizing* the second company. This, in a competitive world, would be unlikely to happen to any company more than once. The imitators could put all their funds behind the promotion of their product. The innovator would have spent his money on research. The patent law is intended to protect the innovator. The record substantiates the fact that patents are not an academic issue. More than three million patents have been granted by the U. S. Patent Office—which is under the jurisdiction of the U.S. Department of Commerce. New additions are being made at the rate of approximately 1500 patents granted per week.[8]

Let us assume that two companies are both working on the same kind of product idea. Company A does not intend to investigate or obtain a patent, whereas Company B has taken all necessary steps to obtain patent protection. Company A is unaware of the fact that company B has a *patent pending*[9] that covers the new product developments of Company A. Therefore, Company A proceeds to produce this new item. Let us assume that the product is an instant success. Company A sells one million units in the first year. Meanwhile, Company B receives its patent on the product. Under some circumstances, Company B can sue Company A for *treble* damages. The triple damage claim, if upheld by the courts, can entitle a company which holds a patent that is infringed upon by another company to triple reimbursement on all losses sustained by that company as a result of the patent infringement. This is a *severe* penalty. It can drastically alter a company's financial solvency. In some cases it can produce bankruptcy.

Patents are granted for the invention of new machines, processes, and products for 17 years from the date that the patent is granted.[10] Design patents which are concerned with the style, ornamentation, and appearance of manufactured articles can be granted for $3\frac{1}{2}$, 7, or 14 years, as requested by the applicant.

Patent Search. The Patent Office maintains records of all patents that have been granted, and these are classified in a thorough fashion. The Patent Office publishes the *Manual of Classification*. It has more than 300 main classes, which are broken down into about 60,000 subclasses. (Copies of the Manual can be purchased from the U. S. Government Printing Office.) Further, on a weekly basis, the Patent Office issues the *Official Gazette* (OG).

---

[8]As of December, 1975.

[9]*Patent pending* means that the patent has been applied for and that the *formal papers* are on file in the Patent Office. The term has no effect in law.

[10]A patent is not renewable except by a Special Act of Congress.

means defining an opening in the flexible wall of the cartridge for receiving an actuator; and

a member positioned in the cartridge between the surface of the supply post and said flexible wall, said member being mounted for pivotal movement in response to the entry of the actuator into said opening between a first position and a second position and being effective when moved from its first position to its second position to flex said one wall outwardly and thereby expand the chamber, said member having a lever arm portion which is located between the opening and the supply post when the member is in its first position so that said lever arm portion is engageable by said actuator to effect movement of said member to its second position.

3,920,198
FILM CARTRIDGE
Robert C. Sutliff, Rochester, N.Y., assignor to Eastman Kodak Company, Rochester, N.Y.
Filed Apr. 30, 1974, Ser. No. 465,456
Int. Cl.² G03B *1/04*; G11B *15/32*
U.S. Cl. 242—194   9 Claims

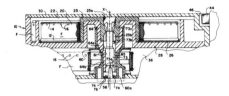

1. In a film cartridge including a supply ring in a supply chamber and a take-up core in a take-up chamber for use with a roll of film having a tendency to become stepped in the axial direction, the improvement comprising:

a control member which is axially moveable from a first, locking position in which said member prevents rotational movement of both the supply ring and the take-up core to a second, release position in which said control member permits rotation of both the supply ring and the take-up core, responsive to the film cartridge being inserted into a camera.

3,920,199
RATE-GYRO STABILIZED PLATFORM
William H. Woodworth, China Lake, and Marc L. Moulton, Ridgecrest, both of Calif., assignors to The United States of America as represented by the Secretary of the Navy, Washington, D.C.
Filed May 3, 1974, Ser. No. 466,564
Int. Cl.² F42B *15/02*
U.S. Cl. 244—3.2   4 Claims

1. In a rate-gyro controlled platform of a missile guidance system, a platform stabilizing network, comprising:

an electronically driven, gimbal mounted, rate-gyro stabilized platform on a supporting structure wherein the rate-gyro is electronically processed to provide an electrical output deviant from a value indicative of the spatial angular rate of change of the platform by a value indicative of the coulomb friction inherent in the gimbal bearings;

circuit means coupled to said output for providing an electrical signal definitive of said value indicative of the cou-

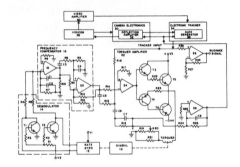

lomb friction, which signal can be used to compensate for said deviation.

3,920,200
PROJECTILE HAVING A GYROSCOPE
John L. Evans, Oakland; C. John DeCotiis, Cranford, and Victor P. Johnson, Fair Lawn, all of N.J., assignors to The Singer Company, Little Falls, N.J.
Filed Dec. 6, 1973, Ser. No. 422,253
Int. Cl.² F41G *7/00*
U.S. Cl. 244—3.16   10 Claims

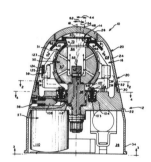

1. A projectile including,

a housing,

an optical tracker, and

a gyroscope disposed within said housing,

said housing having a nose section and a base section forming a chamber enclosing said tracker and said gyroscope, said nose section having a window,

said optical tracker having an optical lens unit and an image detector unit mounted on said gyroscope, said optical unit being arranged to receive an image through said window and to transmit the image to said image detector unit,

said gyroscope comprising,

a stator mounted on said base section within said chamber, said stator having a stator axis of symmetry,

a hollow rotor mounted on said stator for rotation relative to said stator about a spin axis, said rotor spin axis innersecting said stator axis of symmetry at a pivot point,

said stator having an outer surface of spherical shape having a center of sphericity disposed substantially coincident with said pivot point,

anti-friction means disposed between said stator outer surface and said rotor inner surface to permit relative angular movement between said rotor and said stator, said rotor having an outer surface of spherical shape which is

---

FIGURE 4-3. A typical page from the *Official Gazette* of the United States Patent and Trademark Office

The OG lists new patents that have been granted and permits keeping abreast of recent developments in a particular field, From the point of view of avoiding unnecessary litigation this can be most useful. In addition, "searching" can provide real stimulation for totally new ideas. The patent records, and in particular the more recent patents, represent an incredible compilation of creative case histories. Figure 4-3 illustrates a page of patent announcements as these disclosures are typically made in the *Official Gazette*.

The Patent Office has no responsibility for an unsuccessful search. That is to say, if a party overlooks a proper classification within which would be found an infringing patent, it is simply that party's hard luck. However, the Patent Office attempts in every way possible to assist the inventor. Searching is not an operation to be undertaken by the layman. A patent attorney trained in Patent Office classification and knowledge of court rulings is in a much better position to conduct such a search. Large companies usually employ patent attorneys for this purpose. Smaller companies and individuals can easily obtain the services of patent attorneys who, for reasonable fees, will undertake a thorough search. Should the search reveal a possible infringement of a patent, the patent attorney is usually in a position to advise his client or company on the prospects of continuing with the development of the product.

There is only one place where all U. S. patents are arranged by subject matter. This is the Public Search Room of the Patent Office in Washington, D.C. In addition, over 22 libraries, in various parts of the U.S.A., have numerically arranged sets of U.S. patents in bound books. To use these it is first necessary to locate the patents that might be of interest within the subclasses that are relevant. Over 300 libraries have bound volumes of the OG.

Protection of Originality Claim. The right to hold a patent begins with proof of originality. This means that the date of filing for a patent is not significant. It is most important to be able to prove the date when the idea of the invention was first conceived. It is also desirable to be able to prove the dates of written descriptions, blueprints and drawings, working prototypes, and operating tests. Witnesses to these dates are the most effective proof from the point of view of the courts. Thus, even though a patent may not be sought, a company should maintain adequate records of all inventions—properly attested to by witnesses—for its own self-protection.[11]

Working Model. At the time that the patent application is issued the Patent Office can insist that a prototype or working model be furnished with the patent application. This requirement is rarely exercised.

---

[11]As a service to inventors, the Office instituted the "Disclosure Document Program" under which the Office will accept and preserve documents for two years, which may be used as evidence of the dates of conception of inventions. The documents will be destroyed after two years unless they are referred to in related patent applications within the two-year period. Inventors have used various means to attempt to establish such dates, prior to the submission of their patent applications, for use as evidence in any further controversy. This has included the practice of mailing to themselves or to other persons registered envelopes containing disclosure statements.

Patent Application. In addition to the *Formal Papers*, which is primarily a petition for the patent, a description of the invention is required, called the *Specification*, and also an explicit definition of the invention called *Claims*. Drawings will be attached if they provide clarification. Skill is required to write the *Specification*. The description is supposed to be sufficiently clear so that an individual who is skilled in the particular area covered by the patent could construct the invention and utilize it.

Novelty. The patent courts have over the years interpreted the requirement of novelty in a variety of ways. The definition of novelty has varied from something that is a difference imposed on a basic theme to something that is entirely new. In any case, the claims that are made must distinguish the difference between the invention under consideration from all other efforts in this same area.

Utility. The patent law requires that a patentable invention should have utility. Here again semantic problems lead to interpretations which differ over time. It is difficult to determine what constitutes social utility. The issue that must be decided is how to determine what is useful for the public. Historically, the courts have exercised a great deal of influence in determining what utility is—specifically in terms of patent litigation.

Time Limitation. It might be expected that the granting of a patent should obligate the inventor to produce the item in question—in sufficient volume and within a reasonable period of time. After all, only in this way can the fruits of the patent reward be made available to the general public. Surprisingly, the interpretation of the court does not support this point of view.[12] Therefore, if a company obtains a patent on an invention which competes with its present product line, strictly with the intention of keeping it out of production and out of competitors' hands, this does not constitute a violation of the patent laws. There are court rulings that indicate some disposition to modify this position.[13]

---

[12]Chief Justice Stone, in a Supreme Court case construing the Federal Patent Statutes, indicated that prior Court decisions and the Constitution of the United States support the position that "failure of a patentee to make use of a patented invention does not affect the validity of a patent." (*Special Equipment Co.* vs. *Coe, Commissioner of Patents*, Supreme Court of the United States, 324 U.S. 370, 65 Sup. Ct. 741 [1945]).

In defining the nature of a patent grant, the Court stated, "the patent grant is not of a right to the patentee to use the invention, for that he already possesses. It is a grant of a right to exclude others from using it."

Mr. Justice Douglas, in a dissenting opinion, argues that to permit a patentee to suppress the use of one patent to enlarge its monopoly on another is contrary to the limited monopoly control permitted by legislative grace, a block in the development of technology, and irreconcilable with the purpose of the Constitution of the United States, "to promote the Progress of Science and useful Arts." (Art. 1, Sect, 8, Cl. 8.)

[13]In 1961, the U.S. Court of Appeals, 5th Circuit, speculated as follows: "In a close case the existence of a patent only on paper might tip the scale against holding of infringement." (*Edward Values Inc.* vs. *Cameron Iron Works, Inc.*, 286F. 2nd 939, [5th Cir. 1961].) (Note: This does not refer to the Commissioner of Patents with respect to the issuance of a patent.)

When the conditions stated by the patent law are fulfilled, a patent is granted. This guarantees protection in the general case for 17 years. Frequently, companies attempt to extend the period of protection beyond the 17-year period by a procedure that is known as "fencing in." In this case, the basic patent idea is divided into as many components as possible Patents are obtained, one at a time, on each of the component parts. Thus, at the end of the first 17-year period, a second basic notion is patented. The procedure is continued as long as possible. Another form of action with the same purpose is to patent a basic idea and then at a later time to patent improvements of the basic idea. Thus, when the basic idea becomes public property, the first improvement is protected. A company that attempts to produce the basic product without the improvement is operating at a competitive disadvantage which is likely to deter its entering the market.

Only people can obtain patents—not corporations. This means that when a company develops a new idea in its laboratory, the idea must be credited to an individual or individuals. The individuals apply for the patent. The company achieves protection by requiring that its employees sign an agreement—as a condition of employment—which states that all patents obtained by the employee as a result of his work with the company are to be *assigned* to the company by the employee (see Fig. 4-3). Difficulty can develop when a company contends that an individual who is no longer with the company has patented an idea which—it is claimed—was developed during employment with the company, using their facilities and resources. The seeds of a new idea are seldom clearcut.

To conclude, let us briefly analyze some trends. *First*, company size is increasingly correlated with the number of patents that the company holds. Consequently, larger companies hold a disproportionate share of patents. This trend can be explained by the enormous research facilities that are required, at present levels of knowledge, to come up with patentable inventions. *Second*, the percentage of patents granted each year by the U.S. Patent Office to foreign interests continues to grow. This is indicative of the fact that United States research efforts represent a decreasing percentage of world research efforts. *Third*, the emphasis of many companies has shifted from product improvement to cost savings. Also, energy conservation, and efforts to comply with governmental regulations concerning pollution control, food and drug testing requirements, unacceptable product ingredients, etc. have changed the focus of research and development with consequent alterations in the kinds of patent applications that are made.

The growth of international trade has highlighted another aspect of patent coverage. There is no fundamental reciprocity between nations with respect to patent protection. However, an expected outgrowth of the European Economic Community is a common patent system. It has been customary for U.S. companies to apply separately for patent protection in various countries. This is normally done when the company engages in export trade with these other nations. The Common Market policy would probably require only a single patent search and application to be made. The relationship of the U.S.

patent laws to those of the Common Market countries will have significant bearing on future production and operations management developments, both in the U.S. market and in the export trade.

There have been many signs that U.S. organizations are less interested in innovation than their public relations departments allow.[14] Still, life cycle management is much different when a broadly based patent has been obtained than when no patent protection exists at all. With patent protection there is time to build up the size of the market to a point that flow shop activities can be sustained. Viewed in this light, the holding of a patent not only protects against early growth-stage competitive actions but also allows the patent-holding organization to achieve a significant competitive advantage in production efficiency when the patent expires. In the same sense, process patents can offer one organization a flow shop capability that other organizations cannot obtain.

APPENDIX 4-II
Concerning R&D (Optional Material)

Research and development (R&D) are the critical creative functions responsible for initiating new products and services. Total government and industry spending for R&D in the U.S.A. during 1975 was about $34 billion. About 45 percent of this sum was R&D in industry, i.e., $15 billion. Of this $15 billion, less than 4 percent was spent on pure research.

Let us spell out the difference between pure and applied research. Pure research is a generator of ideas. It has no immediate or obvious utility, and is therefore, equatable to the pursuit of knowledge for the sake of knowledge. Pure research findings are equivalent to *new* knowledge. They form a base upon which creative applied research thinking can be launched.

In the laboratory, applied researchers devote their efforts to exploiting pure research results. Only large companies can afford to engage in substantial amounts of pure research. The investments are too large, the risks are major, and the payoff is usually many years away. At the same time, when the payoff is realized, it is frequently very substantial.

Applied research, with relatively immediate commercial advantages, is the major preoccupation of industry. Although this orientation provides short-term benefits, in the long run it leads to economic loss, in the sense of lost opportunities. Accordingly, there is constant social pressure on government to support pure research activities. Nevertheless, in constant dollars, government support of pure research has been decreasing. Also, on a per capita basis, many countries do more pure industrial research than the U.S.A.

Applied research is equivalent to finding ways to use knowledge about physical and social systems in a beneficial or profitable way. Development

---

[14]See, for example, Donald A. Schon, *Technology and Change* (New York: Delacorte Press, 1967).

accompanies applied research and is concerned with the actual application of the applied research to materials, equipment, and people. As we move to heavier involvement with development, an ever greater amount of production and operations management participation is required. Usually, close coordination of research and production personnel is expected during the development phase. We can literally define "development" by this involvement with operations managers.

The R&D function is of critical importance to life cycle management. Each idea forces its own demands in terms of time, money, and talent required to bring it to fruition. Understanding lab work is not a requirement for understanding the relationship of life cycle management and R&D. Similarly, knowledge of specific technology is not a requirement.

R&D is applicable to the service function. Thus, for example, hospital procedures are under constant reevaluation; information retrieval is an area of research that is profoundly affecting library procedures; telephone facilities are constantly being revamped, and the communication industry is one of the largest contributors to the total national research budget.

Some ideas will work and others will not. All R&D work does not succeed. Presumably, if talented people are employed who understand their field, there will be a greater chance of success. But the definition of what constitutes talent is not easy to come by. The use of psychological tests has shown no sign of pinpointing the requisite characteristics for ingenuity and creativity. However, as we proceed along the path from pure research to applied research and then to development, the kind of creativity that is required becomes less difficult to discuss. Also, the ability to forecast the time and effort that will be required to complete a project improves. (See the discussion of Norden's work, pp. 475–76).

Accordingly, it is easier to prepare development budgets than pure research budgets. Budget appropriation and control for R&D is one of the most difficult control areas in an organization. Because the outcome of pure research is essentially unknowable beforehand, the question of how much to allocate to which projects is almost unanswerable. The intangibility dissipates as we move toward and through development stages.

But in all R&D, estimates of time and cost are crucial matters. It has been found that schedules of time and cost for applied research and development are subject to a "slippage factor." Figure 4-4 compares predicted and actual results for the length of time required to complete a project—in terms of manpower allocations that are made. We see that the amount of manpower scheduled increases over a given period of time, then remains constant, and ultimately falls off sharply when the job is near completion. If PERT-type controls are lacking (see pp. 153–60),[15] the actual results seldom conform to the schedule. It takes significantly longer to complete the job than had originally been anticipated. Positive slippage occurs, often of as much as 50

---

[15]PERT-type project control can help alleviate the slippage problem, but it is less effective as the project includes more pure research and less development work.

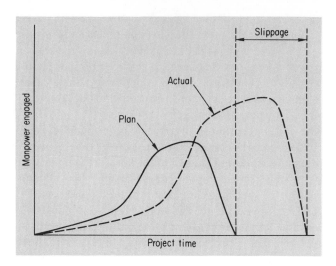

FIGURE 4-4. Typical manpower buildup and phasing out for development project

percent. Because of increased manpower requirements, costs are also much greater than had been anticipated.

Why does slippage occur so generally? It is reasonable to believe that at the beginning of a project the desire to excel in fulfilling the project's requirements causes people to take many more steps than they would permit at a later point when the pressure of a completion date is upon them. As time grows shorter, the project participants dispense with frills and special investigations and they begin to follow the original schedule. Finally, a crash program is undertaken—usually too late. The uniformity of slippage appears to confirm the fact that fundamental behavioral relations are involved.

PROBLEMS
1. Examine the situation of the compact car manufacturer discussed on p. 66. Assume that the price of compacts had risen so that full-size cars were not much more expensive than compacts. Why might this have happened? Consider this problem in terms of labor productivity, total productivity, and price elasticity.

2. What is the pattern of net cash flow of a municipality? Detail some of the major cash inflows and outflows and specify their timing. How does this pattern differ from that of a company selling a product such as toothpaste?

3. Is it likely that the cash flow pattern of a job shop is the same as that of a flow shop? Explain your answer.

4. Give an example of a product or service with which you are familiar that has gone through all 5 stages of the marketing evolution pictured in Fig. 4-1.

5. When would we be indifferent as to whether we should buy an automobile costing $3000 or lease its use at $180 per month? Assume an interest rate of 1 percent per month.

TABLE 4-2 TABLE OF PRESENT VALUES

$$(r = 0.12/\text{yr} = 0.01/\text{mo.})$$

n (months)	$\left(\dfrac{1}{1+0.01}\right)^n$	$\displaystyle\sum_{n=1}^{n}\left(\dfrac{1}{1+0.01}\right)^n$	n (months)	$\left(\dfrac{1}{1+0.01}\right)^n$	$\displaystyle\sum_{n=1}^{n}\left(\dfrac{1}{1+0.01}\right)^n$
1	0.9901	0.9901	13	0.8787	12.1337
2	0.9803	1.9704	14	0.8700	13.0037
3	0.9706	2.9410	15	0.8613	13.8651
4	0.9610	3.9020	16	0.8528	14.7179
5	0.9515	4.8534	17	0.8444	15.5623
6	0.9420	5.7955	18	0.8360	16.3983
7	0.9327	6.7282	19	0.8277	17.2261
8	0.9235	7.6517	20	0.8195	18.0456
9	0.9143	8.5660	21	0.8114	18.8570
10	0.9053	9.4713	22	0.8034	19.6604
11	0.8963	10.3676	23	0.7954	20.4559
12	0.8874	11.2551	24	0.7876	21.2434

6. Assume that a cosmetic manufacturer rushes many new product formulations into the marketplace knowing that most will just recover the initial investment within a year. Thereafter, they must be withdrawn or else they will begin to accumulate an increasing net loss for the company. The reason for this strategy is that about 1 out of 7 times, the new entry become highly profitable over at least a 2-year period. In cash flow terms, discuss what might be the best sequencing of new product releases. Make any other recommendations to management that might be appropriate.

7. Why is ROI regarded so highly by managers as an important measure of performance? In the same context, evaluate brand share, sales volume, and net profit.

8. Determine the present value of an income stream that is associated with a new product, where anticipated revenue changes as follows:

Years after Release	Revenue (*million* $)
1	0.2
2	0.5
3	1.2
4	1.8
5	2.0
6	1.0
7	0.6
8	0.0

(Use the table on p. 70. This assumes that a discounting factor of 0.06 per year is applicable.)

Answer: This is a straightforward problem using the methods described in the text. (See pp. 70–72.)

Year	Revenue (million $)	Discount Factor 6%	Present Worth (million $)
1	0.2	0.943	0.1886
2	0.5	0.890	0.4450
3	1.2	0.840	1.0080
4	1.8	0.792	1.4256
5	2.0	0.747	1.4940
6	1.0	0.705	0.7050
7	0.6	0.665	0.3990
8	0.0	0.627	0.0000
		Total Present Worth =	5.6652

9. Develop a table for $n = 1, \ldots 10$ and $\sum_{n=1}^{n} \left(\dfrac{1}{1 + 0.10} \right)^{n}$ similar in structure to the table for 0.06 shown on p. 70.

Answer: For the student's convenience, we present a table of present worth (for the value of one dollar at the end of n years) in terms of different discounting rates.

TABLE 4-3   TABLE OF CUMULATIVE PRESENT VALUES

$$\sum_{n=1}^{N}\left(\frac{1}{1+r}\right)^{n}$$

Interest Rate (r)

Year n	.030	.035	.040	.045	.050	.055	.060	.065	.070	.080	.090	.100	.110	.120
1	0.9709	0.9662	0.9615	0.9569	0.9524	0.9479	0.9434	0.9390	0.9346	0.9259	0.9174	0.9091	0.9009	0.8929
2	1.9135	1.8997	1.8861	1.8727	1.8594	1.8463	1.8334	1.8206	1.8080	1.7833	1.7591	1.7356	1.7125	1.6901
3	2.8286	2.8016	2.7751	2.7490	2.7233	2.6980	2.6730	2.6485	2.6244	2.5771	2.5313	2.4869	2.4438	2.4019
4	3.7171	3.6731	3.6299	3.5876	3.5460	3.5052	3.4652	3.4259	3.3873	3.3122	3.2398	3.1699	3.1025	3.0374
5	4.5797	4.5151	4.4519	4.3900	4.3295	4.2703	4.2124	4.1558	4.1003	3.9928	3.8897	3.7909	3.6960	3.6049
6	5.4172	5.3286	5.2422	5.1579	5.0758	4.9956	4.9174	4.8411	4.7667	4.6230	4.4860	4.3554	4.2307	4.1115
7	6.2303	6.1146	6.0021	5.8928	5.7865	5.6831	5.5825	5.4847	5.3894	5.2065	5.0331	4.8686	4.7124	4.5639
8	7.0197	6.8740	6.7328	6.5960	6.4633	6.3347	6.2099	6.0889	5.9715	5.7468	5.5350	5.3351	5.1463	4.9678
9	7.7861	7.6078	7.4354	7.2689	7.1080	6.9524	6.8019	6.6563	6.5154	6.2471	5.9955	5.7593	5.5373	5.3285
10	8.5303	8.3167	8.1110	7.9129	7.7219	7.5378	7.3603	7.1891	7.0238	6.7103	6.4179	6.1448	5.8895	5.6505
11	9.2527	9.0016	8.7606	8.5291	8.3066	8.0928	7.8871	7.6893	7.4990	7.1393	6.8055	6.4954	6.2068	5.9380
12	9.9541	9.6634	9.3852	9.1188	8.8635	8.6188	8.3841	8.1590	7.9430	7.5364	7.1611	6.8140	6.4927	6.1947
13	10.6350	10.3029	9.9858	9.6831	9.3938	9.1174	8.8530	8.6001	8.3805	7.9041	7.4873	7.1037	6.7502	6.4239
14	11.2962	10.9207	10.5633	10.2231	9.8989	9.5900	9.2953	9.0142	8.7459	8.2446	7.7866	7.3671	6.9823	6.6286
15	11.9380	11.5176	11.1186	10.7398	10.3800	10.0379	9.7126	9.4031	9.1084	8.5599	8.0611	7.6065	7.1913	6.8113
16	12.5612	12.0943	11.6525	11.2343	10.8381	10.4626	10.1063	9.7682	9.4471	8.8519	8.3130	7.8242	7.3796	6.9744
17	13.1662	12.6515	12.1659	11.7075	11.2744	10.8650	10.4777	10.1111	9.7638	9.1222	8.5441	8.0220	7.5493	7.1202
18	13.7536	13.1899	12.6596	12.1603	11.6900	11.2465	10.8281	10.4330	10.0597	9.3724	8.7562	8.2019	7.7021	7.2502
19	14.3239	13.7101	13.1343	12.5937	12.0858	11.6081	11.1587	10.7353	10.3362	9.6042	8.9507	8.3655	7.8398	7.3663
20	14.8776	14.2127	13.5907	13.0084	12.4627	11.9509	11.4705	11.0191	10.5947	9.8188	9.1292	8.5141	7.9639	7.4700
21	15.4152	14.6983	14.0295	13.4052	12.8217	12.2758	11.7647	11.2856	10.8362	10.0175	9.2929	8.6493	8.0757	7.5626
22	15.9371	15.1674	14.4515	13.7849	13.1635	12.5838	12.0422	11.5359	11.0620	10.2014	9.4431	8.7722	8.1763	7.6452
23	16.4438	15.6207	14.8573	14.1483	13.4891	12.8757	12.3041	11.7709	11.2729	10.3718	9.5809	8.8839	8.2671	7.7190
24	16.9357	16.0587	15.2474	14.4960	13.7992	13.1524	12.5511	11.9915	11.4701	10.5295	9.7073	8.9854	8.3488	7.7849
25	17.4134	16.4819	15.6226	14.8288	14.0946	13.4146	12.7841	12.1987	11.6544	10.6756	9.8233	9.0777	8.4224	7.8438
26	17.8771	16.8907	15.9833	15.1472	14.3759	13.6632	13.0039	12.3932	11.8266	10.8108	9.9297	9.1617	8.4887	7.8963
27	18.3273	17.2857	16.3301	15.4519	14.6437	13.8989	13.2113	12.5759	11.9876	10.9360	10.0274	9.2380	8.5485	7.9432
28	18.7643	17.6674	16.6636	15.7435	14.8989	14.1222	13.4070	12.7474	12.1380	11.0519	10.1169	9.3073	8.6023	7.9851
29	19.1887	18.0361	16.9843	16.0226	15.1418	14.3339	13.5916	12.9084	12.2786	11.1593	10.1991	9.3704	8.6508	8.0225
30	19.6007	18.3924	17.2926	16.2896	15.3732	14.5346	13.7657	13.0596	12.4100	11.2587	10.2745	9.4277	8.6945	8.0559

TABLE 4-4 TABLE OF PRESENT VALUES

$$\left(\frac{1}{1+r}\right)^n$$

Year n	Interest Rate (r) .030	.035	.040	.045	.050	.055	.060	.065	.070	.080	.090	.100	.110	.120
1	0.9709	0.9662	0.9615	0.9569	0.9524	0.9479	0.9434	0.9390	0.9346	0.9259	0.9174	0.9091	0.9009	0.8929
2	0.9426	0.9335	0.9246	0.9157	0.9070	0.8985	0.8900	0.8817	0.8735	0.8574	0.8417	0.8265	0.8116	0.7972
3	0.9151	0.9019	0.8890	0.8763	0.8638	0.8516	0.8396	0.8279	0.8163	0.7939	0.7722	0.7513	0.7312	0.7118
4	0.8885	0.8714	0.8548	0.8386	0.8227	0.8072	0.7921	0.7773	0.7629	0.7351	0.7084	0.6830	0.6588	0.6355
5	0.8626	0.8420	0.8219	0.8025	0.7835	0.7652	0.7473	0.7299	0.7130	0.6806	0.6500	0.6210	0.5935	0.5675
6	0.8375	0.8135	0.7903	0.7679	0.7462	0.7253	0.7050	0.6854	0.6664	0.6302	0.5963	0.5645	0.5347	0.5067
7	0.8131	0.7860	0.7599	0.7348	0.7107	0.6875	0.6651	0.6435	0.6228	0.5835	0.5471	0.5132	0.4817	0.4524
8	0.7894	0.7594	0.7307	0.7032	0.6769	0.6516	0.6274	0.6043	0.5820	0.5403	0.5019	0.4665	0.4340	0.4039
9	0.7664	0.7337	0.7026	0.6729	0.6446	0.6177	0.5919	0.5674	0.5440	0.5003	0.4605	0.4241	0.3910	0.3606
10	0.7441	0.7089	0.6756	0.6440	0.6139	0.5855	0.5584	0.5328	0.5084	0.4632	0.4224	0.3856	0.3522	0.3220
11	0.7224	0.6850	0.6496	0.6162	0.5847	0.5549	0.5268	0.5002	0.4751	0.4289	0.3876	0.3505	0.3173	0.2875
12	0.7014	0.6618	0.6246	0.5897	0.5569	0.5260	0.4970	0.4697	0.4441	0.3972	0.3556	0.3187	0.2859	0.2567
13	0.6810	0.6394	0.6006	0.5643	0.5304	0.4986	0.4689	0.4411	0.4150	0.3677	0.3262	0.2897	0.2575	0.2292
14	0.6611	0.6178	0.5775	0.5400	0.5051	0.4726	0.4423	0.4141	0.3879	0.3405	0.2993	0.2634	0.2320	0.2046
15	0.6419	0.5969	0.5553	0.5167	0.4810	0.4480	0.4173	0.3889	0.3625	0.3153	0.2746	0.2394	0.2090	0.1827
16	0.6232	0.5767	0.5339	0.4945	0.4581	0.4246	0.3937	0.3651	0.3388	0.2919	0.2519	0.2177	0.1883	0.1631
17	0.6050	0.5572	0.5134	0.4732	0.4363	0.4025	0.3714	0.3429	0.3166	0.2703	0.2311	0.1979	0.1697	0.1457
18	0.5874	0.5384	0.4937	0.4528	0.4156	0.3815	0.3504	0.3219	0.2959	0.2503	0.2120	0.1799	0.1528	0.1301
19	0.5703	0.5202	0.4747	0.4333	0.3958	0.3616	0.3306	0.3023	0.2765	0.2317	0.1945	0.1635	0.1377	0.1161
20	0.5537	0.5026	0.4564	0.4147	0.3769	0.3428	0.3118	0.2838	0.2585	0.2146	0.1785	0.1487	0.1241	0.1037
21	0.5376	0.4856	0.4389	0.3968	0.3590	0.3249	0.2942	0.2665	0.2416	0.1987	0.1637	0.1352	0.1118	0.0926
22	0.5219	0.4692	0.4220	0.3797	0.3419	0.3080	0.2775	0.2502	0.2258	0.1840	0.1502	0.1229	0.1007	0.0827
23	0.5067	0.4533	0.4058	0.3634	0.3256	0.2919	0.2618	0.2350	0.2110	0.1703	0.1378	0.1117	0.0907	0.0738
24	0.4919	0.4380	0.3901	0.3477	0.3101	0.2767	0.2470	0.2206	0.1972	0.1577	0.1264	0.1015	0.0817	0.0659
25	0.4776	0.4232	0.3751	0.3328	0.2953	0.2623	0.2330	0.2072	0.1843	0.1460	0.1160	0.0923	0.0736	0.0588
26	0.4637	0.4089	0.3607	0.3184	0.2813	0.2486	0.2198	0.1945	0.1722	0.1352	0.1064	0.0839	0.0663	0.0525
27	0.4502	0.3950	0.3468	0.3047	0.2679	0.2356	0.2074	0.1827	0.1610	0.1252	0.0976	0.0763	0.0598	0.0469
28	0.4371	0.3817	0.3335	0.2916	0.2551	0.2234	0.1957	0.1715	0.1504	0.1159	0.0896	0.0694	0.0538	0.0419
29	0.4244	0.3688	0.3207	0.2790	0.2430	0.2117	0.1846	0.1610	0.1406	0.1074	0.0822	0.0631	0.0485	0.0374
30	0.4120	0.3563	0.3083	0.2670	0.2314	0.2007	0.1741	0.1512	0.1314	0.0994	0.0754	0.0573	0.0437	0.0334

five
premarket and
in-market
production stages

Every product or service must go through the 3 premarket production stages I-A, B, C. These are the preparations required of P/OM before the in-market production stages II-A, B can begin.

I-A   Product and Service Development (Fig. 5-1)
I-B   Process Development (Fig. 5-2)
I-C   Implementation of Operations (Fig. 5-3)
II-A   Operating the System
II-B   Redesigning the Process

We develop a pictorial view of each premarket production stage to explore its characteristics and to learn the involvement of P/OM. Figures 5-1, 5-2, and 5-3 show sequences of activities that are typical of product systems. Without major revision, they could be converted to apply to service systems.

Feasibility Analysis

Our diagrams are PERT-type charts that are now constantly employed by project managers. We shall deal at length with the technical aspects of using PERT charts for project management (see pp. 143–70). However, at this time, we employ the diagrams simply to describe a sequence of activities appropriate for determining the feasibility of the premarket production stages.

Figure 5-1 traces out many of the steps that are critical to the successful *development of new products and services* (Stage I-A). Starting with ④ in

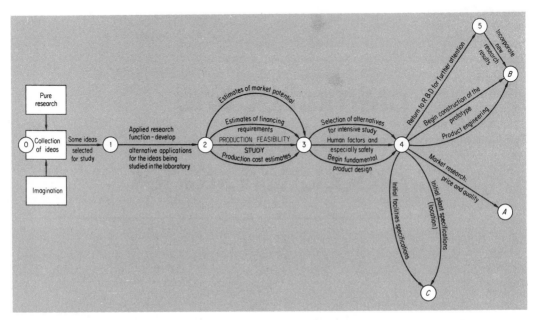

FIGURE 5-1. Model PERT network for the design of a production system: Stage I-A-product and service development

Fig. 5-1 and including most of the paths of Fig. 5-2, we find that the considerations usually required for feasibility analysis of a new product or service appear in the diagram. Feasibility studies are essential to all production and operations management. They start early in the planning process (note ② to ③) and are continued at increasing levels of depth throughout the premarket period of activity. They are responsible for go/no go determinations for the entire activity as well as for parts of it. They lead to major and minor revisions of plans.

Feasibility studies for flow shops (and major projects) are pursued with much greater vigor than those of job shops. This is because the cost of errors in planning the flow shop (and major projects) can be enormous and they are often impossible to correct. This is not generally so for the job shop.

The new product or service can originate with a combination of ideas and research, ⓪ and ①. Not infrequently, the stimulus is a competitive development. The intention is to produce a copy (or "me too" version) of the competitor's product or service. If the originator has no patent protection, the imitator often can benefit substantially by obtaining a reasonable market share without having to invest heavily in research and development. On the other hand, whoever is first to enter the market has distinct advantages.

These notions should be understood by production and operations managers. They explain why financial managers may seem to withhold support from major new undertakings, waiting for competitors to underwrite development costs and test market responses. Conversely, they also explain why marketing managers request unreasonable production delivery schedules in order to assure being first in the marketplace. The key to success is communication of objectives and coordination of efforts between P/OM, financial management, and marketing management. With the above in mind, the activities in Fig. 5-1 speak for themselves.

Figure 5-2 provides network representation for Stage I-B, which is *process development*. Two critical activities should be amplified. The first, test marketing (note Ⓐ → ⑩), is the main premarket activity of marketing. Production must supply sample goods and services in ample quantities to be tested. But this results in a quandary, which is, How can you supply production output to be tested when the production facility is not in place—and,

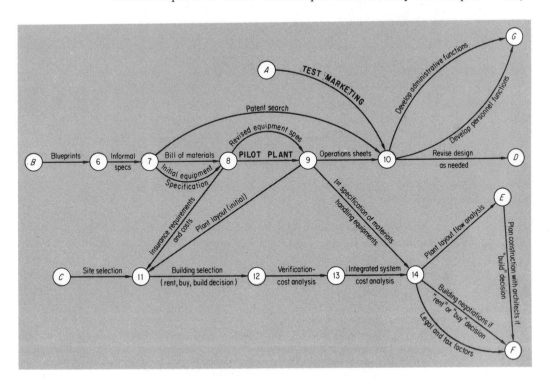

FIGURE 5-2. Model PERT network for the design of a production system: Stage I-B-process development

conversely, how can custom-made output stand in for the real thing so that test market results are credible?[1]

Often, to resolve this dilemma, a pilot plant (note ⑧ → ⑨) is built. The pilot plant is a small-scale copy of the eventual production process. More realistic costs of production can be obtained by using the pilot plant than from custom-made output. Consequently, better pricing strategies can be tested. Also, the output samples bear a reasonable degree of likeness to the actual output of the finalized, full-scale production system.

In Fig. 5-3 we see the third stage of our premarket production activities, called *implementation of operations*. These third-stage steps represent the

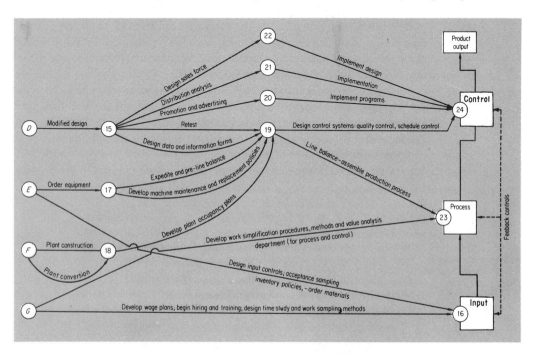

FIGURE 5-3. Model PERT network for the design of a production system: Stage I-C—implementation of operations

activities required to actualize the decisions made in prior stages. Beginning with events D, E, F, and G, the components of the actual facility are assembled and set up in working order. Thus, the end product of the overall planning sequence is the operating system, ⑯ → ㉓ → ㉔. Once assembled, the system must be operated as in Stage II-A. Throughout this book, references will be found to the various activities shown in these PERT diagrams.[2] The

---

[1]The problem is more serious for the flow shop than for the job shop, because the flow shop entails much greater investments. Nevertheless, even in the job shop, significant expenditures may be required, for example, specially trained individuals, costly tools and dies, and materials that cannot be purchased in small quantities.

[2]Almost all of the activities shown in Figs. 5-2 and 5-3 will be explained at some point in the text.

PERT chart is of real informational utility when it comes to providing organization and understanding of many activities. Of course, each activity requires much further clarification and explanation.

The Design of Products and Services

New product or new service development begins with a collection of ideas. Some of these are chosen for further study. Various ways of converting ideas into applications are investigated in the laboratory. Promising alternatives must be checked for such factors as their production feasibility—in a technological sense—production costs, financing requirements, and possible prices and qualities related to marketability. In addition, the human factors concerned with both product and process are considered from various points of view, including attractiveness, ease of use, and safety. From the alternatives, one or more possibilities are selected for further study because of encouraging evaluations. Design is begun in earnest, and a basic decision is reached concerning the product or service design. Thus begins the developmental phase. Occasionally, research is requested for further help and guidance.

Product development requires product engineering, which includes detailed cost specification, the beginning of intensive market research, and the inception of plant and facilities specification. At this point we reach a boundary between product and process development. It is not that the product development phase is finished. Rather, it is *integrated* with the further specification of the process.

Service development frequently requires many of the same steps. Office outputs, for example, should be designed and checked in various ways to verify that they are serving the intended purpose—before the office process is installed. In designing the office, the question arises as to whether it will be essentially a job shop or a flow shop office. Mail order companies, for example, have most of the clerical work so thoroughly routinized that these activities practically constitute a flow shop. As another example, a steamship line must design its output, that is, how much cargo, how many passengers, what kind of cargo, and what kind of service to passengers? How else can the process be designed? The facilities must be developed so that they can provide the specified services.

Prototypes, Pilot Plants, and Test Markets

An important and exciting phase of the development process for products occurs when the output design prototype is made. This is a highly developed model, intended to embody most of the significant characteristics that will be found in the final production line item. Many kinds of prototypes are used. For example, the prototype of an automobile is frequently made of clay. It is a model of the chassis, intended to reveal the styling and appearance of the automobile so that it can be evaluated on a visual basis.

A separate, hand-tooled model of the engine and other moving parts of the system will also be required. At a still later stage, a hand-crafted automobile will be developed that represents a total assembly as it will eventually come from the production line.

Prototypes must be evaluated with care. It is well known to engineers that a reduction in scale can produce certain observable behaviors that do not accurately describe the performance of the intended, final system. When possible, engineers transform the results obtained from experiments with scale models to overcome the inherent distortions. The same kind of thinking should be applied to all prototypes. Differences in physical size must be properly rationalized as they affect performance. Scaled-down energy inputs and outputs may not behave in *linear* proportion to the full-scale system. Materials aging experiments require a reduction of time, as do most fatigue tests, but the effects of artificially compressing time must be completely understood if the prototype is to be used to predict the performance of the full-scale unit operating in real time. Even for styling and appearance, the scaled-down prototype can mislead design judgment.

In the case of a process (for example, a chemical plant) an advanced prototype will take the form of a *pilot plant*. This pilot plant is a scaled-down model of the final plans for the processing unit. It is similar to the final unit in all respects, but on a reduced scale. Pilot plants may involve expenditures of millions of dollars. In such cases, they usually represent models of full-scale units that cost *hundreds of millions* of dollars. If the pilot plant produces negative results, then the plans can be reworked or discarded. The purpose of a pilot plant is to spend a *relatively* small sum of money in order to avoid far larger penalties that could occur if such precautions were not taken.

Since prototypes must be evaluated with care, a *test market* is often set up and supplied with sample production output. It is difficult to design a test marketing situation that incorporates all relevant features existing in the full-scale market. However, by using statistical sampling theory, a reasonable approximation often can be obtained.* A group of people is chosen in the belief that their behavior will approximate the behavior that will be found on a national scale. The test market may be divided into 2 parts on a *matched sample* basis. That is, 2 areas are chosen, supposedly identical and each representing the full market. Both areas are given different alternatives (e.g., taste formulations and package designs) to evaluate. In this way, it

---

*See, for example, Frederick F. Stephan and Philip J. McCarthy, *Sampling Opinions—An Analysis of Survey, Procedures* (New York: John Wiley & Sons, Inc., 1958), and William G. Cochran, *Sampling Techniques*, 2nd ed. (New York: John Wiley & Sons, Inc., 1963).

is possible to obtain information concerning which design alternative is likely to be the most acceptable.

Prototypes, test markets, and pilot plants represent a boundary where research and development, production, finance, and marketing all come together in a crucial *test situation.* Production and operations managers must be thoroughly familiar with the use of such methods for testing technological feasibility, market reactions, and estimates of production costs. Only in this way is it possible to reduce uncertainty before major financial commitments are made. The costs of testing alternative actions can be figured in terms of direct expenditures, which should always be matched against the costs of not conducting such tests (i.e., the penalties of making serious mistakes).

Process Design

Parts 3, 4, and 5 are devoted to problems and issues involved in the operation of projects, flow shops, and job shops, respectively. The efficiency of operations is dependent upon the design of the processes of which they are a part. Therefore, at this point, we wish to generalize about the life-cycle properties and broad systems characteristics of process design.

First, the product line or service mix should be created with the process design in mind. Each should be successively altered (iterative thinking being used) until a best combination is achieved. Iterative thinking is repetitive analysis of a sequence of steps aimed at converging on an acceptable solution. In this case, product or service determines process, which then alters the initial output specifications, leading to further changes in process design, etc. For example, the cost of producing a flashlight battery by a flow shop method is determined to be too high to support the demand required to absorb the flow shop volume. Consequently, a change in design of the battery is proposed, but this change requires an alteration in the process, etc. The use of the systems approach for product/process design can pay off handsomely for the extra work involved.

Second, process design must ultimately deal with every detail of *what* is to be done, *how*, *when*, and *where*. Such detailed study is essential for products. Nothing will occur until a decision has been made for every activity, step by step, that is physically required to produce output. The same requirement cannot always be levied for service systems, where it is often harder to pin down exactly what service is to be rendered. This aspect of designing service systems is especially true when people play an important part in the service process (for example, bank tellers, store checkout clerks, airline reservation personnel, and fast-food order takers). Therefore, before a new service is launched, special stress should be placed on achieving as totally a detailed a description of service elements as is possible.

Third, much greater effort can be justified in designing flow shop processes than can be warranted for designing even relatively high-volume batch jobs in the generalized job shop. Process design goes on continuously in the job shop as new orders are received. Each new job shop order requires some set of operations that can be sequenced together from the modular productive capabilities of the general-purpose equipment on the job shop floor.

Process design and development occur during the premarketing stages of the life cycles of products and services. In conjunction with designing production output, the task is systems-oriented and requires coordination with marketing, finance, etc. Through implementation (Stage I-C) we achieve an operating production process (Stage II-A) that produces the right outputs (i.e., there is demand for them) with high productivity.

Running a system takes one kind of talent. Designing and building the system calls upon another set of talents. *This is the big challenge.* After all, what can be said to be good practice is based upon past practice. Knowledge acquired by experience is that portion of reality which ". . . we partly may compute."[3] But every now and then, the chance to do something in a *new* way appears. No history or easily identified precedent exists for it. The inferences required for assurance cannot be justified. Perhaps others have also seen this possibility, "but know not (the result of) what's resisted."[3]

Success in the design phase prohibits fractionation, segmentation, or splintering the system. Decisions reached in false isolation are the main danger that we face. To help prevent overlooking potentially critical aspects, a number of questions relevant to the design process are raised below.

The list is intended to illustrate the great variety of issues that should be considered in one way or another. Many decisions are not consciously made, and the resulting activities occur by default. Further, the list reveals the interrelationships that bind decisions together, so that a conclusion on one point removes the possibility of deciding about another. It is also evident that some questions are broad while others are narrow. The level of detail should move from the broad to the narrow, so that a decision on detail does not block the possibility of achieving the best solution to a major consideration. The answer to any one of these should involve the total system. Through *synthesis,*[4] a process design of real excellence can emerge.

With Respect to the Output

1. Why has this output been chosen? (Should there be one or more outputs?)
2. Are the attributes of the output completely specified? To what extent are they unique?

---

[3]"What's done we partly may compute. But know not what's resisted." From address to the Unco Guild by Robert Burns, Scotland, circa 1780.
[4]See p. 36.

3. If they are unique, why has no other company done this before?

4. Why does the opportunity exist? (For how long has it existed?)

5. Are the estimates that underlie the choice of the specified output accurate and believable? (Is there consensus on this point?)

6. How will the output be distributed and by whom?

7. How will quality be assessed and assured?

8. How does the production schedule relate to anticipated demands?

9. What mechanisms and policies have been set up for production schedule control?

10. Have proper steps been taken with respect to patent protection?

With Respect to Manpower

11. What are the manpower requirements?

12. Are there trade-offs to be considered between men and machines?

13. Is the relationship between men and machines likely to change because of technological factors? (Alternatively, when will it change?)

14. What are the expected productivities, and what are the commensurate costs?

15. Have the patterns of work been thoroughly studied?

With Respect to Materials

16. Can the choices of input materials be thoroughly justified?

17. Are these choices likely to change because of technological factors?

18. Have all subcontracting possibilities been considered?

19. Are there alternative sources for the same materials? (Have discounts been considered?)

20. Have adequate inventory management policies been developed?

With Respect to the Process

21. What specific equipment and facilities will be needed? (What is available?)

22. How adequately have sources of equipment supply been investigated?

23. How accurately have equipment costs and productivity been estimated?

24. What equipment capacities and sizes have been estimated for the process?

25. What space requirements have been determined for the total process?

26. Is the plant layout based on short- or long-term assumptions?

27. What kind of maintenance should be used—preventive or remedial?

28. How much maintenance will be required? (Has this been considered with respect to equipment selection?)

29. What are the in-process inventory storage requirements? (Do they fluctuate?)

30. Can the process flow that has been designed be totally justified? How flexible and amenable to change are the lines of flow?

31. Is the basis for materials-handling equipment decisions short- or long-term?

32. Have equipment setup times been accurately estimated?

With Respect to Location

33. Has consideration been given to both supply of input materials and demand for output products in locating a plant site?

34. Has the cost of studying the plant location or relocation problem been considered?

35. Have insurance rates and taxes been determined with respect to plant selection?

36. Have the costs, availability, and apparent skills of labor been compared for the various location possibilities? (Has equipment selection been made with this in mind?)

37. What importance have transportation problems and shipping costs played in reaching a location decision? (Can the basis for decision change?)

38. What zoning restrictions and town or state ordinances exist that might affect the location decision? [Do (water, air, noise, etc.) pollution considerations deserve attention?]

39. How available and costly will utility services be, such as sewage, water, oil, gas, heat, and electricity? (Will process demands be stable or grow?)

40. Have incorporation fees and procedures been considered?

41. Has the cost of shutting down and moving been taken into account?

42. What consideration has been given to long-run land values?

43. Have the effects of inflation been taken into account?

44. Have building costs been properly compared with plant purchase and plant rentals?

45. Should climate have any influence on the location decision?

46. Has there been a thorough evaluation of specific site factors, including drainage, exposure, and so forth? (Has ecological impact been evaluated?)

47. What lot dimensions will be required? Has room for expansion been provided?

48. What internal space divisions have been determined?

49. Is a railroad siding a necessary feature? How many floors should the building have?

50. What colors will be used for walls, ceilings, floors, and machines? Have the illumination needs been properly assessed?

51. What construction materials will be used? Who will control the construction schedule?

52. Has the effect of decisions on competitors been properly surveyed?

53. Have all relevant questions been asked? Have all these questions been answered?

54. Is the chosen course of action the best possible way to proceed?

Implementation is greatly facilitated by the use of project management methods which help to organize and schedule all necessary activities and which provide awareness of what is happening as well as controls to rectify problems as they develop. A further requisite is agreement concerning strategies and goals among all managers participating in the implementation process.

Implementing (I-C) the Operating System (II-A)

When the production system is ready to go, most of the fixed costs are already committed. Distribution channels have been secured, and marketing has either started to massively communicate with potential consumers or it is about to do so. In some cases, especially job shop systems, it is possible to let the production system grow in stages, e.g., first distribute the product or service in the Northeast; then (if successful after 6 months) expand to the Midwest, etc. With the flow shop, such stepwise planning is often inefficient. Assessment of competitive actions is essential in all cases to provide strategic timing for actions. Cash flow should be mapped out in accordance with the dynamics of life cycle estimates.

We plan a production system down to the finest possible details of operations. Then we implement our plans. This is a *PROJECT*. When reading Part 3 on Project Management, bear in mind that one of the most important projects is that of designing and implementing any type of production system.

Designing and implementing the production system is one distinct responsibility of production and operations management. Running the system (operating the production process) is a second, distinct type of activity.

Operating the production system means controlling the input/process/output (see node 24 in the PERT network of Fig. 5-3, p. 90). Control is exercised in line with predetermined policies and standards of performance. Productivity must be monitored continuously. Schedules of operations are designed to deliver the desired quantity of product or service output with specific quality levels.

Redesigning the Process (II-B)

The design of products or services can often be changed during their lifetimes by making minor modifications in their processes. This is less true for the flow shop than for the job shop, but it still applies to some extent. The alteration of product or service (called *restaging* when accompanied by changes in marketing strategies) often is needed because of competitive actions. New tools and fixtures, retraining of personnel, and different inventories and equipment can be required, according to the case. In some instances, the extent of change may be nothing more than printing the word "new" on the package.

If flow shop design is the basic configuration, there is less flexibility to make large changes. It is more important for the flow shop than for the job shop, therefore, that the question of what changes might someday be called for be carefully considered and that the original process design allow for them to be achieved. The job shop, on the other hand, is well suited for product or service redesign, since its facilities are general purpose (meaning that they were chosen to be as adaptable as possible for varied production outputs).

Consequently, we find yet another criterion for deciding between the flow shop and job shop. If no changes of consequence are anticipated for the output, or if changes can be predicted that are feasible to allow for in the process design, then the flow shop configuration cannot be eliminated on this score. As the importance of change *increases*, and as the lack of ability to predict what that change might be *increases*, the desirable process configuration moves toward ever greater degrees of job shop flexibility.

PROBLEMS

1. What activities would you convert (and how) to make Figs. 5-1, 5-2, and 5-3 (pp. 88–90) applicable to service systems instead of product systems?

2. How does the market research activity ④ → Ⓐ in Fig. 5-1 concern P/OM? In many organizations, whatever market research is done is unknown to the production department. Does this make sense? Explain. *Answer:* Market research provides answers concerning the qualities of goods and services that people prefer, and the prices that they are willing to pay to obtain these qualities. P/OM can determine the per unit cost advantages of different production systems configurations. Thus, it is essential to know the production cost and quality capabilities before reaching any decision. Consequently, it is a weak managerial system that does not include P/OM inputs when designing the market research questionnaire as well as when analyzing the survey results.

3. What is meant by the statement, "The product line or service mix should be created with the process design in mind"? In this context, explain the use of iterative thinking.

4. The use of seat belts in cars decreases the severity of accidents. Another study indicates that the use of seat belts increases the number of accidents —as a result of increased confidence of drivers who take chances they would not otherwise accept because they are aware of the protection provided by seat belts.

   At an executive meeting (topic: auto design) you are asked to comment on this finding, providing the viewpoint of P/OM.

5. Smoking filtered, low-tar cigarettes should decrease the risk of cancer. There is evidence of the logic of this statement. However, a recent study has shown that smokers of filtered, low-tar cigarettes (feeling more confident that they are safer with these cigarettes) puff more often and inhale more deeply. As a result, their statistical cancer risk has increased. Another recent study indicates that smokers of low-tar cigarettes smoke more cigarettes in order to obtain the same amount of nicotine that they formerly got from regular cigarettes. Thus, their statistical cancer risk has increased.

   At an executive meeting (topic: cigarette product-line design) you are asked to comment on these findings, providing the viewpoint of P/OM.

6. What is the relation of the implementation of a product or service marketing strategy to P/OM?

   Answer: The production facility may not be able to provide quality and/or quantity in line with the expectations of marketing. For example, there have been real situations where the demand has been far too great. Production could not supply the required output volume. Consequently, distribution dried up and demand dropped off permanently. In other cases, output volume requirements have been met but quality was inconsistent. Sometimes costs are high, forcing up prices. Coordination is essential if marketing plans are to be backed up by P/OM capabilities.

7. What kind of pilot plants might be appropriate for
   a. Public transportation systems?
   b. A chain of new hotels?
   c. Fast-food franchisers?
   d. The cosmetic manufacturer?

8. Name some of the pros and cons of using test marketing for each of the systems listed in Problem 7. Explain how test marketing can affect pilot plants and vice versa.

six
the economic advantages of variety

One of the fundamental design questions that management must resolve is what variety of products or services to supply. Given that the strategic answers have been reached in this regard, then various design possibilities exist, and there is real opportunity for introducing consumer choice variety into the line of goods and services offered. Variety has marketing advantages and several economic production benefits as well. The first production benefit is related to the manner in which production capacity is used and the consequent economic utilization of resources. This is the subject we shall be discussing next, where the product-service-mix problem is treated by means of linear programming. The second production benefit stems from high-volume production of certain components or ingredients that are used in as many end products as possible. Such modular production (see pp. 186–89) allows the benefits of flow shop operations to be realized.

Life cycle management involves juggling back and forth between production and marketing questions. Financial goals and constraints are always in the picture. This can be seen very clearly by considering the problem in the box.

> ### What Is Linear Programming?
>
> Linear programming (LP) is a quantitative method for allocating resources. It is widely used by P/OM. A single objective such as profit *or* sales volume is maximized (or if cost, it is minimized).
>
> The objective is achieved by determining how much output of each different kind should be made. Thus, make 200 As, 150 Bs, 30 Cs, etc. This will maximize our profit.
>
> Now, assume that the profit per unit is largest with A-type items. Why not make more of A and less of B and C, etc.? The answer is that constraints exist. The LP model determines the best (optimal) mix for given constraints on resources.
>
> Each output type requires different amounts of the resources (materials, machine time, etc.) that are available. On pp. 103–13 we shall discuss the fundamentals of the technique and explain why this form of mathematical programming is called "linear."

Paintmasters, Inc.

The facilities of Paintmasters, Inc., are in a flow shop configuration. Each time a different color of paint is to be produced, the process is stopped and converted to the next color. There are constraints on ingredients and storage space. The sales department would like to have as many colors as possible in stock. Say that colors $x_1, x_2, x_3, \ldots, x_n$ are feasible mixtures or blends.

The production department calls on its operations management (OM) staff to study the problem. Shortly thereafter, a report is submitted which states that production of 5000 gallons of x_1, zero gallons of x_2, zero gallons of x_3, 1000 gallons of x_4, . . . , etc., will minimize production costs for the company. To find this answer, the OM group used linear programming (LP).

The sales department is understandably unhappy. It has market research personnel who also understand LP. The sales manager calls on the market research group to use the same data but instead of minimizing production costs, to maximize company sales volume. This LP yields a different solution, which is not unexpected. A compromise is required which may or may not be available by asking all parties involved to accept the LP solution that maximizes company profits.

Some of the difficulties cannot be straightened out through the use of LP. For example, consider one aspect of the life cycle characteristics of this product line. One class of paint colors is mature and stable; there is always demand for that class. Another class of colors is faddish; yet another is seasonal. As has previously been said, the sales department would like to have as many colors as possible in stock. To this we can now add the fact that faddish colors are considered particularly important. But production would like to minimize inventories both of raw materials and finished goods. Also, only large quantities of dyes can be purchased at good discounts. Small runs are costly in many ways, but expecially because the process has to be stopped, vats cleaned out, etc., each time the process is stopped. The dilemma is apparent, but it will be resolved because Paintmasters, Inc. must do something. A compromise between the LP solutions and the other factors that prevail will be found.

LP and Variety

The variety issue is intricately bound up with life cycle planning. One approach to the variety problem is by means of the linear programming model. This model provides an economically sound solution (indicating how much of each kind to make). This solution must then be considered in life cycle terms and altered accordingly, possibly by using an iterative procedure.

As we continue, certain points will stand out. It will be seen that LP is particularly well-suited for job shop variety problems. Interdependencies of production, marketing, and finance will become apparent. A difference in the interpretation of the LP solution will be found depending upon whether the facilities have been already purchased or are in the planning stages and could be altered.

Life Cycles and Production Configurations

Depending on marketing needs and production capabilities, variety will be generated in the output. Specifically, when we speak of variety, we refer to the use of the production system to output different end products or services over some given period. How much and what kind of variety is a major issue in life cycle planning, because often the output varieties are brought to the consumer through the same distribution channels. The variety may provide alternative choices to the consumer that are relatively the same and therefore substitutable. When this is the case, such variety speeds up the rate of acceptance of a new product line or service mix; it increases the lifetime of the established set of goods and services; and it postpones the decay of sales volume.

Whether or not the varieties of output are distributed through the same channels and are relatively substitutable, there may be a basic, economic production advantage that can be gained by producing variety. This functional aspect is captured by the LP model.

Flow shops can be designed that produce a high degree of variety. Usually, the only penalty to be paid is the downtime required to switch the line from one output to another. For example, several different blends of coffee could be made and packaged on the same flow system with time out between successive blends to change coffee beans, labels, etc. Petroleum refineries can change the blending formulas of crudes to produce a broad range of fuel outputs on a relatively automatic basis. The point to be remembered is that such output variety can have both marketing advantage and the economic motivation of using production resources in the best possible fashion.

On the other hand, job shop variety is often a function of the orders received that must be processed with as little delay as possible. However, when the job shop configuration is being used to add to inventory rather than fill an order, then the advantages of variety that we have already mentioned remain entirely applicable.

The LP Model

The most fundamental model to determine optimum variety is linear programming.[1] The LP model is capable of maximizing the attainment of one objective (say profit) subject to a set of constraints being met. The set of constraints includes all other objectives (such as not exceeding the production capacity of each department, using no more raw materials than are held in inventory, etc.).

The objective is achieved by employing different activities in various amounts—which requires using up/specific amounts of limited resources. Thus, each possible product or service design that can be made with existing facilities (or possibly with a new facility configuration) is an activity that can be considered as a separate variable by the model. According to the number of units of each design that will be made, the limited resources of departmental capacities will be used up. In the simplest case (which applies to a very large number of real situations) we use linear forms to express the way in which resources get used up, i.e., the same amount of resource is required for each unit of a particular design that is made. The same reasoning applies to profit, which is to be maximized. Each unit sold of a particular design contributes an equal amount of profit. It is assumed that all units are sold. This is basic to the structure of the LP model.

---

[1] Optimal from a process point of view and not in terms of consumer psychology.

> **The Variety Problem as a Function of the Level at Which It Is Viewed**
>
> At the global level, the variety problem is one of *diversification.* With respect to diversification, a major issue is the extent to which an organization's assets are convertible. Where there is high resource convertibility, the company's planning can be very flexible. We know that management ability is highly transferable. Technological knowledge may be the least convertible managerial resource, but the manager is generally quite flexible with respect to the kind of technological system that he might manage, especially within the categories of flow shop, job shop, and project.

At the next level, operating within the accustomed framework of limited resources, a company must determine its optimal product or service mix. The optimal mix is defined as that mix of products and services, using the existing resources and facilities of the company, which will maximize benefits, such as profit. For the determination of optimal mix, the financial, marketing, and production managers must pool their knowledge.

The next step down could be called the level of product style, having less to do with alternative uses of resources and facilities. At this third level, the questions asked concern the number of flavors, colors, package design alternatives, etc., that should be considered for a *particular item*. Thus, for sales promotion reasons that operate in terms of consumer psychology the question is, How many tastes, images, styles, or variations on a theme should be developed? Choice potential seems to interact with the consumer's selection process, thereby producing a greater sales volume than could otherwise be obtained. This is due to the fact that a varied offering can offset boredom for the individual consumer while appealing to a larger number of specialized segments of consumers. Thus, if *you* get tired of vanilla you can try chocolate, but also there are some people who only like chocolate. The company would lose both types of chocolate sales if it offered only vanilla. Conversely, variety costs money. There are more items to stock, more records to keep, more materials to buy (at lesser quantities, e.g., red, yellow, and blue paint, so that discounts will be lower), and so on. And there are line changeover costs.

There are an optimal number of varieties. The product and service-mix models of linear programming can help to determine what this level should be. However, the LP method is not genuinely suited for the (third-level) style problem nor for the (first-level) diversification problem. In both of these cases, the concept of using up limited resources must be stretched to fit the situation. Even so, as a first approximation, the LP model can be used for both first- and third-level problems.

It is ideally suited for second-level problems, where the various activity outputs use up different amounts of the same resources. For example, there are problems where the scarce resource is machine time, and the production mix can be different numbers of nuts and bolts; where the scarce resources are land and fertilizer, and the potential activities are the production of different amounts of peas and beans; where the scarce resources are teachers and rooms, and the decision must be made concerning the mix of graduate students and undergraduates. It is easy to draw similar comparisons for drill presses and milling machines, for different petroleum crude stocks to be blended at the refinery, or perfume blends, or whiskey blends, and for cattle or poultry feed mixtures, which must deliver sufficient nutrition at minimum cost.

The explanation of the linear programming technique is facilitated by employing an example. The situation can be kept manageable by considering the possibility of a 2-product line. Assume that the company makes only P_1 at the present time. Two departments are required to make the product. First, the press shop blanks, draws, and forms the part.[2] Then the item is sent to the second department, where it is chrome plated. (Although it applies here, specific production order is not a requirement of the method.)

The full capacity of the first department is utilized when 10 units of P_1 are made per day. On the other hand, only $83\frac{1}{3}$ percent of the plating department's capacity is used. Presume that this results from the fact that the minimum plating tank capacity that could be purchased was capable of handling less than 10 units per day. The next largest size, accommodating 12 units per day, was purchased. The departmental *capacities* are the *resource constraints* in this particular linear programming problem. The item called P_1 returns a profit of $3 per unit.

The manager, wishing to get fuller utilization of his equipment, and knowing that marketing has been pushing for greater line variety, suggests that the company consider adding another product to the present line, using only the existing facilities. The new product, which marketing has designated as P_2, is developed; a prototype is made and test marketed. The relevant cost and capacity utilization estimates are made. The marketing department feels that the new product should be sold at a lower price than P_1. It is known that P_2 costs less to make. Twenty units could be made in the press shop with full equipment and manpower utilization, but only 12.5 of such units could be processed per day by the plating department if it made only P_2. Thus, for P_2, the capacity of the plating tank is the dominant constraint. Working together, the managers agree that the per-unit profit of P_2 will be $2.

All the above information is summarized in the table below. These questions have to be answered: (1) Should P_2 be added to the line? (2) If so, how many units per day of P_2 (called x_2) should be made?

	x_1 Units/Day of P_1	x_2 Units/Day of P_2	Restriction of Full Utilization
Department 1 (press shop)	10%/unit	5%/unit	100%
Department 2 (plating)	$8\frac{1}{3}$%/unit	8%/unit	100%
Objective: (Maximize) profit	$3.00/unit	$2.00/unit	

We read the table as follows:

x_1 = the number of units of product-type P_1 that we will make per day

x_2 = the number of units of product-type P_2 that we will make per day

---

[2] Blanking is cutting out of the metal stock the flat piece in the size that is needed; drawing and forming refer to operations used to shape the part (such as a door knob formed from a flat metal blank).

Each unit of the P_1 type that is made uses up 10 percent of the daily capacity of department 1 and $8\frac{1}{3}$ percent of the daily capacity of department 2. Each unit of P_2 consumes 5 percent of the daily capacity of department 1 and 8 percent of the daily capacity of department 2. If we make only P_1—as is presently done—we can produce a maximum of 10 units (department 1 is the limiting resource). If we make only P_2, we can produce a maximum of 25 units every 2 days (department 2 is the limiting resource).

We should note at this point that if we could only make one or the other, then we would prefer to make P_1 because it promises a daily profit of $30, as compared to $25 for P_2. Although we can make more of P_2 than of P_1, we cannot make sufficiently more to counterbalance the fact that P_2 has a lower profit per unit. Neither making only P_1 nor making only P_2 will provide full utilization of all plant facilities and resources. Therefore, we can consider a mixture that might provide better utilization of capacity. Better utilization might, but also *might not*, provide a greater profit. The product mix is subject to the departmental constraints, and our objective remains to maximize profit.

Because of the size of this problem, it is relatively easy for a production manager to determine what should be done without recourse to linear programming. Various methods can be used to solve this problem. For example, an algebraic approach could be used. Normally, complex problems would be solved by means of a matrix method, such as the simplex algorithm of linear programming. The simplex algorithm is presented as optional material in Appendix 6-I.

Many computer programs are available for solving LP problems. However, to understand what is involved in obtaining a solution, the method that best serves to explain, and which can be used in this case is the *geometrical* resolution of the problem.

First, let us refer to the previous table so that we can construct the following inequations.[3]

$$10x_1 + 5x_2 \le 100$$
$$8\tfrac{1}{3}x_1 + 8x_2 \le 100$$

These inequations fit the constraint format of the linear programming model. They state the way in which each department's capacities will be utilized for different production schedules of P_1 and P_2.

The inequations express the fact that it is impossible to utilize more than 100 percent of any department's capacity. Thus, for example, if $x_1 = 10$, then department 1 is fully utilized. On the other hand, if $x_1 = 5$ and $x_2 = 5$, then only 75 percent of the first department's capacity has been used up. We say that the remaining 25 percent is departmental *slack*.

---

[3]The symbol $\le$ is read *equal to or less than*, expressing the fact that any combination of x_1 and x_2 which does not use up more than 100 percent of each department's capacity can be considered.

By substituting different values for x_1 and x_2 we can determine whether either departmental constraint has been violated and also what profit would result from such a plan. The objective is to maximize profit, that is, MAXIMIZE $[3x_1 + 2x_2]$. Furthermore, we can never produce negative quantities of a product, thus:

$$x_1 \geq 0, \qquad x_2 \geq 0$$

These inequations express the fact that negative amounts of production cannot be allowed to occur by our model since they have no basis in reality.

Table 6-1 shows a number of different combinations of x_1 and x_2 values that might be tried. Several of the plans violate the departmental restrictions. For this particular set of trial and error plans, maximum profit of 32.20 is obtained with the fifth plan, which is a feasible product-mix strategy, i.e., it does not violate any of the inequations.

TABLE 6-1 EVALUATION BY TRIAL AND ERROR

Plan	x_1	x_2	Department 1 Slack	Department 2 Slack	Profit
Plan$_1$	5	5	25%	18.3%	$ 25
Plan$_2$	10	5	violation	violation	violation
Plan$_3$	5	10	0%	violation	violation
Plan$_4$	6	5	15%	10%	28
Plan$_5$	7.83	4.35	0%	0%	32.20

Even with Small Problems, Trial and Error Is an Inefficient Approach

It is inefficient for solving problems but is useful for learning. Care to try some other combinations? We suggest a few possibilities. Please supply some of your own.

Plan	x_1	x_2	Department 1 Slack	Department 2 Slack	Profit
Plan$_6$	0	0	100%	100%	$ 0
Plan$_7$	7	5	5%	$1\frac{2}{3}$%	31
Plan$_8$					
Plan$_9$					
Plan$_{10}$					

Refer now to Fig. 6-1. All of the plans in Table 6-1 can be found on it. The 2 solid lines that cross each other within the first quadrant[4] represent the 2 departmental constraints. Each line is labeled with its appropriate equation.

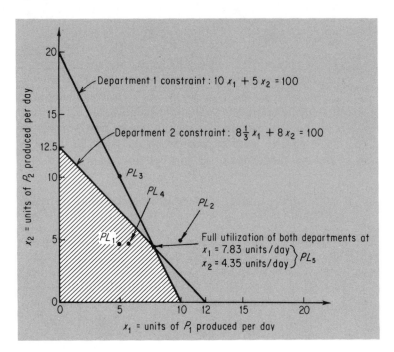

FIGURE 6-1. Feasible solution space for the product-mix problem
Points PL_1 through PL_5 refer to the five plans shown in Table 6-1.

The area under each of the 2 constraint lines is the equivalent of the mathematical statement of an inequation that has the directional sense of less than ($<$). Thus, all points that fall in the first quadrant and meet the requirements of both constraints must lie within the crosshatched area or on its perimeter. We call this *feasible solution space*. The first quadrant is defined by the feasibility constraints, $x_1 \geq 0$, $x_2 \geq 0$. Any combination of x_1 and x_2 that forms an allowable product mix must be part of the crosshatched space or on the bounding lines that enclose the space. It is simple enough to check and see that any combination of values for x_1 and x_2 that falls on a solid line produces *100 percent utilization* of whichever department that line describes. Thus, each solid line stands for the full utilization of the respective department. We should also note that for this case there is only 1 combination of x_1 and x_2 values that yields full utilization of both departments' capacities. It is the crosspoint of the two solid lines.

---

[4]The first quadrant has only positive values of x_1 and x_2. It is, by convention, the upper right-hand portion of any graph.

> **Question:**
>
> Let us ask a question but defer the answer until later.
> Why does it not automatically follow that any combination of x_1 and x_2 that fully utilizes all production capacity (the crosspoint, in this case) would be the optimal product-mix solution?

Our purpose is to maximize profit. At least one point in the feasible solution space will achieve this result. It is unnecessary to use trial and error methods to determine which point will maximize the profit. We shall superimpose a *family* of dashed profit lines on top of the previous figure. This is shown in Fig. 6-2. Each of the dashed parallel lines represents many different combinations

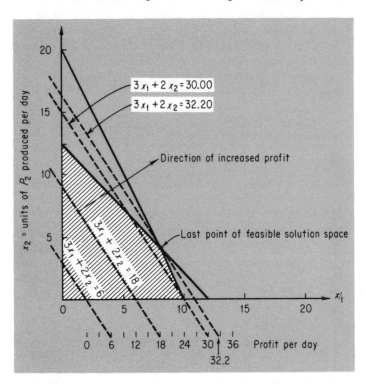

FIGURE 6-2. Family of dashed profit lines superimposed on the feasible solution space

of x_1 and x_2. All combinations of x_1 and x_2 that fall on any particular profit line produce one and only one specific level of profit. Thus, consider the line $3x_1 + 2x_2 = 18$. Here, profit always equals 18. If we substitute any one pair of x_1 and x_2 values that falls along this line, that combination (or product mix) will produce a profit of $18. Note that all the points that lie on this profit line of $18 fall within the feasible solution space. This is not true when profit equals $30.00 or $32.20.

We can obtain a profit of $18 in many ways. Is it possible to obtain even greater profit? Let us consider the profit line that is labeled $30. If we test the profit of each x_1, x_2 pair that falls on this line, we find that they all yield a profit of $30. In this case, however, as previously noted, part of this line does not fall within the feasible solution space. Those x_1, x_2 combinations that are outside of the feasible space cannot be used for the product mix. Nevertheless, because some points do meet the departmental capacity constraints, a profit of $30 could be obtained. However, as we shall see, this is still not the maximum possible profit.

As we consider other profit lines further upward and toward the right, the profit level increases. *We should, therefore, choose that member of the family of (parallel) profit lines which is the last one to touch the feasible solution space as the isoprofit[5] lines move upward.* This last profit line to touch the feasible space is the line of maximum profit. For this example, it occurs at the intersection of the two department constraint lines. The production values for this solution are $x_1 = 7.83$ and $x_2 = 4.35$. With this solution, there is no departmental slack for either department. The profitability is $32.20 per day.[6]

---

[5]Each isoprofit line is a line of equal profit. There is one such line for every possible profit level. We have shown just a few.

[6]The values of x_1 and x_2 in this solution are fractional. If this violates the sense of the solution, then we must utilize the technique of *integer* programming. Frequently, it is quite satisfactory to round off fractional numbers so that a reasonable, discrete solution is obtained which is very close to optimal and which meets the system's constraints.

Answer:

Now, let us answer the question that was previously posed, but left unanswered. We shall do this by raising a different question. What would the optimal product mix be if the relative profitabilities of the different units in the product mix were changed? Let us consider an example where the profitability of the first product has been made equal to $2 per unit and the profitability of the second item has been raised to $3 per unit. This produces a change in the solution, as is shown in Fig. 6-3. This solution leaves 37.5% [i.e., $100 - (5 \times 12.5)$] unused capacity in department 1. Even so, because of the orientation of the profit line, profit can be maximized only by ignoring the attraction of full utilization of facilities.

The real issue is one of appraising the value of the resources as they contribute to the profit objective. LP methods help a great deal in such evaluation.

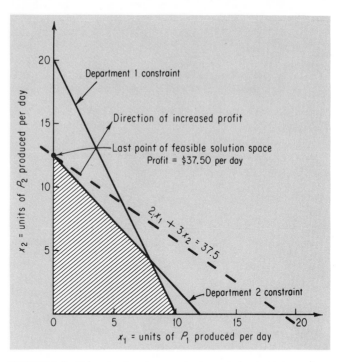

FIGURE 6-3. The optimal product mix for the profit maximization problem changes when P_1 produces $2 of profit per unit and P_2 produces $3 of profit per unit. Thus: maximize $2x_1 + 3x_2$. The solution is: produce 12.5 units of P_2 and no P_1. Total profit = $37.50 per day.

We can show that: (1) a solution must always occur at a vertex; and (2) as a special case, the solution can occur simultaneously at two adjacent vertices. When this happens, all points on the line that connects the vertices will also be optimal product mix solutions. The search for a solution is simplified because it must occur at a vertex.[7]

Let us illustrate this point by considering a cost minimization problem. In this case, the solution is obtained by determining the last possible cost line to leave the solution space as we move down and toward the left with our cost lines (see Fig. 6-4). The objective is to minimize the cost function. For cost minimization, the feasible solution space is ≥ the constraints, and the optimum solution is associated with the last possible cost line to leave that space, moving down and left.

To give meaning to the 2 constraints being used in our cost minimization example, replace department 1 capacity resources with vitamin B_1 requirements for cattle feed and (in the same sense) department 2 with vitamin B_{12}. There are 2 ingredients that we are considering purchasing which contain

---

[7]This is an accurate statement, even when more than one solution point exists.

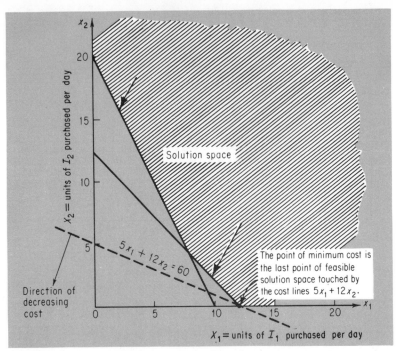

FIGURE 6-4. For cost minimization, the feasible solution space is $\geq$ the constraints, and the optimum solution is associated with the last possible cost line to leave that space, moving down and left. Assume that I_1 costs \$5 per unit and I_2 costs \$12 per unit; then, minimize $5x_1 + 12x_2$. The solution is: purchase 12 units of I_1 and no I_2. Total cost = \$60 per day. Nothing less costly will satisfy the minimum vitamin constraints. We have obtained 120 units of vitamin B_1 and the required 100 units of B_{12}.

the 2 B vitamins in different amounts. We will buy x_1 of the first ingredient I_1 and x_2 of the second ingredient I_2. Table 6-2 summarizes this situation, and adds some additional information.

TABLE 6-2

	I_1 x_1 Pounds/Day of Ingredient 1	I_2 x_2 Gallons/Day of Ingredient 2	Minimum Vitamin Requirements per Day
Vitamin B_1	10 units of vitamin B_1/pound	5 units of vitamin B_1/gallon	100 units
Vitamin B_{12}	$8\frac{1}{3}$ units of vitamin B_{12}/pound	8 units of vitamin B_{12}/gallon	100 units
Objective: (Minimize) cost	\$5/pound	\$12/gallon	

The inequations are now written:

$$10x_1 + 5x_2 \geq 100 \, . \quad (x_1, x_2 \geq 0)$$

$$8\tfrac{1}{3}x_1 + 8x_2 \geq 100$$

And cost is to be minimized:

Objective: MINIMIZE $[5x_1 + 12x_2]$.

It should be evident that linear programming is not a substitute for ingenious product planning or creative new product development. The character of the product or service mix is strictly a function of whatever components the operations manager has been able to conceive. If the various products that are competing for available capacity are individually excellent, then the product or service mix will produce a large profit. Otherwise, the best that can be done may not be good enough. The same applies to ingredients as well as other formulations of the LP model.

Functional Interdependencies

Marketing, finance, and production must get together whenever LP is used. The estimates of the profit coefficients require sales price strategy as well as confirmation that linearity will be a good enough description of the market's response to $x_1, x_2, \ldots$, etc., quantities of goods or services. Especially, when new products or services are to be offered, such estimates can only come from marketing.

Underlying every LP, there is a process with specific capabilities and requirements. The resource utilization coefficients of the process (often called *technological coefficients*) can be quite different, depending on the fixed investments required for the particular production configuration that is used. Constraints can describe limits to production capacity, including labor and machines, as well as raw materials, energy, and capital. Decisions concerning all of these require close coordination between finance and production. With LP, the effects of using different processes on all of these factors can be explored.

The assumption of linear constraints as well as the specification of the resource utilization coefficients is a production and operations management responsibility. Using methods engineering and value analysis (see pp. 336–37) it may be possible to improve the resource utilization coefficients by decreasing them so that greater output can be obtained. Such changes in the constraint coefficients could lead to other solutions. This result, which might change the product or service mix, would be of more than casual interest to marketing.

Functional interdependencies begin with the selection of the objective function and the set of constraints. Different solutions will be obtained in most cases for each of the following: profit maximization, cost minimization, sales volume or brand share maximization, inventory minimization, productivity maximization, etc.

Together, all members of the management team can assess the degree to which a linear model fits the actual circumstances. Even if minor deviations from linearity exist, LP generally provides a good enough solution. For certain kinds of major distortions, the LP model is easily modified to take account of nonlinearities, e.g., when profit increases at a decreasing rate with increasing sales volume. In other circumstances, nonlinear programming must be used.

APPENDIX 6-I
The Simplex Algorithm for Linear Programming (Optional Materials)

There are straightforward mathematical methods that are computer programmable for solving linear programming problems. One of the first, and easiest to understand of these methods, is the simplex method. We can understand this mathematical approach by observing the following general operations:

   I. Begin by selecting any vertex of the area or volume that is formed when 2 or more axes are involved. (The Cartesian coordinates of the 2-dimensional geometric approach must be extended when more than 2 types of products or ingredients are to be mixed.)

  II. Test to determine whether an improvement in profit can be made by moving to another vertex.

 III. If improvement is possible, attempt to find the best possible change to make.

 IV. Make the indicated change, i.e., choose the new, improved vertex solution. Operations II through IV are repeated until condition V occurs.

  V. Stop, because the test (in II) reveals that no further improvement is possible.

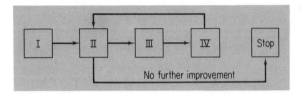

FIGURE 6-5.

The simplex method is now described specifically.

A. We begin with a set of m inequations and n unknowns. (For this example $m = 3$ and $n = 4$.)

$$6x_1 + 4x_2 + 8x_3 + 2x_4 \leq 24$$
$$2x_1 + 6x_2 + 4x_3 + 8x_4 \leq 36$$
$$8x_1 + 2x_2 + 6x_3 + 4x_4 \leq 40$$

Although the numbers are hypothetical, their use simplifies our explanation of the method.

B. Then we appoint slack variables x_5, x_6, x_7. The slack variables are used to convert our inequations into equations; see D below. Since $m = 3$, there are 3 slack variables.

C. Next, we write the appropriate objective function. (For this illustration the objective is maximization of profit Z, and the numbers are hypothetical.)
MAXIMIZE:

$$Z = 5x_1 + 4x_2 + 6x_3 + 3x_4 + (0)x_5 + (0)x_6 + (0)x_7$$

D. The inequations are converted to equations.

$$6x_1 + 4x_2 + 8x_3 + 2x_4 + x_5 \qquad\qquad = 24$$
$$2x_1 + 6x_2 + 4x_3 + 8x_4 \qquad + x_6 \qquad = 36$$
$$8x_1 + 2x_2 + 6x_3 + 4x_4 \qquad\qquad + x_7 = 40$$

E. The feasibility conditions include the slack variables.

$$x_j \geq 0 \quad (j = 1, 2, 3, 4, 5, 6, 7)$$

F. We can now construct the first simplex tableau. We shall explain the table in detail.

ϕ_i	c_i	x_i	x_1	x_2	x_3	x_4	x_5	x_6	x_7	b_i
ϕ_5	0	x_5	6	4	8	2	1	0	0	24
ϕ_6	0	x_6	2	6	4	8	0	1	0	36
ϕ_7	0	x_7	8	2	6	4	0	0	1	40

		c_j	5	4	6	3	0	0	0
		BFS_1	0	0	0	0	24	36	40
		c_j^*	c_1^*	c_2^*	c_3^*	c_4^*	c_5^*	c_6^*	c_7^*

There are 3 boxes in the tableau: upper left with columns ϕ_i, c_i and x_i; upper right with columns $x_1, x_2, x_3, \ldots, x_7$, and b_i; and bottom with rows marked c_j, BFS$_1$, and c_j^*. In the upper right box are the coefficients of the constraints, also ones and zeros, which form a special submatrix, and the values of b_i: 24, 36 and 40, which represent the amount of each resource (row) that is available. We shall explain the use of all of these designations.

If we multiply each row entry by the column heading and then add the products, we derive the equations shown in D. For row 1,

$$6x_1 + 4x_2 + 8x_3 + 2x_4 + x_5 + (0)x_6 + (0)x_7 = 24$$

The Simplex Method: Step by Step[8]

The first simplex tableau (in F above) was constructed as follows:
Step 1. Enter the appropriate values in the upper right-hand box. Thus:

x_1	x_2	x_3	x_4	x_5	x_6	x_7	b_i
6	4	8	2	1	0	0	24
2	6	4	8	0	1	0	36
8	2	6	4	0	0	1	40

Step 2. The top row of the bottom box is obtained directly from the profit coefficients of the objective function.

$$Z = 5x_1 + 4x_2 + 6x_3 + 3x_4 + (0)x_5 + (0)x_6 + (0)x_7$$

Since 0 profit is associated with a slack variable, we have 0 coefficients for x_5, x_6, and x_7.

Step 3. We derive the row marked BFS$_1$ (basic feasible solution number 1). This is the second row of the bottom box. There are always m columns which when taken together form an identity matrix (square matrix, all elements are zero except the elements of the principal diagonal[9] which are all unity). For each unit diagonal element, enter the corresponding value of the

---

[8]We are showing only maximization procedures. Minimization procedures with the simplex are similar but not identical. **Note:** While proceeding through the following 12 steps, continuous reference to the first simplex tableau (in F) is essential.

[9]In the upper right-hand box, note the elements under columns x_5, x_6, and x_7. They produce a matrix

100
010
001

The diagonal with all 1s is the principal diagonal.

resource constraint in the BFS row. Thus:

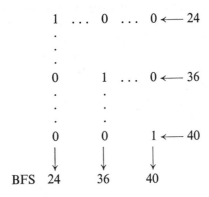

$$
\begin{array}{ccc}
1 & \cdots \quad 0 & \cdots \quad 0 \longleftarrow 24 \\
\vdots & & \\
0 & 1 & \cdots \quad 0 \longleftarrow 36 \\
\vdots & \vdots & \\
0 & 0 & 1 \longleftarrow 40 \\
\downarrow & \downarrow & \downarrow \\
\text{BFS} \quad 24 & 36 & 40
\end{array}
$$

All other entries in the BFS row are 0.
Thus, the values in the bottom box are

c_j	5	4	6	3	0	0	0
BFS_1	0	0	0	0	24	36	40
c_j^*	c_1^*	c_2^*	c_3^*	c_4^*	c_5^*	c_6^*	c_7^*

Step 4. The column marked x_i (upper left box) contains the variables that correspond to the unit elements of the principal diagonal. Thus:

$$
\begin{array}{cccc}
x_i & x_5 & x_6 & x_7 \\
 & \downarrow & \downarrow & \downarrow \\
x_5 \longleftarrow & 1 & 0 & 0 \\
 & \vdots & \vdots & \vdots \\
x_6 \longleftarrow 0 & \cdots & 1 & 0 \\
 & \vdots & \vdots & \vdots \\
x_7 \longleftarrow 0 & \cdots & 0 & \cdots \quad 1
\end{array}
$$

These are the same variables that have resource constraint values entered in the BFS row.

At the outset, the x_i column lists the slack variables (see the upper left box in F above). This is always a convenient way to begin. The first basic feasible solution, BFS_1, will then be modified and new variables will replace the slack variables in the x_i column. *At each stage the variables in the x_i column repre-*

sent the activities that are included in the solution. The corresponding row values
of the b_i's are the activity levels of each variable.

Step 5. The column marked c_i (upper left box) contains the coefficients of
the objective function for the corresponding x_i variables. The same values
appear in the c_j row under the appropriate column headings—in this case
under x_5, x_6, and x_7. To begin with, these values are 0, 0, 0 (see the tableau
in F above).

Step 6. Compute c_j^* for each column. Using the first column as an example,
we obtain the sum of the cross products

$$
\begin{array}{cc}
c_i & x_1 \\
0 \times 6 = 0 \\
0 \times 2 = 0 \\
0 \times 8 = \underline{0} \\
\text{Sum} = 0
\end{array}
$$

and subtract the sum from the x_1 column value in the c_j row. Thus $5 - 0$
$= 5$. This calculation follows for all of the columns.

$$c_1^* = 5 - 6(0) - 2(0) - 8(0) = 5$$
$$c_2^* = 4 - 4(0) - 6(0) - 2(0) = 4$$
$$c_3^* = 6 - 8(0) - 4(0) - 6(0) = 6$$
$$c_4^* = 3 - 2(0) - 8(0) - 4(0) = 3$$
$$c_5^* = 0 - 1(0) - 0(0) - 0(0) = 0$$
$$c_6^* = 0 - 0(0) - 1(0) - 0(0) = 0$$
$$c_7^* = 0 - 0(0) - 0(0) - 1(0) = 0$$

Then we complete the bottom box:

c_j	5	4	6	3	0	0	0
BFS$_1$	0	0	0	0	24	36	40
c_j^*	5	4	6	3	0	0	0

Step 7. Select the *largest positive* c_j^*. The variable heading that column is to
be put into the next BFS, i.e., BFS$_2$. For our numerical example, it is $c_3^* =$
6, so x_3 will be put into BFS$_2$.

Step 8. For that column, divide each resource constraint b_i by the appropriate row coefficient. Call these ratios ϕ_i. Select the *smallest positive* ϕ_i.
The row variable x_i identified with the smallest positive ϕ_i is to be taken out
and excluded from the next BFS. Thus,

$$\phi_5 = \tfrac{24}{8} = 3, \qquad \phi_6 = \tfrac{36}{4} = 9, \qquad \phi_7 = \tfrac{40}{6} = 6\tfrac{2}{3}$$

The smallest positive ϕ_i is 3, so x_5 is to be removed—to be replaced by x_3.

Step 9. We have selected a column to put in and a row to take out. Take the coefficient at the intersection of this row and column. Divide all entries of that row—in the upper right-hand box—by the intersection value. For our example, the coefficient is 8.

We calculate the new values for row one:

$$\tfrac{6}{8} \quad \tfrac{4}{8} \quad \tfrac{8}{8} \quad \tfrac{2}{8} \quad \tfrac{1}{8} \quad \tfrac{0}{8} \quad \tfrac{0}{8} \quad \tfrac{24}{8}$$

or

$$\tfrac{3}{4} \quad \tfrac{1}{2} \quad 1 \quad \tfrac{1}{4} \quad \tfrac{1}{8} \quad 0 \quad 0 \quad 3 \qquad \leftarrow\text{new row 1}$$

Note: We have in this way brought a 1 into the column of the variable to be put in.

Step 10. We must next reduce all other entries in the column of x_3 to zero. To do this for the ith row, multiply all of the row elements derived in Step 9 by the coefficient of the ith row, in that column. For row 2 this is 4, and for row 3 it is 6. Then subtract this modified row from the ith row. For our example, the new row 1 is completed in Step 9. The new row 2 is calculated below:

$$
\begin{array}{cccccccc}
2 & 6 & 4 & 8 & 0 & 1 & 0 & 36 \leftarrow\text{old row 2}\\
-4(3/4) & -4(1/2) & -4(1) & -4(1/4) & -4(1/8) & -4(0) & -4(0) & -4(3) \\
\hline
-1 & +4 & 0 & +7 & -1/2 & 1 & 0 & 24 \leftarrow\text{new row 2}
\end{array}
$$

The new row 3 is calculated:

$$
\begin{array}{cccccccc}
8 & 2 & 6 & 4 & 0 & 0 & 1 & 40 \leftarrow\text{old row 3}\\
-6(3/4) & -6(1/2) & -6(1) & -6(1/4) & -6(1/8) & -6(0) & -6(0) & -6(3) \\
\hline
+3.5 & -1 & 0 & +2.5 & -3/4 & 0 & 1 & 22 \leftarrow\text{new row 3}
\end{array}
$$

Step 11. We can now construct the tableau for BFS_2. Column x_i would be changed by substituting x_3 and x_5. All of the entries are changed in the upper-right-hand box. The old second row is replaced by the elements of the *new row 2*. The *new first row* is the one derived in Step 9. The old third row is replaced by the *new row 3*. We can now complete all other assignments in the tableau, using the rules as before. This is BFS_2.

ϕ_i c_i x_i	x_1	x_2	x_3	x_4	x_5	x_6	x_7	b_i
ϕ_3 6 x_3	$\tfrac{3}{4}$	$\tfrac{1}{2}$	1	$\tfrac{1}{4}$	$\tfrac{1}{8}$	0	0	3
ϕ_6 0 x_6	-1	4	0	7	$-\tfrac{1}{2}$	1	0	24
ϕ_7 0 x_7	3.5	-1	0	2.5	$-\tfrac{3}{4}$	0	1	22
c_j	5	4	6	3	0	0	0	
BFS_2	0	0	3	0	0	24	22	
c_j^*	$\tfrac{1}{2}$	1.0	0	1.5	$-\tfrac{3}{4}$	0	0	

where the c_j^* values were derived as follows:

$$c_1^* = 5 - \tfrac{3}{4}(6) - (-1)(0) - 3.5(0) = \tfrac{1}{2}$$
$$c_2^* = 4 - \tfrac{1}{2}(6) - 4(0) - (-1)(0) = 1.0$$
$$c_3^* = 6 - 1(6) - 0(0) - 0(0) = 0$$
$$c_4^* = 3 - \tfrac{1}{4}(6) - 7(0) - 2.5(0) = 1.5$$
$$c_5^* = 0 - \tfrac{1}{8}(6) - (-\tfrac{1}{2})(0) - (-\tfrac{3}{4})(0) = -\tfrac{3}{4}$$
$$c_6^* = 0 - 0(6) - 1(0) - 0(0) = 0$$
$$c_7^* = 0 - 0(6) - 0(0) - 1(0) = 0$$

Thus, for the next iteration, we will bring x_4 into BFS$_3$, because it has the largest positive value. What do we take out? Running the ϕ_i test, we obtain

$$\phi_3 = \frac{3}{1/4} = 12, \qquad \phi_6 = \frac{24}{7} = 3\tfrac{3}{7}, \qquad \phi_7 = \frac{22}{2.5} = 8\tfrac{4}{5}$$

We choose the smallest positive ϕ_i, which in this case is ϕ_6. We will remove x_6 and replace it with x_4.

Step 12. Objective Z: At each step, the profit Z can be calculated by adding the products of rows c_i and BFS(j). Thus, for the first tableau:

$$Z_1 = (5 \times 0) + (4 \times 0) + (6 \times 0) + (3 \times 0)$$
$$+ (0 \times 24) + (0 \times 36) + (0 \times 40) = 0$$

The optimal solution is reached when all c_j^* are equal to 0 or take on negative values.

We have not reached the optimal solution, so further iterations are required, but they will not be done here. It is recommended for those students wishing to master the simplex algorithm that they continue to work on the example.

We calculate the profit for BFS$_2$:

$$Z_2 = (5 \times 0) + (4 \times 0) + (6 \times 3) + (3 \times 0)$$
$$+ (0 \times 0) + (0 \times 24) + (0 \times 22) = 18$$

Note that at each successive calculation of Z_n, the value of profit must either increase or remain unchanged. It cannot decrease unless a mistake has been made.

PROBLEMS 1. To what extent can the essential elements of the diversification problem be modeled by LP?

2. What is the solution to the following LP problem (based on the two-department example, pp. 105–11)?

	x_1 *Units/Day of P_1*	x_2 *Units/Day of P_2*	*Restriction of Full Utilization*
Department 1 (press shop)	10%/unit	5%/unit	100%
Department 2 (plating)	11%/unit	6%/unit	100%
Objective: (Maximize) profit	$3/unit	$2/unit	

Explain the result.

3. What is the solution to the following LP problem (based on the two-department example, pp. 105–11)?

	x_1 *Units/Day of P_1*	x_2 *Units/Day of P_2*	*Restriction of Full Utilization*
Department 1 (press shop)	10%/unit	5%/unit	100%
Department 2 (plating)	$8\frac{1}{3}$%/unit	8%/unit	100%
Objective: (Maximize) profit	$3/unit	$1.50/unit	

Explain the result.

4. Apply the 54 questions listed on pp. 94–97 to Paintmasters, Inc. Assume that management is considering relocating to a better sales distribution area, and altering the process so that it automatically outputs specified quantities of any color. A recent technological change accounts for this new process capability. Make further assumptions as required.

5. Explain the economic consequences of variety.

6. The fundamental theorem of LP states that there cannot be more activities used in the final solution than the number of constraints. Why is this notion important?

Answer: Assume that an organization has 10 items in its product line, but can only identify 3 viable constraints on capacity and input materials. An investigation is warranted, which should reexamine constraints and check on the linearity assumptions. If the number of constraints is correct and linearity holds, and if several of the varieties are not relatively identical in resource requirements and price, then there is strong reason to advise this organization to decrease the extent of the product line.

7. A greeting card manufacturer, Cardmasters, Inc., wishes to diversify its line. The designers have been experimenting with a new plastic material.

It is available in thin sheets and lends itself to some unusual effects. The designers have come up with 2 alternative card designs—both of which appear to be totally acceptable. Because special equipment is required to print and cut this new material, the production manager wants to carefully consider the advantages of either card or the possibility of making both of them. The following data have been made available to him.

	Card A	Card B
Time to print card on one special machine	2.4 min	2.4 min
Time to cut and fold card on one special machine	4.8 min	1.6 min
Material required	80 in.^{2}	240 in.^{2}
Estimated profit per card	$0.70	$0.80

The company works a 40-hour week and has 833 square feet of the material on hand and cannot obtain more in the near future. Assume no cutting waste and the requirement that the job be completed within 1 week. What product mix should the production manager plan to use? Discuss your answer.

Answer: This is a straightforward linear programming problem. The card printing machine creates the following restraint:

$$2.4x_A + 2.4x_B \leq 2400$$

where $x_A =$ the number of A-type cards that will be made
$x_B =$ the number of B-type cards that will be made

and there are $2400 = (60)(40)$ minutes in a week.
The cut and fold requirements may be expressed as

$$4.8x_A + 1.6x_B \leq 2400$$

The material restraints are

$$80x_A + 240x_B \leq 120,000$$

where $120,000 \approx (833)(144)$ square inches of material.
Plotting these three lines, we can develop the area that includes all of the feasible solutions (i.e., those which do not violate any of the constraints). Then, by drawing the profit lines,

$$0.70x_A + 0.80x_B = K$$

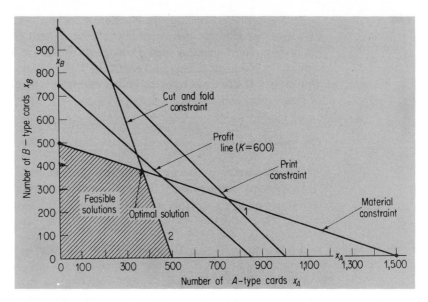

FIGURE 6-6.

we may locate the line with largest K which has at least one point in common with the feasible solution space. In our example this point occurs at the intersection of the cut and fold constraint and the material constraint. The coordinates of this point are

$$x_A = 375, \qquad x_B = 375 \quad \text{cards}$$

The maximum profit that can be obtained with this product mix will be $562.50.

SUMMARY OF PART 2

Chapter 4

Life cycle management is a conceptual framework that provides a dynamic view of the interactions of marketing and production with each other as well as with finance, R&D, personnel, etc. It emphasizes stages of product and service life that require different kinds of production and operations management support. It also stresses change and thereby the planning of the production process. Cash flow analysis is introduced as a means of enabling management to track life cycles and plan for a balanced system. The relevance of present value discounting for evaluating the time stream of net income is then discussed. A broad view is taken of management's use of different payoff period criteria.

Two appendices conclude the chapter. Appendix 4-I offers some information about patents and the patent law, because patentability totally alters the life cycle circumstances in such a way as to encourage flow shop operations with the consequent economic benefits of high-volume production systems. Appendix 4-II discusses research and development, because R&D is a source of innovation and renewal.

Chapter 5

The premarket production stages of product and service development (I-A), process development (I-B), and implementation of operations (I-C) lead to on-going production and distribution of the product or service to the market. Operating the production system (II-A) and redesigning the process (II-B) are also discussed.

A feasibility analysis requires that all essential activities be identified. This is best accomplished using PERT-type networks.

Differentiation is provided between job shops and flow shops at premarket stages, emphasizing design of the product or service and design of the process. In a similar vein, the redesign of existing production systems poses different problems and presents different opportunities depending upon whether the configuration is a job shop or a flow shop.

Chapter 6

The economic advantages of variety are discussed. Also the relationship of variety to life cycle management is explained. Linear programming is introduced, and the geometric method for solving an LP problem is developed. Linear programming is a model that allocates scarce resources to particular activities so as to maximize the attainment of specific managerial objectives. The activities so designated represent the variety of the solution. Thus, we might determine that a certain job shop should produce eight different items, although it is able to make eighty. To use LP properly, an organization must be highly coordinated, since there is always some (and usually there is much) functional interdependence in setting goals, providing data and estimates and in checking out the appropriateness of using a linear model.

An appendix concludes the chapter. It presents a step-by-step approach for using the simplex algorithm for solving LP problems, based upon an example.

REFERENCES
PART 2

ALDERSON, WROE, *Marketing Behavior and Executive Action*. Homewood, Ill.: Richard D. Irwin, Inc., 1957.

AMSTUTZ, A. E., *Computer Simulation of Competitive Market Response*. Cambridge, Mass.: The M.I.T. Press, 1967.

ASIMOW, MORRIS, *Introduction to Design*. Englewood Cliffs, N.J.: Prentice-Hall, Inc., 1962.

BIERMAN, HAROLD and SEYMOUR SMIDT, *The Capital Budgeting Decision*, 2nd ed. New York: The Macmillan Company, 1966.

CHASE, R. B. and N. J. AQUILANO, *Production and Operations Management (A Life Cycle Approach)*, 2nd ed. Homewood, Ill.: Richard D. Irwin, 1977.

DREYFUSS, HENRY, *Designing for People*. New York: Simon & Schuster, 1955.

FORRESTER, JAY, *Industrial Dynamics*. Cambridge, Mass.: M.I.T. Press, 1961.

FRIEDLAND, SEYMOUR, *The Economics of Corporate Finance*. Englewood Cliffs, N.J.: Prentice-Hall, Inc., 1966.

GERLACH, J. T. and C. A. WAINWRIGHT, *Successful Management of New Products*. New York: Hastings House, Publishers, 1968.

GHISELIN, BREWSTER, *The Creative Process*. New York: The New American Library of World Literature, Inc., 1960.

GLEGG, G. L., *The Design of Design*. Cambridge, England: Cambridge University Press, 1969.

GORDON, W. J. J., *Synectics*. New York: Harper & Row, Publishers, 1961.

GREEN, P. E. and D. S. TULL, *Research for Marketing Decisions*, 3rd ed. Englewood Cliffs, N.J.: Prentice-Hall, Inc., 1974.

HARRIS, R. D. and M. J. MAGGARD, *Computer Models in Operations Management*, 2nd ed. New York: Harper & Row, 1977.

HERTZ, DAVID B., "Risk Analysis in Capital Investment," *Harvard Business Review* (January–February 1964), pp. 95–106.

JOHNSON, ROBERT W., *Financial Management*, 3rd Ed. Boston, Mass.: Allyn and Bacon, 1966.

KAUFMANN, A., M. FUSTIER, and A. DREVET, *L'Inventique, Nouvelles Méthodes de Créativité*. Paris: Entreprise Moderne D'Édition, 1970.

LONGMAN, K. A., *Advertising*. New York: Harcourt Brace Jovanovich, Inc., 1971.

LUCE, R. DUNCAN, *Individual Choice Behavior*. New York: John Wiley & Sons, Inc., 1959.

MACHLUP, FRITZ, *The Production and Distribution of Knowledge in the United States*, Princeton, New Jersey: Princeton University Press, 1962.

MAO, JAMES C. T., *Quantitative Analysis of Financial Decisions*. London, England: Macmillan & Co., Ltd., 1969.

MAYER, MARTIN, *Madison Avenue U.S.A.* New York: Harper & Row, Publishers, 1958.

MILLER, DAVID W. and MARTIN K. STARR, *Executive Decisions and Operations Research*, 2nd ed. Englewood Cliffs, N.J.: Prentice-Hall, Inc., 1969.

MONTGOMERY, D. B. and G. L. URBAN, *Applications of Management Science in Marketing*. Englewood Cliffs, N.J.: Prentice-Hall, Inc., 1969.

——, *Management Science in Marketing*. Englewood Cliffs, N.J.: Prentice-Hall, Inc., 1969.

MORTON, J. A., *Organizing for Innovation*. New York: McGraw-Hill Book Company, 1971.

NEWTON, NORMAN T., *An Approach to Design*. Cambridge, Mass.: Addison-Wesley Press, Inc., 1951.

QUIRIN, G. DAVID, *The Capital Expenditure Decision*. Homewood, Ill.: Richard D. Irwin, Inc., 1967.

SANDKULL, BENGT, *Innovative Behavior of Organizations, The Case of New Products, S$_i$AR*. Lund, Sweden: Student litteratur, 1970.

SCHON, DONALD A., *Technology and Change*. New York: Delacorte Press, 1967.

SHUBIK, MARTIN, *Strategy and Market Structure: Competition, Oligopoly, and the Theory of Games*. New York: John Wiley & Sons, Inc., 1959.

SMITH, VERNON, *Investment and Production*. Cambridge, Mass.: Harvard University Press, 1966.

STARR, MARTIN K., "Product Planning from the Top Variety and Diversity," University of Illinois Bulletin, Vol. 65, No. 144, Proceedings, *Systems: Research and Applications for Marketing*, July 26, 1968, pp. 71–77.

——, *Product Design and Decision Theory*. Englewood Cliffs, N.J.: Prentice-Hall, Inc., 1963.

STOCKTON, R. STANSBURY, *Introduction to Linear Programming*, 2nd ed. Boston: Allyn and Bacon, Inc., 1963.

TERBORGH, GEORGE, *Business Equipment Policy*. Washington, D.C.: Machinery and Allied Products Institute, 1958.

TURBAN, E. and J. R. MEREDITH, *Fundamentals of Management Science*. Dallas, Texas: Business Publications, Inc., 1977.

VAN HORNE, JAMES C., *Financial Management and Policy*. Englewood Cliffs, N.J.: Prentice-Hall, Inc., 1971.

VASZONYI, A., *Scientific Programming in Business and Industry*. New York: John Wiley & Sons, Inc., 1958.

WALTERS, J. E., *Research Management: Principles and Practice*. Washington, D.C.: Spartan Books, 1965.

WESTON, J. F., *The Scope and Methodology of Finance*. Englewood Cliffs, N.J.: Prentice-Hall, Inc., 1966.

WILLIAMS, J. D., *The Compleat Strategyst*. New York: McGraw-Hill, Inc., 1954.

3 project management

This section of the text deals with project management. There is no exact definition for a project, because there are many types of work situations that are recognizable as projects. Chapter 7 looks at some of these and at the general character of projects.

Gantt charts have been used to manage projects in the past. PERT and critical path methods are introduced in Chapter 8. This stronger project management approach is of relatively recent vintage (1957). There is a specific methodology to be learned, and the text provides all the details.

Project management using PERT allows control over resource allocations that was unavailable with Gantt charts. This is explained in Chapter 9, where three kinds of trade-offs for resource leveling are discussed.

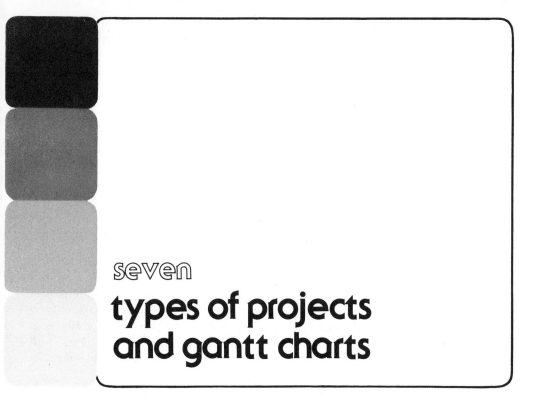

seven
types of projects and gantt charts

The flow shop is most effective and efficient, yielding high-volume output at a minimum cost, but it is not a feasible design configuration if demand is too low. There is the job shop, which is not as cost effective as the flow shop. However, it can be made efficient, producing output of high variety at a relatively low volume. Then there is the project.

Neither flow shop nor job shop configurations can take care of what needs to be done when the circumstances for a project exist. What are those circumstances? Output volume is usually one, unique, complex system. Per unit costs of the output can be gigantic, but there is only 1 unit (or at best a few). There is no variety, since there is only 1 output. Productivity is measured by how many people take how long to complete the project.

Projects are not rare. Every individual deals with projects of different levels of complexity, such as moving into a new home, building a cabinet, constructing a hi-fi set from a kit, or making a dresss from a pattern.

Organizations encounter the need for project management whenever they consider introducing a new product or service.

Thus, development work requires project management. Whether the ultimate production system is going to be a flow shop or a job shop (or some combination of the two), in all cases project management is needed to formulate, design, and actualize plans.

The two main types of P/OM activities are (A) planning, designing, redesigning, and implementing the system and (B) operating the system. A-type activities must be employed to start up (or change) any kind of production system. But there are many types of institutional projects other than that of setting up a production process.

Some organizations do nothing but manage projects, i.e., that is the business in which they have specialized. These projects can be as varied as NASA's developing the Saturn rocket, building the BART transportation system in San Francisco, constructing a supertanker in Korea, converting the telephone system to electronic switching centers, starting up a chain of fish and chips franchisers in the northeast United States, building the Alaska pipeline, or designing and starting up petroleum refineries all over the world.

The life cycles of products and services start with the introduction of a new design. If there is sufficient demand at the market price, then the product or service, if properly managed, becomes mature. It becomes established in production procedures and well-known in the marketplace, with a loyal following. All of this was discussed in Part 2. The point that we now wish to make is that the definiton of a project poses quite special conditions, which arise regularly for *all* organizations, e.g., museums, mines, and manufacturers.

Most organizations are ill prepared for project occasions, because their managers consider their primary function to be something else. A conflict exists. The training and skills (and perhaps the mental set and innate abilities) of flow shop managers differ from those of job shop managers. Both differ from those of project managers.

The issue, then, is how to prepare an organization that sees itself as a flow shop or as a job shop for those project management responsibilities that most surely will occur. Let us look at several examples.

1. When we talk about setting up decision rules for inventories, we incorporate the standards and procedures that will be used by management to operate the inventory system. Setting this up is a project.
2. Consider what is involved in carrying out the decision to build a new facility that requires major investment outlays for construction and equipment. Both building and financing are interrelated projects. (We shall examine the specifics of inventory situations in Part 6, Materials Management. As for facility decisions, they will be treated in Part 7, Facilities Management.)
3. A major market research study is to be conducted in order to assess the value of listing nutritional information on the labels of food products. This study, starting with data collection and ending with analytic reports, is a project.

Our present purpose is not to talk about specific project situations, but to highlight the extent to which variations exist. Our ultimate purpose is to introduce the methods that are applicable for managing complex projects.

Awareness of the Project Management Role

Models that organize the complex information required to know *when* to do *what* in a project have been available for more than 25 years. Then why is it that some projects are completed without the benefit of these models? The answer is that often managers do not know about project models, because they are trained and specialized in operating prodction systems and not in project management. Also, they do not recognize their projects for what they are. They see them as important but temporary distractions from the main line of activities. Thus, production personnel tend to view operations as their primary concern; market researchers view questionnaire formulation, sample selection, and statistical analysis as their primary concern; public managers are concerned about politics and dissatisfied constituencies; financial managers concentrate on debt ratios, price earnings, inflation, and taxes. In all these cases, the concerns are valid, but they obscure the project management roles played by all of these individuals. On the other hand, companies that specialize in managing projects are fully conversant and adept at using the most appropriate forms of project models.

Coordinated Project Management

Project management models are neither difficult to understand nor to use. But there are some basic rules to follow.

1. Project objectives must be clearly stated. They should be reduced to the simplest possible terms. There are often many participants in a project, and unless the knowledge about objectives is shared by all participants, the project is likely to encounter many reverses. Much time will be spent in finding out what everyone is trying to do.
2. Expertise is required to outline the steps of the project designed to deliver the specified results. Accurate time and cost estimates for all project activities are essential. Slippage from schedule can sometimes mean real trouble, whereas at other times it can be tolerated. Project management requires that you know which is which.
3. Duplication of activities should, in general, be eliminated. Under some circumstances, however, *parallel path* activities are warranted. Namely:
   a. If a major conflict of ideas exists and there is urgency to achieve the objectives, then it is sometimes reasonable to allow two or more groups to work independently on the different approaches. Pre-

planned evaluation procedures should exist so that as soon as it is possible the program can be trimmed back to a single path.

b. At the inception of a program—during what might be called the exploratory stage—parallel path research is frequently warranted and can be encouraged. All possible approaches should be considered and evaluated before large commitments of funds have been made.

c. When the risk of failure is high, for example, survival is at stake, or when the payoff incentive is sufficiently great with respect to the costs of achieving it, then parallel path activities can be justified for as long a period of time as is deemed necessary to achieve the objectives.

d. Otherwise, duplication should be avoided.

4. Project management should carefully evaluate the sequence of activities that constitutes the program. An effective organization should be set up to monitor and control accomplishments as compared to expectations.

5. One person should be responsible for all major decisions. This project manager must understand the nature of the problem and the technological, marketing, and production constraints. Multiple decision makers can produce chaotic conditions.

6. The project moves through many phases. Different functional areas of interest must be integrated and coordinated. For example, a supplier's inventory policy can create delivery delays; insufficient quality controls can result in defective parts, which can stop a cascade of interdependent activities; national distribution of a new product requires extensive backup stock; sales levels are affected by promotional and advertising timing, which must be coordinated with production output.

The coordination problem requires great skills in managing a complex information system. Existing project management methodology can help.

1. It can categorize and summarize a mass of information that is important to the project manager.

2. It can organize problem areas, making all relevant variables explicit so that administrators can communicate with each other about the project.

3. It can produce predictions of cost and time for every project stage.

4. It can structure projects, so that details will not be forgotten, so that actions will be taken in appropriate sequence, so that intelligent allocations of resources will be made, and so that control over the development of the project will be insured.

5. Alternative strategies can be *tested* by various methods to determine how sensitive a particular strategy is to technological uncertainties and to the actions that competitors might take.

6. It can assess the effects of possible errors in estimates and predictions.

Degree of Repetition

As can be observed from the brief listing above, project decisions result in actions that are seldom repeated under similar circumstances. Thus, the decision to move a plant to a new geographic area is a major commitment that is best described as a *project*. As each step is accomplished or a stage is completed, it is unlikely to be repeated ever again in the same form. Developing the first space station shuttle is a project, long-term and nonrepetitive. Contrast this with the decision to place an order for materials that are used by a flow shop to make a high-volume production item. Such ordering decisions are made repeatedly. Accordingly, as we shall show in Part 6, there are particular inventory models for flow shops, others for job shops, and still others for projects.

We can see why the type of methodology employed for projects as compared to systems with repetitive operations would be different. The flow shop has preprogrammed decision rules, which are repeated over and over again. Job shop methodology lends itself to a repetitive sequence of different decision situations. When repetition exists, there is a reasonably stable system, providing historical evidence that can be used for forecasting future events. Also, gradual changes in strategies can be introduced, because penalties accumulate over a period of time. No such gradual changes are available for the project.

Degree of Reversibility

By the nature of "big" projects, large investments are required. This means that a mistake can be serious. A company can be competitively crippled or rendered bankrupt. There exist *ruin thresholds* in long-term planning situations where a single decision can push the company across a threshold from which there is no return. Short-cycle decisions, if repeated over and over again, can also result in ruin when the decision repeatedly imposes even a small penalty on the company. But generally, *corrective action* can be taken so that a new and better decision is substituted for the old one. If it is noticed that rejects, customer returns, back orders, machine-idle time, set-up costs, or absenteeism are increasing, steps can be taken to correct these weaknesses long before any one-way doors are passed. Nonreversibility characterizes project management and the flow shop, distinguishing them from the job shop, which has much output flexibility as well as good resale value for facilities.

Project decisions are frequently founded upon nothing more than opinion. If differences of opinion exist, the *reasons* for the differences are vital. The reasons may be expressible only in qualitative terms. This in no way permits an executive group to dismiss differences of opinion. Reasons for disagreements about complex project decisions are exceedingly difficult to uncover. Almost without exception, systematic explication is an absolute necessity.

Belief in predictions and estimates may well be of a low order. Nevertheless, some set of predictions and estimates is essential. Every project requires them. Two considerations, especially applicable to long-term planning situations, can be derived when the degree of belief in predictions is low.

First, there should be a preference for decisions that promise greater flexibility. That is, other things being equal, decisions that permit corrective actions to be taken at a future date are preferred to decisions that cannot be changed once they are made. A strategy that can produce a catastrophic outcome—although with very small likelihood—will be avoided, even though it has a higher potential benefit. This is because the penalty for irreversibility is likely to outweigh simple profit or benefit considerations. Second, there is a preference for decisions that promise a reasonably good expected outcome, across a broad spectrum of "likely" situations that may arise, as compared to decisions that produce exceptionally good expected outcomes with situations that are unlikely to occur.

The Gantt Project Planning Chart

Project planning is a critical function. Serious errors can lead to the destruction of the enterprise. It is, therefore, not surprising that a great deal of both theoretical and practical effort has been expended to define and develop methods that can adequately deal with the kinds of problem involved in these potential ruin situations.

In the early 1900s, an objective method for project planning was develped by Henry L. Gantt, a colleague of Frederick W. Taylor, the acknowledged father of production methods and measurement. The problems that Gantt and production people of his time were faced with had considerably less complexity than the problems that are presently encountered in project management. For his time and situation, Gantt's method was sufficient.

In our present-day world, Gantt's trial and error approach provides a means of organizing our thinking, but it does not satisfy the need for controlling complex situations, where seemingly small errors can produce crises. Furthermore, Gantt's method requires great amounts of computational time to handle problems of even an average level of complexity. Except for relatively small operations, the Gantt project planning approach is passé. However, it has not been forgotten, because the methods that Gantt developed form the fundamental basis for far more elaborate computer-driven planning programs. A great number of computerized, project planning models have become available in recent years. They are far superior to the older methods. Yet many flow shop and job shop managers, when faced with a project, still use the Gantt chart to manage that project, if they use any systematic method at all.

Figure 7-1 pictures a Gantt Project Planning Chart.[1] The intentions of the project planner (as revealed in this figure) are twofold.

---

[1] Also, see Fig. 7-3.

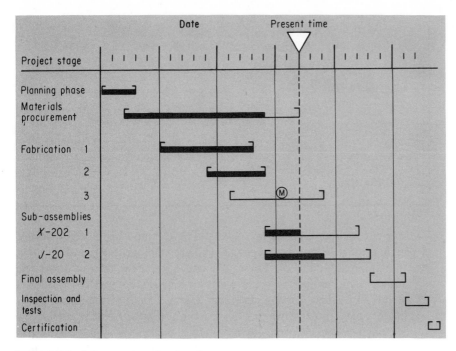

FIGURE 7-1. A Gantt project planning chart

First, to set down—a priori—the steps of work that must be followed in order to bring to fruition a nonrepeating set of activities that constitutes the project system.

Second, to monitor the way in which the steps of the plan are being carried through, that is, to *track the status* of the project over a period of time. These two purposes permeate all project management. They can be translated as: (1) making of the plan; and (2) carrying the plan to completion.

In all projects there are *technological sequences* that constrain the arrangement of steps with which a project shall be accomplished. Sometimes (rarely) there are few such constraints on the arrangement to be used. Usually, the sequence of steps to be taken will be determined at the discretion of the project planner, who must know and take into account the technological restrictions. From the set of all *possible* arrangements we would like to find the best one.

Gantt Chart Symbols

There are some conventional symbols used in the construction of Gantt charts. Within any organization, it is not unusual to find these modified in accordance with the particular circumstances of that organization. This flexibility is warranted as long as all users within the organization are aware of the modifications.

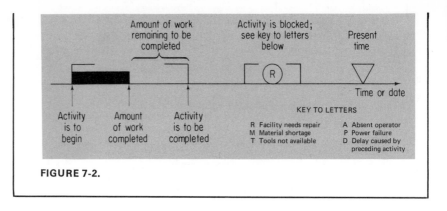

FIGURE 7-2.

It is quite apparent that certain steps can be accomplished faster or slower, depending upon the number of people who are employed, the kinds of facilities that are used, and so on. The way in which resources are allocated to the various steps of a project will determine how long it takes to accomplish each phase and how much it will cost. Taken together, both of these points spell out the fact that for any given project there is at least *one best sequence* to be followed and *one best allocation of resources* to the various stages with respect to a specific set of objectives. The Gantt method requires that the intuition and good judgment of the project manager be responsible for approximating such an optimal project plan.

The Evolution of Project Planning Methods

At the time of the building of the *pyramids* some foresight had to be exercised. The planning methods that were used have been lost to us, but there is no doubt that some planning method was employed. To begin with, the project of building a pyramid was conceived. Then, in logical order, the builders had to specify where to build, what materials to use, what labor would be required at each stage (that is, labor to select the site, to clear it, to bring in the necessary materials, and then to construct the pyramid). If the plan that was determined were to be carried through efficiently, then each of the stages would properly have to dovetail with the others. If not, at various stages materials might be lacking, or an adequate supply of manpower would be missing. From the point of view of the Egyptians, the logistics of the problem were enormous. Materials had to be carried from great distances, and at these faraway locations, individual quarrying operations had to be set up. Work gangs, therefore, were required at the quarries to transport these giant blocks and, finally, at the building site to construct the pyramid. It is evident that many of these operations coexisted in time, so a general administration was required to see to it that the total operation was properly integrated.

Now the steps to build a pyramid represent a good example of the kind of elements that are involved in present-day projects. But the design, construction, and carrythrough of an Apollo moon shot, or the development of a large manufacturing system require coordination and dovetailing to a much greater degree. In the first place, many more factors are involved, and second, time losses are now of extreme importance. It is true that if the construction teams on the site of the pyramids were not supplied with sufficient building materials, a penalty was suffered. Enormous quantities of food had to be transported to these locations in order to keep the indentured slaves alive. This effort taxed the resources of the Egyptian kingdoms. However, there was no competition, no legal contracts with penalties to be paid if a job was not completed at a stated time, and no best time to get into orbit.

Gantt project planning methods might have been able to help the pyramid builders, but they cannot succeed in our present complex, project-planning efforts. Because of competitive factors, we recognize that the ability to reach the marketplace as quickly as possible with a new product or service can be a major influence on its success or failure. Excessive planning periods pose the threat of producing an obsolete product if project development takes too long. In the aircraft industry and in the computer field, delay in carrying out a major plan can produce long-lasting, harmful results.

Figure 7 3 illustrates a specific project, namely bringing to market a new car. The project manager begins by listing the required stages or jobs that are the component building blocks of the project. These must be sequenced in some sensible order if the project is to be completed. The first of these stages can allow for further development of the project design. In such a case, the Gantt chart is later redrawn if an improved sequence of activities can be found.

Lensmasters, Inc.

Design of the sequence of activities often must conform to more than technological feasibility. Here is an example.

This company is well established in the contact lens field but is playing follow the leader when it comes to the new soft contact lens, which has gradually been obtaining a significant share of the contact lens market. After much procrastination, a licensing agreement has been worked out so that Lensmasters can produce and distribute soft lens by paying a reasonable royalty.

To get into production and distribution, a Gantt planning chart was drawn up, which lists in sequence all of the activities that must be undertaken. There is a problem, however. The way that the Gantt chart was constructed,

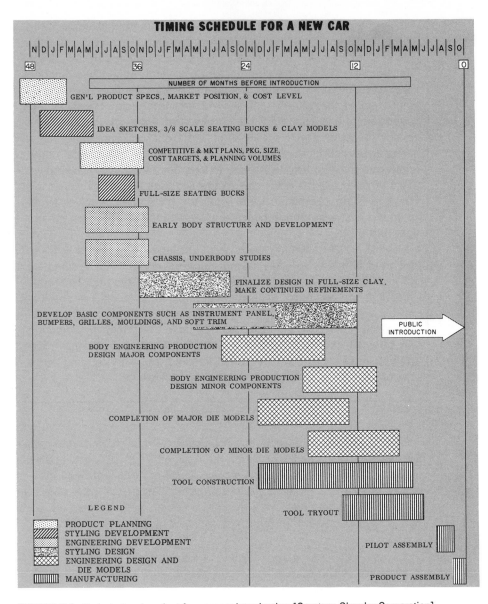

FIGURE 7-3. Project planning chart for new car introduction [Courtesy Chrysler Corporation]

it turns out that most of the activities required to make the soft lens production line operational occur at about the same time.

The manager says that although it is true that all of these activities could be done almost simultaneously, he does not have sufficient personnel to commit to the project at one time. In consequence, he returns the Gantt chart to its originators and requests that they find a new sequence of activities such that the call on his resources will be leveled instead of peaked.

(Resource leveling might be a desirable way of structuring activities in some cases. In others, it might pay for a company to mount a major effort, doing as many things as possible simultaneously, so as to get into the marketplace before the competition.)

The construction of the chart represents a preplan. In the planning phase, adjustments are made to the basic set of steps, the order in which they are to to be used, the allocation of resources to each step, and the estimated times for completing each job. As a general rule, materials, plant, facilities, labor, power, and so forth are required. A statement of actual, or desirable, resource availability allows for intelligent planning of the activity sequence. Once these steps have been completed, the planning process moves on to the detailed level of assigning specific resources and facilities in order to produce the chosen end result. Elapsed time to complete all the steps is usually considered to be of major consequence.

That is where the second purpose of the Gantt chart appears. Running along the top of the chart is a *time scale*. This time scale can be general, in the sense that it represents a sequence of days, or weeks, or months. On the other hand, calendar dates can be associated with the time scale so that it represents particular points in time. The former approach is useful when estimates of total time involved are required and when the starting point in real time is unknown. For example, assume that capital has to be raised to finance the project, but no one can estimate when the necessary monetary assets will be acquired. Plans will be launched at the completion of this stage, but because the completion date of that stage cannot be set, only an abstract time plan can be constructed.

Usually, cost and time estimates are supplied for completing all steps in the project. Such estimates are based upon specific commitments to a particular pattern for the allocation of resources. When a starting date is specified, calendar time can be utilized for the time scale. When real time is used, then it is very convenient to use the project plan as a check or control over what is actually happening so that revisions in the basic plans can be developed as required. There are penalties for delays occurring as a result of poor integration of the planning elements. We cannot afford to have a press shop staffed and waiting with all the necessary tools and dies at their disposal while the research laboratory is still determining the proper materials to be used. Opportunity costs such as these can occur in many different ways in the project planning cycle. The project manager can do a lot to reduce such opportunity costs.

The left-hand column listing all the stages is, in fact, the *operational sequence* of activities required for the design of our system.[2] It is the project's plan. If we make a mistake here we may cost ourselves out of business. It is also essential to bear in mind that a competitor may have a project plan similar to ours—or destructive to ours. If his is without error, or if he meets

---

[2]This may be the construction of a building, the development of a new service, the publication of a book, magazine, or catalog, or bringing out a new car (as in Fig. 7-3).

his objectives on time and we do not, or if he is able to achieve the completion of various steps in less time than it takes us, or if he is a better project planner than we are and finds ways to run various steps in parallel while we sequence them, it is likely that we will suffer many penalties as a result of our inadequacies. Figure 7-1 indicates that a number of the steps can be operating simultaneously even though they begin at different times. To recognize this fact, observe the number of project activities that are intersected simultaneously by any given time line. Sometimes a fraction of a job must be completed before the next step can begin. Often, stages can begin simultaneously. When the constraints are technological, it is not strange if, in a particular case, two-thirds of one prior stage and one-eighth of another prior stage must be completed before a third stage can be started.

Accomplishments: Planned vs. Actual

How does the plan measure up to the *actuality*? The darkened portion of each activity box represents the percentage of completion of each phase at a particular point in time designated by the time arrow. With succeeding days, the dark portion is lengthened until at completion the box is entirely filled. Thus, we have a running record of accomplishments.

The true course of projects never runs perfectly smoothly. Unexpected situations arise and difficulties may delay certain phases of the project. Typically, while some things lag, others spurt, and so some phases are ahead of schedule; others are behind. Specifying the activities of a project and the estimated times is a prior operation, but it is also an on-going operation. Constant refinement with new data is called for. Regular review is needed in order to adjust and update the running record of accomplishment. In rare instances an entirely new project sequence must be developed because of difficulties that arise.

It will be noted that in Fig. 7-1 the arrow appears on the second day of the fourth week. Usually that arrow is moved along on a daily basis, in effect saying, "This is today." We look down at each of the activities and see that the dark bars indicate how much of the job has been completed. The materials procurement stage lags; the second subassembly, J-20, is ahead of schedule. One has not even begun (Fabrication 3), although according to plan it should have almost been done.

We have now reviewed the elements of project planning in terms of the Gantt chart. It is an effective way of keeping track of what has happened in terms of what we thought should have happened. It is also a suitable control and accounting device. But what is lacking is that there is no suitable way of using the Gantt chart to determine how resources might have been allocated in a superior fashion. For example, for two parallel activities, x and y, if manpower had been shifted from activity x to activity y, it might have been possible to accomplish y in a shorter period of time. Correspondingly, x would have taken longer. Is this better? Another possibility would be to permit certain delays to occur in order to reduce costs. With the Gantt chart we have not succeeded in associating costs with the various activities nor with the overall project. As previously stated, problems amenable to Gantt chart methods cannot possess the complexities familiar in present-day project management situations. Let us, therefore, consider a relatively new project planning approach, commonly termed the *critical path method*.

PROBLEMS

1. A crash vaccine production activity has been instituted. Roughly 200 million doses are to be readied for the inoculation program, which starts in 8 months. The flow shop is associated with such high production volumes (and rates). Nevertheless, the characteristics of a project are very much in evidence. What is the best classification in this case? Explain.

2. List three projects and explain why they qualify as such. Describe the character of these projects, being careful to differentiate them from flow shops and job shops.

3. It has been stated in the text that there are 2 main types of P/OM activities, viz.,
(A) Planning, designing, redesigning, and implementing the system.
(B) Operating the system.
Describe the different kinds of managerial activities that would be best associated with each. Do you think that all of the A activities belong together, or would you create a third category?

4. A mass producer of paper products plans to construct another plant. A consulting firm with a strong project orientation has been retained to oversee the activities of the site selection and plant design committee. The committee is composed of executives with flow shop experience.
How should the members of the committee be made aware of the special characteristics of project management?

5. In certain projects, it is considered advisable to duplicate specified activities. Thus, 2 groups would be charged with completing the same activity.
Would you allow the groups to be in communication with each other? Explain your answer, making certain to identify the objectives of such parallel path activity.

6. Why should 1 person be responsible for all major project decisions? How does the flow shop differ from the project in this regard?
Answer: Coordination is an absolute requirement for successful project management. In the flow shop, much of the coordination has been pre-designed and is incorporated in the system.

7. "Sunk costs" are those which cannot be recovered by a decision to stop (or alter) a project. Discuss the degree of reversibility and ruin thresholds of projects in terms of "sunk costs."

8. Using Fig. 7-3 (p. 138), analyze the Gantt chart, "Timing Schedule for a New Car." Why are major die models completed before minor die models?

Should competitive marketing plans be finished two years before public introduction? Tool tryout is started before tool construction is finished; does this make sense? Raise additional questions of this type and try to answer them.

9. With reference to the Gantt chart in Fig. 7-3 (p. 138), how can we be sure that no step has been omitted by mistake? What way is there to tell that the sequence of activities in Fig. 7-3 is as good as can be had?

Answer (to both parts of the question): Consult as many knowledgeable people (including consultants) as can be identified. Check Gantt and PERT charts of prior introductions. The Gantt chart in Fig. 7-3 is more of a public relations piece than a viable project management approach. A detailed PERT-type system of activities would be used in actual practice.

eight
critical path
methods

The weaknesses of the Gantt Project Planning Chart provided the focus for significant developments in the planning of complex projects. A method was required that would permit optimal or near-optimal sequencing and utilization of resources. An appropriate methodology was found in the area of *network analysis*. Starting about 1957, a number of different approaches to large-scale project planning were begun at different locations and for different reasons. The reassuring thing about these efforts is the fact that in spite of a variety of names that emerged to label each system, they all turned out to be fundamentally alike. A rash of acronyms such as those that follow began to appear in literature devoted to the planning area.

PERT   Program Evaluation Research Task[1]
CPM   Critical Path Method
PRISM   Program Reliability Information System for Management

---

[1]See R. L. Martino, *Project Management and Control*. New York: American Management Association, 1964.

PEP	Program Evaluation Procedure
IMPACT	Integrated Managerial Programming Analysis Control Technique
SCANS	Scheduling and Control by Automated Network Systems
ICON	Integrated Control
MPACS	Management Planning and Control System
PAR	Project Audit Report
PLANNET	Planning Network
RAMPS	Resources Allocation and Multi-project Scheduling
LESS	Least Cost Estimating and Scheduling
SPERT	Schedule Performance Evaluation and Review Technique
TOES	Trade-off Evaluation System
TOPS	The Operational PERT System

The differences between the approaches arise primarily as a consequence of the original job for which the method was developed.[2] All of them share the notion of a critical path, and it is for this reason that we have chosen to call this chapter "Critical Path Methods" (CPMs). It is the only sensible choice of a name if the descriptive power of a name is of consequence. As for the remaining labels, PERT is the most familiar of all the above to project managers, and we shall, therefore, discuss the PERT variant of critical path methods.

Constructing PERT Networks

Three steps are required to utilize network models.

1. All the elements, jobs, steps, tasks, activities, and so on that are required to bring the project to fruition must be detailed.

2. A precise sequencing order must be determined that is based on technological feasibility, administrative capabilities, equipment and manpower availabilities, and managerial objectives. The rationale for sequential constraints should be made explicit.

3. The time (and cost) to perform each task or activity must be estimated. The method of estimation for time and cost must be detailed, and related to specifications of quality.

When all this information has been assembled, a PERT network can be constructed. Figure 8-1 presents an example of such a network.

---

[2]PERT was developed by the U.S. Navy Special Projects Office in conjunction with Booz, Allen and Hamilton. It was one of the first of the network methods, and was used for the Polaris project.

CPM was developed by E.I. duPont de Nemours and Company and Remington Rand at about the same time as PERT and was used to plan the construction of a plant. These are the two approaches on which our discussion centers.

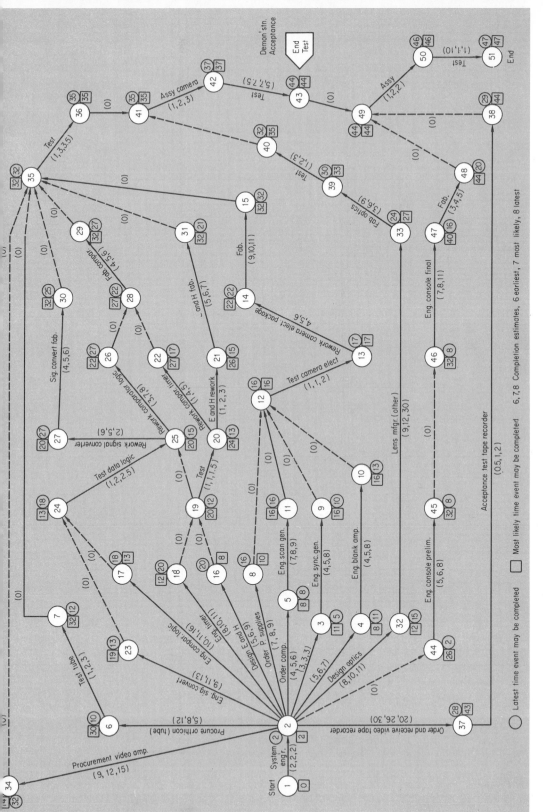

FIGURE 8-1. Datomatic reader—PERT/COST network for datomatic reader ["Datomatic Reader" (9-609-053) was written by Associate Professor William J. Abernathy, Harvard University, Graduate School of Business Administration. Reproduced by permission.]

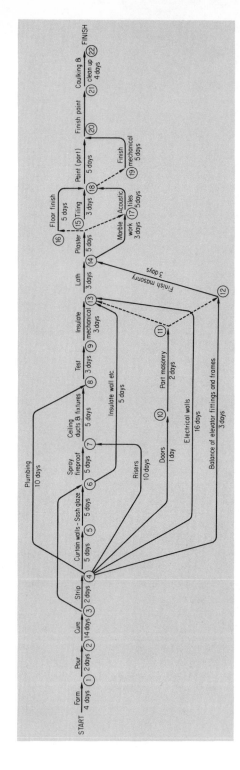

FIGURE 8-2. CPM diagram for a construction of a typical floor in a multistory building [Reprinted from *Engineering News-Record* (copyright, McGraw-Hill, Inc., January 26, 1961, all rights reserved.]

Detail is essential for the success of the CPMs. Jobs must be broken down into the elemental activities of which they are comprised. Activities cannot be overlooked without adversely affecting the results. Various estimates are required for each activity, with the result that for normally complex projects, a gigantic amount of information is generated. Fortunately, computer programs have been developed that readily handle the information required for most network systems.

Many applications of critical path methods can be found for production management projects (note that CPM was developed to manage the project of constructing a production process facility). A service organization may wish to develop a new service center. In the construction industry, CPM is well known (for example, see Fig. 8-2). Work on a government project often hinges on willingness and ability to use PERT.[3] In all these cases, as well as countless others, CPMs are useful. We use the network approach as a means of unifying the totality of activities, problems, decisions, and operations that constitute the project management field. Thereby, we have a planning tool that is operational from the very inception of enterprise activity.

Network Representation
(Where Activities Are Labeled on the Nodes)

Project planning begins with a list of all essential activities; then, it is necessary to describe precedence relations, i.e., which activities *must* go before or follow other activities.

A network of arrows and nodes can be drawn to represent a specific sequence of project activities. Such a network can be constructed by considering each activity to be a node (i.e., each of the small circles in Fig. 8-3 is a node).

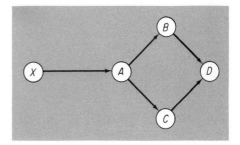

FIGURE 8-3. The activities X, A, B, C, and D have been arranged according to a specific set of precedence relations

The arrows (also called *arcs*) describe the order or precedence of the activities. We call this an *activity-oriented network*.

Figure 8-3 is equivalent to a list of project activities, each of which has

---

[3]Government agencies have found critical path methods so useful that they frequently require this approach from companies working on government contracts. This is particularly true when an integrated effort on the part of several companies is needed.

been numbered and arranged according to precedence. Thus:

Activity	Which Activities Must Immediately Precede
X	none
A	X
B	A
C	A
D	B, C

Another Way of Drawing Networks
(Where Activities Are Labeled on the Arcs)

An alternative technique exists for drawing networks. In this case, the activities are represented by the arcs (for example, refer to Fig. 8-4 and 8-5).

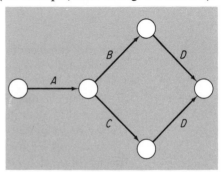

FIGURE 8-4. An infeasible, event-oriented network

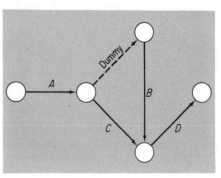

FIGURE 8-5. The infeasible event-oriented network in Fig. 8-4 can be made feasible using a dummy activity

The nodes are *events* that mark either the beginning of 1 or more activities or the completion of 1 or more activities, or both. We call this an *event-oriented network*.

It is easier to draw up an activity-oriented network, where the activities are represented by nodes. However, for the computational requirements of

PERT, it is necessary to employ an event-oriented network having nodes that can be identified with specific starting and finishing times. The reason for this requirement will become evident when we discuss critical path computations (pp. 153–60). For the moment, let us note that every event node in the PERT network will be identified with a 2-part scorecard of event calendar dates or clock times.

There is a problem in drawing some event-oriented networks. For example, if 2 activities, say B and C in Fig. 8-4, are preceded by the same activity A, and are followed by another common activity D, then the event-oriented network would require that 2 arcs be labeled activity D. This cannot be permitted for computational reasons. The PERT network algorithm cannot deal with 2 separate arcs both being called by the same name D. Therefore, we must redraw this network and insert what is called a *dummy activity*, represented by a dashed line in Fig. 8-5. Now, there is only 1 activity D, and the specified precedence relations are correct. The dummy activity is associated with 0 time for completion. Please note that the dummy activity could have gone to C instead of B, just as well.

Finding the right dummy activities, when required, is not difficult. The need for them will be apparent, and the appropriate construction can be developed by trial and error.

Activity Cycles

In planning a project, some activities go through a cycle of steps, repeating themselves many times at increasing levels of detail. But cycles are not permitted in PERT networks; they must be depicted in extensive form, as shown in Fig. 8-6.

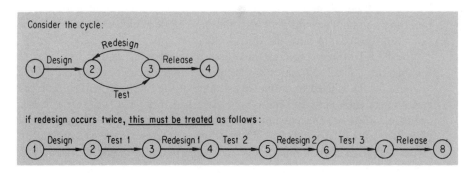

FIGURE 8-6. PERT networks must be developed in extensive form

Many different arrangements of activities and events are possible. Projects of realistic size can have thousands of interrelated activities. Whenever materials, parts, subassemblies, or particular procedures come together for a new activity, an event circle must be used to signify that the previous activity has been completed. Still, the definition of an activity is subjective. Depending on his style, the project manager may use few or many activities to represent the same project elements.

Time Estimation

Estimation is an important and interesting procedure that is intimately related to the well-being of individuals and organizations. Essentially, it means *to calculate approximately*. We are all taught from grade school on to calculate precisely; otherwise, our homework or test problem is marked wrong. There are few, if any, courses devoted to improving one's skill in making rough calculations, or judgments that are based upon opinions formed by tentative evaluations.

Management relies upon its ability to estimate. Continually, it must take action before hard data are available. Yet few organizations track the estimating capabilities of their employees. Such tracking is not hard to do. If historical records are maintained (as possible) of [Estimate minus actual result equals error] it would be possible to grade estimators in terms of:

1. How close is the average error to zero.
2. How dispersed are the errors.
3. Do the errors tend to be overestimates or underestimates.

There are basically different methods for obtaining estimates. First is one person's opinion derived from experience. Second is the pooling of several individuals' opinions derived from experience. Many different pooling techniques are available.[4] Third, several parameters of estimation are requested from an individual, and these are combined by a computing formula.[5] Here too, the pooling of several persons' opinions can be achieved. For PERT, the estimation procedure is of the third kind.

The PERT system requires that three parametric estimates be made for each activity. These estimates are then used as parameters of an estimating formula, which is used to derive an estimate of the time that will be required to complete each activity. The planner is asked to supply: (1) an optimistic estimate, called a; (2) a pessimistic estimate, called b; and (3) an estimate of what is most likely, called m.[6] These three estimates are then combined to give *an expected elapsed time*, called t_e. The formula for achieving the combi-

---

[4]The most obvious pooling technique is to obtain the average value, but many other approaches exist.

[5]Parameters are variables which have specific values that determine (in this case) the final estimate that is used.

[6]To understand why "the most likely" is not a sufficient estimate of activity time, consider the following example. If the vendor delivers on time, then 2 days are required; however, if the vendor cannot deliver on time, then 7 days are required. It is *most likely* that the vendor will deliver on time; therefore, 2 days is most likely, but hardly the best estimate of activity time.

nation is

$$t_e = \tfrac{1}{6}(a + b) + \tfrac{2}{3}(m)$$

This formula uses more information than a single estimate for activity time.[7]
The range, or spread between shortest and longest times, should provide additional insight into activity time, but practically speaking there is ample
evidence both pro and con. A possible distribution for these three elapsed
time estimates is shown in Fig. 8-7. Because estimates can be checked against

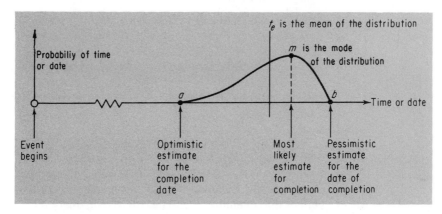

FIGURE 8-7. A *possible* distribution for the elapsed time estimates (There is no assurance
that the three estimates *a*, *m*, and *b*, falling at these positions on the time scale of the distribution,
will provide a better estimate of the mean than a simple, direct estimate of activity time.)

actuality it should be possible to determine eventually what is best for a particular kind of project. In any case, at the heart of the issue is the need to
develop some reasonably good estimate for the expected elapsed time required
for the completion of an activity.

---

[7]The three values *a*, *b*, and *m* are used to estimate the mean of a unimodal Beta distribution. This procedure does not apply to a U-shaped Beta distribution (see p. 152). For the
unimodal distribution, if *a* and *b* are equally spaced above and below *m*, then $m = t_e$.
That is:

$$t_e = \tfrac{1}{6}[(m - x = a) + (m + x = b)] + \tfrac{4}{6}(m) = m.$$

When *a* and *b* are not symmetric around *m*, t_e is moved in the direction of the greatest interval.

An Estimation Dilemma

It is not unusual that either one outcome is highly probable or
quite a different one is likely. A bimodal distribution, as shown in Fig.
8-8, prevails. We must question whether the mean of the distribution
t_e, in this case, is a better estimate than the most likely estimate for
completion *m*.

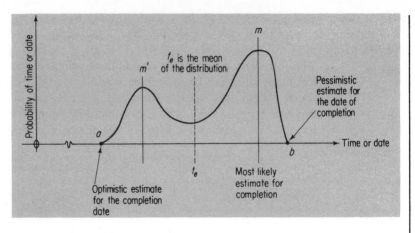

FIGURE 8-8. A bimodal distribution can be the basis for the elapsed time estimate

We would choose m, and test the effect on our plans of the true time being m'. We note also that m is a longer period than m'. Our preference is to use the least desirable (or worst case) estimate. Consequently, if m and m' were in reverse positions, we would have yet another dilemma to cope with. Management must always decide on the best way to deal with such problems. Perhaps the project manager should alter the design of this activity so that the estimation quandary can be removed. He should do this only if the distinction between m and m' seriously affects the project as a whole.

In addition, an estimate of the variances associated with the expected value of elapsed time is also frequently supplied for the PERT system. Variance (represented by σ^2) is a measure of the spread of a distribution. A tall and thin distribution has an almost 0 variance; whereas a flat and shallow distribution has a large variance. The square root of variance, called the standard deviation (and represented by σ), often is used to represent the spread of a probability distribution. An important statistical rule supports the fact that the sum of the variances of a number of consecutive estimates of sequenced *independent* activities measures the variance of the total sequence. The independence referred to is with respect to activity times, i.e., how long it should take to accomplish each operation; not with respect to starting and finishing times by the clock and the calendar. For example, if 3 estimates, t_{e_1}, t_{e_2}, and t_{e_3} are made, each of them having a particular variance measure $\sigma_1^2, \sigma_2^2, \sigma_3^2$, then the variance of the sum of these estimates is given by $\sigma_1^2 + \sigma_2^2 + \sigma_3^2$. This relationship is depicted in Fig. 8-9. The formula for the variance of the distribution[8] (shown in Fig. 8-7) is given by $\sigma^2 = [\frac{1}{6}(b-a)]^2$.

---

[8]Associated with the estimate of the variance of a beta distribution.

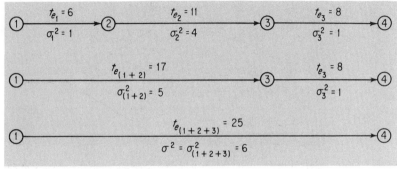

FIGURE 8-9. The variance σ^2 of combined estimates is equal to the sum of the variances of the individual estimates of *independent* activities.

Critical Path Computations

Let us examine the situation for Lensmasters, Inc. At the outset, they must engage in 3 basically different activities. These are

A. Obtain inputs: materials and skills (activities A_1, A_2, and A_3).
B. Construct soft lens production process (activities B_1 and B_2).
C. Develop distribution channels (activities C_1, C_2, and C_3).

Some constraints exist: namely, A_2 must be completed before either A_3 or B_2 can begin; also A_3, B_2, and C_3 must be completed before product launch (called L) can occur. This network information is illustrated in Fig. 8-10. In addition, the estimates for the duration or elapsed time t_e of each activity are shown on their respective arcs (in working days).

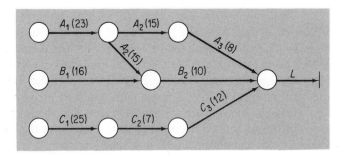

FIGURE 8-10. The network for launching Lensmaters' new soft contact lens (with elapsed time estimates t_e in days)
A dummy variable will be required, since A_2 appears twice in the network.

The network in Fig. 8-10 is not acceptable. The same activity, A_2, appears twice. Therefore, a dummy activity is created, as shown in Fig. 8-11, which

153

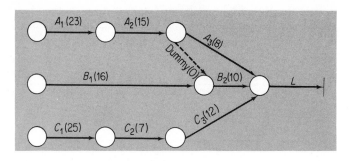

FIGURE 8-11. A dummy activity has been added to the network of Fig. 8-10. The dummy is associated with $t_e = 0$.

solves the problem. Note that the following unique paths exist in Fig. 8-11's network:

Top path: A_1, A_2, A_3
Dummy path: A_1, A_2, Dummy, B_2
Middle path: B_1, B_2
Bottom path: C_1, C_2, C_3

Every event node in the PERT network will be identified with the following 2-part scorecard of event calendar dates or clock times.

$$\boxed{\begin{array}{c|c} T_E & T_L \end{array}}$$

$T_E =$ earliest possible starting time

$T_L =$ latest allowable starting time

We obtain *cumulative* total times for *each* network path, moving along the particular path from the beginning of the project to the end. Call these values T_E. Each cumulative total T_E gives the earliest possible clock time that the next event can begin. In Fig. 8-12, the scorecard of event dates (or times) described above has only the "earliest start up" times entered. It will be noted that as we sum along different paths, until we arrive at a junction node (e.g., where the dummy activity and B_1 meet) that the joining branches can carry a different cumulative number to that node (in this case, 38 and 16). Whenever this condition arises at a junction node, *we accept the largest value of T_E*, i.e., 38. All further accumulation proceeds with this larger number, which is the earliest possible starting time for the next event in the network. The scorecard value of T_E at the last node in the network represents expected *project completion* time. It also represents the earliest possible time that the product launch can begin, viz., after 48 working days. This last value of T_E is a measure of the maximum cumulative time of any path in the network; that is, the longest time sequence of activities in the network.

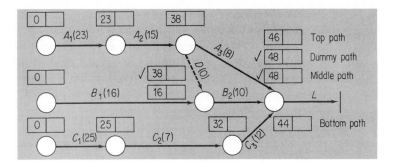

FIGURE 8-12. Lensmasters' network showing the scorecoard of event times at each node

Values for T_E (which is the earliest possible clock time that each event can begin) are indicated.

What we now want to know is, Which of the 4 unique paths (previously listed) accounts for the longest time sequence of activities? That path is called the *critical path*.

To determine the critical path, start with the largest cumulative total. In our case, this is $T_E = 48$, which is the estimated time for project *completion*. We now move backwards through the network. Successively we subtract expected elapsed activity times, t_e. The values derived by subtraction, called T_L (the second box in the scorecard of event times), are assigned to their respective event nodes. Each subtraction ($T_L - t_e$) is based on the last T_L and the preceding t_e. The starting value of T_L is taken as the largest value of T_E, in this case 48. In Fig. 8-13, the values of T_L are recorded in the scorecard of event times.

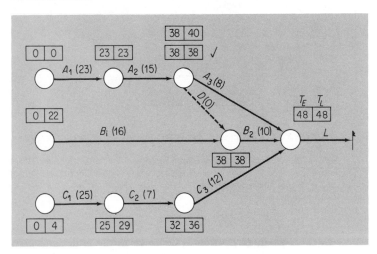

FIGURE 8-13. Lensmasters' network showing the values of T_E and T_L

T_L is the latest possible clock time at which an activity can be started in order for the project to be completed on time.

155

In some instances, when moving backwards, 2 or more arcs converge on a node such that the values of T_L produced by subtraction are not equal. (For this example, such convergence occurs at A_2's completion node, where T_L can equal either 38 or 40.) Then, *we accept the smallest value of T_L*, i.e., 38, and continue our subtractions with this smallest number. The values of T_L are measures of the latest allowable clock time at which the next activity can be started in order to complete the project in accordance with its critical path time.

The critical path is A_1, A_2, D, B_2, based upon the t_e sums $23 + 15 + 0 + 10 = 48$. This is the longest time path through the network, which is the definition of the critical path. In large, complex networks, the critical path can seldom be found by inspection. From the new project management models, an algorithm is available that computes slack time at each node of the network. Slack time is the slippage (or wasted time) that can be tolerated in an activity without change of the project completion time.

Measure of Slack

The difference, $T_L - T_E$, can be obtained for each event node. It describes the amount of *slack* that exists at that node in the network. See Fig. 8-14,

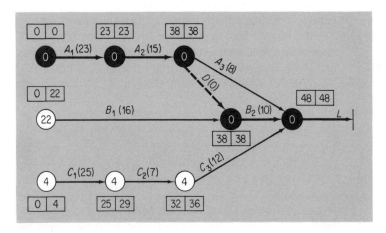

FIGURE 8-14. Lensmasters' network showing the values of $T_L - T_E$ (in the node circles)
($T_L - T_E$) is the slack time available for the activity that follows. The critical path has ($T_L - T_E = 0$) for all its activities. In this example the nodes along the path A_1, A_2, D, B_2 are all associated with 0 slack time; therefore, it is the critical path, marked with the darker line.

where the values $T_L - T_E$ are shown in the node circles. Where slack exists, activities can start later or take longer than planned. Thus, an activity's time estimate can slip by the amount of slack that exists in its part of the network, and yet the total job can still be completed on time. The critical path (or paths) can be recognized by the fact that at every node of the critical path, $T_L - T_E$

$= 0$. In Fig. 8-14, we observe that $T_L - T_E = 0$ for all of the nodes comprising the path A_1, A_2, D, B_2, which is the critical path. All activities in the bottom path have slack of 4, meaning that any 1 of them (but only 1) can slip behind by 4 days without changing the target time of project completion. Slack normally applies to an entire path, but sometimes to just 1 activity. Thus, activity A_3 can slip by its own slack of 2 days[9] and similarly activity B_1 has leeway of 22 days. You will remember, management's concern in the Lensmasters' situation was that to launch their new product, everything seemed to have to be done at the beginning, and at the same time. Now we know that this is not required. B_1 can wait until the twenty-second day. A_1 must begin on time so that A_2 can be completed before B_2 starts. C_1 can begin four days late, followed by B_1 18 days later. Figure 8-15 depicts the project schedule. Note that if the project work schedule in Fig. 8-15 is followed, then

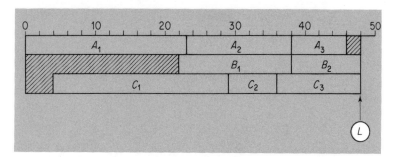

FIGURE 8-15. Lensmasters' project work schedule

3 paths through the network have become critical paths.[10] Only activity A_3 can be allowed to slip without increasing the time to launch. This is because all slack (except A_3's) has been removed by delaying the start of work for both the B and C branches by the total amount of existing slack. Lensmasters' management might not like that situation, preferring to delay B-branch activities by (say) 10 working days and C-branch activities by (say) only one day.

Knowing which activities have slack is important. Assume that A_1, B_1, and C_1 all begin at the same time. Then, it would be wasteful to do any expediting[11] for activities A_3, B_1, C_1, C_2, and C_3, unless the situation had changed and one or more of them had now joined a critical path. The major emphasis of project control should be assigned to the critical path that directly affects the project completion date. This information was not available from the Gantt chart.

---

[9]In this example, activity A_3 connects 2 nodes, both on the critical path. As a result, its slack cannot show up, since all nodes along the critical path have 0 slack. The computation of A_3's slack must be computed independently.

[10]This calls our attention to the fact that more than 1 path through any project network can be critical.

[11]This well-known term was *first used* by Henry Kaiser in connection with maintaining the critical shipbuilding schedules of World War II.

Distribution of Completion Times

The method we have been using is often called PERT/TIME. Time is the only factor under consideration. It is one of the fundamental dimensions of the planners' objectives. With this idea in mind, let us extend the time concept by employing the variance measures shown in parenthesis for each arc in Fig. 8-16. We sum the variances, proceeding along the critical path. Thus, for the

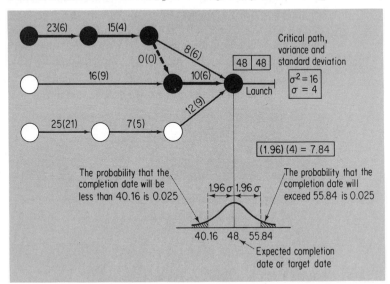

FIGURE 8-16. Lensmasters' Project Network, where the estimates t_e are shown as before but now, in addition, the variance of the estimates are included in parentheses. Also, the distribution of completion times around the expected time of 48 is shown. There is 0.05 probability that the actual completion time will not fall in the range of times 55.84 days to 40.16 days.

final event that signals completion of the job we can obtain not only the expected time for project completion but also an estimate of the variance around this expected value. Figure 8-16 shows a distribution with both tails cut off at the limit of 1.96 standard deviations (plus and minus from the mean value). Each tail contains the probabilities of an event occurring approximately 25 out of 1000 times.[12] The right-hand tail contains long completion dates. The left-hand tail contains short completion dates. Thus, moving 1.96 standard deviations (1.96σ) in either direction gives us a range of times for

---

[12]This assumes that a normal distribution applies, which would be the effect of considering many beta distributions combining to form a single distribution for the project as a whole.

Number of Standard Deviations (σ) $\pm$ from the Mean	Probability that the Actual Time Falls Within the Specified Range
1σ	0.680
1.64σ	0.900
1.96σ	0.950
3σ	0.997

Why Is the Completion Time So Important?

There are 3 dimensions for assessing projects. These are completion time, total cost, and quality of results. All 3 are important but it is often the case that the targeted date for finishing the project is the first factor considered.

This is not surprising for planetary probes, where a "window" is open at very specific, and often rare, times. The so-called "window" is defined by such factors as closeness to Earth, relative trajectories, and so forth. In the same sense, seasonal factors may produce a "window" for the Alaska pipeline, offshore exploratory drilling, or even laying sewer pipes.

Even when the "window" concept does not apply, "as soon as possible" frequently does. Projects usually involve heavy investments that do not start paying off until the project is completed. When viewing project costs against such large investments, managers prefer to spend more now to decrease completion time so that a positive cash flow (or other benefits, e.g., hospital beds) can be obtained "as soon as possible."

In bidding situations, project completion time is a major determinant (or requirement when specified) for being awarded the job. It is not unusual for contract terms to include some pretty stiff penalty clauses relating to failure to bring the project in on time.

---

job completion within which there is a 95 percent probability that the actual completion date will fall. Stated another way, we have determined, utilizing a 1.96σ criterion, an earliest and latest project completion date.

The Effect of Estimated Variance

Let us compute the expected completion time of each unique path in the network and its total variance. First, however, we should note that it is statistically correct to sum the variances associated with each activity when the expected activity times are derived from well-behaved distributions such as the normal distribution or the beta distribution.

Path	Expected Completion Time	Total Variance	95% Range (1.96σ)
1 A_1, A_2, A_3	46 days	16	38.16–53.84
2 A_1, A_2, D, B_2 (critical path)	48 days	16	40.16–55.84
3 B_1, B_2	26 days	15	18.40–33.59
4 C_1, C_2, C_3	44 days	35	32.40–55.60

The variance of the fourth path is so large that the upper limit of 55.60 is almost the same as the upper limit of the *critical path* (55.84). If the activities along the critical path proceed about as expected, but the fourth path activities take excessive times, then completion will not occur within 48 working days. Completion, dominated by the new critical path, C_1, C_2, C_3, may require as much as 55.6 days, and this can occur within the 95 percent probability range. This means that careful managerial attention should be paid to the marketing and distribution activities of the fourth path, since these activities can dominate the present critical path and cause the targeted completion date of the project to be missed.

Schedule Control

At any stage of the project, the manager can ask for a progress report. Each activity, on a regular basis, reports where it stands. The computer can print out, on command, those activities that are ahead and those that are behind, as well as measures of degree. If a shift in the critical path occurs, it is reported. New slack values appear. Control over schedule is excellent. The network is continually updated to reflect project progress.

Thus, the project methods that we have been describing have greatly improved the manager's knowledge of what is going on with all project activities, at any time. In the next chapter, we learn that resource management is yet another benefit derived from the new techniques.

PROBLEMS

1. Convert the figure below, where activities are labeled as nodes, into an an equivalent figure where activities are labeled on arcs.

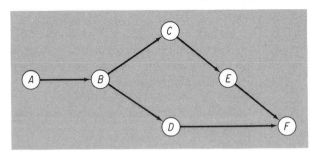

FIGURE 8-17.

2. Project management requires many estimates and relies on the quality of these estimates. Discuss the importance of estimation. How does it count?

3. If an organization wishes to track the estimating capabilities of its employees, how would it go about doing this?

4. What weaknesses of the Gantt project planning technique are overcome by critical path methods?

5. What weaknesses characterize both the Gantt project planning technique and the critical path methods?

6. Draw up an appropriate PERT diagram for the following projects:
   a. A football play
   b. Moving a piano
   c. Dictating a letter
   d. Having a group of 3 people solve the following problem as rapidly as possible with full accuracy:

$$\frac{(10.314)^4}{(6.501)^2} + \frac{(3.241)^3}{(1.008)^5}$$

Answer: A possible PERT diagram for the arithmetic problem *d* is shown in Fig. 8-18.

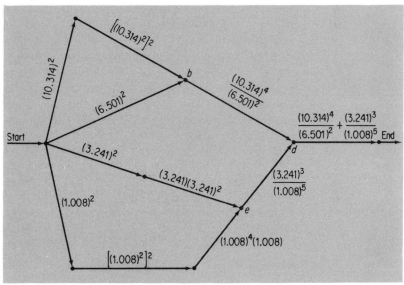

FIGURE 8-18.

We see that up to nodes *c* and *d*, 4 individuals could be utilized. After this, only 2 problem solvers would be required, and at node *d*, the staff requirement is reduced to 1 person. If numerical estimates of required times are associated with these activities, a critical path can be defined. It is interesting to compare actual times against these estimates.

Similar networks and analytic procedures can be developed for the other examples specified in this problem.

7. Convert the Gantt-type project planning chart (Fig. 7-3) into an appropriate critical path diagram. Make whatever assumptions you require. Discuss the advantages of each form of representation.

Answer: It might be said that a PERT diagram has higher dimensionality than a Gantt chart. It requires more detailed information for its construction. Converting a Gantt chart to a PERT chart reveals the significance of this statement far more directly than any set of words. Nevertheless, we can depict the relationship as being somewhat analogous to that of a three-dimensional pyramid as compared to a drawing of the same pyramid.

Current industrial practice dictates that a group that is intimately familiar with the project construct an appropriate critical path diagram. (We can hardly qualify ourselves in this regard with respect to Fig. 7-3) We may, however, attempt to convert the Gantt chart into a PERT diagram by making some approximations concerning the starting and finishing times of an activity. It is frequently useful to introduce delay, that is, an activity having no cost but which takes up a certain amount of time. The PERT diagram might then look something like Fig. 8-19.

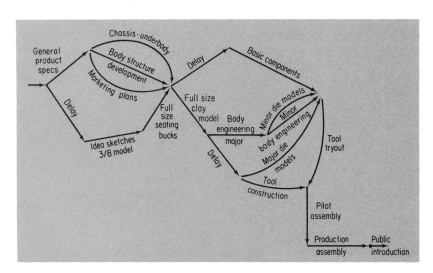

FIGURE 8-19.

nine
resource leveling

The fundamental idea of resource leveling is to smooth out the commitment of resources (pattern of work) and to balance demand for resources among activities over time.

The PERT project method allows us to determine whether a better arrangement of resource utilization might be found. For example, if cash flow to the project is sporadic, the project manager might prefer to smooth this demand for cash over time. Also, if among a set of relatively simultaneous activities, a few are receiving the greatest percentage of project expenditures, it might (or might not) be desirable to level the resource allocations. Once the decision is made to level or smooth, trade-off techniques can be designed to address the specific objectives.

Trading Off Resources over Time

A project that experiences oscillating calls on its resources is hard to manage. For example, if an enormous labor force is required for some (project) work intervals while during other intervals there are few people working, then an effort should be made to level work force requirements over time. It is costly and disruptive to make major changes in project group size. Also, a facility is designed with specific occupancy in mind, and the task of managing a project is impeded by very uneven resource demand patterns.

To better understand the resource leveling problem over time, refer to Fig. 4-2 on p. 68. The figure illustrates the cash flows of n different products or services and their cumulative total cash flow. Negative cash flows (outflows) most often occur during the R&D project stages. The organization must manage its cash flows so that it never runs short of cash to pay employees, buy materials, etc. If the outflow becomes too large, then one or more projects may have to be eliminated or stretched out. Consider Fig. 8-14 on p. 156. Lensmasters could stretch out this project by changing the target interval for completion from 48 to (say) 60 days. The rate of spending for a project of length T can be reduced by stretching T. Leveling can also be achieved by scheduling activities at different times, as allowed by slack conditions. It is always important to make such decisions with the total portfolio of projects that are underway in mind, and to recognize that resources can be traded off between projects—as well as within any specific project.

Trading Off Resources between Activities

The critical path concept is basic to the notion of resource leveling. What is not critical is slack. The existence of slack is an important basis for reallocation of resources and leveling. Shortly, we shall examine a situation where work force assignments to network activities will be shifted from slack path activities to critical path activities. This will produce a decrease in the length of the critical path. It will also result in a greater demand for the use of resources, and the demand will tend to be smoother and more constant over time. The resources can include the work force, materials, equipment, administrative time, and cash to pay both direct and indirect costs.

Trading off resources between activities does not have to result in a shorter critical path. Instead, better resource leveling sometimes might be achieved by moving resources from the critical path to slack paths. This would increase the length of time required to complete the project. Another option exists, namely, to maintain the critical path activities as they are, but to schedule their work at a slower rate. This has the effect of committing fewer resources per unit of time and lengthening the critical path.

The resource leveling activity is an important P/OM responsibility. There are budgetary constraints, and they must be met. Thus, the project managers consistently query, Can the budget be met? They also ask from the viewpoint of efficient use of resources, Would there be an advantage in trading slack path resources to the critical path, or vice versa (if either can be done)?

Let us now specifically consider the goal of reducing the length of the critical path. Alteration of the project design that reduces the time of the critical path would either: (1) decrease the amount of slack that exists in the other branches of the network by trading off their resources to the critical path or (2) employ additional resources. The new resources might be obtained by trading them off from other projects or by increasing the total available budget.

We shall examine the latter alternative (2) in the next section entitled Trading Off Costs and Times. Therefore, turning to the first option, let us assume that the length of time it takes to complete each activity is *linearly* related to the number of workers employed on the job. If the required skills are interchangeable between activities, we could then bring the entire network into better balance by shifting work force resources from slack activities to the critical path. This has been done for a simple example, which is represented in Fig. 9-1.

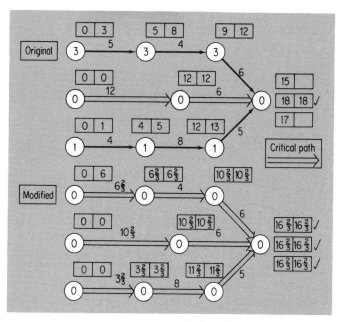

FIGURE 9-1. An orginal project network which is modified by trading-off resources to remove all slack
A perfectly balanced PERT network is achieved because we have permitted the resources to be fractionated. The target date has been improved by 1-1/3 time units.

In Fig. 9-1, the project as *originally* configured has a project completion time of 18. All activities in the upper branch of the project network share a slack of 3; in the lower branch they share a slack of 1. The critical path is the middle branch. Our objective is to trade off resources from slack activities to the critical path, which will reduce the time for completion of the critical path and increase the time of the slack paths, thereby decreasing the amount of slack.

This has been accomplished in the *modified* network of Fig. 9-1, where all of the paths are critical. In Fig. 9-2 we detail the modification steps that result in all paths being critical.

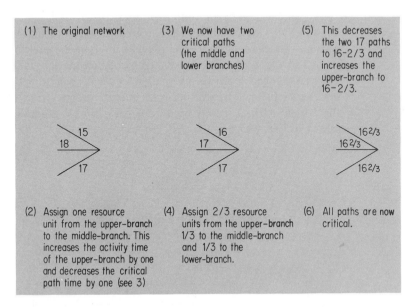

(1) The original network

(3) We now have two critical paths (the middle and lower branches)

(5) This decreases the two 17 paths to 16-2/3 and increases the upper-branch to 16-2/3.

(2) Assign one resource unit from the upper-branch to the middle-branch. This increases the activity time of the upper-branch by one and decreases the critical path time by one (see 3)

(4) Assign 2/3 resource units from the upper-branch 1/3 to the middle-branch and 1/3 to the lower-branch.

(6) All paths are now critical.

FIGURE 9-2. Steps of network modification to decrease slack

In general, we cannot hope to achieve such perfect balance because men, machines, and other resources cannot be fractionated at will, and because all skills and facilities are not readily interchangeable between branches. But to the extent that changes can be made, we usually do achieve considerable improvement in the time performance of the system.[1] The ability to recognize slack paths, and to trade off resources in the manner that we have described above, makes critical path methods significantly more useful than the older methods associated with the Gantt project chart. The paths of greatest slack provide the best opportunities for improving the target date of the project. On the other hand, they also point to places where effort would be wasted in expediting work to meet scheduled deadlines.

Sometimes it is possible to utilize whatever expediting and control facilities exist to improve the variance along the critical path. By doing this, we do not change the target date, but instead we reduce the risk of substantially deviating from the target date.

---

[1] Perfect balance may be undesirable. It raises every activity to critical status, imposing enormous burdens on the project manager, who must deal with every instance of slippage as being crucial to project completion.

Trading Off Costs and Times

Another way to level resources (or alternatively, to peak their use) is by means of trade-offs of costs and time. For activities along the critical path, it is often possible to reduce their duration by spending more money. Activities that are not on the critical path can afford to be lengthened in time. The project manager may save money by withdrawing resources from slack activities. Such savings could be funneled to critical path activities of the same project or to other projects.

Let us examine the alternatives of the "crash" program with peaked resource requirements and the "normal" program with leveled resource needs. Assume that the project planners desire to run the project on a crash basis, i.e., minimum time. This often entails additions to the project budget. Alternatively, another major objective is to minimize cost. This will stretch out project time and relieve budgetary pressures. The relationships of cost and time have received considerable investigation. Various time-cost systems have been developed and others are being developed to attempt to resolve this problem, which we recognize as one of conflicting multiple objectives.

The PERT/COST/TIME system starts in the same way as does PERT/ TIME. That is, we construct the representative network of activities and events. However, in this case we have developed two different estimates for each activity. These are (1) a minimum time estimate and its cost and (2) a minimum cost estimate and its time. Figure 9-3 shows the way in which these factors might be related for each of the network activities A, B, C, D illustrated in Fig. 9-4.

First, the minimum cost estimate is used for each activity, and the critical path is determined for those data. The result will be a completion date that

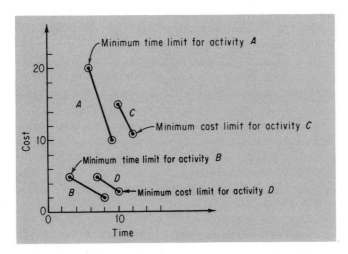

FIGURE 9-3. Some representative COST/TIME relationships where the (weak) assumption is made that linearity prevails over the specified range. The end points are assumed to be limits.

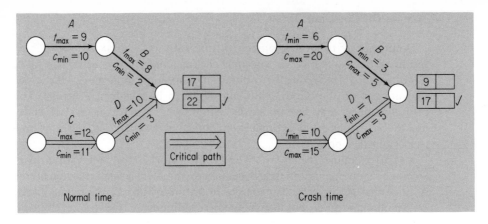

FIGURE 9-4. Comparing normal and crash time networks

is based upon minimum cost requirements for completing the project. This completion date and the length of time required to complete the project under minimum cost conditions may be too great to be tolerated. Then the minimum (crash) time network can be examined. For the comparison, see Fig. 9-4.

For minimum cost and normal time, the bottom path C, D is the critical path, requiring 22 days with a cost of 14. Slack along the upper path A, B is $T_L - T_E = 22 - 17 = 5$ days.

For minimum time (crash program), the bottom path C, D remains critical, but project completion time has been reduced by 5 days to 17 days. The cost has increased by 43 percent to 20. The crash program has not removed slack; it has increased to 8 days. If the top path A, B had not been crashed, then both paths A, B and C, D would be critical at 17 days. By trading off resources between activities (if possible) an even better reduction in total project time might be achieved.

Now, assume that management has stated that total project time should be as close to 20 days as possible. Normal time project planning misses the mark by $+2$ days, and the crash program overshoots the objective by -3 days.

Accordingly, alternative times, requiring greater costs, can then be substituted for chosen minimum cost activities *along* the normal time critical path. In this way, the critical path can be shortened until such time that: (1) another path becomes critical or (2) a satisfactory compromise with the original critical path is achieved.

As a rule of thumb, we make compromises for those activities along the critical path where the ratio of increasing costs for the activity with respect to decreasing time for the activity is smallest. Thus, we select that *critical path activity* where $|\Delta \text{ cost}| \div |\Delta \text{ time}|$ is *smallest*. Then the next biggest ratio is used, and so on, until a satisfactory compromise between time and cost is achieved. If the critical path switches, we make our next alterations along the new path.

For our example, the smallest measure of the ratios (of the absolute values) $|\Delta\ \text{COST}| \div |\Delta\ \text{TIME}|$ applying *only* to the critical path is associated with activity D. Thus:

Activity	Increase (Δ Cost)	Decrease (Δ Time)	|Δ Cost| ÷ |Δ Time|
C	+4	−2	2
D	+2	−3	$\frac{2}{3}$

For activity D, $t_{\max} = 10$, $t_{\min} = 7$; using the normal time network, set t_e at 8, which produces the required critical path of 20. What cost c_e results? Making the required change for activity D, when $t_e = 8$, $c_e = 4\frac{1}{3}$ (see Fig. 9-3).[2] The critical path is now C, D with final $T_E = 20$ and cost $= 15\frac{1}{3}$. The slack for the upper path A, B is $T_L - T_E = 3$. Figure 9-5 depicts this solution.

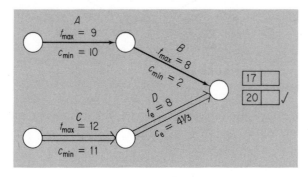

FIGURE 9-5. The trade-off solution

The PERT/COST/TIME method can be modified to meet the particular requirements of a given project. It can be used to level the demand on financial resources as well as on manpower, facilities, energy, etc. It is not an optimizing technique. Instead, it is a logical attempt to utilize reasonable trade-offs between cost and time, where they count, in order to obtain an approximation to an optimal result. Where quality, cost, and time can be formally related, an extension of these trade-off notions is not difficult to construct.

---

[2]If the graph of Fig. 9-3 is not used, the calculation is

$$\frac{c_{\max} - c_{\min}}{t_{\max} - t_{\min}} = \frac{2}{3} = \frac{c_e - c_{\min}}{t_{\max} - t_e} = \frac{c_e - 3}{10 - 8} = \frac{c_e - 3}{2}$$

whence $c_e = \frac{4}{3} + 3 = 4\frac{1}{3}$.

Conclusion

Trade-off models in project planning represent one of the most advanced aspects of P/OM capabilities. Projects are the means by which progress is achieved. The present is altered, hopefully in a constructive fashion. The methods we have discussed do not assure the quality of the future. That remains a social issue.

PROBLEMS

1. Explain the difference between resource leveling over time and between activities.

2. Staging a play has been treated by project planning methods. Assume that the network in Fig. 9-6 is a reasonable description of the production and rehearsal activities that must be completed before the play can open.

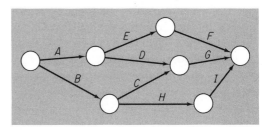

FIGURE 9-6.

We have also tabled the estimates for crash times and normal times in the network.

Activity	t_{min}	t_{max}	c_{min}	c_{max}
A	5	9	5	12
B	10	12	4	10
C	3	8	9	15
D	6	7	3	8
E	4	14	12	20
F	5	7	9	12
G	2	3	6	11
H	7	10	2	9
I	3	5	7	9

a. Find the critical paths for both normal time and crash time.
b. What slack exists in each case? What are the cost differences?
c. Assume that the director wants a target date halfway between the

required total project times of crash and normal planning. Use resource leveling with cost and time trade-offs to achieve the objective.

3. How can resource leveling over time and between activities be applied to the project of filming a movie? Note the degrees of freedom that exist for the time order of scenes.

4. Consider a number of projects that are being done together as a portfolio. The portfolio includes a range of risks and expected returns on investment. When examining possibilities for resource leveling, would you tend to concentrate resources on low risk/low return, average risk/average return, or high risk/high return projects? Explain your answer in terms of trading off resources over time, between activities, and between costs and times.

5. The Delta Company manufactures a full line of cosmetics. A competitor has recently brought out a new form of hair spray that shows every sign of sweeping the market and destroying Delta's position in the market. The sales manager asks the production manager what the shortest possible time would be for Delta to reach the market with a new product packed in a redesigned container. The production manager sets down the following PERT structure:

Activity	Initial Event	Terminal Event	Duration
Design product	1	2	
Design package	1	3	
Test market package	3	5	
Distribute to dealers	5	6	
Order package materials	3	4	
Fabricate package	4	5	
Order materials for product	2	4	
Test market product	2	7	
Fabricate product	4	7	
Package product	7	5	

a. Construct the PERT diagram.
b. Estimate the durations that you think might apply in a reasonable way. Alternatively, use the hypothetical estimates provided in the answer, part **b.**
c. Determine the critical path.
d. Neither the sales manager nor the production manager is satisfied with the way the project is designed, but the production manager insists that because of the pressure of time the company will be forced to follow this plan. In what ways does this plan violate good practice?
e. By trading off resources would it be possible to reduce your critical path time?

Answer:

a.

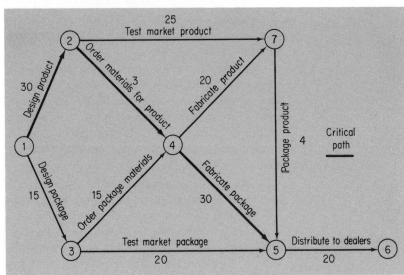

FIGURE 9-7.

b.

Activity	Duration (*days*)
Design product	30
Design package	15
Test market package	20
Distribute to dealers	20
Order package material	15
Fabricate package	30
Order materials for product	3
Test market product	25
Fabricate product	20
Package product	4

c. For the hypothetical expected times in **b**, the critical path is shown as a heavier line in the PERT diagram in **a**.

d. The project has several serious flaws. Materials for both the product and the package are ordered while they are still being individually test-marketed. (The notion of separate test markets for the product and the package deserves to be severely criticized. Few marketing situations could justify a procedure that violates the systems concept in such an obvious way.) Then, in addition, fabrication of the product and package is scheduled to begin before the respective test markets have been completed. This does not permit any improvements suggested by the test market to be incorporated into the product. A further discrepancy arises from the fact that the product is to be packaged before the activity, "fabricate package," is completed. This difficulty would have to be cleared up before the project schedule could be approved. It is doubtful that any amount of time pressure could secure the release of this project as it stands.

e. It should, of course, be possible to reduce the critical path time by trading resources from branches with slack to the critical path activities. For instance, the design of the package might be extended so that more effort could be devoted to product design. Other trade-off possibilities would also be considered, but not until the network design is finalized and approved.

SUMMARY OF
PART 3

Chapter 7

We begin with relevant differentiating characteristics of projects. This is followed by some history of project management. We have introduced the Gantt chart, and have explained how it is used.

Chapter 8

Critical paths methods are introduced, including:

1. The construction of PERT networks.
2. Methods and Problems of activity time estimation.
3. How to use the $(T_L - T_E = 0)$ algorithm of 0 slack to determine the critical path.
4. Working with variance measures of activity times to target completion time within a range x percent of the time.
5. How to expedite slippage by means of schedule control, but only when necessary (i.e., it is seldom used for slack time activities).

Chapter 9

Resource leveling is introduced, and the following concepts are explained.

1. Resource leveling by trading off resources to get a more even balance among project activities.
2. Resource leveling by trading off resources to decrease the overall project completion time.

3. Resource leveling and resource peaking through the use of cost/time trade-off functions to change project completion times and to gain sensible cost control over project activities.

Of course, there is more to project management, but anyone understanding what we have described in Part 3 can put into practice a major capability to deal effectively and productively with project systems.

REFERENCES
PART 3

ARCHIBALD, R. D. and R. L. VILLORIA, *Network Based Management Systems* (*CPM/PERT*). New York; John Wiley & Sons, 1967.

BATTERSBY, A., *Network Analysis for Planning and Scheduling*, 2nd ed. New York: St. Martin's Press, Inc., 1967.

EVARTS, H. F., *Introduction to PERT*. Boston: Allyn & Bacon, Inc., 1964.

IANNONE. A., *Management Program Planning and Control*. Englewood Cliffs, N.J.: Prentice-Hall, Inc., 1967.

KELLEY, J. E., JR., "Critical Path Planning and Scheduling: Mathematical Basis," *Operations Research*, IX, No. 3 (May-June, 1961), 296–320.

LEVIN, R. I. and C. A. KIRKPATRICK, *Management Planning and Control with PERT/CPM*. New York: McGraw-Hill Book Co., Inc., 1966.

MILLER, R. W., *Schedule, Cost, and Profit Control with PERT*. New York: McGraw-Hill Book Co., Inc., 1963.

MALCOLM, D. G., J. H. ROSEBOOM, C. E. CLARK, and W. FAZER, "Application of a Technique for Research and Development Program Evaluation," *Operations Research*, VII, No. 5 (Sept.-Oct., 1959), 646–669.

RADCLIFFE, B. M. ET AL., *Critical Path Method*. Chicago: Canners Publishing Co., 1967.

STOCKTON, R. STANSBURY, *Introduction to PERT*. Boston: Allyn and Bacon, Inc., 1964.

WIEST, J. D. and F. K. LEVY, *A Management Guide to PERT/CPM*. Englewood Cliffs, N.J.: Prentice-Hall, Inc., 1969.

flow shop
management

4

Flow shop management is uniquely involved with preplanning what is to be done. All aspects of the input/output process are predesigned with engineering skills, and the commitment to equipment investments is often substantial. Usually, flexibility to change a flow shop process is designed out of the system—not intentionally, but as a result of the special steps that are taken to increase productivity. For example, equipment is specially designed to do one particular job and to accept work automatically from a preceding machine that is also specially designed to feed its successor equipment. That is what is meant by interdependent, special-purpose equipment, where the parts of the process are useless without the whole, and where specific computer control programs are designed to run such equipment. Chapter 10 describes the characteristics of flow shops. Modular production and group technology (pp. 186–89) are introduced as ways to help circumvent the usual rigidity of highly mechanized and automated production systems. Chapter 11 presents the line balancing problem and uses an example (Filmasters, Inc.) to explain the concepts and techniques for developing efficient work routines. Heuristic line balancing is also discussed with examples. Appendix 11-I (optional material) explores the stochastic line balancing problem. Appendix 11-II (optional material) treats a flow shop simulation with stochastic characteristics.

ten

the flow shop is a high-productivity system

What is to be done (the job) can vary from processing mail orders to treating patients; from making pencils to processing film. But what is to be done is not as significant as the *way* it is done. When a flow shop configuration can be employed, many units can be processed both quickly and cheaply with built in assurance of *stable quality* levels. The equipment is in place; the process is predesigned and routinized. Because the process is dedicated to repetition, there is ample opportunity to remove "bugs," stabilize performance, and evenly maintain quality standards.

Certain jobs have few, if any, options as to how they should be done; other jobs have many options. In what manner do specific job characteristics affect the potentials for process design? Flow shops satisfy high-demand volume, which is not so seasonal that much of the time most of the output is going into inventory. To qualify, flow shop products and services should benefit from capital-intensive rather than labor-intensive process design. Where labor is used, the jobs are highly repetitive and run contrary to oft-cited present-day demands of labor for job enlargement and the removal of boringly limited, repetitive tasks. (There are pros and cons as well as advocates and opponents for both sides. See pp. 491–92, in Chapter 20.) For flow shop outputs, process decisions have already been made. If decisions as well as creative insights, artistic hunches, and the personal touch must be exercised during the product or service process, then the flow shop configuration is inappropriate.

Technological Differentiation

Although no one situation is ever identical to another, the reason that production and operations management can be applied to diverse sets of operations is that certain principles concerning how things can be done are easily transferable. They are *independent of the particular job.*

From a technological point of view, major differences exist between the management of the production function in the chemical industry as compared to the machine tool industry. The same can be stated for comparisons between other industries: between hospital and library management, between different forms of transportation systems, and so on. These differences in physical systems can hardly be called trivial. They represent *technological differentiation.* Knowledge of technology is, at best, only partially transferable between industries. Yet, from a management point of view, these differences can be subsumed under the three production system classes: flow shop, job shop, and project.

Within each of these headings, there are finer classifications that can be useful. For example, the process of transforming input materials into the output product may require *manual* or *machine* operations; *chemical reactions* or *materials shaping* might be involved; perhaps the process is *extractive, transport, communications, energy supply, raising livestock,* or *agriculture.* More detailed breakdowns could specify press shop operations, casting, weaving, or harvesting. We can also categorize systems by their specific output, for example, health, skills, suits, cereals, refrigerators, and gasoline.

Sometimes it is useful to separate technologies in terms of the input materials, such as coffee beans, crude oil, and iron ore. Adequate classification is always a problem because of the highly specialized nature of each industry, and even of companies within an industry. The appropriate body of knowledge that comprises the technology begins with the broadest physical principles, but rapidly encompasses enormous amounts of detail when engineering and production applications are included.

The study of P/OM cannot avoid involvement with technology, nor should it attempt to do so. But the utility of treating specific technological systems in detail is of dubious value for understanding the management problems. The important distinction in process management is between production systems configurations.

The Flow Shop and the Job Shop

Basically, the flow shop consists of a set of facilities through which work flows in serial fashion. The operations are performed repeatedly. The job shop, on the other hand, is not a serially utilized facility. Jobs follow different processing patterns through the facilities in batch fashion. Figure 10-1 provides an illustration of the difference.

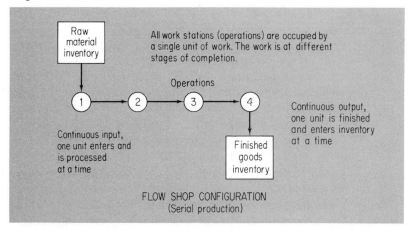

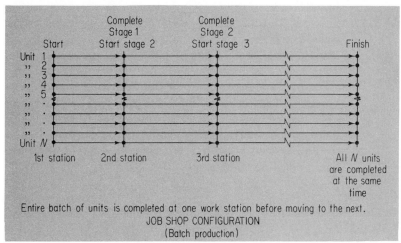

FIGURE 10-1. Serial versus batch processing

Items in the flow shop enter the finished goods inventory one after another, whereas they enter in batches for the job shop. The flow shop is (more or less) what has frequently been referred to as mass production. In some cases, when almost no processing patterns are ever repeated, the job shop is called a *custom shop* (everything is custom made to order). Mostly, the flow shop is designed to make for stock; the job shop makes to order (or to stock where many different items are stocked in relatively small quantities). Which is why flow shop facilities tend to be *special-purpose* equipment, well designed to deliver the high volume of output needed. Job shop facilities are *general-purpose* equipment capable of being outfitted with various tools, dies, and fixtures to do a variety of different jobs at the same basic facility.

An intermittent flow shop exists when there is a call for high production volumes on a periodic or recurring basis. The characteristic of serial production must dominate the process; however, the system does not operate all of the time. Consequently, a cross between general- and special-purpose equipment is used. Generally, this is equipment that involves high setup costs, but once set up, operates in a highly efficient manner. Low production volumes do not justify the expensive setups of such equipment. For most P/OM purposes, the intermittent flow shop can be treated as a flow shop.

Modularity (previously mentioned) enables the output volume of certain parts to be increased to the point where flow shop processing is feasible. Serial production has benefits: it encourages division of labor efficiencies gained from specialization; there are economic scale advantages in using special-purpose equipment; volume production permits highly coordinated promotional, advertising, and marketing activities; and flow-shop inventories can be lower than those of job shops, where unfinished batches of items must be stored.[1]

When demand permits, the continuous (or serial) flow shop is used because it is the most *efficient production configuration*. Less production-efficient, while being a greater producer of product diversity, the job shop treats operations in batches. Each new job consists of a set of such batch-type operations. The movement of each of the batches must be planned for, and it must be kept in mind that these jobs tend to interact with each other, *competing for facilities*. Repeated planning is costly. Consequently, the scope and precision of each job shop plan will necessarily be less than for continuous flow systems where a single, large planning investment is warranted by high production volume.

What Is Line Balancing?

The major flow shop problem is to attain the required output rate (say of *x* parts per hour) with the greatest possible efficiency. The total job is divided into operations, and operations are grouped together at stations. Work moves successively from one station to another. All stations are occupied with job components at different stages of completion. If all stations work an equal amount of time, then no stations are idle while others are working. This is the most efficient arrangement. Figure 10-2 depicts a flow shop with

---

[1]The findings of The Boston Consulting Group are in line with this (see pp. 28–29).

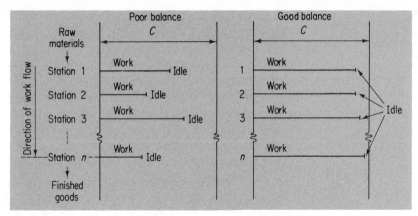

FIGURE 10-2. A flow shop with *n* stations—two versions
C (the cycle time) is the time allotted at each station before the paced-conveyor moves the work along to the next station. Different operations are being performed at each of *n* stations.

n stations, where two versions are shown. On the left, the work load is poorly balanced, i.e., there is considerable idle time. On the right, the balance is good. There is significant idle time in the poor balance arrangement; probably a better design can be found with a different number of stations, different cycle time, (see the caption of Fig. 10·2) and different assignment of operations to stations.

Types of Flow Shops

The kind of line balancing that is required will differ according to the type of flow shop that exists. We shall examine three independent dimensions for characterizing flow shops.

1. How much of a commitment can be made? If demand is large and likely to be stable over a long enough period of time to write off the investment entirely and still make a contribution to overhead and profit, then a total commitment might be made.[2] The degree of commitment can range from fully automated *paced-flow* systems (usually based on the mass production of items carried by a fixed-speed conveyor) to situations in which the demand for a group of *similar* items is relatively continuous, varying in quantity over time. By similarity of items, we mean that essentially the same production routing and flow are required for each of the items that are run through the system in successive sequences. Line balancing is a matter of grouping facilities and workers

---

[2]In public systems, instead of contribution to overhead and profit, we require sufficient public benefit to warrant total commitment (e.g., to a highly productive, flow shop hospital or post office).

in an efficient pattern. For high-volume production of identical items, costly mathematical studies, using linear or dynamic programming,[3] can be justified to achieve line balance. On the other hand, intermittent flow systems are often designed using heuristic procedures and techniques appropriate for partial commitment to flow shop planning.

2. How mechanized is the process? If the system is labor intensive (as in many assembly lines), then rest time must be allowed at worker-dominated stations of the conveyor-paced process. If the system is capital equipment intensive, then engineering design must provide perfect synchronization between successive stations of the flow shop.

3. How much random activity occurs? If workers are trained to do highly specialized tasks, they may work slowly at times and faster at others. Generally they can compensate for deviations so that the paced-line requirements are fully met. When this is not the case, either:
   a. The line must be stopped (so that all stations except the delinquent one must wait).
   b. Unfinished work will come off the line which must receive special treatment for completion.
   c. A special emergency crew will roam from station to station to remedy problems.

Factors other than human variance can account for the need to line-balance stochastic systems.[4] The methods for stochastic line-balancing will be discussed briefly in Chapter 11 and then intensely in the optional materials of Appendices 11-I and 11-II. These discussions have been separated from the main body of the text because they are highly technical and specialized. In the main body of Chapter 11 we shall examine deterministic line-balancing.

Synthetic and Analytic Flow Shops

Progressive assembly or production line work is a synthetic function, as illustrated in Fig. 10-3. Synthetic means that many inputs combine to form a lesser number of outputs. In a deterministic system,[4] all operations at each station are assumed to require predetermined fixed times. In Fig. 10-2, poorly balanced operations have been rebalanced so that equal time is spent at each station. Consequently, a paced conveyor belt can be used.

---

[3]Dynamic programming is a method for examining a great number of alternatives, such as line balancing arrangements. Programming rules eliminate certain combinations by recognizing that they are dominated by others; for example, their costs can never be lower than other combinations that have already been identified. The dynamic program selects the best option.

[4]Stochastic systems are those where random behaviors occur over time. For example, the time to complete a task may vary with the quality of input materials, which cannot be controlled entirely. Deterministic systems do not possess this random quality, and, consequently, all specified times occur exactly each time that they are repeated. It should be noted that the flow shop design is intended to remove stochastic behavior from the system.

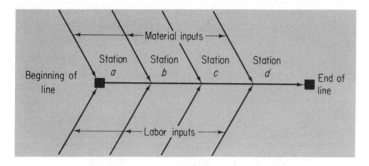

FIGURE 10-3. Synthetic production function

Sometimes an analytic production function is the technological requirement. *Analytic process* means that few inputs are treated to produce a greater number of outputs. Analytic systems can result in several flow systems. Usually, the processing is highly mechanized and, therefore, deterministic schedules prevail. For an example of an analytic production function, see Fig. 10-4 and note the chocolate processing flow diagram in Fig. 10-5.

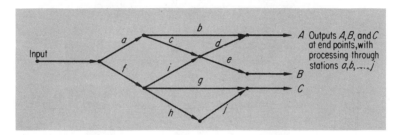

FIGURE 10-4. Analytic production function

We see that in the case of the analytic system, the basic raw material is broken down, transformed, and decomposed into various products and by-products. Figure 10-5 pictures the flow of materials as exemplified by a typical analytic industry. In this case, the raw material is the cocoa bean. From it, 6 different products are derived, viz., cocoa, chocolate-flavored syrup, semi-sweet chocolate chips, semi-sweet chocolate, milk chocolate bars, and milk chocolate kisses. Flow charts of this type can be exceedingly helpful for process development of analytic systems. In synthetic operations, on the other hand, various materials and parts are fed into the main stream, where they are joined together to form a basic unit. For example, Fig. 10-6 shows an automobile assembly line. Each component is brought into the production line at the appropriate point, after which it loses its separate identity.

Synthetic processes lend themselves to flow systems. So do analytic processes except when some of the outputs are low-volume extracts and

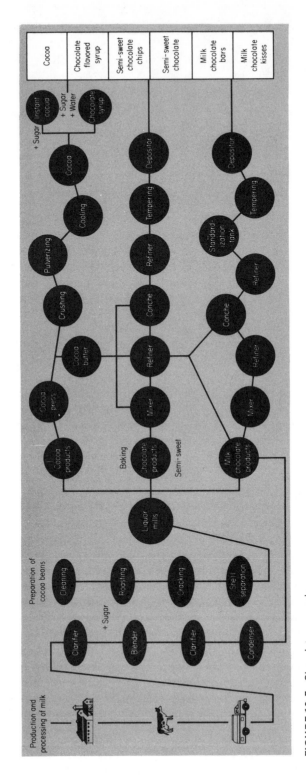

FIGURE 10-5. Chocolate processing
[Copyright Hershey Foods Corporation, Hershey Chocolate & Confectionary Division, Hershey, Pa., 17033, U.S.A.]

HOW AN AUTOMOBILE IS ASSEMBLED

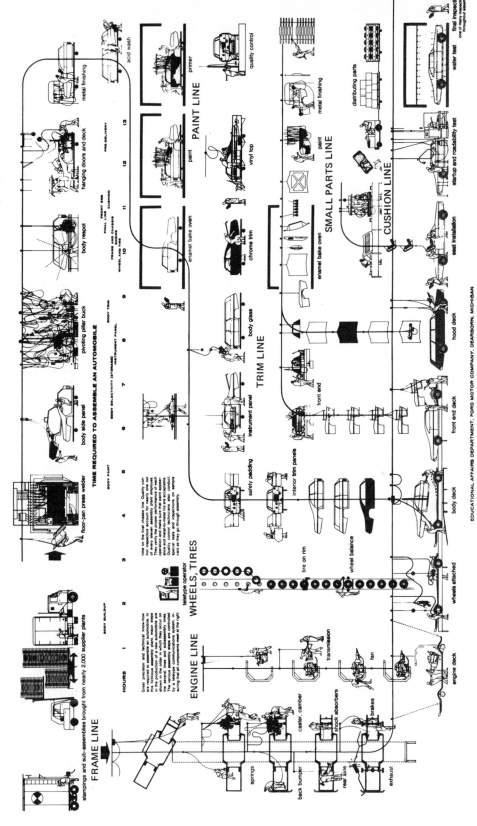

FIGURE 10-6. How an automobile is assembled [Courtesy of Educational Affairs Department, Ford Motor Company, Dearborn, Michigan]

by-products. These latter situations tend toward job shop or intermittent flow shop configurations. Most processes *combine* both analytic and synthetic operations. This would even be true for the examples we have used. However, they can be distinguished as being *essentially* analytic or synthetic.

The stations through which materials flow have *special-purpose facilities*, designed strictly for the limited product line under continuous flow. (Clearly, such configurations present different problems to the planner than do those comprised of *general-purpose equipment* that can accommodate the many different operations of the job shop.) Serial production configurations involve successively differentiated stages (such as *a*, *b*, *c*, and *d* in Fig. 10-3) based on their *division of labor*. This arrangement offers at least two advantages:

1. Items produced serially can be shipped continually, thereby reducing inventories.
2. Specialization usually increases efficiency and productivity.

> There is . . . the familiar economic principle that specialization implies trade and that neither without the other creates an ongoing process of economic development. If there was specialization without trade the tailor would starve and the farmer would go naked. On the other hand, of course, without specialization, trade itself cannot take place for there would be nothing to trade. It is one of Adam Smith's astonishingly acute perceptions that "the division of labor depends on the extent of the market." The division of labor, however, itself increases the extent of the market simply because we get specialization in traders and in trade itself, which facilitates further specialization in production, which facilitates further trade and so on in a magnificent process of disequilibrating feedback.[5]

Modular Production and Group Technology

Some goods and services lend themselves naturally to flow shop production. Others could not be pressed into the flow shop system even if all competitors withdrew from the market, because the life cycle is too short and demand is limited to small runs. Yet there are times when a conversion can be made from job shop operations to intermittent and even permanent flow shop status. The change can take place gradually and partially.

It is always easier to design toward an ideal when one is starting from scratch than when one is attempting to bring about change. On the other hand, when one is starting up a new system, without the determination to achieve a flow shop, it is more likely that a job shop will result. At least 2 reasons for this can be cited. First, there is a job shop tradition (mentality) in the world, based upon pre-1950 technology (which was before economical and powerful computer capabilities and before the development of computer-

[5]Kenneth E. Boulding, "The Specialist with a Universal Mind," *Management Science*, **14**, 12 (August, 1968), B647–B653.

controlled equipment).[6] Second, it is easier to settle for a job shop that promises enough profits than to persevere for a flow shop that has potential for even more. At the same time, it should be reiterated: Not every good and service can be produced by a flow shop for both economic and technological reasons. We point, instead, to those opportunities that do so often exist, but are overlooked.

One approach to achieving flow shop operations is the use of the *modular production* concept. By this is meant *specialization* in the production of particular parts or activities that can then be included as components of more than 1 product or service.[7] The reason for wanting to achieve such *commonality* is that 1 part or operation, if used in several products or services, can accumulate sufficient demand volume to warrant investment in a flow shop.

> The principle of modularity is to design, develop, and produce the minimum number of parts (or operations) that can be combined in the maximum number of ways to offer the greatest number of products (or services).

The matrix in Table 10-1 illustrates this principle, using products and parts. With N different kinds of parts, a total of M different product configurations is derived. Some of these products require several units of a single part; for instance, PR_4 requires two of PA_2, and PR_j requires two of PA_i. The maximum possible variety, i.e., maximum M, that can be obtained with N different parts may be very large. This is especially so when we include both the different possible combinations of the parts and varying numbers of them in combination. Our objective is to have M as large as possible and N as small as possible.

Of course, many of the theoretical possibilities cannot exist and would have no appeal as a product choice for any consumer. But the basic idea of modular design is to have an inventory of parts that can partake in many appealing product configurations. (The same sort of matrix as shown in Table 10-1 must have been designed long ago for the first Erector set. Industry is now taking seriously a fundamental principle long embodied in many children's toys.) A useful measure of the effective degree of modular design might be, therefore, the ratio of the number of products (columns) that can be generated from a given number of parts (rows), i.e., objective: MAX M/N.

Group technology provides another aspect of these same concepts. It refers to specialization in *families* of similar parts. For example, we can

---

[6]This is "programmable" general-purpose equipment. It is computer-controlled to do, in sequence, many different jobs, and to coordinate activities with one or more other facilities. See "Computer-Managed Parts Manufacture," by Nathan H. Cook, *Scientific American*, Vol. 232, No. 2 (February 1975). (Although a completely automatic factory still lies in the future, important advances have been made in fully automatic systems for the batch manufacture of a variety of complex components.)

[7]The roots of such efforts exist in the well-developed concept of standard parts, e.g., screw threads and light bulbs.

TABLE 10-1 MATRIX OF SPECIFICATIONS FOR THE KIND AND NUMBER OF PARTS TO BE COMBINED FOR EACH OF A GIVEN NUMBER OF DIFFERENT END PRODUCTS

Variety of Parts	Variety of Products							
	PR_1	PR_2	PR_3	PR_4	. . .	PR_j	. . .	PR_M
PA_1	1	0	1	1	. . .	0	. . .	0
PA_2	0	1	1	2	. . .	0	. . .	0
PA_3	0	0	0	0	. . .	1	. . .	0
PA_4	0	1	1	0		0		0
.	.	.	.	.		.		.
.	.	.	.	.		.		.
.	.	.	.	.		.		.
PA_i	0	0	1	0	. . .	2	. . .	0
.	.	.	.	.		.		.
.	.	.	.	.		.		.
.	.	.	.	.		.		.
PA_N	0	0	0	1	. . .	1	. . .	1

PA_i denotes the part identified by the stock number i.

PR_j denotes the product variation listed in the finished goods catalog as j. (As shown above, the product j assembly requires one unit of part 3, two units of part i, and one unit of part N. The sequence of assembly is not indicated.)

PA_N denotes the last part listed in our table.

PR_M denotes the last product variation listed in our table; in this case, it is the product using only one unit of part N.

develop efficient flow shops for gears, cams, springs, etc., all of different sizes but of similar design, having production operations that are essentially the same. The technology required assures minimum transition costs as the production line shifts from one variant to another. A company using group technology to improve the profit margin of its line of products or services might become so efficient in this *specialized family of operations* that it would gradually shift production emphasis until it became a subcontractor to industry and institutions of its most efficient operations.

How Do Modular Production and Group Technology Differ from the Concept of Interchangeable Parts?

Interchangeable parts exist when outputs from a production system can be mixed together in a bin and withdrawn in any order for assembly with other parts that have been similarly produced. This gigantic step (in 1798) that revolutionized the production process seems to have been inevitable. While Eli Whitney was developing the notion of interchangeable parts in the United States, Leblanc was also making the concept operational in France, but neither man was aware of the other's work. The growth in use of modular production and group technology partakes of the same sense of inevitability. They are important, new configuration concepts.

The traditional idea of interchangeable parts can be interpreted as follows: All units made to the specifications of a particular parts classification can be treated as identical. It does not matter whether a given unit was made at the beginning or end of a production run. Any part can substitute for any other part in its row. Note that this interchangeability exists *within* each row of the matrix and not between the rows of the table.

Interchangeable part *modules*, on the other hand, are designed to be highly transferable *between columns*; i.e., an interchangeable module enters into many different product configurations. In contrast, production often tends to isolate the columns.

Group technology *clusters rows* together as families. Thus, because of common equipment, materials, and techniques, it becomes feasible to develop flow shop productivity for the family of parts.

It is not enough to plan for and start up a modular production system. It is necessary to preserve it in a changing economic and competitive environment. This can only be done by forecasting possible futures and accordingly planning to have sufficient flexibility to bring about necessary changes in product or service design that can sustain the product or service in its mature stage of the life cycle.

We deal with forecasting in Chapter 12. Forecasting is essential to the job shop. But it applies here as well, since we have linked the evolutionary changes that affect the flow shop to the consistent changes that characterize the job shop.

PROBLEMS
1. It has been said that organizational bureaucracy operates like a badly designed flow shop. Comment on this thought, reflecting on the extent to which it might be true as well as on those aspects that might be false.

2. How does forecasting apply to the flow shop?

3. Contrast an intermittent flow shop with a regular flow shop. How does it compare with a project?

4. Explain the distinction between analytic and synthetic production processes.

5. Numerically controlled machines (NCMs) can be computer-programmed to do many different jobs. Thus, in effect, general-purpose equipment is transformed into special-purpose equipment. By relating the programming of adjacent facilities, coordination between stations is achieved. Different items can be turned out from a serialized production process.

Explain the relationship of modular production and group technology to NCMs.

6. For what type of products and services does the flow shop appear well suited?

7. For what type of products and services does modular design make sense? How about group technology?

8. Why does the flow shop provide built-in assurance of stable quality levels?

9. The explosion chart shown below is widely used by industry to identify the aggregation of part requirements. How does it relate to modular production and group technology?

	Jobs						
Parts	*X 112*	*PR 5*	*987*	*989*	*TF 5*	*. . .*	*Monthly Requirements*
C32	2	—	—	—	—		120
C325	1	1	1	—	—		180
C45	—	—	4	—	—		320
C47	—	—	1	0	1		100
C549	—	—	1	1	1		130
.							.
.							.
.							.
Monthly Demand	60	40	80	30	20	. . .	

eleven
line balancing methods

The need for a line balancing method arises because many *activities* usually are required to fashion the goods and services that constitute the flow shop's production output. *Activities* are comprised of *operations*, which must be assigned to work *stations*. For balance, the stations will be equally loaded with work, i.e., total operation times at each station should be about the same. But equal work assignments at stations are not easily achieved because:

1. Most of the operations must be done in specific sequences.
2. Operation times follow production necessities, and there is only minimum flexibility to alter these times.
3. The productive capabilities of people and equipment differ; they do not work at the same rate.

The Precedence Relations of Work Stations

The flow shop is a balanced sequence of operations. For example, raw materials enter station 1 at 9 AM. Stations 2, 3, 4, etc., are idle. Between

9:00 and 9:03 the raw materials are worked on at station 1 and move to station 2 at 9:03. At the same time, new raw materials enter station 1. Then at 9:06 station 3 begins to operate. We continue in this way until all stations are actively engaged. Every 3 minutes raw materials enter at station 1 and finished goods leave the final station. In the above description, we have *started up* the flow shop.

How do we determine the ordering of stations? Sometimes it is easy to specify which operation must follow another. For example, we must first prepare the surface before we paint it. At other times, there are different operation orderings that could be used. An example of this is the repetitive "job" of preparing a patient for a specific hospital treatment. Certain operations must precede others, but many parts of the sequence are flexible.

Figure 11-1 illustrates a precedence diagram for treatment x that utilizes 42 operations. There are three teams of doctors, technicians, and nurses. The

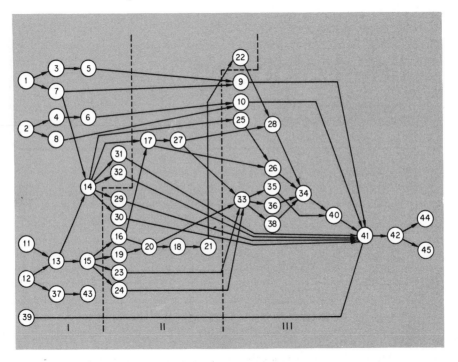

FIGURE 11-1. Precedence diagram for a repetitive hospital treatment administered by three medical teams

first 2 teams move from place to place according to the location of the patient. The third team is always located in the operating room. The diagram can be read as follows: Operation 1 (performed by team 1) is followed by operations 3 and 7 (same team). Operation 7 is followed by operation 9 (performed by the third team in the operating room). Operation 9 is followed by operation 41 (same team), etc.

The medical teams tell us that this "job" could be accomplished in alternate ways. The decision of how to sequence these steps should be the result of careful consultation by experienced practitioners. Like any flow shop, once decisions are made they are difficult and costly to change. There are psychological commitments as well as investments in facilities that can lock routines into place. That is why the system should be carefully examined before a final design sequence is selected. To assign activities to each team, this precedence diagram has been partitioned into 3 sections. Each can be considered as a station.

The problem is a big one. We are not going to solve it, since it would take too much time and obscure the basic concepts in a welter of detail. It has been introduced to show the kind of complex problems that we are concerned with and with which we can cope. A much smaller problem will be introduced in the next section. Real line balancing problems are seldom so small.

Filmasters, Inc.

This mail order film processor has developed a new, computer-controlled color process that promises to improve the quality of work while speeding up film developing and printing time. The company executive committee has agreed to run a flow shop operation starting with the receipt of films in the mail to the return of finished work by mail. Accordingly, it has had the plant manager list the various *operations* (call them $i = 1, 2, \ldots, k$) for the process. For each operation, an *operation time* t_i has been estimated (as shown in Table 11-1), and an ordering of the sequence of operations has been determined (illustrated by the precedence diagram of Fig. 11-2).

TABLE 11-1 FILMASTERS' OPERATION TIMES

Operation (i)	Operation Time (t_i), Minutes
1	0.4
2	0.5
3	0.6
4	0.7
5	0.5
6	1.0
7	0.6
8	0.1
9	0.4

This information is essential for line balancing. Now, in addition, Filmasters' executive committee must indicate the level of productivity that is expected, e.g., 40 orders processed per hour.

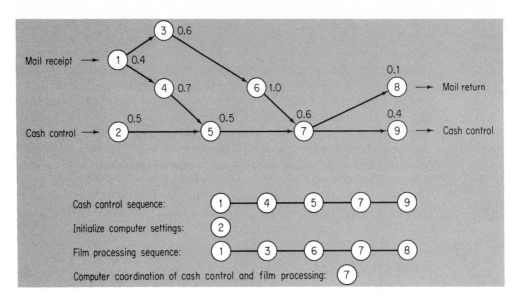

FIGURE 11-2. Filmasters' precedence diagram

The number 40 was arbitrarily chosen by us, but it would be quite specifically chosen by Filmasters, representing the expected demand level of 320 orders per 8-hour day or 1600 orders per week. If more orders than that are received, there will be a waiting line, which will begin to disappear when less than 320 orders are received per day.[1] Mail order film customers do not like to wait too long, so the probability that more than 320 orders will be received each day should be low.

Cycle Time

How many work stations should Filmasters have? How should operations be assigned to stations? How well balanced will the flow shop be? The answers to these questions depend on the required productivity rate; also, on the precedence constraints and the operation times.

Productivity can be directly translated into *cycle time C*, which is the time allowed for the job to remain at each station (see Fig. 10-2). Thus, if N orders are to be processed in a work period of T minutes, we have $N/T = 1/C$. The productive rate of the line is measured by $1/C$ as well as by orders processed (or, in general, items produced) per unit time. For our example, 40/60 (orders ÷ minutes per hour) equals $1/C$. Hence $40C = 60$ and $C = 1.5$ minutes.

---

[1]With a processing capacity of 320 orders per day, if 400 are received on a particular day, then a waiting line of 80 orders will result. Then, if on the following day, 260 orders are placed, the backlog of 80 will be reduced to 20 orders waiting.

Reference to Table 11-1 indicates that the selected productivity of 40 orders per hour may be possible. Every operation time is shorter than the cycle time of 1.5 minutes, so one or more operations can be completed at a station. We shall assume that the operation times cannot be shortened, having been chosen as the smallest reasonable components into which the total job can be subdivided.[2] Let us then find out what productivity rates are possible—under conditions of perfect balance.

The number of stations n must always be an integer. We cannot have $2\frac{1}{2}$ work stations. For each integer number of stations, there is an associated cycle time. In Table 11-2, we have added all the operation times ($\sum_i t_i$) and found the sum to be 4.8 minutes. ($\sum_i t_i$ is called the *total work content time*.) Thus, each order processed by Filmasters requires 4.8 minutes of work.

**TABLE 11-2 FILMASTERS' TOTAL WORK CONTENT TIME
AND LONGEST OPERATION TIME (t_{max})**

Operation (i)	Operation Time (t_i), Minutes
1	0.4
2	0.5
3	0.6
4	0.7
5	0.5
6	1.0 (t_{max})
7	0.6
8	0.1
9	0.4
	$4.8 = \sum_i t_i$

Line balancing cannot decrease the total work content time. However, the number of stations used will determine how many orders are being worked on at the same time (although each at different stages of completion). This, in turn, will determine the rate at which orders are finished, i.e., the production rate. If we divide the total work content time by the integer number of stations, we shall determine the number of minutes spent by an order at each station and, accordingly, the number of minutes elapsing between completion of orders. Equation (11-1) gives the cycle time.

$$C = \frac{\sum_i t_i}{n} \tag{11-1}$$

where n equals the integer number of work stations.

---

[2]Later, however, we shall allow changes in operation times resulting from technological factors and from running identical parallel operations.

In Table 11-2, we have marked the sixth operation with t_{max}, because it is the longest operation time. Cycle time cannot be smaller than t_{max}. If it were, then the single operation must be completed at more than one station, which is not allowed. Also, cycle time must be equal to or less than $\sum_i t_i$ [the latter follows from Eq. (11-1), where the smallest integer value of n is one]. Thus, we have

$$t_{max} \leq C \leq \sum_i t_i \tag{11-2}$$

Table 11-3 presents Filmasters' possible cycle times C and hourly productivity rates $N/T = 60(1/C)$ for all possible integer number of stations. *Warning: This is based on perfect balance, which may not be able to be achieved* (see Fig. 11-4).

TABLE 11-3 FILMASTERS' POSSIBLE CYCLE TIMES, C,
AND HOURLY PRODUCTIVITY RATES, $N/T = 60(1/C)$
FOR ALL INTEGER NUMBER OF STATIONS, n

n	$C = \sum_i t_i/n$	$N/T = 60(1/C)$
1	4.8 minutes	12.5 orders/hour
2	2.4	25.0
3	1.6	37.5
4	1.2	50.0
*5	0.96	62.5
*6	0.80	75.0
*7	0.69	87.5
*8	0.60	100.0
*9	0.53	112.5

*Not feasible, since $C < (t_{max} = 1.0)$

Filmasters' expectation of processing 40 orders per hour seems possible with 4 stations, which with perfect balance can process 50 orders per hour. This allows leeway of 10 orders per hour under circumstances of less than perfect balance. Another possibility is to set up more than 1 parallel production line. For example, with perfect balance, 2 production lines with 2 stations each would also be able to process 50 orders per hour.

Question: What happens if we reduce t_{max} from 1.0 to 0.7 by improving the technology of this film development step?

Answer: With perfect balance, if that could be achieved, 3 stations would suffice, with a cycle time of exactly 1.5 minutes. Perfect balance is not an unreasonable goal if all operations are mechanized, or if sufficient allowance has already been made in estimating operation times for rest of workers.

To obtain this answer we should note that t_{max} is now 0.7 at operations (4) and (6). Also, $\sum_i t_i$ would now be 4.5 minutes. Table 11-4 presents C and N/T for all integer numbers of stations.

TABLE 11-4 FILMASTERS' CYCLE TIMES AND
PRODUCTIVITY FOR ALL INTEGER NUMBER OF
STATIONS, n; GIVEN THAT t_{max} IS
REDUCED FROM 1.0 TO 0.7

n	C	N/T
1	4.5 minutes	13.3 orders/hour
2	2.25	26.7
3	1.5	40.0
4	1.13	53.3
5	0.90	66.7
6	0.75	80.0
*7	0.64	93.3
*8	0.56	106.7
*9	0.50	120.0

*Not feasible, since $C < (t_{max} = 0.7)$.

Question: What happens if we reduce t_{max} from 1.0 to 0.5 by installing 2 developing units in parallel for operation (6)? Develop your own table for this answer.

Developing Station Layouts

The procedure for developing station layouts is based on the use of precedence diagrams. We proceed as follows. Place in station I (the first column) all operations that need not follow others. Reference to Fig. 11-2, which is Filmasters' precedence diagram, shows that operations (1) and (2) can be placed in station I. Then place in station II operations that must follow those in I [i.e., (3) and (4); note that (5) must follow (4) and, therefore, cannot be in the second station). Continue to the other columns in the same way. Thus, in Fig. 11-3 we have forced Filmasters' operations into the maximum number of stations required by operation sequence, not by operation times.

We observe that while sequence is fully specified, column position is not. For example, operation (2) could be done as well in station II. Note also that, for this first feasible set of 5 stations (which is the maximum number that can be required), 5 is determined by the longest chain of sequenced operations, not in time but in the number of operations.

There exist many orderings that satisfy the precedence requirements. Intracolumn movement is totally free between operations that are mutually

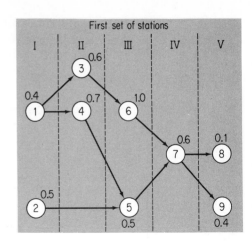

FIGURE 11-3. Filmasters' precedence diagram with 5 stations

independent (not connected by arrows). For example, at station II, operation (3) could be done before operation (4) or vice versa. Also, elements can be moved sidewise from their columns to positions to their right without disturbing the precedence restrictions. Thus, operations (3) and (6) could be done at the same work station, with (3) always preceding (6). The first kind of flexibility is called *permutability of columns*, and the second kind is called *lateral transferability*.

Let us see how well we have done. With these 5 stations we have a cycle time of 0.96 minute. The total operation times, idle times, and violations of cycle time at each station are shown in Table 11-5.

TABLE 11-5 FILMASTERS' FIVE-STATION LAYOUT IS NOT FEASIBLE
CYCLE TIME = 0.96

	Station				
	I	*II*	*III*	*IV*	*V*
Operations	(1), (2)	(3), (4)	(5), (6)	(7)	(8), (9)
Total operation time	0.9	1.3	1.5	0.6	0.5
Idle time	0.06	—	—	0.36	0.46
Violations of cycle time	—	0.34	0.54	—	—

We have violated the condition[3] that $C \geq (t_{max} = 1.0)$ (see $n = 5$ in Table 11-3). The cycle time of 0.96, being less than $t_{max} = 1.0$, is not permissible. Also, we have overassigned the second and third stations. This is not allowable. In fact, we require a cycle time of 1.5 to accommodate station III. We have a lot of idle time at the fourth and fifth stations.

---

[3]Equation (11-2) on p. 196.

A feasible but inefficient assignment pattern is illustrated in Table 11-6. (By "feasible" we mean that no violations of cycle time have occurred.)

TABLE 11-6 A FEASIBLE BUT INEFFICIENT LINE BALANCE
WITH FIVE STATIONS
CYCLE TIME = 1.5

Station	i	t_i	Station Sum	Cumulative Sum	Idle Time
I	1	0.4			
	2	0.5	0.9	0.9	0.6
II	3	0.6			
	4	0.7	1.3	2.2	0.2
III	5	0.5			
	6	1.0	1.5	3.7	0.0
IV	7	0.6	0.6	4.3	0.9
V	8	0.1			
	9	0.4	0.5	4.8	1.0

Total idle time is 2.7 minutes out of a total work time of $5 \times 1.5 = 7.5$ minutes. This is 36 percent idle time. If we decrease the number of stations, can we balance Filmasters' flow shop? Shortly, we shall turn to a method for line balancing, and we shall see then what must be done. First, however, let us consider perfect and imperfect balance.

Perfect Balance and Balance Delay

If the cycle time C is fixed by design (e.g., 1.5 minutes for Filmasters), then the number of stations *under perfect balance* would be $\sum_i t_i/C = n$, or $4.8/1.5 = 3.2$ stations. This is not a possible solution. The integer number of stations, $n = 3$ or $n = 4$ might qualify; the former if a lower production rate can be accepted, and the latter if higher productivity (probably reduced by idle time) is preferred. Even if the number of stations, given perfect balance, turned out to be an integer, such perfect balance may not be achievable, because the jigsaw puzzle of operation times cannot be fitted together so that all operations are self-contained within 1 station or another (i.e., there is no way to group operations into stations such that the total operation times at all stations are equal).

Aside from the number problem, technological factors exist that do not let operations be put together. Sometimes workers or facilities cannot be shifted between stations in such a way as to let total idle time equal zero. These physical restrictions often are referred to as *zoning* constraints.

When perfect balance is not available, we measure the system's inefficiency (or imperfect balance) by a quantity d, called the balance delay.[4]

$$d = 100(nC - \sum_i t_i)/nC \qquad (11\text{-}3)$$

This equation for balance delay d can be better understood by observing that balance delay is 0 for all cycle times listed in Tables 11-3 and 11-4. That is because $nC = \sum_i t_i$, for all values of n. Similarly, for the cycle time specified by Filmasters (1.5 minutes) we have $n = 3.2$ for perfect balance. Therefore, $d = 100[(3.2)(1.5) - (4.8)]/(3.2)(1.5) = 0$. Realistically, we must use $n = 4$ with cycle time of 1.5 minutes, then balance delay would be $d = 100[(4)(1.5) - (4.8)]/(4)(1.5) = 20$ percent. This is illustrated in Fig. 11-4 to show that balance delay is the total idle time of all stations as a percentage of total available working time of all stations.

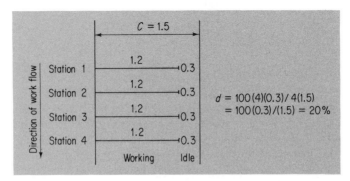

FIGURE 11-4. Filmasters' flow shop with balance delay of 20 percent

Heuristic Line Balancing

Heuristic models are based on applying logical rules to the solution of problems. They are used when strictly mathematical approaches cannot succeed or are too costly to employ. The line balancing problem provides a good example. Complex formulations of linear programming and other mathematical models have been devised to obtain solutions to the line balancing problem, but heuristic approaches are faster and offer more latitude for testing alternative hypotheses.

If the product or service output of the flow shop is expected to have a long and stable life cycle, then engineering design will override (possibly incorporating) the mathematical approaches to line balancing. The technological approach using engineering knowledge of materials, mechanics, and elec-

---

[4]The term "balance delay" refers to unproductive periods at the stations, which we have also called idle times. Balance delay is a systems measure of idle time.

tronics alters operation times and creates facilities that are equivalent to many fully integrated and coordinated stations. On the other hand, when the output life cycle is not stable over a long time, shorter-term flow shops (including intermittent designs) are needed, and these are ideally suited for heuristic resolution.

Heuristic Models

Heuristic comes from the Greek word, *heuriskein*, meaning to discover. The term has been used by Simon and Newell* to describe a particular approach to problem solving and to decision making. Heuristic models utilize logic and common sense derived by observation and introspection. These models replace mathematical ones when formal, analytic methods have little promise of being operational.

The essence of the heuristic approach is in the application of selective routines that reduce the size of a problem. Thus, for example, the production problem of assembly line balancing can be treated by reducing the total system to a series of simpler line balancing problems that can be studied analytically.† Another kind of reduction is used in which a relatively simple rule is applied repeatedly until all decisions that must be made have been made.

Looking at heuristic procedures in another way, sensible rules can be used to simulate the decision-making pattern of managers as they would normally operate in the system. The advantages of this approach are consistency, speed, and the ability to cope with more data and larger systems than is otherwise possible. Once the basic decision-making pattern is developed, it can be expanded and applied to greater system segments. Accordingly, for situations that do not lend themselves to mathematical analysis, the heuristic approach is an attractive alternative. The key is to trace out and then embody the thinking process that an intelligent decision maker would use to resolve the specific type of problem. Heuristic models do not guarantee an optimal result. Instead, they are designed to produce relatively good strategies subject to specific constraints. *For the line balancing problem,* we will talk about a number of heuristics and illustrate one in particular, so that all the above points will become evident.

---

*H. A. Simon and A. Newell, "Heuristic Problem Solving: The Next Advance in Operations Research," *Operations Research,*" Vol. 6, No. 1 (January–February, 1958), pp. 1–10.

†Fred M. Tonge, "Summary of a Heuristic Line Balancing Procedure," *Management Science,* Vol. 7, No. 1 (October, 1960), pp. 21–39.

Kilbridge and Wester's Heuristic

Kilbridge and Wester[5] proposed a heuristic procedure that assigns a *number* to each *operation* describing how many *predecessors* it has. This is easily accomplished by referring to the appropriate precedence diagram. The operations are then rank-ordered according to the number of predecessors each has. The number 0 is ranked first in line; next comes 1, then 2, etc. The first operations assigned to stations are those with the *lowest predecessor numbers*, i.e., 0, then 1, then 2, etc. This procedure is illustrated in Tables 11-7 and 11-8.

Using the data for Filmasters, let us balance a 3-station configuration where $n = 3$ and $C = 4.8/3 = 1.6$ minutes [Equation (11-1), p. 195].

We count the number of predecessors for each operation (see Fig. 11-2) and list them in Table 11-7.

TABLE 11-7 OPERATIONS RANKED BY THE NUMBER
OF PREDECESSORS

Operation	Number of Predecessors	t_i
1	0	0.4
2	0	0.5
3	1	0.6
4	1	0.7
5	3	0.5
6	2	1.0
7	6	0.6
8	7	0.1
9	7	0.4

Operations are assigned to stations in the order of the least number of predecessors. This means, for station I, we first select operations (1) and (2). They have a total operation time of 0.9. Since $n = 3$, then $C \doteq 1.6$, so we can introduce either operation (3) with $t_i = 0.6$ or operation (4) with $t_i = 0.7$ into station I. Where ties exist, another rule applies. Choose first the longest operation times *that can be used*. Short operations are saved for ease of manipulation at the end of the line. In this way, earliest stations are given the least idle time possible. Operation (4)'s time of 0.7 is larger than operation (3)'s time of 0.6; therefore, operation (4) is assigned to station I. This results in a total time of 1.6 for station I, which is fully packed with no idle time.

Turning to station II, we find that, of the remaining operations, (3) has the least number of predecessors. Next comes operation (6). Together, they

[5]M. D. Kilbridge and L. Wester, "A Heuristic Model of Assembly Line Balancing," *Journal of Industrial Engineering*, Vol. 12, No. 4 (July–August, 1961), pp. 292–98.

have a total activity time of 1.6. Therefore, station II is also fully packed. If operation (6) had been too long to fit in station II, then operation (5) would have been chosen, but operations (7), (8), and (9) must be saved for a later station assignment because of precedent constraints. Thus, when an operation with the next smallest number of predecessors has too large an operation time to be included in the station, we select that operation with the next smallest number of predecessors that fits within the station time and precedent constraints.

Continuing in this way, we obtain 3 fully packed stations having no idle time (see Table 11-8).

TABLE 11-8 CYCLE TIME = 1.6

Station	i	t_i	Station	Cumulative Sum	Idle Time
I	1	0.4			
	2	0.5			
	4	0.7	1.6	1.6	0
II	3	0.6			
	6	1.0	1.6	3.2	0
III	5	0.5			
	7	0.6			
	8	0.1			
	9	0.4	1.6	4.8	0

The precedence diagram (Fig. 11-5) can then be subdivided accordingly. These 3 perfectly balanced stations can be used—if the technology permits (and this is probable because the precedence constraints have been observed), if facilities permit, and if operator movements permit. This is an excellent

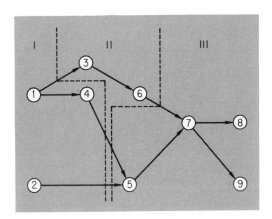

FIGURE 11-5. Filmasters' three-station assignment (Kilbridge and Wester's heuristic)

solution, but production output is 37.5 orders per hour and not the 40 orders that Filmasters has set as the objective. If rest time is needed at the stations, then cycle time could be increased to (say) 1.7 or 1.8 minutes, but this would further decrease productivity to 35.3 or 33.3 orders processed per hour.

Some Additional Heuristics

Another heuristic suggested by Helgeson and Birnie[6] is to assign to stations first those operations whose *followers* have the *largest total time*, i.e., the sum t_i of all successors. They call their approach the *ranked positional weight method*. In Table 11-9, each operation of the Filmasters' example is associated with a weight equal to the sum of all operation times that follow it. The operations are then ranked by descending order of the weight measure. Check Fig. 11-5 to find weights. For example, operations (3), (4), (5), (6), (7), (8) and (9) (not 2) follow operation (1). The sum of these operation times is 3.9, the weight given to operation (1) in Table 11-9. Similarly, operations (8) and (9) follow operation (7). The sum of their operation times is 0.5, which is the weight for operation (7) in Table 11-9.

TABLE 11-9 CYCLE TIME = 1.6

Station	Operation in Ranked Order	Weight	t_i	Station Sum	Idle Time
I	1	3.9	0.4		
	3	2.1	0.6		
	2	1.6	0.5	1.5	0.1
II	4	1.6	0.7		
	5	1.1	0.5	1.2	0.4
III	6	1.1	1.0		
	7	0.5	0.6	1.6	0
IV	8	0	0.1		
	9	0	0.4	0.5	1.1
				4.8	1.6

Subject to the cycle time of 1.6 minutes, in the attempt to get 3 stations, operations are assigned that do not violate precedence or zoning constraints. When the total time for a station is exceeded, the attempt is made to find a

---

[6]W. B. Helgeson and D. P. Birnie, "Assembly Line Balancing Using the Ranked Positional Weight Technique," *Journal of Industrial Engineering*, Vol. XII, No. 6 (November–December, 1961), pp. 394–398.

feasible operation further down the list that can be included. This was not possible with station 1. The heuristic requires that operations (1) and (3) be included as part of station I. Operations (2), (4), and (6) are the only ones that might then be included for completion without violating precedence. We could have operations (1), (3), and (4), but their total time is 1.7 minutes; for (1), (3), and (6), it is two minutes.

This approach does not yield 3 stations but results in 4 stations operating under the cycle time of 1.6. The fourth station's unused capacity is particularly poor. Balance delay is $d = 100(4 \times 1.6 - 4.8)/(4 \times 1.6) = 25$ percent. It should be noted that this same result can be obtained by adding up the total idle time in Table 11-9 and dividing it by total station time, i.e. $1.6/(4 \times 1.6)$. Four stations might be used with a cycle time of 1.5 minutes if a feasible station assignment can be found. Can this be done? Answer: Yes, a better solution can be obtained in this way, again using the Helgeson and Birnie heuristic (see Table 11-10 and Fig. 11-6). The Kilbridge and Wester solution for $n = 3$ is much better, however. It has a fewer number of stations with no idle time.

**TABLE 11-10 CYCLE TIME = 1.5;
BALANCE DELAY = 1.2/(4 × 1.5) = 20 PERCENT**

Station	i	Weight	t_i	Station Sum	Idle Time
I	1	3.9	0.4		
	3	2.1	0.6	1.0	0.5
II	2	1.6	0.5		
	4	1.6	0.7	1.2	0.3
III	5	1.1	0.5		
	6	1.1	1.0	1.5	0
IV	7	0.5	0.6		
	8	0	0.1		
	9	0	0.4	1.1	0.4
				4.8	1.2

Tonge[7] describes a learning (reward and penalty) procedure that selects a heuristic randomly from a catalog of heuristics. The sequence of selections provides the basis for assigning operations to stations. When the selected heuristics produce improved solutions (i.e., less idle time), they are rewarded by increasing the likelihood that they will be selected the next time. When they produce poorer solutions, a penalty is imposed that decreases such

[7]Fred M. Tonge, "Assembly Line Balancing Using Probabilistic Combinations of Heuristics," *Management Science*, Vol. 11, No. 7 (May, 1965), pp. 727–735.

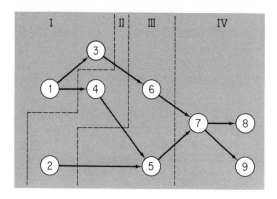

FIGURE 11-6. Filmasters' four-station assignment (Helgeson and Birnie's heuristic)

likelihoods. Among the set of heuristics employed to choose the next operation were

- A. Longest operation time, t_i.
- B. Largest number of immediate followers.
- C. Operation i chosen at random.

In effect, the choice of heuristic is determined by $p(A)$, $p(B)$, and $p(C)$. These probabilities of choice sum to one, and, initially, they are all equal, i.e., $\frac{1}{3}$. Then, according to the balance delay achieved by successive iterations, particular probabilities are increased as they appear to contribute to improved performance. Tonge concludes that this probabilistic approach results in fewer work stations than using any one individual heuristic alone or a purely random choice of operations.

Arcus randomly generated feasible sequences using probability assignments based on precedence, zoning, and feasibility relations. In addition, he used heuristic weighting to improve his results. The computer program generates 1000 sequences, and the 1 out of a 1000 sequences that is chosen is the one that requires the minimum number of stations.[8] Especially for large problems, the *objective of minimizing work stations for a given cycle time* makes good sense.

Obviously, there is reasonable expectation that a number of alternative configurations will require the same minimum number of stations, so there is additional leeway for interpretation. All these heuristics attempt to organize those operations that are free to move, recognizing that some operations can-

[8] It is reported that the generation of 1000 sequences for a system of 70 operations on an IBM 7090 required 30 minutes. A. L. Arcus, "Comsoal: A Computer Method of Sequencing Operations for Assembly Lines," see Elwood S. Buffa, ed., *Readings in Production and Operations Management* (New York: John Wiley & Sons, Inc., 1966), pp. 336–360.

not move because they are constrained by the partial ordering determined by precedence relations.[9]

Beyond Deterministic Estimates

There is yet another dimension to the line balancing problem if we allow operation times to be randomly variable within limits, i.e., stochastic. To illustrate, Filmasters' operation (6) might require as little as 0.8 minute sometimes and as much as 1.3 minutes at other times, with an average time of 1.0 minute. Accordingly, we would consider the costs of stopping the line plus other methods of dealing with the situation when a station exceeds its time. There are various line balancing algorithms that minimize overall costs under stochastic conditions.[10]

Perfect Balance and the Stochastic Problem

No manager would wish to approach too closely the state of perfect balance. After all, the t_i's are seldom entirely fixed but are random variables. The more that human effort is involved on the line, the more this statement applies. Thus, some idle time is purposely maintained so that the cycle time will not be exceeded. With a paced line, exceeding the cycle time often means that the conveyer must be stopped and all $n - 1$ stations will be idle waiting for the other station to catch up; or the part can be removed from the line, creating a queue (or waiting line) for the station that slipped behind; or a special worker can be assigned who can shift from station to station to provide extra help where needed. Each situation has its own characteristics that determine what might be the best thing to do.

As a rule of thumb, managers frequently load their stations within 90 percent of their full utilization. This provides a degree of leeway for rest and changing pace. Also, it takes some of the pressure off the workers that a perfectly balanced system incurs. The resulting product quality is improved, and the costs of inspection rejects are decreased. The total cost concept should include the additional terms related to costs of exceeding cycle times when this occurrence is a possibility. We should not overlook the fact that the line-balancing problem refers to the way in which machines and human components of a production line are matched with respect to their characteristic production rates. The machines can be counted upon for relatively deterministic t_i's, whereas the human operators of the system have significant variability.

---

[9]For an excellent summary of line balancing approaches see E. J. Ignall, "A Review of Assembly Line Balancing," *Journal of Industrial Engineering*, Vol. 16, No. 4 (July–August, 1965), pp. 244–254.

[10]For a good example, see Fred N. Silverman, "The Effects of Stochastic Work Times on the Assembly Line Balancing Problem," August 19, 1974 (unpublished dissertation).

There is a substantial literature on the effects of stochastic behavior on a systems performance where inventories build up when a successor operation works more slowly than the preceding one. In Appendices 11-I and 11-II, which are optional materials, we turn our attention to this subject.

1. The flow shop is designed to remove stochastic behaviors. Explain this statement and comment on whether the objective is usually fully accomplished.

2. Draw a precedence diagram for changing a tire. Discuss the way in which this job could be done with a flow shop configuration. Suggest a possible division of labor that would produce a reasonable line balance.

3. Draw a precedence diagram for making a deposit at the bank. How can this job be accomplished by tellers in flow shop configuration? Suggest a possible division of labor that would produce an acceptable line balance. What effect would customers wishing to make withdrawals have?

4. For the Filmasters' example, see pp. 193–197. Assume that Fig. 11-2 still applies as the precedence diagram, but the operation times in Table 11-1 are changed as follows:

Operation (i)	Operation Time (t_i), Minutes
1	1.4
2	1.5
3	1.6
4	1.7
5	1.5
6	2.0
7	1.6
8	1.1
9	1.4

   a. What productivity rates are possible with perfect balance?
   b. Develop the station layout for $n = 5$. What idle time and violations of cycle time occur (see Table 11-5 on p. 198)?
   c. Develop a feasible station layout. Describe its productivity and balance delay.

5. With respect to line balancing:
   a. What does permutability of columns mean?
   b. What does lateral transferability mean?
   c. To what do zoning constraints apply?

6. What is the difference between deterministic and stochastic line balancing?

7. Solve Filmasters' problem multiplying all operation times by 10 (pp. 193–95). Use the Kilbridge and Wester heuristic for productivity of 20 finished units per eight-hour day.

Answer: To begin with, we convert to an hourly basis, i.e., $\frac{20}{8} = 2\frac{1}{2}$ units per hour. Then, cycle time must be $60/2.5 = 24$ minutes, whence we derive the number of stations ($n = \sum_i t_i/C = 48/24 = 2$). The total work content is 48 and $t_{max} = 10$. The cycle time must be $10 \leq C \leq 48$. When $n = 2$, the value of C is given by $\frac{48}{2} = 24$. This assumes zero balance delay. Using Kilbridge and Wester's heuristic, we have

Station	i	t_i	Station Sum	Cumulative Sum
I	1	4		
	2	5		
	3	6		
	4	7	22	22
II	6	10		
	5	5		
	7	6		
	8	1	22	44
III	9	4	4	48

This is obviously a poor arrangement. One alternative would be to include operation (9) in the second station (II). This would necessitate changing the cycle time to 26 or greater. Possibly, by shifting manpower or changing technology a decrease in some t_i could be obtained (say, operation (6)'s time). Another arrangement would be to shift operation (6) to the first station (I) and put operation 4 in the second station. This would produce station times of 25 and 23, respectively.

The balance delay in the case of $C = 25$ with $n = 2$ is

$$d = \frac{100(2 \times 25 - 48)}{(2)(25)} = 4 \text{ percent}$$

If C were increased to 27 for flexibility,

$$d = \frac{100(2 \times 27 - 48)}{(2)(27)} = 11.1 \text{ percent}$$

8. Find the solution for Filmasters (pp. 202–3), using the Kilbridge and Wester heuristic with $n = 4$. What is the cycle time? What is the productivity rate? How much idle time results? What do you recommend, 3 stations or 4? How about working 9 hours per day with $n = 3$? Was rest allowance made for workers so that the perfect balance (achieved with $n = 3$) is realistic? If the system is totally mechanized (there are no

workers), can we speed up certain operations so that an output rate of 40 per hour is achieved? Is it possible to design a balanced flow shop that can deliver hourly output rates of 37.5, 40, 42.5 at the flick of a switch?

9. A flow shop system has been balanced as follows:

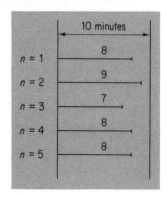

FIGURE 11-7.

All the work is done with 5 stations.

a. What is the productive output per hour?

b. What is the balance delay?

10. With respect to Problem 9 above, if perfect balance is assumed, how many stations would be required?

_____

The following problems relate to the Appendixes

11. In the bulk mail-sorting problem (pp. 217–22) assume that the process rates are exponential but different $\lambda = 8$, $\mu = 10$. What kind of in-process storage will be needed?

12. If the bulk mail-sorting operations did not combine to form exponential distributions at each station, but instead were constant, what then is the line balancing problem?

Answer: Station I needs $60/(\lambda = 3) = 20$ seconds per unit whereas station II needs $60/(\mu = 4) = 15$ seconds per unit. Consequently, a paced conveyor would have to stay the longer time of 20 seconds at both stations leaving station II idle $5/20 = 20$ percent of the time. The solution, if possible, is to move a 2 (or 3) second operation from station I to station II resulting in 18 seconds at station I and 17 seconds at station II.

13. Omega Company, manufacturer of a mid-price line of calculators, requires a comparison of production configurations A (Fig. 11-15) and B (Fig. 11-17). The value of each finished unit is $40. Materials cost $10 per unit. Costs at the first A facility are $3/hr., and at the second, they are $50/hr. The process rate of the first A facility is 8 units/hr. It is 10 units/hr. at the second. For B, both inputs are 4/hr.; outputs are 5/hr.; and all 4 facilities cost half the amounts in A. All facilities have exponential process times and storage costs of $2 per unit per hour. Which configuration should be used?

APPENDIX 11-I
Queueing Aspects of Line Balancing (Optional Material)

Let us now consider what happens when stochastic behavior characterizes the t_i's (i.e., the operation times are statistically distributed), which is not unusual.

It should be noted that we are dealing with a series of stations, every one of which can be considered to be an input-output process. Each station provides service through its combined activities. Some one or several things come to the station to claim service. Thus, we have a provider of service and a user of that service.

Queueing models[11] are ideal representations of systems that provide service. Let us consider a fundamental queueing (service) model. Figure 11-8 shows a single-channel (one service facility) system, where λ is the input rate and μ is the output (or processing) rate.

FIGURE 11-8. A single-channel service system

We can expand this model to a multiple-channel service system with M service facilities (see Fig. 11-9). Multiple-channel service systems exist within stations of line balanced processes, wherever a station has several facilities dedicated to the same set of activities.

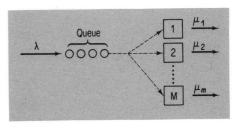

FIGURE 11-9. An *M*-channel service system

Knowledge of the structure of queueing models is fundamental to understanding stochastic line balancing. Therefore, we shall now examine queueing in greater depth. Queueing models are concerned with the following generalized situations:

1. The system provides a specific service. The service facilities might be composed of such diverse units as drill presses, milling machines, turret lathes, drop forges, plating tanks, airplane seats, hospital operating

---

[11]The word "queue" literally means a tail-like plait of hair worn behind; a pigtail. The word is now commonly used to describe a waiting line for service (e.g., in Britain, a group of people lining up while waiting for a bus).

tables, supermarket checkout counters, tellers' windows, toll booths, shipping docks, airport runways, restaurant tables, telephone trunk lines, and machine repairmen.

2. Units arrive to receive the service. These can include materials to be machined or plated, travelers, patients, shoppers, customers, ships, airplanes, gourmets, and machines that have broken down. The diversity of these applications is incredible—which is why we have emphasized our interest in goods and services, public and private sectors, especially with regard to achieving flow shop productivity whenever possible.

3. There is an expected or average rate of servicing the units; for example, on the average, 5 units are serviced per hour. We call this expected servicing rate μ. There is a distribution of servicing rates around a mean value. That is, sometimes more than 5 units are serviced per hour—at other times, less than 5 units receive service.

4. There is an expected rate of arrival of the units for servicing, for example, on the average, 3 units require service per hour. We call this expected arrival rate λ. There is a distribution of arrival rates around a mean value. That is, sometimes more than 3 units arrive, sometimes less.

5. *Because we are dealing with distributions*, a greater than average number of units can arrive for servicing. It is equally possible that a run of units will require longer than average servicing times. Under such circumstances a queue or waiting line can develop, even though the process has ample capacity and is capable of providing more service than is normally demanded, that is, $\mu > \lambda$. At other times, less than the expected number of units can arrive or shorter than average servicing times can occur. This produces idle time for service facilities.

6. We have as a guide to the probable behavior of a single-channel system the ratio $\rho = \lambda/\mu$. It is called the *process utilization factor*. We must also know or make assumptions about the shapes of the distributions around the expected values of λ and μ.

7. When the service units are arranged in job shop configuration, then each one stands alone as an individual input/output system providing batch service. However, when the flow shop configuration is used, then the various service units are interrelated, and the outputs of one system become the inputs to another. This requires careful coordination and matching of the stochastic behaviors of systems that are in communication with each other.

Measures of Service Effectiveness

For the successful operation of any production process, management must decide how much service capacity is required, what type of facilities will provide optimum service, and how to group facilities in a production line. These problems are particularly demanding for the flow shop.

Whatever the specific situation, some *measures of effectiveness*, such as the ten shown below, are useful to evaluate the service system. Others may be found that are better suited to particular situations.

1. The average *number of units* in a queue. We shall call this L_q.

2. The average *number of units* in the system, called L. (This includes the number in the queue and the number in service.)

3. The average *waiting time* or delay before service begins, called W_q.

4. The average *total time* spent by a unit in the system, called W. (This total delay is the sum of waiting time and service time.)

5. The *probability* that *any* delay or waiting will occur, called $P(n > M)$, where n equals the total number of units in the system, and M stands for the number of service facilities.

6. The *probability* that the total delay will be greater than some value of t, $P(W > t)$. (A comparable expression could be written for W_q.)

7. The *probability* that n units will be in the system (where M of them will be in service, given M channels) called P_n.

8. The probability that all service facilities will be idle, called P_0. (Note: $n = 0$ in 7 above.)

9. The expected percentage of idle time of the total service facility,
$$\bar{I} = \frac{M}{M}P_0 + \frac{(M-1)}{M}P_1 + \cdots + \frac{(M-n)}{M}P_n + \frac{(M-M)}{M}P_M.$$ (Again, note that P_n equals the probability that n units will be in the system, both waiting for and receiving service from M facilities.)

10. The probability of turn-aways, resulting from insufficient waiting line accommodations, P_N, where $N - M$ represents the maximum number of units that can be stored or accommodated on the waiting line at any moment.

Having evaluated the characteristics of a process (or components of a process) in terms of these or other measures of effectiveness, it is possible to achieve highly productive systems. Without such measures, the production and operations manager will be hard pressed to achieve even a reasonably good systems design. The reason for this is that the situation is simply far too complex for intuition to cope with it. Even using queueing models, one does not obtain optimum performance. Queueing models are descriptive. They cannot be optimized. Consequently, the manager designs one or more production systems and then tests them by the measurement of adequate queueing criteria. Changes are made based on test results, and the system is retested. This goes on until a satisfactory system configuration is obtained.

Queue Accommodations

A natural restriction on queue size exists if the storage facilities needed to accommodate a waiting line are limited. For example, the size of a doctor's waiting room provides a physical upper limit on queue length. Similarly, on a production line, the in-process inventory will be limited by the amount of storage space that can be made available between operations. Figure 11-10 depicts the fact that only an inventory limited to N items can be carried between operations A and B.

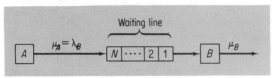

FIGURE 11-10. There is a limitation (N) on the size of the in-process inventory between operations A and B.

We know that because of variability in both arrival and service rates a queue can form under even the most favorable process utilization ratio, p. When this queue has grown to size N, several different things can happen. Following are some examples:

The $N + 1$ arrival is turned away—which could mean it is taken to an outside storage depot. In the case of a person arriving at the doctor's office when it is completely filled up, the individual becomes a self-motivated turn-away.

The $N + 1$ arrival does not leave the first service facility, A, but stays there until the queue in front of B can accept it. In this way, A is blocked for other service and forced to be idle. This is equivalent to shutting down operation A until the "bottleneck" is cleared up. The problem is particularly relevant to the flow shop. Consequently, adjacent facilities must be coordinated so as to minimize the probability that bottleneck events occur.

The design of the production process must take these possibilities into account. It is unusual that a large in-process inventory can be tolerated; accordingly, some disposition must be made of excessive in-process inventories, or they must be prevented. In some production lines no queue is permitted.[12] Thus, only when all operations have been completed at each facility is the production line permitted to advance. This is illustrated by Fig. 11-11. For such lines a breakdown of any one facility will close down the

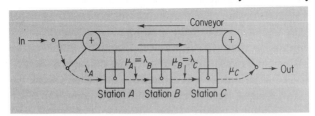

FIGURE 11-11. A production system where no waiting line is permitted

[12]Especially where the facilities are arranged for continuous production and there is an uninterrupted flow of materials through the total process (as contrasted with batch production).

entire line until repairs are made—unless duplicate facilities have been made available.

We see that our discussion is converging on the production fundamentals of line balancing and plant layout. There are many variations of facility arrangements. Figure 11-12 is meant to provide just a few possibilities. Each of these three variants would perform quite differently even though they all have the same number of A- and B-type facilities.

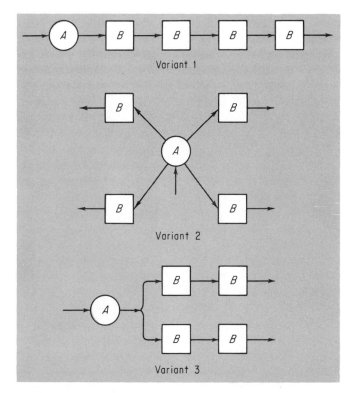

FIGURE 11-12. Alternative arrangements of facilities produce different systems' performances. Thus, three possible arrangements are shown for a system with one A facility and four B facilities.

Arrival and Service Distributions

Our initial line balancing analysis was based on the assumption that activity times were deterministic. Now we are considering what happens when we allow activity times to vary; i.e., they are stochastic. We must examine two important questions concerning the probability distributions of activity times.

1. Are the arrival and service rate distributions stable over time? A rough criterion to use with respect to this requirement would be that the distribution shapes, obtained in successive periods of time, are similar. In other words, the distribution of the first sample period as compared with that of the second sample period is essentially the same. These data can then be pooled. Although such a criterion lacks rigor, it can be of practical utility if used with care. A more satisfactory criterion is supplied by statistical control theory (see pp. 558–64). We cannot work with unstable distributions, and we shall not consider these cases in our discussion.

2. What are the shapes of the distributions? Figure 11-13 illustrates a number of possible distributions. These are cumulative probability

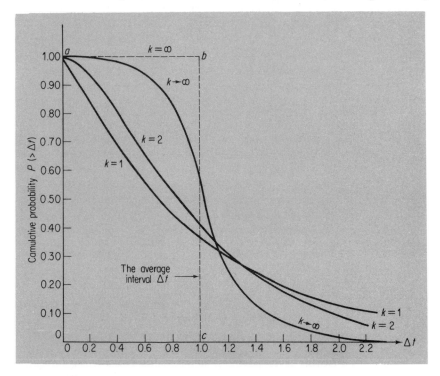

FIGURE 11-13. Some theoretical cumulative probability distributions
As the parameter k approaches infinity, the distribution takes on the shape abc.

distributions. A point on any one of the curves is the probability that the arrival or service interval will be greater than the (x-axis) interval Δt. Accordingly, there is 100 percent probability that the interval will be greater than zero for all distributions, and this makes sense. For the $k = 1$ curve, there is a 50 percent probability that the interval will be greater than 0.69315 ($e^{-0.69315} = 0.5$) and a 36.78 percent probability that the interval will be greater than 1 hour ($e^{-1} = 0.3678$).

Frequently, some member of this family of theoretical curves will provide a reasonably good approximation to the observed distribution. The curve marked $k = 1$ in the figure is an *exponential distribution*. It is identified with the case of *pure randomness*. Pure randomness exists if there are no sequential patterns of long and short intervals. The exponential distribution is observed when the intervals between arrivals or the service intervals are entirely independent of the length of all previous intervals. In effect, the succession of intervals is the outcome of a random process. A process of this type is exemplified by the succession of heads and tails of a coin. The coin has no memory of prior outcomes. The output rates of behavioral systems are often of this type. The distribution associated with $k \rightarrow \infty$ is more characteristic of machines. It is approaching a constant interval value.

On the other hand, here are some examples that would not satisfy this requirement: A pieceworker's rate increases with practice and decreases with fatigue, producing a cyclical pattern over the day; the speed of a machine increases as it heats up, and the temperature rises as a function of use; a maintenance crew always attempts to beat the servicing times of another crew; finally, the accident rate of an individual increases because of the psychological phenomenon of accident proneness. The lack of independence is more frequently associated with the man component in the system than with machines, but it can be found with machines.

Many situations are reasonably well described by the $k = 1$ type of distribution. We shall limit our attention to exponential distributions, but with the full realization that process design and line balancing may involve an enormous variety of types of distributions, all of which must be properly treated for satisfactory control.

A Line Balancing Example

Fundamental differences exist between continuous and intermittent production processes. We are familiar with such relatively continuous processes as canning, bottling, refining, and the (so-called) mass production capabilities of the automobile companies. Other goods and services, such as printing of books and newspapers,[13] making clothing and toys, delivering mail, and providing patient care, require different degrees of intermittent production (ranging from a pure job shop form to reasonable candidates for planning a flow shop). For job shop systems, the major production problem is to find the best way to assign jobs to machines. The various methods available to help resolve this problem are discussed in Chapters 12, 13, and 14.

With the flow shop, if the station assignments are not properly designed, serious bottlenecks can develop, resulting in extremely inefficient operations. Machine breakdowns can stop the entire line and cause a backing up of

---

[13]Computer typesetting moves the publishing industry much closer to a flow shop configuration.

in-process inventories. There is only so much storage space between stations. A complete study of equipment characteristics is required.

Line balancing can be handled by simulating *throughput*[14] in the system, all the random factors that can affect the process being taken into account. Such simulations can be well worth the time and effort required if a large process investment is being tested. See Appendix 11-II, which treats simulation. Another approach, which we shall now examine, utilizes the mathematical and statistical models derived from queueing theory. To give substance to our discussion, let us consider the flow shop problem of sorting bulk mail (see Fig. 11-14).

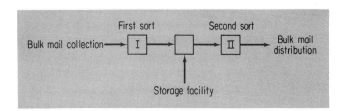

FIGURE 11-14.

Our production line consists of only two stations, called I and II. The technological sequence will be fixed: I goes first, II goes second. Thus, I is Sort mail *by* region, and II is Sort mail *within* region. We shall assume that station I has an expected production output rate of 3 units per minute. This, in turn, describes the expected load on station II, which has an assumed process rate of 4 units per minute. Furthermore, we shall not restrict the in-process inventory accommodations between the first and second mail-sorting stages. Figure 11-15 depicts this arrangement, called Case A (where $\lambda = 3$ is the output rate of I and, consequently, the input rate to II; and $\mu = 4$ is the process or service rate of II).

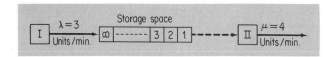

FIGURE 11-15. Sorting system: Case A

Although station II's output capacity is greater than I's, a queue can develop. This might occur if I speeds up while II remains constant at the expected value. It could also be that a queue of in-process inventory develops because II slows down while I performs according to expectation. If both events occur simultaneously, then the resultant queue can be quite formidable.

---

[14]These are the flows of information, materials, energy, and all resources that are used by the transformation process.

The average number of units in the queue would be[15]

$$L_q = \frac{\rho^2}{(1 - \rho)}$$

where
$$\rho = \frac{\lambda}{\mu} = \frac{3}{4} = 0.75$$

Then

$$L_q = \tfrac{9}{4} = 2.25$$

We can also determine the probability distribution $\{P_n\}$, where P_n equals the probability that a total of n units is in the system. Some units would be waiting for service[16] from station II, the remaining unit being served by II. When $n = 0$, station II is idle. When $n = 1$, station II is working and the in-process inventory is zero. When $n = 2$, one unit is waiting for station II to become available, and so forth. We know:[17]

$$P_n = (1 - \rho)\rho^n$$

Then, we can prepare Table 11-11 for station II.

Figure 11-16 depicts the resulting probability distribution that n units are in the system. The area of the tail of this distribution (crosshatched) is the probability that the *queue length* will exceed some designated value of $n - 1$. (We have called this tail area α.) When there are n units in a single channel system, one unit is being serviced. Therefore, the queue length is $n - 1$, which for this example is equal to 8 with a probability $\alpha = 0.0563$ that the queue length will exceed this value.

Thus, the in-process inventory can be expected to be greater than 8 more than 5 percent of the time. If only 8 units can be stored between stations I and II, then at least 5 percent of the time the flow shop will have to be shut down. This is undesirable, and steps must be taken to decrease the probability of exceeding 8 units in queue or of providing more storage space between stations I and II.

Many other performance characteristics of this system are also apparent. Station II will be idle 25 percent of the time. We know this from the fact that

---

[15]This relationship applies when:

1. There is a very large source of mail to be sorted.
2. There are unlimited accommodations for a waiting line.
3. Service is granted on a FIFO (first-in, first-out) basis.
4. There is a single service channel.
5. The arrival and service distributions are both exponential.

[16]These units comprise the in-process inventory.

[17]The same conditions hold as were listed in footnote 15. For these and other queueing formulations see: P. M. Morse, *Queues, Inventories and Maintenance* (New York: John Wiley & Sons, Inc., 1958); D. R. Cox and W. L. Smith, *Queues* (London: Methuen & Co., 1961); T. L. Saaty, *Elements of Queueing Theory* (New York: McGraw-Hill Book Co., Inc., 1961).

TABLE 11-11

n	P_n		Probability Density	Cumulative Probability
0	P_0	$= (1 - \rho)$	$= 0.2500$	0.2500
1	P_1	$= (1 - \rho)\rho^1$	$= 0.1875$	0.4375
2	P_2	$= (1 - \rho)\rho^2$	$= 0.1406$	0.5781
3	P_3	$= (1 - \rho)\rho^3$	$= 0.1055$	0.6836
4	P_4	$= (1 - \rho)\rho^4$	$= 0.0791$	0.7627
5	P_5	$= (1 - \rho)\rho^5$	$= 0.0593$	0.8220
6	P_6	$= (1 - \rho)\rho^6$	$= 0.0445$	0.8665
7	P_7	$= (1 - \rho)\rho^7$	$= 0.0334$	0.8999
8	P_8	$= (1 - \rho)\rho^8$	$= 0.0250$	0.9249
9	P_9	$= (1 - \rho)\rho^9$	$= 0.0188$	0.9437
10	P_{10}	$= (1 - \rho)\rho^{10}$	$= 0.0141$	0.9578
·	·		·	·
·	·		·	·
·	·		·	·
n	etc.		etc.	etc.

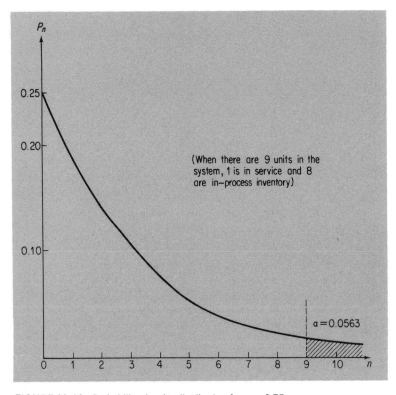

(When there are 9 units in the system, 1 is in service and 8 are in—process inventory)

$a = 0.0563$

FIGURE 11-16. Probability density distribution for $\rho = 0.75$

$P_0 = 0.25$. Station II's output will be

$$\text{Expected output} = (1 - P_0)\mu = (0.75)(4) = 3 \text{ units per minute}$$

which is equal to $3(60) = 180$ units per hour.

The use of line balancing to resolve the bulk mail sorting problem assumes realistic meaning when the manager begins to associate costs and value with the system's performance characteristics. Thus, for example, he might assemble the following information:

Expected output	180 units per hour
Output value	$0.50 (postage) per unit of dispatched bulk mail
Cost of station I[18]	$30.00 per hour
Cost of station II[19]	$50.00 per hour
Storage cost	$5.00 per bulk mail unit per hour

Then, the net value of the configuration shown in Fig. 11-15 (called Case A). would be

$$\text{Net value (\$/hr)} = \text{total output value} - \text{total input costs}$$

$$= \left(\begin{array}{c}\text{output value} \\ \text{per unit}\end{array}\right)\left(\begin{array}{c}\text{expected output} \\ \text{per hour}\end{array}\right) - \text{total input costs}$$

$$= (\text{output value})(1 - P_0)\mu(60) - (\text{storage cost})L_q$$

$$- \text{cost of stations}$$

$$= (\$0.50)(180) - [(\$5.00)(2.25) + \$30.00 + \$50.00]$$

$$= \$90.00 - \$91.25 = -\$1.25$$

The job shop method of sorting may well have resulted in an even greater loss than $1.25 an hour. We cannot jump to any conclusions about how bad is bad until we have compared this flow shop arrangement with the net value per hour of the presently used method.

In any case, the manager does have another idea in mind. He would like to test an alternative to see which balanced configuration is superior (see Fig. 11-17, which is called Case B).

For Case B, 2 slower station I-type sorters, having the same combined output as the Case A facility, will be used; these are called I_1's. The combined cost of the 2 slower stations is $15 less per hour than that of the faster station. Also, for Case B, two slower station II-type sorters, each having half the

---

[18] The cost factors of the facilities would be straightforward to compute if the facilities are salaried individuals; for machines and man-machine combinations, an approximate cost figure can still be found.

[19] *Ibid.*

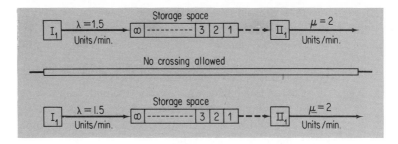

FIGURE 11-17. Sorting system; Case B

output of the Case A facility, will be used; these are called II_1's. The combined hourly cost of these 2 slower stations is the same as that of the faster station.

The manager's idea is to try 2 slower parallel sorting operations. Cross-overs are not allowed between channels; i.e., each I_1 is specifically paired with one II_1 and cannot supply the other one.

The relevant equations are the same as those used for Case A:

For each subsystem $(I_1 \rightarrow II_1)$:

$$\rho = \frac{1.5}{2} = 0.75$$

Therefore,

$$L_q = 2.25$$

$$P_0 = 0.25$$

$$\text{Expected output} = (1 - P_0)\mu = (0.75)2 = 1.5 \text{ units/min}$$

which is equal to $1.5(60) = 90$ units/hour.

The combined expected waiting line is $2L_q = 4.50$. The combined output is $2(90) = 180$ units per hour. Then the net value for the total system is

$$\text{Net value (\$/hr)} = (\$0.50)(180) - [(\$5.00)(4.5) + \$15.00 + \$50.00]$$

$$= \$90.00 - \$87.50 = +\$2.50$$

Presumably, the Case B design would be chosen unless still other alternatives existed.[20]

We have tried to present a simple description of the kind of thinking that occurs in the stochastic line balancing problem. Far more complex situations, including many activities and stations and a variety of alternative arrange-ments, can occur.

---

[20]Other alternatives might also have been requested if none of the designs yielded a satisfactory measure of value.

APPENDIX 11-II

Flow Shop Simulation with Stochastic Station Times
(Optional Material)

It has been proposed that a 2-station system be used to sort bulk mail in a flow shop configuration (see Fig. 11-18). The output rates of the first and second stations are expected to vary as shown in Table 11-12.

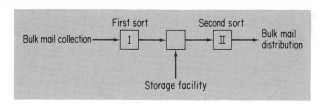

FIGURE 11-18.

TABLE 11-12

	Output Rate	Interval between Inputs to Station II	Probability	Monte Carlo Number
Station I	2 units/min	0.500 minutes	0.10	00–09
	3	0.333	0.50	10–59
	4	0.250	0.30	60–89
	5	0.200	0.10	90–99
		Service Duration at Station II		
Station II	2 units/min	0.500 minutes	0.10	00–09
	3	0.333	0.30	10–39
	4	0.250	0.50	40–89
	5	0.200	0.10	90–99

The average output rate for station I is 3.4 units per minute and for station II it is 3.6 units per minute. Since II processes at a faster rate than I, it might be supposed that the storage facility between I and II, *which is of limited size,* would not become a constraint on the output of station I. That is, station I must stop working when the storage queue gets larger than N.

Output rates are easily converted to "intervals between inputs from station I and to service durations at station II" by taking the reciprocals (as in column 2 of Table 11-12). Column 3 gives the probability distribution estimates, and these are converted into Monte Carlo numbers (column 4) for the following reason.

We want to simulate a random process. In this case, we need to generate sequences of input intervals from station I and service intervals at station II that conform to the respective probability distributions of each station. Monte Carlo numbers enable us to do this. However, we shall begin our discussion with colored chips mixed together in a bowl. Then we shall show how these colored chips can be used to explain the Monte Carlo process. We count out colored chips in the quantities shown in Table 11-13.

TABLE 11-13

	Station I			*Station II*	
Input Intervals	*Color*	*Quantity*	*Service Intervals*	*Color*	*Quantity*
0.500 min	Green	10	0.500 min	Yellow	10
0.333	Red	50	0.333	Orange	30
0.250	Blue	30	0.250	Purple	50
0.200	Black	10	0.200	Brown	10

Mix station I's chips in a bowl marked I. Mix station II's chips in a separate bowl, marked II. Withdraw a single chip from each bowl. Say they are blue and yellow. This means that the first interval between inputs to station II was 0.250 minute (blue). Then, 0.500 minute (yellow) elapses before station II completes its sorting operations on this same unit. The sequence of colors withdrawn from bowl I will represent the sequence of input intervals from station I. The sequence of colors withdrawn from bowl II will represent the sequence of service durations at station II.

Replace the chips in their respective bowls (we do not want to change the probability distributions). Make sure that the chips are well mixed in each bowl (we want to be certain that every chip has an equal likelihood of being picked). Continue picking and replacing chips in the same way until an adequate simulation sample has been achieved. (A good criterion for adequate is that the frequency count of the actual colors withdrawn matches the estimated probability distribution.)

Figure 11-19 graphically depicts what has occurred and makes it easy to

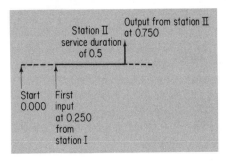

FIGURE 11-19.

visualize what can happen next. If the second chip withdrawn from bowl I is red, blue, or black, it will signify that a second input will arrive at station II before the first input unit has been completed. Consequently, the second arrival will have to wait. Specifically, if the second bowl I chip is red, then the unit arrives at $0.250 + 0.333 = 0.583$ and must wait $0.750 - 0.583 = 0.167$ minute. On the other hand, if the second bowl I chip is green, then the unit arrives at $0.250 + 0.500 = 0.750$ just as station II has completed sorting the first unit, and there is no waiting.

To complete our analysis of "what if's—," first, assume that the storage facility between stations I and II can accommodate only one unit and that two more units are completed at station I before station II has completed servicing the first unit (one at $0.250 + 0.200 = 0.450$, a bowl I *black* chip— the second at $0.450 + 0.250 = 0.700$, a bowl I *blue* chip); then station I must shut down from 0.700 until 0.750. At 0.750, station II begins servicing the waiting unit and thereby unblocks the storage facility, which accepts the unit that has been held at station I.

Second, assume that station II completes servicing the first unit at 0.750 and that a second unit arrives at that time which is serviced in 0.200 minutes (a bowl II *brown* chip). This means that station II will be idle at $0.750 + 0.200 = 0.950$ if anything but a bowl I black chip is drawn. In Fig. 11-20, the third input is a bowl I *red* chip, arriving at station II at $0.750 + 0.333 = 1.083$.

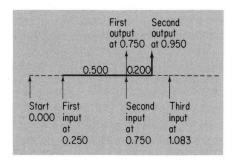

FIGURE 11-20.

To understand Monte Carlo numbers, replace the colored chips with numbered chips. This is shown in Table 11-14. Instead of green chips, we now have chips numbered 00–09. There were 10 chances to pick a green chip. Now there are 10 chances to pick a chip numbered 00–09, associated with an input interval from station I of 0.500 minute. Similarly, there are 50 chances of picking a chip numbered 10–59. This is the right proportion of station I input intervals of 0.333.

Because we have numbers instead of colors, we can do away with the necessity for chips. Instead, we use a table of random numbers (Table 11-15, p. 226–227). The character of the numbers in the table is that they have been randomly generated; i.e., any digit 0 through 9 is as likely to appear as any

TABLE 11-14

Station I				Station II			
Input Interval	Color	Monte Carlo Numbers	Quantity	Service Interval	Color	Monte Carlo Numbers	Quantity
0.500 min	Green	00–09	10	0.500 min	Yellow	00–09	10
0.333	Red	10–59	50	0.333	Orange	10–39	30
0.250	Blue	60–89	30	0.250	Purple	40–89	50
0.200	Black	90–99	10	0.200	Brown	90–99	10

other. Therefore, following some systematic pattern of reading the numbers (i.e., vertically, diagonally, horizontally) so that we do not introduce bias in the way numbers are selected, we read off successive pairs of digits.[21] Of every 2 pair, the first is equivalent to an input interval from station I, and the second is equivalent to a service interval at station II.

TABLE 11-15 RANDOM NUMBERS

05621	64483	38549	62908	71579	19203	83546	05917	51905	10052
03550	59144	59468	37984	77892	89766	86489	46619	50263	91136
22188	81205	99699	84260	19693	36701	43233	62719	53117	71153
63759	61429	14043	49095	84746	22018	19014	76781	61086	90216
55006	17765	15013	77707	54317	48862	53823	52905	70754	68212
81972	45644	12600	01951	72166	52682	97598	11955	73018	23528
06344	50136	33122	31794	86423	58037	36065	32190	31367	96007
92363	99784	94169	03652	80824	33407	40837	97749	18364	72666
96083	16943	89916	55159	62184	86208	09764	20244	88388	98675
92993	10747	08985	44999	36785	65035	65933	77378	92339	96454
95083	70292	50394	61044	65591	09774	16216	63561	59751	78771
77308	60721	96057	86031	83148	34970	30892	53489	44999	18021
11913	49624	28510	27311	61586	28576	43092	69971	44220	80410
70648	47484	05095	92335	55299	27161	64486	71307	85883	69610
92771	99203	37786	81142	44271	36433	31726	74879	89348	76886
78816	20975	13043	55921	82774	62745	48338	88348	61211	88074
79934	35392	56097	87613	94627	63622	08110	16611	88599	02890
64698	83376	87524	36897	17215	74339	69856	43622	22567	11518
44212	12995	03581	37618	94851	63020	65348	55857	91742	79508
82292	00204	00579	70630	37136	50922	83387	15014	51838	81760

---

[21]We would use successive triplets of digits 000–999 if the probabilities are stated to three places, etc.

TABLE 11-15   RANDOM NUMBERS (Continued)

08692	87237	87879	01629	72184	33853	95144	67943	19345	03469
67927	76855	50702	78555	97442	78809	40575	79714	06201	34576
62167	94213	52971	85974	68067	78814	40103	70759	92129	46716
45828	45441	74220	84157	23241	49332	23646	09390	13032	51569
01164	35307	26526	80335	58090	85871	07205	31749	40571	51755
29283	31581	04359	45538	41435	61103	32428	94042	39971	63678
19868	49978	81699	84904	50163	22625	07845	71308	00859	87984
14294	93587	55960	23149	07370	65065	06580	46285	07884	83928
77410	52195	29459	23032	83242	89938	40510	27252	55565	64714
36580	06921	35675	81645	60479	71035	99380	59759	42161	93440
07780	18093	31258	78156	07871	20369	53947	08534	39433	57216
07548	08454	36674	46255	80541	42903	37366	21164	97516	66181
22023	60448	69344	44260	90570	01632	21002	24413	04671	05665
20827	37210	57797	34660	32510	71558	78228	42304	77197	79168
47802	79270	48805	59480	88092	11441	96016	76091	51823	94442
76730	86591	18978	25479	77684	88439	35112	26052	57112	91653
26439	02903	20935	76297	15290	84688	74002	09467	41111	19194
32927	83426	07848	59327	44422	53372	27823	25417	27150	21750
51484	05286	77103	47284	05578	88774	15293	50740	07932	87633
45142	96804	92834	26886	70002	96643	36008	02239	93563	66429
12760	96106	89348	76127	17058	37181	74001	43869	28377	80923
15564	38648	02147	03894	97787	35234	44302	41672	12408	90168
71051	34941	55384	70709	11646	30269	60154	28276	48153	23122
42742	08817	82579	19505	26344	94116	86230	49139	32644	36545
59474	97752	77124	79579	65448	87700	54002	81411	57988	57437
12581	18211	61713	73962	87212	55624	85675	33961	63272	17587
00278	75089	20673	37438	92361	47941	62056	94104	45502	79159
59317	31861	62559	30925	23055	70922	47195	29827	68065	95409
59220	42448	70881	33687	53575	54599	69525	76424	98778	10459
00670	32157	15877	87120	13857	23979	38922	62421	03043	19602

We shall now run a hand simulation of the 2-station bulk mail flow shop for sorting that was introduced at the beginning of this appendix. The simulation consists of choosing successive pairs of random numbers and matching these against the input interval and service interval Monte Carlo numbers shown in Table 11-12. The first random number pair indicates the interval until the next arrival at station II; the second random number pair tells how long service will take. When a sufficient sample is drawn, the bottleneck effect of limited storage between stations can be assessed, the idle time of station

II can be estimated, and the overall quality of this flow shop configuration can be observed to determine whether an acceptable line balance has been achieved.

If we use a left to right scan of a random number table (only the first line of which is shown here), our first 2 pair of digits are 05 and 62, representing an input interval of 0.500 and a service duration of 0.250.

05621   64483   38549   62908   71579   19203   83546

The simulation continues in Table 11-16 (especially note Arrival Time, Completion Time, Idle Time, and Queue Size).

TABLE 11-16

Sample Number	Random Numbers	Input Interval	At Station II			Idle Time	Queue Size
			Arrival Time	Service Duration	Completion Time		
1	05, 62	0.500	0.500	0.250	0.750[a]	0	0
2	16, 44	0.333	0.833[a]	0.250	1.083	0.083[a]	0
3	83, 38	0.250	1.083	0.333	1.416	0	0
4	54, 96	0.333	1.416	0.200	1.616[b]	0	0
5	29, 08	0.333	1.749[b]	0.500	2.249[c,d]	0.133[b]	0
6	71, 57[e]	0.250	1.999[c,d]	—	—	0	1[c]
7	91, 92[f]	0.200	2.199[d,f]	—	—	0	2[d]
6			2.249[d,e]	0.250[e]	2.499[d]	0	1[e]
7			2.499[f]	0.200[f]	2.699	0	0[g]
8	03, 83	0.500	2.699	0.250	2.949	0	0
.							
.							
.							
etc.							

[a]Station II is idle from 0.750 until 0.833 (0.083 minute).
[b]Station II is idle from 1.616 until 1.749 (0.133 minute).
[c]Station II is busy, so arrival must wait from 1.999 until 2.249 (0.250 minute).
[d]A second unit joins the line at 2.199. We shall assume that there is storage space for it; otherwise, station I would have to stop at 2.199 and wait until 2.499 before it could begin again. One unit waits from 1.999 until 2.249 (0.250 minute); the other unit waits from 2.199 until 2.249 (0.050 minute).
[e]The random number 57 in the sixth sample indicates a service duration of 0.250. Thus, the sixth arrival begins to be serviced at 2.249.
[f]The seventh arrival waits from 2.199 until 2.499 to be serviced. The random number 92 indicates a service duration of 0.200.
[g]The line is cleared of waiting units. To this time, station II has been idle a total of 0.216 minute. The waiting line has been occupied by a single unit for 0.200 minute, and by two units for 0.050 minute for a total waiting time of 0.300. There has been no shutdown of station I.

Thus, we see that all of the different performance characteristics of our system can be simulated. Complex assumptions can be made that would defy strictly mathematical analyses. For example, to this point, we have assumed that the input and service intervals are independently distributed, but if this is not so, and they are conditional upon each other or on prior states, then these conditional dependencies can be modeled in a simulation. With a computer simulation program, it would not be difficult to simulate Filmasters' line balancing problem or any much more complex situations involving hundreds of activities (e.g., note the reference to Arcus' heuristic, p. 206.)

SUMMARY OF PART 4

Chapter 10

The line balancing problem arises in the flow shop because operations must be partitioned into nearly equal work assignments to avoid idle time at specialized facilities. This applies to labor-intensive systems as well as to primarily mechanized systems, which explains why much line balancing work has been focused on assembly line balancing, where workers and their equipment are paced by the conveyor belt. In Chapter 10 we expand the concept of the flow shop as a high-productivity system. The design of modular production systems and the application of group technology to families of parts are treated as relevant means to achieve the high-volume production required to justify the flow shop.

Chapter 11

The problem and resolution of deterministic line balancing is presented. An example is built around the precedence diagram of Filmasters', Inc., and its related situation. The calculation of cycle time is established (equal to total work content time divided by the number of stations) as well as its limits (no less than the longest operation time; no more than total work content time). It is shown how productivity and cycle time relate. The concepts of perfect balance and balance delay are dovetailed with the development of station layouts and the application of special heuristic methods of achieving line balance.

The stochastic line balancing problem is introduced in Appendix 11-I as optional material. Its relationship to queueing models is examined with sufficient detail to allow an analytical maximum profit solution to the choice between alternative bulk mail sorting flow shop configurations. In Appendix 11-II, as optional material, simulation as a line balancing method is explored in sufficient detail to allow an example to be fully worked out.

With this understanding of flow shops, we proceed in Part 5 to study job shops.

REFERENCES PART 4

ALFORD, L. P. (ed.), *Cost and Production Handbook*, 3rd ed. New York: The Ronald Press Company, 1955.

ANSOFF, H. I. (ed.), *Business Strategy*. Middlesex, England: Penguin Books, 1969.

ASHBY, W. R., *An Introduction to Cybernetics*. New York: John Wiley & Sons, Inc., 1956.

BAUMOL, WILLIAM J., *Economic Theory and Operations Analysis*, 2nd ed. Englewood Cliffs, N.J.: Prentice-Hall, Inc., 1965.

BECKETT, J. A., *Management Dynamics, The New Synthesis*. New York: McGraw-Hill Book Company, 1971.

BEER, STAFFORD, *Cybernetics and Management*. New York: John Wiley & Sons, Inc., 1959.

———, *Decision and Control*. New York: John Wiley & Sons, Inc., 1967.

BELLMAN, R., *Adaptive Control Processes*. Princeton, N.J.: Princeton University Press, 1961.

——— and R. KALABA, *Mathematical Trends in Control Theory*. New York: Dover Publishing, 1964.

BLACK, GUY, *The Application of Systems Analysis to Government Operations*. New York: Frederic A. Praeger, Inc., 1968.

BONINI, C. P., R. J. JAEDICHE, and H. W. WAGNER, *Management Controls: New Directions in Basic Research*. New York: McGraw-Hill Book Company, 1964.

BOSTON CONSULTING GROUP, *Japan in 1980: The Economic System and Its Prospects*. London: The Financial Times Ltd., 1974.

BOWMAN, EDWARD H. and ROBERT B. FETTER, *Analysis for Production and Operations Management*, 3rd ed. Homewood, Ill.: Richard D. Irwin, Inc., 1967.

BROOM, H. N., *Production Management*. Homewood, Ill.: Richard D. Irwin, Inc., 1962.

BROWN, R. G., *Smoothing, Forecasting and Prediction*. Englewood Cliffs, N. J.: Prentice-Hall, Inc., 1962.

BUFFA, ELWOOD S., *Modern Production Management*, 3rd ed. New York: John Wiley & Sons, Inc., 1969.

——— (ed.), *Readings in Production and Operations Management*, New York: John Wiley & Sons, Inc., 1969.

CHERRY, COLIN, *On Human Communication*. New York: John Wiley & Sons, Inc., 1957.

COCHRAN, W. G. and G. M. COX, *Experimental Designs*. New York: John Wiley & Sons, Inc., 1950.

COOMBS, C. A., *Theory of Data*. New York: John Wiley & Sons, Inc., 1964.

CYERT. R. and J. MARCH, *A Behavioral Theory of the Firm*. Englewood Cliffs, N.J.: Prentice-Hall, Inc., 1967.

DE LATIL, P., *Thinking by Machine: A Study of Cybernetics* (Trans. Y. M. Golla). Boston: Houghton Mifflin Company, 1957.

DOOLEY, ARCH R. ET AL., *Casebooks in Production Management, Basic Problems, Concepts, and Techniques*. New York: John Wiley & Sons, Inc., 1964.

EILON, SAMUEL, *Elements of Production Planning and Control*. New York: The Macmillan Co., 1962.

FELLER, W., *Probability Theory and Its Applications*, Vol. 1, 2nd ed. New York: John Wiley & Sons, Inc., 1957.

FISHER, R. A., *The Design of Experiments*. Edinburgh, Scotland: Oliver & Boyd, Ltd., 1947.

FORRESTER, J. W., *Industrial Dynamics*. New York: John Wiley & Sons, Inc., 1961.

GARRETT, LEONARD J. and MILTON SILVER, *Production Management Analysis*, New York: Harcourt Brace Jovanovich, Inc., 1966.

GAVETT, J. WILLIAM, *Production and Operations Management*, New York: Harcourt Brace Jovanovich, Inc., 1968.

GEORGE, JR., CLAUDE S., *Management for Business and Industry*, Englewood Cliffs, N.J.: Prentice-Hall, Inc., 1970.

GOETZ, B. E., *Quantitative Methods: A Survey and Guide for Managers*. New York: McGraw-Hill Book Company, 1965.

HALL, A. D., *A Methodology for Systems Engineering*. Princeton, N.J.: D. Van Nostrand Co., Inc., 1962.

HEGELSON, W. B. and D. P. BIRNIE, "Assembly Line Balancing Using the Ranked Positional Weight Technique," *Journal of Industrial Engineering*, Vol. 12, No. 6 (November–December, 1961), pp. 394–398.

HENDERSON, B. D., *The Experience Curve—Reviewed* (a series of pamphlets). Boston: The Boston Consulting Group, 1974.

HOLT, C. C., F. MODIGLIANI, J. MUTH, and H. SIMON, *Planning Production Inventories and Work Force*. Englewood Cliffs, N.J.: Prentice-Hall, Inc., 1960.

IGNALL, EDWARD J., "A Review of Assembly Line Balancing," *Journal of Industrial Engineering*, Vol. 16, No. 4 (July–August, 1965), pp. 244–254.

IRESON, W. GRANT and EUGENE L. GRANT (eds.), *Handbook of Industrial Engineering and Management*. Englewood Cliffs, N.J.: Prentice-Hall, Inc., 1957.

KILBRIDGE, M. and L. WESTER, "A Heuristic Method of Assembly Line Balancing," *Journal of Industrial Engineering*, Vol. 12, No. 4 (July–August, 1961), pp. 292–299.

KLIR, J. and M. VALACH, *Cybernetic Modelling*. Princeton, N.J.: D. Van Nostrand Co., 1967.

LEVITT, T., "Production-Line Approach to Service," *Harvard Business Review,* Vol. 50, No. 5 (September-October, 1972), pp. 41-52.

McGARRAH, ROBERT E., *Production and Logistics Management*. New York: John Wiley & Sons, Inc., 1963.

McKEAN, R. N., *Efficiency in Government through Systems Analysis*. New York: John Wiley & Sons, Inc., 1958.

McMILLAN, C. JR. and R. F. GONZALES, *Systems Analysis: A Computer Approach to Decision Models*, 2nd ed. Homewood, Ill.: Richard D. Irwin, Inc., 1968.

MAYER, R. R., *Production Management*. New York: McGraw-Hill, Inc., 1962.

MORSE, PHILLIP M., *Queues Inventories, and Maintenance*. New York: John Wiley & Sons, 1958.

MUTH, J. F. and G. L. THOMPSON, *Industrial Scheduling*. Englewood Cliffs N.J.: Prentice-Hall, Inc., 1963.

NAYLOR, T. H. ET AL., *Computer Simulation Techniques*. New York: John Wiley & Sons, Inc., 1968.

NILAND, POWELL, *Production Planning, Scheduling, and Inventory Control*. New York: The Macmillan Company, 1970.

OPTNER, S. L., *Systems Analysis*. Englewood Cliffs, N.J.: Prentice-Hall, Inc., 1960.

PANICO, J. A., *Queueing Theory*. Englewood Cliffs, N.J.: Prentice-Hall, Inc., 1969.

PIERCE, JOHN F. (ed.), *Operations Research and the Design of Management Information Systems*. New York: Technical Association of the Pulp and Paper Industry, 1967.

ROSCOE, EDWIN SCOTT, *Organization for Production*, 3rd ed. Homewood, Ill.: Richard D. Irwin, Inc., 1963.

SAATY, T. L., *Elements of Queueing Theory*. New York: McGraw-Hill Book Co., 1961.

STARR, MARTIN K. (ed.), *Management of Production*. Middlesex, England: Penguin Books Ltd., 1970.

———, *Management: A Modern Approach*. New York: Harcourt Brace Jovanovich, 1971.

TIMMS, HOWARD L. and MICHAEL F. POHLEN, *The Production Function in Business: Decision Systems for Production and Operations Management*, 3rd ed. Homewood, Ill.: Richard D, Irwin, Inc., 1970.

job shop
management

Job shop management is dependent on good forecasting, which in turn is dependent on the backup of an adequate information system. This is not true of the flow shop, where information systems have been predesigned, where demand predictions have been made, and where output volume is fixed by that. Chapter 12 introduces the job shop and treats some basic facts about how to forecast.

Job shop planning starts at the aggregate level; that is, all the different kinds of jobs that might be done in some period of time (forecast needed) are lumped together to determine work force and equipment requirements. Chapter 13 deals with the aggregate scheduling model.

Shoploading is the assignment of different kinds of work to various departments or machine centers. This scheduling activity is also unique to the job shop. (So many service activities are done by job shop process configurations that we remind the reader to think in terms of services as well as goods.) Tasks are ultimately assigned in specific order to individuals and machines (called sequencing). The concern of Chapter 14 is shoploading and sequencing.

There are three appendices of optional material in Part 5. The first (Appendix 13-I) applies linear programming and the transportation method to the aggregate scheduling problem. Appendix 14-I develops the general assignment model for matching jobs with individuals, departments, machines, etc. Appendix 14-II extends the sequencing model so that it is applicable for scheduling work at more than one facility.

Throughout this text, the flow shop is advocated for its high productivity. At the same time, we recognize that under many circumstances, especially service situations, the flow shop is not feasible. Accordingly, we stress the powerful techniques that are available for making the job shop as efficient and productive as possible.

Aggregate scheduling and the requisite forecasting capabilities, as well as shop loading and sequencing, are not applicable to the flow shop. However, in some cases, especially where high volume is needed to generate inventory, the use of aggregate scheduling for the intermittent flow shop configuration may be justified. Such circumstances in no way alter the applicability of the materials of Chapter 13. For the purposes of aggregate scheduling, the intermittent flow shop can be treated as a job shop when it shares resources with many other kinds of work. However, it should be remembered that intermittent flow shops have higher productivity than job shops because their work routines have been serialized; see Fig. 10-1, p. 179.

twelve
forecasting
for the job shop

The job shop requires managers who know how to juggle production schedules. Often many pressing problems arise, and they all must be solved within minutes of each other.

Complexity of the Job Shop

As a rule, the job shop manager has direct and immediate contact with many customers. This is because the job shop regularly produces to fill specific orders. Some job shops also produce for finished goods inventory where stable and sufficient demand exists, but this must be fitted into the schedule just as if it were an order by a customer.[1] One's own inventory department manager can be as demanding as an outside customer.

Contrast these conditions with those of the flow shop, where the process

---

[1] A significant difference between goods and services is the inability to build an inventory of "finished" services.

has been predesigned and debugged, where production materials are ordered long in advance in substantial quantities, and where requisite skills are fully cataloged and well-practiced. The flow shop produces inventory that is usually distributed to warehouses, then to retailers, and finally to the ultimate consumer. Flow shop volume often is so large that an organization for distribution of the output is an inherent requirement. (For distribution of the job shop output, if an organization is needed, it will usually have quite a different form, being designed for the distribution of smaller quantities.) Although problems can and do arise in the flow shop, they are more orderly, often mechanical, and far better anticipated than those of the job shop.

The job shop produces relatively small amounts of diverse outputs requiring many different materials, skills, setups and takedowns, jigs, fixtures, repair routines, and so forth. In a job shop of any size, hundreds and even thousands of jobs can be going on.[2] They are at different stages, being produced in varying quantities, which means that there is no fixed schedule of equipment utilization, so *scheduling work* becomes of the greatest importance.

Information management is essential. *Bottlenecks* removed from the flow shop by design must be kept to a minimum in the job shop by schedule control. Each order carries its own delivery date. The salesperson's promised delivery date should not be given without confirmation from the production schedulers. Yet it is not unheard of for this to occur, and conflicts arise between sales and production.

An important customer calls in a rush order and the general manager gives it the highest priority—and says, "Do it now." What job (or jobs) should be stopped? Decision problems like this occur regularly, yet they are each special, and unique with respect to the conflicts that must be resolved. A sudden surge of orders occurs for various products or services, and the work force is not sufficient, or raw materials are in short supply, or facilities are inadequate. A waiting line develops. Sales management has good marketing reasons for preferring that certain jobs get done; operations management has good scheduling reasons for its own recommendations, which may not coincide at all with those of sales. What's to be done? Who is to make the decision?[3]

The Information Management Requirement

With all the different jobs to schedule, materials to stock and dispatch, etc., the management of information is a necessity for the job shop. For each job, there are dozens of kinds of data that must be stored, used, checked against, and so forth.

---

[2]In some job shops, there are large order sizes and longer production runs. Such shops straddle the flow and job shop, using intermittent flow shop practices in conjunction with job shop techniques. Everything that we discuss in Parts 4 and 5 remains relevant to this case.

[3]Many of the methods that we will be talking about in Chapters 12, 13, and 14 allow several parties (such as sales and operations) to represent their concerns in reaching a decision.

Figures 12-1 through 12-4 are intended to illustrate the diversity of documents that maintain critical information for the organization. Briefly, we shall consider each of these in turn. (Bear in mind that Fig. 12-2 applies to a service industry—airlines—whereas Figs. 12-1, 12-3, and 12-4 are relevant to manufacture and assembly.)

First, consider the information content of one kind of data required by the job shop, namely, the blueprint. There are usually a number of parts that cannot be made without blueprints. Figure 12-1 illustrates the kind and amount of information that blueprints contain. While this is not scheduling

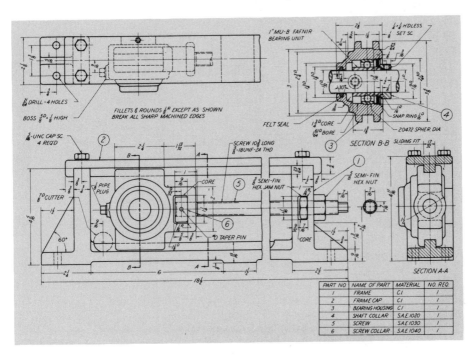

FIGURE 12-1. Blueprint of a conveyor take-up unit [From Warren J. Luzadder, *Fundamentals of Engineering Drawing,* 6th ed. Englewood Cliffs, N. J.: Prentice-Hall, Inc.. 1971, p. 413.]

information, it is related. Only certain machines can be used to make this conveyor take-up unit. Equipment requirements and the quantity to be produced interact with other job requirements in the shop. So blueprint data are essential inputs to the work scheduling decision.

Distinction between Blueprints for Flow Shops, Job Shops, and Projects

Blueprints are unambiguously detailed descriptions of product output and of special equipment and service facilities required for the process. We may note that for the job shop, blueprints of the output

					FINAL
TWA	T R A N S W O R L D A I R L I N E S				
Boeing 707 – 131 – B		ROUTING CHART			
EFFECTIVE August 1,1975		CHART NO. 8		ISSUED 6 – 20 – 75	

					Assignment of aircraft at 0600	
Date	8/1	8/10	8/17	9/1	8/1	8/17
Available	36	36	37	37	BOS 2	
Active	36	36	37	37	BDL 1	
L/M	1	1	1	1	JFK 1	
Spare		1	1		EWR 2	
OHB	3	2	1	2	BAL 2	
					PHL 1	
PT					I AD 1	
UNA					CMH 3	
Other						
Total	40	40	40	40	CVG 1	
Block hours		330:48		338:53	PIT 2	
					ORD 1	
Schedule utilization		9:11		9:09	SDF 1	
Fleet utilization		8:16		8:28	DTW 1	
O – Originate					STL 2	
T – Terminate					MCI 1	
Ⓔ – Enroute					DEN 1.....................2	
PCK – Pilot training check					PHX 1	
L/M – Line maintenance					LAS 1	
PT – Pilot training					LAX 3	
OHB – Overhaul					SFO 4	
					Ⓔ 4	
					TTL 36	37
					TWA Form 448001	

FIGURE 12-2. Equipment routing chart for Boeing 707-131-B aircraft [Courtesy Trans World Airlines]

and of tools, dies, fixtures, casting molds, etc., are critically important and continually referenced.

In the flow shop, blueprints are important during the project management phase of bringing the flow shop into being. At that time, they are used to coordinate precisely the design of facilities and process specifications with output objectives. It is economically feasible to employ highly skilled engineering assistance to obtain the most efficient configurations. Thereafter, use is made of the blueprints only when there is a breakdown. Thus, the project is more like the job shop, requiring frequent reference by technicians to the blueprints.

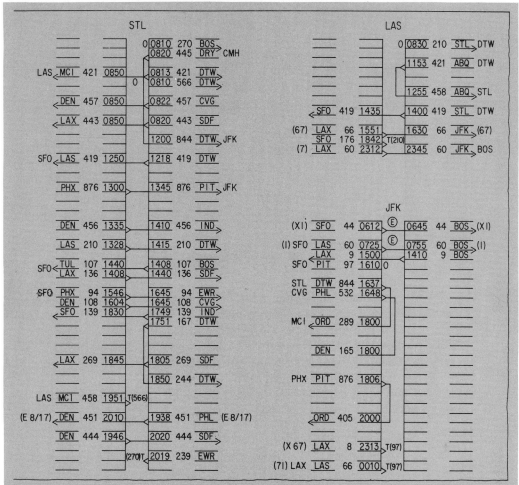

Though this chart is filled with technical matters, the essentials of aircraft routing are apparent. On 8/1 there are 36 aircraft available, plus backups of another 4. Of the 36 planes, 4 are enroute; the remainder at 0600, are at 20 airports, e.g., BOS, BDL, JFK, etc. Also, we show a few of the 26 airport schedules (included on the complete chart) that specify flight number, exact destinations and times of flight (STL, LAS and JFK).

The equivalent of the blueprint in service systems is a carefully detailed statement of methods and procedures, i.e., the service to be provided under all conditions that are likely to be experienced. Indeed, specific documents and forms (that communicate what the job is) characterize the information managed by many nonfabricating and service systems. Consider, for example, post office procedures, hospital care routines, and airline routing systems (see Fig. 12-2).

Another relevant form of information for the job shop is the *bill of materials*. This is illustrated for switch Z33 by Fig. 12-3. The bill of materials lists all parts required to make the item. Also, it details some important characteristics of each part (materials, costs, and operations). Further, note that switch Z33 is used in only one final assembly of a finished product, viz., the

Item Switch Z 33					Sheet No. 1 of 2	
Drawings Z 1-Z 6					Assembly 5 hp motor J	
Part No.	Part name	No./item	Material	Quantity/item	Cost/item	Operations
CH 20	Casing	1	SF 60	0.25 lbs	$0.15	Cast, trim
SJ 64	Drive Sprg	2	Sprg. St.	....	$0.08	Purchase
RH 82	1" Rod	3	1045 St.	4 in	$0.05	Make
⋮	⋮	⋮	⋮	⋮	⋮	⋮
TJ 32	Fitting	1	Ti-6A1-4V	0.10 lbs	$0.85	Forge, anneal

FIGURE 12-3. Bill of materials
The item, switch Z33, is used in the assembly of the 5 HP Motor J.

5-horsepower motor, designated J. With modular production objectives, perhaps switch Z33 could be redesigned and thereby used in other assemblies as well as J. (See footnote 4, which examines the modular potential of the casing CH20; the same reasoning can be applied to the switch Z33.)

Each part listed in the bill of materials has an *operations sheet*. In Fig. 12-4, we show an operations sheet for part no. CH20.[4] It is a fully detailed description of what must be done to make the casing. In general, operations sheets show:

All departments needed to make the part.

All operations and machines (including alternatives when they exist).

All materials, tools and fixtures that are required.

Operation times and setup times for each operation.

Economic order quantity or economic lot size (see pp. 341–51).

The information essential for scheduling is now in our hands. We know what orders are in the shop (item name and quantity). Therefore, we can calculate the total work loads on machines and departments.[5] The loads that result may be unbalanced and then alternative assignments would be tried. Ultimately, some jobs must wait and some facilities must be idle. Schedule decisions will determine which jobs are done first and which facilities work under- or overtime.

---

[4]Note how the CH20 is used for three different items: switches Z33 and Z34, and it also is subcontracted to an outside organization (T102). This is an example of modularity. Assume that a new switch Z35 is being designed. Check to see if the casing CH20 can do the job. If not, see if a new casing can be designed for the Z35 that also could be substituted for all present applications of CH20. Can the new casing be better, less costly, etc., because of its combined volume?

[5]See the discussion of material requirements planning (MRP) on pp. 322–36.

Part No. CH 20				Economic lot size	500	
Part name	Casing			Process time/pce	3.5 h	
Blueprint No.				Set up time	2 h	

Use for	Switch Z 33	Quantity per	1
	Switch Z 34		1
	Sub-contract T 102		50/mo

| Material | SF 60 | Vendor | BQV | |
| % Scrap | 10 | Weight 1/4 lb. per | Cost | $0.15 per |

Operation No.	Operation	Operation* time	Set up* time	Machine No.	Tool No.	Department
1	Cast			M235 (or M237)	DX103	D6
2	Trim			M81	DX104	D8
3	Drill (2) holes			M631 (or M635)	jig X103	D2
4	Broach			M631 (or M635)	jig X1035	D2
5	Tumble			DR3 24	———	DR3

*Look up on Machine card

Inspection ____ ✓

Authorization ____ ✓

FIGURE 12-4. Operations sheet

Contrast the well-balanced, smooth-running line of the flow shop with the multiplicity of decisions that must be made in the job shop and the information that must be kept track of to support these decisions. You begin to perceive why a flow shop manager may have to be a very different kind of person (in style and temperament) than the manager of a flow shop. For career planning, students are advised to take note that the choice between flow shop, job shop, and project is likely to have far more profound influence on their success or failure than the choice of going with Company A or Company B, in the same industry. That is because the character of work in each type of shop is profoundly different, calling upon different skills and attitudes, whereas companies in the same industry generally share similar environments.

Managing the Job Shop: A Single Overall Problem
That Must Be Resolved in Three Steps

We have stressed the role of information management in running the job shop, because at the heart of the problem is the number of combinations of work/facility assignments that can be made. Some of them are good; some terrible; and one or more are best. The computer has altered the organization's capacity to deal with all the data and their combinations, but not enough to allow the entire job shop scheduling problem to be solved in one step.

There are three distinct problem stages that can be identified. They should be solved together as one overall problem, but that cannot be done, because actions that require lead time must be taken before actual orders are in hand. Figure 12-5 shows the 3 problem stages of which the overall problem is comprised.

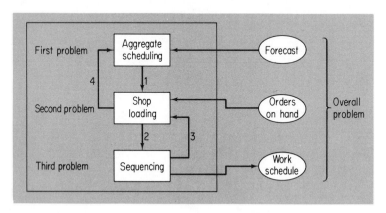

FIGURE 12-5. Three problem stages of the job shop

First, we must determine what labor force, raw materials, supplies, and facilities to have on hand for a chosen *planning period* (say 3 months). This is called *aggregate scheduling*.

Second, we must assign actual work on hand to facilities (called *shop loading*). This is done for an actionable planning period (say weekly or even daily). If many changes arise regularly, then daily shop loading is probably preferable to weekly. Note that work has been assigned to facilities but has not been sequenced as to the order in which it will be done.

Third, sequence the order of work to be done at each facility. (*Sequencing* might always follow shop loading or be done even more frequently.)

The work schedule is derived in this way: shop loading followed by sequencing. This is not an optimal solution, since *interactions* abound. To begin with, work can be sequenced at each specific facility efficiently or inefficiently (see pp. 297–99). If the work already assigned could be shifted between the existing facilities, perhaps even better sequences could be arranged. But usually this will not be done, because the shop has already been loaded on the basis of criteria other than sequencing efficiency (see pp. 277–92). It is too much work to go back and forth between criteria. Thus, the path marked 3 in Fig. 12-5 will not be followed.

Further, an even better sequence might be found, if shop loading and sequencing were treated together (paths 2 and 3 in Fig. 12-5). This could be done by changing the kind and number of facilities that were used to reach the shop loading solution in order to get a better sequencing solution. But the decision about facilities was previously made during aggregate scheduling and with enough lead time to bring plans to fruition. Even if the required lead time is short. for practical, size-of-problem, computational reasons we we do not follow an iterative chain of reasoning[6] (paths 3 and 4 in Fig. 12-5), which would allow aggregate scheduling to be influenced by ·shop loading, which in turn would be influenced by sequencing.

Instead of trying to resolve the overall problem, we solve the three problem stages in order, and believe that we get a good enough solution. The difficulty of trying to solve the overall problem is compounded by the fact that aggregate scheduling must be based on forecasts with a planning period that is sufficiently long to allow facilities and work force plans to be converted to actions.

Forecasting on a regular and continuous basis is a particular requirement of the job shop. It is a distinguishing feature not shared by the flow shop or the project.

Forecasts and Predictions

> To not be able to foretell the future in any way is a more mysterious thought by far than to propose that it can be done to some degree.

Inventory planning and *aggregate scheduling* are two "operations" areas that are highly sensitive to forecast and prediction abilities. That is why we intend to dwell on the forecast and prediction area at this point. A series of events that occur over time is called a *time series*; i.e., sales demand in 3 successive months can be written S_1, S_2, S_3. If the 3 months are yet to come, we must predict values for the time series $\{S_t\}$. If a believable time series $\{S_t\}$ cannot be derived (so that the predicted time series would have little error when compared to actuality), then no method for aggregate scheduling has any merit.

First, let us make clear how we distinguish between forecasting and prediction. *Prediction* is the choice of 1 particular state. It is chosen as the state that is most likely to happen from among a number of different states that appear to have some likelihood of occurring—e.g., betting on one particular horse in a race. The odds on the board are the *forecast*. Turning to another

---

[6]To explain iterative reasoning, a series of decisions is taken, and then the performance of the system, under the new conditions, is evaluated. Corrections in the decisions are made to adjust the system so that actual performance comes closer to expectation. The cycle is repeated as many times as necessary. Linear programming (discussed in Chapter 6) exemplifies such iterative procedures.

example, using meteorology, tomorrow's weather is *predicted* to be fair, based on the *forecast* that there is a 30 percent probability of precipitation.[7]

Aggregate scheduling uses *predictions*, which are frequently derived from *forecasts*. It is important to note that predictions of the behavior of aggregations tend to be more accurate than predictions of the behaviors of the individual components that make up the aggregate. For example, it is easier to predict next year's (total) aggregate sales level for a department store than next month's aggregate sales level, because the longer period has less erratic behavior than the small, short interval sample; it is easier to predict aggregate sales for all floors of the department store than for any one floor, because fluctuations in individual departments tend to cancel each other out. As shown in Fig. 12-6, trajectories of time series over long intervals tend to be smooth; over short intervals, unpredictable.

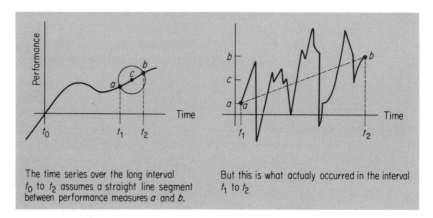

The time series over the long interval t_0 to t_2 assumes a straight line segment between performance measures a and b.

But this is what actually occurred in the interval t_1 to t_2

FIGURE 12-6.

As a result, it is not unusual to study the aggregate system to explain the smaller, component systems' behaviors. Thus, the trend from a to b is quite clear in the aggregate system and not as readily apparent from detailed information collected during the short interval t_1 to t_2. Similarly, the department store manager may estimate quarterly sales in aggregate terms and later proportionately divide this gross prediction into particular product-line sales.

It is usually easier to interpolate or extrapolate on aggregates and later convert to component predictions through proportioning. *Interpolation* is the process of trying to reconstruct an unknown history *between* 2 known points. For example, we know that at t_1 the system was at a and at t_2 it was at b [Fig. 12-7(a)]. *Question:* What had happened at $t_{1.5}$ in between? *Answer:*

---

[7]While this is not a universal distinction, R. G. Brown states, "I use *predict* to refer to . . . subjective estimates, and *forecast* to denote an objective computation." Brown's further explanation is entirely compatible with the definition suggested in this text. See R. G. Brown, *Smoothing, Forecasting and Prediction* (Englewood Cliffs, N.J.: Prentice-Hall, Inc., 1962), pp. 2–3.

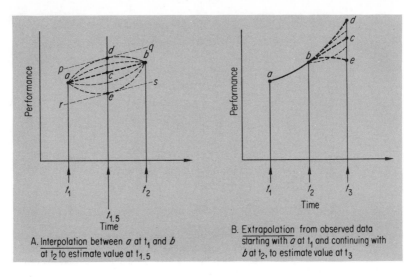

A. Interpolation between a at t_1 and b at t_2 to estimate value at $t_{1.5}$

B. Extrapolation from observed data starting with a at t_1 and continuing with b at t_2, to estimate value at t_3

FIGURE 12-7.

We cannot say exactly; a likely guess is point c on the straight line, and anything greater than point d or less than point e is unlikely. For example, the upper and lower bounds, pq and rs, might express the statistical variation that is believed to apply to 95 percent of all events occurring during the interval of time $t_2 - t_1$. In short, everything that has been observed, or that can be logically postulated, can be used to estimate the value that might have held at $t_{1.5}$. It might (or might not) be reasonable, for example, to suggest that adjacent points will be like each other for inertial reasons; i.e., the system has a tendency to keep performing in the same manner that it has been. The size of the interval $(t_{1.5} - t_1)$ will restrict how much change could have occurred, given that the system went from a to b during the interval $(t_2 - t_1)$. Proceeding in this fashion, we try to find some reasonable rules for interpolating between a and b.

Extrapolation is the process of moving from observed data (past and present) to the unknown values of future points, Fig. 12-7(b). Extrapolation is typical of many forecasting and predicting activities. The same kind of reasoning concerning interval sizes, statistical variation, dynamics of the system, and inertial effect applies as was the case with interpolation.

Given a forecast, the mean or mode of the forecast distribution might be the basis for a prediction of a particular event. Figure 12-8 illustrates a forecast distribution and shows how the mean and mode predictions might differ. Both with and without forecasts, predictions can be based on guesses, linear and nonlinear extrapolations of trends, belief that history repeats itself, or the mode of values based on a collection of expert mathematical models, etc.

Some forecasts (known as *Bayesian forecasts*) are based on *subjective* judgments, whereas *objective* forecasts are derived by *counting* the number of special events and dividing that number by the total number of all events—

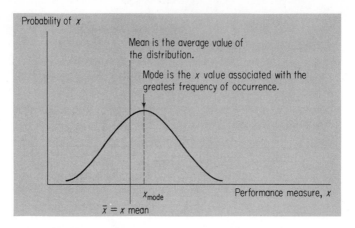

FIGURE 12-8. In the interval $t_3 - t_2$, the performance measure x is believed to be distributed as shown. From this forecast, a prediction for x must be given. Two different rules for prediction that are often used are (1) choose the mean value $\bar{x}$, and (2) choose the mode value x_{mode}.

e.g., out of 10 letters drawn at random, three are A's, so $p[A] = \frac{3}{10}$. If we retain knowledge of the past, we obtain the historical stream of data known as a *time series*. Contrast this with information that has lost its time tag. Such information that is bereft of specific time or even time sequence but is known to belong to a given interval of time is called *cross-sectional data*. The analysis of time series separates out any basic trends in the data that might exist; as well, the analysis isolates any cyclical variation (perhaps seasonal). It also identifies and removes a class of information associated with random variation, often called *noise*. Many methods exist for filtering out noninforming noise so that "pure" trends and "real" cycles can be spotted. Difficulty arises because noise often *hides* fundamental patterns.

Prediction Error

The history of any system of predictions can be recorded as a difference between what was expected to happen and what actually happened—predicted − actual = the error. For *systems of attributes*, where predictions take the form of "yes" or "no" (such as: it is or it is not oilbearing land), we can tally each individual's record to observe who was right *most* of the time. When predictors are chosen, preference can only be given to good predictors if you know who they are. For *systems of variables* (such as estimating next month's sales demand), forecasts of predictive error distributions, such as that shown in Fig. 12-9, could be obtained for each individual.

Although B's prediction errors average out to 0 (because he over- and underestimates equally), A is a better predictor, since we can correct A's bias

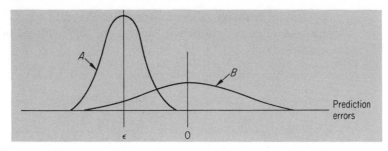

FIGURE 12-9.

by adding ϵ to every prediction made by A. Then the A and B distributions are both centered over 0, and A's variance is less than B's.

Data-based Predictions

A variety of methods exist for making predictions by extrapolation. We shall discuss a number of these.

Historical and Seasonal Predictions

When historical information is available, a simple historical prediction can be made based on the assumption that what happened last year will happen again. Thus, for example, if the demand in the previous January was x, then in the coming January it will also be x. This method is effective only if a stable seasonal pattern exists.

If the aggregate level appears to be changing over a period of time, but the seasonal pattern remains fixed, then a *base series* modification can be used. For example, assume that in the preceding year the quarterly demands were 40, 20, 30, 10. This gives a yearly demand of 100 units. Now, let us assume that in the current year the yearly demand is expected to increase to 120 units. Then the quarterly predictions would be $(40/100)120 = 48$; $(20/100)120 = 24$; $(30/100)120 = 36$; $(10/100)120 = 12$. These quarterly demands total to 120 units.

When there is no seasonal pattern and the system is thought to follow a gradual trend, then a moving average can be used to advantage.

Moving Averages

This method provides a simple means of obtaining a prediction of future values based on past history. The most recent N successive observations of actual events, such as monthly demand, are recorded. The data are regularly updated to maintain recent information. We shall use $\hat{x}_t$ to represent the predicted value of x in period t, and x_t to represent the actual value that occurred. Then

$$\hat{x}_{t+1} = (x_t + x_{t-1} + \ldots + x_{t-N+1})/N$$

$$\hat{x}_{t+2} = \hat{x}_{t+1} + (x_{t+1} - x_{t-N+1})/N$$

It will be noted that each next month's prediction is updated by dropping the oldest month of the series x_{t-N+1} and adding the latest observation x_{t+1}.[8] This yields the equation for $\hat{x}_{t+2}$, above. In this way, new trends are taken into account, and old information is removed from the system.

Here is an example, in which a 4-period moving average is assumed.

Month	Actual, x_t	Predicted, $\hat{x}_t$	Error
1	1	We need four values of x_t before we can make a	
2	3	prediction $\hat{x}_t$ and calculate the error.	
3	4		
4	4		
5	5	3	−2
6	6	4	−2

The first prediction is 3 calculated by $\hat{x}_5 = (4 + 4 + 3 + 1)/4 = 3$. When the actual demand occurs, it turns out to be 5. The prediction has fallen short by 2. Now a second prediction can be made. We add 5 to the moving average series and drop 1 from the first month. The prediction for the sixth month is 4; i.e., $\hat{x}_6 = (5 + 4 + 4 + 3)/4 = 4$. Let us say that instead of the prediction of 4 being correct, the actual result is 6. Then, the following period prediction is 4.75, i.e., $\hat{x}_7 = 4 + \left(\dfrac{6 - 3}{4}\right) = \dfrac{6 + 5 + 4 + 4}{4} = 4.75$. The moving average is slowly increasing with the apparent trend. Such slowness of response will be appreciated only if there is a gradual trend. But the manager is beginning to think that demand stability is disappearing. What should be done?

We can handle this situation in a number of ways. One is to decrease the number of observations N in the moving average. This will make the predictions more responsive to recent events. Try it out with $N = 2$ and see for yourself.

Weighted Moving Averages

A second way to make the prediction more responsive to trends is to use *weighted moving averages*. Let the sum of the weights w_t be 1; thus, $\sum_t w_t = 1$.

---

[8]The moving average method applies to any time period—hours, days, weeks, etc.

Our system of predictive equations becomes

$$\hat{x}_{t+1} = w_t x_t + w_{t-1}x_{t-1} + \ldots + w_{t-N+1}x_{t-N+1}$$

or, specifically,

$$\hat{x}_{t+1} = 0.4x_t + 0.3x_{t-1} + 0.2x_{t-2} + 0.1x_{t-3},$$

for the given weights, 0.4, 0.3, 0.2, 0.1

(Note that the biggest weights are assigned to the most recent observations. This will generally hold true. However, in a rapidly changing system w_t will be much greater ($\ggg$) than w_{t-1}, etc. Thus, $w_t \ggg w_{t-1} \ggg w_{t-2} \ldots$ etc. This is equivalent to reducing the size of N, which was discussed in the section on moving averages.) With the previous method of moving averages, all the w_t were treated as being equal, viz., for $t = 5$:

$$\hat{x}_{t+1} = \tfrac{1}{4}(5) + \tfrac{1}{4}(4) + \tfrac{1}{4}(4) + \tfrac{1}{4}(3) = 4$$

Using the weights (0.4, 0.3, 0.2, 0.1) with the numbers from our previous example, we obtain

$$\hat{x}_{t+1} = 0.4(5) + 0.3(4) + 0.2(4) + 0.1(3) = 2 + 1.2 + 0.8 + 0.3 = 4.3$$

This system is responding more rapidly to the (possible) trend (4.3 vs. 4).

Introducing the new value of 6 (as we did before), we again observe an increase in reaction rate, (5.1 vs. 4.75).

$$\hat{x}_{t+2} = 0.4(6) + 0.3(5) + 0.2(4) + 0.1(4) = 2.4 + 1.5 + 0.8 + 0.4 = 5.1$$

Thus weighted moving averages can track strong trends more accurately.

Prediction through Exponential Smoothing

Often, the use of weighted moving averages is less effective than exponential smoothing, which requires less calculation. Many control systems employ exponential smoothing. It has proven effective for such diverse applications as tracking aircraft and predicting demand levels for inventory systems. The method of exponential smoothing carries the last *average value* of actual observations in memory and combines it with the most recent *observed value*. Thus, $\hat{x}_{t-1}$ is the last prediction made; x_{t-1} is the actual result observed for the period $t - 1$, and $\hat{x}_t$ is the new prediction to be made for period t.

$$\hat{x}_t = \alpha x_{t-1} + (1 - \alpha)\hat{x}_{t-1}$$

According to the weight α that is used, the response rate of the system can be changed markedly. Thus, using the same data as before, we observe the effect on the prediction $\hat{x}_t$ of different values of α.

$\hat{x}_t$	α
0.1(6) + 0.9(4) = 4.2	0.1
0.2(6) + 0.8(4) = 4.4	0.2
0.3(6) + 0.7(4) = 4.6	0.3
0.375(6) + 0.625(4) = 4.75	0.375 ← Moving average result
0.4(6) + 0.6(4) = 4.8	0.4
0.5(6) + 0.5(4) = 5.0	0.5
0.55(6) + 0.45(4) = 5.1	0.550 ← Weighted moving average result
0.6(6) + 0.4(4) = 5.2	0.6
.	.
.	.
.	.
1.0(6) + 9(4) = 6.0	1.0

This simple updating system requires only one operation. Thus, if $\alpha = 0.1$ and the actual result is $x_t = 4.5$, then $\hat{x}_{t+1} = 0.1(4.5) + 0.9(4.2) = 4.23$.

Small values of α are used for noisy, randomly fluctuating systems that have a basic stability, and larger values of α are used for emerging and evolving systems, where a goodly amount of weight can only be placed on the last observation. For many aggregate scheduling systems, α is kept quite small, in the neighborhood of 0.05 to 0.15, to decrease the system's response to random fluctuations.

Regression Analysis for Prediction— Schoolmasters, Inc.

Another important approach for prediction is regression analysis. When future outcomes that are to be predicted appear to be related to other factors that *lead* them (i.e., occur first), then it is possible to predict a sequence of *future* outcomes on the basis of *current* observations of the other factors.

The least-squares technique is a method of regression analysis that can be used to estimate the value of future outcomes, y_{t+k}, if a leading factor x_t can be found.[9] For example, let the sequence of outcomes we wish to predict be the aggregate demand for kindergarten school supplies. Schoolmasters, Inc., (a job shop company producing a full range of kindergarten supplies and distributing them nationally) assumes that the aggregate demand for kindergarten supplies is related to the number of children born 5 years before. For aggregate planning, Schoolmasters has prepared the information shown in Table 12-1.

---

[9]Causality between y_{t+k} and x_t is not assumed. A common causal factor (that is unknown) may be responsible for whatever relationship is found.

TABLE 12-1

Year t	x_t = Number of Children Born in Year t (in millions)	Year t + 5	y_{t+5} = Kindergarten Attendance in Year t + 5 (in millions)
1	3	6	2
2	4	7	3
3	6	8	5
4	4	9	5
5	8	10	6

It is assumed that the number of children born in a given year *leads* kindergarten attendance by 5 years, and we have, therefore, paired the x_t's with the y_{t+5}'s that occurred 5 years later. Schoolmasters will use this relationship to determine its aggregate production schedule.

Let us fit a least-squares line to these data. This line will be an estimate of the way in which kindergarten attendance changes as a result of the number of children born five years before. It can then be used to extrapolate probable kindergarten attendance in the future for known or estimated number of births.

We use what are called *normal equations* (based on the assumption of a *linear* relationship between x_t and y_{t+5}) to derive the least-squares line. It can be shown that the least-squares line minimizes the total variance of the distances of the *observed* points from that line. The *normal equations* achieve this objective.

$$\sum_{t=1}^{t=N} y_{t+5} = aN + \sum_{t=1}^{t=N} x_t \tag{12-1}$$

$$\sum_{t=1}^{t=N} x_t y_{t+5} = a \sum_{t=1}^{t=N} x_t + b \sum_{t=1}^{t=N} x_t^2 \tag{12-2}$$

For our example, $N = 5$, which is the total number of pairs of x_t and y_{t+5}. Table 12-2 assembles the data needed for our analysis.

TABLE 12-2

t	x_t	y_{t+5}	$x_t y_{t+5}$	x_t^2
1	3	2	6	9
2	4	3	12	16
3	6	5	30	36
4	4	5	20	16
5	8	6	48	64
Σ	25	21	116	141

Therefore,

$$21 = a(5) + b(25) \qquad \text{using Eq. (12-1)}$$
$$116 = a(25) + b(141) \qquad \text{using Eq. (12-2)}$$

Solving for a and b, we obtain: $a = \frac{61}{80}$; $b = \frac{11}{16}$. These values are introduced in the least-squares line:

$$y_{t+5} = a + bx_t = +\frac{61}{80} + \frac{11}{16}x_t \qquad (12\text{-}3)$$

This least-squares line and the actual scatter of values around it are shown in Fig. 12-10. To use this line, let us suppose that when $t = 6$, $x_t = 10$. We see that y_{t+5} would be predicted to be 7.6375 million. We would use this line for prediction only if the observed data appear to fit it well, especially in recent years.

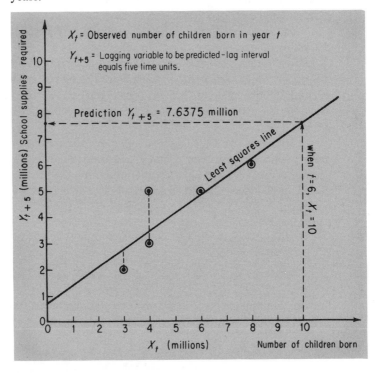

FIGURE 12-10. Least-squares linear relationship between a leading indicator and the variable to be predicted

Different forecasts for the same outcomes frequently exist within a single organization. Sometimes, the production manager derives one forecast; the sales manager derives another; branch managers derive still others. Often a variety of different data bases coexist. Methods for pooling information to provide a stronger prediction should not be ignored. Also, it is of critical importance that all parties share the same forecasts, and, usually, much stronger forecasts can be obtained if both data *and experience* are pooled.

A Small Glossary for Anticipating Events that Change over Time

Time series: A succession of values identified with the time of their occurrence.

Forecasting: Identifying the different things that can happen, and how likely each of the possibilities is.

Predicting: Naming the event that is expected to happen, so that plans can take shape around this event.

Multiple prediction: Naming several events that might occur so that plans and contingency plans can be developed.

Future control: Attempting to modify the future, which would be reflected in altered forecasts and changed predictions.

Using linear regression, Schoolmasters can prepare an aggregate schedule for its job shop. For aggregate scheduling, many different items are treated as though they were of one kind in terms of their demands on resources. Chapter 13 describes the aggregate scheduling function.

PROBLEMS
1. Contrast the relationship of the job shop and the flow shop with respect to their production of output for finished goods inventory.

2. In a large job shop, there are many departments having the same kind of general-purpose equipment, and, therefore, able to do the same kind of job. Of course, some departments are better for certain kinds of jobs than others. The job shop manager wants to choose the best assignments, but to evaluate all possibilities without a method is generally impossible.

   To illustrate, assume that 10 jobs are to be assigned to 10 different departments. How many variations must be evaluated, if all possible arrangements are considered?

3. What is the relationship of the *bill of materials* to the *blueprint*, and what is the relationship of the *operations sheet* to the *bill of materials*?

4. Why is management of the job shop called a single overall problem that must be resolved in 3 steps? Explain the 3 subproblems and discuss the effect of solving them in sequential order.

5. The job shop requires a good information management system. Why is this a requirement? Does it apply to the flow shop? Does it apply to projects?

6. Explain the difference between
   a. Historical and moving average predictions.
   b. Moving average and weighted moving average predictions.
   c. Weighted moving average and exponential smoothing predictions.

7. The Parks Department has a job shop orientation. Crews of park workers are assigned different tasks, which are completed in batches before

another task is tackled. For example, tree care in the previous year required the following number of crew hours.

Month	Crew Hours	Month	Crew Hours
Jan.	110	July	200
Feb.	120	Aug.	220
March	140	Sept.	280
April	180	Oct.	120
May	250	Nov.	100
June	200	Dec.	80

a. Using the moving average method, based on 6 periods, prepare an analysis of prediction error.
Answer:

Month	Total Crew Hours	Prediction	Actual	Error
July	1000	167	200	−33
Aug.	1090	182	220	−38
Sept.	1190	198	280	−82
Oct.	1330	222	120	+102
Nov.	1270	212	100	+112
Dec.	1120	187	80	+107
Jan.	1000	167		

b. Using the moving average method based on 3 periods, prepare an analysis of prediction error. Compare your results with part a results above. Discuss.

c. Using the weighted moving average method, based on 6 periods and weights of 0.1, 0.1, 0.1, 0.2, 0.2, 0.3, prepare an analysis of prediction error. Compare your results with those obtained in parts a and b above. Discuss.

d. Using exponential smoothing, find the α values that would yield the results obtained in parts a, b, and c above. What α value would you choose? Explain your answer.

8. Draw up an appropriate *bill of materials* for producing the following items:

a. A table knife

b. An office stapler

c. A flashlight

Answer: The bill of materials for a product should list all parts that are required for its assembly. It is a useful form of information for both the design and control of the production system. A simplified version of the materials for a flashlight might be

Part No.	Description	Quantity	Cost/Item
10057	Plastic case	1	$0.253
10573	Screw-on battery holder	1	.029
84638	Switch	1	.164
74935	Screws to hold switch	2	.006
67395	Bulb housing	1	.058
93867	Glass front	1	.094
12345	Bulb	1	.132

Similarly, lists can be drawn up for the table knife (simple) and for the stapler (more complex). By assigning part numbers and costs per item, useful bills of materials can be derived.

9. A beach umbrella manufacturer had the following monthly sales in the year just completed:

Month	Sales
1	500
2	800
3	1200
4	2000
5	4000
6	8000
7	10000
8	7000
9	6000
10	1000
11	500
12	300

The company anticipates a growth in next year's sales of 40 percent.
a. Prepare a monthly estimate of sales for the coming year.
b. Why is such a monthly breakdown of sales required?
Answer: **a.** Assuming that the seasonal pattern is stable, we need only increase each month's sales by 40 percent.

Month	1	2	3	4	5	6
Sales	700	1,120	1,680	2,800	5,600	11,200

Month	7	8	9	10	11	12
Sales	14,000	9,800	8,400	1,400	700	420

The prior year's total sales were 41,300 units. With a 40 percent increase the total sales will be 57,820 units, which is the total of the adjusted, monthly (forecast) figures.

b. Monthly forecasts are needed to plan production; to regulate staffing, hiring, and training; to set levels for inventories and to provide storage facilities for purchased materials and for in-process and finished goods; even to determine how much cash should be available to meet immediate needs.

10. A manufacturer of kitchen equipment keeps track of *new housing starts* in his region. He believes that demand for his products follows housing starts by 3 months. Fit a least-square line to the data below, which are based on the manager's assumptions.

Month	Sales Volume	Housing Starts
1	$45,000	260
2	60,000	250
3	62,000	320
4	30,000	380
5	40,000	500
6	45,000	480
7	68,000	320
8	75,000	400
9	80,000	350
10	45,000	250
11	30,000	100
12	25,000	150

Answer:

Month	Housing Starts (H)	Sales (S) 3 Mo. Later	H × S	H²
1	260	30,000	7,800,000	67,600
2	250	40,000	10,000,000	62,500
3	320	45,000	14,400,000	102,400
4	380	68,000	25,840,000	144,400
5	500	75,000	37,500,000	250,000
6	480	80,000	38,400,000	230,400
7	320	45,000	14,400,000	102,400
8	400	30,000	12,000,000	160,000
9	350	25,000	8,750,000	122,500
	3,260	438,000	169,090,000	1,242,200

The equation of the least squares line (see pp. 250–53 of the text) is

$$S = a + bH$$

where a and b can be determined by solving:

$$438{,}000 = a(9) + b(3260)$$

$$169{,}090{,}000 = a(3260) + b(1{,}242{,}200)$$

We find that

$$S = -12{,}947.3 + (170.1)H$$

11. Would you prefer a good prediction or a good forecast? Explain your answer?

Answer: A good forecast will describe all possible states of nature and their probabilities. Based on this forecast, it is possible to select a strategy that maximizes the expected value. The forecast considers all of the various outcomes that are possible and weights their respective likelihoods.

A prediction pertains to a specific state of nature. Since it considers only one happening, it represents the use of less information than a forecast. However, as the prediction improves (until it is perfect), a different counter-form of information is being called upon. Good predictive ability approaches omniscience. A perfect prediction allows the best strategy to be chosen, i.e., that strategy which maximizes the outcome for the single (predicted) state. This strategy may not necessarily have the highest expected value, a fact which is inconsequential, since only one state of nature is considered as possible. Other states are not considered relevant.

A poor prediction lacks information about possible alternatives, and, therefore, a good forecast is worth more than a poor prediction. However, as the quality of the prediction improves, the information for good decision making becomes balanced between the forecast and the prediction. Therefore, a good prediction is preferred to a good forecast. A perfect prediction is the ultimate, and there is no such thing as a perfect forecast.

thirteen

aggregate scheduling

Aggregate scheduling is achieved by lumping all items together to determine work force requirements, general productivity levels, etc.

The Use of Standard Units of Work

By "lumping" we mean that different parts, activities, products, and services are all described and accounted for in terms of an arbitrarily chosen, agreed-upon standard unit of work. Thus, a gallon of Paintmasters' famous velvet white paint (known within Paintmasters as X12) requires two standard units of labor, e.g., a standardized work-force-hour of labor, or of man-machine time. Since the demand for X12 in the next quarter ahead is expected to be 100 gallons, then the X12 contribution to the expected aggregate demand is 200 standard units. This figure will be added to other products' or services' expected needs, also expressed in standard units. The aggregate total will be used for work-force planning. The aggregate schedule that is derived represents an important planning stage for management. It applies to intermittent flow shops and job shops.

A Simple Example of How Planners Aggregate Demands for Different Products (or Services) into Standard Units of Required Production Capacity*

Assume that 4 machines (people, departments, etc.) represent our total production capacity. These machines work at different rates. Machine 2 is fastest. Arbitrarily, it is chosen as the standard machine (S.M.) and assigned an index of 1.0. Machine 1 is half as fast (index 0.5); machine 3 is 80 percent as fast (index 0.8); machine 4 is 60 percent as fast (index 0.6). Each machine is ranked by an index number which when multiplied by the actual machine hours available (say) per week, yields the *standard machine hours* (S.M.H.) available per week. Thus:

Machine	Hours Available per Week	Index	S.M.H. of Supply Available per Week
1	36	0.5	18
2*	54	1.0	54
3	80	0.8	64
4	$33\frac{1}{3}$	0.6	20
			156

*Chosen as the standard machine (S.M.). If machine 1 had been chosen as S.M., the indices would have been 1.0, 2.0, 1.6, 1.2.

There is a total of 156 standard machine hours (S.M.H.) available per week. How many standard hours are demanded?

Next week's demand prediction is shown below:

Job	A	B	C	D	E
Units demanded	300	210	240	1800	400

We use the *productivity rate of the standard machine* for each job.

Job	A	B	C	D	E
Production rate of the standard machine in pieces per S.M.H.	6	7	6	30	25

———————

*We have made some simplifying assumptions, for ease of explanation, but these assumptions do not alter the basic concepts of standard units.

Our computations are guided by the following equation (where dimensions are shown in Italics):

$$\left(\begin{matrix}\text{Demand} \\ \text{in units}\end{matrix}\right) \frac{pieces}{week} \div \left(\begin{matrix}\text{production} \\ \text{rate}\end{matrix}\right) \frac{pieces}{S.M.H.} = \left(\begin{matrix}\text{demand in} \\ \text{standard hours}\end{matrix}\right) \frac{S.M.H.}{week}$$

Specifically, for job A:

$$(300) \frac{pieces}{week} \div (6) \frac{pieces}{S.M.H.} = (50) \frac{S.M.H.}{week}$$

For all of the jobs, we obtain the table below:

Job	S.M.H. of Demand
A	300/6 = 50
B	210/7 = 30
C	240/6 = 40
D	1800/30 = 60
E	400/25 = 16
	196 standard machine hours

Both supply and demand are now converted to the common terms of S.M.H., but we have only 156 standard hours available from our machines. Therefore, 196 − 156 = 40 S.M.H. of demand will not be met.

The same reasoning applies to standard man-hours and to combinations of work force and capital equipment. Various weighting schemes are required to bring the different kinds of estimates of supply and demand into a common framework.

The Use of Forecasts

The first requirement is a believable forecast that can then be used with various methods that exist for achieving aggregate schedules. In fact, for every planning period (say 3 months) the need for new and revised forecasts is recurrent; see pp. 243–53. Paintmasters (a pseudonym for a large, real U.S. company) deserves much credit for having supported the development of aggregate scheduling methods. Their technique of using quadratic equations is explained on pp. 266–71. In Appendix 13-I, pp. 271–75, other approaches are described, namely, the use of linear programming and the transportation method. This is optional material.

Aggregate scheduling gains much of its utility from the advantage of predicting aggregate phenomena as compared to detailed components of the aggregation. The methodology of aggregate scheduling is entirely dependent on a reasonably good ability to forecast and predict, so the previous pages (243–53) devoted to forecasting should be recalled at this time.

An Aggregate Scheduling Model

Job shops require a strong methodological approach for planning ahead. Aggregate scheduling provides such a powerful approach. *Demand* and *production output* are treated in *aggregation* across a variety of different work facilities and output jobs. The aggregate is treated as one job made by one facility operating under several different modes, e.g., regular and overtime production. The organization's facilities are used to satisfy varying demand levels over time in whatever way promises to minimize total costs that vary according to the production schedule that is used. Demands for different outputs are aggregated by considering them all to be demand for the output capacity of the facility. Figure 13-1 portrays seasonal demands for several different items that have been transformed into an aggregate demand for production facilities. Let the demand during period t be called S_t.

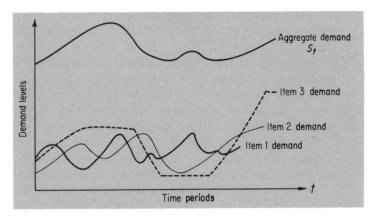

FIGURE 13-1. Determination of aggregate demand as the sum of the demand for three items during time periods t

The amount produced during time period t is called P_t. The facilities and especially the organization's work force can vary over time. We shall call the work force level W_t during time t.[1] An additional variable that we usually wish to control over time is the inventory level I_t. Therefore, given a "good" prediction of aggregate demand S_t over time, the problem to solve is How should we vary P_t, W_t, and I_t so as to optimize the systems performance? Clearly, if the demand predictions are unreliable, then the aggregate method of scheduling is meaningless.

---

[1] At the period before, called $t - 1$, the work force level is W_{t-1}.

261

Two strategies suggest themselves. First, vary W_t so that P_t matches the demand S_t as closely as possible. In Fig. 13-2 this is production pattern B, which exactly satisfies demand for every period in time, i.e., $P_t = S_t$. This is

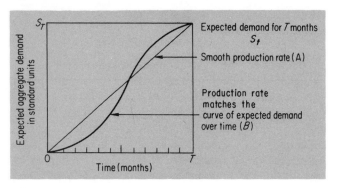

FIGURE 13-2. Expected demand S_T for period T can be satisfied with smooth production (A) or by matching demand seasonality and other fluctuations (B).

the situation where workers are to be hired and fired each time period, according to the expected demand of the time period. The practice could be daily, weekly, monthly, etc. Second, do not vary the work force, thereby keeping P_t constant over time, i.e., $P_t = P$ for all t. In Fig. 13-2 this is pattern A. The latter strategy permits a fixed-volume production output where only routine production sequences need be followed. Compared to a variable-volume shop, fixed-volume creates a more stable job shop environment. The information management problem of the variable-volume job shop system simply compounds the difficulties of the job shop that we have previously discussed. Nevertheless, as we shall see, there are definite circumstances in which variable-volume of output is management's best option. In a job shop system, certain costs disappear when pattern A is followed, but other costs increase.

We expect our solution to represent some combination of changing production rates, changing work force size, varying degrees of overtime utilization, and fluctuating inventory levels. Figure 13-3 captures some of the aspects of this system's interrelatedness.

What happens to the change in the work force level $(W_t - W_{t-1})$ when production pattern B, monthly variation of the work force, is followed, i.e., $P_t = S_t$. (For this illustration, we assume that each worker can produce 10 units in every time period.) Demand in the first period is 420 units, i.e., $S_1 = 420$. (See Table 13-1.) Production in the first period is 420 units, i.e., $P_1 = 420$. Production exactly matches demand, so there is no inventory, i.e., $I_1 = 0$. Cumulative inventory, $\sum_t I_t$, is also 0. We need 42 workers, so $W_1 = 42$. The change in work force size is not relevant for the start-up period. In the second period the work force contracts to 36, which is a reduction of 6. The work force expands to 39 in the third period, etc. Inventory is never produced, so it cannot be accumulated. All orders are filled with minimum delay.

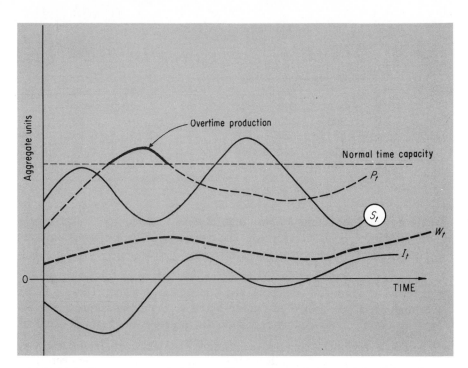

FIGURE 13-3. The aggregate scheduling problem requires period by period solutions that will optimize the total system's performance, recognizing interperiod dependencies.

TABLE 13-1 PATTERN B

t	S_t	P_t	I_t	$\sum_t I_t$	W_t	$(W_t - W_{t-1})$
1	420	420	0	0	42	
2	360	360	0	0	36	−6
3	390	390	0	0	39	+3
4	350	350	0	0	35	−4
5	420	420	0	0	42	+7
6	340	340	0	0	34	−8

Now, let us look at the second case (A-type) where the work force is maintained at a constant level ($W_t = 38$), which means that inventory can fluctuate. At the end of the first period, production has fallen short of demand by $\sum_t I_t = 40$ units. (See Table 13-2.) This back-ordered work is shown as negative inventory. We cannot tell which actual jobs will not be completed, because we are dealing with aggregates. But some jobs—or parts of jobs—are going to be back ordered. These customers are going to be more or less unhappy. It is even possible that some will cancel their orders (leading to the little rhyme, "fill or kill"). Note that in the second period, demand S_t falls 20

263

TABLE 13-2   PATTERN A

t	S_t	P_t	W_t	$(W_t - W_{t-1})$	I_t	$\sum_t I_t$
1	420	380	38	0	−40	−40
2	360	380	38	0	+20	−20
3	390	380	38	0	−10	−30
4	350	380	38	0	+30	0
5	420	380	38	0	−40	−40
6	340	380	38	0	+40	0

units behind production P_t. This adds 20 units to inventory, I_t. These units will be shipped to fill back orders. The remaining 20 back-ordered units are shown in the column of cumulative inventory $\sum_t I_t$ as −20.

Let us now contrast these 2 cases. The constant work force (A-type) has produced 3 instances of supply being less than demand. These total to 90 units. However, back orders never exceed 40. From the cumulative inventory column $\sum_t I_t$ we see that back orders at any time vary between 0 and 40.

There is never positive cumulative inventory, but there could have been. Note that total demand for 6 periods is 2280, which is the same as supply. Yet, with the B-type rule, there is not one back-order occasion, even though demand fluctuates. Thus, in trade for no back orders, we are required to hire 10 workers and lay off 18. Such work force changes have costs.

The question to be answered before deciding how to set up the job shop is Which approach has the lowest expected cost? Other configurations come to mind. For example, what happens if a mixture of policies is used, i.e., if only limited changes of the work force level are allowed?

Question: What result do you obtain if you maintain a constant work force of 39 instead of 38 workers?
Answer:

t	I_t	$\sum_t I_t$
1	−30	−30
2	+30	0
3	0	0
4	+40	+40
5	−30	+10
6	+50	+60

Back orders occur only at the end of the first period. Thereafter, inventory begins to accumulate. There is a cost for carrying inventory. Consequently, this example illustrates another opportunity for cost trade-offs, i.e., the wages of another worker plus the costs of carrying inventory versus reduction in the number of back orders.

Question: What result would have occurred if the demand series $t = 1$ through 6 had occurred in reverse order, i.e., 340, 420, 350, 390, 360, 420, and the work force was held constant at 38? This result is worth discussing.

When P_t varies with S_t, work force adjustment costs occur. This could represent the costs of a constant size work force engaged in overtime, or a fluctuating work force size, with or without overtime.

Let us consider the opposing costs that we have encountered in these cases.

When the production rate over time P_t is smooth, then hiring, training, and other work force adjustment costs, such as overtime, go to 0. Further, when P_t is constant, then demand fluctuations produce inventory costs for overstocks and back-order costs for understocks. The extent of these costs depends on the demand fluctuation. The optimal size for the work force should be determined by the cost trade-offs between, work force adjustment costs, including wages and the over- and understock costs. If production rates match demand rates, then inventory-type costs disappear.

Figure 13-4 illustrates these opposing costs. For such systems analysis

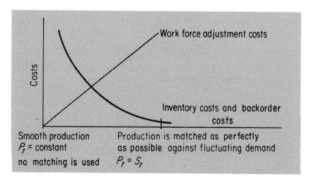

FIGURE 13-4. The x axis represents the degree to which production rates P_t match demand rates S_t.

there is a total cost, composed of inventory costs and work force adjustment costs, which reaches a minimum value for some particular production schedule. Also, a large constant-size work force will decrease back-order costs and increase inventory carrying costs.

The Quadratic Cost Model (HMMS)

Production requirements for many items can be expressed in aggregate figures using *standard processing hours*. Then a reasonable time series of predicted demand (in standard processing hours) is developed. Next, costs of carrying inventory, back orders, work force level changes, and so forth, are estimated. All of these can be united in an aggregate scheduling model, which will produce minimum total cost work schedules.

Work done by Holt, Modigliani, Muth, and Simon (in a paint factory) has provided an important aggregate scheduling model, which we will call the HMMS model.[2] They examined all relevant costs (hiring, layoff, regular and overtime payroll, setup, back ordering, and inventory carrying costs), using both linear ($y = cx$) and quadratic ($y = cx^2$) cost functions as required to provide adequate approximations of the cost systems. Their predictions of sales were based on a method of moving averages, which we have previously covered (pp. 247–49).

The paint factory experienced significant fluctuations in demand, and although large inventories were maintained, outages occurred frequently. As a result, sales were lost or significant overtime and hiring costs were incurred. Worker morale was low and efficiency poor as workers stretched out their jobs during demand downturns.

"HMMS" built a mathematical model that involved minimizing a quadratic total cost equation:

Minimize $\sum_{t=1}^{T} C_t$ where

$$C_t = C_1 W_t + C_2 (W_t - W_{t-1})^2 + C_3 (P_t - C_4 W_t)^2$$
$$+ C_5 P_t - C_6 W_t + C_7 (\sum_t I_t - C_8 - C_9 S_t)^2$$

subject to the necessary inventory constraint:

$$\sum_t I_{t-1} + P_t - S_t = \sum_t I_t$$

This equation is equivalent to the cumulative inventory measure, $\sum_t I_t$ as used in the tables on pp. 263–64. The variables are identified as follows:

C_1 = costs related to payroll, i.e., absolute size of the work force.

C_2 = hiring and layoff costs, in terms of work force *changes*.

---

[2] C. C. Holt, F. Modigliani, J. F. Muth, and H. A. Simon, *Planning Production Inventories and Work Force*. (Englewood Cliffs, N.J.: Prentice-Hall, Inc., 1960).

$C_3, C_4, C_5, C_6 =$ different kinds of overtime costs.

$C_7, C_8, C_9 =$ different kinds of inventory costs.

$S_t =$ demand forecast for period t.

$\sum_t I_t =$ on hand inventory minus back orders at the end of period t.

$P_t =$ the *aggregate* production rate in period t.

$W_t =$ the size of the work force for period t.

To understand how the costs were derived, see Fig. 13-5. Note that the payroll costs $C_1 W_t$ are treated as being linear, whereas the other costs are approximated by quadratic (squared) terms. The quadratic approximations are more realistic than linear ones, which are assumed by other aggregate scheduling models.

The HMMS Model Applied to Paintmasters' Problem

The best way to understand the HMMS aggregate scheduling model is to use it in an example. Because there are a lot of calculations, we shall keep our example small, limiting our analysis to only 2 time periods. Let us contrast the 2 cases that we previously studied.

A. The work force level is kept at constant size.

B. Production output rate matches demand.

Assume that Paintmasters has determined that its costs are as follows:

$$C_1 = 100 \qquad C_4 = 10 \qquad C_7 = 0.1$$
$$C_2 = 3 \qquad C_5 = 2 \qquad C_8 = 60$$
$$C_3 = 0.2 \qquad C_6 = 20 \qquad C_9 = 0.2$$

A. Constant size work force policy (it is assumed that each worker can produce 10 units in each time period)

t	W_t	P_t	S_t	I_t	$\sum_t I_t$
0	38	380	380	0	0
1	38	380	400	−20	−20
2	38	380	350	+30	+10

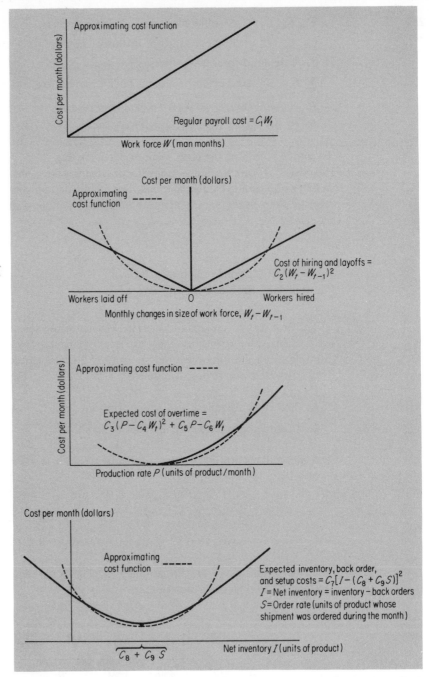

FIGURE 13-5. Hypothetical cost behavior as a function of planning variables [From Charles C. Holt, Franco Modigliani, and Herbert A. Simon, "A Linear Decision Rule for Production and Employment Scheduling," *Management Science*, Vol. 2, No. 1 (October 1955). Reprinted by permission of the Institute of Management Sciences.]

$$C_{t=1} = 100(38) + 3(0)^2 + 0.2[380 - 10(38)]^2 + 2(380) - 20(38)$$
$$+ 0.1[-20 - 60 - 0.2(400)]^2$$
$$= 6360$$
$$C_{t=2} = 100(38) + 3(0)^2 + 0.2[380 - 10(38)]^2 + 2(380) - 20(38)$$
$$+ 0.1[10 - 60 - 0.2(350)]^2$$
$$= 5240$$
$$C_{t=1} + C_{t=2} = 11,600$$

B. The policy that matches production output with demand

t	W_t	P_t	S_t	I_t	$\sum_t I_t$
0	38	380	380	0	0
1	40	400	400	0	0
2	35	350	350	0	0

$$C_{t=1} = 100(40) + 3(2)^2 + 0.2[400 - 10(40)]^2 + 2(400) - 20(40)$$
$$+ 0.1[0 - 60 - (0.2)(400)]^2$$
$$= 5972$$
$$C_{t=2} = 100(35) + 3(-5)^2 + 0.2[350 - 10(35)]^2 + 2(350) - 20(35)$$
$$+ 0.1[0 - 60 - (0.2)(350)]^2$$
$$= 5265$$
$$C_{t=1} + C_{t=2} = 11,237$$

Thus, the B-type policy produces a total cost that is 363 less than the A-type policy. But this does not mean that Paintmasters should match demand and production output. There may be a mixed-policy solution that is even better. For example, consider the use of overtime in periods 1 and 2 (indicated by the fact that P_t is larger than the normal, regular-time output of W_t).

C. A mixture of policies with overtime allowed

t	W_t	P_t	S_t	I_t	$\sum_t I_t$
0	35	390	380	+10	+10
1	36	400	400	0	+10
2	35	350	350	0	+10

$$C_{t=1} = 100(36) + 3(1)^2 + 0.2[400 - 10(36)]^2 + 2(400) - 20(36)$$
$$+ 0.1[10 - 60.2(400)]^2$$
$$= 5693$$

$$C_{t=2} = 100(35) + 3(-1)^2 + 0.2[350 - 10(35)]^2 + 2(350) - 20(35)$$
$$+ 0.1[10 - 60 - 0.2(350)]^2$$
$$= 4943$$

$$C_{t=1} + C_{t=2} = 10{,}636$$

This pattern of aggregate scheduling gives the best result so far. Total cost at 10,636 is 964 less than the policy B result and 601 less than the policy A result. (Note, however, that the $t = 0$ period costs have been ignored. This start-up effect would not apply to on-going systems but could be taken into account, if need be.) We could keep trying different combinations, choosing the best mixed policy we discover. However, we will never know what the optimal result is, and how close we have come to it. A method is required to obtain the optimal solution, and such a method does exist.

The HMMS model can be solved for optimum values of W_t, P_t, and I_t, for each time period $t = 1, 2, 3, \ldots, n$. These solutions (for minimum total cost) will differ according to the planning period n that is used. A better systems solution is obtained as n increases, but the reliability of demand predictions usually decreases as n moves further into the future. As a rule of thumb, the best planning interval would be about a quarter (or 3 months), but specific circumstances could dictate that shorter or longer intervals be used.

The planning interval T in Fig. 13-6 does not have to coincide with the updating interval D. The intervals D and T could coincide, but when predic-

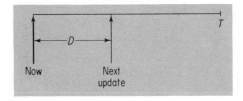

FIGURE 13-6. Every D months the aggregate schedule for the planning period of T months ahead is updated.

tions for the period T should be altered to account for actual occurrences and new information, then D would be smaller than T (e.g., say that monthly updating of the quarterly schedule would be used).

The method for obtaining the optimal solution is fully detailed in the book referenced in footnote 2 in this chapter. It is not a difficult method (although it does surpass the level of mathematics required by this text). To employ the model does not necessitate mathematical capability. The manager would have the equations of the model programmed for computer use, since a great deal of computation is involved.

Paintmasters should derive the same kind of benefits from using the HMMS model as did the company that supported the original research. Employee morale improved, there were lower process and freight costs, smaller inventories, higher sales and numerous intangible benefits.

The complexities of managing a large job shop are awesome. The HMMS model provides a means for organizing the great amount of information that characterizes the job shop, i.e., the composition of aggregate demand forecasts and predictions, the costs associated with overstock, understock, overtime, hiring, laying off, setups, etc. Although other models have been designed that treat aggregate scheduling,[3] none of them is as detailed, thorough, and representative as the HMMS model.

In Figure 12-5, p. 242, we showed the three problem stages involved in managing the job shop. We have just addressed the first problem. Now it is time to move on to the second problem, shop loading, which is the first part of Chapter 14. The second portion of Chapter 14 concerns the third problem, which is sequencing.

APPENDIX 13-I
Linear Programming and Transportation Method
Approaches to Aggregate Scheduling (Optional Material)

A number of practitioners have suggested the use of LP for aggregate scheduling.[4] Generally, the objective function to be minimized is total cost. Here such cost is treated as being reasonably well represented by a linear function consisting of some combination of payroll, hiring, layoff, overtime, and inventory costs. Constraints are set on the availability of regular and overtime production capacity, the amount of capacity that can be added or removed, and restrictions on inventories that are in line with meeting demand (with or without back ordering).

Standard units are required to achieve comparability of inputs and outputs in aggregation. The standard unit will be given in terms of man-hours

---

[3]For example, see Appendix 13-I, where the LP approach to aggregate scheduling is presented as optional material.

[4]J. F. Magee and D. M. Boodman, *Production Planning and Inventory Control* (New York: McGraw-Hill Book Co., Inc., 1967), pp. 369–373. Also, see A. Kaufmann, *Methods and Models of Operations Research* (Englewood Cliffs, N.J.: Prentice-Hall, Inc., 1963), pp. 40–44. Also F. Hanssmann and S. W. Hess, "A Linear Programming Approach to Production and Employment Scheduling," *Management Technology*, Vol. 1, No. 1 (January, 1960), pp. 46–51.

required. Say there are $i = 1, 2, \ldots, k$ planning periods, and that:

$d(i) =$ *predicted* demand in period i.

$p(i) =$ actual regular production in period i; maximum regular production is $p_{max}(i)$.

$y(i) =$ actual overtime production in period i; maximum overtime production is $y_{max}(i)$.

$b =$ overtime cost per unit.

$c =$ inventory carrying charge per period.

$a' =$ cost of adding 1 extra unit of production capacity.[5]

$a'' =$ cost of removing 1 unit of production capacity.[6]

$u(i) =$ units of added capacity in period i.

$v(i) =$ units of subtracted capacity in period i.

$r =$ overtime units that can be produced for each added unit of regular production capacity.

The linear program can be understood by studying the following description of constraints and program objective.

The constraints on regular production can be read as follows: regular production in period 2 must be equal to or less than maximum regular production capacity in period 2 plus the net change in capacity stemming from changes made (plus and minus) in periods 1 and 2.

$$p(1) \leq p_{max}(1) + u(1) - v(1)$$
$$p(2) \leq p_{max}(2) + \sum_{1}^{2} [u(i) - v(i)]$$
$$\cdot$$
$$\cdot$$
$$\cdot$$
$$p(k) \leq p_{max}(k) + \sum_{1}^{k} [u(i) - v(i)]$$

The constraints on overtime production can be read in the same way as the constraints on regular production.

$$y(1) \leq y_{max}(1) + r[u(1) - v(1)]$$
$$y(2) \leq y_{max}(2) + r \sum_{1}^{2} [u(i) - v(i)]$$
$$\cdot$$
$$\cdot$$
$$\cdot$$
$$y(k) \leq y_{max}(k) + r \sum_{1}^{k} [u(i) - v(i)]$$

---

[5] These can be either machine or manpower changes.
[6] *Ibid.*

Inventory Restrictions: $I_0 = 0$, meaning an initial inventory of zero. This is a simple, but not essential, way to begin.

If no back ordering is to be allowed, then the cumulative sum of regular plus overtime production must always be equal to or greater than cumulative demand. Thus, no back-ordering is allowed.

$$p(1) + y(1) \geq d(1) \text{ (because demands must be met)}$$

$$\sum_1^2 p(i) + \sum_1^2 y(i) \geq \sum_1^2 d(i)$$

$$\vdots$$

$$\sum_1^k p(i) + \sum_1^k y(i) \geq \sum_1^k d(i)$$

Constraints on capacity changes: Added capacity in any period must be equal to or greater than the regular production in that period minus the regular production in the preceding period. Capacity subtracted must be constrained in the reverse way.

$$u(1) \geq p(1) - p(0) \quad \text{or} \quad v(1) \geq p(0) - p(1)$$
$$u(2) \geq p(2) - p(1) \quad \text{or} \quad v(2) \geq p(1) - p(2)$$
$$\vdots$$
$$u(k) \geq p(k) - p(k-1) \quad \text{or} \quad v(k) \geq p(k-1) - p(k)$$

Minimize the objective function. The objective function is total cost, which is the sum of added capacity cost plus subtracted capacity cost plus total overtime cost plus aggregate inventory carrying cost.

$$\text{Total cost} = a' \sum_1^k u(i) + a'' \sum_1^k v(i)$$
$$+ b \sum_1^k y(i) + c \left[\sum_{i=1}^k \sum_{j=1}^i \{p(j) + y(j) - d(j)\} \right]$$

These equations suffice to solve the aggregate scheduling problem within the LP assumptions.

We should not lose sight of the fact that some simpler approaches exist as well. E. Bowman formulated a transportation algorithm that is highly efficient for aggregate scheduling with hand computation.[7] The significance of

---

[7]Original citation is E. H. Bowman, "Production Scheduling by the Transportation Method of Linear Programming," *Operations Research*, 4: 1 (February 1956), 100–103. Further discussion will be found in E. H. Bowman and R. B. Fetter, *Analysis for Production and Operations Management*, 3rd ed. (Homewood, Ill.: Richard D. Irwin, 1967), pp. 134–36.

the transportation model is hard to miss. It does not require a square matrix (a slack column or row can be added to balance supply and demand); the solutions are relatively easy to obtain by hand computation. On the other hand, it is linear, since unit costs or profits are not able to be changed as a function of volume; and since each matrix applies to a specific period, no allowance is made for interdependencies over time.

Let us examine the Bowman transportation algorithm for aggregate scheduling. The matrix is as follows:

Sales Periods

	1	2	3	Final Inv.	Slack	Supply
Initial Inv.	0	c	$2c$	$3c$	0	I_0
Regular 1	r	$r+c$	$r+2c$	$r+3c$	0	R_1
Overtime 1	v	$v+c$	$v+2c$	$v+3c$	0	O_1
Regular 2	x	r	$r+c$	$r+2c$	0	R_2
Overtime 2	x	v	$v+c$	$v+2c$	0	O_2
Regular 3	x	x	r	$r+c$	0	R_3
Overtime 3	x	x	r	$v+c$	0	O_3
Demand	D_1	D_2	D_3	I_f	S	Grand total

where c = carrying cost per unit for the interval of time.
r = regular production cost per unit.
v = overtime production cost per unit.
I_0 = initial inventory.
I_f = final inventory.

The regular transportation method (as described in Chapter 17) is used for solution. It should be noted that in this matrix backorders are prohibited (by x).

When back orders are allowed, the matrix appears as below.

	Sales Period					
	1	*2*	*3*	I_f	Slack	*Supply*
I_0	0	c	2c	3c	0	I_0
R_1	r	r + c	r + 2c	r + 3c	0	R_1
O_1	v	v + c	v + 2c	v + 3c	0	O_1
R_2	r + b	r	r + c	r + 2c	0	R_2
O_2	v + b	v	v + c	v + 2c	0	O_2
R_3	r + 2b	r + b	r	r + c	0	R_3
O_3	v + 2b	v + b	v	v + c	0	O_3
Demand	D_1	D_2	D_3	I_f	S	Grand total

It has the additional new cost, b, which is the back-order cost per unit. This problem also can be solved by conventional transportation techniques, as described in Chapter 17.

PROBLEMS   **1.** We expect that seven jobs will be in the shop next week. The demand in units for each job (called D), and the production rate of the standard operator in pieces per standard operator hour (called PR) are given below:

Job	A	B	C	D	E	F	G
D	600	1000	500	50	2000	20	800
PR	60	20	25	10	40	2	40

What production capacity in standard operator hours is required to complete all of these jobs?

2. Why do predictions for aggregate scheduling have an advantage over predictions for disaggregated scheduling of specific jobs?

3. Can the effects of seasonal demands be taken into account for aggregate scheduling? Explain.

4. In some job shop industries, a smooth production rate is preferred; in others, the work force size is altered to match the expected demands. Give some examples of each kind of situation.

5. The canning industry was, at one time, totally dependent on harvest dates. As a result, work force alterations were enormous and sporadic. After careful study, steps were taken to smooth the demand patterns. What measures do you think might have been effective?

6. Actual monthly demands for the past year are available for item Z54, a microswitch.

Month	Demand	Month	Demand
1	621	7	708
2	415	8	615
3	380	9	422
4	763	10	669
5	845	11	810
6	550	12	396

Can you find any useful patterns that will enable you to proceed with an aggregate scheduling problem?

7. With reference to the analyses on pp. 267–70, find the total cost for the following aggregate scheduling policy, D:

t	W_t	P_t	S_t	I_t	$\sum_t I_t$
0	35	380	380	to be filled in	
1	36	390	400		
2	37	370	350		

How does policy D compare with policies A, B, and C? What type of policy is D?

Optional Problem

8. Use the HMMS model with the data in problem 6 grouped into quarterly demands. Assume simple values for all the costs based on reasonable patterns for the curves in Fig. 13-5, p. 268. Determine the optimum values for each of the four quarters of the coming year. *Note:* The solution to this problem requires the use of calculus.

fourteen
shop loading
and sequencing

Shop loading is required to assign specific jobs to equally specific facilities. But shop loading does not specify the order in which jobs should be done at each facility. Sequencing methods provide this ultimate detail. For example, ten patients are assigned to the third floor medical clinic for treatment. In what order should they be processed? The answer can make a big difference. Both shop loading and sequencing epitomize job shop management techniques.

Shop Loading

Shop loading is a highly repetitive job shop, managerial responsibility. The requirement is to determine which facility (machines, equipment, individuals, areas, etc.) will be assigned specific jobs. We say that each facility carries a certain "load," which is why the term "shop loading" is used. Individual jobs and facilities are identified, whereas in aggregate scheduling, jobs are grouped together as demand and facilities are grouped together as supply. Further, demand has to be predicted for aggregate scheduling, while for shop loading, the jobs are real tasks, on hand, that must be done.

Gantt Shop-loading Charts

The first well-known shop-loading methods were based on Gantt charts. Henry L. Gantt recognized that only by means of some formal device could the problem of assigning jobs to facilities be suitably attacked. Gantt charts provided a better tool than anything that had existed before. Figure 14-1 typifies a Gantt load chart. It has a time scale running along the top. The rows are intended to represent machines, departments, or whatever facilities will be required to do the job. The time scale can be labeled in either calendar time or in (say) weeks. The left-hand side of the chart is *now*, whether that be

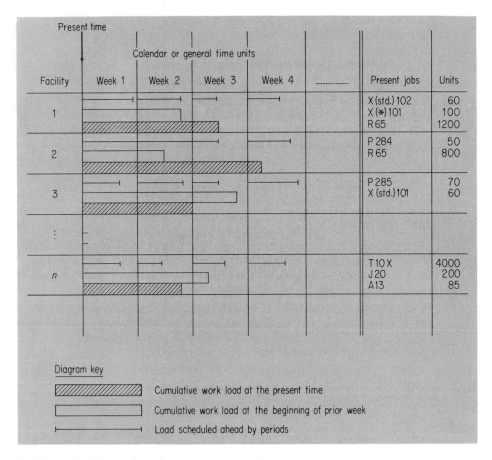

FIGURE 14-1. The Gantt load chart
Cumulative work load is the sum of unfinished jobs at each facility. These jobs are identified by their code names such as R65 and T10X.

May 21 or merely time 0. Bars and lines, running from left to right, convey various kinds of information—as interpreted by the diagram key.

We can read off the cumulative load that exists with respect to each facility. (Note that the load chart does not indicate the sequence for doing the jobs.[1]) The backlog of jobs is shown as it exists at the beginning of the present week[2] and as it existed at the beginning of the prior week. We are interested in this information to find out whether the load and the backlog are increasing, decreasing, or staying about the same. The backlog has increased for facilities 1 and 2; it has decreased for facilities 3 and n.

The way in which the manager has scheduled work in the weeks ahead is also shown on the chart. The criterion of what a good loading is or what a change for the better might be will depend upon the configuration of job shop facilities and the load situation. Thus, the Gantt load chart will reveal whether we have sufficient resources and capacity available to handle the work load that has been accumulating. It also helps to determine whether the load is equally distributed among facilities. Perhaps most important of all, it can point out the fact that the load level is changing.

The Assignment Model—
To Minimize Total Costs

When alternative facilities exist for processing jobs, e.g., when there are 3 jobs that can be done at any 1 of 3 available facilities, but with different costs, then an assignment problem exists. To understand the basic nature of this shop-loading problem, we are going to develop the assignment model in which there are costs for not making the best possible assignments of jobs to facilities. These are called *opportunity costs*. The reason that we cannot always make the best possible assignments is that often jobs compete with each other for available time on those facilities for which they are best fitted with respect to productivity or cost or both. Thus, consider Matrix 1 of cost per part for jobs 1, 2, and 3 at facilities *A*, *B*, and *C*, below.

MATRIX 1 OF COST PER PART

		Facilities		
		A	*B*	*C*
	1	0.10	0.09	0.12
Jobs	2	0.08	0.07	0.09
	3	0.15	0.18	0.20

---

[1] See the Gantt sequencing (or layout) chart on p. 294.
[2] It is also listed (see the column Present Jobs) in Fig. 14-1.

Jobs 1 and 2 achieve their lowest cost per part when made at facility *B*. They are, therefore, in direct competition with each other for the use of this facility. What should be done? First, note that job 3 is best assigned to facility *A*, and it is not competing with any other job for that facility. Yet this assignment cannot be made until we have resolved the conflict between jobs 1 and 2. All the numbers in the matrix are interrelated. Therefore, we must regard this as a systems problem. It might turn out that to best resolve the conflict, job 3 should not be assigned to facility *A*.

The assignment model develops comparisons of penalties that must be paid for making an assignment other than the best possible one. To get these comparisons, we subtract the smallest number in each *row* from all other numbers in that row. This yields Matrix 2.

MATRIX 2

	A	B	C
1	0.01	0	0.03
2	0.01	0	0.02
3	0	0.03	0.05

The numbers in Matrix 2 are the *opportunity costs* per part for not assigning each job to the best possible facility for that job. Wherever there is a zero, we would like to make an assignment, but we cannot do that in this case, because jobs 1 and 2 have their only zero opportunity cost assignment at facility *B*. Also, we are making the assumption that the orders are of the same size; otherwise, we should be thinking in terms of total costs. (See problems 3 and 4, pp. 307–308, in the problem section for further discussion of this point.)

We could, as well, have used column subtraction, which yields the *opportunity costs* at a given facility for assigning jobs that are not the best jobs. Return to Matrix 1; the opportunity costs of each facility with respect to jobs are obtained by column subtraction, as shown in Matrix 3.

MATRIX 3

	A	B	C
1	0.02	0.02	0.03
2	0	0	0
3	0.07	0.11	0.11

Job 2, having all zero opportunity costs in its row, is the preferred job at each facility. Based on our analysis so far, there is no feasible assignment. Therefore, using Matrix 3, subtract the smallest number in each row from all other numbers in that row. This gives us the combined opportunity costs for each job's being assigned to less than the best facility—and each facility's being assigned to less than the best job (Matrix 4).

MATRIX 4

	A	B	C
1	0	[0]	0.01
2	0	0	[0]
3	[0]	0.04	0.04

Note that all jobs could be assigned to facility A with zero opportunity cost. If we would permit this (assuming that there was other work for facilities B and C), then we have a sequencing problem at facility A (i.e., which job goes first, which second, which third?). Sequencing, you will recall, is the third kind of problem in the job shop (see Fig. 12-5, p. 242 and also pp. 293–301 for the discussion on sequencing).

Given that we must assign a job to each facility, there is now 1 feasible set of 0 opportunity cost assignments for this case. They are shown by the squares in Matrix 4. There is only one 0 in column C; job 2 must be assigned there. There is only one 0 in row 3; job 3 must be assigned to facility A. That forces the assignment of job 1 to facility B.

For completeness, let us return to Matrix 2, which was derived by using row subtraction first (i.e., the opportunity costs of each job being assigned to less than the best facility). This time, follow with column subtraction and derive Matrix 5.

MATRIX 5

	A	B	C
1	0.01	[0]	0.01
2	0.01	0	0
3	[0]	0.03	0.03

We have obtained the same assignment solution as in Matrix 4, although the final matrices are not identical. It is always equally correct to use either row or column subtraction first. However, sometimes it turns out to be easier to use one way rather than the other to reduce the matrix to an assignable set of zeroes. There is no way of prejudging this matter beforehand.

There is yet one additional complication. Assume that the initial cost per part matrix is as shown in Matrix 6.

MATRIX 6 OF COST PER PART

		A	B	C
		Facilities		
	1	0.11	0.09	0.13
Jobs	2	0.08	0.07	0.09
	3	0.18	0.15	0.20

After row and column reduction, we obtain Matrix 7.

MATRIX 7

	A	B	C
1	0.01	0	0.02
2	0	0	0
3	0.02	0	0.03

We still cannot make an assignment. Jobs 1 and 3 are both assigned to facility *B* without any other options. Facility *A* and facility *C* have been assigned job 2 without any alternatives. There is no further basis for row and/or column subtraction, since a 0 exists in each row and in each column.

To resolve this situation, remember that each 0 signifies an acceptable assignment. Therefore, we want to move any one of the zeroes to another position in the matrix in order to remove the deadlock.[3] The best place to move a 0 is to the position of the lowest opportunity cost in the matrix. This is 0.01 for job 1 at facility *A*. Thus, to assign job 1 to facility *A* imposes an extra cost of 0.01 to any assignment at facility *B*. Accordingly, we add 0.01 to *all entries* in column *B*. Similar reasoning applies to job 2. An assignment of job 1 to facility *A* imposes an extra cost of 0.01 to any assignment of job 2, so we add 0.01 to *all entries* in row 2. We had to break the deadlock, and we did it with the smallest opportunity cost (i.e., 0.01). Note that at the intersection of row 2 and column *B*, 0.01 is added twice. This results in Matrix 8.

MATRIX 8

	A	B	C
1	0	0.01	0.02
2	0.01	0.02	0.01
3	0.02	0.01	0.03

---

[3]The general methodology for resolving situations that are deadlocked after row and column subtraction is described in Appendix 14-I as optional material.

Whether we use row or column subtraction, we achieve the same final assignments in Matrices 9.

MATRICES 9

	Row Subtraction				Column Subtraction		
	A	*B*	*C*		*A*	*B*	*C*
1	[0]	0.01	0.02	1	[0]	0	0.01
2	0	0.01	[0]	2	0.01	0.01	[0]
3	0.01	[0]	0.02	3	0.02	[0]	0.02

The assignment model captures the essence of the opportunity cost basis for shoploading assignments. Before we go on to a broader modeling use of these concepts, let us try our hand at another assignment problem, which introduces some additional aspects of the methodological strengths of opportunity cost analysis.

**Burgermasters, Inc.—An Assignment Problem Involving
Maximization of Objectives (Rather than Minimization)
where the Load Is Greater than the Capacity**

This fast foods franchiser is planning to open three new, company-owned outlets (*A*, *B*, and *C*). Managers are sought. Out of numerous applicants, four candidates (1, 2, 3, and 4) remain. They have been interviewed and rated with respect to their qualifications for managing each store, on a scale of 0 (worst) to ten (best). The matrix of qualifications is shown below.

MATRIX OF QUALIFICATIONS

		Stores		
		A	*B*	*C*
	1	9	5	6
Candidates for Manager	2	x	10	4
	3	5	8	9
	4	7	7	7

Note: Candidate 2 is unable to be considered for store *A* because of travel distance from home and unwillingness to move.

There are 3 new problems that confront us in this assignment problem.

1. We are asked to maximize the total value of the assignments. For jobs and facilities this could have been to maximize productivity or profit.
2. One of the possible assignments is prohibited.
3. We are forced to choose 3 assignments from among 4 candidates. This could have been 4 jobs to be assigned to 3 facilities.

Let us consider each of these in turn. To maximize the total benefits of a set of assignments, subtract all numbers from the largest number in the matrix, and then proceed with row and column subtraction, etc., as previously. The subtraction of all numbers from the largest has created a set of costs for not doing as well as the best that can be done. Thus, candidate 2 at store *B* has a zero cost, because that assignment is the best that can be obtained.

To handle the blocked assignment, enter a large enough cost to prohibit assignment. These steps have been taken in the matrix below.

	Stores A	B	C
1	1	5	4
2	100	0	6
3	5	2	1
4	3	3	3

Candidates for Manager

To deal with the extra candidate for manager, create a dummy store, called *D*. All costs at the dummy store will be zero, meaning that we are indifferent as to which candidate is assigned to that store. Whichever candidate is so assigned will not be hired. Thus:

	Stores A	B	C	D
1	1	5	4	0
2	100	0	6	0
3	5	2	1	0
4	3	3	3	0

Candidates for Manager

Using column subraction, we obtain a final solution.

	A	*B*	*C*	*D*
1	⊡ 0	5	3	0
2	99	⊡ 0	5	0
3	4	2	⊡ 0	0
4	2	3	2	⊡ 0

	Value in the Original Matrix
Candidate 1 goes to store *A*	9
Candidate 2 goes to store *B*	10
Candidate 3 goes to store *C*	9
	28

There is no set of assignments that can have a higher value than 28 (although often, alternative, equally good assignments do occur in assignment problem solutions).

The Index Method for Shop Loading—
A Heuristic Method

A major weakness of the assignment model is that each job can be assigned to only one facility. That is, jobs cannot be divided. Another weakness is that only one job can be assigned to each facility, even though some jobs may be long and others short. Thus, the sizes of jobs are not properly related to the available working capacity of the facilities. A transportation model has been used to overcome these difficulties, but it requires certain restrictive assumptions that are often not met by reality.[4]

A shoploading technique with assumptions that conform nicely with reality is the index method. It is a heuristic method; therefore, it does not produce an optimum solution. But it has been used in practice with satisfying results.[5] The basic idea behind this method is opportunity cost analysis. In this case, the opportunity costs are viewed in ratio to the value of the best assignment, and these are called *index numbers*.

---

[4]See Martin K. Starr, *Systems Management of Operations* (Englewood Cliffs, N.J.: Prentice-Hall, Inc., 1971), pp. 278–287.

[5]See R. O. Ferguson and L. F. Sargent, *Linear Programming* (New York: McGraw-Hill Book Co., Inc., 1958), pp. 149–159.

A Machine Shop Example

Toolmasters, Inc., is an old established and well-known manufacturer of metal cutting tools (used for lathes, milling machines, drill presses, etc.). The company has employed Gantt charts for shop loading as long as the division manager can recall. The manager has reviewed new techniques for shoploading and has decided in favor of the heuristic approach (the index method). This is not surprising. The activity of shop loading is repeated so often that a relatively fast heuristic that allows multiple job assignments, job assignment splitting, and hand computation is highly desirable.

To begin with, a row of index numbers is computed for each job i with respect to its performance at the places it can be done, e.g., machine centers j.

When the performance criterion is of the cost per part type, the ith row of index numbers will be $(c_{ji} - c_{ji}^*)/c_{ji}^*$ and when the performance criterion is for profit per part, we have $(p_{ji}^* - p_{ji})/p_{ji}^*$. (In both cases, the asterisk represents the ideal machine assignment—lowest cost or highest profit per part.) These index numbers show the relative *penalties* of assigning each of the given jobs to the different machine centers.

In many job shops, for every part that is reordered by certain customers, a schedule card is maintained that presents relevant information concerning processing times and costs on different machines. For example, Toolmasters has the data for Part 4x shown in Table 14-1.

TABLE 14-1 TOOLMASTERS' SCHEDULE CARD FOR CUTTING TOOL 4x.

Part Name—4x

Machine	A	B	C
Time per part (hr)	$\frac{2}{5}$	1	$\frac{4}{5}$
Cost per hour	$4	$2	$3

An order has been received for 100 cutting tools of type 4x. The schedule card is modified to an index card reflecting the order quantity of 100 units. Indices are developed for total time and total cost (see Table 14-2). Examination of the data in Table 14-2 shows that machine A is the most productive facility that can be used, turning out 100 units in 40 hours at a total cost of $160. Machine B is the least productive facility, requiring 100 hours to do the same job; yet it is less costly than machine C. Thus, although machine C can do the entire job in 80 hours, it does so at an expense of $240 versus $200 for machine B.

**TABLE 14-2 TOOLMASTERS' INDEX CARD FOR CUTTING
TOOL 4x; ORDER QUANTITY = 100.**

		Order	
Part Name: 4x		*Quantity: 100*	
Machine	A	B	C
Time per part (hr)	$\frac{2}{5}$	1	$\frac{4}{5}$
Total time (hr)	40	100	80
Cost per hour	$4	$2	$3
Total cost	$160	$200	$240
Total time index	0	$\frac{3}{2}$	1
Total cost index	0	$\frac{1}{4}$	$\frac{1}{2}$

Let us review the calculation of the index numbers. At machine A, each cutting tool requires $\frac{2}{5}$ hour. Consequently, to make 100 units of 4x takes 40 hours. Similarly, the order will spend 100 hours with machine B and 80 hours with machine C. We want to minimize total time, so the best time is 40 hours at machine A. Thus, using $(c_{ji} - c_{ji}^*)/c_{ji}^*$, because as with cost, best is smallest, we obtain

Machine	A	B	C
Total time index	$\dfrac{40 - 40}{40} = 0$	$\dfrac{100 - 40}{40} = \dfrac{3}{2}$	$\dfrac{80 - 40}{40} = 1$

To compute total cost at each facility, we multiply the cost per hour by the total time. The lowest total cost is at machine A. Then we obtain the total cost index numbers.

Machine	A	B	C
Total cost index	$\dfrac{160 - 160}{160} = 0$	$\dfrac{200 - 160}{160} = \dfrac{1}{4}$	$\dfrac{240 - 160}{160} = \dfrac{1}{2}$

Question: What are the total time index numbers for Toolmasters' part 1x?

Given: | Machine | A | B | C |
| :--- | :---: | :---: | :---: |
| Time per part (hr) | $\frac{1}{4}$ | $\frac{1}{5}$ | $\frac{3}{8}$ |

Order quantity—200 cutting tools

Answer:

Machine	A	B	C
Total time (hr)	50	40	75
Total time index	$\dfrac{50-40}{40}=\dfrac{1}{4}$	$\dfrac{40-40}{40}=0$	$\dfrac{75-40}{40}=\dfrac{7}{8}$

In fact, Toolmasters has on hand orders for 5 types of cutting tools, all of which can be made at machines *A*, *B*, and *C*. The *sizes of the orders* are reflected by the total times to complete the jobs, listed in Table 14-3.

TABLE 14-3 TOTAL TIMES (IN HOURS)
TO COMPLETE JOBS

	Machines		
Job	A	B	C
1x	50	40	75
2x	25	40	50
3x	27	30	54
4x	40	100	80
5x	20	100	50

Additional information is required concerning the availability of machines *A*, *B*, and *C* during the next week. Thus, there are 2 machines of each kind. Every machine is able to work 40 hours per week, less preventive maintenance time, which is $2\frac{1}{2}$ hours per week. Accordingly, 75 hours each of *A*-, *B*-, and *C*-type facilities are available in the next week, for a total of 225 hours. From this information, a matrix of total times, total time index numbers, and available times at the facilities is prepared (see Table 14-4). The index numbers have been entered into the little boxes in each cell of the matrix. Available time is the capacity constraint at each center. An investment in another type-*A* machine would be required to increase the total available time at facility *A* to 112.5 hours.

The Heuristic Rule

First assignments are always made to 0 index measures. Then, to satisfy capacity constraints if some machines are overloaded, jobs are shifted to other machines that have the *lowest possible alternative index numbers*. The reassignments are done in the order of increasing index values.

TABLE 14-4

Machines

Job	A	B	C
1x	1/4 50	0 40	7/8 75
2x	0 25	3/5 40	1 50
3x	0 27	1/9 30	1 54
4x	0 40	1.5 100	1 80
5x	0 20	4 100	1.5 50
Available Time	75	75	75

In our example, the assignments based on 0 index would be as shown in Table 14-5.

TABLE 14-5

	Machines		
Jobs	A	B	C
1x		40	
2x	25		
3x	27		
4x	40		
5x	20		
Available time	75	75	75
Assigned time	112	40	0
Excess	+37	−35	−75

Machine *A* is overloaded with an excess of 37 hours (shown as +37 in Table 14-5). Machines *B* and *C* are underutilized (shown as −35 and −75 in Table 14-5).

If we do not use the index method at all, and simply choose an assignment that is feasible (i.e., assigned time at each facility is equal to or less than available time), we could obtain the result shown in Table 14-6. We can use this casually produced result of 205 hours as an *upper bound solution*. That is,

TABLE 14-6

| Jobs | Machines | | |
	A	B	C
1x			75
2x		40	
3x		30	
4x	40		
5x	20		
Available time	75	75	75
Assigned time	60	70	75
Excess	−15	−5	0
Total time = 60 + 70 + 75 = 205 hours			

we do not have to accept any solution that has a total time that is greater than 205. When we obtain a new solution that requires less total time, it will replace 205 as the new upper bound.

Let us now apply the heuristic rule to Table 14-5. We shall shift job $3x$ because in its row the smallest alternative index appears, $\frac{1}{9}$ at $3x$, column B. When we shift $3x$ from A to B, it takes 30 hours to do the job instead of 27

TABLE 14-7

| Jobs | Machines | | |
	A	B	C
1x		40	
2x	25		
3x		30	
4x	40		
5x	20		
Available time	75	75	75
Assigned time	85	70	0
Excess	+10	−5	−75

(see Tables 14-4 and 14-7). The heuristic rule can be applied in several ways at this point. For example, since $\frac{1}{4}$ is now the next best index, at $1x$, A, this would mean that $1x$, B should be shifted to $1x$, A. Generally, however, we refuse to further overload a machine center, and instead, we try to move jobs from it to the best possible alternative positions. Here, for machine A either $2x$, $4x$, or $5x$ could be shifted from A to C. Since $5x$'s index for C is larger than the others, we eliminate it as a choice. And $4x$, when moved, will cause an overload at center C, so move $2x$. The index for job $2x$ at machine B is smaller than at machine C. Therefore, we shall move as much as we can of job $2x$ to machine B and the remainder of job $2x$ to machine C.

This requires *job splitting*. We should note the difference between assigning several jobs to 1 facility (which we have done previously in Tables 14-5, 14-6, and 14-7 and which we could not do with the square matrix of the assignment model) and the splitting of 1 job between several facilities (which we do in Table 14-8).

TABLE 14-8

		Machines	
Jobs	A	B	C
1x		40	
2x		5	43.75
3x		30	
4x	40		
5x	20		
Available time	75	75	75
Assigned time	60	75	43.75
Excess	−15	0	−31.25
Total Time = 60 + 75 + 43.75 = 178.75 hours			

We can assign no more than 5 hours at machine B. The entire job $2x$ requires 40 hours at machine B. We are using only $\frac{5}{40}$ or $\frac{1}{8}$ of this time. Consequently, $\frac{7}{8}$ of the job $2x$ remains to be completed at machine C. Job $2x$ requires 50 hours at machine C. Thus, we assign $\frac{7}{8}$ of 50 hours (or 43.75 hours) to machine C for completion of job $2x$. The result, producing a total job time of 178.75 hours, becomes our new upper bound. It represents an improvement of 12.8 percent over our previous upper bound of 205, in Table 14-6.

Still further improvement is available (if we allow additional splitting), because machine A, which is fast for every job except $1x$, is underutilized. (For the next solution see Table 14-9.)

TABLE 14-9

		Machines	
Jobs	A	B	C
1x		40	
2x	15	5	13.75
3x		30	
4x	40		
5x	20		
Available time	75	75	75
Assigned time	75	75	13.75
Excess	0	0	−61.25
Total Time = 75 + 75 + 13.75 = 163.75 hours			

We have returned 15 hours of job $2x$ to machine A. This completes the available time at machine A. Job $2x$, if done entirely at machine A, consumes 25 hours. We are doing $\frac{15}{25}$ (or $\frac{3}{5}$) of job $2x$ at machine A. Previously, we noted that $\frac{5}{40}$ (or $\frac{1}{8}$) of job $2x$ is completed at machine B. This leaves $1 - \frac{3}{5} - \frac{1}{8}$ (or $\frac{11}{40}$) of 50 hours required by job $2x$ at machine C, i.e., $(11/40) \times 50 = 13.75$ hours. The result reduces the total job time to 163.75 hours, an improvement of 8.3 percent over the previous upper bound of 178.75 hours, or a total improvement of 20.1 percent over the first upper bound of 205 hours.

Question: If no splitting is allowed, can we find a better total time solution than 205 hours?

Answer: We must rearrange Table 14-7, which is not a feasible solution. Shifting all of job $2x$ to machine C is probably the best thing to do.

Jobs	Machines A	B	C
1x		40	
2x			50
3x		30	
4x	40		
5x	20		
Available time	75	75	75
Assigned time	60	70	50
Excess	−15	−5	−25
Total Time = 60 + 70 + 50 = 180 hours			

We reduce total time from 205 to 180 hours; an improvement of 12.2 percent.

Perhaps we could still improve on the 163.75 hour solution, but it is a good one, and likely to be good enough.[6] The index method promises only "approximately optimal" solutions, with a degree of directness that captures the real elements of the shoploading problem and with simplicity that permits large shoploading problems to be resolved by hand, or with inexpensive computer operations.

---

[6]The best solution that we could get, assuming that we had additional capacity at machine A, will be found in Table 14-5 as $112 + 40 = 152$. This represents a 7.1 percent improvement over the 163.75-hour solution. Given the existing capacity constraints, we are willing to say that total time of 163.75 hours is "likely to be good enough."

Sequencing Operations

Loading is accomplished without regard to the *order* or *precedence* with which jobs will be done at a particular facility. Sequencing establishes the *priorities* for jobs in each facility's queue. As will be seen shortly, there are different costs associated with different orderings.

When there are many jobs and facilities, sequencing rules take on considerable economic importance.

Gantt Sequencing Charts

Gantt also developed a chart to formalize the sequencing problem. Let us consider this chart (which Gantt called a *layout chart*). It *reserves specific times* on the various facilities for the particular jobs on hand.

First-in, First-out (FIFO) Sequence Rule

The most natural ordering is that the first jobs into the shop get worked on first. We call this first-in, first-out. It is appealing because it seems to be the *fairest* rule to follow.

However, by at least one measure, it is *unfair*, because it penalizes the *average* customer more than other sequencing rules. Thus, it will benefit customers who submit orders to the same job shop from time to time, if that job shop does not employ the FIFO rule, but uses instead a rational rule.

Sequencing is one of the most highly repetitive decisions made in the job shop. Even if only a small savings can be realized each time by using a rational rule, these savings accumulate to substantial sums over time.

Using the Gantt layout chart, shown in Fig. 14-2, we can sequence specific jobs at particular facilities, for some given period of time. Concurrently, past sequences of work can be monitored to discover the state of completion of those jobs that were scheduled to be run in prior time periods. Thus, Gantt charting provides work schedule control but offers little help in determining what the best work sequences might be.

For each facility, we observe the job schedule and its state of completion. The present date is indicated by the arrow and its associated vertical line. Thereby, the chart is divided into time past, present, and future. Looking ahead, we can observe what the load is but not in the cumulative form of the load chart, *which does not specify sequence*. Thus, the difference between loading and sequencing is that the latter specifies the time of assignments. When one is sequencing, future assignments are specific time reservations on the facility. They block other assignments from being made. Because sequencing charts are revised regularly, assigned time can be unblocked if it appears to permit a better schedule. A little time is usually allowed between jobs, to account for machine maintenance, to absorb divergences from estimates and

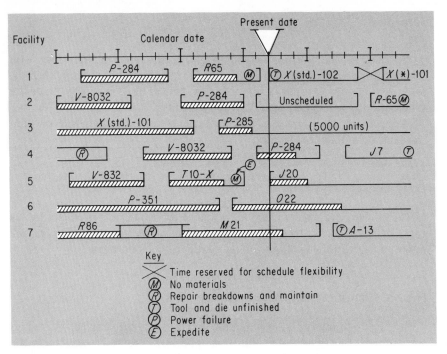

FIGURE 14-2. The Gantt layout chart (a reserved time planning system)
Status: (1) job P-284 is ahead 2 days; (2) job J20 is ahead 3.0 days; (3) job 0-22 is ahead 5.5 days; (4) job M21 is ahead 1.0 day; (5) job R65 is 2 days short of completion—and 2.5 days late waiting for materials (M); (6) job P-285 is 1.5 days short and 1.5 days late (breakdown delay); (7) job T10-X is 1.5 days short and about 3.5 days late (M) and (E).

minor variabilities, and to allow for setups and takedown. Frequently, additional symbols are attached to these charts to indicate why a job has not been completed and to convey other kinds of useful information by means of a succinct shorthand notation. The Gantt layout or sequencing chart must be continually updated; jobs must be rescheduled, so that it can serve its intended function of providing reasonably good work schedules.

Classification of Sequencing Problems

There are at least 4 factors that are essential for classifying sequencing problems.[7] The first describes job-arrival patterns, where the jobs come for service at the facilities. The symbol n refers to the number of jobs that are *waiting* to be sequenced through the facility. Typically, in the job shop, n is a number that varies a good deal. Second, it is necessary to specify the number of facilities, m, through which the jobs must pass. Third, the flow pattern in

---

[7]R. W. Conway, W. L. Maxwell, and L. W. Miller, *Theory of Scheduling* (Reading, Mass.: Addison-Wesley Publishing Co., 1967), p. 1.

the shop must be identified. When a set of jobs follows a fixed ordering, the conditions exist for an intermittent flow shop. On the other hand, when many technological orderings are required, job shop sequencing prevails. The sizes of orders, the number of alternative facilities for doing each job, the length of production runs, the importance of setups and takedowns, etc., are the ultimate determinants of what type of shop exists. Fourth, a variety of criteria exists for evaluating the performance of the schedule.

Evaluatory Criteria

In our discussion, we shall emphasize the sequence evaluation measures of *flow time* and *mean flow time* as defined in the following way. Three jobs (11, 12, and 13) in Fig. 14-3 are sequenced through a facility in that order. Job 11, which goes first, is completed after 5 minutes. Meanwhile, jobs 12 and 13 have waited 5 minutes. Job 13 then must wait an additional 3 minutes (while job 2 is being worked on) before it can begin its own processing.

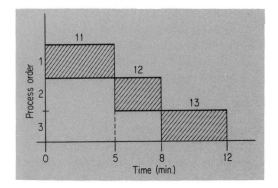

FIGURE 14-3.

We define for job i a waiting time W_i and a processing time t_i. If we assume that job 11 begins at time zero,[8] then the completion time is $C_i = W_i + t_i$. For our three jobs this yields the following table:

Job i	W_i	t_i	C_i
11	0	5	5
12	5	3	8
13	8	4	12
Sums	$\overline{13}$ +	$\overline{12}$ =	$\overline{25}$

---

[8]That is, the release time, often called r_i, equals zero (say at the start of the day).

The $\sum_i C_i$ is the *flow time*, in this case 25, and *mean flow time* would be $\sum_i C_i/n = 25/3$.

Part of flow time and mean flow time is job waiting time W_i. We would like the total waiting time to be as small as possible on the assumption that all customers want to have their orders filled as quickly as possible. Therefore, if we minimize the mean flow, this is equivalent to minimizing the mean waiting time (since the processing times t_i are fixed). If the average completion time $\sum_i C_i/n$ is as small as possible, the average customer's order is delayed the minimum necessary time. This is a primary objective in determining rational sequence priorities.

Other measures are used in evaluating operation sequences. For example, there are promised delivery times. Thus, define d_i as the due date of a job. Then $L_i = C_i - d_i$ is a measure of the lateness of job i. To minimize average lateness, we should minimize mean flow time, assuming that the promised dates are reasonably determined. There are also degrees of facility idleness that may play a critical role in sequence determination.

The fact is, however, that sequencing models become increasingly difficult to handle with optimizing models, as the number of facilities through which the jobs must pass becomes large. Since the jobs take different times at each facility, what is the best sequence at one location may not be best at another. The information problem is enormous. Consequently, heuristics have been developed to try to cope with the level of detail involved in making the highly repetitive sequencing decisions required by many job shops.

n Jobs—One Facility

As we have stated, a common objective of facility sequencing is to minimize mean flow time. For reasons apparent from our previous descussion, in many problems this is equivalent to minimizing average job waiting times; i.e.,

$$\min \frac{\sum_i^n C_i}{n} = \min \frac{\sum_i^n (W_i + t_i)}{n} = \min \frac{\sum_i^n W_i}{n}$$

A simple rule applies. Namely, it can be shown that if a set of n jobs in 1 facility's queue are ordered so that the operations having the shortest processing times t_i are done first, the mean flow time, mean completion time, and mean waiting time will all be minimized. It also turns out that facility idleness is often minimized. Ordering jobs according to shortest processing times is called the SPT rule.

Using this rule, we can rank-order jobs by least t_i, as in Fig. 14-4. Note that the area under the curve is minimized.

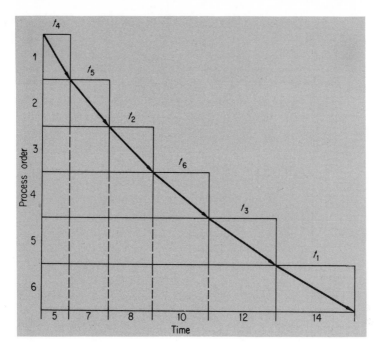

FIGURE 14-4. Jobs ordered by ranked process times

An example of SPT, shortest processing time rule, where $t_4 < t_5 < t_2 < t_6 < t_3 < t_1$. There are $n = 6$ jobs and $m = 1$ facility.

Job i	W_i	t_i	C_i
4	0	5	5
5	5	7	12
2	12	8	20
6	20	10	30
3	30	12	42
1	42	14	56
	109 +	56 =	165

On the other hand, in Fig. 14-5, the jobs are *randomly* ordered without regard to SPT, and the area under the curve is not minimized, nor is mean flow time. The random ordering is quite like the expected sequence of jobs if FIFO is employed, since any job is as likely to enter the shop first as any other.

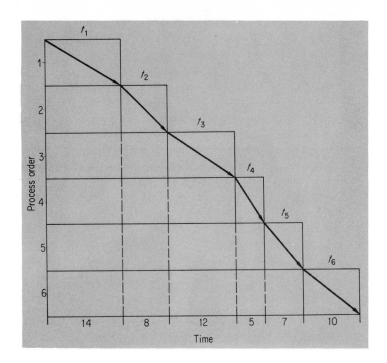

FIGURE 14-5. Jobs are randomly ordered

An $n \times 1$ problem where SPT
is not used. There are $n = 6$ jobs and
$m = 1$ facility.

Job i	W_i	t_i	C_i
1	0	14	14
2	14	8	22
3	22	12	34
4	34	5	39
5	39	7	46
6	46	10	56
	155	+ 56	= 211

The area under the curve in Figs. 14-4 and 14-5 is well approximated by multiplying each job's processing time t_i by the number of jobs waiting (plus the job being worked on). This is the number of process order blocks in each job's column. We can call the product *job time spent in the system*. Thus, for

Fig. 14-4 we have:

$$t_i \times \text{number of jobs waiting} = \text{job time spent}$$
$$\text{and working} \qquad \text{in the system}$$

5 ×	6	=	30
7 ×	5	=	35
8 ×	4	=	32
10 ×	3	=	30
12 ×	2	=	24
14 ×	1	=	14

Total job time spent in
the system = 165

This is the same value that we obtained in Fig. 14-4 for flow time, $\sum_i C_i$. Note how the larger values of t_i are multiplied by the smaller value of the number of jobs waiting and working, i.e., of the sequence 6, 5, 4, 3, 2, 1. When we go through the same multiplication operation for the random ordering of jobs (Fig. 14-5), we obtain

$$t_i \times \text{number of jobs waiting} = \text{job time spent}$$
$$\text{and working} \qquad \text{in the system}$$

14 ×	6	=	84
8 ×	5	=	40
12 ×	4	=	48
5 ×	3	=	15
7 ×	2	=	14
10 ×	1	=	10

Total job time spent in
the system = 211

This is the same value that we obtained in Fig. 14-5 for flow time $\sum_i C_i$. Now, the largest value of t_i happens to be multiplied by the largest value of the number of jobs waiting and working. This is not a logical ordering of the sequence aimed at achieving the minimum possible total job time spent in the system.

With this evidence before us, we can see why ordering jobs by the SPT rule also succeeds in minimizing average delivery lateness L_i. (The purpose is to maximize the fulfillment of delivery promises.)

A Modified SPT Rule Where Sequence Is
Determined by Job Importance and Time

As an additional strength, the SPT rule can be modified to take into account the fact that some jobs are more important than others. This is done by dividing each job time t_i by the relative importance of that job, w_i. Thus, t_i/w_i are rank ordered. The job having the smallest value of t_i/w_i is placed first, etc. An important job will have a large value of w_i, resulting in a small number t_i/w_i, placing the job earlier in the sequence than would otherwise have been the case. In Fig. 14-6, the importance weight, w_i, alters the height of the blocks, and thereby the slope of the arrows. Previously (in Fig. 14-4 and 14-5) the w_i's were all equal to one. Now, the most vertical arrow (i.e., the largest slope) will belong to the job with the smallest ratio t_i/w_i.

With respect to Fig. 14-6, it happens that t_3 is the shortest processing time.

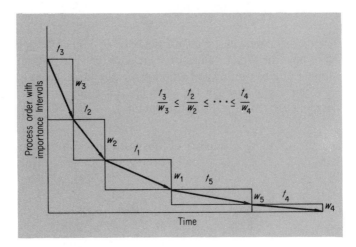

FIGURE 14-6. Jobs ordered by smallest ratios of weighted processing time

In any case, the ratio t_i/w_i is smallest for job 3, and so it is placed first in the sequence. It is clear that this ratio rule assures a smooth (convex) function that will minimize the area under the curve.

The SPT character of the sequencing problem is epitomized by n jobs and 1 facility. But the complexity of sequencing becomes increasingly evident as we consider larger numbers of facilities. Appendix 14-II treats situations with more than 1 facility as optional material.

Information Please, Inc.

This small but growing company receives requests by telephone from clients who seek all sorts of information, such as the number of automobiles registered in Costa Rica in 1976, the soybean crop in Russia in 1950, etc. At first, the company processed orders in FIFO fashion. Then, after it discovered the SPT rule, its efficiency jumped by more than 30 percent. New clients were signed up, and existing clients increased their contract levels.

One problem marred the picture. Estimates of t_i were made by a small group of people whose track records in estimation were excellent, and who, with feedback of how well they had done, continued to improve. So the SPT ordering was very good, but jobs with very high estimates of t_i were continually bounced to the end of job sequences and would get done only when the client complained. The president of Information Please, Inc., decided to resolve this problem by using SPT with weighted processing times. Her decision rule was to set $w_i = 1$ for all new requests for information. Any order that had not begun processing on the first day was given a weighting factor $w_i = 2$ for the second day's sequence decisions, and $w_i = 3$ for the third day's decisions, etc. For example, at the beginning of one particular day, there were 100 requests on hand. One of 15 researchers was carrying the following load.

Job	Estimated t_i (minutes)	w_i	Job	Estimated t_i (minutes)	w_i
1	20	1	6	64	2
2	12	1	7	30	1
3	120	2	8	13	1
4	5	1	9	366	2
5	180	1	10	93	3

Question: How should these be sequenced: first, in line with the (former) straight SPT rule? Second, in accord with the president's decision to use weighted processing times?

Answer: If straight SPT is used, the sequence would be

$$4, 2, 8, 1, 7, 6, 10, 3, 5, 9$$

If weighted processing times are used, the sequence would be

$$4, 2, 8, 1, 7, 10, 6, 3, 5, 9$$

Question: Will the President's modified rule benefit the company? (See problem 12, p. 310.)

APPENDIX 14-I
The Generalized Methodology for the Assignment Model
(Optional Material)

Step 1. Set up the matrix for the assignment model with minimization as the objective.

Step 2. Use row subtraction (arbitrarily chosen before column subtraction).

Step 3. Use column subtraction.

Step 4. Use the minimum number of lines through rows and columns to cover all zeroes. For example,

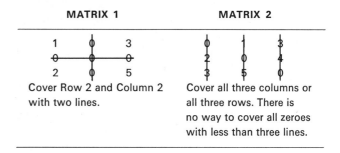

MATRIX 1			MATRIX 2

Cover Row 2 and Column 2 with two lines.

Cover all three columns or all three rows. There is no way to cover all zeroes with less than three lines.

Step 5. If the *minimum* number of marked rows and columns to cover all zeroes is equal to n for our $n \times n$ matrix, then the assignment problem is solved. See Matrix 2 in Step 4. If this is not the case, then go to Step 6.

Step 6. Take the smallest uncovered value and subtract this number from every uncovered number in the matrix including itself. Then add this value to every intersection of the covering lines. Using Matrix 1 in Step 4 as an example, we obtain Matrix 3.

MATRIX 3

0	0	2
0	1	0
1	0	4

Step 7. Use row (or column) subtraction. If the final assignment solution is not obtained (Steps 4 and 5), then repeat Step 6. In this case, we need go no further. Matrix 4 shows the final solution.

MATRIX 4

[0]	0	2
0	1	[0]
1	[0]	4

Note: Often alternative solutions are available.

APPENDIX 14-II
Sequencing with More Than One Facility
(Optional Material)

First Let Us Consider n Jobs with 2 Facilities. The SPT concept still applies when jobs must pass through 2 facilities in a given technological ordering, e.g., facility 1 (*F*1) followed by facility 2 (*F*2) (or, in a medical case, diagnosis followed by treatment, where jobs are people and facilities are doctors).

REQUIRED TIMES

Job (Person)	F1 (Diagnosis)	F2 (Treatment)
a	6	3
b	8	2
c	7	5
d	3	9
e	5	4

S. M. Johnson's algorithm[9] solves this problem for all "no passing" cases in terms of minimum completion time. ("No passing" means that the *order* of processing jobs by the first facility *must be preserved* for all subsequent facilities).

To use the algorithm for the above table, where *F*1 must be first, select the job (or person) with the shortest processing time on either *F*1 or *F*2. If this minimum value is in the *F*2 column, place the person *last* in sequence (here in fifth place); if it is in the *F*1 column, award that person *first* place. For our example, person *b* with 2 in the *F*2 column will be treated last. Remove person *b* from further consideration, then continue in the same way. Select the smallest number remaining in the matrix. If it is in the *F*2 column, assign that person to the last place if available or the next to last place if not; should the number be in the first column, that person gets first or next to first place. (Ties are resolved by randomly selecting either position for assignment.) For the example above, person *b* goes last, person *d* goes first in sequence, person *a*, next to last; person *e* is treated next to next to last; person *c* fills the remaining slot. The minimum total completion time is 31, shown in the Gantt chart on the following page. (See Fig. 14-7.)

---

[9]S. M. Johnson, "Optimal Two- and Three-Stage Production Schedules with Set-up Times Included," *Naval Research Logistics Quarterly*, Vol. 1, No. 1 (March, 1954), pp. 61–68.

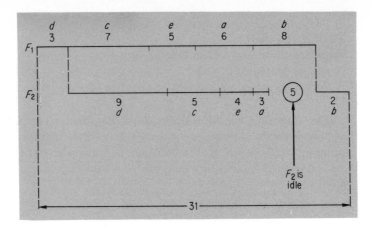

FIGURE 14-7. Gantt chart

Next Let Us Consider n Jobs with 3 Facilities. Johnson proposed a variant of his 2-facility algorithm that will obtain the optimal sequence for 3 facilities—if certain conditions are met. Suppose that we have 3 facilities with the technological ordering $F1$, $F2$, $F3$. As before, no passing is allowed, and we define t_{ij} = processing time of the ith person at facility j.[10] Then if at least 1 of the following restrictions holds, we can apply Johnson's method:

$$\min t_{i1} \geq \max t_{i2}$$

or

$$\min t_{i3} \geq \max t_{i2}$$

In words, the middle facility may not have any operation times that are greater than the minimum operation times of *both* the other facilities. For example, the method can be applied to the matrix of processing times below.

Facility	Person					
	a	*b*	*c*	*d*	*e*	
F1	4	7	5	3	3	Min t_{i1} = 3
F2	2	1	2	0	2	Max t_{i2} = 2
F3	1	1	3	9	2	Min t_{i3} = 1

If there had been a 4 in the $F2$ row, the method we are about to describe could not be used.

We reformulate the problem as a 2-facility system. That is, let $p_i = t_{i1} + t_{i2}$ and $q_i = t_{i2} + t_{i3}$.

---

[10]There is no solution that allows passing which can produce a shorter completion time than the no-passing solution for up to $n = 3$. See Conway et al., pp. 80–83.

For the numbers in the matrix:

	Person				
	a	*b*	*c*	*d*	*e*
$(F1 + F2)p$	6	8	7	3	5
$(F2 + F3)q$	3	2	5	9	4

Then, we proceed as we did before: Person i should precede Person k in the optimal sequence if

$$\min(p_i, q_k) < \min(p_k, q_i)$$

So the optimal sequence is unchanged from the one previously developed for the $n \times 2$ case. Giglio and Wagner applied this method to a series of problems where the restrictive condition did not hold and found that fairly good results were achieved. Of the 20 problems solved, the optimal sequence was achieved in 9 cases, and in 8 others it would have been reached if 2 adjacent jobs in the sequence exchanged positions. More important, the average error—measured from the true optimum that was found by enumeration—was under 3 percent for the twenty problems tested. Therefore, by relaxing the restrictive conditions and applying Johnson's algorithm, we have what amounts to a heuristic method for finding a pseudo-optimum sequence.

Last, Let Us Consider n Jobs with m Facilities. There is no *general* solution for any problem where $m > 2$. But there are *heuristic* approximations of the optimal solution. Campbell, Dudek, and Smith report on the successful performance of a heuristic algorithm that generates a series of sums for each job similar to the two new sets of sums generated in the prior discussion of $n \times 3$ systems.[11] Thus, with m facilities, we can develop $m - 1$ two column sets of job times that can then be treated by the S. M. Johnson $n \times 2$ algorithm, assuming the technological ordering $1 \rightarrow 2 \ldots \rightarrow m$ and no passing. For example, consider the following 6-person, 4-facility problem.

	Processing Time on Facility			
Person	*1*	*2*	*3*	*4*
a	50	43	15	4
b	89	99	95	77
c	7	47	20	98
d	8	64	12	94
e	61	19	65	14
f	1	80	66	78

[11]H. G. Campbell, R. A. Dudek, and M. L. Smith, "A Heuristic Algorithm for the *n* Job, *m* Machine Sequencing Problem," *Management Science*, Vol. 16, No. 10 (June, 1970), pp. B630–B637.

For our first 2-facility subproblem, we need to reformulate the above table so that we are considering the times for facilities 1 and 4 only. Our new table is

Person	Facility 1	Facility 4
a	50	4
b	89	77
c	7	98
d	8	94
e	61	14
f	1	78

Applying the 2-facility algorithm, we get (*fcdbea*) as the solution to our first subproblem.

The second subproblem is based on adding the processing times for facilities (1 + 2), creating the first column below, and then adding the processing times for facilities (3 + 4) found in the second column below.

Person	Facility (1 + 2)	Facility (3 + 4)
a	50 + 43 = 93	15 + 4 = 19
b	89 + 99 = 188	95 + 77 = 172
c	7 + 47 = 54	20 + 98 = 118
d	8 + 64 = 72	12 + 94 = 106
e	61 + 19 = 80	65 + 14 = 79
f	1 + 80 = 81	66 + 78 = 144

Solving this subproblem, we find the solution to be the sequence (*cdfbea*).

The last subproblem to be solved, in this case, consists of facilities (1 + 2 + 3)—that is, the sum of the times on facilities 1, 2, and 3—and facilities (2 + 3 + 4)—that is, the sum of the times on facilities 2, 3, and 4.

Person	Facilities (1 + 2 + 3)	Facilities (2 + 3 + 4)
a	50 + 43 + 15 = 108	43 + 15 + 4 = 62
b	89 + 99 + 95 = 283	99 + 95 + 77 = 271
c	7 + 47 + 20 = 74	47 + 20 + 98 = 165
d	8 + 64 + 12 = 84	64 + 12 + 94 = 170
e	61 + 19 + 65 = 145	19 + 65 + 14 = 98
f	1 + 80 + 66 = 147	80 + 66 + 78 = 224

The solution sequence for this subproblem is the same as for subproblem two, (*cdfbea*). Each of the subproblem sequences is evaluated in terms of total flow time. The results are shown below:

Sequence	Total Processing Time
(*fcdbea*)	512
(*cdfbea*)	487

On the basis of these figures, we would choose the sequence (*cdfbea*) as our quasi-optimal sequence for this problem. Actually, our chosen sequence did not fare badly at all with the true optimum for the problem. By enumeration we would find that the sequences (*cdbfae*) and (*cdbfea*) are optimal with a total processing time of 485. Thus, we could calculate the degree of error as

$$\frac{487 - 485}{485} \times 100 = 0.41 \text{ percent error}$$

PROBLEMS
1. The Gantt load chart (see p. 278) can be used to determine whether the "load" is equally distributed among facilities. The same kind of issue applied to resource leveling for projects. Discuss the relationship of these 2 situations.

2. Do Gantt sequencing (or layout) charts reflect a preference for first come-first served ordering or for the SPT rule? Discuss your answer.

3. Here is a total cost matrix for jobs 1, 2, and 3 at facilities *A*, *B*, and *C*:

	A	B	C
1	1000	900	1200
2	800	700	900
3	1500	1800	2000

Was the opportunity cost analysis in the text (pp. 279–83) of the cost per part matrix appropriate? Explain how you can tell.
Answer: Yes, it was appropriate; in fact, the 2 matrices are equivalent given that each job had 10,000 parts. By finding the minimum cost per part assignment, we also found the minimum total cost solution.

4. In the terms of Problem 3 (above), assume that the order sizes of the jobs are

Job	Size
1	10,000
2	10,000
3	5,000

What assignment do you recommend?

5. The executive offices for 5 vice presidents of a large bank are on the tenth floor of the bank's new building. The president wants to assign the offices in such a way as to maximize total satisfaction. He therefore asks each vice president to rank his preference for the available offices. The president receives the information in the following form:

Office	VP_1	VP_2	VP_3	VP_4	VP_5
O_1	1	1	2	3	2
O_2	5	3	1	2	3
O_3	4	2	5	1	1
O_4	3	5	4	3	4
O_5	2	4	3	5	5

Rank 1 is the most preferred location.
a. What is the best assignment plan?
b. How does this relate to production schedules?

6. Our company has 4 orders on hand, and each must be processed in the sequential order:
Department A—press shop
Department B—plating and finishing
The table below lists the number of days required by each job in each department. For example, Job IV requires 1 day in the press shop and 1 day in the finishing department.

	Job I	Job II	Job III	Job IV
Department A	8	6	5	1
Department B	8	3	4	1

a. Assume that no other work is being done by the departments. Use a Gantt layout chart to try to find the best work schedule. By best work schedule, we mean minimum time to finish all 4 jobs.

b. Find the best sequence, treating each department separately. How does that compare with your Gantt chart solution?

7. Use the assignment method to achieve a satisfactory shop loading arrangement for an intermittent flow shop where the per unit profits are given in the matrix below and relatively continuous production (in the quarter) can be expected for each assignment.

	Machines				
Jobs	A	B	C	D	E
1	19	17	15	15	13
2	12	30	18	18	15
3	13	21	29	19	21
4	49	56	53	55	43
5	33	41	39	39	40

8. For the data in Problem 7 a new machine F has become available that can only work on jobs 1, 2, or 3, with unit profits of 14, 11, and 12. Would it be worthwhile to replace one of the present machines with F? After analysis, what information is still lacking?

9. Use the data below to develop an index shop loading analysis where splitting of assignments is permitted and assumed to have negligible costs. Assume that the objective is to minimize total job times.

	Parts per Hour at Facility				
Job	A	B	C	D	Demand/Week
1	7.5	15	10	20	400
2	4.5	9	6	12	300
3	3	6	4	8	200
Available Hours Per Week	40	40	40	40	

10. Examine several alternative sequences for the following $n \times 1$ system, with 6 jobs and processing times t_i.

i	t_i	i	t_i
a	5	d	9
b	4	e	12
c	6	f	8

Especially study SPT and also the effect of LPT (longest processing time).

11. For Problem 10 above, what effect does the information that jobs a, b, and c are half as important as jobs d, e, and f have on the sequence solution?

12. For the problem faced by Information Please, Inc. (pp. 300–301) determine the mean flow times with and without the president's weighting system. Will the president's policy be helpful?

The following problem relates to Appendix 14-I

13. With respect to Problem 3, relating to the opportunity cost analysis in the text (pp. 279–83), assume that the order sizes of the jobs are

Job	Size
1	10,000
2	20,000
3	5,000

What assignment do you recommend?

Chapter 12

The job shop is the most complex production system. If it can be converted to a flow shop, it should be. But if not, there are many ways of being competitively better, and enjoying the greater marginal advantages. Three job shop problems should be recognized. These are

1. Aggregate scheduling.
2. Shop loading.
3. Sequencing.

The job shop is involved with so many details that it requires great information management capabilities. If management is not on top of the situation, losses occur at all three levels. Cumulatively, these can cripple the organization. Therefore, we develop awareness of blueprints, bills of materials, operations sheets, etc.

At the aggregate scheduling level, forecasting and prediction play a critical role. Consequently, the character of time series is explored. Historical and seasonal predictions, moving averages, weighted moving averages, and exponential smoothing are introduced. Regression analysis is explained within the context of an example.

Chapter 13

The prediction capability having been developed, the aggregate scheduling problem is examined and the quadratic cost model created by Holt, Modigliani, Muth, and Simon (HMMS) is applied to Paintmasters' problem. Appendix 13-I offers a linear programming and a transportation method approach to aggregate scheduling as optional material. (These are weaker models than the HMMS one, but have computational advantages.)

Chapter 14

Shop loading is the next problem level. Gantt's shop-loading chart method is introduced. But then, the real character of shop loading is explained by means of the assignment model, which has as its underpinning the concept of opportunity costs. The character of the assignment model is fully explained in the text by means of examples. Appendix 14-I provides, as optional material, the generalized methodology in more formal terms. With understanding of opportunity costs, as developed by the assignment model, the index method for shop loading, which is a heuristic approach, is applied to the machine shop of Toolmasters, Inc. The index method is a strong and relatively easy way to obtain near-optimal solutions for real shop-loading problems.

The third job shop problem of sequencing is described. Gantt sequencing charts are introduced. Then the logic of the SPT (shortest processing time) sequencing rule is fully developed. It is the keystone concept of the sequencing area. An application of SPT to the scheduling problem of Information Please, Inc., provides further insights about the use of weighted processing times. Appendix 14-II (optional material) treats the sequencing problem when jobs must be sequenced for processing through more than one facility.

**REFERENCES
PART 5**

AGEE, M. H., R. E. TAYLOR, and P. E. TORGERSEN, *Quantitative Analysis for Management Decisions*. Englewood Cliffs, N. J.: Prentice-Hall, Inc., 1976.

BIEGEL, JOHN E., *Production Control*. Englewood Cliffs, N.J.: Prentice-Hall, Inc., 1963.

BOWMAN, E. H. and R. B. FETTER, *Analysis for Production and Operations Management*, 3rd ed. Homewood, Ill.: Richard D. Irwin, Inc., 1967.

BROWN, ROBERT G., *Smoothing, Forecasting, and Prediction of Discrete Time Series*. Englewood Cliffs, N.J.: Prentice-Hall, Inc., 1963.

BUFFA, ELWOOD S. and WILLIAM H. TAUBERT, *Production-inventory Systems: Planning and Control*. Homewood, Ill.: Richard D. Irwin, 1972.

BUFFA, E. S., *Modern Production Management*, 3rd ed. New York: John Wiley & Sons, Inc., 1969.

————, ed., *Readings in Production and Operations Management*. New York: John Wiley & Sons, Inc., 1966.

CONWAY, RICHARD W., WILLIAM L. MAXWELL, and LOUIS W. MILLER, *Theory of Scheduling*. Reading, Mass.: Addison-Wesley Publishing Company, 1967.

DOOLEY, A. ET AL., *Basic Problems, Concepts and Techniques, Casebooks in Production Management*, rev. ed. New York: John Wiley & Sons, Inc., 1968.

DORFMAN, ROBERT, PAUL A. SAMUELSON, and ROBERT M. SOLOW, *Linear Programming and Economic Analysis*. New York: McGraw-Hill Book Company Inc., 1958.

EILON, S., *Elements of Production Planning and Control*. New York: The Macmillan Company, 1962.

ELMAGHRABY, S. E., *The Design of Production Systems*. New York: Reinhold Publishing Corp., 1966.

FERGUSON, ROBERT O. and LAUREN F. SARGENT, *Linear Programming: Fundamentals and Applications*. New York: McGraw-Hill Book Company, Inc., 1958.

GARRETT, L. J. and M. SILVER, *Production Management Analysis*. New York: Harcourt Brace Jovanovich, 1968.

GAVETT, J. W., *Production and Operations Management*. New York: Harcourt Brace Jovanovich, 1968.

GEORGE, C. S., *Management in Industry*, 2nd ed. Englewood Cliffs, N.J.: Prentice-Hall Inc., 1964.

GOLD, BELA, *Foundations of Productivity Analysis*. Pittsburgh, Penn.: University of Pittsburgh Press, 1955.

HOPEMAN, R. J., *Systems Analysis and Operations Management*. Coulmbus, Ohio: Charles. E. Merrill Publishing Co., 1969.

HOTTENSTEIN, M. P., *Models and Analysis for Production Management*. Scranton, Penn.: International Textbook Co., 1968.

HOLT, C. C., F. MODIGLIANI, J. F. MUTH, and H. A. SIMON, *Planning Production Inventories and Work Force*. Englewood Cliffs, N.J.: Prentice-Hall, Inc., 1960.

IRESON, W. G. and E. L. GRANT, eds., *Handbook of Industrial Engineering and Management*, 2nd ed. Englewood Cliffs, N.J.: Prentice-Hall, Inc., 1970.

JOHNSON, R. A., W. T. NEWELL, and R. C. VERGIN, *Operations Management*. Boston: Houghton Mifflin Company, 1972.

JOINT ECONOMIC COMMITTEE, CONGRESS of the UNITED STATES, "Measures of Productive Capacity," July 24, 1962.

MacNIECE, E. H., *Production Forecasting, Planning, and Control*, New York: John Wiley & Sons, 1961.

MAGEE, J. F. and D. M. BOODMAN, *Production Planning and Inventory Control*, 2nd ed. New York: McGraw-Hill Book Company, 1967.

MUTH, JOHN F. and GERALD L. THOMPSON, eds., *Industrial Scheduling*. Englewood Cliffs, N.J.: Prentice-Hall, Inc., 1963.

NILAND, POWELL, *Production Planning, Scheduling, and Inventory Control*. New York: The Macmillan Co., 1970.

Progress in Operations Research, Vol. I, Russell L. Ackoff, ed., 1961; Vol. II, David B. Hertz and Robert T. Eddison, eds., 1964; Vol. III, Julius Aronofsky, ed., 1969. New York: John Wiley & Sons, Inc.

SCHEELE, EVAN D., ET AL., *Principles and Design of Production Control Systems*. Englewood Cliffs, N.J.: Prentice-Hall, Inc., 1960.

STARR, M. K., ed., *Management of Production*. Middlesex, England: Penguin Book, Ltd., 1970.

———, *Systems Management of Operations*. Englewood Cliffs, N.J.: Prentice-Hall, Inc., 1971.

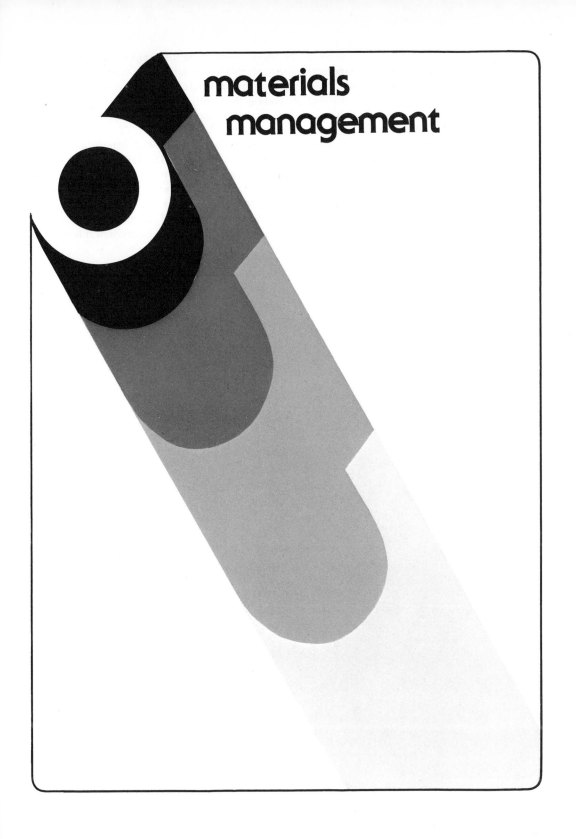

materials
management

In Chapter 15, materials planning is shown to be different for the flow shop, the job shop, and projects. Although this is not surprising, what is required is the understanding of how to deal with each kind of situation. Further, Chapter 15 examines the information system that unifies the materials management function. It goes on to study material requirements planning (MRP) and value analysis for choosing alternative materials.

Of critical importance is the difference between MRP (material requirements planning) and (OPP) order point planning. The latter subject is the concern of Chapter 16. MRP is *most often* appropriate for the job shop and for projects. OPP is *most often* appropriate for the flow shop. Neither approach to materials planning is exclusively reserved to any form of process configuration. Consequently, it remains for Chapters 15 and 16 to explain why one system would be preferred to another, so that P/OM can know when it is correct to apply either.

fifteen
materials planning

Materials of many kinds are inputs to all process configurations for both products and services. Consequently, materials planning is essential for high productivity and cost advantages.

The specifications of materials must be defined exactly. They must be ordered at the right price, delivered on time, and inspected for faults. Information about materials must be managed with skill. Stock outages can delay or even halt production of both goods and services. The costs of mistakes can be exorbitant. They can also be relatively trivial, depending upon the kind of process configuration being used.

Materials Management Is Different for the Flow Shop, the Job Shop, and Projects

The management of materials calls upon different rules (and decision models) for different production configurations. That is, certain kinds of problems are posed by materials requirements of flow shops that are not the same for job shops and projects.

Flow Shop

The flow shop needs a continuous supply of a limited and unchanging set of materials. The line has to be shut down if stock outages occur. On the other hand, carrying very large amounts of inventory can be extremely costly. Because of large order quantitites placed long in advance of delivery, substantial quantity discounts can usually be obtained.

Knowing when to order and how much to order is crucial. Therefore, an order point policy (OPP) that specifies "when" and "how much" to order for each item, *independent* of what is happening to other items, makes sense. Order point planning will be discussed in Chapter 16.

There is considerable experience and familiarity with vendors. For new flow shop lines, much vendor competition can be expected. Vendors actively compete to supply the materials requirements of high-volume demand systems.

Job Shop

The job shop has a varied and changing set of material requirements. These may include certain materials that are repeated with some degree of regularity and others that are "last-minute" orders. Generally, the job shop requires smaller order quantities of more kinds of materials than the flow shop. Consequently, smaller discounts can be obtained, and tracking of stock levels creates a more demanding information management problem.

The use of material requirements planning (MRP) involves having a good information system to track, for each particular job, the components needed. Also, the time when those components are needed. MRP will be discussed later in this chapter (see pp. 332–36).

Many vendors can be involved, and changes from one to another are not unusual. A single decision that deviates from optimal materials planning cannot do much harm. Only the cumulative effects of repeated divergencies from acceptable results can impose severe penalties over a period of time. From time to time, a job can be delayed while corrections are made. Most jobs are small, and the consequences for delay are slight. This is not true of the flow shop, and it is seldom true of the project, where delays usually impose severe penalties.

Projects

Projects such as ships or buildings have stages when certain materials are used that will not be used again. Since the activity stages are nonrepetitive, the majority of orders are placed only once. Nevertheless, material requirements planning can be used successfully to track the timing of materials needed for specific project activities. The order point concept would apply only to those project materials that are used consistently and uniformly throughout the project. Order point policies would be appropriate when demands are independent of the specific project activities, e.g., lubricants for machines, food for workers, and light bulbs. In contrast, if MRP logic is used, the right amount of cement can be ordered, to be delivered on time, for a specific construction job of known dimensions.

Often, much work on project materials is subcontracted to suppliers who are familiar with aspects of the materials requirements of particular project stages. Cost of materials may be less critical than on-time delivery. Frequently, the materials required are unique, and there is little experience in producing them. Discounts for quantity purchases are relatively rare, whereas special setup charges are not unusual. Careful follow-up with suppliers is essential when experience with the vendors is limited. Also, the vendors may have little familiarity with the materials they are supplying, which can lead to production difficulties in the vendors' shops.

The differentiation we have just drawn is representative, but hardly complete. Materials management requirements are affected by working experience with vendors, vendors' knowledge of the products and services they supply, quantities ordered both in total amount and per order, the continuity of demand, the number of competing vendors and the importance of the orders to them, the requirement to use bidding, the quality ranges that can be tolerated, etc.

The Materials Information System

Material inputs produce direct costs. These costs often constitute a major share of operating costs. Thus, the material inputs are associated with the variable-cost line of the break-even chart (see pp. 16–22). This area of materials cost control is critical to production and operation managers.

Many companies have been moving toward an organizational integration of the information required for materials control. In the past, a variety of materials management activities existed as individual operations, each attended by managers who seldom communicated with each other. Eventually, in the search for greater effectiveness, a single, central materials control department has appeared in numerous organizations.

Today, many organizations have a vice president in charge of materials control. The responsibilities vested in a materials control department include at least four subfunctions, namely, purchasing and vendor relations, inventory stock control, acceptance sampling for quality control, and accounting to pay the bills. Each function interfaces with the others and with many other departments within the organization. Coordination of activities is essential, which is why we have stressed information management once again.

Let us examine Fig. 15-1. It is a flow diagram which depicts the various communications that unite the materials management area. We observe the many forms of communication that must flow between the organizational units in order that an integrated materials control department may be

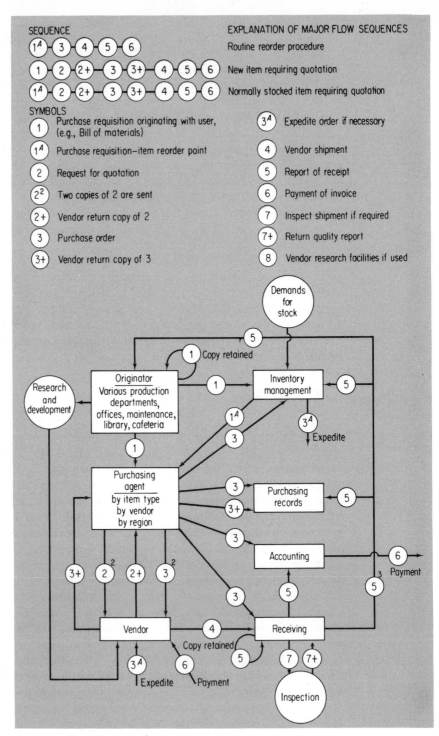

FIGURE 15-1. A detailed flow diagram of materials management

achieved. In addition, the materials control department communicates with research and development, with the production department, with other operating dividisions of the company, and in many ways with outside organizations, including the vendor's R&D department.

The Purchasing Function

The purchasing division occupies a vital and unique position. Through its procurement function the organization operates as a *customer*. Accordingly, it is susceptible to the marketing strategies of the vendors from whom it obtains the materials that are required for its operations.

Depending upon the *extent* to which the company requires outside suppliers, because it does not self-produce for all its needs, the importance of the buying function increases. For example, a mail order company produces a very small fraction of the materials that it offers for sale.

Buyers in such enterprises are responsible, in large measure, for the success of their companies. Commensurate with this responsibility is the remuneration which such buyers receive. At the same time, they must accept the risk of making errors such as overestimating demand or paying too high a price. The penalties of errors can be high.

The purchasing function is deeply involved with human behavior. Relations with vendors cannot be pinned down to a formula. They can affect "deals" that are made, favors that are rendered, and the continuity of suppliers. Purchasing operations are immersed in a maelstrom of human relations. There are many mechanical aspects to the achievement of a successful purchasing function, but the human factors cannot be overlooked. Buyers can succeed in achieving special arrangements because of friendly relationships that exist. These are not dishonorable relationships, because they include the evaluation of both buyer and vendor of the long-term stability and goodwill of their relationship. However, in the business environment of North America, personal friendships are not considered to be a reasonable basis for enterprise decisions. In other business environments, for example, Latin America and the Middle East, personal friendships are considered to be business assets that reduce risk and have monetary value. Part of this cultural difference can be traced to the importance placed upon legal contracts in North America that does not exist elsewhere. Because of the enormous growth of international operations, these factors can play a significant role in determining the success of management in handling the affairs of subsidiaries outside the United States.[1]

Purchasing records provide a history of what has been done in the past, what costs were involved, who the major suppliers were, as well as the costs,

---

[1]For a useful discussion of these points, see Edward T. Hall, "The Silent Language in Overseas Business," *Harvard Business Review*, Vol. 38, No. 3 (May–June, 1960), pp. 87–96.

discounts, quality levels, and delivery periods for specific items. But purchasing is a function that is not even roughly similar in many different companies. Differentiated skills exist that emphasize types of materials and vendor purchasing *traditions*. It would be impossible to discuss all the intricate relationships that have been developed by buyers and vendors in order to achieve maximum satisfaction for both parties. One important procedure, however, should be mentioned. It is called *vendor releasing*. In this case, a buyer contracts for a substantial number of units and thereby obtains discount prices. The vendor agrees to ship fixed or varying amounts of the purchased material at stated intervals. Often, only the approximate shipping quantitities for each time period are agreed upon. Generally, the buyer is in a position to change the quantities, from time to time, if he does so with sufficient notice. We can observe how an arrangement, such as vendor releasing, is dependent upon a reasonable forecast of demand and a reasonably accurate specification of the vendor's lead time.[2] It requires a fairly long-term commitment to obtain the benefits of quantity discounts. Job shops that use large quantities of certain basic materials can employ vendor releasing to obtain discounts that approximate those of the flow shop.

Bidding

Sometimes, a number of vendors are requested to submit a bid for the cost of supplying particular equipment or supplies. The bids will include delivery dates and quality specifications, so there is more than one criterion upon which to rate the competing vendors.

The bid system is commonly associated with governmental acquisitions of materials. But it is also familiar in situations where industrial organizations have no prior vendor arrangements and in which costly purchases are to be made. Bidding is applicable only when a competitive market exists for the goods or services that are to be acquired.

There are bidding models that indicate that as the *number of competitors increases*, the size of the winning bid decreases.[3] The reason is that different costing systems, capacity and load conditions, skills, and facilities exist for each bidder. As a result, the range of bids will increase. On the basis of this reasoning, the procurement manager would seemingly want as many bidders as possible. But there is an opposing force at work. As the number of bidders increases, the cost of ordering rises, since each bid must be evaluated not only for costs but for the many intangible factors that must affect the ordering decision. Perhaps, for example, the lowest bidder will promise to meet a delivery schedule that evaluation indicates is unlikely to be fulfilled. Also,

---

[2]Lead time, or lag time, is the interval that elapses between the placement of an order with the vendor and the receipt of the ordered goods.

[3]See David W. Miller and Martin K. Starr, *Executive Decisions and Operations Research*, 2nd ed. (Englewood Cliffs, N.J.: Prentice-Hall, Inc., 1969), pp. 425–437.

too many bidders may make the expected profit so low that qualified suppliers refuse to join the bidding, leaving the field open to the less qualified.

A company does not, of necessity, choose to make its purchases from the organization presenting the lowest bid. Price is seldom the only factor that should be taken into consideration when one is awarding a contract. Among other things, it is necessary to consider the guarantees of quality, the experience of the vendor, the certainties of delivery, and the kind of long-term supplier-producer relationship that is likely to develop. Transportation costs further complicate the picture. A high bid received from a vendor that is two miles away may be less costly—after transportation—than a lower bid from a potential supplier located 3000 miles away. Thus, it is not enough to compare bids on an FOB point of origin basis.[4]

Bidding is applicable for project procurement policies and for start-up (or reevaluation of) purchase arrangements for the flow shop. It is less relevant for the job shop, although it does make sense when substantial amounts of materials are involved. Bidding is always useful when there is suspicion that special purchasing deals are being made between suppliers and company personnel.

Inventories of Critical Parts

In the flow shop (and sometimes for projects) certain parts will fail, which can shut down the line or seriously delay project completion. An entire refinery can be shut down. The cost of lost production may well run into millions of dollars. Should spares of all critical parts be kept in stock? If so, how many of each kind? How likely is it that a spare part kept in stock for an emergency is, in fact, a reject—a faulty part—that will fail immediately upon use?

Often, severe *technical* problems are involved in purchasing critical parts for the maintenance function of complex technological systems. Buyers must be familiar with production equipment and its requirements. They must also be able to evaluate the failure characteristics of the merchandise they acquire. A rational plan should be developed for purchasing and stocking such items. Inventory policies for critical parts are a function of the type of maintenance that is used, that is, *preventive* or *remedial* maintenance or a combination of the 2. In many systems, the technical basis used for purchasing decisions can be exceedingly critical. When reliability and failure are of major importance, the purchasing function is frequently assigned to a scientifically trained individual. This is particularly necessary when technical engineering specifications are used.

---

[4]FOB Detroit. This familiar expression is read "freight on board, Detroit." It means that the price is quoted without shipping charges from Detroit to whatever point of destination is involved.

City Hospital's Decision Model for
Critical Part Inventories

An important class of maintenance inventories is identified with the fact that at the time a major facility is purchased, critical spare parts can be obtained inexpensively. Later on, however, if it turns out that an insufficient supply of these critical parts was acquired, the cost of obtaining additional spares is much higher. (By *critical*, we mean that if the part fails, the entire unit ceases to function in an acceptable fashion.)

To illustrate, assume that City Hospital is purchasing an emergency generator for the operating room in its new wing. Engineering data indicate that a particular critical part has a probability of i failures p_i over the lifetime of the machine.

There is a cost c for each spare part purchased at the time that the generator is acquired. When a spare part must be purchased *at a later time*, because not enough were originally purchased, the cost is estimated to be c' (which includes renting a generator as a temporary replacement and the large cost per replacement part charged by the vendor, who must treat the spare part request as a special order).

For a simple example of this model,[5] let $i = 1, 2, 3$, meaning that at least 1 failure must occur and that no more than 3 failures can occur over the lifetime of the generator. Also, assume that the probability of failure is distributed as follows:

$$p_1 = \tfrac{1}{2}$$
$$p_2 = \tfrac{1}{3}$$
$$p_3 = \tfrac{1}{6}$$

The sum of these probabilities equals one, as it should. Further, let $c = \$5$ and $c' = \$400$. The question that we wish to answer is, How many spare parts k should be ordered at the time of the original purchase? We note that the spare part is inexpensive if purchased initially. However, the failure of the part without a replacement is a relatively critical event, costing 80 times the price of the spare.

A decision matrix can be constructed to represent this problem.[6] See Table 15-1.

The minimum expected cost is obtained by ordering 3 spares. This result could have been anticipated. At least 1 failure must occur (in line with the given probability distribution); therefore, at least 1 spare would be ordered in any case. Further, the cost of obtaining a spare *after* the initial order is so

---

[5]We could complicate the problem considerably by adding a charge for carrying a part in stock, by changing the probabilities of failure according to when a failure had occurred, by allowing more than one spare to be reordered after failure, etc. All such issues, and others as well, can be treated in a realistic, but more complicated, model. For our example, we have assumed that whenever a failure occurs, the probabilities of additional failures remain unchanged.

[6]Refer to the previous development of the decision matrix, pp. 38–43.

**TABLE 15-1 FAILURE COST MATRIX FOR THE CITY HOSPITAL
GENERATOR**

		\multicolumn{3}{c}{*Number of Failures i Occurring During Generator's Lifetime*}		
	p_i	1 $\frac{1}{2}$	2 $\frac{1}{3}$	3 $\frac{1}{6}$	*Expected Cost*
Initial number	k ⎰1	5	5 + 400	5 + 800	271.67
of spare	⎱2	10	10	10 + 400	76.67
parts ordered	3	15	15	15	15.00 (min.)

much greater than *with* the initial order, that obvious advantage accrues to
the latter; i.e., order 3 spares with the generator.

Let us review the steps required to obtain the expected values in the table
above. The outcome entries in the matrix are computed by two different
relationships. First, when the number of failures equals or is less than the
number of parts originally ordered with the generator, the cost is simply kc.
Second, when the number of failures is greater than the number of parts
originally ordered, the cost is $kc + (i - k)c'$. For example, if three failures
occur ($i = 3$) and only two parts were originally ordered ($k = 2$), then the
cost is $(2 \times 5) + (3 - 2)400 = 410$. After the matrix of total costs is completed, the expected values are obtained in the usual fashion.[7]

$$\text{Expected cost for } k = 1: \quad 5(\tfrac{1}{2}) + 405(\tfrac{1}{3}) + 805(\tfrac{1}{6}) = 271.67$$
$$\text{Expected cost for } k = 2: \quad 10(\tfrac{1}{2}) + 10(\tfrac{1}{3}) + 410(\tfrac{1}{6}) = 76.67$$
$$\text{Expected cost for } k = 3: \quad 15(\tfrac{1}{2}) + 15(\tfrac{1}{3}) + 15(\tfrac{1}{6}) = 15.00$$

City Hospital should order 3 spare parts with the generator. When those
parts arrive, they should be inspected with care to make certain that they
will be able to do the job—if and when called upon.

---

[7]For similar decision matrix computations, see pp. 43–51.

Question: What would the decision be if zero failures are expected with 0.97 probability and the other failure rates are all 0.01 ?
Answer: The matrix would now be:

	\multicolumn{4}{c}{(*i*)}	
p_i	0 0.97	1 0.01	2 0.01	3 0.01	*Expected Cost*
k ⎧0	0	400	800	1200	24
⎪1	5	5	405	805	17
⎨2	10	10	10	410	14 (min.)
⎩3	15	15	15	15	15

which means that we would shift from ordering three spares to two spares.

Question: If $c = 5$, $c' = 20$, and $p_1 = \frac{1}{2}$, $p_2 = \frac{1}{3}$, $p_3 = \frac{1}{6}$, how many spares should be ordered? Note that the initial acquisition cost remains the same but is now only $\frac{1}{4}$ the failure replacement cost.

Answer: The failure cost matrix is

		(i)		
	1	2	3	
p_i	$\frac{1}{2}$	$\frac{1}{3}$	$\frac{1}{6}$	*Expected Cost*
$k \begin{cases} 1 \\ 2 \\ 3 \end{cases}$	5 10 15	25 10 15	45 30 15	$18\frac{1}{3}$ $13\frac{1}{3}$ (min.) 15

which signifies a change wherein two spares should be ordered instead of three.

The decision matrix lends itself nicely to representing this static[8] form of inventory problem where there is a one-time purchase. This is not a flow shop inventory model but is applicable to the job shop and to the project manager. Note that variability of demand (e.g., the spare parts failure distribution) is only one way in which uncertainty about the order size can arise. Other causes are work rejects requiring additional parts to be made to fill an order, materials spoilage, and pilferage. All such factors can be accounted for with probability estimates and the decision matrix methodology.

Classification of Inventory Systems

There are many significant distinctions between types of inventories that need to be made. First, as in the case of City Hospital, there are items that are functionally critical to operations, no matter how much or how little they cost. The lack of one spare engine part could ground a 747 aircraft. The need for a gasket might severely slow down a refinery.

Second, there are items that are important because their dollar volume is high. These can be a few expensive items, many inexpensive ones, or mixtures of both kinds. A significant division of all items under materials manage-

---

[8]"Static" is defined in the next section.

ment is based on the recognition that some few items have high dollar volumes and many others have substantially lower dollar volumes. Figure 15-2 portrays the not unusual case where 25 percent of all items carried in the inventory account for as much as 75 percent of the company's total dollar volume.

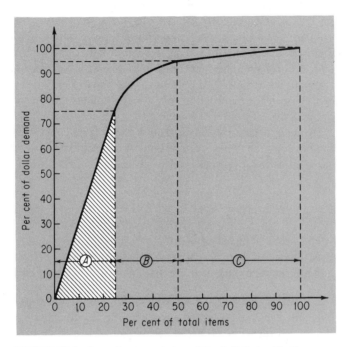

FIGURE 15-2. General representation of the *A-B-C* classification
The lion's share of dollar demand is produced by a small percentage of items.

For example, say that a hotel carries an inventory of 1000 different items, for which it spends $1 million annually. It might well be that about 250 of these items would cost approximately three-quarters of a million dollars. This is called the A class of inventory items.

Since *dollar volume* relates directly to inventory costs, *potential savings* available as a result of better inventory policies will be far greater in the A class than in any other. This is particularly apparent when it is pointed out that the *cost of inventory studies* tends to be proportional to the *number of items* under consideration. The B class (another 25 percent of all items) may account for 15 or 20 percent of dollar volume. Thus, for the hotel, another 250 items might account for $200,000. The C class often deals with no more than 5 to 10 percent of the company's total dollar volume, although 50 percent of all items inventories belong in that group. Therefore, 500 hotel items involve about $50,000. There is no commitment to provide class breaks at 25 and 50 percent nor a need to abide by three classes. It is essential, however, that the operations manager recognize the unequal contributions of different items in his inventory, and the fact that *equivalent effort should not be spent* on improving the inventory policies of all items.

Another important classification is based on the difference between *static* and *dynamic* situations. In the *static* case, only one inventory decision can be made. City Hospital's spare parts model is a static case. A well-known problem that is often cited to explain the static situation is the "Christmas tree problem." The Christmas tree dealer can place only a single order for trees. Then, on Christmas day, it is learned whether the estimation was exactly right, or over or under. In the case of overestimated demand, *salvage value* is sometimes available.[9] For example, a department store that overbuys on toys, shipped from abroad in time for the holiday season, can often sell those toys at a discount after the selling season is finished.

Dynamic situations do not require these same considerations, because the demand for such items is continuous. The problem, as we shall see, becomes one of adjusting inventory levels so as to balance the various costs that apply.

Inventory Costs

The heart of inventory analysis resides in the identification of relevant costs. There are many kinds of cost that apply to the inventory situation. We shall now itemize some of those that are most frequently encountered.

1. Cost of Ordering. Each time a purchase requisition is drawn up, both fixed and variable costs are incurred. The fixed costs of ordering are associated with the salaries of the permanent staff of the order department. We also include investments in equipment and properly assigned overhead charges. Fixed costs are not affected by the inventory policies that are followed. The variable cost component consists of the purchase requisition form, the cost of sending this purchase requisition to the vendor; in fact, any costs that increase as the number of purchase requisitions increases. Not to be overlooked are opportunity costs associated with alternative uses of both time and equipment. Thus, the ordering cost for a self-employed shopkeeper must take into account the fact that he could be redecorating his windows, talking longer with a customer, or using his time in some other fruitful manner.

Then, by definition, as the number of orders increases, the fixed costs remain constant and the variable costs increase. For example, a company may be able to process 100 orders per week. If a new inventory policy requires that 150 purchase requisitions—on the average—be processed in a week, then the ordering department must be enlarged. The increase in labor costs and equipment and overhead is considered to be additional variable cost. In this way the ordering cost is determined on top of a base ordering system.

---

[9]Salvage values can readily be added to the decision matrix by decreasing costs in appropriate quantities for those cells where demand is less than supply.

2. *The Cost of Carrying Inventory.* It is well known that organizations strive to maintain the minimum necessary inventories. We frequently hear that in times of uncertainty companies begin to cut back on their inventory. Why is this so? The answer is that a company maintains an investment in the form of inventory. Its capital is tied up in materials and goods. If the capital were free, alternative uses might be found for it. For example, the company could take this freed capital and put it in the savings bank, thereby earning interest on the money. It should be noted that the interest charges are a variable cost which depend upon the number of units stocked, the price per unit, and the interest rate that is determined to be applicable. Somewhat more speculative investments could be made in stocks. The company could purchase additional equipment and expand capacity, or even use this money to diversify. Thus, we see that an opportunity cost exists. By holding inventory the company foregoes investing its capital in alternative ways. These opportunity costs account for a large part of the costs of carrying inventory.

Inventory carrying costs must also include the expense of storing inventory. As was the case for the ordering department, costs should be measured from a fixed base. We must consider only the variable cost component associated with storage—the costs over which the operations manager can exercise control in terms of the inventory policies. Thus, if a company has shelf space for 1000 units but can get a discount if it stocks a maximum of 2000 units, then to get this discount it must expand storage capacity, or rent additional space. An appropriate inventory cost analysis must be made to determine whether or not the discount should be taken. The extra costs incurred are a variable cost component associated with holding inventory.

Items that are carried in stock are subject to pilferage losses, obsolescence, and deterioration. These costs represent real losses in the value of inventory. Pilferage is particularly characteristic of certain items. Small items, for example, are more likely to disappear than large ones. Tool cribs are provided with attendants and frequently kept locked when the plant is shut down for the night and over the weekend. Tools have general appeal and almost universal utility. They are small enough to filch—ergo, the tool crib concept. Department stores suffer enormous pilferage losses; hotels lose ashtrays and towels; pencils and stamps disappear in company offices. Thus, pilferage losses add substantially to the carrying costs of many organizations.

Obsolescence can occur quite suddenly because of technological change. Or it can be the kind of loss that is associated with style goods, toys, and Christmas trees. Out of season and out of style, these items lose value and must be sold at a special reduced rate. The problem of determining how much inventory to carry will be affected by the nature of the inventories and the way in which units lose value over time.

An additional component of the carrying cost includes both taxes and insurance. If insurance rates and taxes are determined on a per unit basis, then the amount of inventory that is stocked will determine directly the insurance and tax components of the carrying costs.

A Sample Determination of Carrying Cost

As a guide, we can furnish the following table. Hypothetical figures have been entered that are similar to the carrying cost computations of many companies in the United States. Each situation is different, so the accountants and operating managers must assess those costs that apply to their situation.

Category	Percent
Loss due to inability to invest funds in profit-making ventures, including loss of interest	14.00
Obsolescence	3.00
Deterioration	3.00
Transportation, handling, and distribution	2.00
Taxes	0.25
Storage cost	0.25
Insurance	0.25
Miscellaneous	0.25
Pilgerage (highly variable)	—
C_c = Carrying cost expressed as a percentage of the product's cost, per year	= 23.00

---

3. Cost of Out of Stock. If a company cannot fill an order, there is usually some penalty to be paid. Sometimes, the customer goes elsewhere, and the penalty is the value of the order that is lost. If this customer is annoyed because he had to do without or find a new supplier and he continues to hold a grudge against the company, then the loss of a sale plus the loss of goodwill must be translated into a cost. If the buyer is willing to wait to have his order filled, then the company treats this situation as a back order. Back orders cost money. They can annoy the customer, even though he appears to be willing to wait. Many times, a company will attempt to fill the customer's order with a more expensive substitute. The cost factor is not difficult to determine in this case. Whatever the system, fill or kill,[10] back ordering, material substitutions, and so on, some costs of being out of stock will occur. The lost goodwill cost is considered to be one of the most significant and one of the most difficult to evaluate.

4. Other Costs. The above named costs are the ones that usually are considered most relevant in the determination of inventory policy. Many

---

[10]No back orders allowed.

other costs also play a part in specific cases. Thus, for example, there are systemic costs associated with running the inventory system, costs of delays in processing orders, costs of discounts not realized, setup costs, costs of production interruptions, salvage costs, and expediting costs. In some instances, one or more of these costs will dominate the inventory policy evaluation.

Differentiation of Costs for Flow Shops, Job Shops, and Projects

For the flow shop, the cost of ordering is low, because orders for the same items are placed with regularity. On the other hand, the carrying cost of inventory tends to reflect the profitability of the industry. The reason for this relationship is that the carrying cost rate C_c is larger where reinvestments in the process or in marketing and distribution can continue to bring excellent profitability and ROI's (return on investment). Out-of-stock costs are generally severe. The line may have to shut down or run at some fraction of total capacity. For this reason, large safety stocks are usually held in the inventory, no matter how high the carrying costs may be. Depending on the particular kind of flow shop, pilferage costs will vary. Because materials at different stages of completion are moved from station to station, only the last station has access to the finished goods. Consequently, flow shop pilferage can be controlled to a great extent.

For the job shop, the cost of ordering is often high. The right vendor has to be located for various jobs that call for special materials, new components, etc. The carrying costs will tend to be lower than those of the flow shop to the degree that the job shop is less profitable. But over ordering to provide protection against rejects, etc., leaves an increasing accumulation of small amounts of materials and components that eventually can be sold as salvage. This increases the costs of obsolescence. Pilferage costs also can turn out to be quite high because of the lesser degree of control that can be exercised over smaller amounts of many items. Out-of-stock costs are more or less significant (depending on the situation) but far less so than for the flow shop.

For the project, the cost of ordering can be extremely high. Bidding, which is expensive, is often used. Project managers must buy from a variety of vendors with whom they have had little experience. Because the purchases are essentially one-time, minimum effort is made to bring efficiency and control to the purchasing function. Carrying costs are relatively unimportant, because the inventory is quickly used up; where this is not the case, items are sold for salvage without being held as obsolete inventory. Pilferage may be a significant cost. Out-of-stock costs can be very large, especially if the outages apply to activities along the critical path. The importance of being on time with the project has led to the development of critical path methods that permit a great deal of control over out of stocks. Though these project control methods are costly, they are warranted by the high out-of-stock costs. They help minimize (or entirely eliminate) the number of outages to which the high out-of-stock costs can be applied.

Material Requirements Planning (MRP)

The MRP approach[11] to materials planning makes eminent good sense when demand is infrequent for many different end products. MRP is a management information system. It can keep track of many items. MRP is also applicable when demand, over time, changes size; i.e., demand is not smooth but is lumpy. These descriptions of demand are typical of job shop experience, and include the intermittent flow shop.

In addition, MRP should be used for items and ingredients that are components of the end product. "Material requirements planning calculates requirements for new materials, semi-finished materials or components (parts, subassemblies) based on plans to make the item that these materials go into."[12] We have made reference on a number of occasions to the part composition of end products. For example, see p. 188 for the matrix of modular production and p. 190 for the (parts) explosion chart. The Gozinto chart (see p. 429) is another illustration of the P/OM concern for cascades of end products from components, and components from subcomponents, etc.

For our present purposes, consider the bill of materials (Fig. 12-3, p. 240). It lists all of the parts which go into a specific end product. To explain MRP, let us consider switch Z33 which is part of the end product, 5-HP motor J. First, we draw up the end-product *master schedule*, entering the required production quantities; see Table 15-2.

TABLE 15-2 MASTER SCHEDULE FOR 5-HP MOTOR J

Past Due	Week									
	1	2	3	4	5	6	7	8	9	10
	—	60	—	—	—	80	—	—	40	—

---

[11]MRP has drawn attention only in recent years. However, Orlicky indicates that he and others began its development around 1960. Also, he states, "the number of MRP systems used in American industry gradually grew to about 150 in 1971, when the growth curve began a steep rise as a result of the 'MRP Crusade,' a national program of publicity and education sponsored by the American Production and Inventory Control Society (APICS)." (See Joseph Orlicky, *Material Requirements Planning*. New York: McGraw-Hill Book Company, 1975, p. ix.).

[12]G. W. Plossl and O. W. Wight, "Designing and Implementing a Material Requirements Planning System," *Material Requirements Planning Systems*. Presentations at APICS 13th International Conference by J. A. Orlicky, G. W. Plossl, and O. W. Wight, Cincinnati, Ohio, October 8, 1970.

For *each* part, we draw up the appropriate *component materials plan* (see Table 15-3). Our immediate interest is switch Z33, 1 unit of which is required for each 5-HP motor J. Note that the time between order and delivery (called *lead time*) is 2 weeks.

TABLE 15-3 COMPONENT MATERIALS PLAN FOR SWITCH Z33

Lead Time = 2 Weeks	Past Due	Week									
		1	2	3	4	5	6	7	8	9	10
Gross requirements		—	60	—	—	—	80	—	—	40	—
Stock on hand (SOH)		80	20	20	20	20	—	—	—	—	—
Net requirements		—	—	—	—	—	60	—	—	40	—
Planned order release		—	—	—	60	—	—	40	—	—	—

The production schedule calls for 60 5-HP motor J's in week 2, 80 in week 6, and 40 in week 9. We have 80 units of switch Z33 on hand in week 1. Because 60 J-type motors are scheduled for week 2, the stock on hand (SOH) for switch Z33 will decrease to 20 in week 2. That level of SOH will continue through week 5 when it will be used up, leaving a net requirement of 60 units.

Lot Sizing Policies

We can plan ahead, ordering the 60 units of switch Z33 two weeks in advance, i.e., in week 4 (called *planned order release*). Similarly, we must place an order for 40 units of switch Z33 in week 7 to accommodate the production schedule of week 9. Our ordering policy is *lot for lot*. That is, when the gross requirement for the 5-HP motor J is X, order X units of switch Z33 two weeks in advance.

We should, in fact, call this policy lot for lot with corrections for errors. (This policy, without errors, has zero carrying costs. If set up costs are low, it is a preferred lot sizing policy.) Without errors, we should never have any SOH. But in week 1, the record begins with 80 units of SOH. The reason is that in a prior period, the actual gross requirements fell short of expectations. As a result, excess stock exists which takes 5 weeks to fully dissipate. Carrying charges for this inventory may be high, if the cost per unit for switch Z33 is large.

The *planned order release policy* we have just described tracked net requirements. No attention was paid by that method to the setup costs of each new production run, or to the carrying costs of excessive inventory when the expected gross requirements exceed the actual gross requirements.

We can design a lot sizing policy (called minimum total cost policy) that balances setup (or ordering) costs and carrying costs.[13] To explain, let the unit cost of switch Z33 equal $10. The carrying cost rate will be 1 percent per month, and setup cost to produce switch Z33 is $15.

In Table 15-4, we list monthly net requirements. Then we sum these in the column titled "cumulative lot size." Thus, if we produce enough for the first month only, the lot size is 20 units. If we produce enough for the first 4 months, then the lot size will be 150 units, etc.

TABLE 15-4

Month	Net Requirements	Cumulative Lot Size	Weeks Carried	Carrying Cost	Policy: Order for Months
1	20	20	0	0	1
2	40	60	1	$4	1 + 2
3	60	120	2	$16	1 + 2 + 3
4	30	150	3	$25	1 + 2 + 3 + 4

For each policy, we determine the carrying cost. Thus, if we produce enough for only the first month, there are no carrying costs. Producing for 2 months entails no carrying charges for the first 20 units consumed in month 1, and $4 for the second month. Thus:

$$20 \text{ units} \times \$10/\text{unit} \times (0.01) \times 0 \text{ months carried} = \$0$$
$$40 \text{ units} \times \$10/\text{unit} \times (0.01) \times 1 \text{ month carried} = \$4$$
$$\text{Total} = \$4$$

Producing 120 units for three months requires:

$$20 \text{ units} \times \$10/\text{unit} \times (0.01) \times 0 \text{ months carried} = \$0$$
$$40 \text{ units} \times \$10/\text{unit} \times (0.01) \times 1 \text{ month carried} = \$4$$
$$60 \text{ units} \times \$10/\text{unit} \times (0.01) \times 2 \text{ months carried} = \$12$$
$$\text{Total} = \$16$$

To determine the carrying cost of producing 150 units for 4 months' requirements, we simply add the 3-month total to the carrying cost of the fourth month's net requirements.

---

[13]As will be explained in Chapter 16, when setup (or ordering) costs are equal to carrying costs, total cost is minimized (see pp. 341–46).

$$30 \text{ units} \times \$10/\text{unit} \times (0.01) \times 3 \text{ months carried} = \$9$$

$$\text{Carried forward from 3-month lot size policy} = \underline{\$16}$$

$$\$25$$

The setup cost of $15 is closest to the carrying charges of $16 for a lot size of 3 months' requirements. Consequently, we would produce 120 units at this time. Future computations and results might differ markedly. If this approach is used, both the ordering interval and the quantity ordered will vary over time.

Another possible lot sizing policy is to determine a *fixed order quantity*. This is done by using the EOQ model, which is discussed in Chapter 16, pp. 341–46.[14] The ordering interval then varies according to net requirements.

MRP as an Information System

The appeal of MRP is that its logic extends down the tree of components, subcomponents, etc. For our switch Z33, referring to the bill of materials on p. 240, we now develop net requirements for casing CH/20, drive spring SJ/64 (2 units required per switch), 1-in. rod RH/82 (three units required per switch).

When a change occurs in the gross requirements for 5-HP motor J, the effect cascades all the way down the materials planning tree. *Computer support of this information system is essential.*

A properly organized information system will spot the fact that switch Z33 is also used in other end products than 5-HP motor J. The net requirements for switch Z33 should represent all uses, and the planned order release should reflect the merged net requirements statement.

Updating and Correcting

The master schedule for end products and the component materials plan are updated regularly by a *time shift*. Accordingly, in a weekly schedule, the past week would be dropped and the next week added. As this is done, the computer signals all planned order release dates that have been reached for which orders are to be placed. Deliveries are recorded as increases to stock on hand (SOH). Changes in gross requirements are made according to the latest information.

There are two options for updating. The first of these is called "regeneration." In effect, an entirely new master plan is set up; the old one is discarded. The second approach, called "net change," modifies the existing plan. In a large job shop, both systems demand highly systematic information manage-

---

[14]Nine alternatives are treated by Orlicky; see pp. 120–133 of his book, previously referenced. None of the nine alternatives is clearly superior to all others.

ment. Each has advantages and disadvantages, but overall, the "net change" system has greater appeal, because it identifies the effects of specific changes.

MRP or OPP

We have identified the situations in which MRP is most likely to be the best materials planning route to follow. There are equivalent generalizations that can be made about when not to use MRP and to instead apply order point planning (OPP) techniques, described in Chapter 16.

First, when demand is independent of the production schedule, as it often is for finished goods of flow shops, maintenance supplies, etc., OPP should be used.

Second, with serial production, where process materials must be on hand at all times, OPP should be used.

Third, when demand is fairly regular and continuous, as opposed to being lumpy and sporadic, OPP and MRP should be compared to decide which way to go. If there are many interdependent components, the probability is good that some form of MRP will be beneficial.

Also, it should be noted that various combinations of MRP and OPP are possible. The advantage of bringing them together is that order point planning accents the use of forecasts, while material requirements planning focuses on the interdependencies of components and end products. Materials management that uses both tracks of reasoning is bound to benefit.

Value Analysis (Alternative Materials Analysis)

As a part of materials planning, we include value analysis. The fundamental notion of value analysis is that the quality of the production output must be maintained while at the same time the cost of the output should be decreased. Value analysis is applied to all materials used by the production or service (e.g., materials used by hospitals) process. To distinguish value analysis from *methods analysis*,[15] the latter is primarily concerned with process improvement and only incidentally with materials. We could, and perhaps should, call value analysis "materials analysis." It is inevitable that value and methods analysis must share some common ground; they tackle the same kind of problems, and they provide similar kinds of problem resolution.

Undoubtedly, the surge of interest in value analysis can be explained by the fact that materials technology has been undergoing rapid and dramatic changes. New materials are constantly being made available through research efforts.

---

[15]Methods analysis is the systematic examination of all operations in any process in search of a better way of doing things, e.g., combining operations or eliminating unnecessary operations, making work easier, etc. Method analysts are widely employed by both government and industry.

Also, materials *shortages* have been experienced with increased frequency. As a result, many organizations are faced with the need to make swift alterations in the composition of their products and services. Alternate formulations are prepared by R&D and kept ready for anticipated contingencies. Material shortages hit particularly hard at the flow shop.

With growing frequency, governmental agencies have prohibited the use of well-established materials. The food industry has experienced bans on cyclamates, food dyes, preservatives, etc. The detergent industry has been forced to reformulate its products several times because of ecological effects of phosphorous and enzyme additives. We can expect the announcement of new governmental restrictions to continue and grow in number.

If proper value (alternative materials) analyses have been done, then materials alternatives do not have to be hastily sought when either shortages occur or governmental edicts forbid the use of specific materials.

The procedures of value analysis are applied to established products as well as to new ones. The essence of value analysis is embodied in well-structured *organization of the approach*. This is evidenced by the consistent application of a set of relevant questions. For example:

1. What is this product or service intended to do?
2. How much does it cost to provide this product or service?
3. What materials are used?
4. What other materials could be used?
5. How much does the suggested alternative cost?

The taxonomy of quality, explained on pp. 527–34, reveals that the problems of defining what a product or service is intended to do are enormously complex and not well understood. Accordingly, the utility of value analysis will be dependent upon the knowledge and creative insight that the individuals who are doing these studies can bring to bear. The value analysis approach has been designed to release such insights by providing a structural framework to encourage the development of alternative strategies.

The starting point is the examination of an existing output. The purposes or functions of this output are divided into primary and secondary classes. Significant functions are then related by analogy to other items and then to materials that are thought to provide similar properties.

It is through the *analogic method* that material alternatives are derived. Thus, for example, we might develop comparisons between different joining methods, which include adhesion, cohesion, welding, brazing, and mechanical fastenings such as screws, nuts and bolts, lock washers, cotter pins, and nails. Harking back to decision theory, we find that *both methods analysis* and *value analysis* are primarily intended as a means for *discovering new tactical alternatives*. Any approach that suceeds in improving this aspect of decision making is of real importance when properly used. But we must always guard against investments in efficiency studies before effectiveness issues have been thoroughly considered.

1. How does materials planning differ for the flow shop, the job shop, and the project?

2. With respect to MRP, what is meant by time-phased requirements planning?

3. With respect to MRP, what is the difference between updating by "regeneration" as compared to the "net change" method? Discuss the pros and cons of each.

4. The master schedule for "end product" P is as follows:

Week	Gross Requirements
1	400
2	200
3	200
4	300
5	500
5	100
7	600
8	400

Stock on hand for p_1, a component of P, is 700.
   a. Develop the planned order release schedule for p_1, assuming a lot for lot sizing policy (with corrections for stock on hand).
   b. The cost of a unit of p_1 is $12. The carrying cost rate is 0.25 percent per week. The setup cost to produce p_1 is $48. Lead time is two weeks. Using the minimum total cost policy, determine the appropriate planned order release schedule.

5. Contrast goods and services with respect to "in-process" and "finished" inventories.

6. With what lines of the break-even chart are material inputs associated?

7. Should your company get a computer before or after you organize to introduce material requirements planning? Discuss.

8. List some of the items inventoried by the administration of your school. Do you think they employ the concept of an ABC-type distribution?

9. Assuming that your company has a long history of bidding for jobs, prepare a study that would be useful in evaluating the results to date and in achieving improvements in bidding.
   Answer: A table of the bids offered for all jobs can be compiled. The individuals responsible for the bid should be listed along with a column for pertinent remarks. A column should be left for entry of the company's actual performance on all jobs that have been received, undertaken, and completed. As much as possible, estimates should be made of the winning bidder's costs, after his completion of the project—for those cases where

our company has not been awarded the job. This table, when a sufficient sample has been taken, can be very useful for the analysis of the company's bidding procedures.

10. For the spare-part failure model on pp. 323–26, assume that a salvage value of $2 now exists. Would this alter the solution to the problem?

11. Let us return to City Hospital's problem of how many spares to order with their emergency generator, when $c = 5$ and $c' = 20$. What set of probabilities for $i = 1$, 2, and 3 failures will produce equal expected costs for all three strategies $k = 1$, 2, and 3?

    Answer: Solve the 4 equations

$$5x_1 + 25x_2 + 45x_3 = V$$
$$10x_1 + 10x_2 + 30x_3 = V$$
$$15x_1 + 15x_2 + 15x_3 = V$$
$$x_1 + x_2 + x_3 = 1$$

and you will derive $x_1 = \frac{1}{4}$, $x_2 = 0$, $x_3 = \frac{3}{4}$, and V (the expected value) $= 15$. This last point is obvious from the bottom row of the decision matrix.

12. As production and operations manager of a large company producing copying machines, how do you react to the announcement that the vice president in charge of materials management has set up a value analysis group under the head purchasing agent?

sixteen
order point
inventory systems

Order point planning (OPP) has been in use for many years. The fundamental economic order quantity (EOQ) model (also called the *square root model*) can be traced back to early industrial engineering endeavors, with very practical concerns.[1]

The major mathematical work which underlies present order point models was developed in the 1940s and 1950s.[2] At first, the field emphasized the mathematical aspects of the inventory models at the expense of the inventory problems themselves. However, since 1960, a great deal of effort has gone into making the mathematical methods applicable to real situations.

[1]See, for example, Benjamin Cooper, "How to Determine Economical Manufacturing Quantities," *Industrial Management*, Vol. 72, No. 4, pp. 229–233, 1926; and Raymond E. Fairfield, *Quantity and Economy in Manufacture* (Princeton, N.J.: D. Van Nostrand Company, Inc., 1931).

[2]See, for example, Aryeh Dvoretsky, J. Kiefer, and Jacob Wolfowitz, "The Inventory Problem," *Econometrica*, Vol. 20 (1952), pp. 187–222, 450–66, and Kenneth J. Arrow, Theodore E. Harris, and Jacob Marschak, "Optimal Inventory Policy," *Econometrica*, Vol. 19 (1951), pp. 250–272.

The Economic-Order-Quantity Model (EOQ)—
For Batch Delivery

Let us see how the costs we have defined operate in an inventory system where deliveries of purchased supplies are made at regular intervals. The delivery quantities will be in batches of x units (the order quantity). Also, we shall assume that the production system uses up the inventory at a constant rate and that there is no variability in this rate or in the delivery intervals. Because of the assumptions that we have made, all units ordered will be used up. There will be no salvage costs for excess units, and no stock outages can occur. (Later, we shall take the steps necessary to allow for variability in both the rate of use of inventory and in the delivery interval.)

The conditions that have been proposed apply to many production system configurations. For example, they are applicable to the flow shop, which receives batch deliveries of an item. They are also relevant for the job shop or the project where the question arises: Should all of the needed inventory be purchased at one time?

This is not like the static inventory problem that we considered previously, because *certainty* exists in this inventory system. That is, all inventory purchased will be used up, and no shortage of supplies can occur. Our objective, therefore, is to balance opposing costs so that an optimal inventory procedure can be followed. The logic of our approach is now described.

Figure 16-1 pictures the relationship of the order quantity x, with variable *ordering costs* and *carrying costs*. Let x equal the number of units purchased per order. We see that as the number of units that are purchased at one time

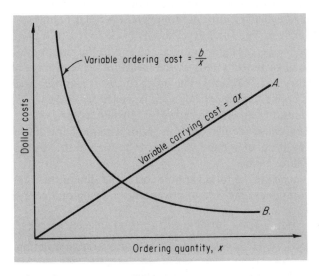

FIGURE 16-1. Variable ordering costs and carrying costs as a function of the order quantity x

increases, the carrying costs rise. This is line *A*. On the other hand, as the number of units per order increases the number of orders that must be placed in a year will decrease. This declining ordering cost is line *B*. Thus, if the demand for a particular item amounts to 500 units per year,[3] we could order all 500 units at one time. Only one order would have to be placed per year. The 500 units would gradually decrease from the beginning to the end of the year so that an average of approximately 250 units would be carried in stock for that year. Figure 16-2 portrays the withdrawal pattern. The carrying cost rate must be applied to the average dollar value of the 250 units. Only one order is to be made, so the ordering cost would be incurred only once.

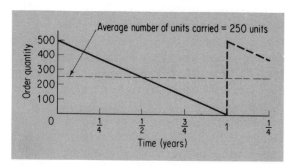

FIGURE 16-2. Continuous withdrawal pattern when *x* = 500 and only one order is placed per year. The demand is 500 units per year.

Now let us consider the policy of ordering twice a year. There would be 250 units ordered with each of two purchase requisitions. These 250 units get used up regularly[4] until nothing is left. At that point, the next order of 250 units arrives. The stock level shoots back up to a full bin of 250 units. Then the decline begins again until, at the end of the year, nothing is left. We now have half of the 250 units as the measure of the average number of units of inventory, viz., 125 units. The ordering cost is incurred twice, but the carrying cost is applied to the smaller average inventory of only 125 units. Figure 16-3 illustrates this, and it also shows what would happen with five orders per year. Each purchase requisition consists of a request for 100 units. The average number of units on hand would now be 50, and the variable cost per order is incurred five times.

In each case the total variable cost is the sum of the total variable ordering cost component and the total variable carrying cost component. Thus:

$$\text{Total variable cost} = \text{total variable carrying cost}$$
$$+ \text{total variable ordering cost}$$

---

[3]For the job shop or the project, the time interval can be set consistent with the activity schedule, e.g., a month, 10 days, or a week.

[4]Meaning at a uniform, continuous rate. If this assumption is not met precisely, it is seldom a serious problem so long as all units get used up in the period.

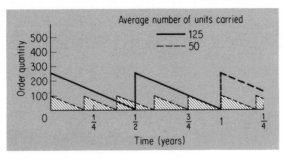

FIGURE 16-3. Continuous withdrawal pattern when $x = 250$ and two orders are placed each year; also when $x = 100$ and five orders are placed each year.

The basis of inventory theory is to write an appropriate cost equation including all possible variable costs, such as obsolescence, pilferage, and so on, if they apply. Then we proceed to minimize this total variable cost equation with respect to the order size x. It is quite clear that different costs result from different ordering policies. The smallest possible carrying charges would occur when we placed 500 orders for one unit at a time. On the other hand, a small ordering cost could be achieved by ordering only once.

Figure 16-4 shows the plot of the total variable cost equation. It is the sum of the two cost factors, ordering cost B and carrying cost A. This equation

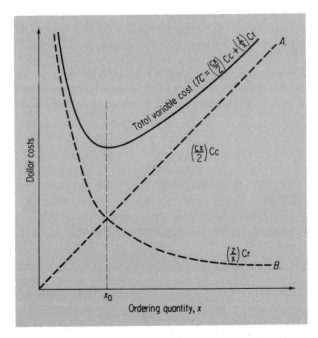

FIGURE 16-4. The total cost resulting from different ordering policies, x, is the sum of the carrying costs, line A, and the ordering costs, line B.

has a minimum (that is, total variable cost is minimized) when $x = x_0$, which is called x optimal.

Let us write the explicit equation for total variable cost.

1. The average number of units carried in stock is $x/2$, where x is the number of units purchased per order.
2. The average dollar inventory carried is $cx/2$, where c is the per unit cost of the item.
3. The total carrying cost per year[5] would be $(cx/2)C_c$, where C_c is the carrying cost rate, applied as a percentage of the product's cost per year (as previously described). This is the first term of the total-cost equation.
4. The number of orders placed per year[6] is z/x, where z is the total demand per year, and x is as has been defined previously.
5. The total ordering cost per year[7] will then be $(z/x)C_r$, where C_r is the variable cost per order. This is the second term of the total-cost equation.

We then describe the total variable cost TC as follows:

$$TC = \left(\frac{cx}{2}\right)C_c + \left(\frac{z}{x}\right)C_r$$

We can minimize this equation by plotting the points for each cost component and then adding them together (see Fig. 16-4). Also, we could use trial and error methods, by substituting different values of x into the total variable cost equation until the minimum value of TC is obtained. Both of these approaches are cumbersome and fortunately unnecessary.

Using one simple fact, we can find the value of x_0. That fact is: the minimum total cost always occurs at the crosspoint of lines A and B.[8] Therefore, if we set $(cx/2)C_c = (z/x)C_r$, and solve for x, we obtain the economic order quantity:

$$x_0 = \sqrt{\frac{2zC_r}{cC_c}}$$

---

[5] As previously mentioned, the time interval can be adjusted to be consistent with the activity schedule.
[6] Ibid.
[7] Ibid.
[8] This statement applies to all equations of the form $y = ax + b/x$.

The Lion's Den

This famous student lounge is managed by a business student who learned about the EOQ model in a P/OM course. The manager decided to try out EOQ on one item with the idea of extending its use to other items if satisfied. Accordingly, the following estimates for determining the optimal order quantity for napkins were derived.

$$\text{Carrying cost rate} = C_c = 0.06 \text{ per year}$$
$$\text{Price} = c = \$0.005 \text{ per napkin}$$
$$\text{Demand} = z = 3000 \text{ napkins per month}$$
$$= 36{,}000 \text{ napkins per year}$$
$$\text{Cost per order} = C_r = \$2 \text{ per order}$$

Then, the total variable cost equation could be written and simplified.

$$TC = \left(\frac{0.005x}{2}\right)0.06 + \left(\frac{36{,}000}{x}\right)2 = 0.00015x + \frac{72{,}000}{x}$$

The manager used the EOQ formulation

$$x_0 = \sqrt{\frac{2zC_r}{cC_c}} = \sqrt{\frac{2\,(36{,}000)\,(2)}{(0.005)\,(0.06)}} = \sqrt{480{,}000{,}000} = 21{,}909$$

and thereby determined that 21,909 napkins should be ordered at one time (actually 22,000, since orders must be placed in units of 1000). This represents about $7\frac{1}{3}$ months' supply. The present policy is to order 3000 napkins on a monthly basis.

Since there was such a great difference in policy indicated, the manager decided to compare the total variable costs for each policy. Thus:

$$x = 3000 \qquad TC = 0.00015(3000) + \frac{72{,}000}{3000} = \$24.45$$

$$x_0 = 22{,}000 \qquad TC_0 = 0.00015(22{,}000) + \frac{72{,}000}{22{,}000} = \$6.57$$

Indeed, there is a big difference, but such small sums were involved that the manager wondered whether EOQ was worth the bother. Then he thought, "I spend 36,000(0.005) = \$180.00 a year on napkins. By using the EOQ policy, I save \$24.45 − 6.57 = \$17.88, which is almost like a 10 percent discount on the purchase price. If I can do as well on many other purchased items, it will add up to a substantial overall saving." (Still, there was a nagging thought: "Where am I going to store a seven months' supply of napkins?")

This inventory model provides the *economic order quantity*, EOQ. It has great utility in itself, and, at the same time, is the most important equation in all inventory theory. Upon it is built a variety of models that reflect the interplay of additional relevant factors. But this foundation model, which is useful for flow shops, job shops, and projects, signals the square-root relationship between optimal order size and all of the factors that influence what is optimal.

Even when risk exists in the system, the EOQ model can be employed, and then a *reserve stock level* would be added (see pp. 354–60). Other modifications of this model permit stock outages to occur at some fixed level. Discounts can be examined to see whether it would benefit the company to take advantage of them (see pp. 351–53). When the inventory is self-supplied by the production system, rather than purchased from an external vendor, the model can be converted to indicate the optimal run size. This variant, called the economic lot size model, is the subject of the next section. For all these cases, and many others as well, the appropriate value of x_0 that will produce a minimum cost can be readily determined by equation and not by intuition.

The Economic Lot Size Model (ELS)—
For Continuous Delivery (not continuous production)

Having investigated the relationship that describes the optimal order quantity when purchase orders are delivered (by an outside vendor or one's own shop) in batches, let us now consider a comparable problem—identical in all respects, except that the vendor provides continuous delivery, or, more likely, the company is its own supplier, providing continuous delivery. Figure 16-5 illustrates the difference between batch and serial delivery systems.

We call this formulation the economic lot-size model, ELS, because the production run quantity is called a "lot." Figure 16-6 depicts the variations in stock level over time for the continuous delivery situation. The sharp, sawtooth form that applied to the EOQ case, where a total shipment of stock was delivered at one point in time, has been replaced by a gradual stock buildup. There is continuous withdrawal, so the stock level reaches a maximum and then begins to decline. We can see why the ELS model (which determines production run size) is of primary interest to a supplier or self-supplier, whereas the EOQ model (which determines the order quantity) captures the interest of the purchaser. The key to understanding the role of the ELS model is that it provides continuous delivery with discontinuous production. Thus, it epitomizes the intermittent flow shop, which is sometimes used to supply inventory required by the paced-flow shop. Such intermittent flow shops will often be encountered in the job shop, but only rarely for project systems.

Yet, the ELS model (as will be shown) really runs the gamut from the continuous production of the flow shop to very short production runs. When the vendor delivers the economic order quantity to the buyer, the production of the required batch can be thought of as instantaneous. Let us develop the model so that we can examine these relationships. As we have stated, x_0 is the optimal run size.

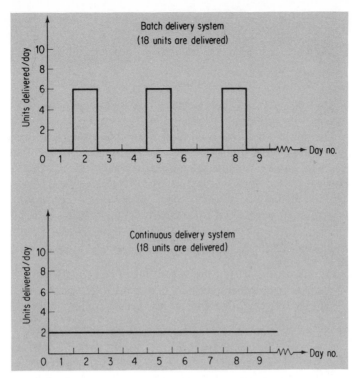

FIGURE 16-5. Contrasting batch and continuous delivery systems

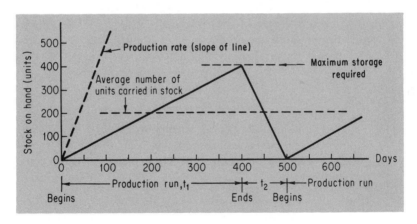

FIGURE 16-6. The economic lot size model, ELS, used to determine the optimal production run
It also can be used to study the effect of varying the production rate.

The cost of an order is no longer relevant. In its place we substitute C_s, which is the setup cost. Usually it is much larger than the order cost. The setup cost is composed of at least two parts: (1) the cost of labor required to

347

prepare the facility for the new production run and (2) the cost of lost production occasioned by the facility's being down while being prepared for the new job. In addition, we shall name two other variables:

$$p = \text{production rate in units per day}$$

$$d = \text{demand rate in units per day.}$$

The optimal run size is derived in a manner similar to the derivation of the economic order quantity.

Our total variable cost equation is

$$TC = \left(\frac{cx}{2}\right)\left(\frac{p-d}{p}\right)C_c + \left(\frac{z}{x}\right)C_s$$

where $\left(\frac{p-d}{p}\right)\frac{x}{2}$ can be shown to be the average number of units carried in the inventory. Setting the two terms of the equation for total variable cost equal to each other (because minimum total variable cost occurs at the x value, where the 2 lines in Fig. 16-4 cross), we obtain the value for x_0.

$$x_0^2 = \left(\frac{2zC_s}{cC_c}\right)\left(\frac{p}{p-d}\right)$$

and

$$x_0 = \sqrt{\frac{2zC_s}{cC_c}\left(\frac{p}{p-d}\right)}$$

Furthermore, the production run x_0 must equal pt_1 (where t_1 = the length of time of the production run). Since $x_0 = pt_1$, we can solve for t_1 as follows:

$$t_1 = \frac{x_0}{p}$$

We know that the period of each cycle $t = t_1 + t_2 = x_0/d$ (where t_2 = the length of time between production runs). For a graphical explanation of t_1 and t_2 see Fig. 16-6 on p. 347. The explanation of this equation follows from the fact that

$$x_0 = dt$$

which means that the optimal run size must satisfy the demand per day times the number of days of the cycle. Then,

$$t_2 = t - t_1 = \frac{x_0}{d} - \frac{x_0}{p} = x_0\left(\frac{p-d}{pd}\right)$$

so we are now able to compute production run time t_1 and the time between production runs t_2.

This company produces inexpensive ball point pens, using a flow shop configuration. The ink cartridges are made on an intermittent flow shop where different colors are run successively. Blue ink is the major color, having by far the largest share of sales. Penmakers has obtained new equipment for producing the ink cartridges and wishes to recalculate the optimal production run size for blue cartridges.

The following data have been assembled.

$$\text{Yearly demand} = z = 200{,}000 \text{ per year} = 250d$$
$$\text{Daily demand} = d = 800 \text{ per day} = z/250$$

(*Note:* We are assuming 250 working days per year. Consequently, daily demand d multiplied by 250 days is equal to yearly demand. From this we can determine the value of d.)

$$\text{Daily production} = p = 1800 \text{ per day}$$
$$\text{Setup cost} = C_s = \$20 \text{ per setup}$$
$$\text{Carrying cost rate} = C_c = 0.15 \text{ of the unit cost per year}$$
$$\text{Unit cost} = c = \$0.06 \text{ per cartridge}$$

The optimal lot size x_0 would be

$$x_0 = \sqrt{\frac{(2)(200{,}000)(20)(1800)}{(0.06)(0.15)(1000)}} = \sqrt{\frac{(144)(10^8)}{9}} = \frac{(12)(10^4)}{3}$$
$$= 40{,}000 \text{ cartridges}$$

The production run time is

$$t_1 = \frac{x_0}{p} = \frac{40{,}000}{1800} = 22.22 \text{ days}$$

The cycle period is determined:

$$t = t_1 + t_2 = \frac{x_0}{d} = \frac{40{,}000}{800} = 50 \text{ days}$$

and so the period between runs is

$$t_2 = x_0 \left(\frac{p - d}{pd}\right) = 40{,}000 \left(\frac{1000}{800 \times 1800}\right) = 27.78 \text{ days}$$

This means that Penmakers will have about 28 days to run all other color cartridges. Fitting them on to the line will not be an easy task. An approach that can be followed to determine the optimal run sizes for a sequence of items produced serially on the same facility is described in Appendix 16-I, (pp. 364–366) as optional material.

The Range of ELS—from EOQ
to Continuous Production

Consider the ELS equation for optimal run size:

$$x_0 = \sqrt{\frac{2zC_s}{cC_c}\left(\frac{p}{p-d}\right)}$$

If d is almost equal to p, then $(p-d)$ approaches 0. This means that x_0 becomes very large, approaching infinity as the difference between d and p approaches 0. This result makes sense. In effect it states: If the demand rate is as great as the production rate, then run the process continuously. There is no inventory buildup, and the line in Fig. 16-6 showing stock on hand runs flat against the x axis. On the other hand, if p is very much greater than d, that is, $p \gg d$, then x_0 equals EOQ. The increasing stock on hand line rises almost perpendicularly as in Fig. 16-2 and 16-3. The producer is literally able to supply the order quantity on demand, much as is the case when delivery is received from an outside vendor. This result is also reasonable. The condition that is given approximates the state of being able to receive total replenishment upon request.

Lead Time

For both economic order quantity (EOQ) and the economic lot size (ELS) systems, the lead time required to supply items for inventory must be known In Fig. 16-7, the lead time or replenishment time is called LT; the reorder point (RP) is the stock level at which a new order should be placed.

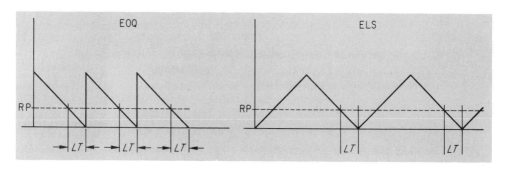

FIGURE 16-7. When lead time (*LT*) is known, at a specific level of stock (*RP*), a new order is placed.

Consider the EOQ case. The obvious components of lead time include the period for recognition of the fact that it is time to reorder; the interval for doing whatever clerical work is needed (vendor releasing has advantages here—see p. 322); mail or telephone intervals for communicating with the vendor; then, recognition of the order by the vendor, who will see whether the requested items are in stock, and if not, will set up to make them. Next, the vendor ships the items, so there is delivery time. The items are delivered but must be processed by the receiving department, which may require inspection. Until the items are entered on the warehouse stock cards, the lead time continues. Similar descriptions could be given for the ELS case, where the sometimes illusory advantages of dealing within your own firm, and thereby having greater control, appear.

It should be noted that when the EOQ model is applied to self-supply with batch production, appropriate lead times should be included in the schedule.

Lead times can be variable. When they are, estimates must be made of the variability, and appropriate steps must be taken to include the effects of variability in the analyses. Usually, a larger estimate of lead time than the expected value is used, e.g., (1.5)LT.

Quantity-discount Model

If a quantity discount is offered, should it be taken? When does the discount potential override the selection of the optimal undiscounted order quantity x_0? By using sets of total-cost equations,[9] it is possible to analyze whether or not a quantity discount that is offered should cancel out the x_0 value associated with the undiscounted minimum total cost.

The discounting situation is directly reflected by the following schedule:

Quantity (x Units)	Cost per Unit	Total Cost
$x = 0$ to x_1	c	$TC(c)$
$x = x_1$ and greater	c' (c' less than c)	$TC(c')$

Consulting Fig. 16-8, we see that 2 total cost equations are drawn. Note that each curve includes its own respective dollar volume cost (cz for the first curve and $c'z$ for the second curve), since dollar volume cost is a variable factor of the discount problem.

The top curve $TC(c)$ is based on an undiscounted cost c. The bottom curve $TC(c')$ is applicable when a discount is available, *but it is only applicable at and above the quantity needed* to obtain the discount. Let x_j be the specified quantity required to obtain the discount. If x_j is x_1 in Fig. 16-8, then the discount must be taken. In fact the order quantity should be increased from x_1 to x_b, which intersects point b. Point b is the minimum total cost that can be obtained in the discount region.

Note that the top curve applies from $x = 0$ to $x < x_1$; the bottom curve applies for $x \geq x_1$. Figure 16-9 illustrates this discontinuity. The cost of point

---

[9]We did not forget to say total variable costs, since for discount analysis it is imperative to include the *new variable*, cost of goods purchased.

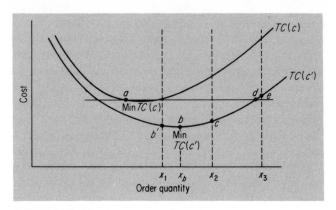

FIGURE 16-8. The discount model involves more than one total-cost equation, but when the discount is specified, only one discontinuous curve applies.

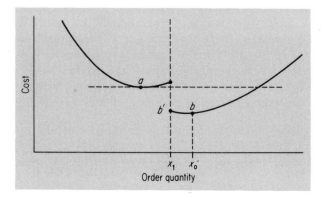

FIGURE 16-9. An example of a specific discounting situation where x_0 is the indicated order quantity so the discount should be taken

b is lower than that of point b'. In Fig. 16-8, when x_j is specified at x_2, then point c provides a lower cost then point a. Point a is the minimum total cost without the discount. Point c is the lowest total cost that is available in the discount region. So x_2 units should be purchased. Again with reference to Fig. 16-8, if $x_j = x_3$, the interesected cost point is e, which is a greater cost than a. Therefore, the order quantity corresponding to point a should be used.

The same reasoning can be extended to more than one price break for quantity discounts, and a purely mathematical approach can be used as well.[10] If the quantity specified for discount intersected point d, the manager (theoretically) would be indifferent between buying the small amount at point a or buying the large amount at point d. In fact, the manager would consider

[10]Martin K. Starr and David W. Miller, *Inventory Control: Theory and Practice* (Englewood Cliffs, N.J.: Prentice-Hall, Inc., 1962), pp. 84–86.

a variety of intangibles such as: is the item ordinarily hard to get; is there possibility of a strike; could we corner the supply to our competitive advantage? Is there a speculative advantage? All of these notions could favor point *d*. On the other hand, does this item spoil easily, does it require a lot of storage space, does it experience a high pilferage rate? These last thoughts are more likely to favor purchasing the smaller quantity associated with point *a*.

Question: Travelmasters, Inc., present their customers who have purchased travel arrangements with a soft canvas shoulder-strap bag. The company that furnishes these bags to Travelmasters has suggested that if the order quantity is doubled, it would discount the cost per bag by 20 percent. At present Travelmasters buys 600 imprinted bags at a time (a 2 months' supply) for $1.50 per bag. Should the discount be taken?

Answer: Since this is a small company, we shall assume a carrying cost rate of 5 percent per year (equivalent to the investment return of a commercial bank). Ordering cost will be set at $3. Then:

$$x_0 = \sqrt{\frac{2(3600)(3)}{(1.5)(0.05)}} = 536.66$$

Without the discount, Travelmasters is buying about the right quantity. With the discount, the optimal ordering quantity would be

$$x_0' = \sqrt{\frac{2(3600)3}{(1.2)(0.05)}} = 600$$

The discount begins at $x = 1200$, so the optimal order quantity with the discount does not fall in the appropriate discount region. Still, we must compare the total cost at the optimal order quantity $x_0 = 536.66$ with the total cost at the discount boundary $x = 1200$.

$$TC(x_0 = 536.66) = \frac{1.5}{2}(0.05)[536.66] + \frac{3600}{[536.66]}(3) + 3600(1.5)$$

$$= \$5440.25$$

$$TC(x = 1200) = \frac{1.2}{2}(0.05)[1200] + \frac{3600}{[1200]}(3) + 3600(1.2)$$

$$= \$4365.00$$

Therefore, by all means, Travelmasters should accept the discount, buying 1200 canvas bags at a time and thereby saving $1075.25 per year.

The economic lot-size model and the economic order quantity model are based on the assumption that there will be no variability in demand. In most practical instances this assumption cannot be sustained. As a result, a class of inventory models has been designed to cope with situations where the demand level fluctuates.

These models apply to both the intermittent flow shop and to the paced-flow shop as well. In the latter case, variability of demand can arise from changes in the number of rejects, as this affects order shipments. It can also occur if the paced-conveyor rate is changed from time to time. In general, these models do not apply to job shops where there is no continuity of demand (therefore, the same can be said about projects). Static inventory models (see pp. 324–28) do apply. When there is continuous but lumpy demand for the job shop, the methods of MRP should be used.

The Need to Handle Demand Variability

The department store is an excellent example of a mixture of inventory situations. Some items are ordered once. What is left over is discounted and remaindered (salvage). Shortages cannot be made up.

Other items are stocked regularly, and the demands for these vary greatly. The buyer properly orders the economic order quantity, but has on hand some extra stock (called reserve stock) so that when demand is heavier than expected, customers' orders can still be filled. There is extra carrying cost for the reserve stock, so two questions must be answered: How much reserve stock should be carried? When should an order be placed?

Many companies use perpetual inventory systems to determine when they should order next. The perpetual inventory system works as follows: Withdrawal quantities are entered on the item's stock card each and every time that a unit is withdrawn from stock. The withdrawal quantity is subtracted from the previous stock level to determine the present quantity of stock on hand. A *minimum level* is designated as the *reorder level* for each item. This reorder point quantity is marked on the respective stock card. When the minimum level has been reached, then an order is placed for the economic order quantity, x_0.

The level of stock represented by the reorder point (RP) is equal to the expected demand *in the lead time* (LT), plus what is called the reserve stock or buffer stock (BS).[11] This buffer has been designed to absorb a certain percentage of the fluctuations in demand that are likely to occur for each particular item. The buffer stock is geared to provide some chosen level of protection against stock outages. The level that is chosen is based on the balance of out-of-stock costs and carrying costs associated with the buffer stock. We have drawn Fig. 16-10 to illustrate the way in which a perpetual inventory system operates. Note that when demand is heavy, the RP is reached quickly.

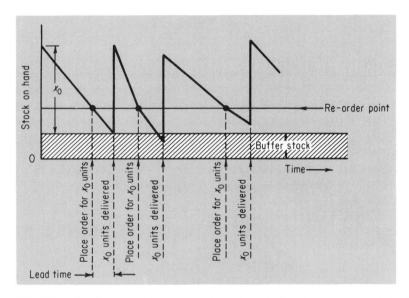

FIGURE 16-10. A perpetual inventory system where stock on hand is recomputed with each withdrawal

---

[11]This rule always applies when the lead time is equal to or less than the optimal period between reorders (t_0), i.e., $LT < (x_0/z = t_0)$. However, a rule that covers all situations, including the cases where $LT \geq t_0$, is now given. The reorder point RP should be calculated as follows: $RP = BS +$ fractional part of $\left[\frac{LT}{t_0}\right]x_0$. The fractional part of $\left[\frac{LT}{t_0}\right]x_0$ is equivalent to the expected demand in the lead time period, less deliveries that occur in the lead time period. Deliveries are represented by integer values of $\left[\frac{LT}{t_0}\right]$.

Perhaps the best way to explain the equation above is by an example. Assume that the lead time LT is two days, and the optimal period between reorders is $t_0 = x_0/z = 110/60 = 1.83$ days. Thus:
$$t_0 = 1.83 \text{ days} < LT = 2 \text{ days}$$
Buffer stock is specified as $BS = 20$ and $x_0 = 110$ has also been given. Therefore,
$$RP = 20 + \text{fractional part of } \left[\frac{2}{1.83}\right]110.$$
The fractional part of $\left[\frac{2}{1.83}\right] = 1.09$ is 0.09, whence
$$RP = 20 + 0.09(110) = 29.9, \text{ or } 30 \text{ units.}$$

The calculation of the reorder point is not difficult to accomplish. First, as has been noted, stock must be provided to cover the expected demand *in the lead time period*. Call this *S*. Then additional buffer stock is to be provided which gives some specified level of protection against *going out of stock* in the same lead time interval. Call this additional inventory *BS*. Figure 16-11 depicts the situation for a probability distribution of demand in the lead time period.

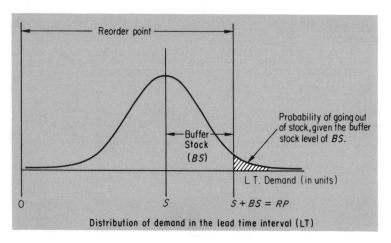

FIGURE 16-11. Determination of the reorder point (*RP*)
It is *S* + *BS* units where *S* is expected demand in the lead time interval.

Storemasters, Inc. (I)—An Example of the Perpetual Inventory System in Use

This department store chain intends to install computerized, perpetual inventory control for all *A*-type items (see pp. 327–28) in its inventory. For a trial run, they have decided to use a high-volume face cream in the cosmetics department. This face cream has an expected demand per day of 20 jars. Sometimes the demand goes as high as 30 and infrequently it drops as low as 10 jars.

The lead time between placing an order with the supplier and receiving the replenishment stock is regular, since the supplier's warehouse is nearby and this face cream is in continuous production. Lead time is 2 days. Accordingly, we know that the expected demand *in the lead time interval* is 40 jars.

To this number 40 (which matches *expected demand* in the interval elapsing between placing the order and receiving it, inspecting it, and putting it in stock) we want to add buffer stock to protect against outages caused by greater than expected demand. By keeping appropriate records, it is determined that the demand in any 2-day period exceeds 60 jars only once out of every hundred 2-day periods that we have studied. Storemasters has decided that it is desirable to be protected at this level. That is, only once in a hundred lead time periods (of 2 days) will Storemasters be unable to fill a customer's order for face cream. Thus, it has been determined that the *reorder point* will be 40 + 20 = 60 jars. Further, that buffer (or reserve) stock is 20 jars.

Notice that the reorder point analysis is independent of the calculation of the economic order quantity. This is true because out-of-stock protection is solely a function of expected demand in the lead time period and the variability of extra demand in the lead time period.[12] Storemasters has determined the reserve stock without using estimates of real costs for being out of stock. It is better to use real costs, but if we lack them, it is entirely feasible to estimate how often we are willing to allow stock outages.[13]

To illustrate how the perpetual inventory system works, we will simulate daily demand and track the stock level to determine when to place an order. Let us suppose that the economic order quantity has been determined to be $x_0 = 110$ jars. An order has just been received and we have on hand 110 jars.

TABLE 16-1

Day	(Begining of Day) Stock on Hand	Simulated Demand	Units Ordered at Reorder Point	Order Received
1	110	25		
2	85	30		
3	55	20	110	
4	35	15		
5	20 + 110 = 130	36		110
6	94	18		
7	76	22		
8	54	25	110	
9	29	17		
10	12 + 110 = 122	19		110
11	103	25		
12	78	32		
etc.	etc.	etc.		

In this simulation, the average daily demand is 23.67 (our expectation is 20). Two orders have been placed in 12 days [our expectation is $(12 \times 20)/110 = 2.18$]. (Note: For this calculation, expected demand for 12 days is divided by x_0.) Stock on hand dropped as low as 12 on the tenth day, but this was immediately replenished by the receipt of the second order. Although the

---

[12]This statement does not strictly apply to the case where $LT \geq t_0$ (see footnote 11). Whenever the lead time period includes a delivery, we subtract the delivered number of units x_0 from the reorder point RP. Thus, the economic order quantity does affect the reorder point analysis, but only because a delivery of this amount has been made. The fractional part of LT/t_0 remains independent of the calculation of EOQ.

[13]It is also useful to point out that lead time can vary (although we have held it constant). With variable lead time, we would increase the size of the reserve stock.

simulation is simple, it does reveal to Storemasters the operation of the perpetual inventory system.

The Two-bin System for Perpetual Inventory Control

The two-bin system provides a clever way of continuously monitoring the order point in a perpetual inventory system. Figure 16-12 is almost self-explanatory in this regard.

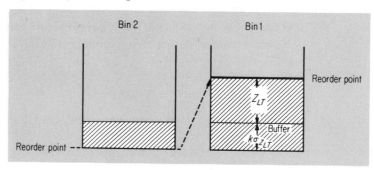

FIGURE 16-12. A two-bin perpetual inventory system
When Bin 2 is depleted, an order is placed for the EOQ.

When a replenishment order is received, Bin 1 is filled to the reorder point level. The remainder of the order is placed in Bin 2. If Bin 1 is at the reorder point level, all of the incoming items are placed in Bin 2. When Bin 2 is emptied, a new order is placed. The two-bin system is not feasible for many kinds of items, but when it is, a great deal of clerical work is eliminated.

Periodic Inventory Systems

Periodic systems are based on the determination of a *fixed* and regular review period. Some items may be reviewed once a week, others once a month, semi-annually, or yearly. The optimal period is determined by $x_0/z = t_0$. Usually, certain items have shorter review periods than others.[14] These would be items with large demands. Thus,

$$t_0 = \frac{x_0}{z} = \frac{1}{z}\sqrt{\frac{2zC_r}{cC_c}} = \sqrt{\frac{2C_r}{cC_c z}}$$

However, even if the demand level is relatively high, the time between reviews may be short, because, for example, the cost per unit c is high.

At each review, the stock on hand is determined. An order is then placed for a *variable* quantity. This quantity is larger than usual when demand has

[14]Although t_0 is most often a fraction of a year, it may be greater than a year.

been greater than expectation. It is smaller than usual when demand has been less than expected. Thus, in the case of the periodic inventory model, the review period is fixed, but the order quantity is variable. Figure 16-13 illustrates the way in which a periodic ordering system functions.

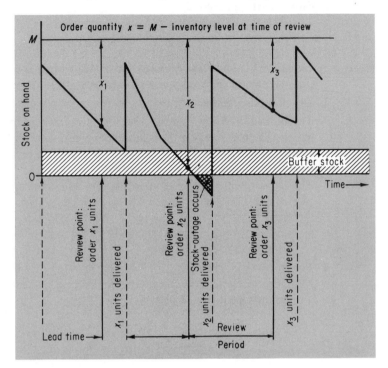

FIGURE 16-13. A periodic inventory system where stock on hand is computed only at fixed intervals
At that time, an order *x* of variable size is placed.

The target level *M* is determined by calculating the expected demand in a *review period plus one lead time interval*. To this is added buffer stock, which offers protection against excessive demand in a *review period plus one lead time interval*. It may be noted that the same kind of reasoning applies in this case as was explained when Fig. 16-11 was introduced.

When the optimal order quantity x_0 is subtracted from the target level *M*, the remaining stock size is somewhat larger than the reorder point of the perpetual inventory model. It is greater because the planning period for *M* must be 1 review period plus 1 lead time interval. Extra inventory has to be carried, and this is an added cost of using the periodic inventory system.

On the other hand, the clerical costs of the perpetual model are higher than those of the periodic model.[15] The clerical cost advantage of the periodic

---

[15]The use of the two-bin system, when it is feasible, can reduce the clerical cost of operating a perpetual inventory system, because the reorder point signal is automatic. Many items, however, cannot be stored in bins and do not lend themselves to this arrangement.

model disappears, however, when on-line, real-time computer systems operate the perpetual model's calculation requirements. As a result, there is a distinct trend toward perpetual systems and away from periodic ones. For calculations of the periodic inventory system, see (as optional material) Appendix 16-II, pp. 366–367.

PROBLEMS
1. Explain why the 2-bin, perpetual inventory system is particularly appropriate for small items, such as nuts and bolts. Could it be used for liquids?

2. Develop the arguments pro and con for order point models.

3. The Bureau of Water Testing uses a chemical reagent that costs $500 per gallon. The use is regular at $\frac{1}{3}$ gallon per week. Carrying cost rate is considered to be 12 percent per year, and the cost of an order is $125.
   a. What is the optimal order quantity?
   The Department of Maintenance Supplies could make this reagent at the rate of $\frac{1}{8}$ gallon per day, at a cost of $300 per gallon. The setup cost is $150.
   b. How has your answer changed? What course of action do you recommend?

4. For the data in Problem 3, the vendor, learning that the Department of Maintenance Supplies is considering making the reagent, has now offered a discount schedule, as follows:

c	x_j
$500	1
450	2
450	3
400	4
400	5
380	6 and up

Should any of these discounts be taken?

5. Modify Storemasters' perpetual inventory model (see pp. 356–58) as follows: Face cream has an expected demand of 15,000 jars per year (or 60 jars per day). Lead time is 3 days. It has been determined that demand in any 3-day period exceeds 200 jars only once out of every hundred 3-day periods. This outage level (of 1 in a 100 LT periods) is considered acceptable by P/OM. The economic order quantity has been derived as 2820 jars.
   Set up the perpetual inventory system.

6. Use the information given in Problem 5, plus the fact that it has been determined that demand in any 50-day period exceeds 4000 jars only

once out of every hundred 50-day periods. This outage level (of 1 in a 100 LT periods) is considered acceptable by P/OM.

Set up the periodic inventory system.

7. Compare the results derived in Problems 5 and 6 above. What are your recommendations, taking into account all of the characteristics of perpetual and periodic inventory systems?

8. If, in a dynamic inventory problem under certainty, the costs are

$$c = \$10 \text{ per item}$$
$$C_c = 16 \text{ percent per year}$$
$$z = 5000 \text{ units per year}$$
$$C_r = \$10 \text{ per order}$$

What is the optimal order quantity? Now, assume that you are going to make this same item with equipment that is estimated to produce $p = 30$ units per day. Also, c then equals $6 per item and $C_s = \$150$ per setup. How has your answer changed? What would you do?

Answer: The optimal order quantity is

$$x_0 = \sqrt{\frac{2zC_r}{cC_c}} = \sqrt{\frac{2(5000)10}{10(0.16)}} = 250$$

To compare this result with self-supply, given the decreased cost per item and the increased setup cost as compared to order cost, we have

$$\sqrt{\frac{2zC_s}{cC_c}\left(\frac{p}{p-d}\right)} = \sqrt{\frac{2(5000)150}{6(0.16)}\left(\frac{30}{30 - \frac{5000}{250}}\right)}$$
$$= 2165$$

The optimal run size with self-supply is more than 8 times the optimal order quantity. The run time would be: $t_1 = 2165/30 = 72.17$ days. Average inventory under self-supply conditions is

$$\frac{y}{2} = \frac{(p-d)t_1}{2} = \frac{10(72.17)}{2} = 360.85 \text{ units}$$

If the item is ordered from a vendor, the average inventory is 125 units. Average dollar inventory for the self-supply situation is $2165.10, whereas for the outside purchase it is $1250. When we compare yearly total costs TC, we find that with outside suppliers, total cost is $400 + 5000(10) = \$50,400$; with self-supply, the total cost is $693 + 5000(6) = \$30,693$.

On the face of it, we should use self-supply. However, many other factors are important that are not included in these equations—for example, skills and abilities that are available within the company, the existing demand levels with respect to existing capacity, etc.

9. The C & B Food Company bottles instant coffee, which it purchases periodically in quantities of 120,000 lb. The coffee mixture costs C & B $2.40 per lb. The company ships 1,2000,000 one-pound bottles of instant coffee per year to its distributors. The demand is constant and continuous over time. What carrying cost (in percent per month) is implied by the above policy if an order costs $100 on the average? Discuss your result.

Answer: From the economic order quantity inventory model we know

$$x_0 = \sqrt{\frac{2zC_r}{cC_c}}$$

where in this case:

$$x_0 = 120,000 \text{ lb (We are assuming optimal}$$
$$\text{procedures to impute } C_c.)$$

$$z = 1,200,000 \text{ lb}$$

$$C_r = \$100$$

$$c = \$2.40$$

Substituting and solving for C_c, we obtain

$$C_c = \tfrac{1}{144} = 0.7 \text{ percent per year}$$

This implied carrying cost does not consider possible fluctuations in coffee market prices which may determine C & B's buying pattern during the year. In any case, the percentage is far too low. It is obvious that C & B is not following an optimal ordering policy.

10. What production run lengths would you recommend for the following items?

i	z_i (per year)	C_{s_i}	c_i	p_i (per day)
1	200	100	6	10
2	400	50	10	12
3	600	20	15	14
4	800	80	9	20

where $C_c = 0.24$ per year and $z_i = 250d_i$.

Could all of these items be scheduled to run on the same equipment? Discuss.

11. A quantity discount schedule has been offered for the situation discussed in Problem 8. It is

c	x_j
10	up to 300
9	300 to 499
8	500 and up

Should either of these discounts be taken?

Answer: We must determine the relevant portions of the total cost function with discounted costs.

For $c = \$9$

$$x_0 = \sqrt{\frac{2(5000)10}{9(0.16)}} = 263.5 \text{ units}$$

For $c = \$8$

$$x_0 = \sqrt{\frac{2(5000)10}{8(0.16)}} = 279.5 \text{ units}$$

From the results in Problem 8 we know that for $c = \$10$, $x_0 = 250$ units. This is the only real minimum optimal value, since the others violate the quantity discount breaks. As shown in Fig. 16-14, we must still investigate the total costs at the quantity breaks. [Note that in this case $TC = (cx/2)C_c + (z/x)C_r + zc$.]

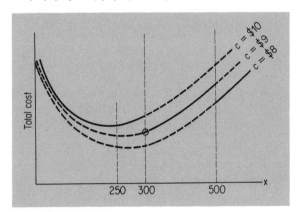

FIGURE 16-14

	c = *10*	c = *9*	c = *8*
x_0	250	263.5*	279.5*
TC at x_0	$400 + (10)(5000)	*	*
TC at x = 300	*	$383 + 9(5000)	*
TC at x = 500	*	*	$420 + (8)(5000)

*not relevant

Clearly, we should order 500 units at $8 per unit, with $TC = \$40{,}420$.

12. Under what circumstances would you prefer a periodic inventory system to a perpetual system?

13. For Storemasters' use of the perpetual inventory system, it has been decided to run an additional 12 days of simulated demand. The numbers to be used are

Day	13	14	15	16	17	18	19	20	21	22	23	24
Demand	32	25	19	17	25	22	18	36	15	20	30	25

Describe your results.

14. Cardmakers' manager of the greeting card production department has been buying 2 roles of acetate at a time. They cost $200 each. Card production requires 10 rolls per year. Ordering cost is estimated to be $4 per order. What carrying cost rate is imputed?

Answer:

$$2 = \sqrt{\frac{2(10)4}{200C_c}}$$

$$4 = \frac{2(10)4}{200C_c}$$

$$C_c = 0.10$$

which seems reasonable.

———————

The following problem relates to Appendix 16-I

15. Referring to Problem 10, determine the production run lengths necessary for all items to be scheduled on the same equipment. Compare your results with those obtained in Problem 10.

APPENDIX 16-I
Multi-Item Flow Shop Systems (Optional Material)

It is not unusual for a variety of *different* items to *follow one another* in serial fashion through the system. This is an intermittent flow shop, all items being produced on the same equipment, in the same sequence, but requiring some new setups as each different item begins production. Our previous discussions concerning sequencing models might well be applied here. Given that a best sequence of items is known (or if the order of processing is not relevant to cost), then a simple formulation has been suggested concerning the amount of each item to run.[16] There are *n* different products that are all

———————

[16]See J. F. Magee and D. M. Boodman, *Production Planning and Inventory Control*, 2nd ed. (New York: McGraw-Hill Book Co., Inc., 1967), pp. 354–356.

made on the same equipment, and each product is made only *once* in the cycle. Using i to denote specific products, we find that the optimal run sizes would be

$$x_{o_i} = \sqrt{\frac{2z_i^2 \sum_i^n C_{s_i}}{\sum_i^n (cC_c)_i z_i \left(1 - \frac{d_i}{p_i}\right)}}$$

As an example, let us treat Penmakers' case (pp. 349–50) where blue, red, and green ink cartridges are to be made in the sequence blue, red, green. It will be noted that red has a high setup cost, since it follows blue, which stains the equipment more than the other colors.

	Blue	Red	Green
z	200,000	150,000	100,000
d	800	600	400
p	1,800	1,800	1,800
C_s	20	100	40
C_c	0.15	0.15	0.15
c	0.06	0.06	0.06

Then[17]

$$x(\text{blue})_0 = \sqrt{\frac{2(4 \times 10^{10})160}{2600}} = 70,164.64 \quad \begin{cases} t = 87.70 \\ t_1 = 38.98 \\ t_2 = 48.72 \end{cases}$$

$$x(\text{red})_0 = \sqrt{\frac{2(2.25 \times 10^{10})160}{2600}} = 52,623.48 \quad \begin{cases} t = 87.70 \\ t_1 = 29.23 \\ t_2 = 58.47 \end{cases}$$

$$x(\text{green})_0 = \sqrt{\frac{2(1 \times 10^{10})160}{2600}} = 35,082.32 \quad \begin{cases} t = 87.70 \\ t_1 = 19.49 \\ t_2 = 68.21 \end{cases}$$

We note that our previous optimal solution for blue cartridges (see p. 349) has now been altered by the constraints of the red and green cartridges, which must be able to run on the same equipment when the blue cartridges are not running. This matching of run–nonrun time has been accomplished.

---

[17]The denominator of the expression for x_{o_i} is calculated as follows:

$$(0.009)(2 \times 10^5)\frac{(1000)}{1800} + (0.009)(1.5 \times 10^5)\frac{(1200)}{1800} + (0.009)(1 \times 10^5)\frac{(1400)}{1800} = 2600$$

$$t_2(\text{blue}) = 48.72 = t_1(\text{red}) + t_1(\text{green}) = 29.23 + 19.49$$
$$t_2(\text{red}) = 58.47 = t_1(\text{blue}) + t_1(\text{green}) = 38.98 + 19.49$$
$$t_2(\text{green}) = 68.21 = t_1(\text{blue}) + t_1(\text{red}) = 38.98 + 29.23$$

To accomplish this, Penmakers is paying a higher total variable cost, but the serial production intermittent flow shop is fully utilized.

APPENDIX 16-II
Storemasters, Inc. (II)—An Example of the Periodic
Inventory System in Use (Optional Material)

As has been stated (pp. 356–58), the management of Storemasters intends to install a computerized, perpetual inventory system for all A-type items in its inventory. Presently, a hand-calculated, periodic inventory system is in use. It works as follows (we use the high-volume face cream in the cosmetics department for our example):

The review period $t_0 = x_0/z = 110/20 = 5.5$ days. This was approximated by the inventory manager as 5 days.

M is calculated by:

$$M = \text{Expected demand in the review period plus}$$
$$1 \text{ lead time interval} + \text{buffer stock to}$$
$$\text{protect against a fixed level of outages}$$

Let us illustrate this for Storemasters' face cream data. First, the expected demand in a review period (5 days) plus 1 lead time interval (2 days) is $7 \times 20 = 140$ jars. Second, to this is added the buffer stock, which must protect against some percentage of stock outages during 1 review period plus 1 lead time interval (7 days). The company had determined that the demand in any 7-day period exceeded 190 jars only once out of every hundred 7-day periods. This level of protection was considered satisfactory and was used for the calculation of M. Thus, the buffer stock was determined to be $190 - 140 = 50$ jars, and $M = 190$ jars.[18]

Let us simulate the behavior of the periodic model, using the same data that were employed by Storemasters to examine the applicability of the perpetual inventory model (p. 357).

We observe how few calculations must be made with the periodic inventory model. At the end of each review period, total demand is added up and an order is placed for this quantity. Alternatively, the stock on hand can be subtracted from M (190, in this case). There is no need to keep a running total, as was required for the perpetual inventory model.

---

[18]When variable lead times exist, additional reserve stock should be carried to provide protection against stock outages caused by material delivery delays.

Day	Simulated Demand	Total Demand in Review Period	$=$ (M − Stock on Hand) Reorder Quantity	(End of Day) Stock on Hand
review		115	190 − 75 = 115	⑦⑤
1	25			50
2	30			115 + 20 = 135
3	20			115
4	15			100
5	36			64
review		126	190 − 64 = 126	⑥④
6	18			46
7	22			126 + 24 = 150
8	25			125
9	17			108
10	19			89
review		101	190 − 89 = 101	⑧⑨
11	25			64
12	32			101 + 32 = 133
etc.	etc.			etc.

SUMMARY OF
PART 6

Chapter 15

Materials management is characterized by many techniques for controlling inventory levels. These models differ for the flow shop, the job shop, and the project. Information flows are numerous, and many combinations of ordering patterns must be dealt with, especially for the job shop. Accordingly, we look at the various functions of materials management, including purchasing, and the bidding of vendors for orders.

The inventory model for critical parts is shown to be a decision matrix where the appropriate costs must be derived. An example is developed for City Hospital's acquisition of an emergency generator.

Inventory systems are classified by the ABC system, which separates high dollar volume items (called *A*-type) from all others. Thus, two major classes of inventory problems that deserve careful attention are *A*-type inventories and critical parts.

Also, the difference between static and dynamic inventory problems is discussed. The critical parts model exemplifies the static classification, whereas many inventory situations require a sequence of ordering decisions over time (these latter are dynamic).

Inventory costs are carefully explained, because they are essential to understand certain aspects of material requirements planning (MRP). They are also fundamental to the development of order point policies (OPP) in Chapter 16. Differentiation is provided for the way in which inventory costs are reflected by the flow shop, the job shop, and the project. Material requirements planning methods are explained, including the lot sizing problem. An example of how MRP dovetails the master requirements schedule of an "end product" with its component materials plans is presented. MRP is an information system, and the consequences of this fact are explored.

Then, value analysis is briefly described in its role of choosing the best alternative materials for each job. The effects of material shortages and governmental restrictions on undesirable ingredients are included in the discussion.

Chapter 16

The economic order quantity model (EOQ) for batch delivery is developed. An example (The Lion's Den) is included. Next, the economic lot size model (ELS) for continuous delivery (not continuous production) is explained and shown to be a model that spans the gamut between very short production runs and continuous production. Penmakers furnishes an example of the ELS model. As optional material, the example is expanded in Appendix 16-I, which explores multi item flow shop systems, where a sequence of items is produced on the same equipment.

Lead time (between ordering and receiving the items in stock) is shown as the basis for determining that stock level which, when reached, signals that an order should be placed. It is called the reorder point (*RP*) and is applied to both the EOQ and the ELS models.

The question, How do you know when to take a quantity discount? is answered. Travelmasters' problem is used as an example.

The order point characteristics of the perpetual inventory system are developed. Simulation is used to explore Storemasters' interest in installing a perpetual inventory system for their face cream. The 2-bin system for perpetual inventory control is described. This is followed by an explanation of order point planning with the periodic type of inventory system. In Appendix 16-II, as optional material (pp. 366–67), Storemasters' example is used again with simulation to show how the periodic inventory system works.

REFERENCES
PART 6

ALFANDRY-ALEXANDER, MARK, *An Inquiry into Some Models of Inventory Systems.* Pittsburgh, Penn.: University of Pittsburgh Press, 1962.

ALJIAN, GEORGE W., ed., *Purchasing Handbook.* New York: McGraw-Hill Book Co., Inc., 1958.

AMERICAN MANAGEMENT ASSOCIATION, *Managing the Materials Function.* Report No. 35, Mfg. Division, AMA, N.Y., 1959.

AMMER, DEAN S., *Materials Management.* Homewood, Ill.: Richard D. Irwin, Inc., 1962.

ARROW, K., S. KARLIN, and H. SCARF, *Studies in the Mathematical Theory of Inventory and Production.* Stanford, Calif.: Stanford University Press, 1958.

Brown, R. G., *Decision Rules for Inventory Management.* New York: John Wiley & Sons, Inc., 1965.

———, *Statistical Forecasting for Inventory Control.* New York: McGraw-Hill Book Co., Inc., 1961.

Buchan, J. and E. Koenigsberg, *Scientific Inventory Management.* Englewood Cliffs, N.J.: Prentice-Hall, Inc., 1962.

Buffa, E. S., *Operations Management: Problems and Models*, 2nd ed. New York: John Wiley & Sons, Inc., 1968.

Cady, E. L., *Industrial Purchasing.* New York: John Wiley & Sons, Inc., 1945.

Cook, T. M. and R. A. Russell, *Introduction to Management Science.* Englewood Cliffs, New Jersey: Prentice-Hall, Inc., 1977.

England, Wilbur B. *Procurement*, 4th ed. Homewood, Ill.: Richard D. Irwin, Inc., 1962.

Fetter, Robert B. and Winston C. Dalleck, *Decision Models for Inventory Management.* Homewood, Ill.: Richard D. Irwin, Inc., 1961.

Gavett, J. W., *Production and Operations Management.* New York: Harcourt Brace Jovanovich, 1968.

Hadley, G. and T. Whitin, *Analysis of Inventory Systems.* Englewood Cliffs, N.J.: Prentice-Hall, Inc., 1963.

Hanssmann, F., *Operations Research in Production and Inventory Control.* New York: John Wiley & Sons, Inc., 1961.

Heinritz, S. F. and P. V. Farrell, *Purchasing: Principles and Applications*, 5th ed. Englewood Cliffs, N.J.: Prentice-Hall, Inc., 1971.

Hillier, F. S. and G. J. Lieberman, *Introduction to Operations Research.* San Francisco: Holden-Day, Inc., 1967.

Holt, C., F. Modigliani, J. Muth, and H. Simon, *Planning Production, Inventory and Work Force.* Englewood Cliffs, N.J.: Prentice-Hall, Inc., 1960.

Hottenstein, M. P., *Models and Analysis for Production Management.* Scranton, Penn.: International Textbook Co., 1968.

McGarrah, R. E., *Production and Logistics Management.* New York: John Wiley & Sons, Inc., 1963.

Magee, John F. and David M. Boodman, *Production Planning and Inventory Control.* New York: McGraw-Hill Book Co., Inc., 1967.

Massé, P., *Les Reserves a la Regulation de I'Avenir* dans la Vie Economique, 2 vol. Paris: Hermann, 1946.

Miles, L. D., *Techniques of Value Analysis.* New York: McGraw-Hill Book Co., 1961.

Moran, P. A., *The Theory of Storage.* London: Methuen & Co., Ltd., 1959.

Morse, P. M., *Queues, Inventories, and Maintenance.* New York: John Wiley & Sons, Inc., 1958.

Niland, Powell, *Production Planning, Scheduling, and Inventory Control.* New York: The Macmillan Company, 1970.

Orlicky, Joseph, *Material Requirements Planning.* New York: McGraw-Hill Book Co., 1975.

Plossl, G. W. and O. W. Wight, *Production and Inventory Control.* Englewood Cliffs, N.J.: Prentice-Hall, Inc., 1967.

PRICHARD, J. and R. H. EAGLE, *Modern Inventory Management*. New York: John Wiley & Sons, Inc., 1965.

RICHMOND, S. B., *Operations Research for Management Decisions*. New York: The Ronald Press Co., 1968.

STARR, MARTIN K. and DAVID W. MILLER, *Inventory Control—Theory and Parctice*. Englewood Cliffs, N.J.: Prentice-Hall, Inc., 1962.

TEICHROEW, D., *An Introduction to Management Science*. New York: John Wiley & Sons, Inc., 1964.

WAGNER, H. M., *Statistical Management of Inventory Systems*. New York: John Wiley & Sons, Inc., 1962.

WELSH, W. E., *Tested Scientific Inventory Control*. Greenwich, Conn.: Management Publishing Co., 1961.

WHITIN, THOMSON M., *The Theory of Inventory Management*, 2nd ed. Princeton N.J.: Princeton University Press, 1953.

WIGHT, OLIVER W., *Production and Inventory Management in the Computer Age*. Boston, Mass.: Cahners Books, 1974.

facilities
management

In the text of Chapters 17 and 18, we refer to *facilities* and mean by this term to consider inclusively office buildings, plants, hospitals, airline terminals, laboratories, libraries, warehouses, schools, etc., and the equipment they contain. In other words, facilities are the structures and their contents arranged to promote the operations and activities of projects, job shops, and flow shops, which are the processes of P/OM.

First we discuss (in Chapter 17) the location/site facility selection problem. This is the broadest problem in the facilities management area. It is a problem composed of two parts that interact; first, the facility location problem and second, the specific facility (site) that is chosen.

Then (in Chapter 18) we deal with the equipment of facilities and how they are selected. Finally, we treat the question of how facilities should be arranged, i.e., the facility layout problem.

Investments in facilities, such as structures and equipment, are generally large. Consequently, much attention has been devoted to improving decision-making capabilities with regard to facilities management. But these decision areas are complicated and resistant to quantitative description, let alone optimization.

Approaches that estimate expected return on investment (ROI) are among the most applicable techniques in use for industrial decisions (see Chapter 4). Cost minimization would be the policy followed by not-for-profit institutions subject to constraints guaranteeing adequate service levels. Such institutions might prefer to maximize the benefits they offer, subject to cost constraints, but this is difficult to formulate, because benefits are often intangible and hard to quantify. Still, some systematic approaches have been developed, and we shall discuss these in the materials of Part 7.

seventeen
facility selection

The facility selection process consists of 2 different decision problems (the nature of the facility and its location). These can be highly interrelated.

Service industries locate close to their customers. Service institutions locate close to their clients. Municipal governments provide service to those who live within the municipality. They do not extend police and fire protection beyond the tax-paying boundary. Federal service often requires regional offices to be effective.

A *refinery* can be located at the oil fields close to its raw material sources. It could also be located adjacent to its market. Reference to Fig. 17-1 shows that petroleum refining is an analytic process. (See pp. 182–86, where analytic and synthetic processes are discussed.) The raw material is crude oil from the well, which is refined into a number of finished products. Flow charts of this type can be exceedingly helpful for process development of analytic systems. It is evident that quite different cost structures result, depending upon how far the refinery is from the wells, and, in turn, how distant the customers are from the multitudes of finished product.

Petroleum Refining

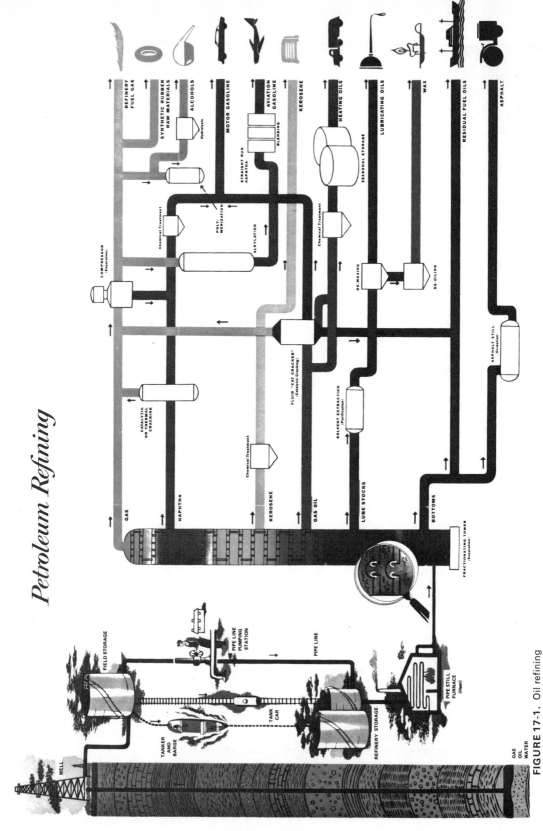

FIGURE 17-1. Oil refining

It should be noted that in the United States very little crude oil moves by tank car from the field to a refinery. Also, in the United States, naphtha from a fractionating tower is generally separated into two fractions—one that goes directly to motor gasoline after chemical treatment and the other that is reformed for octane improvement prior to blending into motor gasoline. [Courtesy of Exxon USA's Refining Department]

An automobile *factory*, where parts are stamped, etc., can be located close to its source of process inputs, including materials and energy. The heavy manufacturing operations can be separated from the required assembly operations. Then the latter can be located close to the markets that purchase the process outputs. Multiple facilities pose additional questions concerning the division of functions between several facilities. Although such problems are complex, we know that there is some *optimal locational arrangement of facilities*. The question is: How do we go about determining this optimal arrangement?

Decisions regarding the location of facilities usually require consideration of many factors. Sometimes, however, one major factor completely overrides the others. Let us look at some factors, bearing in mind that they are interactive parts of the multiple-criteria, facility selection decision problem.

Location Factors

We shall discuss the following factors, which can play a large role in location decisions:

1. Process inputs
2. Process outputs
3. Process requirements
4. Personal preferences
5. Tax and legal factors
6. Site and plant availabilities

With respect to the first 2 factors, we are primarily concerned with *shipping and transportation costs*.

Location Dependent upon the Process Inputs. Such dependency is typically the case where bulky or heavy raw materials are essential inputs for the production process. Thus, as previously mentioned, analytic-type industries are likely to locate near the source of their materials, because in this way they can minimize their overall transportation costs. These overall transportation costs include shipping inputs to the facilities and shipping outputs from them. (In Chapter 10, pp. 179–86, we examine the characteristics of analytic and synthetic systems from the viewpoint of batch versus flow processes. Now, we consider the facility location decision in these same terms. In the analytic system, the basic raw material is broken down, transformed, and decomposed into various products and by-products. If there is one location from which inputs arrive and many widely separated destinations to which they are shipped, it is likely that a location near the input source will turn out to have economic advantages.

In synthetic operations, on the other hand, various materials and parts are fed into the mainstream, where they are joined together to form a single basic unit.[1]

In addition to materials that are process inputs, we also have human resource inputs, which are discussed in Part 8. Work force costs are one of the most important factors in the determination of a suitable plant location for certain labor-intensive industries. Service industries are particularly sensitive to this factor. Companies that employ large work forces have been known to change their locations to take advantage of a lower wage scale. This motive impelled New England textile firms to close up shop in the North and move South. However, with increasing mechanization, the labor problem has been alleviated for all industries. There has also been a reduction in differential wage rates by regions of the country and between national and foreign locations. Taken together, these changes have reduced the dependency of the location decision on the cost of labor.[2]

In addition to the advantage of lower wage rates for similar skills, there are more subtle costs of human resources. Foremost is the *availability* of manpower and, in particular, of various skill levels within a particular region. Movement from a high-skill, high-wage-rate area to a low-skill, low-wage-rate area can be accomplished only when sufficient process mechanization is achieved. The computer has altered the skill requirements of both blue- and white-collar functions.

Technological progress and computer data processing permit a company to trade off higher machine investments for lower wages and for less manpower and lower skills. A trade-off potential is created between manpower and machine power, which makes the location decision less dependent on the expense of both indirect and direct labor. Work force cost evaluation also includes consideration of turnover rates, absenteeism, and employee reliability, as well as costs of hiring and training workers. Some of these considerations were essential in Chapter 13, where aggregate scheduling was treated. Different production schedules will be used according to the costs we have just discussed.

We see that plant location (a system's design-type problem) interacts with the management of operations. The size of a labor market and the attitudes of workers and their labor unions can figure heavily in some plant location decisions. These considerations are likely to affect location decisions with respect to urban labor markets as compared to suburban and rural markets. From various sources, demographic information by areas—such as population size, education, and income—can be pooled with industrial data concerning hourly earnings, right-to-work laws, and so forth. Such a data base allows the manager to be well informed when reaching a location decision.

---

[1]See Fig. 10-6, p. 185, for auto production and assembly as an example of a synthetic industry.

[2]International wage differentials present something of an illusion. Tariffs, cost of materials, international exchange rates, taxes, and other factors tend to balance out over time what appear to be immediate substantial advantages.

Location Dependent upon the Process Outputs. The location of the company's markets can be significant under certain circumstances; e.g., service industries must be near their market. The assembly functions of synthetic industries (p. 183) frequently locate near the market, because many raw materials must be gathered together from diverse locations and assembled into large-scale single units.

Location Dependent upon Process Requirements. Many processes require special environments. When the technology of the process requires large amounts of water, then only a location where such water resources are available can be considered. Another common process requirement concerns the need for substantial amounts of power. There are not too many locations that could supply such power. Accordingly, the size of the location problem is immediately cut down.

Certain processes produce disagreeable odors and in other ways pollute the environment. For such cases, both urban and suburban locations are automatically ruled out. Noise and other community irritants will be treated in a similar fashion. Sometimes, a process is responsive to factors such as temperature, humidity, and weather conditions in general. To a great extent, internal weather conditioning obviates such factors. But this is not always the case. High salinity in the air, arising as a result of a coastal location, must be taken into account when materials and equipment would be adversely affected by such a condition. An additional aspect of the relevancy of weather conditions, which is quite frequently overlooked, can be noted. If a process requires highly skilled individuals to perform certain operations, then absenteeism can be a significant deterimental factor. For such cases, it might be desirable to locate in a region where the common cold would be a less virile destroyer of time. Within some reasonable period for development, space factories will orbit earth, providing gravity-free and particle-free environments. Thus, many unique circumstances exist wherein process requirements with respect to environment override all other considerations.

Location Dependent upon Personal Preferences. Occasionally the entrepreneurs or chief executives prefer a given location for entirely personal reasons. Not infrequently, once it has been decided to relocate an operating facility, strong monetary incentives must be used to encourage company personnel to relocate with the company. The cost of moving personnel and inducing them to do so must be balanced against the costs of building a new group with the same level of skills and company loyalty in the new location. Frequently, the preferences of the firm's top executives to move (or remain where they are) will take precedence over considerations that otherwise might be considered more important.

Location Dependent upon Tax and Legal Factors. Because of high taxes applicable to the corporation, personal income taxes, sales taxes, etc. desirable locations with respect to other variables will be bypassed. In fact, a favorable tax structure provides such basic motivation that many decisions are made to locate a new plant or to relocate a going operation solely for this reason.[3] In addition to tax advantages, communities attempt to attract industries by providing industrial parks or properly zoned land at advantageous rates. Although some communities desire any kind of industrial growth, most attempt to attract only certain types of industries. Others have been reluctant and even hostile toward any industrial development. Companies that fail to perceive community attitudes frequently rue this oversight.

---

[3]One example of such location decisions was effectively used by Puerto Rico, where Operation Bootstrap attracted many new companies because of tax incentives.

Location Dependent upon Site and Plant Availabilities.

There is a complex problem that exists, namely, when should we make the decision? At any point in time a list of available sites can be compiled. Some sites already have a structure built on them that can either be purchased or rented. Other sites require building. Assume that the desirability of each site could be evaluated with a single measure and that a ranked order list of sites has been developed. Figure 17-2 illustrates such a list, where E_1 is considered to be best, E_2 is next best, etc. At any point in time, a new opportunity

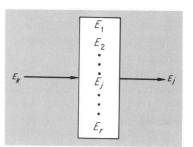

FIGURE 17-2.

can arise. Thus, E_k is shown as a new arrival. The quality of E_k can be measured, and it will be placed in its proper rank order in the list.

Sites must be removed from the list when some other organization rents or buys them, i.e., E_j. Then the question is, when is E_1 good enough so that it can be chosen as a location? If the manager waits, his best choice may disappear; if he does not wait, the day after he commits the company to a new location, a preferred one may appear. This decision problem can be modeled, but the probability estimates that a new opportunity will arise or an existing opportunity disappear are hard to obtain. The quality criteria for ranking $E_1, E_2, \ldots$, etc., can be developed. Although the manager may not be able to achieve a real application of this model, he or she gains insight by thinking of the problem in this way.

Facility Factors

The manager must be able to define the type of structure that is desired to house the product's or service's production. Sometimes the choice of building and the choice of location are related; often they are not. Dependency occurs when there is a need to *rent* specialized and *unique* structural configurations that exist only in certain places. *Building* one's own facility removes much of the pressure, as does the requirement for a general facility configuration rather than a highly individualized one.

Facility Selection Differs for the Flow Shop, the Job Shop, and the Project

In many flow shop situations there is little ambiguity concerning the shape and form of buildings and basic facilities. There is heavy investment in the design of the process, and it is quite clear what kind and shape of structure will be adequate to house that process. Project design also tends to constrain the kind of facilities that can be used. Building rather than renting may be required. Job shops have greater flexibility and more choices available. Therefore, flow shops and projects tend to be located without consideration of the rental opportunities, and their costs, whereas job shop locations may well be determined by such factors.

Specific product and service industries are often associated with particular kinds and shapes of structures. It is not our intention to catalog these here, since a great deal of technological information and understanding of real process details would be required to explain them.

In general terms, when renting, building, or buying, one must consider a great many elements. Expert assistance from architects and building engineers should be obtained to insure the proper evaluation of an existing facility or to plan a new structure. Among the elements to be considered are:

Is there enough floor space?
Is the space open with wide bays so that machines, men, and materials handling equipment can be effectively arranged and utilized?

How Many Stories Are There? Early factories were multistoried. With the development of improved transportation, particularly the automobile, plants could be located outside the central city on less expensive land. The one-story building followed. It is usually preferred unless sufficient reasons can be found to justify multistory buildings, which are more expensive to construct, especially when floor loads are high because heavy equipment must be supported. In certain industries, gravity feed conveyors are used. In such cases, multiple storied buildings are necessary.

What Kind of Roof Is Used? This was a very important question at one time (say pre-1950). Thereafter, heat, air conditioning, and lighting technologies advanced to the point where an assist from roof design seemed unnecessary. Roof shapes permit at least a degree of control over illumination, temperature, and ventilation.[4] Architectural factors again became important in the 1970s when fuel shortages developed, energy prices soared, and all organizations became conscious of light, power, and heat bills. Apart from such considerations, if the process requires hoists and cranes, then high roofs and ceilings are needed.

What Type of Construction Should Be Used? The answer given will in large measure determine the feasibility of converting an old building to conform to a new set of specifications. This answer will be the major determinant of both new construction costs and the speed of construction. In all cases, building codes must be observed. Industrial parks usually require a degree of conformity with respect to construction and appearance. Such factors as foundations, floors, walls, and windows are part of the architectural design of a building. They affect layout flexibility and building convertibility. In addition, insurance rates will be dependent upon the type of construction that is used. The considerations mentioned concerning light, power, and heat bills also are very relevant to the type of construction used.

What Kind of Maintenance Requirements Will There Be? The maintenance of flow shop facilities is critical, immediate, and costly. For the job shop, it is less demanding. Older buildings usually have greater costs for maintaining the structure.

What Determines Resale Value? The resale value of a facility may be an important determinant. In general, *special purpose facilities* designed for a unique process make special structural demands and create a lower resale value than *general purpose facilities*. The latter accept process requirements that are not unique but fit a pattern which is satisfactory for many different kinds of processes.

---

[4]For examples, the sawtooth roof construction was extensively used in the 1930s to provide even illumination of work spaces; irrigation of flat rooftops was used for temperature control.

What Conveniences Should the Building Have? If the building is located at a distance from the city, it might be essential to provide a parking lot as well as cafeteria facilities. Many companies require a medical room or a plant hospital on the premises. There must be adequate rest rooms. In some instances an auditorium is included in the plans. Railroad sidings or ship docking facilities may be of major importance. If this is the case, the construction or rental plan must take such factors into account.

What Appearance Should the Building Have? Different architectural styles appear at different points in time. Attitudes and policies of management will strongly influence these decisions. Some executives consider appearance to be a frill, whereas others take it so seriously that they insist on illumination of the building at night and the provision for an impressive view from the air. There is no question that a beautiful building increases employee pride in their company and can influence the consumer's evaluation of the company. On the other hand, how these truisms affect productivity and profit remains an intangible factor.

Should We Rent, Buy, or Build? The answer to this question depends upon what is available. If a suitable building exists, then its cost can be compared with costs that would be incurred if a new building were constructed. Rent or buy alternatives depend upon what is offered. An interesting aspect of this problem is the question: How long should we wait to see what buildings become available? (See p. 378.) If no suitable structure exists, then an appropriate facility must be constructed. Airline terminals are built for this reason. In the communications field, radio and TV stations are built to specifications. Unused power generating plants are not found in rentable condition. Clearly, when there is nothing available to meet the need, it must be built. On the other hand, when the process requirements are not unique, many suitable facilities usually can be found. This would apply to office space, which is commonly rented.

The problem of buying, renting, or building should be resolved by means of a comparison of costs based on present worth analysis. To accomplish this we make use of discounting procedures; see pp. 67–72.

Cost Determinants

A facility selection decision represents an attempt to minimize costs, including *opportunity costs.* For example, there is a cost of staying put and not moving to a new location. The investigation required to choose a new facility has a cost all its own that should be considered explicity, rather than its being taken for granted.[5]

---

[5]The collection of relevant data is facilitated through the cooperation of regional Chambers of Commerce, which are able to provide such information, usually without cost. But location studies are not free. The costs rise as the number of locations investigated increases.

The facility selection problem involves long-term, nonrepetitive commitments. The many relevant risk factors are seldom able to be analyzed properly. The decision requires a sizable investment and creates heavy sunk costs.[6] It involves other costs as well.

Let us consider two kinds of fundamental cost factors, namely, *tangible* costs and *intangible* costs. The latter are distinguished by the fact that it is almost impossible to *measure* them. They can only be judged intuitively. Although it is difficult to measure many of the tangible costs, nevertheless, to some extent, they can all be measured. Among the *tangible* costs are:

The cost of land. This cost is often thought of as an investment.

The cost of renting, buying, or building. A discount analysis, such as is shown on pp. 70–72, can be helpful.

Transportation costs of bringing raw materials and fuels to the facility and transportation costs of moving finished goods to the market. Transport costs affect the determination of lead times, size of reserve stocks, economic order quantities, and discounts taken or foregone. Also, these costs should be included in the determination of market price, which affects demand volume and, consequently, shipping quantities. Thus, using iterative reasoning, we return to the costs of transportation. We shall shortly develop a transportation model that assumes that the transportation costs are established. This model then determines optimal shipping patterns, where optimal is defined as the minimum total cost of transportation.

Power and water costs. With increasing fuel shortages, the availability of power, let alone its price, becomes an issue. Water costs often include purification.

The cost of taxes and insurance. Return on investment (ROI) should be calculated after taxes.

Labor costs. The trade-off costs for different man/machine configurations should be investigated.

The cost of moving, including production stoppage costs incurred during relocation. Inventory buildups can help offset the effects of production stoppages for the intermittent and paced-flow shop. Work in the job shop and project would be delayed.

In determining an optimal facility selection, intangible costs place a severe burden on the manager. Let us consider some of these.

Competition for labor within a restricted labor market introduces a cost that changes over time. It will vary as a function of the attractiveness of a particular region for all industries. The situation is dynamic. When an attractive general location exists, a number of companies begin to move to this area in order to take advantage of its opportunities. Saturation must occur, and at

---

[6]That is, nonrecoverable costs.

some point competition for the available labor resources can become significant; paradise is transformed into limbo.

Union attitudes are exceedingly important, but difficult to evaluate. It is seldom possible to do more than intuitively assess such conditions. Militant unions develop reputations that are widely known, but a change of leadership or policy within the union can significantly alter the stereotype. Shifts in the economy and changes in the welfare and fortune of a particular industry will bring about rapid shifts in union attitudes.

Community attitudes are not measurable. Small enclaves of resistance to industrial developments must not be overlooked, particularly when such groups are led by a few individuals who are influential members of the community. It is possible to document specific instances where companies have fully developed plans to move into a new community only to discover that a strong and militant group exists that is prepared to resist the move. Because of its investment in reaching the decision that has been made, and because some executives become outraged at being thwarted, some companies have occasionally attempted to fight this battle. Even if the company legally succeeds in installing itself, the enmity that has been aroused can prove to be a lasting penalty. For example, the company may discover that bus service has been suspended on routes from the city to the plant location; the community may rezone the plant location so that fire protection is denied. This can produce a dramatic rise in insurance rates until the company is able to develop its own fire protection unit. Other possible sources of difficulty include the municipality's withholding adequate sewage facilities and the passage of new zoning laws that can prevent company expansion, even on its own land.

Problems of this type can also arise when a community becomes disillusioned with the company because of unexpected pollution, noise, or other undesirable process outputs. The various forms that inimical relations can take is limited only by the powers of the city fathers. Community relations should be considered as an integral part of every facility selection decision problem. A company that does not make clear to the community the degree to which the environment will be contaminated by operations should not be surprised to find promised favors withdrawn and local groups agitating for its removal.

Local and state ordinances must be taken into account. There is no direct way to attach a cost to such rulings. Knowledgeable legal assistance is required to interpret the situation so that it can be evaluated. Each location possibility poses its own economic considerations in terms of such costs as workmen's compensation payments, unemployment insurance, waste disposal laws, pollution and smoke control requirements, noise abatement rules, and other nuisance regulations.

The costs of weather and other natural phenomena should not be overlooked. Such events as hurricanes, earthquakes, and floods can produce heavy penalties. These are acts of nature and cannot always be avoided. At the same time, they are less unexpected in certain areas than in others. Companies in low-lying areas near rivers have higher probabilities of being flooded; similarly, well-known earthquake and hurricane zones exist. Normal weather conditions also produce costs that can be associated with specific locations. Companies locating in the North must be prepared to pay for heating equipment and costly fuel bills. Industries locating in the South may require investments in air conditioning as well as concomitant power expenses. Other costs related to weather concern the maintenance of plant and the deterioriation of equipment.

How can all these factors be related? Assuming that we could measure all the costs, then we would write an equation of the general form:

$$\text{Total costs} = f(\text{tangible, intangible, and opportunity cost factors})$$

and we would minimize the equation.

All matters that might interact with the facility selection decision, such as plant layout, output productivity and costs, maintenance and machine replacement costs, market demand, transportation costs, and competitive actions, would be included in the equation. Because we do not have this capability, the method outlined in the next section becomes all the more attractive. It is a multiple-criteria method for evaluating tangible and intangible costs simultaneously. The comparison among strategic alternatives is akin to the opportunity costs of doing one thing which thereby prohibits doing the other.

Facility Selection Using Dimensional Analysis

Decisions related to intangible cost systems present great difficulties. Several means of resolving these problems can be suggested.

Entirely subjective decisions can be made. A quasi-objective approach can be utilized which requires that *preference measures* be stated for various factors that describe different aspects of the system's performance. Weights or index numbers can be used to express preference. These measures are then used to make a comparison in some objective manner, so that a choice can be made.

Tangible costs can be measured, but to mix them with intangible costs, we must place weights of relative importance on both kinds of costs. Then we combine them all, treating measured values as though they are also preferences.

The major difficulty in evaluating alternative facilities is the fact that conflicting objectives, having quite different dimensions, must be combined, somehow, to provide a reasonable basis for evaluation.

We reject the idea of initially using an entirely subjective approach, because the human mind cannot carry the rich detail that is involved in a problem of this type. We propose a method that will organize the information that is relevant to the decision. Thus, one or more managers can study what is known, what is agreed upon and what is not, what appears to require additional research, what is considered important, whether consensus exists about what is important, etc. Further, we propose that this method provide a solution that can be accepted or rejected by the one or more managers concerned. The decision may be to accept a solution rejected by the method. This is entirely reasonable, because it is an informed decision.

Let us first develop an example, and then the method in terms of the example.

Ristormakers, Inc.

Assume that in searching for a new plant location, this large-scale transistor manufacturer develops 2 plans based on 6 factors. Three of these are tangible, i.e., directly measurable, and the other three are intangible. With respect to the latter, at best, they can be assigned a scale position (say) between 1 (best) and 6 (worst). (The discussion could have included many more of the factors we previously discussed without changing in any way the significance of what we are about to say.) Let Plan 1 specify building a plant in Boston, while Plan 2 specifies building a plant in Camden. Assume that the proposals have been evaluated as shown in Table 17-1.

TABLE 17-1 A COMPARISON BETWEEN ALTERNATIVE PLANT
LOCATIONS FOR RISTORMAKERS

Factors	Boston Plan 1	Camden Plan 2	Weight*
Building costs and equipment costs—yearly depreciated value	$500 000	$300,000	4
Taxes (per year)	$ 50,000	$ 20,000	4
Power cost (per year)	$ 20,000	$ 30,000	4
Community attitude	1	2	1
Product quality as a function of worker morale and skill	2	3	5
Flexibility to adapt to situations that are likely to occur	1	6	3

*The larger the weight, the more important the dimension is considered to be relative to the other dimensions.

Dollars must be added together. Using discounting (pp. 414–16), we can make dollars apply to the same period of time. Companies will have different measures for the relative importance of dollars, depending upon their assets.

Thus, Ristormakers' management evaluates dollars with a weight of 4, which indicates more importance than any other factor—except product quality as a function of worker morale and skill (which is weighted 5). Of course, such weighting is arbitrary, but it is not random. The executive committee, composed of five top executives, all agreed on the evaluation in Table 17-1. Such agreement lends supports to the use of these particular numbers. If factors such as community attitude, product quality, and flexibility could be associated with a dollar value, there would not be a dimensional problem to resolve. Everything could be measured in dollars, and there would be no need for weights. However, it must be recognized that these latter elements represent *intangible costs*. The attempt to estimate such costs in dollars would prove arduous with little conviction that the results are satisfactory. On the other hand, it is possible for the manager to rank the relative merits of the two plans for each intangible factor.

The example utilizes a scale from 1 to 10 to measure factor outcomes (the value of 1 represents the "best possible" result and the value of 10, the least desirable). This is because the table is written in terms of costs. (The value 10 would be optimal if the table had been constructed in terms of profit.) Thus, with respect to community attitude, Plan 1 is preferred to Plan 2, although, on the whole, both of them seem to be considered desirable. With respect to flexibility, Plan 2 is inferior to Plan 1.

Let us turn to the third column in the table—captioned "Weight." These weighting factors (or index numbers) represent the relative importances of the set of outcome objectives being analyzed. According to the weights that have been assigned, product quality is the most important consideration, whereas community attitude is least important. Flexibility is rated as being slightly less important than costs. This arrangement of weighting values would change if the company's capitalization were altered or if the planning objectives were modified. The numbers that we have used represent assignments for a particular set of individuals and circumstances.

Various approaches can be used for obtaining the weights. These include:

1. Using the estimates of that individual who is responsible for this decision.
2. Using an average value, obtained by pooling the opinions of a number of Ristormakers' executives who have different responsibilities with respect to the decision.
3. Employing an informal blending of the opinions of Ristormakers' executives to develop a set of estimates and weights that are agreeable to all concerned parties.

A noteworthy characteristic of the third approach is that it creates an opportunity for the project participants to *communicate* with each other about the facility decision. They can do this:

First, with respect to which factors are likely to be critical determinants of the decision.

Second, concerning the estimates of the outcomes for each of the factors, a set of which must be supplied for each of the alternative plans.

Third, with respect to the selection of the weights which indicate the relative importance in each executive's mind for the critical factors required to evaluate the system.

For problems of this kind, the multiplication method of evaluating alternatives by means of weighting factors is frequently used.[7]

This approach, which Ristormakers' management has decided to employ, was chosen because it is particularly suitable for dealing with intangible factors. The company's profits are not good. In boom years, the profit and loss statement has pleased stockholders, but given average or poor economic conditions, the company's performance has been marginal. As the controller pointed out, the problem has not been with the hard numbers. Ristormakers uses flow shop production, and the lines have been well balanced. It has been the inefficiencies of intangibles that have corroded profits. Perhaps, just because of the rigorous line design, worker morale has been poor; in turn, the community has not been supportive.

Our approach requires that location preference be expressed as a ratio of the products of the outcomes raised to powers for each plan. We compare the plans in ratio with each other. The comparison measure is R.

$$R = \frac{\text{preference for location 1}}{\text{preference for location 2}} = \left(\frac{O_{11}}{O_{21}}\right)^{w_1} \left(\frac{O_{12}}{O_{22}}\right)^{w_2} (\cdots) \left(\frac{O_{1j}}{O_{2j}}\right)^{w_j} (\cdots) \left(\frac{O_{1n}}{O_{2n}}\right)^{w_n}$$

Estimates are supplied to describe the values of the various outcomes that each location will produce. For the ith alternative location we would measure each factor outcome: $O_{i1}, O_{i2}, \ldots, O_{ij}, \ldots, O_{in}$. Each outcome is then weighted for its relative importance. Call the weighting factors $w_1, w_2, \ldots, w_j, \ldots, w_n$.

Note that the ratio R is a *pure number*, meaning that it has no dimensional involvement.[8] If all outcomes are measured in the same dimension, e.g., dollars, then this approach would incorrectly treat a single outcome as though it were many outcomes having a variety of dimensional properties.

---

[7]See, for example, the use of this method to evaluate alternative aircraft designs as used by a major aircraft manufacturer, L. Ivan Epstein, "A Proposed Measure for Determining the Value of a Design," *The Journal of the Operations Research Society of America*, Vol. 5, No. 2 (April 1957) pp. 297–299. Also, C. Radhakrishna *Rao, Advanced Statistical Methods in Biometric Research* (New York: John Wiley & Sons, Inc., 1952), p. 103; also, see Walter R. Stahl, "Similarity and Dimensional Methods in Biology," *Science*, Vol. 137, No. 20 (July, 1962), pp. 205–212, and P. W. Bridgman, *Dimensional Analysis* (New Haven: Yale University Press, 1922); this is also available in paperbound edition, 1963.

[8]Thus, for example, $\dfrac{(\$)^{w_1}(\text{quality})^{w_2}}{(\$)^{w_1}(\text{quality})^{w_2}} = \text{pure number}$.

In Ristormakers' numerical example presented in Table 17-1, all costs are based on a 1-year period, so we can add them together. This yields $570,000 and $350,000 respectively for alternatives 1 and 2. Accordingly, the comparison we are seeking is

$$R = \frac{\text{preference for location 1}}{\text{preference for location 2}} = \left(\frac{570,000}{350,000}\right)^4 \left(\frac{1}{2}\right)^1 \left(\frac{2}{3}\right)^5 \left(\frac{1}{6}\right)^3 = 0.002$$

$$= \frac{1}{500} = \frac{\text{costs of Plan 1}}{\text{costs of Plan 2}}$$

On the basis of this result, Ristormakers choose location 1 because the ratio is less than 1. The costs of location 2 (in the denominator) are greater than the costs of location 1 (in the numerator). Accordingly, we choose the alternative in the numerator.

The method of evaluation that we have employed is useful for a wide range of project-type decisions. It would be appropriate for product-design decisions, process and service design decisions, equipment selection, and plant-location plans. Ristormakers' executive committee accepts the Boston location. If it had not, there would be some good explanations as to why the model's solution was rejected.

Facility Selection Using the Transportation Model

When transportation costs *dominate* the facility location problem, then a relatively straightforward model exists for analyzing this situation. By transportation costs, we mean the combined costs of moving raw materials to the plant and of transporting finished goods from the plant to one or more warehouses. To develop and illustrate the model, let us return to the Ristormakers case. In Table 17-1 (p. 385) we did not consider transport costs. Let us now do so. It is determined that on the average, the cost of moving raw materials to the Boston location is $6 per production unit; it is $3 to Camden. The cost of shipping from the Boston location to the distributor's warehouse is $2 per unit; from Camden, it is $4 per unit. These data are shown in Fig. 17-3. Total transportation costs for the Boston location are $8 per unit; for Camden they are $7. Therefore, we would choose Camden.

Now, let us complicate the problem by creating two distributors' warehouses (called markets) and by allowing the *possibility* of multiple facilities. Figure 17-4 illustrates this situation, which fits the pattern of a simple distribution problem. The question is, which facilities should ship (how much) to which warehouses? This problem can be resolved most rapidly by means of the generalized transportation algorithm, which is described (as optional material) in Appendix 17-II (see pp. 399–407). We shall solve the problem here by means of some useful heuristic[9] procedures with trial and error.

---

[9]For the definition of heuristic, see pp. 200–201.

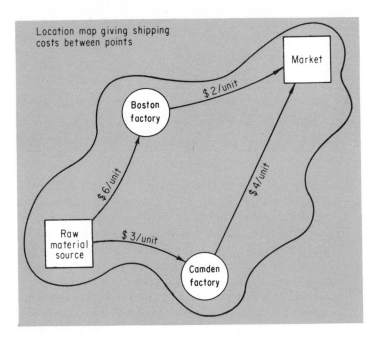

FIGURE 17-3. Plant location problem (where only one market and one raw material source exist)

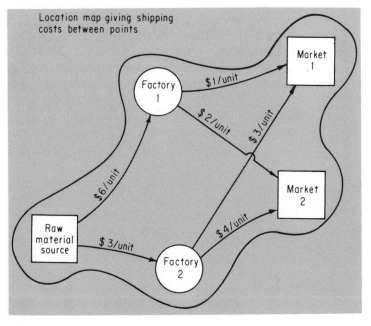

FIGURE 17-4. Plant location problem—factory 1, factory 2, or both? (where two markets and one raw material source exist)

TABLE 17-2

Factory (F_i)	Raw Material Transport Costs	Market (M_j)		Supply
		M_1	M_2	
F_1	$6/unit	$1/unit	$2/unit	90 units/day
F_2	$3/unit	$3/unit	$4/unit	90 units/day
	Demand	40 units/day	40 units/day	

Using the costs specified in Fig. 17-4, we can prepare a transportation matrix, where the matrix cell entries are the costs of transporting finished goods from factory i to market j. (*Note:* Factories are distinguished by rows, $i = 1, 2$; markets are represented by columns, $j = 1, 2$.) In the case of Ristormakers, $i = 1$ stands for Boston location and $i = 2$ represents Camden. Also, we have added the description of supply and demand. Thus, each market demands 40 units per day to be shipped from either F_1 or F_2, or a combination. Both factories can be designed so that they will have a maximum productive capacity of 90 units per day. Which *location* should be chosen for Ristormakers' factory? We allow the possibility of choosing both.

In the first place, we note that total daily supply potential exceeds total daily demand by 100 units, assuming that both factories operate at full capacity. (We shall not permit this to occur.) To correct the theoretical imbalance between supply and demand, we create a slack, or *dummy market* (DM), to absorb 100 units per day. The market does not really exist. Therefore, whichever factory is assigned the job of supplying the dummy market is, in effect, eliminated as a location.[10] For example, a possible pattern of shipments is shown in Table 17-3. If this were the optimal solution, we would interpret this matrix as stating that F_2 is the best location because it supplies the real markets, M_1 and M_2. Further, that F_1 should be eliminated because it has been assigned the task of supplying the dummy market, which does not exist. We also note that the excess capacity of F_2 has been allocated to the dummy, which means that F_2 will work at $\frac{8}{9}$ of capacity, supplying only real demand.

TABLE 17-3

Factory	Market			Supply
	M_1	M_2	DM	
F_1			90	90
F_2	40	40	10	90
Demand	40	40	100	180

---

[10]We have used *dummies* before; see pp. 283–85.

Is this result really the best solution? The best solution will result in minimum total transportation costs, so we must test to find out if there is any better arrangement. The matrix of total transportation costs would be as shown in Table 17-4. The raw material transportation costs have been added to the finished goods transportation costs. Any shipments to the dummy market cost $0, because it does not exist.

TABLE 17-4 TOTAL TRANSPORT COSTS PER UNIT

		Market	
Factory	M_1	M_2	*DM*
F_1	6 + 1 = $7	6 + 2 = $8	$0
F_2	3 + 3 = $6	3 + 4 = $7	$0

Heuristic Total Cost Procedures for Solving the Transportation Problem[11]

Let us take a number of steps that raise some questions for which we will find the appropriate answers.

Step 1. Start with *any* solution that balances supply and demand. (We have done this in Table 17-3 above.)

Question: What is the *total cost* of the shipping plan described in Table 17-3? The cost is calculated directly. There are 40 units shipped from F_2 to M_1 at $6 per unit, or $240, and an additional 40 units are shipped from F_2 to M_2 at $7 per unit, or $280. The *total cost* is $240 + $280, which equals $520 per day.

Step 2. Choose the lowest-cost, nonassigned cell, and find out what the effect of moving 1 unit to that cell will be. That is, will *total shipment costs* increase or decrease? Make sure that the supply and demand totals are unchanged. This requires subtracting and adding one unit at appropriate places in the matrix.[12] If no saving is obtained, go to the next lower cost cell and do the same. Test every assignment alternative.

Question: Can we lower the cost of $520 by shipping one unit from F_1 to M_1? If we ship one unit from F_1 to M_1, we must rearrange the total shipping schedule, as shown in Table 17-5. The *total cost* of this shipping arrangement is: ($7 × 1) + ($6 × 39) + ($7 × 40) = $521 per day. Because 1 unit shipped from F_1 to M_1 produces a greater *total cost*, more than 1 unit shipped in this way will be even worse.

---

[11]See the footnote on p. 388.
[12]The stepping-stone method is developed (as optional material) in Appendix 17-I, but for small matrices, the operations can be performed by eye.

TABLE 17-5

Factory	Market M_1	M_2	DM	Supply
F_1	1		89	90
F_2	39	40	11	90
Demand	40	40	100	

Can we lower the *total cost* by shipping 1 unit from F_1 to M_2? See Table 17-6.

TABLE 17-6

Factory	Market M_1	M_2	DM	Supply
F_1		1	89	90
F_2	40	39	11	90
Demand	40	40	100	

The *total cost* result is $(\$8 \times 1) + (\$6 \times 40) + (\$7 \times 39) = \$521$ per day. Once again, no decrease in *total cost* has been found. Because no other possibilities exist for alternate shipping routes, we conclude that the original solution was optimal. The location to be chosen is factory 2 in Camden.

Step 3. If a decrease in *total cost* is obtained, then *ship as many units as possible* to the location where 1 unit produced a decrease. Always ship as many units as possible.[13] To illustrate, assume that a starting assignment pattern (Step 1) had been selected as shown in Table 17-7.

Step 1.

TABLE 17-7

Factory	Market M_1	M_2	DM	Supply
F_1	40		50	90
F_2		40	50	90
Demand	40	40	100	180

---

[13]Appendix 17-I (optional material) also addresses the question, What is the maximum number of units that can be shifted from one assignment to another? (See pp. 397–99.)

Question: What is the *total cost* of the shipping plan described in Table 17-7? The *total cost* is ($7 × 40) + ($7 × 40) = $560 per day.

Step 2. The lowest, nonassigned cost is $6 at F_2, M_1. Table 17-8 illustrates the pattern for testing one unit at the $6 location.

TABLE 17-8

Factory	Market			Supply
	M_1	M_2	DM	
F_1	39		51	90
F_2	1	40	49	90
Demand	40	40	100	

The new *total cost* is ($7 × 39) + ($6 × 1) + ($7 × 40) = $559.

Step 3. We have decreased *total cost*; therefore, move as many units as possible to the new location.[14] We can move 39 units from F_1, M_1 to F_2, M_2. Then we must increase F_1, DM by 39 and decrease F_2, DM by 39. Table 17-3 shows the resulting shipping assignment.

As we know from our previous tests of the matrix, we cannot improve upon this result, but if we did not know this fact, we would continue testing.

The heuristic procedure that we have been using consists of evaluating the difference in *total costs* that would result from alternative shipping patterns for 1 unit. If a savings could be made by shifting the pattern, then we would put as many units as possible into the preferred shipment pattern.[14] For small enough matrices, we can evaluate every nonassigned entry, but we call our method heuristic because we do not employ the stepping-stone rule for shifting assignments and can, therefore, have difficulty in finding the optimal assignment. There is no problem in identifying the optimal assignment, however. When every empty cell is evaluated, and none of them produces a decrease in *total cost*, then the optimal solution has been found. The generalized transportation method presented as optional material in Appendix 17-II (pp. 399–407) evaluates all nonassigned cells systematically. The northwest corner method (see pp. 394–95) assures that the right number of shipments will be included in the solution. The stepping-stone method, presented in Appendix 17-I as optional material, assures that each next change in the assignment pattern will produce equal or lower total costs. Let us now consider a slightly more elaborate example, where up to three factories might supply 2 markets.

The cost entries in Table 17-9 are *total* transportation costs *per unit*. Assume that Ristormakers has an *actual* operating factory F_1, which has

---

[14]See footnote 13, pp. 392.

TABLE 17-9

Factory	Market			Supply
	M_1	M_2	DM	
F_1	\$7/unit	\$8/unit	\$0/unit	50 units/day
F_2	\$6/unit	\$7/unit	\$0/unit	90 units/day
F_3	\$8/unit	\$10/unit	\$0/unit	90 units/day
Demand	40 units per day	40 units per day	150 units per day	230 units per day

a maximum capacity of 50 units per day. The demand for the product is greater than the supply, viz., 80 units per day. The locations F_2 and F_3 are under serious consideration. Whichever is chosen, it has been decided to install a production capacity of 90 units per day. As before, we assume that transportation costs dominate the plant location decision. Let us make our initial assignment pattern conform to the northwest corner method described below (see Table 17-10). (Again, supply and demand are balanced with a dummy market, DM.)

TABLE 17-10

Factory	Market			Supply
	M_1	M_2	DM	
F_1	40	10		50
F_2		30	60	90
F_3			90	90
Demand	40	40	150	230

We use the northwest corner method. Begin in the upper left-hand corner of the matrix and allocate as many units as possible to F_1, M_1. This is 40 units. More than 40 units would exceed demand. We assign as many units as are *allowed* by whichever constraint dominates, i.e., the row contraint of 50 units or the column constraint of 40. In this case, it is the column constraint, so 40 units are entered at F_1, M_1. But F_1 still has 10 units of unassigned supply. These 10 units can be assigned at F_1, M_2. All of F_1's supply is now allocated.

However, M_2 still requires 30 units. These are assigned from F_2 (we move down in the matrix and to the right). F_2 then has 60 unallocated units remaining. These are assigned to DM (and, therefore, they will not be made or shipped). To complete the matrix, F_3's supply of 90 units must be allocated. We place them in the F_3, DM cell.

The *northwest corner method* will always satisfy the requirement for an initial, feasible solution, but so would a procedure that starts at any corner.

Whatever method is used to obtain an initial, feasible solution, it must produce $M + N - 1$ assignments given a matrix with M rows and N columns.[15] This number does not only apply to initial solutions; it applies to all intermediate solutions, and the final and optimal solution as well.

Heuristic Marginal Cost Procedures for Solving the Transportation Problem

We now test to find out whether a cost reduction can be achieved. There are four possible changes that could be made in the shipping pattern of Table 17-10.

1. We could shift 10 units from F_1—M_2 to F_1—DM. Thus, see Table 17-11. If more than 10 units were shifted, this would create a negative shipment at the intersection of F_1—M_2, which is a situation that could not be tolerated. Similar restrictions exist with respect to other changes.

TABLE 17-11

Factory	Market			Supply
	M_1	M_2	DM	
F_1	40		10	50
F_2		40	50	90
F_3			90	90
Demand	40	40	150	230

2. We can shift 30 units from F_2—M_2 to F_2—M_1.
3. We can shift 30 units from F_2—M_2 to F_3—M_1.
4. We can shift 30 units from F_2—M_2 to F_3—M_2.

Let us evaluate the change in *marginal cost* that will result from shipping one unit from F_1 to DM.

---

[15]The number of shipments used should never exceed $M + N - 1$, where

M = the number of markets and N = the number of factories.

Thus, for the example above, we have $3 + 3 - 1 = 5$, which is the number of shipments derived by means of the northwest corner rule. We can never obtain a better solution with more than five shipments and usually we would obtain a worse one. Although the logic of this point is indisputable, the most convincing demonstrations can be derived by working through a few simple examples, e.g., one factory and many markets or two factories and many markets.

There is an exception which results in *less* than $M + N - 1$ assignments, called the state of degeneracy. This condition is a purely technical problem, which can always be resolved by adding a negligible amount to an appropriate row or column total. There is no exception that results in more than $M + N - 1$ assignments.

1. Ship 1 unit from F_1 to DM $+\$0$
2. Ship 1 less unit from F_1 to M_2 $-\$8$
3. Ship 1 more unit from F_2 to M_2 $+\$7$
4. Ship 1 less unit from F_2 to DM $-\$0$

TOTAL $-\$1$

The total cost can be reduced one dollar by making this change. Each of 10 units can be shipped for $1 less per unit. This is a total cost reduction of $10. Proceeding in the same fashion, we find the change in *marginal cost* for the other three options discussed above.

1. Shipping 1 unit from F_2 to M_1 produces zero change.
2. Shipping 1 unit from F_3 to M_1 would result in extra expense of $2.00 per unit.
3. Shipping 1 unit from F_3 to M_2 would result in extra expense of $3.00 per unit.

Accordingly, we choose the first option and shift 10 units from F_1—M_2 to F_1—DM. The new transportation matrix has already been shown in Table 17-11.

TABLE 17-12

	Market			
Factory	M_1	M_2	DM	Supply
F_1	40	(+1)	10	50
F_2	(−1)	40	50	90
F_3	(+1)	(+3)	90	90
Demand	40	40	150	230

We have tested this arrangement to see if any other savings can be made (Table 17-12). The *marginal cost* changes that would result from further modification of the shipping pattern are shown in the circles of the matrix in Table 17-12. Additional improvement is possible. Forty units can be shifted from F_1—M_1 to F_2—M_1. We would then have:

TABLE 17-13

	Market			
Factory	M_1	M_2	DM	Supply
F_1	(+1)	(+1)	50	50
F_2	40	40	10	90
F_3	(+2)	(+3)	90	90
Demand	40	40	150	

The *marginal cost* analysis shows that no further improvements can be obtained. Because factories 1 and 3 ship only to the dummy, they will be eliminated. The solution also states that factory 2 will operate at $\frac{8}{9}$ of capacity.

We can see how the transportation method can be of real help to companies such as Ristormakers. Say there were production differentials at the various locations. For example, low taxes or high worker productivity at one location may result in a lower per unit production cost. This can be added in with shipping costs, making each row's costs higher by the per unit production costs of the supplier. In Table 17-14, per unit production costs of the three facilities differ. This is a modification of Table 17-9, where the production costs are equal and, therefore, ignored. (Note that the dummy market's costs remain 0 because we do not want to bias assignments to the dummy with costs that never actually appear.)

TABLE 17-14

Factory Costs	Factory	Market			Supply
		M_1	M_2	DM	
($/Unit)			($/Unit)		(units/day)
20	F_1	27	28	0	50
28	F_2	34	35	0	90
12	F_3	20	22	0	90
Demand (units/day)		40	40	150	230

Ristormakers could analyze alternative warehouse (market) locations. They could also study the effects of using different modes of transportation for the same route, e.g., train vs. plane vs. truck. The production cost differentials will play their parts.

The limitations of the transportation method should also be understood by management. The model is linear and does not reflect the many other factors that influence location decisions. Intangible factors have been ignored by this method. When the intangibles are critical, then the transportation cost differentials of the various alternatives can be combined with other costs and used with the intangible factors in a dimensional analysis.

APPENDIX 17-I
The Stepping-stone Concept of the Transportation Model
(Optional Material)

Given that an assignment of shipments has been made, 2 questions arise.

1. How do we evaluate the effect on costs of shipping 1 unit to a non-assigned location of the transportation matrix? Logically, if a savings can be made by this change, then we would want to ship as many units

from the source to the new destination, as possible. This leads to the second question.

2. How do we determine the maximum number of units that can be shifted from one assignment to another?

The stepping-stone approach is most easily described by example. Using the northwest corner approach (see pp. 394–95), we obtain the following initial assignment, where cost per unit of shipping is indicated within the box in the upper right-hand corner of every shipping assignment possibility.

	M_1	M_2	DM	Supply
F_1	7 40	8 10	0	50
F_2	6	7 30	0 60	90
F_3	8	10	0 90	90
Demand	40	40	150	230

To evaluate the effect on costs of reassigning shipments (Question 1), choose any nonassigned cell and:

1. Move horizontally (along that row) until an assigned shipment is located that has another assignment in its same column. Thus, to evaluate the effect on costs of shipping one unit to F_3, M_1, move to F_3, DM (90).
2. Move vertically until an assigned shipment is located that has another assignment in its same row. Continuing with our example, move from F_3, DM (90) to F_2, DM (60).
3. Repeat Step 1. In this case, move from F_2, DM (60) to F_2, M_2 (30).
4. Repeat Step 2. In this case, move from F_2, M_2 (30) to F_1, M_2 (10).
5. Repeat Step 1. In this case, move from F_1, M_2 (10) to F_1, M_1 (40).
6. We continue this pattern, until we return to the starting point. In this case, the starting point was F_3, M_1 (no entry, but testing). We move from F_1, M_1 (40) to F_3, M_1 (to be evaluated).

The specific cost evaluation for 1 unit is as follows:

Add 1 unit to F_3, M_1	Added cost $8
Remove 1 unit from F_3, DM	Subtracted cost 0
Add 1 unit to F_2, DM	Added cost 0
Remove 1 unit from F_2, M_2	Subtracted cost $7
Add 1 unit to F_1, M_2	Added cost $8
Remove 1 unit from F_1, M_1	Subtracted cost $7

The net change is $+\$16 - \$14 = +\$2$, which would increase costs. Therefore, no shipment will be made to F_3, M_1. The pattern of change is shown in Fig. 17-5.

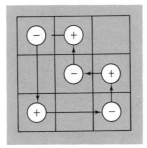

FIGURE 17-5.

This is called the stepping-stone method, because assigned shipments are the only "stones" that can be counted as part of the path, and only horizontal and vertical paths are permitted. There is always 1 path, and only 1 path that will complete a circuit. This statement is valid for any shipment pattern that conforms to the $M + N - 1$ requirement of the (linear) transportation model (see p. 395). Occasionally, a "degenerate" shipping pattern arises, where the number of assignments is less than $M + N - 1$. In this case, the symbol epsilon (ϵ) should be added to the missing stepping stone. Epsilon is evaluated as so close to zero that it will not affect the final solution, but it will allow the path circuit to be completed. (See footnote 15 in this chapter.)

We now turn to Question 2. How do we determine the maximum number of units that can be shifted from one assignment to another?

We are talking now about shipping amounts and not costs. The smallest number of units, associated with the subtracted costs $\ominus$, is the maximum number of units that can be shifted. Thus, in our example, these are (90 at F_3, DM), (30 at F_2, M_2), and (40 at F_1, M_1). Consequently, no more than 30 units can be entered at F_3, M_1. If more than this number of units were assigned to F_3, M_1, then a negative shipment assignment would occur at F_2, M_2, which is infeasible.

APPENDIX 17-II
The Generalized Transportation Method (Optional Material)

Many forms of problems can be well represented by the transportation model. Therefore, it is worthwhile to become familiar with an alternative to the stepping-stone method (previously described on pp. 397–99). This generalized method provides insight concerning the nature of the cost structure of the transportation model, and especially the role of opportunity costs in leading to a solution. A side benefit is that the generalized method is faster for obtaining solutions by hand computation.

Let us quickly review the basic idea of the transportation method, namely: A supply of resources is to be allocated to users of those resources, in such a way as to find a pattern of allocation that minimizes costs or maximizes profits. Each source, shipper, or producer can split its allocations among users. The output of several sources can be assigned to a single user. These relations are reflected in the matrix below, where the cost of shipping one unit from a particular producer P_i to a specific consumer C_j is stated as c_{ij}.

		Consumers							
		C_1	C_2	C_3	$\cdots$	C_j	$\cdots$	C_m	Supply
	P_1	c_{11}	c_{12}	c_{13}		c_{1j}		c_{1m}	s_1
	P_2	c_{21}	c_{22}	c_{23}		c_{2j}		c_{2m}	s_2
	P_3	c_{31}	c_{32}	c_{33}		c_{3j}		c_{3m}	s_3
Producers	$\cdot$								$\cdot$
	P_i	c_{i1}	c_{i2}	c_{i3}		c_{ij}		c_{im}	$s_i.$
	$\cdot$								$\cdot$
	P_n	c_{n1}	c_{n2}	c_{n3}		c_{nj}		c_{nm}	s_n
	Demand	d_1	d_2	d_3	$\cdots$	d_j	$\cdots$	d_m	

Constraints on producers' supplies (in a given time period) are indicated by s_i values and consumers' demands are shown by d_j's.

First, let us consider a 2×2 transportation matrix, with the given values for supplies and demands for the period, and unit costs of allocation, as shown.

	C_1	C_2	Supply
P_1	4	6	600
P_2	2	5	400
Demand	300	700	1000

The minimum cost allocations can be determined by (first) finding any feasible allocation pattern (i.e., a pattern that properly matches supply and demand totals); (second) by examining the effects of making changes in that pattern; (third) making changes that assure improvement; and (fourth) stopping when no further improvement can be obtained. The similarity to linear programming rules is hardly accidental. Transportation models can always be solved by LP methods.

A. How do we quickly derive a jumping-off solution?

B. How can the patterns of reassignment be rapidly evaluated?

C. How do we determine the maximum amount that can be reassigned?

Let us consider each of these questions, in turn, using a larger example (Matrix I) as our basis for discussion.

MATRIX I

	C_1	C_2	C_3	Supply
	4	6	3	
P_1	50			50
	2	5	8	
P_2	50	110		160
	7	3	2	
P_3		190	60	250
	4	5	6	
P_4			140	140
Demand	100	300	200	600

Total cost $= 50(4) + 50(2) + 110(5) + 190(3) + 60(2) + 140(6) = 2380$

To answer A, we use the northwest corner method, described on pp. 394–95. Thus, starting in the upper left-hand corner, as many units are assigned to P_1C_1 as is *allowed* by whichever constraint dominates, i.e., the row constraint of 50 or the column constraint of 100. In this case, it is the row constraint, so 50 units are entered at P_1C_1, but the C_1 column still has 50 units of unfilled demand. These can be assigned at P_2C_1; however, all of P_2's supply is not yet assigned. In fact, 110 units can be assigned at P_2C_2, which leaves 190 units of C_2's demand to take care of. Continuing in this way, we complete the total matrix of assignments.

For Question B, the net costs of all assignments that have not been made can be determined by the stepping-stone method. This method has been discussed in Appendix 17-I; see pp. 397–399.

Instead, we shall now explain the generalized method of transportation analysis. (Also called the modified, or MODI, method.)

Step 1. Write out the matrix of *actual costs*, $\{c_{ij}\}$—(Matrix II).

Step 2. Create a new matrix (Matrix III) where only those costs are entered that represent assignments, as in Matrix I with its northwest corner assignments. Circle each assignment's cost.

MATRIX II

	C_1	C_2	C_3
P_1	4	6	3
P_2	2	5	8
P_3	7	3	2
P_4	4	5	6

MATRIX III

	C_1	C_2	C_3
P_1	④		
P_2	②	⑤	
P_3		③	②
P_4			⑥

Step 3. We develop row and column costs for Matrix III, such that every circled entry equals the sum of its row cost plus its column cost. The first cost we choose is 0. It can be entered for any row or column (Matrix IV). Thereafter, all other row and column costs are determined by the numbers in the matrix.

MATRIX IV

	C_1	C_2	C_3	Row Costs
P_1	④			0
P_2	②	⑤		−2
P_3		③	②	−4
P_4			⑥	0
Column Costs	4	7	6	

1. Arbitrarily, we assign the 0 cost to row P_1.

2. Then the cost assigned to column C_1 must be 4, since $0 + 4$ must equal ④ at P_1, C_1.

3. The cost assigned to row P_2 must be -2, since $-2 + 4$ must equal ② at P_2, C_1.
4. The cost assigned to column C_2 must be 7, since $-2 + 7$ must equal ⑤ at P_2, C_2.
5. The cost assigned to row P_3 must be -4, since $-4 + 7$ must equal ③ at P_3, C_2.
6. The cost assigned to column C_3 must be 6, since $-4 + 6$ must equal ② at P_3, C_3.
7. The cost assigned to row P_4 must be 0, since $0 + 6$ must equal ⑥ at P_4, C_3.

Step 4. Now, complete Matrix IV by entering calculated costs in all empty matrix cells. Each entry equals the sum of the row cost plus the column cost. For example, the cost at P_2, C_3 is equal to $-2 + 6 = 4$. This yields Matrix V.

Step 5. From Matrix II, cell by cell, subtract Matrix V. Zeros will occur at every circled entry. This produces Matrix VI, which is the *opportunity cost matrix* that would have been derived from calculations of every stepping-stone path in Matrix I.

FIRST ITERATION

MATRIX V

	C_1	C_2	C_3	Row Costs
P_1	④	7	6	0
P_2	②	⑤	4	-2
P_3	0	③	②	-4
P_4	4	7	⑥	0
Column Costs	4	7	6	

MATRIX VI THE OPPORTUNITY COST MATRIX

	C_1	C_2	C_3
P_1	0	-1	-3
P_2	0	0	$+4$
P_3	$+7$	0	0
P_4	0	-2	0

Step 6. Change Matrix I assignments, by selecting the largest negative value in Matrix VI (this is -3 at P_1, C_3) and assigning as many units as possible to it. The biggest per unit cost saving can be made in this manner, i.e., a net decrease of \$3 for each unit shipped to P_1, C_3. Matrix VII presents the new assignment pattern.

MATRIX VII

	C_1	C_2	C_3	Supply
P_1			50	50
P_2	100	60		160
P_3		240	10	250
P_4			140	140
Demand	100	300	200	600

Total Cost

$50 \times 3 = 150$

$100 \times 2 = 200$

$60 \times 5 = 300$

$240 \times 3 = 720$

$10 \times 2 = 20$

$140 \times 6 = \underline{840}$

2230

Now, to answer Question C: How do we determine the maximum amount that can be shifted? This is answered in Appendix 17-I (see pp. 397–399). Also, Fig. 17-6 shows the pattern of units shifted, and below, we describe the specific operations.

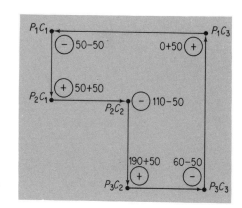

FIGURE 17-6. The pattern for transferring units to $P_1 C_3$

How many units can be entered at $P_1 C_3$? The pattern for unit changes must be examined in terms of how many units are presently assigned to each "take out" position (indicated by negative signs in Fig. 17-6's network). The smallest such number with a negative sign is the answer. Otherwise, some assignments would become negative, which violates the feasibility condition. Thus, no more than 50 units (at $P_1 C_1$) can be reassigned.

Having completed the reassignment of 50 units to $P_1 C_3$, we must now go through Steps 1 through 6 again. We continue reassigning until no more negative numbers appear in Matrix VI; i.e., no further improvement is possible. This is done below:

SECOND ITERATION

MATRIX V′

	C_1	C_2	C_3	Row Costs
P_1	1	4	③	3
P_2	②	⑤	4	4
P_3	0	③	②	2
P_4	4	7	⑥	6
Column Costs	-2	1	0	

MATRIX VI′

	C_1	C_2	C_3
P_1	+3	+2	0
P_2	0	0	+4
P_3	+7	0	0
P_4	0	-2	0

This time, we began our computations for Matrix V′ by placing the zero in Column 3. From Matrix VI′, we see that as many units as possible should be shipped to P_4, C_2, where an opportunity cost of -2 exists.

From Matrix VII, we derive Matrix VII′ based on shifting 140 units from P_4, C_3 to P_4, C_2. Thus:

SECOND ITERATION

Total Cost

$50 \times 3 = 150$

$100 \times 2 = 200$

$60 \times 5 = 300$

$100 \times 3 = 300$

$150 \times 2 = 300$

$140 \times 5 = \underline{700}$

1950

MATRIX VII′

	C_1	C_2	C_3	Supply
P_1			50	50
P_2	100	60		160
P_3		100	150	250
P_4		140		140
Demand	100	300	200	600

We evaluate this pattern to see if any further improvement is possible.

MATRIX V″

	C_1	C_2	C_3	
P_1	1	4	③	4
P_2	②	⑤	4	5
P_3	0	③	②	3
P_4	2	⑤	4	5
	−3	0	−1	

MATRIX VI″

	C_1	C_2	C_3
P_1	+3	+2	0
P_2	0	0	+4
P_3	+7	0	0
P_4	+2	0	+2

The answer is no; all opportunity cost evaluations are positive. Total cost has decreased with each new iteration, from a northwest corner assignment total cost of 2380 to a first iteration total cost of 2230, to a second iteration total cost of 1950, to a third iteration STOP. We have reached the final solution; there is no total cost available that is less than 1950.

Had a 0 opportunity cost appeared in the cost evaluations of Matrix VI″ (other than the assigned zeros), this would have signified that alternatives existed. It would be up to the operations manager to decide which of the minimum cost alternatives he preferred. We note that our final solution has six assignments; thus, it meets the condition $M + N - 1 = 4 + 3 - 1 = 6$.

When supply and demand are not equal, a dummy slack variable, having *all* 0 unit costs can be created to take care of this situation. The dummy, whether it be needed for the rows or columns, is not simply a computational convenience; it has decision-making significance for the manager.

Finally, if we wish to use the transportation model to achieve profit maximization rather than cost minimization, the rule concerning which new assignment is preferred is reversed. The largest possible plus-valued opportunity cost evaluation is chosen to be entered in the network. The procedure stops when all evaluations are negative.

The significance of the transportation model is hard to miss. It does not require a square matrix; the solutions are relatively easy to obtain by hand computation. On the other hand, it is linear, since unit costs or profits are not able to be changed as a function of volume, and since each matrix applies to a specific period, no allowance is made for interdependencies over time.

The generalized transportation method, once understood, is fast. It works by setting a 0 opportunity cost on all entries in the assignment that is being evaluated. Then row and column opportunity costs are developed in order to determine the per unit opportunity costs of all possible shipment entries that are not in the assignment. If any of the nonassigned possibilities reveals a negative opportunity cost, the largest of these is entered, and a new assignment pattern is developed and tested for further possible improvement. The underlying basis of the solution to any transportation problem is the opportunity costs of shifting assignments between rows and columns, i.e., suppliers and producers.

PROBLEMS
1. Why is it that the procedures (total cost and marginal cost) for solving the transportation problem (see pp. 391–97) are called heuristic?
2. For the matrix below, use trial and error methods to answer questions b, c and d.
   a. Ignoring the boxes marked with x's, what kind of shipping assignment has been made?
   b. What is the maximum number of units that can be shipped to x_1?
   c. What is the maximum number of units that can be shipped to x_2?
   d. What is the maximum number of units that can be shipped to x_3?
   (For parts b, c, and d, show the revised shipping assignment.)

		To 1	2	3	4	
	A	30	x_1		x_2	30
	B	40				40
	C	10	40			50
From	D		20	10		30
	E			20	40	60
	F				20	20
	G	x_3			10	10
		80	60	30	70	240

3.

MATRIX 1	1	2	3
A	10	6	
B		12	2
C			12

MATRIX 2	1	2	3
A	10		6
B		12	2
C		6	6

To evaluate different shipping assignment patterns, Matrix 1 was changed to Matrix 2 by adding 6 units at A_3. As a result, three cells have been altered.

407

a. What problem does this suggest?

b. If instead 2 units had been put in at A_3, what shipping pattern would have resulted?

c. How many cells would have been altered?

d. Why is the shipping pattern suggested in part b preferred?

4. Based on heuristic reasoning, what is the optimal assignment for the transportation problem below?

MATRIX OF SHIPMENTS
(with northwest corner assignments)   **MATRIX OF SHIPPING COSTS**

	1	2	3	Supply
A	10	6		16
B		12	2	14
C			12	12
Demand	10	18	14	42

	1	2	3
A	6	10	5
B	8	3	7
C	9	4	2

5. In the shipping matrix below, the manager wishes to shift 6 units from A_1 to A_2.

	1	2	Supply
A	6		6
B	12	6	18
Demand	18	6	24

a. What happens to the shipping matrix as a result of this move? What is that condition called?

Optional Part:

b. To use the stepping-stone method, described in Appendix 17-I, what must the manager do to the matrix?

6. The industries listed below tend to form high-density clusters in specific geographic areas. Is there a rational explanation?

a. Steel

b. Automobiles

c. Stock yards

d. Textiles

e. Electronics
f. Aircraft
g. Rubber
h. Motion pictures
i. Books
j. Cigarettes

Answer: Many factors can operate to create geographic clustering. The obvious answers may not be correct or may be only partial explanations of complex, multidimensional systems of factors. One possible variable that is seldom considered is that of "follow the leader." A company might assume that, since a competitor is operating successfully in a given area, it too can move to that area with less risk being involved because of the prior precedent and empirical evidence that the area is at least satisfactory. The next company in this industry faced with a location problem now sees 2 companies operating in this area and moves there with even less trepidation. By the time that the fifth company is looking around for a location, the decision to move anywhere but to this same region is fraught with danger, because it runs contrary to practice and time must be spent explaining why. Area advantages can change, improving or deteriorating as a result of clustering and other factors.

Bearing the above remarks in mind, we find steel locating close to its supply of coal. Similarly, automobiles, stock yards, textiles, rubber, cigarettes, and grains have located close to the sources, or shipping centers, of some of the major inputs that these industries require. At least in part, this is due to the high cost of transporting these input commodities. Electronics, aircraft, motion pictures, and books, on the other hand, require people with special skills, and therefore would tend to locate in areas where it is easiest to attract these people. (Either because they already live there or because they would like to live there.)

7. The Omicron Company has 2 factories, A and B, located in Wilmington, Delaware and San Francisco, California, respectively. Each has a production capacity of 550 units per week. Omicron's markets are Los Angeles, Chicago, and New York. The demands of these markets are for 150, 350, and 400 units, respectively, in the coming week. A matrix of shipping distances is prepared, and the shipping schedule is determined to minimize total shipping distance. Estimate the distances and solve this problem on that basis.

Answer: Using the approach outlined in pp. 395–97, we must first estimate the shipping distances (in thousands of miles) as follows:

	Los Angeles	Chicago	New York
(A) Wilmington	3.0	1.0	0.3
(B) San Francisco	0.4	2.0	3.0

An initial solution can be determined by the northwest corner rule (NWC). (Note that the use of a dummy market is required to compensate for the fact that supply exceeds demand. Also, the distances assigned to the dummy are 0.)

	Los Angeles	Chicago	New York	Dummy	Supply
(A) Wilmington	150	350	50	0	550
(B) San Francisco	0	0	350	200	550
Demand	150	350	400	200	1100

This NWC allocation produces a shipping schedule with a total distance of

$$1000\,[150(3) + 350(1) + 50(0.3)$$
$$+\ 350(3) + 200(0)] = 1{,}865{,}000 \text{ miles.}$$

If we modify the NWC allocation, we could, for example, ship 350 units from San Francisco to Chicago. This eliminates the 350 units to be shipped from San Francisco to New York, as well as the 350 units from Wilmington to Chicago. We now have 400 units going from Wilmington to New York. The change in total distance would be

$$1000[350(2) - 350(3) + 350(0.3)$$
$$-\ 350(1)] = -595{,}000 \text{ miles}$$

which is a substantial improvement. The new matrix is then

	Los Angeles	Chicago	New York	Dummy	Supply
(A) Wilmington	150	0	400	0	550
(B) San Francisco	0	350	0	200	550
Demand	150	350	400	200	1100

In the same way, a further saving can be made by shifting 150 San Francisco units from Chicago to Los Angeles. Thus:

	Los Angeles	Chicago	New York	Dummy	Supply
(A) Wilmington	0	150	400	0	550
(B) San Francisco	150	200	0	200	550
Demand	150	350	400	200	1100

A check of the matrix will reveal that no further distance savings can be obtained by shifting any units, so this must be the optimal arrangement. The minimum total distance is

$$1000\,[150(0.4) + 150(1) + 200(2)$$
$$+ 400(0.3)] = 730{,}000 \text{ miles}$$

8. Omicron decides to build a third plant. The strongest contenders are Chicago, Illinois and Cleveland, Ohio. The new plant would have a productive capacity of 400 units. Keeping the market demands unchanged from Problem 7 above, what should Omicron do?

9. Use the dimensional method described on pp. 384–88 to resolve the following long-term decision problem. An equipment choice is to be made between 2 alternative computer designs, and the following data have been obtained:

	Design 1	Design 2
Cost	$0.5 million	$0.6 million
Speed	2	1
Memory	3	2
Flexibility	4	5
Size	50 square feet	40 square feet

Characteristics are scaled so that large numbers are less desirable than small numbers. Establish your own weighting factors for each of the cases below, and comment on the way that the choice changes as a function of the particular point of view that is employed.

a. The computer manufacturer in terms of the potential market.
b. A mail order company where the unit will control inventory.
c. A NASA-systems manufacturer operating under government contract, where the unit will be used for scientific calculations.

Answer: For a mail order company (b), memory size and cost are very important; speed is relatively important (depending upon the specific circumstances); physical size and flexibility play secondary roles. An appropriate set of weighting factors might be:

Item	Factor
Cost	5
Speed	3
Memory size	6
Flexibility	1
Size	1

Using the methods of pp. 387–88, we can write:

$$\frac{\text{Preference for design 1}}{\text{Preference for design 2}} = \left(\frac{0.5}{0.6}\right)^5 \left(\frac{2}{1}\right)^3 \left(\frac{3}{2}\right)^6 \left(\frac{4}{5}\right)^1 \left(\frac{50}{40}\right)^1 = \frac{9375}{256} > 1$$

We would, therefore, choose design 2 in this case.

Similar analysis applies to the other examples. Here, too, assigning values and estimating weights can lead to interesting discussions, which ultimately produce results similar to the one above. The computer manufacturer might stress flexibility, or size or memory, etc., depending upon its marketing philosophy. Actual company product lines exist that represent such differences in market segmentation. The weapons-system manufacturer will not care about cost but is likely to emphasize size and flexibility.

10. For the supply and demand situation, shown with costs in the matrix below, what is the optimal transportation pattern?

	C_1	C_2	Supply
	4	6	
P_1	100	500	600
	2	5	
P_2	200	200	400
Demand	300	700	1000

Note: Problems 2, 3, 4, 5, 7, 8, and 10 can also be solved by the Stepping-Stone method (Appendix 17-I) or the Generalized Transportation method (Appendix 17-II).

eighteen
equipment selection and facility layout

Equipment Selection

The selection of equipment necessary to do the job precedes facility layout. Ideally, facility layout would then precede facility selection. In fact, it would dictate facility construction, but it would not influence facility location. Many times, however, the facility layout must be arranged and rearranged to fit a particular structure that has previously been selected by management. Of course, P/OM has a pretty good idea of the equipment that will be required at the chosen facility, and therefore, of the general adequacy of a particular structure. Still, it is not unusual to find that equipment selections must bend to fit the selected facility. We do have methods (applicable to the job shop or the project) that enable the manager to choose between alternative facilities that do essentially the same job, but at different costs and rates, etc.

Our methods are general and do not get involved with technology, although relevant estimates about equipment performance are required from engineers and equipment manufacturers. For the flow shop, equipment selection is much more intricately bound up with technology, and consequently,

413

decision making about flow shop equipment requires the direct participation of technological experts.

Discounting Analysis—Selecting among Equipment Alternatives

Previously, on pp. 68–72, we developed a buy or rent analysis. Now, we shall look at the question of how to choose equipment on an economic basis. We assume that technological features of the equipment are identical. If this is not the case, then it is necessary also to employ dimensional analysis, much in the same way that it was previously used for facility selection (see pp. 384–88).

Let us determine the real cost of equipment alternatives when several relevant factors change over time. For example, if we want to compare alternative facilities that have different expected service lifetimes and/or different operating costs that change as a function of usage and age, we apply discounting functions at all of the appropriate points in the time streams of payments.

To illustrate, Tiremasters, Inc. is planning to install an entirely new materials-handling system. The company has received two proposals for different arrangements of hand trucks, fork-lift trucks, cranes, and conveyors. Each alternative represents an integrated materials handling system.

TABLE 18-1

	Materials Handling System A	Materials Handling System B
Estimated service life	3 years	2 years
Investment	$25,000	$20,000
Discount factor	6 percent per year	6 percent per year
Operating cost per year	$2,000	$1,000

Operating costs in Table 18-1 must be related to optimal run sizes for the equipment served by the materials-handling facilities. Comparisons are sometimes made where the costs for one alternative are based on an efficient system, while the costs for the second alternative are based on an inefficient system. Equipment manufacturers have been known to use the following kind of argument when trying to sell their products. "You have nothing to lose in buying this equipment. If the savings obtained as a result of using the new equipment are not sufficient to pay for it, then we will gladly take it back and make a full refund." A manufacturer's salesman can base this offer on his observation that the operations on the present equipment are inefficient.

When the new equipment is installed, a thorough study will be made of how to properly utilize it. This will include efficient work routines and optimal production runs. Then, the advantage of the new machine, at least in part, is connected with the development of optimal work routines rather than with the superiority of the new equipment derived from fundamental technological advances. If a study of the use of the present equipment is made, savings could also be realized. It is only on the basis of equally efficient use of equipment that an intelligent comparison of alternative facilities can be made.

The required comparison of the alternative materials-handling plans, *A* and *B*, is given below. The smallest common period for systems *A* and *B* is 6 years. During that period of time, system *A* will turn over twice, and system *B* will turn over 3 times. Then, using the discounting data (p. 70), for system *A* (2 cycles), we derive Table 18-2.

TABLE 18-2

End of Year	Investment A	Discounted Operating Costs	Total Discounted Cost	Average Cost per Year
0	$25,000 × 1.000 = $25,000		$25,000	
1		$2000 × 0.943 = $1886	26,886	$26,886
2		2000 × 0.890 = 1780	28,666	14,333
3	$25,000 × 0.840 = $21,000	2000 × 0.840 = 1680	51,346	17,115
4		2000 × 0.792 = 1584	52,930	13,233
5		2000 × 0.747 = 1494	54,424	10,885
6		2000 × 0.705 = 1410	55,834	9,306

And for system *B* (3 cycles), we obtain Table 18-3.

TABLE 18-3

End of Year	Investment B	Discounted Operating Costs	Total Discounted Cost	Average Cost per Year
0	$20,000 × 1.000 = $20,000		$20,000	
1		$1000 × 0.943 = $943	20,943	$20,943
2	$20,000 × 0.890 = $17,800	1000 × 0.890 = 890	39,633	19,817
3		1000 × 0.840 = 840	40,473	13,491
4	$20,000 × 0.792 = $15,840	1000 × 0.792 = 792	57,035	14,259
5		1000 × 0.747 = 747	57,782	11,556
6		1000 × 0.705 = 705	58,487	9,748

We have discounted both investment sums and operating costs. Year by year these have been added together to give total discounted cost. Tiremasters could make its comparison of alternatives A and B with these figures. At the end of 6 years,[1] system A has accumulated total discounted costs of $55,834, which is $2653 less than system B's total.

However, average costs are frequently used as the basis for comparison. These are the total costs divided by the number of years of the cost accumulation. Using either the total discounted costs or the average yearly determination of cost, Tiremasters would select materials-handling system A.

The steps that have been followed are quite straightforward. System A requires an initial investment of $25,000. Because it is paid at the beginning of the first year, it is already at present value. At the end of the first year $2000 has been paid out in operating costs. The $2000 is discounted to a value of $1886. In fact, the operating costs are paid out over the period of a year; therefore, a more accurate computation might be based on monthly operating charges which are appropriately discounted with the monthly discount factor. We observe that at the conclusion of the first year the average yearly costs for system A are $26,886. This is equal to the total costs for a 1-year period of time.

Next, we add the second year's operating costs, properly discounted, and again as though the costs were incurred at the end of the second year. These amount to $1780. The second year's operating costs are then added to the previous year's total costs, giving a figure of $28,666. For average yearly costs—over a 2-year period—we divide by 2. This results in a figure of $14,333. We continue our computations in the same way until the total cycle period of 6 years is covered. If the equipment has salvage value at the time it is replaced, then the salvage amount, properly discounted, is subtracted from the total accumulated cost.

Other techniques can also be used for determining an optimal selection of equipment and facilities. Among such techniques we should include the break-even chart (especially when it is applied in its decision matrix form) and the dimensional analysis approach described on pp. 384–88.

The MAPI Method for Equipment Replacement

The Machinery and Allied Products Institute of Washington, D.C. has done a great deal to organize the data requirements comprehensively, and to design a method of analysis for the job shop, machine replacement problem.[2] The approach, called the MAPI method, is widely utilized by industry.[3] A

---

[1]It should be noted that when the facilities under consideration have different estimated service lives, then we must always use the smallest common cycle of these lifetimes.

[2]With minor modifications, the MAPI method can be used for startup equipment selection from a given set of alternatives.

[3]See George Terborgh, *Business Investment Management, A MAPI Study and Manual* (Washington, D.C.: Machinery and Allied Products Institute and Council for Technological Advancement, 1967).

critical requirement of this method is that costs should be based on the process performance and should not be measured for an individual facility in isolation from the system.

The important differences between the MAPI approach and that of discounting are:

1. MAPI does not assume technological equivalence. Allowance is made for differences in the quality of output, and in the productivity of the process. Both of the above relate to changes in revenue. The MAPI system includes changes in operating costs, but so does the discounting method.

2. The discounting approach highlights the effects of different payment rates over time, whereas MAPI concentrates on 1-year advantage. (We should note that MAPI can be modified to permit longer-term views, taking into account some discounting effects.)

Examining the MAPI Summary Form, Sheet 1, Fig. 18-1, we observe that operating advantage is measured in terms of the effect of the proposed project (where the project is meant to be interpreted as the investment in a new facility) on revenue and on operating costs. Figure 18-2 demonstrates how initial investment and terminal value are used to determine a measure of after-tax return. This measure is, in fact, a kind of urgency rating, being a relative measure of the return on investment (ROI). When the measure on line 40 is large, there is justification to go ahead with the proposed project.

Hampton Mills, Inc. Hampton Mills' management has learned about a new computer-controlled stitching machine. The plant manager has asked his operations management department to complete a MAPI comparison with the present equipment. This has been done. A report follows.

To Mr. Hampton: We believe that the computer-controlled stitcher should be purchased to replace the present equipment. We shall explain our recommendation, introducing the necessary data as we proceed, indicating, where useful, the appropriate lines in the MAPI figures attached.

1. We evaluate the replacement of the present equipment by a new computer-controlled stitcher. The installed cost of the new system is $29,800 less the initial tax benefit ($2100) determined for this investment. The resulting net cost is $27,700 (Line 26).

2. The disposal value (after tax adjustments) of the present system components is $4000 (Line 27). No capital additions are required or contemplated if the proposed change is not made. For some cases, extensive repairs might be necessitated if a replacement is not made, but we are not considering ourselves to be faced with such a situation.

3. The initial net investment (Line 26 minus 27) is $23,700 (Line 28).

4. The comparison period *P* is 1 year. Note the use of *P* in Line 32.

MAPI SUMMARY FORM
(AVERAGING SHORTCUT)

PROJECT___Computer Controlled Stitcher_____

ALTERNATIVE___Continuing as is_____

COMPARISON PERIOD (YEARS)   (P)_____1_____

ASSUMED OPERATING RATE OF PROJECT (HOURS PER YEAR)   _____1,200_____

I. OPERATING ADVANTAGE
(<u>NEXT-YEAR</u> FOR A 1-YEAR COMPARISON PERIOD,* <u>ANNUAL AVERAGES</u> FOR LONGER PERIODS)

A. EFFECT OF PROJECT ON REVENUE

		INCREASE	DECREASE	
1	FROM CHANGE IN QUALITY OF PRODUCTS	$	$	1
2	FROM CHANGE IN VOLUME OF OUTPUT			2
3	TOTAL	$ X	$ Y	3

B. EFFECT ON OPERATING COSTS

		INCREASE	DECREASE	
4	DIRECT LABOR	$ 900	$	4
5	INDIRECT LABOR	150		5
6	FRINGE BENEFITS	190		6
7	MAINTENANCE	200		7
8	TOOLING	80		8
9	MATERIALS AND SUPPLIES		16,800	9
10	INSPECTION			10
11	ASSEMBLY			11
12	SCRAP AND REWORK			12
13	DOWN TIME			13
14	POWER	40		14
15	FLOOR SPACE		1,000	15
16	PROPERTY TAXES AND INSURANCE	320		16
17	SUBCONTRACTING			17
18	INVENTORY		1,100	18
19	SAFETY			19
20	FLEXIBILITY			20
21	OTHER			21
22	TOTAL	$ 1,880 Y	$ 18,900X	22

C. COMBINED EFFECT

23	NET INCREASE IN REVENUE (3X − 3Y)	$	23
24	NET DECREASE IN OPERATING COSTS (22X − 22Y)	$ 17,020	24
25	ANNUAL OPERATING ADVANTAGE (23 + 24)	$ 17,020	25

* Next year means the first year of project operation. For projects with a significant break-in period, use performance after break-in.

FIGURE 18-1. MAPI summary form [This form is excerpted from *Business Investment Policy* (Machine and Allied Products Institute, 1967.)]

5. We now calculate the next-year operating advantage to be gained. First, we determine that the project promises no effect on revenue (Lines 1, 2, 3 and 23).

6. Assuming one shift with 30 operating hours per week, and 40 weeks per year for the new equipment, we obtain 1200 operating hours per year.

7. We now move to the consideration of the facility change on operating

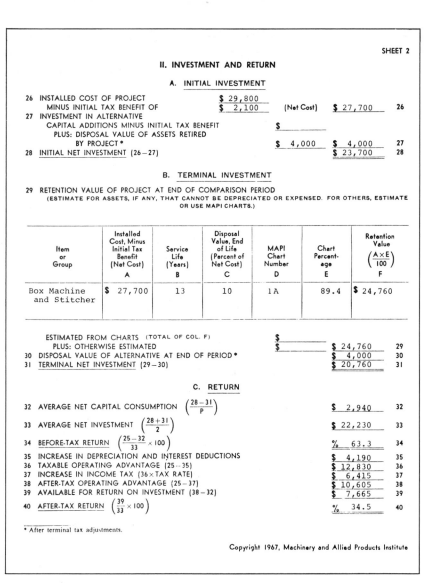

FIGURE 18-2. MAPI investment and return form [This form is excerpted from *Business Investment Policy* (Machine and Allied Products Institute, 1967.)]

costs. These are Lines 4 through 22. For our example, there has been an increase of $900 in direct labor and an increase in indirect labor of $150. Maintenance costs are increased by $200, and downtime is unaffected. We charge ourselves for increased fringe benefits ($190), tooling ($80), power ($40), and property taxes and insurance, *estimating* this increase to be $320. On the other hand, costs for materials and supplies decrease by $16,800. Floor space costs decrease by $1000 and inventory costs decrease by $1100.

8. The total increase in operating costs is $1880; total decrease is $18,900.
9. The net decrease in operating costs is $17,020 (Line 24).
10. The resultant next-year operating advantage is also $17,020 (Line 25).
11. Now we look at the calculation of the terminal investment (Fig. 18-2). Refer to columns A through F as well as the MAPI Chart No 1A (Fig. 18-3) for a 1-year comparison ($P = 1$) and sum-of-digits depreciation

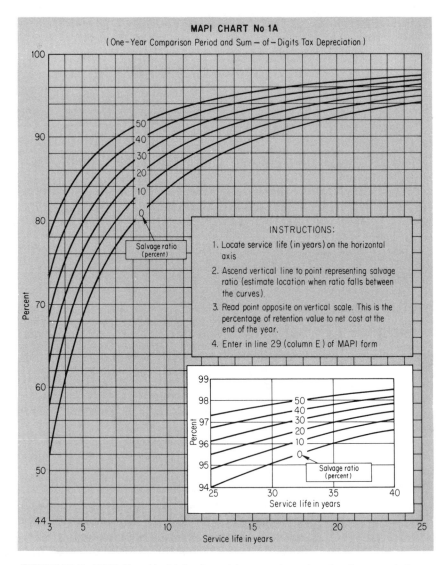

FIGURE 18-3. MAPI Chart No. 1A for determining retention value of project at end of comparison period
(In this case, a 1-year period where sum-of-digits tax depreciation is used. Charts for other conditions are available.) [This chart is excerpted from *Business Investment Policy* (Machine and Allied Products Institute, 1967).]

(see Appendix 18-I, which is presented as optional material). Other MAPI charts are available for alternative depreciation methods.[4]

Column A: Installed cost of computer-controlled stitcher, less initial tax benefit, is $27,700 (Line 26).

Column B: Service life has been estimated to be 13 years.

Column C: *Estimated* salvage value after 13 years is $2770, which is 10 percent of the net cost shown in Column A.

Column D: We use the most appropriate MAPI chart. Three basically different forms of depreciation can apply; see Fig. 18-4. What we require is a percentage to apply to the required investment based on depreciation, machine wear,[5] and salvage value. We have chosen the 1-year, sum-of-digits case, found on Chart No. 1A., illustrated in Fig. 18-3. We apply this accelerated method of depreciation [option (c) in Fig. 18-4] to our situation.

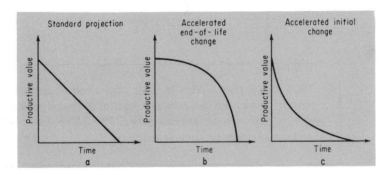

FIGURE 18-4. Three different patterns that describe the way in which the productive value of a facility can change over time

Column E: For our assumptions, we obtain a chart percentage of 89.4 percent, or the decimal fraction 0.894.

Column F: This is ($27,700)(0.894) = $24,760, which is shown on Line 29.

12. The return on investment, after taxes, is now calculated (see Line 40 of Fig. 18-2).

13. The after-tax return, as a percentage, is determined to be 34.5. This is a large enough figure to command immediate management attention. The numerical procedures for deriving this number are clearly delineated in Fig. 18-2.

14. On the basis of the figure of 34.5 percent, we recommend replacing the present facility with the new computer-controlled stitcher.

---

[4]Terborgh, *A MAPI Study and Manual.*
[5]This refers to the way in which the facility declines as a profit producer because of technological factors. See Fig. 18-4.

Line 40 is a measure of investment urgency. Available investment funds can be used in many different ways. There is competition between alternative facilities, dividends to stockholders, increased salaries or wages, improvement studies and so forth. If we can obtain a measure of the relative urgency (or desirability) of alternative investments, then we can determine a reasonable guide for action. The MAPI measure (Line 40) expresses the first-year, after-tax funds that are available for return on investment (Line 39) as a percentage of the average net investment (Line 33). By using this measure of effectiveness, or modifications of it, one can examine the various process alternatives in a reasonable manner.

Rational policies will dominate the design and control of the process. The major advantage of the MAPI method is that it permits a simple and consistent method to be applied for evaluating all company facilities—and this in terms of an appropriate measure of effectiveness, viz., return on investment (ROI). The fact that taxes are considered is an important strength of the MAPI procedure. Too frequently, taxes are overlooked in the equipment selection process.

> *Our objective:* This book is organized to reveal in an entirely operational way the sequence of reasoning that is needed to produce and run high-productivity systems. The MAPI calculations are an excellent example of such reasoning.

Plant Layout

The choice of a facility interacts with the process being used. Once the process has been specified and the appropriate types of equipment have been selected, it is then necessary to arrange all the system's components in an *optimal layout*. In some job shop cases, the plant may have already been selected. For most flow shops and some projects, the plant location choice is affected by layout considerations. For every kind of system, careful thought has been given to the selection of specific machines and to the number of such machines needed to provide adequate capacity. The possible connections for material flows between the machines have been surveyed, and the sensible placement of operators and the number of operators have also been discussed. Usually, however, alternatives exist. The list of alternatives interacts with layout decisions. Facility alternatives constrain layout, and layout alternatives constrain facilities. This is not easy to show, because the layout problem, even *with fixed equipment selections*, is still extremely complex.

Trial and Error Approach to Layout with Graphics

Decisions concerning the arrangement of specific elements are what we refer to as the *layout problem*. The solution to the line-balancing problem provides direct guidelines and constraints. For shop loading, often specific facilities are grouped into *machine centers*. This helps the operations manager by giving him fewer elements to think about. Although physical models of the plant floor and the selected equipment are frequently helpful in guiding arrangement, intuition underlies their use (see Fig. 18-5).

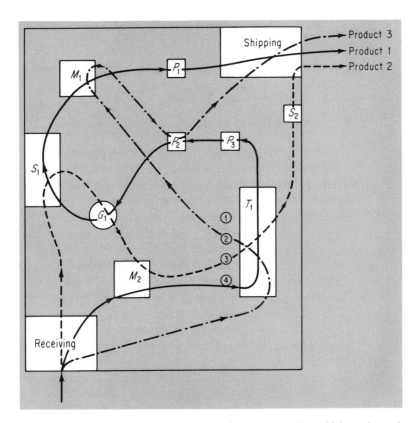

FIGURE 18-5. Flow process layout diagram for a system with multiple product-mix requirements

Models can be 2- or 3-dimensional. Often, 2-dimensional floor plans with cutouts, or templates, representing the various pieces of equipment are used. When conveyors are employed, overhead space requirements may be important, and 3-dimensional models are preferred. These techniques are useful for *approaching a satisfactory* layout, but they do not hold out any promise of finding an optimal layout (as explained below).

Can an optimal layout really be found? For the job shop, it is not productive to seek an optimal arrangement. There are too many possible layout variables and combinations of facilities and work spaces. There is no way to search through them all. Figure 18-5 illustrates the kind of complexity that we are addressing.

As the production process approaches total mechanization and, ultimately, complete automation, technological constraints operate. The flow-shop configuration warrants large study investments, so the notion of an optimal layout becomes more tenable. For the general case, however, it is desirable to talk about obtaining *a satisfactory* layout.

What is a satisfactory layout? Some of the possible measures of a layout's effectiveness are

1. The capacity of the system under different arrangements.[6]
2. The investment and operating costs of various production configurations.
3. The flexibility to change a layout as required.

The layout problem is complicated by the question of whether we shall make do with an existing plant or build a new one to our specifications. Frequently, when a plant-rental arrangement is used, basic structural changes either are prohibited or are not economically sensible. When an existing structure has been purchased, it may not be economically feasible to knock down walls, add sections, and make other structural changes. Such alterations require investment in plant, and such investments must be justified in terms of alternative uses of these funds. The relative permanency desired for any physical arrangement of components is a matter that arises here. If a continuous production line is to be set up, it obviously presents different conditions than would be encountered with a job-shop system.

Given some knowledge of the plant construction, a well-known basic approach to the plant layout problem makes use of schematics, such as flow-process diagrams, flow-process charts, and various forms of dimensional models; all decisions that follow are clearly dominated by intuition. (See Figs. 18-6, 18-7, 18-8, 18-9, and 18-10.) It is reasonable to work with both the flow diagram and the process chart. Thus, for example, an initial layout and system is conceived (e.g., Figs. 18-6 and 18-7). Then, various changes are proposed as challengers. Figures 18-8 and 18-9 are representative of proposed improvements.

In general a satisfactory resolution of the plant layout problem is considerably expedited by the use of flow-process layout diagrams, as shown in Figs. 18-6 and 18-8. These diagrams describe the flow of food shelves for a

---

[6]For flow and project shops, it is essential to balance the output rates of consecutive operations. This is the line-balancing problem; see pp. 191–207.

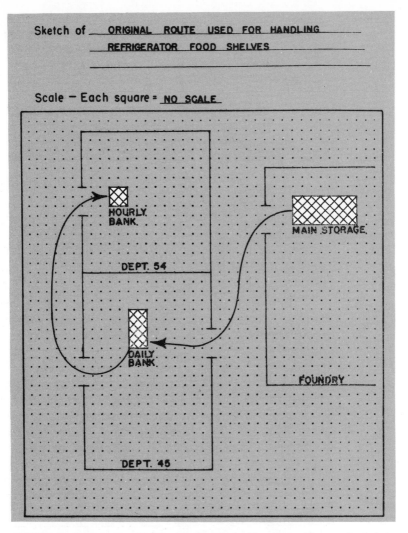

FIGURE 18-6. Flow diagram for original method of handling refrigerator food shelves from bulk storage to plating department [From Marvin E. Mundel, *Motion and Time Study*, 4th ed. (Englewood Cliffs, N.J.: Prentice-Hall, Inc., 1970), p. 60.]

refrigerator manufacturer. The flow path is superimposed on the floor plan. Alternative arrangements of layout produce different flow patterns. Changes in layout are normally made until a satisfactory flow pattern is achieved. In conjunction, appropriate flow-process charts are developed to describe those characteristics of the system's flow that do not lend themselves to visual representation, e.g., Figs. 18-7 and 18-9. Note that special symbols are used to indicate different categories of systems behaviors. Figure 18-10 presents the key for interpreting these symbols. There is no totally uniform convention with respect to such symbols, and in practice, many variations will be found.

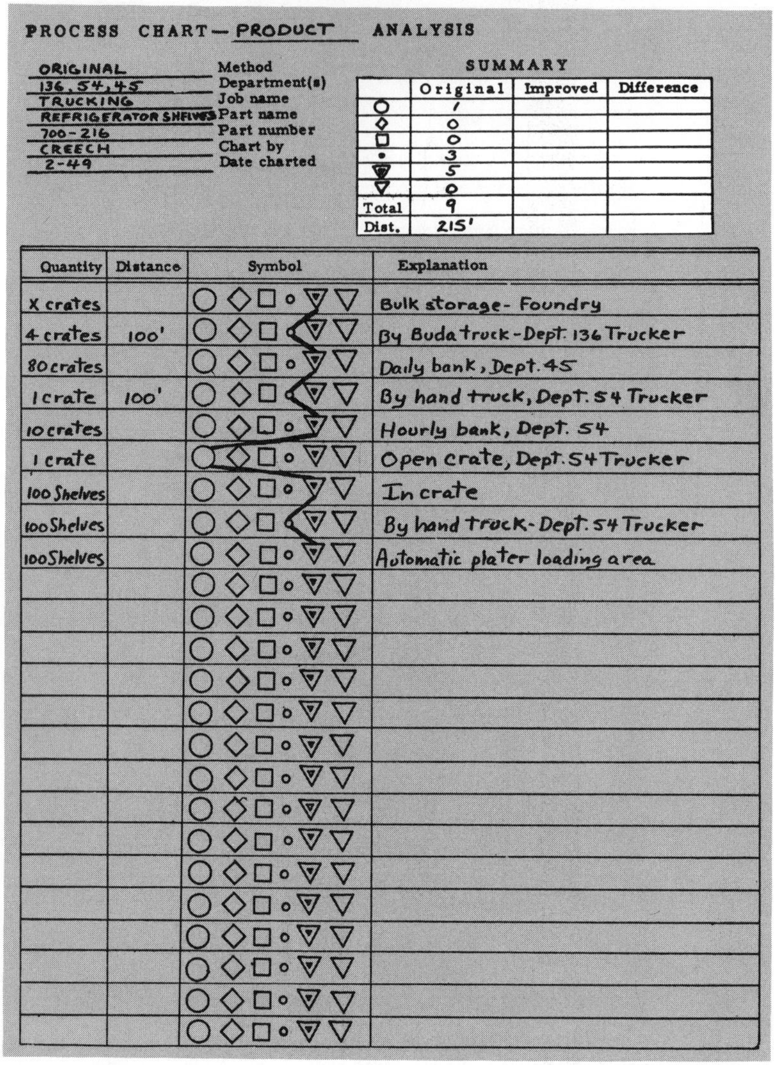

PROCESS CHART—*PRODUCT* ANALYSIS

ORIGINAL _____ Method
__136, 54, 45__ Department(s)
__TRUCKING__ Job name
__REFRIGERATOR SHELVES__ Part name
__700-216__ Part number
__CREECH__ Chart by
__2-49__ Date charted

SUMMARY

		Original	Improved	Difference
○		1		
◇		0		
□		0		
●		3		
▽		5		
▽		0		
Total		9		
Dist.		215'		

Quantity	Distance	Symbol	Explanation
X crates		○ ◇ □ ○ ▽ ▽	Bulk storage- Foundry
4 crates	100'	○ ◇ □ ○ ▽ ▽	By Buda truck - Dept. 136 Trucker
80 crates		○ ◇ □ ○ ▽ ▽	Daily bank, Dept. 45
1 crate	100'	○ ◇ □ ○ ▽ ▽	By hand truck, Dept. 54 Trucker
10 crates		○ ◇ □ ○ ▽ ▽	Hourly bank, Dept. 54
1 crate		○ ◇ □ ○ ▽ ▽	Open crate, Dept. 54 Trucker
100 Shelves		○ ◇ □ ○ ▽ ▽	In crate
100 Shelves		○ ◇ □ ○ ▽ ▽	By hand truck - Dept. 54 Trucker
100 Shelves		○ ◇ □ ○ ▽ ▽	Automatic plater loading area

FIGURE 18-7. Process chart-product analysis for original method of handling refrigerator food shelves from bulk storage to plating department [From Marvin E. Mundel, *Motion and Time Study*, 4th ed. (Englewood Cliffs, N.J.: Prentice-Hall, Inc., 1970), p. 61.]

The summary box of the flow process chart permits rapid comparison of various layout plans. Thus, Fig. 18-9 illustrates a proposed revision. The summary box of the proposed method reveals that 2 kinds of improvements will result if the original layout arrangement is changed. These include 1 less transport and 2 less uncontrolled storage stages. The travel distance has been decreased by 140 feet. If the first layout is in actual use, then it is necessary to compare the cost of making the change with the reduction in operating costs that can be achieved. The comparison requires the use of an appropriate discounting formulation so that the stream of savings can be properly evaluated.

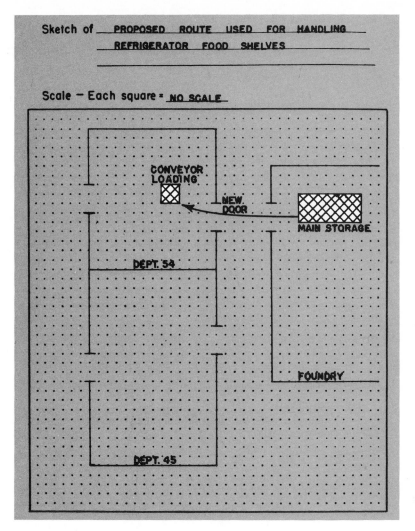

FIGURE 18-8. Flow diagram for the proposed method of handling refrigerator food shelves
Note that a wall has been broken through to yield direct access to the conveyor. [From Marvin E. Mundel, *Motion and Time Study*, 4th ed. (Englewood Cliffs, N.J.: Prentice-Hall, Inc., 1970), p. 62.

It is frequently more practical to begin the layout plan in an environment that is totally divorced from the spatial constraints of reality. An assembly diagram, also called a Gozinto (goes-into) Chart, is a flow diagram concerned neither with real time nor real space. Only sequence is presented. Generally, service activities, such as transportation and storage are excluded. An example of a Gozinto Chart is shown in Fig. 18-11. Using this chart, one can determine an intelligent arrangement of facilities based on the essential sequential requirements of the process.

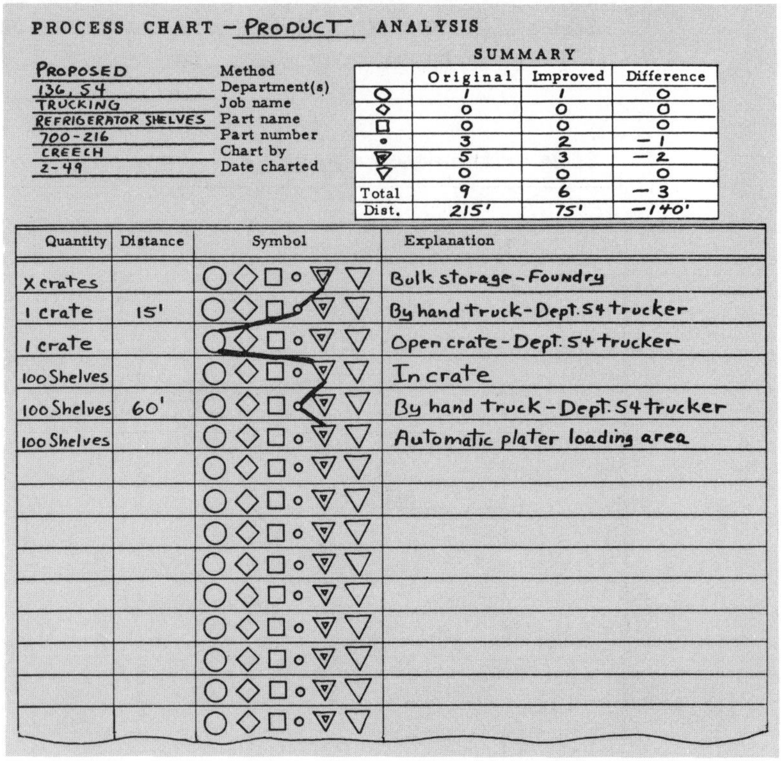

PROCESS CHART — _PRODUCT_ ANALYSIS

PROPOSED	Method
136, 54	Department(s)
TRUCKING	Job name
REFRIGERATOR SHELVES	Part name
700-216	Part number
CREECH	Chart by
2-49	Date charted

SUMMARY

	Original	Improved	Difference
○	1	1	0
◇	0	0	0
□	0	0	0
•	3	2	− 1
▽ (filled)	5	3	− 2
▽	0	0	0
Total	9	6	− 3
Dist.	215'	75'	−140'

Quantity	Distance	Symbol	Explanation
X crates		○ ◇ □ ∘ ▽ ▽	Bulk storage – Foundry
1 crate	15'	○ ◇ □ ∘ ▽ ▽	By hand truck – Dept. 54 trucker
1 crate		○ ◇ □ ∘ ▽ ▽	Open crate – Dept. 54 trucker
100 Shelves		○ ◇ □ ∘ ▽ ▽	In crate
100 Shelves	60'	○ ◇ □ ∘ ▽ ▽	By hand truck – Dept. 54 trucker
100 Shelves		○ ◇ □ ∘ ▽ ▽	Automatic plater loading area
		○ ◇ □ ∘ ▽ ▽	
		○ ◇ □ ∘ ▽ ▽	
		○ ◇ □ ∘ ▽ ▽	
		○ ◇ □ ∘ ▽ ▽	
		○ ◇ □ ∘ ▽ ▽	
		○ ◇ □ ∘ ▽ ▽	
		○ ◇ □ ∘ ▽ ▽	
		○ ◇ □ ∘ ▽ ▽	
		○ ◇ □ ∘ ▽ ▽	

FIGURE 18-9. Process chart-product analysis for proposed method of handling refrigerator food shelves from bulk storage to plating department [From Marvin E. Mundel, _Motion and Time Study,_ 4th ed. (Englewood Cliffs, N.J.: Prentice-Hall, Inc., 1970), p. 61.]

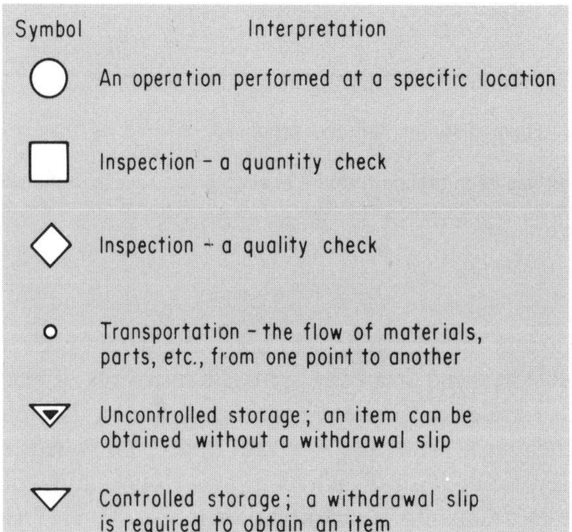

Symbol	Interpretation
○	An operation performed at a specific location
□	Inspection – a quantity check
◇	Inspection – a quality check
∘	Transportation – the flow of materials, parts, etc., from one point to another
▽ (filled)	Uncontrolled storage; an item can be obtained without a withdrawal slip
▽	Controlled storage; a withdrawal slip is required to obtain an item

FIGURE 18-10. Symbol key for flow process chart

428

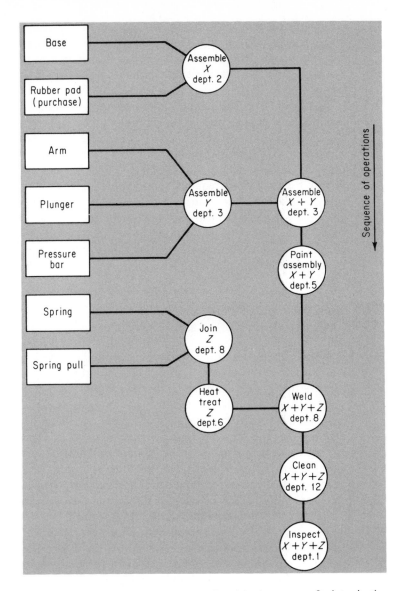

FIGURE 18-11. An assembly sequence chart (also known as a Gozinto chart)

This chart fully details which parts (e.g., base, arm, plunger) are made and which are purchased. (Only the rubber pad is purchased.) Following the lines, from left to right, we learn which parts enter into each subassembly, and where, i.e., subassembly X in department 2, Y in department 3, and Z in department 8. Then, X and Y are joined together in department 3 and painted in department 5. After heat treating in department 6, subassembly Z is welded to subassembly ($X + Y$) in department 8, cleaned in department 12, and inspected in department 1.

429

The relevance of MRP is underscored by the cascade of interdependent components shown in Fig. 18-11. That is why we referred to the Gozinto chart on p. 332. Also, we observe the job shop nature of this work, wherein batches of components and subassemblies move through 7 different departments.

The layout problem is. much more complicated when a common set of facilities must be shared by multiple products that require different flow paths and sequences through the system. For example, Fig. 18-5 portrays a flow-process layout diagram where alternate routes must be followed by the several products in the company's product mix. To find layout plans that are satisfactory for such cases requires considerable juggling of the facilities. As a rule, the product that contributes the *greatest percentage to total profit* is given preferential treatment, and the others less so in accordance with their value to the company. At least, this *heuristic* simplifies the problem. With one major product being processed (flow-shop configuration), it is reasonable to route that product on a *minimum cost path*.

The Minimum Cost Path Layout
(Using the Mayor's Office as an Example)

When we consider the layout problem in mathematical terms, we find that it is surprisingly large and complex. This is true, even though we dismiss many of the factors that being intangible are reserved ordinarily for intuition. The layout problem for an average size job shop, strictly in cost terms, is recognized to involve consideration of billions or trillions of alternatives. This explains why the intuitive approach has been so widely used for job-shop layout decisions. It is always possible (even probable) that intuition will overlook some excellent solutions, but one thing is certain, while optimality may be missed by the manager, an illogical and inappropriate solution will not be accepted by him. Let us see why the formal analysis of the layout problem for the job shop is so demanding.[7]

The mayor's office is an excellent example of a job shop. The office is composed of work centers that are responsible for different functions, such as typing, filing, phoning, copying and so forth. Work flows back and forth between centers. Although there is a pattern, it is one rich with combinations and variations.

The mayor has brought in a management consulting firm to study the layout problem. The head consultant explains to the 160 individuals who work in the mayor's office—at different civil service levels with an assortment of job descriptions—that the layout study will include tangible and intangible factors, but the first crack at the problem will be to determine which work

---

[7]Clearly, the layout problem of a flow shop or a project shop would be different from a job shop. The layout, in these cases, would actually interact with the line-balance solutions and project trade-off solutions that we derived in earlier chapters. So it is most often the job shop layout problem to which we address ourselves.

paths are used the most, and what distances work has to travel. Ultimately, a set of locations will be chosen to which the work centers will be assigned so as to minimize the costs of shuffling work around.

Let us get more specific. Here is how the mayor's consultants view the problem.

Define the *job shop* as consisting of *N work centers*, WC_j ($j = 1, 2, \ldots, N$), and *N* locations, L_i($i = A, B, \ldots, N$). Each work center has a fundamentally different activity, and each location is clearly defined.

There is a distance $d_{ii'}$ between any 2 locations and a work flow rate of $F_{jj'}$ between any 2 work centers. Also, there is a cost $C_{jj'}$ for handling work between centers. (It is the cost per unit of flow per unit of distance moved.)

As an example, let us assign work centers 1 and 2 to locations *A* and *B*, respectively. The distance between *A* and *B* is 10 feet in either direction, i.e., $d_{AB} = d_{BA} = 10$ feet (see Matrix 1). The work flow rate between centers 1 and 2 is 100 ($1 \rightarrow 2$) plus 40 ($2 \rightarrow 1$). (See Matrix 2.) Thus, $F_{12} + F_{21} = 140$. Assume that all handling costs (including C_{12} and C_{21}) are equal to 1 per unit of flow per unit of distance moved.

The cost of locating work centers 1 and 2 at locations *A* and *B*, with respect to each other, is

$$FC_{12} = C_{12}(d_{AB}F_{12}) + C_{21}(d_{BA}F_{21})$$

where $FC_{jj'}$ is the total work flow cost between work centers *j* and *j'*. For our illustration

$$FC_{12} + FC_{21} = 1(10 \times 100) + 1(10 \times 40) = 1400$$

After assigning all work centers to locations, we determine the sum of all total flow costs for that configuration, i.e., $\sum_j \sum_{j'} FC_{jj'}$. This is the grand total of handling costs for the specific layout. Our objective is: *Minimize materials-handling costs.*

Given a specific office, its configuration will constrain the way in which work centers can be assigned to office space.[8] Assume that 5 office spaces are designated. The question is, how to assign 5 work centers to these locations? Figure 18-12 portrays a floor layout with 5 work centers assigned to specific locations. (More complex illustrations would involve several floors of an office building, or materials handling in a large manufacturing job shop.)

The office is a job shop with many different flow patterns. Its layout problem is complicated, because a variety of work flows through a common set of facilities. There are many different flow paths and sequences through

---

[8]For example, there are security constraints for the computer center and privacy requirements for the filing center. The telephone center should be isolated from the typing pool, etc. Similar constraints exist in other layout situations. For manufacturing, machinery can be assigned only to certain areas. Cranes may require special height clearance; upper floors are needed for gravity conveyors; press shops cannot be located near offices because of noise; receiving and shipping should logically be close to truck docks and rail spurs, etc.

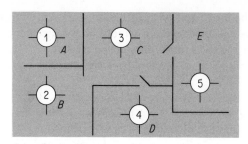

FIGURE 18-12. The floor layout of the mayor's office with 5 work centers 1, 2, 3, 4, and 5 (e.g., filing, typing pool, reproduction equipment, etc.) assigned to 5 office locations *A, B, C, D,* and *E*

the system, e.g., Fig. 18-5. The material being handled is mostly information in different forms.

Matrix of Distances. Divide the mayor's office into locations. (See Figure 18-12.) Next, measure either the time or distance required to transport work from one location to another. It is now possible to construct a matrix that shows the appropriate time or distance for transporting work between any 2 locations of the office. An example is Matrix 1.

MATRIX 1   DISTANCES $d_{ii'}$ BETWEEN LOCATIONS L_i
OF THE OFFICE (IN FEET)

		To Location				
		A	B	C	D	E
	A	0	10	20	32	40
	B	10	0	16	18	20
From location	C	20	16	0	12	15
	D	32	18	12	0	10
	E	40	20	15	10	0

The diagonal of the matrix is 0, because it is assumed that within a location no travel is required. Also, as a general rule, the matrix will be symmetrical; that is, the distance from *A* to *B* will be equal to the distance from *B* to *A*. This is not always the case, for example, if an "up" escalator connects 2 floors while stairs are used to go down; or in a factory, if unidirectional (e.g., gravity) conveyor systems connect some of the plant locations.

Work Flow Rates. Although the distances between locations may be small, the frequency with which work travels between stations is high. Therefore, an efficient layout, which assigns work centers to office locations in a near-optimal fashion, can produce substantial savings when compared with

an arbitrary assignment method. For the mayor's office, measures of work
flows between stations yields Matrix 2.

**MATRIX 2 WORK FLOW RATES $F_{jj'}$ BETWEEN WORK CENTERS
WC_j AND $WC_{j'}$ (IN NUMBER OF UNITS PER DAY)**

		To Work Center				
		1	2	3	4	5
	1	x	100	60	80	20
From	2	40	x	50	10	90
Work	3	80	90	x	60	30
Center	4	120	10	40	x	70
	5	110	5	5	30	x

Matrix 2 is seldom symmetrical. For example, there is no reason to expect
as much work to move from the filing center to the typing pool as vice versa.
The diagonal of Matrix 2 is blocked because although the rate of work trans-
fers within each center can be measured, such work is assumed to travel zero
distance. Since a cost is associated with moving a unit of work a given distance, internal transactions will have zero cost. Consequently, they will not
affect our solution.

The mayor's consultants decided to evaluate first the present configuration. That is, the work centers are presently assigned to the office locations
as follows: 1*A*, 2*B*, 3*C*, 4*D*, 5*E* (see Fig. 18-12). Matrix 3 represents the total
daily work flows (number of units times distance traveled) for the present
configuration. It is obtained by multiplying the distance between the assigned
work centers by the work flow rates between them.

**MATRIX 3 TOTAL DAILY WORK FLOWS ($F_{jj'} \times d_{ii'}$) BETWEEN
WORK CENTERS j AT PRESENTLY ASSIGNED LOCATIONS i
(IN TOTAL UNIT FEET TRAVELED PER DAY)**

		To Work Center				
		1	2	3	4	5
	1	0	1000	1200	2560	800
From	2	400	0	800	180	1800
Work	3	1600	1440	0	720	450
Center	4	3840	180	480	0	700
	5	4400	100	75	300	0

Because we have been told to consider all costs to be 1 per unit foot
traveled, Matrix 3 is also a matrix of total work flow costs. Bearing this in

mind, we now have a picture of what the present assignment configuration means. The mayor's office is paying heavily for work flows from centers 5 and 4 to center 1, as well as from center 1 to center 4. Perhaps there is no better arrangement, but that fact is hardly certain. There are 5! ways (i.e., 120) to assign 5 work centers to 5 locations, and we have just looked at 1 of these.

Costs for Distance Traveled. We need 1 more matrix to complete our analysis (namely, the costs per unit for distance traveled). It could be that all work flows have the same handling costs. We have assumed a unit cost to this point. If, however, cost differentials do exist, then the matrix of costs (per unit of flow per unit of distance moved) must be multiplied cell by cell with the matrix of total daily work flows. Matrix 4 presents an example of a matrix with cost differentials, and Matrix 5 (the result of multiplication with Matrix 3) is the matrix of total work flow costs.

MATRIX 4 COSTS PER UNIT OF FLOW PER UNIT OF DISTANCE TRAVELED BETWEEN WORK CENTERS j AT PRESENTLY ASSIGNED LOCATIONS i (IN DOLLARS PER WORK UNIT PER FOOT MOVED)

| | | To Work Center | | | | |
		1	*2*	*3*	*4*	*5*
From	1	x	0.8	1	0.5	0.5
Work	2	0.8	x	1	1	1
Center	3	1	1	x	0.8	0.8
	4	0.5	1	0.8	x	1
	5	0.5	1	0.8	1	x

MATRIX 5 TOTAL DAILY WORK FLOW COSTS $FC_{jj'}$ (IN DOLLARS)

| | | To Work Center | | | | |
		1	*2*	*3*	*4*	*5*	
From	1	0	800	1200	1280	400	
Work	2	320	0	800	180	1800	Total Costs
Center	3	1600	1440	0	576	360	= $16,600
	4	1920	180	384	0	700	
	5	2200	100	60	300	0	

The large costs associated with work flows from centers 5 and 4 to center 1, and from center 1 to center 4 have been reduced, but they still appear formidable. Relocation analysis would still appear to be worthwhile. (See Problem 8, p. 447.)

Let us return to Matrix 3 and, assuming that equal unit flow costs are appropriate, determine the total costs for this case. Matrix 6 presents this information and, in addition, shows the total costs that originate with a center (row sums) and total costs that culminate with a center (column sums).

MATRIX 6 TOTAL DAILY COST OF WORK FLOWS BETWEEN CENTERS, $FC_{jj'}$

		To Work Center						
		1	2	3	4	5		
	1	0	1000	1200	2560	800	5560	
From	2	400	0	800	180	1800	3180	Total costs
Work	3	1600	1440	0	720	450	4210	= $23,025
Center	4	3840	180	480	0	700	5200	
	5	4400	100	75	300	0	4875	
		10,240	2720	2555	3760	3750	23,025	

It is striking that work center 1 completes almost 45 percent of all transactions (10,240/23,025 = 0.44). Perhaps some basic redesign is called for—a point that will hardly be lost on the mayor's consultants. Also, the mayor will be surprised to learn that the total costs of handling work between centers 1 and 4 (3840 + 2560 = 6400) and between centers 1 and 5 (4400 + 800 = 5200) are so large (see Matrix 7). The office layout should be changed.

Improving Layouts

Two heuristics come to mind when one is searching for rules by which to improve the office (or plant) layout.

1. Assign the centers with large work flow rates between them to locations as close as possible.
2. Assign the centers with small work flow rates between them to locations as distant as possible.

The mayor's consultants try to apply these rules. First, in Matrix 7, they have summed all the costs of each pair of work centers.

**MATRIX 7 SUMS OF DAILY PAIRED WORK
CENTER FLOW COSTS $FC_{jj'} + FC_{j'j}$**

	To and from Work Center					
	1	2	3	4	5	
1	0	1400	2800	6400	5200	
2		0	2240	360	1900	Total costs
3			0	1200	525	= $23,025
4				0	1000	
5					0	

The biggest number in Matrix 7 relates work centers 1 and 4. Accordingly, work center 1 is placed at location *A* and work center 4 is placed at location *B*. (Note in Matrix 1 that 10 is the shortest distance between any 2 locations, but it is also available at *D* and *E*. That alternative should also be tried, as should others which seem to merit analysis. We should bear in mind that our approach is heuristic and, therefore, could bypass a clue that might yield a superior solution.) Centers 1 and 5 have large flow costs; thus, work center 5 is placed at location *C*. Similar reasoning assigns work center 3 to location *D*. This forces work center 2 to location *E*. However, we would have placed work center 2 as far from center 4 as possible, because the work flows between them are the smallest in the matrix, so we achieve the benefits of both heuristics with this move.

The assignment is 1*A*, 2*E*, 3*D*, 4*B*, 5*C*. Matrix 1 times Matrix 2 now becomes Matrix 8. Thus:

MATRIX 8

		Location Distances						Work Flow Rates						Total between Center Work Flows				
														A	B	C	D	E
														1	4	5	3	2
	A	*B*	*C*	*D*	*E*		1	4	5	3	2							
A	0	10	20	32	40	1	x	80	20	60	100	1	0	800	400	1920	4000
B	10	0	16	18	20	4	120	x	70	40	10	4	1200	0	1120	720	200
C	20	16	0	12	15	5	110	30	x	5	5	5	2200	480	0	60	75
D	32	18	12	0	10	3	80	60	30	x	90	3	2560	1080	360	0	900
E	40	20	15	10	0	2	40	10	90	50	x	2	1600	200	1350	500	0

Assuming that equal unit flow costs apply, we derive Matrix 9, which is similar in concept to Matrix 7.

MATRIX 9 TOTAL DAILY COST OF COMBINED WORK FLOWS BETWEEN CENTERS

			Work Center			
	1	2	3	4	5	
1	0	5600	4480	2000	2600	
2		0	1400	400	1425	Total costs
3			0	1800	420	= $21,725
4				0	1600	
5					0	

There has been a substantial decrease in cost ($1300, or almost 6 percent) but it is possible that greater decreases could be achieved. We have tried only 2 configurations out of 120 possibilities. Of course, our improved version was based on a reasonable heuristic, so it should be better than an alternative picked at random. Yet, other layouts exist which conform with the general idea of the heuristic, and these should be tried.

CRAFT (Computerized Relative Allocation of Facilities Technique)

The simple heuristics we have used up to this point are not sufficiently powerful to cope with a big problem. Total enumeration is out of the question for a big problem. However, a strong heuristic approach exists. It was developed by G. C. Armour and E. S. Buffa,[9] and called CRAFT (Computerized Relative Allocation of Facilities Technique).

The improvement algorithm is based on exchanging the locations of pairs of work centers, and for each exchange computing the alteration in materials-handling costs.

This is demonstrated for the case of Olympic Studios that follows.[10] There are $n(n-1)/2$ such pairs, *starting with any one* machine center. The best exchange is made, and then the procedure continues, starting with a different work center.

For example, with 4 centers 1, 2, 3, and 4 (starting with 1), the first iteration of $n(n-1)/2 = 4(3)/2 = 6$ pair exchanges would be:

Exchange Number	① 2 3 4	Exchange Pair
1	2 1 3 4	1,2
2	3 2 1 4	1,3
3	4 2 3 1	1,4
4	1 3 2 4(*)	2,3
5	1 4 3 2	2,4
6	1 2 4 3	3,4

Say that the fourth exchange 1 3 2 4 is best (*). Then the second iteration begins with any center except 1, which has been used already. Arbitrarily, let us choose 2.

[9]Gordon C. Armour and Elwood S. Buffa, "A Heuristic Algorithm and Simulation Approach to the Relative Location of Facilities," *Management Science*, Vol. 9, No. 2 (January, 1963), pp. 294–309. Also, see, Elwood S. Buffa, Gordon C. Armour, and Thomas E. Vollmann, "Allocating Facilities with 'CRAFT,'" *Harvard Business Review*, Vol. 42, No. 2 (March–April, 1964), pp. 136–58.

[10]An actual, successful application of CRAFT to a movie studio layout is cited in the *Harvard Business Review* article mentioned in footnote 9.

Exchange Number	1	3	②(2)	4(**)	Exchange Pair
1	2	3	1	4	2,1
2	1	2	3	4	2,3
3	1	3	4	2	2,4
4	3	1	2	4	1,3
5	4	3	2	1	1,4
6	1	4	2	3	3,4

Say that the best $^{(**)}$ is still 1 3 2 4. We must now begin the third iteration with either center 3 or 4. Arbitrarily, let us choose 4. The best arrangement found by the third iteration is the starting point of the fourth and final iteration, which tests all pairs in terms of center number 3.

As an upper limit $n^2/2$ computations are required with each of n iterations (which also is a reasonable upper limit), whereas total enumeration requires $n!$ computations.[11] As reported in the articles cited in the footnote, the algorithm is effective and provides substantial savings over an intuition-based layout.

---

[11]At $n = 4$, the break-even-point is reached; thereafter $n!$ grows far more rapidly than $n[n(n-1)/2]$.

Olympic Studios—A Simplified Application of CRAFT

Olympic is a well-known film studio that moves sets and personnel between locations regularly. The moves are costly but necessary, since at each location a different kind of work center operates, i.e., space available, camera setups, supporting props, etc.

Olympic's management wants to determine the best layout, invest in it, and stick with it. Assume that 3 locations (*A*, *B*, and *C*) exist with distances (in feet) between them as shown in Display 1.

DISPLAY 1

		A	To B	C
	A	0	4000	2000
From	B	4000	0	3000
	C	2000	3000	0

Filming activities are sequenced through 3 work centers (1, 2, and 3) with monthly flow *costs* per unit distance as shown in Display 2.

DISPLAY 2

		To		
		1	*2*	*3*
	1	x	$50	$70
From	2	$20	x	$40
	3	$30	$80	x

With these data, we may be able to improve upon the existing assignment, which is 1*A*, 2*B*, 3*C*. The total monthly flow cost matrix (in thousands) for the existing layout is derived by multiplication (Display 3).

DISPLAY 3

	A 1	*B* 2	*C* 3	
1	0	200	140	Total monthly cost
2	80	0	120	= $840,000
3	60	240	0	

Using CRAFT for our heuristic, start with work center 1 and exchange locations as shown in Display 4.

DISPLAY 4

Variation	*Location* A B C	*Total Monthly Flow Costs** *(in thousands)*
Original	① 2 3	$840
First exchange	2 1 3	820 ⟵
Second exchange	3 2 1	890
Third exchange	1 3 2	900

We take the best of these results ($820,000, which occurred with the first exchange) and start the series of exchanges with work center 2. This is shown in Display 5.

DISPLAY 5

Variation	Location A B C	Total Monthly Flow Costs* (in thousands)
Start	② 1 3	$820 ←
First exchange	1 2 3	840
Second exchange	3 1 2	850
Third exchange	2 3 1	920

We can stop. Because of the small number of work centers and locations ($n = 3$), we have ended up enumerating all $n!$ possible arrangements of work centers and locations. With values of n larger than 4, this will not occur. CRAFT has been of great help to Olympic Studios. The heuristic technique produces $20,000 of savings a month ($840,000 − 820,000 = $20,000). Note also how bad a solution might have been achieved by chance, i.e., the worst case is 2A, 3B, 1C with total monthly flow costs of $920,000.

*These flow costs are computed in the same way that Display 3 was derived. For the work sheet, see Appendix 18-II (optional material).

APPENDIX 18-I
Depreciation Methods (Optional Material)

Over time, a process ages. It must be constantly renewed and updated. Otherwise, there is increasing risk that it will become obsolete. As an expression of this fact, accounting practice attempts to design and apply a depreciation procedure that captures the essence of the way in which the value of a company's facilities changes with *use* and *age* over a period of time.

We must understand the relevance of alternative methods of depreciation with respect to equipment replacement. In Fig. 18-13, 3 different methods for calculating depreciation are illustrated. Each of these has its own characteristic advantages and disadvantages.

Straight-line depreciation is applied, for example, to a 10-year period. This linear function has the property of decreasing by the same amount each year. That amount is simply N/T, where N is the initial facility cost and T is the facility lifetime over which it will be amortized. Thus, at any time t the undepreciated portion will be $N - tN/T$.

The method called *declining balance* involves nonlinear change that is

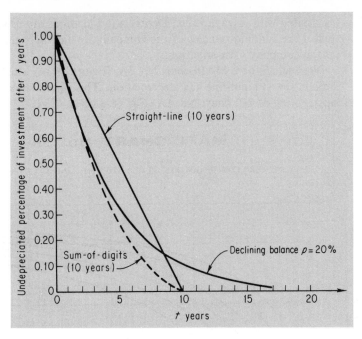

FIGURE 18-13. Three alternative depreciation methods

achieved by taking a fixed percentage p of the undepreciated balance every year. Thus, at any time t the undepreciated portion will be $N(1-p)^t$. For example, consider a machine costing $1000 with $p = 0.20$. After 3 years, the undepreciated portion will be $512. At the end of 10 years it will still be approximately $107. Therefore, the declining-balance method does not fully write off the investment by the end of the 10-year period. Instead, it approaches the full write-off asymptotically, but never reaches it.

The third method is called the *sum-of-digits method*. In this case, for a 10-year period we obtain the sum of $10 + 9 + 8 + 7 + 6 + 5 + 4 + 3 + 2 + 1$, which equals 55. At the end of the first year we depreciate the principal N by an amount $(10/55)N$. For the second year's depreciation we use $(9/55)N$; third-year depreciation equals $(8/55)N$. The total amount depreciated over the ten-year period will be $(10/55)N + (9/55)N + \ldots + (1/55)N$. This is equal to $(55/55)N$—that is, full depreciation. We observe that for each succeeding year the fraction used decreases. In order to determine the denominator value for the sum-of-digits method for a period of T years, we can utilize the formula $T(T+1)/2$. Thus, we obtain for $T = 10$ years, $10(11)/2 = 55$.

The straight-line method should be used when the facility is used up in equal amounts over a period of time. This method does not penalize any 1 year in particular. The remaining 2 methods penalize the initial years more than the latter ones. The declining-balance method leaves some amount of undepreciated value at the time of intended replacement, which can be associated with salvage value. Depreciation methods are usually designed to reflect the funding policies of the company for facility replacement, as well as the company's tax situation.

We include here MAPI chart No. 3A, (Figure 18-14) which permits calculations for straight-line tax depreciation. This figure should be viewed as augmenting MAPI chart No. 1A (Fig. 18-3 on p. 420).

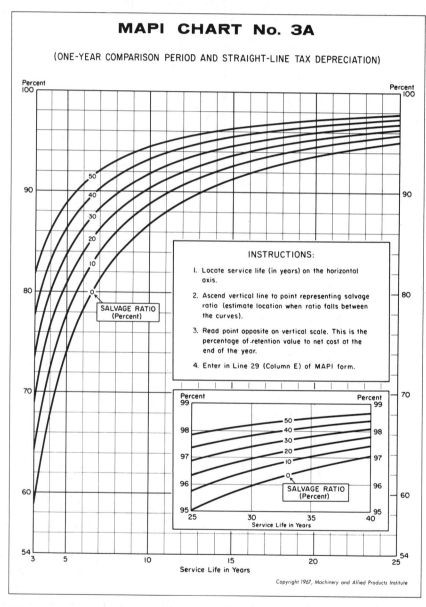

FIGURE 18-14. MAPI Chart No. 3A for determining retention value of project at end of comparison period (In this case, a 1-year period where straight-line tax depreciation is used. Charts for other conditions are available.) [This chart is excerpted from *Business Investment Policy* (Machine and Allied Products Institute, 1967.)]

APPENDIX 18-II
Work Sheet for CRAFT Computations (Optional Material)

A	B	C
2	1	3

$$\begin{vmatrix} 0 & 4 & 2 \\ 4 & 0 & 3 \\ 2 & 3 & 0 \end{vmatrix} \times \begin{vmatrix} x & 20 & 40 \\ 50 & x & 70 \\ 80 & 30 & x \end{vmatrix} = \begin{vmatrix} x & 80 & 80 \\ 200 & x & 210 \\ 160 & 90 & x \end{vmatrix} = 820$$

A	B	C
3	2	1

$$\begin{vmatrix} 0 & 4 & 2 \\ 4 & 0 & 3 \\ 2 & 3 & 0 \end{vmatrix} \times \begin{vmatrix} x & 80 & 30 \\ 40 & x & 20 \\ 70 & 50 & x \end{vmatrix} = \begin{vmatrix} x & 320 & 60 \\ 160 & x & 60 \\ 140 & 150 & x \end{vmatrix} = 890$$

A	B	C
1	3	2

$$\begin{vmatrix} 0 & 4 & 2 \\ 4 & 0 & 3 \\ 2 & 3 & 0 \end{vmatrix} \times \begin{vmatrix} x & 70 & 50 \\ 30 & x & 80 \\ 20 & 40 & x \end{vmatrix} = \begin{vmatrix} x & 280 & 100 \\ 120 & x & 240 \\ 40 & 120 & x \end{vmatrix} = 900$$

A	B	C
3	1	2

$$\begin{vmatrix} 0 & 4 & 2 \\ 4 & 0 & 3 \\ 2 & 3 & 0 \end{vmatrix} \times \begin{vmatrix} x & 30 & 80 \\ 70 & x & 50 \\ 40 & 20 & x \end{vmatrix} = \begin{vmatrix} x & 120 & 160 \\ 280 & x & 150 \\ 80 & 60 & x \end{vmatrix} = 850$$

A	B	C
2	3	1

$$\begin{vmatrix} 0 & 4 & 2 \\ 4 & 0 & 3 \\ 2 & 3 & 0 \end{vmatrix} \times \begin{vmatrix} x & 40 & 20 \\ 80 & x & 30 \\ 50 & 70 & x \end{vmatrix} = \begin{vmatrix} x & 160 & 40 \\ 320 & x & 90 \\ 100 & 210 & x \end{vmatrix} = 920$$

PROBLEMS 1. Discount analysis is suggested as a means of comparing alternative equipment that is equivalent technologically.
   a. What does technological equivalence mean?

b. If the equipment being compared is not technologically equivalent, what *two* methods might be used as a basis for making the selection?

2. Smokestack output contamination has been regulated by local ordinance. The cost of Company A's electronic precipitator is $8000. It will last 5 years. Maintenance costs are $1000 per year. The alternative is Company B's chemical filtering system, which costs $12,000, lasts 10 years, has operating cost of $500 per year and maintenance charges of $100 per year. Both systems meet the ordinance requirements. Which system do you recommend for the Northwest Paper Company, which uses a conservative 6 percent discount factor for all present value analyses?

3. A small drill press is valued at $1000. It is expected to last 2 years. It costs $4000 per year to operate. A larger drill press can be purchased for $3000. It will last 4 years. It costs $3000 per year to operate. Which drill press should we purchase? (Use a 6 percent discount factor.) Comment on your result.

4. At City Hospital, 2 miniaturized insertable cameras are under consideration for surgical support. Camera A costs $800 and has operating costs of $0.10 per picture. Camera B costs $1200 and has operating costs of $0.08 per picture. The forecast (in pictures demanded per year) is

1st Year	2nd Year	3rd Year	4th Year	5th Year
5000	6000	8000	8000	10,000

City Hospital estimates its return on available funds at 6 percent per year.

a. Approximately at what point in time are the 2 cameras equivalent in value?

b. What is the average cost per year of each camera at the end of the fifth year?

Answer: An analysis similar to that in Problem 3 applies to this problem, except that the yearly operating cost must be computed on the basis of the projected use of the camera. Thus:

End of Year	Camera A	Discounted Operating Cost	Total Cost	Average Cost
0	800(1.000) = 800		800	
1		500(0.943) = 472	1272	1272
2		600(0.890) = 534	1806	903
3		800(0.840) = 672	2478	826
4		800(0.792) = 634	3112	778
5		1000(0.747) = 747	3859	772

End of Year	Camera B	Discounted Operating Cost	Total Cost	Average Cost
0	1200(1.000) = 1200		1200	
1		400(0.943) = 377	1577	1577
2		480(0.890) = 427	2004	1002
3		640(0.840) = 538	2542	847
4		640(0.792) = 507	3049	762
5		800(0.747) = 598	3647	729

a. After $3\frac{1}{2}$ years both cameras have a total cost of about $2795. After that, camera B has lower average costs.

b. The average cost per year of camera A = \$772; of camera B, \$729.

5. Using the matrix below, assign 1 machine center to each location, in such a way as to minimize the total assignment costs. Determine the best layout for the system.

MATRIX OF COSTS FOR EACH ASSIGNMENT

Locations

		1	2	3	4	5	6
	A	16	25	9	16	7	14
	B	12	22	5	14	9	32
Machine Centers	C	35	41	13	8	14	8
	D	26	14	24	10	31	14
	E	40	15	15	26	16	18
	F	28	11	6	18	19	22

Hint: Use the assignment method (see pp. 279–85).

6. For replacement of facilities, use the example of the MAPI approach given in the text, pp. 417–22, but make the following change:

a. Column B—estimated service life—5 years.
   How does this alteration affect the after-tax return? Discuss. Now, go back to the original example and answer the following questions:

b. What tax rate has been used in Line 37?

c. Change the tax rate by cutting it in half. What effect does this have?

7. *Question:* Referring to the CRAFT heuristic (pp. 437–40), how many assignments of 4 work centers to floor locations can be made with a 4-story building? (No splitting of work centers is allowed.)

Answer: 4! = 24

Question: How many CRAFT exchanges can be made each time that a new work center is selected as the basis for exchanging?

Answer:
$$\frac{4 \times 3}{2} = 6$$

Develop a scenario of exchanges to include at least 2 iterations. The matrix of distances between locations is:

	A	B	C	D
A	0	1	2	3
B	1	0	1	2
C	2	1	0	1
D	3	2	1	0

And, the matrix of total daily flow costs, per unit distance traveled, between work centers is:

	1	2	3	4
1	0	8	10	5
2	8	0	10	10
3	10	10	0	8
4	5	10	8	0

Question: How many of the 24 possibilities did you obtain? Our scenarios follow:

	A	B	C	D		Total Costs
START	①	2	3	4		162
1	2	1	3	4		172
2	3	2	1	4		174
3	4	2	3	1		
4	1	4	3	2		
5	1	3	2	4	← one of the best	154
6	1	2	4	3		
START	1	3	②	4		
1	2	3	1	4		
2	1	2	3	4		
3	1	3	4	2		
4	4	3	2	1		
5	1	4	2	3		
6	3	1	2	4		

Answer: In these scenarios, there are 12 unique layouts. Work out the costs for these.

8. Using the cost data of Matrix 4 (p. 434), try to find the layout for the mayor's office that has the lowest total daily flow cost.

9. Tree Top Nurseries has found an ideal greenhouse. The owner has offered to rent or sell it under the following conditions.
   a. Rent of $6000 per year.
   b. Buy immediately for $48,000.
   Tree Top's management has decided that a 9-year comparison of the alternatives is reasonable. They estimate the worth of the greenhouse at the end of nine years to be $8000. The interest rate of 6 percent is used to evaluate all Tree Top investments. What should be done?

10. Complete the total enumeration of all possible arrangements for the 3×3 layout problem described by the 2 matrices below. Work out a few examples of total daily flow cost.

	Location Distances				Work Flow Rates		
	A	B	C		1	2	3
A	—	25	40	1	—	2	5
B	25	—	10	2	1	—	3
C	40	10	—	3	6	4	—

(Assume unit costs.)

11. Finding the best locations for police and fire stations is a pressing urban problem. Discuss the nature of this problem and what variables are likely to be important. How does this compare to the facility layout problem?

12. Explain why, in a job shop, the matrix $[F_{jj'}]$ might have few 0 entries, whereas, in a flow shop, the matrix might have 1 entry per row.
    Answer: The job shop is based on the existence of flexible routines between *all* work centers. In other words, a well-designed job shop can be identified by its utilization of many flow paths for jobs. In the flow shop, on the other hand, specific routines are emphasized and, where possible, unidirectional flows between locations such as $A \rightarrow B \rightarrow C \rightarrow D \rightarrow$ etc., are not confounded with flow potentials such as $B \rightarrow A$ and $A \dashrightarrow C$. Special-purpose machines underscore these flow shop designs.

The following problem relates to Appendix 18-I.

13. Compare straight-line depreciation (20 years) with the equivalent sum-of-digits result. What salvage value would remain after 20 years with a 10 percent rate for the declining balance method? Assume an investment of $10,000.

Answer: For a $10,000 investment the three methods of depreciation yield the following results:

End of Year	Straight-line Depreciation	Balance	Sum-of-digits Depreciation	Balance	Declining Balance (at 10 percent) Depreciation	Balance
1	$500	$9500	$953	$9047	$1000	$9000
2	500	9000	905	8142	900	8100
3	500	8500	857	7285	810	7290
4	500	8000	810	6475	729	6561
5	500	7500	762	5713	656	5905
6	500	7000	714	4999	591	5314
7	500	6500	667	4332	531	4783
8	500	6000	619	3713	478	4305
9	500	5500	571	3142	431	3874
10	500	5000	524	2618	387	3487
11	500	4500	476	2142	349	3138
12	500	4000	428	1714	314	2824
13	500	3500	381	1333	282	2542
14	500	3000	333	1000	254	2288
15	500	2500	285	715	229	2059
16	500	2000	238	477	206	1853
17	500	1500	191	286	185	1668
18	500	1000	143	143	167	1501
19	500	500	95	48	150	1351
20	500	0	48	0	135	1216

The sum-of-digits method starts out fast and then slows up. In the eleventh year the rate of straight-line depreciation overtakes the decelerating rate of the sum-of-digits approach. Both methods provide full depreciation at the end of the twentieth year, whereas the 10 percent declining balance method has an undepreciated residual at the end of the twentieth year that is greater than 10 percent of the original investment.

SUMMARY OF PART 7   Facilities management consists of three problems that interact with each other. These are the facility selection problem, the equipment selection problem, and the facility layout problem.

Chapter 17

With respect to facility selection, we examine the differences between analytic and synthetic processes. Then we detail a number of factors that influence the location decision. Next, factors that dictate the design of the facility are introduced. Cost determinants of facility selection are discussed.

Because intangible costs mix with measurable costs, the real facility selection problem transcends simple cost and profit analysis. As a result, we introduce a method of facility selection using dimensional analysis. This method is applied to the search for a new facility by Ristormakers.

If shipping costs are important (of raw materials to the producer or of finished goods to the market), then the transportation model can be applied. This model is explained with a heuristic approach. In the optional appendices, the stepping-stone concept of the transportation method is presented (Appendix 17-I), and the generalized transportation method is explained (Appendix 17-II).

Chapter 18

The equipment selection problem is explained. A continually encountered decision problem is how to choose between alternative equipment that is similar in a technological sense, but which differs in investment levels, operating costs, and length of life. To resolve this problem, discounting analysis is used. As an example, Tiremasters choice between alternative materials-handling systems is studied. Then the MAPI method for choosing between alternative equipment is detailed. The MAPI approach expands the selection problem of alternative equipment to include different technological capabilities and the resulting consequences. Hampton Mills' opportunity to replace their present stitchers with computer-controlled equipment is examined on a tightly controlled cost basis. The decision to go to the new equipment is not arrived at lightly. In Appendix 18-I, optional material on depreciation methods (an important consideration of the MAPI method) is presented.

The problem of plant layout is first explored with graphic methods of trial and error. This is followed by a more quantitative approach using the mayor's office as an example. Without any complex mathematics, the way to improve layouts is fully detailed. One of the best heuristics available for the layout problem (called CRAFT) is completely described and illustrated with the case of Olympic Studios. (A work sheet for the CRAFT computations referred to in the text is given in Appendix 18-II.)

PART 7
REFERENCES

APPLE, JAMES M., *Plant Layout and Materials Handling*, 2nd ed. New York: Ronald Press, 1963.

COOK, T. M. and R. A. RUSSELL, *Introduction to Management Science*, Englewood Cliffs, N. J.: Prentice-Hall, Inc., 1977.

DEAN, JOEL, *Managerial Economics*. Englewood Cliffs, N.J.: Prentice-Hall, Inc., 1951.

ISARD, WALTER, *Location and Space-Economy*. New York: John Wiley & Sons, Inc., 1956.

KARASKA, G. J. and D. F. BRAMHALL, *Location Analysis for Manufacturing: A Selection of Readings.* Cambridge, Mass.: M.I.T. Press, 1969.

MAGEE, JOHN F., *Physical Distribution Systems.* New York: McGraw-Hill Book Company, 1967.

MASSÉ, PIERRE, *Optimal Investment Decisions.* Englewood Cliffs, N.J.: Prentice-Hall, Inc., 1962.

MILLER, RICHARD B., *Plant Location Factors United States*, Monograph, Noyes Development Corporation, 188 Mill Road, Park Ridge, N.J. 07656, 1966.

MOORE, JAMES M., *Plant Layout and Design.* New York: The Macmillan Company, 1962.

MUTHER, RICHARD, *Practical Plant Layout.* New York: McGraw-Hill Book Company, 1955.

REED, RUDDELL, Jr., *Plant Layout.* Homewood, Ill.: Richard D. Irwin, Inc., 1961.

STARR, M. K., *Systems Management of Operations.* Englewood Cliffs, N.J.: Prentice-Hall, Inc., 1970.

human resource management

The most trying problem that P/OM has faced over the years has been the question of how to deal with the work and pay of people in the system.

Such topics as

Worker evaluation (how to measure the productivity of workers)

Job improvement (how to design or redesign the job)

Job evaluation (how to determine the contribution of each job to the organization)

Wage determination (how to convert job evaluations into wage scales)

have always concerned managers. But the concern intensified as the industrial revolution moved into the twentieth century. Organizations grew larger and more impersonal, unionism expanded, and budgetary and other accounting controls added a new dimension to managerial responsibility.

Chapter 19 treats the measurement of workers' productivity in the job shop, flow shop, and project (worker evaluation). Chapter 20 examines job improvement, job evaluation, and wage determination.

In addition to economic considerations, the management of human resources concerns a variety of *human factors* that do not lend themselves to quantification in dollars and cents. Yet they are not less important. They deal with the safety, comfort, and efficiency of human beings at their work place.

Human factors are a major field of study in their own right. They extend to consumers who use products and services as well as workers who are the consumers of work-place facilities and equipment. Chapter 21 discusses human factors.

nineteen

the measurement
of workers'
productivity

The evaluation of workers has never been simple. The answer to the question how much output is reasonable can be readily given for machines, but it is elusive for human beings.[1] We shall see why this is so as we proceed with this chapter.

The contribution of human resources to the total cost of goods and service outputs is usually a sizable component. This is particularly emphasized in the service sector, which has been growing at an extremely fast rate, but it also remains true in the production of goods. Therefore, the problem of measuring human resource (labor) costs has received widespread and continuous attention over many years.

By and large, the problem remains critical. Whenever people play a significant part in the system, the difficulty in measuring productivity remains an impediment. As a result, union-management relations have developed in an

---

[1] See, for example, A. Abruzzi, "Formulating a Theory of Work Measurement," *Management Science*, Vol. 2, No. 2 (January, 1956), pp. 114–130; also S. B. Littauer and A. Abruzzi, "Experimental Criteria for Evaluating Workers and Operations," *Industrial Labor Relations Review*, Vol. 2, No. 4 (July, 1949), pp. 502–526.

atmosphere of confrontation stemming from the uncertainty of all parties concerning the parameters for measuring the performance of the work force.

Measuring Worker Performance

The search for a measure of worker performance and its value has led to *production standards*. What is a production standard? It is an *accepted* criterion for the amount of work to be accomplished in a given period of time. These standards state specifically what the expected productivity is for a particular job. However, the output rate for any one worker is variable. Furthermore, differences exist between workers. How, then, are these standards established? *Which individual is the standard worker?*

Before we examine alternative approaches for the resolution of such problems, let us question why standards are needed. The answer is that the manager must be able to compute the real costs of production efforts. Let us list some production activities that require reasonable estimates of labor costs to be made.

1. The break-even chart needs believable estimates. *Direct labor* is part of the variable cost component. *Indirect labor*, administration, and creative endeavors, such as research, are part of the fixed cost component.

2. For the decision matrix, these estimates are required to determine a minimum cost strategy or for the purpose of defining a maximum profit strategy. For the facility, the plant selection problem requires estimates of labor costs in different areas of the country.

3. For aggregate scheduling and shop loading, labor costs are a significant dimension.

4. In Chapter 6 the question of an optimal product mix was discussed. To find such a mix we were required to estimate the relative profitabilities of various items that competed for production capacity. For a sensitive system, small errors in estimating labor costs can produce sufficiently different estimates of profit per piece to change the entire aspect of the company's product mix.

5. When new product and service alternatives are evaluated, estimated labor costs are reflected in proposed price levels, estimated sales volume, and estimated profitability. How can we choose between alternative new products unless it is possible to estimate the labor cost per part and, thereby, the expected profitability?

6. A major decision involves the extent to which a company should mechanize its operations and move toward the flow shop configuration. This problem boils down to a comparison between labor costs and machine costs for approximately the same services. Without reasonably good estimates of the respective costs per part, decisions to

employ a flow shop or a job shop cannot be based on sound foundations.

7. Many organizations are in areas that traditionally bid for new jobs. With increased government spending, the use of bidding has spread. More companies utilize subcontracting than ever before. Bidding systems frequently require estimates that totally predate experience with the process. If the company hopes to remain solvent, let alone make sufficient profit, it must be able to estimate with a high degree of precision what the labor cost component will be for the job. If it is unable to do this, it is usually not advisable to enter a bid.

We have given just a few examples of the way in which labor costs affect the manager's performance. Why do we make such a special case for labor costs? Because they are among the *least certain elements* in the system. We are able to predetermine the costs of purchased materials, power, insurance, and machine and equipment costs. These factors do not introduce the same kind of uncertainty that the labor cost estimates do. The problem of estimating how much labor will be required to turn out a given volume of output is involved with *behavioral factors*, as is the complex problem of determining consumer demand levels. Behavioral elements are not well understood. The language of behavioral modeling is tentative and vague.

As the production configuration becomes more like a flow shop, the importance of the labor estimation problem is reduced. If for no other reason than to achieve increased levels of certainty, the manager tends to choose machines in place of labor whenever the trade-off costs are about the same. However, as if in compensation, new problems have arisen. There has been growth in the wage rates of indirect, administrative, sales promotional, and creative personnel. (The computer has helped offset some of these.) The problem of assigning such overhead costs to the output has not been satisfactorily resolved. In addition, uncertainties in consumer demand exact a greater toll when highly automatic processes are utilized. Mistakes are costly because these facilities demand high investment and are relatively inflexible. In any case, the problem of how to measure the productive capacity and related costs of the labor component remains a major issue. Let us consider some of the ways in which this problem can be approached.

Time Studies—The Razormaker Corporation

Jobs differ from one another and so do people. In order to find a common ground for setting standards and for evaluating the efforts and outputs of workers, it was necessary to begin the analysis on a very elementary level. Originally, *production studies* were used. These represented situations where the worker was *constantly* observed over a long period of time. The approach can be compared to 100 percent inspection. Both the job and the worker were studied with patient detail. This method has such shortcomings that it is now almost a historical curiosity. The primary weaknesses are high cost, unreliable results, and belligerent subjects.

The 100 percent sample, in almost every situation where it was used by the operations management field, eventually gave way to sampling procedures.[2] Present-day time studies are based on sampling methods derived from developments begun in the 1920s. Work sampling procedures led to time and motion studies. Instead of tracking the worker continuously, time and motion studies obtained a *sufficient sample of observations* to answer such questions as how long does it take to do a job, and what is the expected daily output of a worker.

First, the person doing the time study observes the overall job. Next, the job is broken down into basic elements. These, when added together, form the *job cycle*. This cycle should be relatively short and used repetitively. It will constitute the major portion of the worker's job. For long-cycle jobs, time study methods are difficult to apply. The character of a short-cycle, repetitive job will be illustrated by a razor packing operation of the Razormaker Corporation (see Fig. 19-1).

A *stop watch* is employed to time the cycle elements. A number of different kinds of such watches are available. Each is designed for particular types of applications as well as to satisfy personal preference. We shall differentiate only between the *continuous* and *snap-back* methods for using stop watches. The snap-back approach is used to time each work element directly. (See the columns headed Δ in Fig. 19-1.) When an element is completed, the watch hand is returned to 0 to begin timing the next element. Continuous readings are cumulative and require subtraction to determine element times. (See the columns headed 1, 2, *A*, *B*, *C*, and *D* in Fig. 19-1.) The snap-back system usually requires a larger sample for the same precision that can be obtained from the continuous method. However, as we shall shortly observe, precision is a strange word to apply to the time study area.

Usually, the stop watch is attached to a *time study board*, which holds an observation, or time study sheet. Such a time study sheet is shown in Fig. 19-1. The illustration presents a completed time sheet that lists the kind of information usually obtained. There is as much information as possible about the operation that is being observed. Note that the work elements of the job as well as a diagram of the razor packing layout are furnished. Also, the name of the operator, the machine that is being used, the setup being used, the materials, the speed and feed rates, and, in general, whatever information characterizes and categorizes the total job are given. The need for all these data follows from the point that a time study done under 1 set of conditions may not apply to another set. Thus, if the job is being done on a type *A* facility, it cannot be assumed that a similar production standard will apply to a type *B* facility. Change of materials, locations, and a host of other fac-

---

[2]Appendix 19-I presents as optional material the determination of an adequate time study sample size, pp. 476–77.

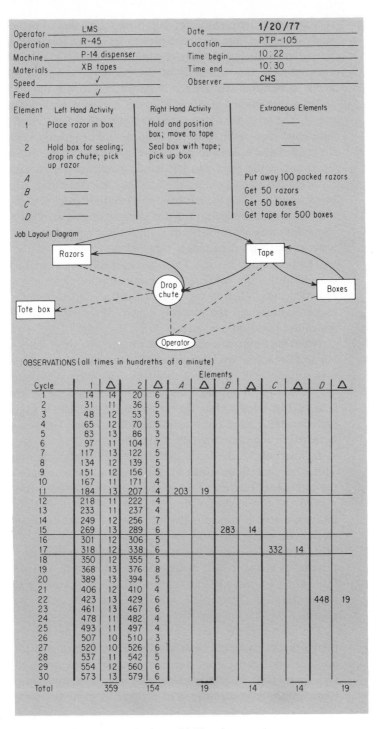

Operator ___LMS___ Date ___1/20/77___
Operation ___R-45___ Location ___PTP-105___
Machine ___P-14 dispenser___ Time begin ___10:22___
Materials ___XB tapes___ Time end ___10:30___
Speed ___✓___ Observer ___CHS___
Feed ___✓___

Element	Left Hand Activity	Right Hand Activity	Extraneous Elements
1	Place razor in box	Hold and position box; move to tape	—
2	Hold box for sealing; drop in chute; pick up razor	Seal box with tape; pick up box	—
A	—	—	Put away 100 packed razors
B	—	—	Get 50 razors
C	—	—	Get 50 boxes
D	—	—	Get tape for 500 boxes

Job Layout Diagram

OBSERVATIONS (all times in hundreths of a minute)

Elements

Cycle	1	△	2	△	A	△	B	△	C	△	D	△
1	14	14	20	6								
2	31	11	36	5								
3	48	12	53	5								
4	65	12	70	5								
5	83	13	86	3								
6	97	11	104	7								
7	117	13	122	5								
8	134	12	139	5								
9	151	12	156	5								
10	167	11	171	4								
11	184	13	207	4	203	19						
12	218	11	222	4								
13	233	11	237	4								
14	249	12	256	7								
15	269	13	289	6			283	14				
16	301	12	306	5								
17	318	12	338	6					332	14		
18	350	12	355	5								
19	368	13	376	8								
20	389	13	394	5								
21	406	12	410	4								
22	423	13	429	6							448	19
23	461	13	467	6								
24	478	11	482	4								
25	493	11	497	4								
26	507	10	510	3								
27	520	10	526	6								
28	537	11	542	5								
29	554	12	560	6								
30	573	13	579	6								
Total		359		154		19		14		14		19

FIGURE 19-1. A time study sheet with 30 cycles
The operation (R-45) is to package razors.

457

tors can, and frequently do, interpose themselves. Further, to check on a study by replication, it is necessary to set up the job conditions in as similar a fashion to the initial study conditions as possible. When time study results are contested, the variability of study conditions and/or their variance with actual conditions are frequently introduced to win the argument.

Let us examine Fig. 19-1. This job has been broken down into two elements. The activities of the *left* and *right hands* are described for each element. Element 1 requires that the left hand should be placing a razor in a box while the right hand holds and positions the box so that the razor can be inserted. Presumably, the right and left hand operations are coordinated. Element 2 finds the left hand holding the box for the right hand, which must seal the box with tape. Then the left hand releases the box over a chute, which carries the box away. The layout for this job as pictured on the time sheet does not show distances of the operator from the work place and materials. Often the exact layout with distances is supplied.

The time study begins: The observation for element 1 in the first cycle is entered in the first column; the observation for element 2 in the first cycle is recorded next. Then, cycle 2 begins, and so forth. It can be seen that these element values are continuously timed. The sample size is 30 cycles, all of which are listed on our sheet.

After the observations have been made, the time study computations are begun. The initial cycle required 0.20 minute. Of this, Element 1 consumed 0.14 minute and element 2 took the remaining 0.06 minute.[3] The second cycle ends at 0.36 minute. This means that the second cycle consumed $0.36 - 0.20 = 0.16$ minute. For the second cycle, element 1 required 0.11 minute and element 2 used the remaining 0.05 minute. The rest of the values are obtained in the same way, by subtraction.

In addition to the basic cycle, the time sheet lists *extraneous elements*. These are operations which must be done *every now and then*. For example, the extraneous element *A* is the requirement that after 100 razors have been packed and dropped into the chute, the tote box they fall into must be taken away. Element B concerns the fact that the worker must interrupt the basic work cycle every 50 razors to get a new supply of razors to work on. The other extraneous elements are equally easy to comprehend. We see that the extraneous elements will break into the short-cycle system regularly. Therefore, when we include them, the total job is not really short-cycle, but of longer duration. Elements 1 and 2 constitute the *major subcycle* within this system.

The longest cycle is element *D*, which occurs once every 500 boxes. It is, therefore, the shortest, *common-cycle* time for *all* elements in the system. This point is significant; even the shortest-cycle, repetitive jobs usually include very long-cycle, extraneous elements. The time study inspector must catch these longer-cycle elements and include them in the study. Thus, we have

---

[3]The stop watch used is a decimal-minute type. It is read directly in hundredths of a minute.

included observations that are relevant to the extraneous elements in our data. (As shall be seen shortly, *work sampling* is an effective method for coping with the problem of the long-cycle factors.)

Productivity Standard

Using time study data, we can develop a productivity standard for job shop operations and for worker performance in the line balanced flow shop. Clearly, there is a difference in the degree of measurement effort that would be sanctioned for these 2 cases. The job shop worker might spend several days with a particular job and then move to another. Another time study would be taken to determine a productivity standard for the new job. On the other hand, the razor packer is most likely part of an assembly operation for the Razormaker Corporation, which manufactures razors on a flow shop basis. It is probable that a number of workers are doing the same packaging operation. In this event, a productivity standard must be set carefully to represent the expected output of all workers similarly engaged.

The need for the productivity standard is to determine the expected output rate of each worker, and thus to know how many workers are required and to be able to estimate the labor cost component of the finished products or services. Let us, therefore, examine Fig. 19-1, which is a summary of the information previously collected.

TABLE 19-1 RAZORMAKER CORPORATION—TIME STUDY SUMMARY

Element	1	2	A	B	C	D	
Total time observed	359	154	19	14	14	19	
Number of observations	30	30	1	1	1	1	
Expected cycles per observation	1	1	1/100	1/50	1/50	1/500	
Average time or selected time*	11.97	5.13	0.19	0.28	0.28	0.04	
Allowances or leveling factors	0.95	1.00	1.00	1.00	1.00	1.00	
Adjusted time or normal time*	11.37	5.13	0.19	0.28	0.28	0.04	
Correction for rest and delay	110%	110%	110%	110%	110%	110%	TOTAL
Standard time*	12.51	5.64	0.21	0.31	0.31	0.04	19.02

*In hundredths of a minute.

459

All the elements, 1, 2, *A*, *B*, *C*, and *D*, are listed. Total times are collected for each element as they appeared in the 30-cycle period. Those are the column sums for each element, including the extraneous factors.

The *total time* for element 1 is 359; for element 2 it is 154; it is 19, 14, 14, and 19, respectively, for the extraneous elements *A*, *B*, *C*, and *D*. The number of observations for each element is recorded. There are 30 such observations for elements 1 and 2. By chance, during this period of time, each extraneous element occurs once. The third row of our summary sheet lists the number of occurrences that can be expected per cycle. We divide the first row by the second and multiply this quotient by the third row. In this way, an *average time*, or *selected time*, is developed for each of the operations that constitute the job. For example, dividing 359 by (30) and then multiplying by 1, we obtain 11.97 hundredths of a minute, or 0.1197 minute for element 1. For element 2, we obtain 0.0513 minute, and so forth.

Now we come to one of the most disagreeable jobs in the time study system. This is the choice of an *allowance* or *leveling factor*. Whom should the time study inspector observe? Generally, an average worker is chosen, operating under standard conditions, with presumably routinized method. But if the subject appears to work at something more or less than an average rate, a leveling factor, or allowance, must be applied. The *allowance* is applied to *average* or *selected time*, whence we obtain *adjusted time*, or *normal time*. This is simply the product of the average time and the allowance. Thus, if the leveling factor is 110 percent, meaning that the observed worker is faster than normal, then the adjusted time will be larger than the average time, meaning that the normal (slower) worker can be expected to take a longer than observed time. In the case of the operator who is working at 95 percent of normal, in the judgment of the time study inspector, multiplication produces a normal time that is smaller than the selected time, meaning that the average worker can go faster. For the average worker the leveling factor is 100 percent. This leaves the resulting system of numbers unchanged.

In Table 19-1, only element 1 diverges from average. On this aspect of the job, the worker is rated as slower than average. The leveling factor 0.95 is multiplied by the selected time 11.97 to obtain the adjusted time of 11.37.

Because of leveling, our efforts to achieve precise measures and our hopes for precision may seem to have been a waste of time. But this is not exactly the case. The leveling estimate introduces a different kind of measurement error than do the time study errors. Clearly, we would prefer neither type of error. But these 2 types of errors tend to cancel each other.

On what basis does the time study inspector decide whether a worker is performing above, below, or exactly at the normal level? The answer is that time study inspectors, after much practice, can exhibit far more agreement among themselves than would occur by chance, even though the concept of a standard basis for allowances is vague, undefined, and subjective. Training in leveling is accomplished in many ways. One of the most successful is by means of motion pictures, where the projector has a variable speed control.

Even if we could accept leveling with equanimity, we must now add an additional *rough* correction. This is the *rest and delay* correction factor. Usually, it is assigned values that range from 5 percent to 15 percent, depending upon the character of the job, the degree of personal needs, and so on. The adjusted, or normal, time is multiplied by the rest and delay factor. In this way we derive the *standard time*, which is the basis of the production standard. We note that the standard times are listed along the bottom row of the summary box. Each element, including the extraneous elements, has its standard time. The sum of all the elemental standard times is the *standard time of the operation*. In our example this is 0.1902 minute.

The Expected Cost of the Operation

$$\text{Productivity standard} = \frac{60 \text{ min}}{\text{hour}} \times \frac{100 \text{ boxes}}{19.02 \text{ min}} \cong 316 \text{ boxes per hour}$$

We divide 60 minutes per hour by the operation's total standard time. This tells us that approximately 316 boxes per hour is the expected output rate for the job. That is, 60/0.1902 equals a *productivity measure* of 316 boxes per hour. If the wage rate for this class of job is $2 per hour, then the labor cost component for the operation would be $2/316 = $0.006, or the *expected cost of the operation* is a little more than a half-cent apiece.

Primary weaknesses of time study are the definition of an average worker, applying the leveling factor, applying the rest and delay correction, and not recognizing influential extraneous elements. Ingenious answers have been found for some of these problems. Time study is a *skill*. To begin with, the use of the stop watch requires training and practice. The same applies to leveling. Time study practitioners seldom break down elements into less than 0.04 minute, because less than this interval is difficult to observe. The major criticism of time study centers around leveling, but another problem worthy of consideration is the fact that the worker's performance may not be stable in the Shewhart sense (see pp. 558–59). Also, the fact that the worker is not necessarily interested in participating in the study and may have no desire to provide an accurate production standard of performance is another criticism. The expert time study inspector is supposed to sense this and make appropriate changes in the leveling factor. One can question who will win such a contest—the observer or the observed? Another issue of importance to the time study field is, How many cycles should be observed? This question is addressed in Appendix 19-I, because it is a technical question that swerves us from our basic line of discussion. Also, when workers begin a job that they have not done for a while (even overnight), they improve their productivity through repetition. This phenomenon called "learning" is discussed as optional material in Appendix 19-III. The time study should not begin until the worker's learning ceases and performance has stabilized.

The methods of time study, *in spite of the inherent problems, are widely used by industry*. The need for this kind of information is *fundamental*. At the same time, for many applications, such as for long-cycle systems and for pre-estimating jobs that do not yet exist, other methods had to be developed. We shall now consider some of these.

Work Sampling—State Court House

It may seem strange, at first thought, that certain kinds of workers cannot account for the way in which they spend their time. This applies, for example to office workers, research personnel, creative staff, and managers themselves. Recognition of this problem led the manager of the State Court House to employ work sampling,[4] a method for determining, with reasonably accuracy, the percentage of time that the labor force is engaged in different tasks.

The State Court House budget has been slashed by the state legislature by 30 percent. This measure was not directed specifically against the State Court House. Financial difficulties afflict the state as a whole, and all state functions have been similarly affected. The manager of the State Court House has decided to use an operations management technique (viz., work sampling) to resolve the problem.

The alternative is a political solution—which is to dismiss all persons hired in the last six months. That policy would produce the least repercussions. However, the manager believes that the problem is longer term and that productivity is the issue. Among the people hired within the last 6 months, many are highly productive and others are not. At the same time, many employees with years of service are unproductive.

The manager's decision is to study the efficiency of the Court House by means of work sampling. No one is to be dismissed unless he or she is clearly nonproductive. (A certain percentage of individuals meet that description.) Meanwhile, normal attrition will reduce the payroll gradually. At the same time, all outside help is to be discontinued. The manager projects that first year performance will break even with budget and thereafter that the State Court House will have budget to build up inventories that were depleted, to invest in capital improvements, etc.

Let us examine the work (or operations) sampling method. The ideas that are fundamental to work sampling were derived at about the same time as techniques for sampling the quality of materials (see pp. 536–37).[5] Just as in

---

[4]Also called operations sampling.

[5]In the 1930s, Tippett reported on his experiments with work sampling in English textile factories. At about the same time, Morrow was utilizing this same type of technique in factories in the USA.

the case of materials sampling, the observations to be made represent less than a 100 percent study. Therefore, the observations must be *random* and of sufficient number that an accurate picture can be constructed of what is going on in the system.

The State Court House will divide its day into 450 intervals, each of which is a working minute. On a purely random basis, the manager agrees to select 54 of these 450 intervals; these will constitute the sample. Thus, if 450 numbered chips were thrown into a bowl—where the chips are numbered consecutively from 1 to 450—then by drawing 54 chips at random from the bowl, we could determine a set of *observation assignments for* each day.

A method simpler to use than the bowl of chips requires *tables of random numbers* (see Appendix 11-II, pp. 226–27) and Monte Carlo number assignments. A random-number table has the important characteristic that there is no pattern whatever to the numbers listed in the table. The numbers are generated by a process that is comparable to withdrawing numbered chips from the bowl. This is true if the procedure of drawing numbers from the bowl is completely unbiased—and every number has an equal chance of being picked at each selection.[6]

The Monte Carlo assignments could be made as follows. We wish to sample 54 out of 450 minute intervals. This is 0.12 of the total number of daily intervals. Then, let the Monte Carlo numbers 00–11 stand for Take an observation; and the Monte Carlo numbers 12–99 stand for No observation is to be taken. We now draw 450 pairs of random numbers in succession. As we read successive numbers from the table, we determine whether we are supposed to take an observation. Thus, assume the following random numbers:

$$62831 \qquad 04609 \qquad 83826 \qquad 57106 \qquad 38640$$

Reading these off in pairs from left to right,[7] we find the information in Table 19-2.

Because all random numbers are equally likely, on the average, 12 out of 100 (or 1.2 out of 10) random numbers will signify that an observation should be made. The sample that we have drawn has delivered 3 out of 10, but this is in the nature of statistical systems. Sometimes they will be high, sometimes low; in the long run, the results will average out.

The purpose of this method is to insure that a good sample is drawn, i.e., one which neither observer nor worker can anticipate. Only in this way can the observations be unexpected and the situation that is observed be known to be unstaged, unpremeditated, and representative. Thus, a good approximation of what takes place in the State Court House will be available. Following the directives of the random numbers, the observer makes an appearance at the work place at the third, fifth, tenth, and so on, intervals. The observer makes the observations, records them, and departs.

---

[6]For a comprehensive discussion of Monte Carlo procedures, see pp. 223–26.

[7]The table of random numbers can be read in any direction consistently, including along table diagonals.

TABLE 19-2

Time Interval	Random Number	Monte Carlo Interpretation	Working	Idle
1	62	No observation		
2	83	No observation		
3	10	Observation	x	
4	46	No observation		
5	09	Observation	x	
6	83	No observation		
7	82	No observation		
8	65	No observation		
9	71	No observation		
10	06	Observation		x
.	.	.		
.	.	.		
.	.	.		
etc.	etc.	etc.		

The purpose of the observations, for the State Court House example, has been to determine how much of the time workers are engaged or idle. If a particular project or operation were the observation base, then categories of what was being done might be used. When a sufficient sample has been taken, ratios can be formed as descriptive measures of what goes on in the system. For example, assume that for a particular day, 45 observations have been made. Forty times, the individual was found to be busy. Then 40/45, or 8/9, of the time the operator can be assumed to have been engaged in a productive task.

The manager's idea of work sampling is not to catch the workers off guard. Rather, it is to map out their activities and to help them utilize their time more fully. A more elaborate study than the one we have just described will help the State Court House manager to make this point. Rather than just observing whether workers are idle or busy, the expanded analysis notes *how* the work force spends its time. This is more appropriately called *operations sampling* than *work sampling*.

	Filing	Phoning	Typing	Other	Total
Number of times observed	60	182	30	28	300
Percent of total	20	61	10	9	100

The State Court House manager has discovered that 61 percent of the time state workers are on the telephone. It is unlikely that this heavy commitment to the telephone is strictly business. The manager decides to remove the telephone from each person's desk. A central telephone, with controls on incoming and outgoing calls, is to be installed. This is one of the manager's decisions. Another one is to centralize filing, appoint a file maintenance manager and allow only file clerks access to the files. These decisions may be wrong, but they are based on a reasonable assessment of work load requirements.

Many study variations can be made on this basic theme. The sampling study is designed to reveal what many workers and executives cannot tell, namely, how they spend their time. A 100 percent sample could not provide as reliable a picture, because the constant pressure of observers creates bias and distortion that sampling methods eliminate.[8]

We have tried to show how work sampling can be of real value when properly utilized. The State Court House manager will increase the productivity of the operation if he or she rejects the political solution in favor of the economic solution. This manager has not dealt with time studies of specific jobs. *Time studies are of little help when noncyclical jobs or long-cycle jobs are involved.* In these cases, it is extremely difficult to measure, or even approximate, productive outputs. For those situations where either work sampling or time studies can be used, work sampling offers attractive advantages, such as the fact that time study requires great skill, whereas the work sampling observer can be relatively unskilled. Further, all extraneous elements that can enter the short-cycle job are not always picked up by time study. A properly designed *work sampling study will frequently prove to be a more effective way of dealing with special extraneous factors* that characterize the job shop. To apply work sampling for the determination of time standards (see Problem 5 at the end of this chapter), we ask first, What should the job be like, e.g., what percentage of time is spent in filing, phoning, typing, etc.? From the work sampling study, we know what the job is like now. By redesigning the job, i.e., removing phones, buying faster filing systems, setting new policies, etc., the observed work is brought closer to the time standard objectives set by management. Also, for later job evaluation, see pp. 493–96, it is important that the job should actually be what management thinks it is.

Innovative work patterns can be created. This applies to the flow shop as well as the job shop. Public management work modes do not have to conform to a job shop pattern, per se. We hope that many of them (including State Court House) will be converted to flow shop operations without losing the human touch.

Synthetic Time Standards

It is difficult to obtain accurate measures of a fair day's output under many circumstances. There is also the problem of preparing estimates for jobs that have not been physically actualized. Both of these motives led to the develop-

---

[8] As with time studies, the question arises as to what is an adequate sample size. Appendix 19-II (presented as optional material) sheds light on this question.

ment of *synthetic*, or *predetermined* time standards. Casting about for some way of categorizing the work measurement field, we can generalize, as follows:

1. Time study is applicable for short-cycle, repetitive operations that are *presently* being performed and can, therefore, be observed.
2. Work sampling can be used for long-cycle, repetitive operations that are *presently* being performed so that they can be observed. The cycle must be stable, or else the sample has no meaning.
3. Synthetic (or predetermined) time studies can treat nonrepetitive, noncyclical jobs as well as jobs that are not *yet being done*, so that they cannot be observed.

The basis of synthetic time standards is the fact that every job is composed of a set of elements that are *common to all jobs*. The unique feature of a particular job is the way in which this common alphabet of elements is used and the way in which the elements are arranged. Frank Gilbreth was one of the first management pioneers to describe such an alphabet of job elements or modules. He called these modules *therbligs* and named 17 of them. For example,[9]

Grasp: Begins when hand or body member touches an object. Consists of gaining control of an object. Ends when control is gained.

Position: Begins when hand or body member causes part to begin to line up or locate. Consists of hand or body member causing part to line up, orient, or change position.

Assemble: Begins when the hand or body member causes parts to begin to go together. Consists of actual assembly of parts. Ends when hand or body member has caused parts to go together.

Hold: Begins when movement of part or object, which hand or body member has under control, ceases. Consists of holding an object in a fixed position and location. Ends with any movement.

From this beginning, A. B. Segur, who had worked with Gilbreth, developed his system of Motion-Time-Analysis (MTA), which was a work measurement procedure utilizing predetermined, standard, work element times. MTA was based upon the fundamental notion that "Within practical limits the times required of all expert workers to perform true fundamental motions are constant."[10]

---

[9]Marvin E. Mundel, *Motion and Time Study, Principles and Practices*, 4th ed. (Englewood Cliffs, N.J.: Prentice-Hall, Inc., 1970), pp. 243–248.

[10]J. H. Quick, J. H. Duncan, and J. A. Malcolm, Jr., *Work-Factor Time Standards, Measurement of Manual and Mental Work* (New York: McGraw-Hill Book Co., Inc., 1962), p. 4.

Once the standard modules, or work elements, were named, then it was possible to study thousands of different operations in which each of these elements appeared. Motion pictures were made of many different kinds of jobs, and these in turn were analyzed to determine the appropriate statistical distribution of element times. Expected standard times were obtained in this way. Tables of such standard times for various work elements are shown in Fig. 19-2. This is the system of synthetic standards known as MTM, the methods-time-measurement system.[11]

Another well-known system is that of *Work-Factor*, for which tables of standards are also available.[12] The Work-Factor system has been computerized, which eliminates a great deal of the work required to establish production standards with predetermined times. The computer operation also has significant advantages in reducing the effort required to revise and update comprehensive standard data. Operations times are computed rapidly, and with great accuracy. The system also permits a reduction in the effort required for effectively designing motion patterns in the simplification of work (see pp. 485–87).

Using predetermined standards, we can derive a standard time for a job.[13]

1. Describe the job completely and isolate the work elements; this is *analysis*.
2. Determine the appropriate times for each element as specified by the system that is being used.
3. Add the times together; this is *synthesis*, requiring that the isolated work elements be independent of each other or that any existing interactions be taken into account so that the sum truly reflects the total time for the job.

An example of how synthetic times are used to determine production standards, to develop estimates, and to compare alternatives is shown in Fig. 19-3.

Some advantages of synthetic time standards, as compared to those derived from conventional time study methods, are:

1. The leveling factor problem is bypassed. It is already included in the synthetic time standard, because rating differences are averaged out across many jobs and many operators. In short, *no rating factor is required* with these systems.
2. Distortions that arise because of observer bias and interaction between the observer and the worker can be controlled and removed from the synthetic times, which is not the case for time studies.

---

[11]Harold B. Maynard, G. J. Stegemerten, and John L. Schwab, *Methods-Time-Measurement* (New York: McGraw-Hill Book Co., Inc., 1948).

[12]J. H. Quick, et al., *Work-Factor Time Standards, Measurement of Manual and Mental Work*, pp. 435–446.

[13]The time measurement units, TMU for MTM, are given in terms of 0.00001 hour; for Work Factor the time unit is 0.0001 minute.

METHODS-TIME MEASUREMENT
MTM-I APPLICATION DATA

1 TMU	=	.00001	hour		1 hour	=	100,000.0 TMU
	=	.0006	minute		1 minute	=	1,666.7 TMU
	=	.036	seconds		1 second	=	27.8 TMU

Do not attempt to use this chart or apply Methods-Time Measurement in any way unless you understand the proper application of the data. This statement is included as a word of caution to prevent difficulties resulting from mis-application of the data.

**MTM ASSOCIATION
FOR STANDARDS
AND RESEARCH**
9-10 Saddle River Road
Fair Lawn, N.J. 07410

TABLE I — REACH — R

Distance Moved Inches	Time TMU				Hand In Motion		CASE AND DESCRIPTION
	A	B	C or D	E	A	B	
3/4 or less	2.0	2.0	2.0	2.0	1.6	1.6	**A** Reach to object in fixed location, or to object in other hand or on which other hand rests.
1	2.5	2.5	3.6	2.4	2.3	2.3	
2	4.0	4.0	5.9	3.8	3.5	2.7	
3	5.3	5.3	7.3	5.3	4.5	3.6	**B** Reach to single object in location which may vary slightly from cycle to cycle.
4	6.1	6.4	8.4	6.8	4.9	4.3	
5	6.5	7.8	9.4	7.4	5.3	5.0	
6	7.0	8.6	10.1	8.0	5.7	5.7	
7	7.4	9.3	10.8	8.7	6.1	6.5	
8	7.9	10.1	11.5	9.3	6.5	7.2	**C** Reach to object jumbled with other objects in a group so that search and select occur.
9	8.3	10.8	12.2	9.9	6.9	7.9	
10	8.7	11.5	12.9	10.5	7.3	8.6	
12	9.6	12.9	14.2	11.8	8.1	10.1	
14	10.5	14.4	15.6	13.0	8.9	11.5	
16	11.4	15.8	17.0	14.2	9.7	12.9	**D** Reach to a very small object or where accurate grasp is required.
18	12.3	17.2	18.4	15.5	10.5	14.4	
20	13.1	18.6	19.8	16.7	11.3	15.8	
22	14.0	20.1	21.2	18.0	12.1	17.3	**E** Reach to indefinite location to get hand in position for body balance or next motion or out of way.
24	14.9	21.5	22.5	19.2	12.9	18.8	
26	15.8	22.9	23.9	20.4	13.7	20.2	
28	16.7	24.4	25.3	21.7	14.5	21.7	
30	17.5	25.8	26.7	22.9	15.3	23.2	
Additional	0.4	0.7	0.7	0.6			TMU per inch over 30 inches

TABLE II — MOVE — M

Distance Moved Inches	Time TMU			Hand In Motion B	Wt. Allowance			CASE AND DESCRIPTION
	A	B	C		Wt. (lb.) Up to	Dynamic Factor	Static Constant TMU	
3/4 or less	2.0	2.0	2.0	1.7				
1	2.5	2.9	3.4	2.3	2.5	1.00	0	
2	3.6	4.6	5.2	2.9				**A** Move object to other hand or against stop.
3	4.9	5.7	6.7	3.6	7.5	1.06	2.2	
4	6.1	6.9	8.0	4.3				
5	7.3	8.0	9.2	5.0	12.5	1.11	3.9	
6	8.1	8.9	10.3	5.7				
7	8.9	9.7	11.1	6.5	17.5	1.17	5.6	
8	9.7	10.6	11.8	7.2				**B** Move object to approximate or indefinite location.
9	10.5	11.5	12.7	7.9	22.5	1.22	7.4	
10	11.3	12.2	13.5	8.6				
12	12.9	13.4	15.2	10.0	27.5	1.28	9.1	
14	14.4	14.6	16.9	11.4				
16	16.0	15.8	18.7	12.8	32.5	1.33	10.8	
18	17.6	17.0	20.4	14.2				
20	19.2	18.2	22.1	15.6	37.5	1.39	12.5	
22	20.8	19.4	23.8	17.0				
24	22.4	20.6	25.5	18.4	42.5	1.44	14.3	**C** Move object to exact location.
26	24.0	21.8	27.3	19.8				
28	25.5	23.1	29.0	21.2	47.5	1.50	16.0	
30	27.1	24.3	30.7	22.7				
Additional	0.8	0.6	0.85				TMU per inch over 30 inches	

TABLE III A — TURN — T

Weight	Time TMU for Degrees Turned										
	30°	45°	60°	75°	90°	105°	120°	135°	150°	165°	180°
Small — 0 to 2 Pounds	2.8	3.5	4.1	4.8	5.4	6.1	6.8	7.4	8.1	8.7	9.4
Medium — 2.1 to 10 Pounds	4.4	5.5	6.5	7.5	8.5	9.6	10.6	11.6	12.7	13.7	14.8
Large — 10.1 to 35 Pounds	8.4	10.5	12.3	14.4	16.2	18.3	20.4	22.2	24.3	26.1	28.2

TABLE III B — APPLY PRESSURE — AP

FULL CYCLE			COMPONENTS		
SYMBOL	TMU	DESCRIPTION	SYMBOL	TMU	DESCRIPTION
APA	10.6	AF + DM + RLF	AF	3.4	Apply Force
APB	16.2	APA + G2	DM	4.2	Dwell, Minimum
			RLF	3.0	Release Force

MTMA 101
PRINTED IN U.S.A.

Copyright 1973

FIGURE 19-2. Time values for various classifications of motions [Copyrighted by the MTM Association for Standards and Research. No reprint permission without written consent from the MTM Association, 9-10 Saddle River Road, Fair Lawn, New Jersey 07410]

TABLE IV — GRASP — G

TYPE OF GRASP	Case	Time TMU	DESCRIPTION	
PICK-UP	1A	2.0	Any size object by itself, easily grasped	
	1B	3.5	Object very small or lying close against a flat surface	
	1C1	7.3	Diameter larger than 1/2"	Interference with Grasp on bottom and one side of nearly cylindrical object.
	1C2	8.7	Diameter 1/4" to 1/2"	
	1C3	10.8	Diameter less than 1/4"	
REGRASP	2	5.6	Change grasp without relinquishing control	
TRANSFER	3	5.6	Control transferred from one hand to the other.	
SELECT	4A	7.3	Larger than 1" x 1" x 1"	Object jumbled with other objects so that search and select occur.
	4B	9.1	1/4" x 1/4" x 1/8" to 1" x 1" x 1"	
	4C	12.9	Smaller than 1/4" x 1/4" x 1/8"	
CONTACT	5	0	Contact, Sliding, or Hook Grasp.	

EFFECTIVE NET WEIGHT

Effective Net Weight (ENW)	No. of Hands	Spatial	Sliding
	1	W	W x F_C
	2	W/2	W/2 x F_C

W = Weight in pounds
F_C = Coefficient of Friction

TABLE V — POSITION* — P

CLASS OF FIT		Symmetry	Easy To Handle	Difficult To Handle
1—Loose	No pressure required	S	5.6	11.2
		SS	9.1	14.7
		NS	10.4	16.0
2—Close	Light pressure required	S	16.2	21.8
		SS	19.7	25.3
		NS	21.0	26.6
3—Exact	Heavy pressure required.	S	43.0	48.6
		SS	46.5	52.1
		NS	47.8	53.4

SUPPLEMENTARY RULE FOR SURFACE ALIGNMENT

P1SE per alignment: >1/16 ≤1/4"	P2SE per alignment: ≤1/16"

*Distance moved to engage—1" or less.

TABLE VI — RELEASE — RL

Case	Time TMU	DESCRIPTION
1	2.0	Normal release performed by opening fingers as independent motion.
2	0	Contact Release

TABLE VII — DISENGAGE — D

CLASS OF FIT	HEIGHT OF RECOIL	EASY TO HANDLE	DIFFICULT TO HANDLE
1—LOOSE—Very slight effort, blends with subsequent move.	Up to 1"	4.0	5.7
2—CLOSE—Normal effort, slight recoil.	Over 1" to 5"	7.5	11.8
3—TIGHT—Considerable effort, hand recoils markedly.	Over 5" to 12"	22.9	34.7

SUPPLEMENTARY

CLASS OF FIT	CARE IN HANDLING	BINDING
1—LOOSE	Allow Class 2	
2—CLOSE	Allow Class 3	One G2 per Bind
3—TIGHT	Change Method	One APB per Bind

FIGURE 19-2a. *Cont.*

TABLE VIII — EYE TRAVEL AND EYE FOCUS — ET AND EF

Eye Travel Time = 15.2 x $\frac{T}{D}$ TMU, with a maximum value of 20 TMU.

where T = the distance between points from and to which the eye travels.
D = the perpendicular distance from the eye to the line of travel T.

Eye Focus Time = 7.3 TMU.

SUPPLEMENTARY INFORMATION

— Area of Normal Vision = Circle 4" in Diameter 16" from Eyes

— Reading Formula = 5.05 N Where N = The Number of Words.

TABLE IX — BODY, LEG, AND FOOT MOTIONS

TYPE		SYMBOL	TMU	DISTANCE	DESCRIPTION
LEG—FOOT MOTION		FM	8.5	To 4"	Hinged at ankle.
		FMP	19.1	To 4"	With heavy pressure.
		LM	7.1	To 6"	Hinged at knee or hip in any direction.
			1.2	Ea. add'l inch	
HORIZONTAL MOTION	SIDE STEP	SS—C1	*	<12"	Use Reach or Move time when less than 12". Complete when leading leg contacts floor.
			17.0	12"	
			0.6	Ea. add'l inch	
		SS—C2	34.1	12"	Lagging leg must contact floor before next motion can be made.
			1.1	Ea. add'l inch	
	TURN BODY	TBC1	18.6	——	Complete when leading leg contacts floor.
		TBC2	37.2	——	Lagging leg must contact floor before next motion can be made
	WALK	W—FT	5.3	Per Foot	Unobstructed.
		W—P	15.0	Per Pace	Unobstructed.
		W—PO	17.0	Per Pace	When obstructed or with weight.
VERTICAL MOTION		SIT	34.7	——	From standing position.
		STD	43.4	——	From sitting position.
		B,S,KOK	29.0	——	Bend, Stoop, Kneel on One Knee.
		AB,AS,AKOK	31.9	——	Arise from Bend, Stoop, Kneel on One Knee
		KBK	69.4	——	Kneel on Both Knees.
		AKBK	76.7	——	Arise from Kneel on Both Knees.

TABLE X — SIMULTANEOUS MOTIONS

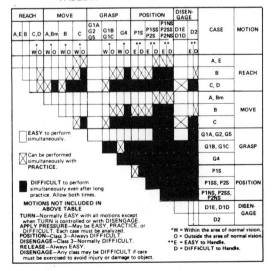

EASY to perform simultaneously.

Can be performed simultaneously with PRACTICE.

DIFFICULT to perform simultaneously even after long practice. Allow both times.

MOTIONS NOT INCLUDED IN ABOVE TABLE
TURN—Normally EASY with all motions except when TURN is controlled or with DISENGAGE.
APPLY PRESSURE—May be EASY, PRACTICE, or DIFFICULT. Each case must be analyzed.
POSITION—Class 3—Always DIFFICULT.
DISENGAGE—Class 3—Normally DIFFICULT.
RELEASE—Always EASY.
DISENGAGE—Any class may be DIFFICULT if care must be exercised to avoid injury or damage to object.

*W = Within the area of normal vision.
O = Outside the area of normal vision.
**E = EASY to Handle.
D = DIFFICULT to Handle.

469

TABLE 1 — POSITION — P

Class of Fit and Clearance	Case of † Symmetry	Align Only	Depth of Insertion (per ¼")			
			0 >0≤1/8"	2 >1/8≤¾	4 >¾≤1¼	6 >1¼≤1¾
21 .150" — .350"	S	3.0	3.4	6.6	7.7	8.8
	SS	3.0	10.3	13.5	14.6	15.7
	NS	4.8	15.5	18.7	19.8	20.9
22 .025" — .149"	S	7.2	7.2	11.9	13.0	14.2
	SS	8.0	14.9	19.6	20.7	21.9
	NS	9.5	20.2	24.9	26.0	27.2
23* .005" — .024"	S	9.5	9.5	16.3	18.7	21.0
	SS	10.4	17.3	24.1	26.5	28.8
	NS	12.2	22.9	29.7	32.1	34.4

*BINDING—Add observed number of Apply Pressures.
DIFFICULT HANDLING—Add observed number of G2's.

†Determine symmetry by geometric properties, except use S case when object is oriented prior to preceding Move.

TABLE 1A — SECONDARY ENGAGE — E2

CLASS OF FIT	DEPTH OF INSERTION (PER 1/4")		
	2	4	6
21	3.2	4.3	5.4
22	4.7	5.8	7.0
23	6.8	9.2	11.5

TABLE 2 — CRANK (LIGHT RESISTANCE) — C

DIAMETER OF CRANKING (INCHES)	TMU (T) PER REVOLUTION	DIAMETER OF CRANKING (INCHES)	TMU (T) PER REVOLUTION
1	8.5	9	14.0
2	9.7	10	14.4
3	10.6	11	14.7
4	11.4	12	15.0
5	12.1	14	15.5
6	12.7	16	16.0
7	13.2	18	16.4
8	13.6	20	16.7

FORMULAS:

A. CONTINUOUS CRANKING (Start at beginning and stop at end of cycle only)

$$TMU = [(N \times T) + 5.2] \cdot F + C$$

B. INTERMITTENT CRANKING (Start at beginning and stop at end of each revolution)

$$TMU = [(T + 5.2) F + C] \cdot N$$

C	=	Static component TMU weight allowance constant from move table
F	=	Dynamic component weight allowance factor from move table
N	=	Number of revolutions
T	=	TMU per revolution (Type III Motion)
5.2	=	TMU for start and stop

FIGURE 19-2b. *Cont.*

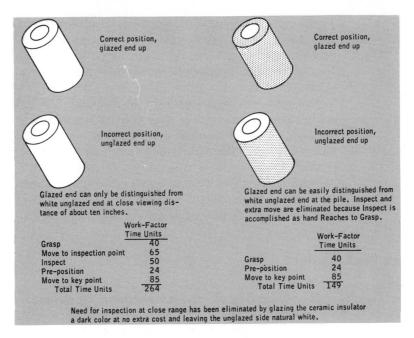

FIGURE 19-3. Time reduction through elimination of visual inspection [From J. H. Quick, J. H. Duncan, and J. A. Malcolm, *Work-Factor Time Standards* (New York: McGraw-Hill, Inc., 1962), p. 417.]

3. Time studies are normally based upon an established job. For all new jobs there is a learning period for the worker. During this period, observations are unreliable. Even on established jobs, workers improve their productivity after start-up. The problems of using time studies where learning occurs are bypassed through the use of predetermined time standards.

4. The cost of determining production standards is reduced.

5. The synthetic production standard is founded upon element times derived from very large samples of observations. This increased reliability of the standard time cannot be obtained with time studies, because it is out of the question to utilize such large samples for studying any one particular job.

6. The speed of preparing cost estimates, as well as their reliability for new jobs, new products, and so on, is improved. Production schedules can be quickly determined and modified. Product-mix analyses can be expedited similarly.

The Work-Factor system includes time values and techniques for measuring *microminiature assembly operations* performed under high-powered microscopes, both with hand tweezers and micromanipulators. A system called Mento-Factor has extended the use of predetermined time values to include mental functions involved in the performance of work. Mento-

Factor embodies some 450 fundamental mental process times, representing such functions as: proofreading, visual inspection, calculations, reading, problem solving with slide rule, tool design problems, and scanning blueprints. No synthetic time standards are applicable to human mental process functions in creative areas.

New jobs occur regularly in the job shop, but with different frequencies, according to the character of work done by a particular shop. Thus, for the job shop, the use of synthetic time standards is essential. At best we can see occasional application of the synthetic time methods to the flow shop and the project.

The productivity of the flow shop is measurable in terms of its line balance. But a different approach is required for the project. In the next section we examine the way in which productivity of projects can be discussed.

Project Productivity

The productivity of indirect labor, including clerical, administrative, and supervisory positions, is difficult to define and measure. And it is even more difficult to measure the productive output of a project team. Yet this is a crucial measurement because of the large quantities of money that are spent on projects, such as construction and research and development.

Let us define productivity as some number of units of project accomplishment *per period of time*. We shall assume that environmental and work force conditions remain relatively stable over each particular interval. Thus, we shall measure productivity per phase rather than in the aggregate. An average measure of productivity can then be obtained for the total project. Underlying this definition is the belief that project tasks can be divided into unit phases or accomplishment units. We would like to maximize the productivity of the project team in each phase so that the total job can be completed in the minimum possible time. A short development time is often crucial for competitive reasons.

To minimize project completion time we must employ just the right number of workers. However, another basic objective is to achieve project completion at a reasonable, if not a minimum, cost. It has been observed that the most efficient team size with respect to cost will frequently require a smaller group of research workers than would be needed for maximum group productivity. In other words, group size for minimum cost is smaller than for minimum project development time. Thus the definition of an optimal group size is dependent on the manager's objectives.[14]

Figure 19-4 illustrates the point that has just been made. The horizontal axis represents the number of workers engaged in any particular phase of project development. For the entire project, consisting of various phases, manpower commitments can be regulated to control project progress and performance. The vertical axis is *measured in* 2 ways: productivity (the solid

---

[14]Reference to pp. 167–69 on PERT/COST should be illuminating now.

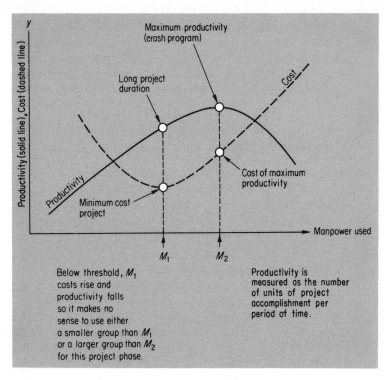

The figure contains the following labels:

y

Productivity (solid line), Cost (dashed line)

Maximum productivity
(crash program)

Long project
duration

Cost

Productivity

Cost of maximum
productivity

Minimum cost
project

Manpower used

M_1 M_2

Below threshold, M_1
costs rise and
productivity falls
so it makes no
sense to use either
a smaller group than M_1
or a larger group than M_2
for this project phase.

Productivity is
measured as the number
of units of project
accomplishment per
period of time.

FIGURE 19-4. Cost and productivity interrelations that underlie the cost/time analysis of any project phase

line) and cost (the dashed line). As stated, minimum cost occurs before the point of maximum productivity is reached. Cost is determined by the number of workers and the time required to complete the job. Thus, if we have 2 workers earning $12,000 per year and it takes them 6 months to complete this development phase, then the total cost of this phase of the project is $12,000. On the other hand, if 4 workers are employed, each earning $12,000 per year, and it takes them 4 months to complete the project phase, then the cost of doing this job is $16,000. Minimum cost in this example occurs when 2 workers are used instead of 4.

How is productivity affected? Because 4 workers complete the project phase in 4 months, their efforts place them higher on the productivity curve than the 2-person group. Let us assume that 4 worker's produce the maximum number of accomplishments per hour. This is the team size that can finish the job first. More or less than 4 workers will have a somewhat lower overall team productivity. With this in mind, it is not surprising that 2 workers might have something more than half the productivity of 4. So for our specific example, the 4 person team can accomplish the job in the minimum amount of time but at a higher total cost as compared to the 2 person team.

Which result do we want? If our objective is to minimize time, then 4 are indicated. If our objective is to strike some efficient balance between the cost of doing the job and the time for completion, something less than the maxi-

mum productivity group size is indicated. This result is exceedingly important
when we are dealing with sizable projects and development programs consisting of many phases, each of which requires substantial team sizes. Frequently, because of marketplace competition, great urgency is attached to
obtaining maximum productivity and, thereby, minimizing the total time to
accomplish the job.

Overstaffed Projects

There is a natural tendency to overestimate project manpower requirements. The result of this can be detrimental. Productivity drops off when
more than an optimal number of individuals are involved on the job. This
can be explained in a number of ways, including use of the old adage: "Too
many cooks spoil the broth." For those who prefer a logical explanation:
productivity falls off above a certain group size because of communication
and supervision problems.

Overstaffing is a consequence of many basic urges of management. It is
only natural to think that a "massive" effort can produce results faster than
a minimum cost effort. As we have seen, it is frequently true that minimum
cost will not coincide with minimum completion time. But the "massive"
effort is likely to overshoot the mark and result in both project delay and
additional costs. Our discussion should signal care in preparing research and
development budgets. Further, in synchronizing development programs with
production, greater forecast accuracy can be obtained if attention is paid to
the relationships of time and cost.

What can happen if management overestimates manpower requirements?
Assume that a group size is chosen that is somewhat larger than would be
required for maximum productivity. As a result of this choice, project costs
are greater than was expected and the job takes longer than the required
time. The result is paradoxical. The project manager believes that manpower
requirements have been underestimated. The manager attributes the additional cost to the additional time required to complete the project. The next
time that a similar job must be undertaken on a tight schedule the manager
will employ even more people. This pushes the results further to the right on
our curve in Fig. 19-4. Productivity drops even lower; a longer time is required to accomplish the job; costs are greater than ever. Instead of correcting the error, the manager is led further astray.

Cost and time estimates are predicated on historical records. Thus, over
time, project budgets increase. More and more workers are allocated to each
job. We see that a special form of Parkinson's Law[15] is in operation. Parkinson observed that work expands to fill up time available for its completion,
which is another way of saying that people create work that would not otherwise be done. In turn, we require more people to handle the jobs that have
been created. The process is self-perpetuating. When we couple this with the

---

[15]C. N. Parkinson, *Parkinson's Law* (New York: Houghton Mifflin Company, 1957).

productivity paradox that we have just described, we can understand why many organizations have experienced great difficulties in controlling expenditures on new product and service development.

Norden[16] indicates that the development function gives rise to certain patterns that are independent of the specific nature of the project. These patterns that Norden has found allow manpower requirements, time, and costs to be forecast with reasonable precision. Norden has identified five basic subcycles that underlie most development projects. These are shown in Fig. 19-5. This work is especially focused on the development part of R&D.

We have covered a range of issues concerned with how to measure the productivity of individual workers and project groups. However, these meas-

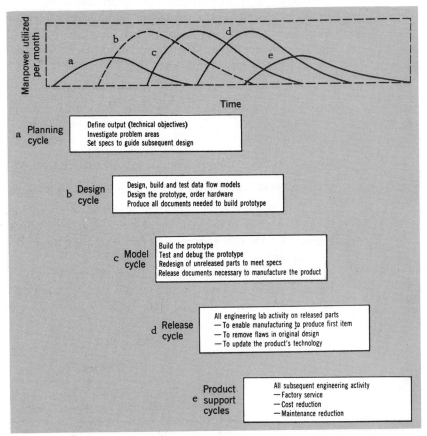

FIGURE 19-5. Typical manpower pattern of an engineering project [From Peter V. Norden, "Resource Usage and Network Planning Techniques," *Operations Research and Development*, ed. Burton V. Dean (New York: John Wiley & Sons, Inc., 1963), p. 160.]

---

[16]Peter V. Norden, "Resource Usage and Network Planning Techniques," *Operations Research in Research and Development*, Burton V. Dean, ed. (New York: John Wiley & Sons, Inc., 1963), pp. 149–169. See also an updated version of this material in Peter V. Norden, "Useful Tools for Project Management," in *Management of Production*, ed. Martin K. Starr (Middlesex, England: Penguin Books Ltd., 1969), pp. 71–101.

urements of productivity should always be thought of as "before" and "after," that is, before job improvement and after it is accomplished. Job improvement is the first topic of Chapter 20, which follows.

APPENDIX 19-I
Time Study Sample Size (Optional Material)

Time study methods are based on sampling. Therefore, a statistical question arises concerning how large a sample should be taken. The formula given below is predicated on the assumption of a degree of accuracy in time studies that is not warranted by the requirements for leveling and rest and delay factors. However, statistical measurement error is of a different sort, and it can be controlled. Therefore, on this basis we have at least some means for setting a proper sample size. Thus,

$$N' = \left[\frac{40\sqrt{N\sum\limits_{i=1}^{i=N} x_i^2 - \left(\sum\limits_{i=1}^{i=N} x_i\right)^2}}{\sum\limits_{i=1}^{i=N} x_i} \right]^2$$

where x_i is the ith observation for a particular element, N is the number of cycles observed up to this point, $\sum\limits_{i=1}^{i=N} x_i$ is the sum of all N of the x_i measures, and N' is the number of cycles that *should be* observed. Specifically N' is the required number of cycles to be observed so that we obtain *95* percent confidence that the true element time lies within the range $\bar{x} \pm 0.05\bar{x}$, which is ± 5 percent of the observed average time.

Because the job can comprise many different elements, we must use the element that will dominate the sample size by requiring the largest value of N'. The largest N' derived from Table 19-3 is $N'(2) = 66.7$.

TABLE 19-3

Reading i	Element			
	1 $x_i(1)$	2 $x_i(2)$	1 $x_i^2(1)$	2 $x_i^2(2)$
1	14	6	196	36
2	11	5	121	25
3	12	5	144	25
4	12	5	144	25
5	13	3	169	9
	62	24	774	120
$\bar{x}$:	$\frac{62}{5} = 12.4$	$\frac{24}{5} = 4.8$		

For element 1: $N'(1) = \left(\dfrac{40\sqrt{5(774) - (62)^2}}{62}\right)^2 = 10.8$

For element 2: $N'(2) = \left(\dfrac{40\sqrt{5(120) - (24)^2}}{24}\right)^2 = 66.7$

Having completed a partial study, the time study inspector will check to find out how much further to go. If a value for N' is obtained that is larger than N, observations must continue to be taken. This sample size evaluation procedure is repeated until the largest value of N' is equal to or less than the actual number of observations made, that is, Max $N' \le N$.

Our example begins with $N = 5$ observations of the two elements. We find that N' for element 2 dominates the sample size. It specifies 66.7 readings. Because we have taken only 5 readings, we must enlarge the sample size. We take another 5 readings and then test again. In this way, we keep collecting observations until we find that Max N' is equal to or less than N.

TABLE 19-4

Reading i	Element			
	1 $x_i(1)$	*2* $x_i(2)$	*1* $x_i^2(1)$	*2* $x_i^2(2)$
1	14	6	196	36
2	11	5	121	25
3	12	5	144	25
4	12	5	144	25
5	13	3	169	9
6	13	4	169	16
7	12	5	144	25
8	12	5	144	25
9	14	4	196	16
10	13	5	169	25
	126	47	1596	227

$$\bar{x}_1 = 12.6 \qquad \bar{x}_2 = 4.7$$

$$N'(1) = \left(\frac{40\sqrt{10(1596) - (126)^2}}{126}\right)^2 = 8.5$$

$$N'(2) = \left(\frac{40\sqrt{10(227) - (47)^2}}{47}\right)^2 = 6.6$$

Since Max $N' = 8.5$, which is equal to or less than $N = 10$, we may stop.

APPENDIX 19-II
Work Sample Size (Optional Material)

Designing a study that will reveal *needed* information with measurable reliability that cannot be obtained in a less expensive way is the essence of the work sampling, or operations sampling, technique. But how large a sample is needed? The same question was asked previously with respect to time studies. The answer that we now give is in the same vein. We have

$$N = \left(\frac{k}{s}\right)^2 p(1 - p)$$

where

$N = $ The number of observations to be taken to provide a sufficient sample. A sufficient sample is defined by management in terms of k and s.

$k = $ The number of normal standard deviations required to give a confidence measure of α. When $k = 1$, $\alpha = 68$ percent; when $k = 2$, $\alpha = 95$ percent; when $k = 3$, $\alpha = 99.7$ percent. (See p. 158.)

$\alpha = $ The likelihood that the true value of p falls within the range $p \pm s$.

$s = $ The accuracy range specified by management such that the true value of p falls within the range $p \pm s$.

$p = $ The fraction of total observations that an activity is observed to occur. When using this formula, we need only compute N for the one activity that dominates the sample size requirements.[17] This will be the activity whose observed p is closest to $\frac{1}{2}$.

An example is the most direct way to reinforce the above explanation. We shall use the State Court House office sampling figures that were given on p. 464. The phoning activity has a value of p that is closest to $\frac{1}{2}$, viz., $p = 0.61$. Let $k = 2$ and $s = 0.05$. Then

$$N = \left(\frac{2}{0.05}\right)^2 (0.61)(0.39) = 381$$

Because only 300 observations were made, it is necessary that an addition be made to the sample. We shall presume that 100 more observations are taken and that $p(\text{phoning}) = \frac{240}{400} = 0.60$. Then

$$N = \left(\frac{2}{0.05}\right)^2 (0.6)(0.4) = 384$$

---

[17]It should be noted that the sample formula given on p. 476 was based on an interval of the type $p \pm sp$. If we had used that relationship here, our sample size formula would be

$$N = \left(\frac{k}{s}\right)^2 \left(\frac{1-p}{p}\right)$$

The dominating activity, in this case, will be the one with the smallest p value.

This is smaller than the actual sample of 400. Therefore, the sample size is sufficient and we can stop.

APPENDIX 19-III
The Learning Curve

The worker's productivity rate improves with practice. (Rates of output deteriorate between practice intervals.) Learning is responsible for the observed improvement. After a while, with continued practice, learning reaches a productivity plateau where the time to produce a unit is about constant. This is shown in Figure 19-6.

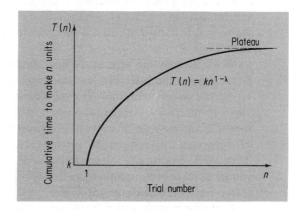

FIGURE 19-6.

The equation, $T(n) = kn^{1-\lambda}$ is read as follows:

$T(n) = $ *cumulative* time to make n units, consecutively;

$k = $ time required to make the *first* unit $n = 1$;

$n = $ trial number, i.e., the number of units made; and

$\lambda = $ the learning coefficient, $0 \leq \lambda < 1$.

We observe that when $\lambda = 0$, the cumulative time $T(n)$ increases linearly (kn), and there is no plateau. As $\lambda \to 1$, the "plateau effect" becomes accentuated. With learning, leveling-off is always expected to occur. The value of λ, therefore, reflects the speed with which the "plateau effect" is felt.

Often, average time measures are used to describe learning. Thus,

$$\bar{T}(n) = \frac{T(n)}{n} = kn^{-\lambda}$$

The same terms apply, as before. When $\lambda = 0$, $\bar{T}(n) = k$, which is the condition for nonlearning. Figure 19-7 illustrates $\bar{T}(n)$.

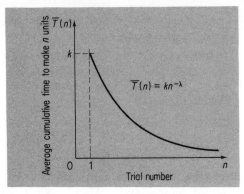

FIGURE 19-7.

Attempts such as these to describe one of the most complex of all human phenomena in quantitative terms has been shown to work with some reasonable level of predictive success.[18] Especially, in labor intensive situations, the results can be useful. Many refinements exist including S-curves and learning functions that include variables to describe the character of the job to be done.[19]

When workers are used in the flow shop, the effect of learning is marked. For example, the assembly line start up times will decrease as the workers repeat the same operations. The learning effect is also important for the job shop. If orders for work are too small, then the advantages of learning (i.e., lowering the cost per piece) will not be achieved. Cost bids for work must take learning into account by pricing jobs at the average productivity rate. Time study begins after the worker stabilizes at the plateau level. In some instances there are multiple plateaus, i.e., learning starts again after a stable interval of continued practice.

Learning models suffer from some serious flaws. The learning function that is used must be matched to the particulars of the specific situation. Empirical knowledge is essential.[20] Forgetting as a function of the pattern of intervals between trials deserves serious attention, and little is known about this aspect of the problem. Still, in project planning, as Norden has shown (pp. 475–76), the learning model has introduced a great deal more predictive ability than had previously existed. And it is clear that we need to understand more about the learning situation. What effect does job enlargement have on learning rates? What is the significance, in time studies, of the assumption that a worker can be tested at a stable point of "normal" activity? Finally, what part does learning play in the empirically observed decrease in per unit costs reported by The Boston Consulting Group (see pp. 28–29).

Despite their liabilities, there is general agreement that learning models bring the *behavioral* and the *quantitative* together.

[18]C. C. Pegels, "On Startup or Learning Curves: An Expanded View," *Management of Production*, edited by Martin K. Starr (London, England: Penguin Books Ltd., 1970), pp. 183–95.

[19]Martin K. Starr, *Management: A Modern Approach* (New York: Harcourt Brace Jovanovich, Inc., 1971), pp. 236–39.

[20]Nicholas Baloff, "Estimating the Parameters of the Startup Model—An Empirical Approach," *The Journal of Industrial Engineering*, Vol. 18: No. 4 (April, 1967), 248–53.

1. Frederick W. Taylor thought that the relationship between the well-designed job, the best worker, and the reasonable wage scale could be determined by logical analysis and intelligent experiment. The concept of the well-designed (specialized and efficient) job has been attacked. The notion of best workers—and therefore, fewer good workers—has been fought. A guaranteed wage and pay not related to productivity have been suggested as the only reasonable wage scale. Discuss.

2. Output volume determines wages. Wages are a major factor of worker motivation. Motivation conditions worker performance with respect to output volume. Figure 19-8 illustrates this feedback relationship. However, additional inputs (arrows) have been added to the figure to indicate that other factors also affect output volume, wages, and worker motivation. Describe these "other" factors.

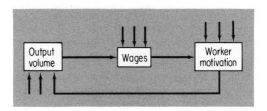

FIGURE 19-8.

3. We have been commissioned to study the activities of a research laboratory. It has been decided that work sampling should be used, because the continued presence of an observer would alter the behavior patterns of the research teams. Do you agree? Discuss.

4. For the study described in Problem 3, what categories of activities might apply? How often should observations be made? Would you use random sampling or make your observations at set times that are known to the researchers?

5. The following data have been collected by the Razormaker Corporation, using operations sampling to study Operation R-45 (see Fig. 19-1, p. 457).

Activity	Description	No. of Times Observed
1	Place razor in box	212
2	Seal box, etc.	90
A	Put away 100 boxes	10
B	Get 50 razors	8
C	Get 50 boxes	7
D	Get tape	12

How do these figures compare with those derived by the time study (see p. 459)? Discuss.

6. Figure 9-3 (p. 167) shows the cost/time trade-offs for PERT network activities. Compare these relationships with the one that is shown in Fig. 19-4 (p. 473) describing the cost and productivity interrelations that underlie the cost/time analysis of any project phase. Are the relationships consistent? Are they the same? Explain your answer.

7. New street lights are to be installed along Parker Avenue. A team of 5 workers can complete the job in 6 months. On the other hand, with 10 workers, completion can be achieved in 3 months. The workers are paid $1000 per month. For maximum project productivity, which team arrangement will you choose? For minimum project cost, which team arrangement is preferred? What is your recommendation?

8. Why is there a tendency to overestimate project manpower requirements?

9. Foodpackers, Inc. packs figs with syrup in jars. The imported figs are weighed out in lots of 1 pound. There are 12 figs to the pound, on the average. The figs must be inserted in a jar to which a portion of fig syrup is added. Then the jar is sealed with a twist cap.
   a. Analyze the job. Develop what you consider to be a good sequence of work elements.
   b. Sketch the process flow and layout.
   c. Use an operation chart to detail the work involved (see p. 488).
   d. Prepare a time sheet.
   e. Assume that the time study has been taken and supply your own hypothetical data for these observations. Then determine the standard time for the job. (Use at least ten cycles.)
   Answer: The purpose of this question is to permit the development of a relatively thorough analysis of time study methods. An adequate answer would be far too involved to present here. Nevertheless, the fundamental structure is shown.
   a. The basic components of the job are: get the figs to the scale; weigh the figs; get the jar; put the figs in the jar; get the syrup; add the syrup; get the cap; seal the jar with a twist; remove the jar.
   b. The process flow chart might be constructed something like the one shown in Fig. 19-9. The flow can then be adapted to a specific floor plan layout.

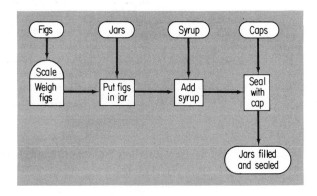

FIGURE 19-9.

c. A simplified operation chart might be:

	Left Hand	Right Hand
Element 1	get figs and put them on scale until correct weight is achieved	get a jar
Element 2	put figs in jar	clamp jar and get syrup
Element 3	get cap	add syrup
Element 4	screw on cap	unclamp jar
Element 5	move toward figs	put jar on conveyor

d. & e. A time chart is a convenient form for recording the elapsed time of each of the 5 elements of the process during successive cycles. Pertinent information concerning who is being observed, who is observing, where, when, and so forth should also be set down.

TABLE 19-5 FIG PACKING TIMES (IN HUNDREDTHS OF A MINUTE)

		Element				
		1	2	3	4	5
Cycle	1	15	8	7	10	10
	2	13	8	8	11	10
	3	15	7	8	12	10
	4	17	9	9	11	11
	5	12	9	6	10	10
	6	14	7	7	10	9
	7	14	8	6	9	9
	8	13	8	6	9	10
	9	15	7	8	9	11
	10	16	9	7	10	9
Total time		144	80	72	101	99
No. of obs.		10	10	10	10	10
Exp. cycles		1	1	1	1	1
Average time		14.4	8.0	7.2	10.1	9.9
Allowance		1	1	1	1	1
Normal time		14.4	8.0	7.2	10.1	9.9
R&D Correction		1	1	1	1	1
Standard time		14.4	8.0	7.2	10.1	9.9

Far more complex data can be employed. The method we use follows the one developed in Fig. 19-1 and Table 19-1 of the text. Then, the total standard time for the job would be $14.4 + 8.0 + 7.2 + 10.1 + 9.9 = 49.6$ hundredths minutes $= 0.496$ minute per jar.

So: $\dfrac{60}{0.496} \approx 2(60) = 120$ jars per hour— standard output.

10. The President of Foodpackers learns about predetermined time standards. He calls you in and asks for a report on the applicability of synthetic time methods to check the above times. Develop the appropriate report.

The problem below relates to material in Appendix 19-III.

11. With respect to the learning model on pp. 479–80, let $k = 10$ minutes and $n = 2$. Let λ vary. What values would $T(n)$ and $\bar{T}(n)$ have? Develop appropriate curves for $T(n)$ and $\bar{T}(n)$ given $k = 10$. Discuss your results.

twenty
job improvement, job evaluation, and wage determination

In many cases, time study of an existing job leads to job improvement. However, it is counterproductive to develop time standards for work that is known to be badly designed. Instead, work simplification[1] should be used first to come up with as good a job as possible. Then the application of time studies and productivity measures can lead to further improvement, which might not otherwise be attained.

Work Simplification (Methods Study)

The notion that work patterns could be studied and improved was the core from which modern P/OM evolved. Frederick Taylor, Henry Gantt,

---

[1]We can identify work simplification as an important part of methods study. The latter term is widely used (see pp. 336–37) to describe industrial engineering efforts to improve productivity, decrease costs, and increase worker satisfaction with the job. However, methods study encompasses a broader range of techniques than work simplification. Much of the material of Chapter 19, for example, would be considered part of the methods engineer's work.

Frank Gilbreth, Lillian Gilbreth, and others recognized that intuitive and judgmental methods of managing could be assisted by "scientific" analysis. The form that the analysis took was based on the premise that *if the parts were improved, then the whole must be better*. We now know that analysis can go just so far, and that, in fact, it can mislead us. We talk about the *system*, and wherever we use analysis we subsequently require synthesis. We reject efficiency without the simultaneous consideration of effectiveness.

We should avoid doing better and better what we shouldn't be doing at all.

This caution does not, however, reduce the *utility of work simplification when properly applied*. After all, efforts to improve efficiency represent investments. Like all investment alternatives, the burden of proof that an efficiency study is the best possible way to proceed falls upon those who would use it. But it must also be remembered that diminishing utility is likely to set in when what is already quite efficient is asked to be more so. The desire for efficiency and *perfection* is frequently more a matter of personal values than of systems rationality. When this is not the case, work simplification, job evaluation, value analysis, and methods analysis are legitimate and desirable investments for company funds.

It was from this basic urge to improve "things" that production management methodology began to search for new ways to look at the process. It was recognized that the process was composed of operations and that the operations could be further broken down, until such *micromotion units* as therbligs were created as sort of the ultimate in microcategorization.

Micromotion units are very small divisions of work, for example, wrist movements in *grasping*, finger motions in *releasing*, eye motions alone in searching, head movement in *searching*. Such micromotions were identified as the components of all work, and they could be put together in different ways to create different operations. Thus, the Gilbreths recognizing the interchangeability of finely categorized operations between jobs, developed 17 such job elements.[2] They called them "therbligs," which is almost Gilbreth spelled backwards. (Recall pp. 466–67 in Chapter 19.)

On the one hand, classification was a fundamental tool of the work simplification analyst. On the other hand, a means to organize and sequence these data was required. The fundamental method used was the visual representation of work flows. Such schematics typify the contributions of the early scientific management pioneers. Many of these charting techniques are still used because they are the best way for coping with the complexities of work.

As in any method that relies heavily on categorization, an important decision is *how fine* or *how broad* to make the categories. The choice was made to develop analytic tools for each of the various levels that would be encountered. Thus, the *process chart* was relatively *macro* in its view of the system

---

[2]F. B. Gilbreth, *Primer of Scientific Management* (New York: D. Van Nostrand Company, 1914).

487

*Job
Improvement,
Job Evaluation,
and Wage
Determination*

(see Figs. 18-7 and 18-9, pp. 480–482). Essentially, it charted the space-sequence flow of materials through the various stages of the production transformation process.

At the next level of detail come *operation charts*. In this case, observation is concentrated on a specific worker and the particular work station. Frequently, the level of analysis is in accord with the element interval requirements of time study methods. An example of this kind of schematic is shown in Fig. 20-1.

The *right and left hand movements* could be traced in terms of as fine a breakdown as the therblig classes, or with equal facility at grosser levels. Various symbols were developed to facilitate visual orientation and communication. There is nothing fixed or unalterable about these charts and the symbols used. Practice has produced the general form, which can be regarded as a standard. Modifications should be made according to requirements. The charts are intended to be *data organizers* that permit *intelligent evaluation of the situation* so that reasonable alternative arrangements of process and operations can be achieved. In common practice, a chart that portrays present conditions is compared with charts for one or more competing alternative plans.

Man-Machine Systems[3]

Another familiar work simplification chart is concerned with the operating characteristics of the *man-machine system*. This is the *man-machine time chart*, which encourages visual analysis of the way in which man-machine operations are coordinated. In Fig. 20-2 we observe that both the operator and the machine are idle 50 percent of the time. The problem seems to stem from the fact that the machine cannot be used during the *make ready* or the *put away* operations. In other words, the primary machine function must be interrupted, both to prepare and to remove successive parts. *If this were not true, then the more efficient arrangement shown in Fig. 20-3 could be used. Here, after the first cycle, both man and machine are 100 percent utilized.*

Let us now assume that a different facility, machine *B*, can be used where make ready and put away idle the facility but can be simultaneously performed. Then, if a helper is supplied to the operator, the machine utilization can be increased from $\frac{1}{2}$ to $\frac{2}{3}$. Both the operator and the helper have only $\frac{1}{3}$ utilization factors. This is shown in Fig. 20-4. Let us examine the use of these charts in the context of an example.

Foodpackers, Inc. runs an efficient job shop, canning and packing foods that change according to season, market prices, etc. The cans, jars, and boxes span a broad range of shapes and sizes. Consequently, general-purpose packing equipment characterizes the production system. The company derives its profit margin by setting up the most efficient job shop routines that are possi-

---

[3]This generic use of the term *man* refers to either sex in any number.

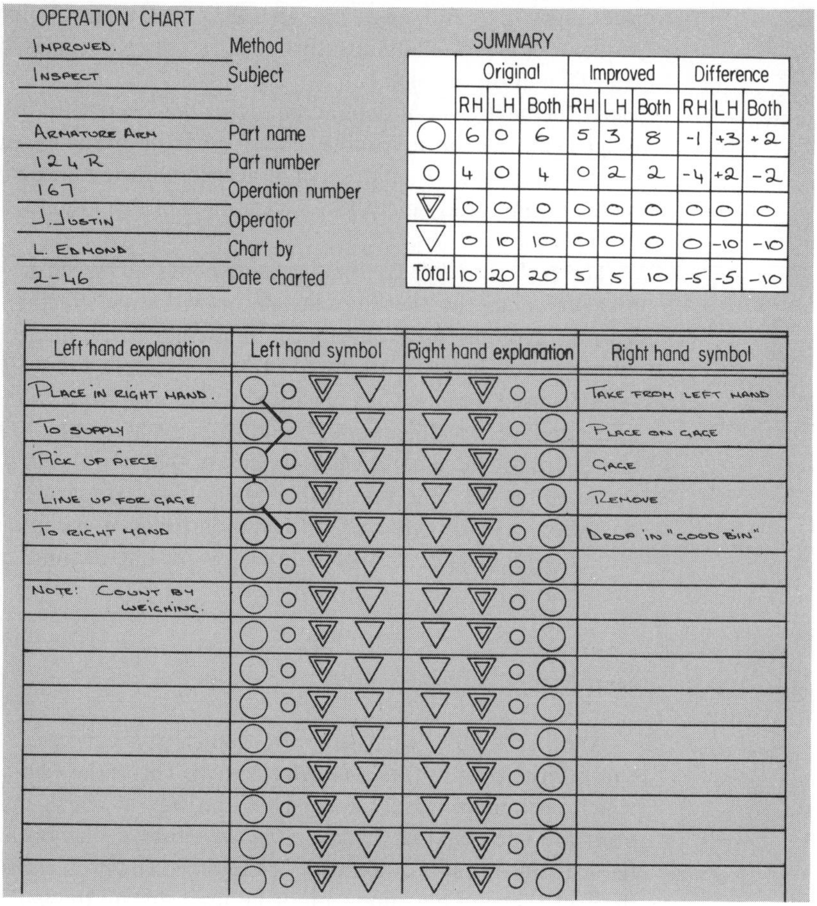

OPERATION CHART

	Method
IMPROVED.	Method
INSPECT	Subject
ARMATURE ARM	Part name
124 R	Part number
167	Operation number
J. JUSTIN	Operator
L. EDMOND	Chart by
2-46	Date charted

SUMMARY

	Original RH	LH	Both	Improved RH	LH	Both	Difference RH	LH	Both
◯	6	0	6	5	3	8	-1	+3	+2
o	4	0	4	0	2	2	-4	+2	-2
▽ (filled)	0	0	0	0	0	0	0	0	0
▽	0	10	10	0	0	0	0	-10	-10
Total	10	20	20	5	5	10	-5	-5	-10

Left hand explanation	Right hand explanation
PLACE IN RIGHT HAND.	TAKE FROM LEFT HAND
TO SUPPLY	PLACE ON GAGE
PICK UP PIECE	GAGE
LINE UP FOR GAGE	REMOVE
TO RIGHT HAND	DROP IN "GOOD BIN"
NOTE: COUNT BY WEIGHING.	

FIGURE 20-1. Operation chart for inspect relay armature arm (improved method) using form with preprinted chart symbols [From Marvin E. Mundel, *Motion and Time Study,* 3rd ed. (Englewood Cliffs, N.J.: Prentice-Hall, Inc., 1960), p. 204.]

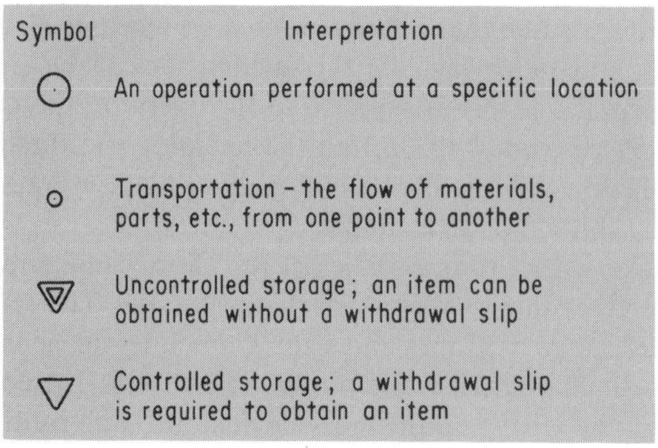

Symbol	Interpretation
◯	An operation performed at a specific location
o	Transportation – the flow of materials, parts, etc., from one point to another
▽ (filled)	Uncontrolled storage; an item can be obtained without a withdrawal slip
▽	Controlled storage; a withdrawal slip is required to obtain an item

Symbol key for operation chart (Figure 20-1)

488

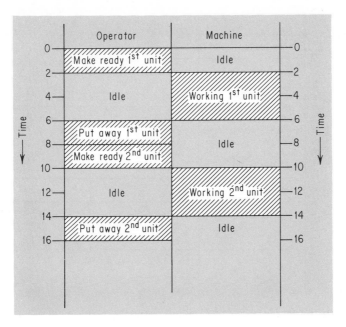

FIGURE 20-2. Man-machine time chart—Machine A, Plan 1, see p. 490

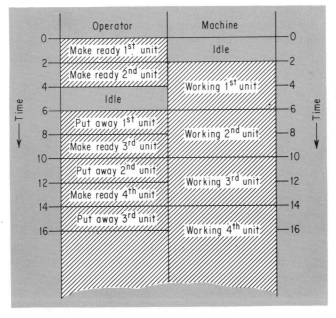

FIGURE 20-3. Man-machine time chart—Machine A is modified to permit 100 percent utilization of both operator and machine

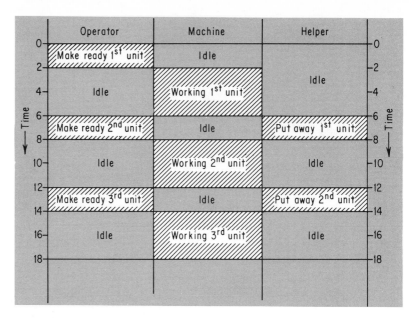

	Operator	Machine	Helper
0	Make ready 1st unit	Idle	
2			Idle
4	Idle	Working 1st unit	
6	Make ready 2nd unit	Idle	Put away 1st unit
8			
10	Idle	Working 2nd unit	Idle
12	Make ready 3rd unit	Idle	Put away 2nd unit
14			
16	Idle	Working 3rd unit	Idle
18			

FIGURE 20-4. Man-machine time chart—Machine B, Plan 2

ble. Many times, the operational sequences approach the productivity of an intermittent flow shop. The balancing of workers with simple machine functions lies at the heart of Foodpackers' success.

A bulk shipment of figs has arrived from Tunisia, and two plans are being considered for packing them in 1-pound boxes. Consult Figs. 20-2 and 20-4 for Plans 1 and 2, which are detailed below. The relevant costs are

$$\text{Operator's wage} = \$6.00 \text{ per hour}$$
$$\text{Helper's wage} = \$3.50 \text{ per hour}$$
$$\text{Machine } A\text{'s cost} = \$10.00 \text{ per hour}$$
$$\text{Machine } B\text{'s cost} = \$14.50 \text{ per hour}$$
$$\text{Value of output} = \$3.00 \text{ per box}$$

We analyze the situation in the following way:

Plan 1: Machine A is utilized 50 percent of the time. It takes 4 minutes to pack a box. Therefore, 7.5 boxes are packed per hour.[4] These are sold for $22.50. From this revenue we subtract the sum of machine A's hourly cost and the hourly wage of the operator; that is, $22.50 − $16.00 = $6.50, which is a measure of gross profit per hour for plan 1.

Plan 2: Machine B is utilized $66\frac{2}{3}$ percent of the time. Therefore, 10 boxes can be packed per hour. These are valued at $30. We subtract machine B's

---

[4]Thirty working minutes of machine time per hour ÷ 4 minutes per box = 7.5 boxes per hour.

491

*Job
Improvement,
Job Evaluation,
and Wage
Determination*

hourly cost and the hourly wages of both the operator and his helper. This gives $30 — $24 = $6 of gross profit per hour. *Therefore, Select Plan 1.* Food-packers must persistently use such planning, because its profit margin is tight. After subtracting the cost of figs, boxes, and fillers, there is not much left over. Efficiency of operations spells the difference between profit and loss.

We can see how closely related work simplification is to time study analysis. Before production standards are set, *jobs should be studied* and brought to a point where common sense and good judgment can no longer be readily used to improve the operations. Nevertheless, at a particular moment in time an individual may get a sudden insight as to how a well-studied job can be further improved. In recent years, there has been deemphasis on work simplification in certain industries, because job shop lots are decreasing in size; line changeovers to new and modified outputs are becoming more frequent; high-level mechanization and automation require intense preplanning that obviates the need for on-going improvement of operations; and more elaborate methodologies of operations research and management science have appeared, which compete for investment study dollars with the older work simplification methods.

Job Enrichment

The work arrangement between operator and machine in Fig. 20-3, p. 489, has the operator working constantly. The only relationship the operator has is with the machine. On the other hand, in Fig. 20-4, p. 490, the operator and helper are idle at the same time and can communicate with each other, if the machine is not too noisy. It is also possible that the operator and helper could talk with other operators and helpers who are idle at the same time. Still, the job is repetitious and the individuals tend to be isolated by the need to tend the machine.

A great deal has been said and written that contends that such isolation runs counter to people's desires to work with other people on nonroutine tasks or, if routine, on tasks that are complex enough not to repeat every few minutes. Because of the economic benefits of specialization, organizations have designed many jobs that are highly repetitive and very narrow in scope. Workers have complained about the dehumanizing quality of the work place.[5]

Thus, with respect to the flow shop, as more stations are added, productivity rises; however, cycle time gets shorter, placing an increasing burden on station workers, who have shorter jobs to do with greater frequency. The quality of work can deteriorate under such circumstances. Worker dissatisfaction can increase. (For example, the Vega plant of General Motors at

---

[5]There is also research evidence that a significant number of workers prefer simple, highly repetitive tasks.

Lordstown suffered a long and difficult strike shortly after it was built because of worker dissatisfactions with the flow shop pace.)

During the 1970s, a number of organizations redesigned their production lines so that workers would do many jobs. For example, Volvo of Sweden began experimenting with teams that built the entire car. Other organizations decreased specialization in their line-balancing analysis, thereby increasing the size of each work station. Most of the complaints center around the paced-flow shop as well as its intermittent forms rather than the job shop, but there are tedious aspects about the job shop as well. The project is, however, immune. If there is any criticism on the part of project workers, it is the continual crises and exceptions that afflict their nonroutinized workdays.

It is not clear yet how broadly acceptable such concepts as *job rotation* (where workers exchange jobs with each other) and *job enlargement* will be. The extent to which *worker participation* in decision making will be endorsed by both public and private organizations is also uncertain. The ultimate criterion is whether the objectives of the organization can be met with less specialization and with less authority over workers.

Wage Plans and Incentives

The problem of determining human resource costs has two parts. First, what is fair or a reasonable output? That is, how much service should be rendered or how many pieces should be expected per unit of time? Chapter 19 was devoted to answering this question, and the first part of this chapter (re job improvement) is also relevant. The second problem deals with the question: What is fair wage for fair output?

The difficulty of answering the second question is underscored by such further queries as: How can we equate the work done by a secretary and a punch press operator? What is a reasonable salary for the research director as compared to the operations manager? If 2 people work equally hard, but one turns out 10 pieces while the second turns out 20 pieces, should we pay them equal salaries? Should a person be paid for time or for physical output?

All these questions seem to hinge on 2 points that can be studied rationally. First, what value does the company derive from its human resources? Second, considering the factor of supply and demand for the kind of services that the organization requires, how much should it pay?

Now we turn to the second aspect of the 2-part problem. With respect to a "fair" wage, the manager is concerned with the motivational forces which affect creativity and productivity. The fact that behavior can be influenced by various inducements (for example, monetary incentives), whereas machines cannot be, points up a major difference between the 2 and is still another aspect of man-machine relations.

A startling case history was obtained in the 1930s by a study group from Harvard at the Western Electric Company in Chicago. The original study concerned levels of illumination and their effect on productivity. It was dis-

493

*Job
Improvement,
Job Evaluation,
and Wage
Determination*

covered that whether the illumination was raised or lowered productivity was improved. The key discovery was that employees responded positively to the management's *interest and attention*. This response level overrode the functional effects of the illumination level. Such complex behavior provides important differentiation between man and machine.

Motivation can be both positive and negative. We usually associate the latter with poor employee morale. On the face of it, one would suppose that an average level of morale existed from which positive and negative deviations could be measured. Of course, there is no standard to use in this way. With discussions of *incentives and motivation*, the major difficulty is the measurement problem. Nevertheless, accepting the lack of precision involved, we recognize that incentives exist as a real causal factor affecting worker behavior.

Incentives include wages, job title, size of office, recognized organizational importance, ability to participate in decisions, vacations, leisure time, and the variety of tasks assigned. For the most part, these categories represent intangible qualities that escape definition and measurement. Thus, we speak of leadership, knowing that an undefinable characteristic is involved. It is a characteristic that is intimately involved with the subject of motivation and incentive. We lack a yardstick by which to measure it. One of the few ways to set an objective standard for the control of incentives is through wage plans.

What is an equitable wage? Do we measure real wages in terms of the *cost of living*, or do we compare monetary wages as they are found in different parts of the country? Is it reasonable to compare, for a given industry, rural with urban wages? There has been a continuing attempt to relate monetary wages to real wages. For this reason the minimum wage as fixed by law has been steadily increased over the years in order to keep pace with a rising cost of living.

From each company's point of view there is some level of wages that is optimal. High wages remove dollars that could otherwise be invested in expansion possibilities. Salary increases might cause dollars to be withheld from stockholders. This action produces unpredictable results on the stock market. It generally lowers the credit ratings that banks will offer. Low wages, on the other hand, discourage highly skilled and able personnel; produce negative motivation, increase turnover rates, and increase recruitment costs.[6] From the company's point of view, therefore, neither high nor low wages are desirable. Rather, a wage rate that produces a balanced system of costs is desired.

Each wage rate is part of a set of wage rates that apply to different jobs. Balance is necessary here too, in the relationship of jobs to each other and the wage rates they earn. This brings us to job evaluation as a necessity for the determination of an equitable wage.

---

[6]This can be related to the costs associated with $W_t - W_{t-1}$ in aggregate scheduling (see pp. 266–68).

There are several different but reasonable approaches to the problem of *job evaluation*. One way is to use purely qualitative evaluations. A second possibility calls for the ranking of jobs in terms of their contribution to the organization. A third approach is based upon an explicit point system. The purely qualitative approach is overly susceptible to personal bias. Because of this, it is disappearing from use. Ranking is certainly superior, but ranking does not indicate how much one job differs from another. Let us, therefore, consider the most elaborate of the named approaches, that is, the point system. A job is classified in terms of a number of factors required for the job.

Job Factors

1. Intelligence
2. Physical skill
3. Physical effort
4. Responsibility that must be assumed in order to accomplish the job
5. Working conditions, including the environment and other human factors relevant to job accomplishment

Any job can be described in terms of these attributes. Each task requires a varying amount of each factor. By assigning point values to each factor it is possible to derive a total score for any job. The score is equivalent to a monetary wage rate. It is intended to reflect the requirements of the job in terms of the significant factors. Presumably, in this way an approach is made to the problem of determining true worth to the company. After all, the real issue in a rational, laissez-faire society is: What is a particular job, or set of operations, worth to the organization? For machines, the costs are easily derived. For people, the problem has been intelligently approached, but never totally resolved.

To convert job point levels into appropriate wage rates, the key-job concept is often used. Certain key positions exist that are commonly found in the industry. These might include the position of secretary, foreman, and skilled tool and die-maker in a metal-working firm; or secretary, flight attendant, and pilot for an airline. The key jobs are carefully studied in terms of the kind of factors listed above. Then, a job rating is assigned. Based upon an industry-wide, geographical analysis of the going wage rates for key positions, a curve can be drawn such as that shown in Fig. 20-5. We see that first the key jobs are located on this graph. Then, a curve is put through the key job points. It follows that all other jobs can be assigned appropriate wage rates by estimating their positions on the curve between the key job points.

To illustrate the use of the point system and the key-job concept, assume that 4 key positions are identified in hospital management. We shall call these 4 jobs *A*, *B*, *C*, and *D*. Each position has been evaluated and given the number of points shown in Table 20-1. The ratings are based on job requirements

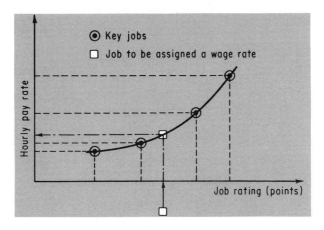

FIGURE 20-5. The key-job curve where hourly pay rate is related to the job's rating

for intelligence (1), physical skill (2), physical effort (3), responsibility (4), and working conditions (5).

It will be noted that a maximum of 220 points is available to be assigned to any position. A job demanding the utmost intelligence can receive 50 points. A job that is done under the worst possible working conditions would be assigned 20 points. (This might be a highly repetitious job if the organization considers job enlargement essential.) The assignment of the maximum number of points available from each job factor is a management judgment of the contribution that each factor makes to the achievement of organizational objectives. The assignment of a given number of points from each factor to a particular job is also a management judgment based on the job evaluation.

TABLE 20-1 POINT ASSIGNMENTS AND AVERAGE WAGE RATES
FOR KEY POSITIONS

| Key Jobs | Maximum Number of Points Available, Shown Above Each Category | | | | | Total Points of Job | Average Hospital Wage Rate/Week for Key Position |
| | 50 | 40 | 30 | 80 | 20 | | |
	1	2	3	4	5		
A	20	20	30	10	20	100	$200
B	50	10	10	60	0	130	$400
C	40	40	10	70	15	175	$700
D	25	20	10	10	10	75	$150

The key-job curve derived from Table 20-1 is shown in Fig. 20-6.

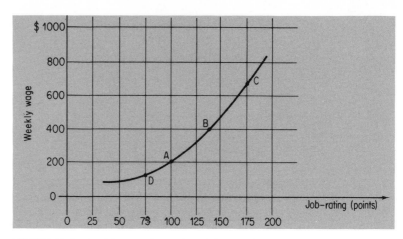

FIGURE 20-6. Key-job curve for the hospital positions

Now, consider a non-key job *E*, which has been rated with 150 points. Consulting Fig. 20-6, we see that job *E* would be associated (by interpolation, see pp. 244–45) with a weekly wage of $500.

Although this is a relatively straightforward method for pricing jobs, many additional factors intervene. These include the use of incentive plans, merit rating systems, the importance of seniority, the effect of cost-of-living factors, the supply and demand both regionally and nationally for certain skills, and the notion of a guaranteed annual wage. We shall turn particular attention to the question of wage incentives.

Before proceeding further, let us recapitulate the steps required to establish a wage rate structure:

1. Develop relevant job factors, and assign each one its maximum point value.
2. Classify jobs in terms of the relevant factors, and assign each job its point allocation.
3. Select key jobs and determine appropriate wage rates from industry data.
4. Draw key-job curve.
5. Assign wage rates to non-key jobs by interpolation and extrapolation.
6. Take special factors into account such as seniority, merit ratings, and incentive plans.

Many jobs can be assigned a wage only according to the amount of *time* that the worker contributes. This is characteristic of executive and administrative positions. It is also true of creative and research jobs. Indirect labor, by definition, cannot be paid on the basis of production output. This applies to most clerical operations. Only those jobs that are directly associated with the volume of production can be paid for on the basis of physical output.

Various models that are suitable for the analysis of employee motivation have been developed.[7] They are concerned with the methods used to obtain maximum worker participation. They are designed, on the one hand, to provide equitable distinction between workers who expend different amounts of energy and contribute different benefits to the company. On the other hand, they are intended to provide a balanced system of wages for the company. Many different plans or models have been conceived. We shall mention only a few.

1. *Straight Piecework Model:*

$$W = HA\left(\frac{O_A}{O_S}\right)$$

where

$H =$ hourly rate in dollars per hour.

$A =$ actual time worked in hours per week.

$O_A =$ actual output per hour in pieces per hour.

$O_S =$ standard output per hour in expected number of pieces per hour.

$W =$ weekly wage rate in dollars per week.

H/O_S is the rate in dollars per piece of completed work and is derived in terms of an output standard (from time studies) and a wage standard (from job evaluation). The worker, however, has no security with this fundamental wage plan. Weekly wages decrease proportionally as actual work output falls.

2. *Piecework Model with a Guaranteed Base:*

$$\text{for } O_A \leq O_S \quad W = HA$$

$$\text{for } O_A > O_S \quad W = HA\left(\frac{O_A}{O_S}\right)$$

In this case, the worker is guaranteed at least a weekly wage rate of $W = HA$. And, as in 1 above when actual output becomes greater than standard output, take-home pay increases above the base level HA.

3. *General Incentive Model:*

$$\text{for } O_A \leq O_S \quad W = HA$$

$$\text{for } O_A > O_S \quad W = HA\left[1 + k\left(\frac{O_A}{O_S} - 1\right)\right]$$

Here again, the minimum is established at $W = HA$. Now, however, we observe that the incentive given is proportional to the size of the coefficient k. For O_A greater than O_S, some fraction of the value of the extra production

---

[7]Historically, we find great interest in this subject concerning the development of incentive plans. Frederick W. Taylor, Henry Towne, Henri Fayol, and others were concerned with incentive, profit sharing, work definition, work division, authority and responsibility, and the questions of satisfactory pay.

of the worker is paid to him as both reward and incentive. The value of k depends upon the plan that is used. For example, there is the Halsey 50-50 plan where $k = \frac{1}{2}$. In the 100 percent bonus plan,[8] $k = 1$. In the Bedaux plan, $k = \frac{3}{4}$. Many other plans also have been tried. The history of these plans, their results, and the subsequent design of new and improved plans is an area of specialization in itself.

---

[8]This is equivalent to the piecework model with a guaranteed base.

Foodpackers' Figpacking Labor Cost

Using a key job curve, Foodpackers' figpacking operation is rated at $H = \$6$ per hour. As previously derived (p. 490), the standard output per hour with plan 1 is $O_S = 7.5$ boxes per hour. One of Foodpackers' best pieceworkers averages 12 boxes per hour over a 40-hour week; i.e., $O_A = 12$ and $A = 40$.

Using either the straight piecework model or the piecework model with a guaranteed base, we obtain the same result, namely, wages are

$$W = (6)(40)\left(\frac{12}{7.5}\right) = \$384 \text{ per week}$$

If the actual output had matched the standard output, then wages would have been

$$W = (6)(40)\left(\frac{7.5}{7.5}\right) = \$240 \text{ per week}$$

If the actual output had been only six boxes per hour, then wages would fall (if the straight piecework model is used) to

$$W = (6)(40)\left(\frac{6}{7.5}\right) = \$192 \text{ per week}$$

The weekly wage would be supported at $240 if the piecework model with a guaranteed base applied.

Last, if the general incentive wage model was used with the Halsey 50–50 plan where $k = \frac{1}{2}$, then

for actual output, $O_A = 12$,

$$W = (6)(40)\left[1 + \frac{1}{2}\left(\frac{12}{7.5} - 1\right)\right] = \$312$$

for actual output, $O_A = 7.5$,

$$W = (6)(40)\left[1 + \frac{1}{2}\left(\frac{7.5}{7.5} - 1\right)\right] = \$240$$

for actual output, $O_A = 6$,

$$W = (6)(40)\left[1 + \frac{1}{2}\left(\frac{6}{7.5} - 1\right)\right] = \$216$$

499

*Job
Improvement,
Job Evaluation,
and Wage
Determination*

These computations are intended to illustrate the kind of differences that exist between the various wage plans.

Question: What is the smallest weekly take-home pay that can be earned with each of these plans?

Answer: For the straight piecework model:

$$W = (6)(40)\left(\frac{0}{7.5}\right) = 0$$

For the piecework model with a guaranteed base:

$$W = (6)(40) = \$240$$

For the general incentive model with $k = \frac{1}{2}$:

$$W = (6)(40)\left[1 + \frac{1}{2}\left(\frac{0}{7.5} - 1\right)\right] = \$120$$

Wage incentives are powerful motivators, but they are not the only motivators, as was indicated by the section of text devoted to job enrichment (pp. 491–92). Job factor disincentives also exist. These were lumped together in the job factor category 5 (on p. 494) which was "working conditions, including the environment and other human factors relevant to job accomplishment" In Chapter 21, we shall examine some of these human factor considerations.

PROBLEMS

1. How do the micromotion divisions of work, such as therbligs, relate to the basic motions of synthetic time standards such as MTM (see pp. 465–72)?

2. What is the relationship of work simplification to methods study?

3. Compare the purpose of *process charts* (pp. 480–82) with that of *operation charts* (p. 488) and discuss the differences.

4. The Volvo Company of Sweden has utilized job enlargement for the production of some of its automobiles. What does this mean? How does the production process differ from that of a paced-conveyor flow shop?

5. How does the concept of job enrichment affect the economic advantages to be gained from specialization through division of labor? What other factors might influence productivity?

6. What was learned from the Hawthorne experiment? How does it apply, in general, to human resource management?

7. Job improvement can lower the costs of output. This may enable an organization to drop its prices and/or increase the quality of its product line or service mix. Then the managers of other organizations must ask themselves why their costs are not competitive. However, especially in the

job shop, the cost of studying the job and the work place may offset the economic advantages to be gained from improvement. This is less likely with respect to the intermittent flow shop. Explain.

8. Airborne, Inc. has decided to use the point-based, key-job curve system to set its employees' wages. Four key jobs were identified and rated with points. (See the table below.)

Job	Job Point Rating	Industry Wage (*Annual*) for Key Jobs
Secretary	10	$12,288
Flight attendant	15	$20,240
Engineer	30	$44,096
Pilot	40	$60,000

a. Derive the wages for ground crew with a 25-point job rating.
b. Derive the wages for ticket office personnel with a 12-point job rating.

9. Assume that the man-machine situation on pp. 484–90 is now as follows: Both *make ready* and *put away* can be accomplished only when the machine is idle. These operations cannot be performed simultaneously. Two machines are used and are to be tended by a single operator. The element times are unchanged. Use a man-machine time chart to find the best way of handling this situation.

Answer: The man-machine time chart depicting the optimum configuration under the given condition would be:

	Machine 1	Operator	Machine 2
0			
	Idle	Make ready 1	
2			
	Work	Idle	Idle
4			
	1	Make ready 2	
6			
		Put away 1	Work
8	Idle		
		Make ready 3	2
10			
	Work	Put away 2	
12			Idle
	3	Make ready 4	
14			
		Put away 3	Work
16	Idle		
		Make ready 5	4
18			

501

*Job
Improvement,
Job Evaluation,
and Wage
Determination*

If this configuration is used, each machine will be idle one-half of the time (the operations of make ready and put away are being performed at these times). On the other hand, the operator is being utilized 100 percent of the time. The arrangement is optimal if the worker's wage is much greater than the cost of idle machine time.

10. Company X is about to undertake a program to encourage its employees to suggest new products and revisions of present design. A strong incentive is provided. The company employs 5000 workers, and it is expected that the number of suggestions per year will average about one per man. If the average working year is 250 days, there will be about 20 suggestions per day to be screened. The suggestions are to be sorted by the sales division. Only marketable ideas will be forwarded to operations management. It is decided that production will use an initial screening process in order to quickly eliminate the unworkable suggestions. Those ideas that pass the screening will then be subjected to a more intensive feasibility study.

   a. Develop a logical procedure that operations management can follow in order to achieve its objectives. Make sure that you include all questions required by the decision process.

   b. Estimate the number of employees required to administer such a program.

   Answer: A committee should be formed. The size of the committee that will be able to cope with the work load will be a function of the expected number of suggestions that the sales division will consider to be marketable and therefore pass back to the production department. If the sales division really does its job, the number of ideas that must be reviewed by the production department will be considerably cut down. On the other hand, if real cooperation does not exist, sales may just pass most of the ideas along to production in order to avoid investing a great deal of their time in the suggestion procedure. Then, at a later stage, after production has provided the initial filtering, the sales division could veto ideas that would not be marketable. This approach would overburden production and waste their time. Someone, however, has to provide the initial filter. On the other hand, if the sales division has been appointed to serve as the initial filter in the system, the sales division could erroneously reject good ideas, figuring that too many ideas superficially accepted and sent along to the production division would lead to complaints that might reach top management. This high rejection procedure has its built-in troubles too. It is likely to anger the workers who have submitted suggestions, leading to an increased number of grievances and generally poor morale. Both of these costs would be experienced by the production division alone.

   Here we see an example of how divisional boundaries can produce unexpected distortions unless a systems point of view prevails such that cooperation and understanding can flow across the boundaries.

   a. Specifically, P/OM would begin by asking questions to check out the technological feasibility of the various projects that have been suggested. Once it is established that a specific product can be made or a specific service can be offered, then a production study that relates costs to qualities could be undertaken. The economic feasibility of the production process would have to be assessed in terms of the market potential for various price and quality combinations. (An elaborate answer to this question can be framed in terms of PERT diagrams.)

b. Let us assume that the following table applies:

Period of Time = 100 days

Number of Suggestions	Level of Activity	Average Time Spent per Suggestion	Total Time
2000	Sales division	$\frac{1}{5}$ hour	400 hours
1000	Production—1st Level	$\frac{1}{2}$ hour	500 hours
100	Production—2nd Level	10 hours	1000 hours
1	Production—3rd Level	40 hours	40 hours

According to this set of estimates, one idea emerges every 100 days for serious consideration by the engineering, production and sales departments. To achieve this, the sales division must contribute 4 hours per day, whereas the production department must use almost two men on this function to achieve the required 15.4 hours per day.

11. Two man-machine plans are compared in the text (pp. 489–91). For what value of output would these plans be equal?
Answer:

$$7.5p - 16.00 = 10p - 24$$

$$p = \$3.20 \text{ satisfies the conditions.}$$

12. In Razormakers' cafeteria, the tables are tightly packed together. This was done, given the limited available space, to allow 90 percent of all employees to eat at the same time. Now, an employee complaint has been filed. How should this matter be handled?

13. An employee group has petitioned Razormakers' management to introduce "flexitime." Flexitime is one of several names used to describe a plan whereby workers can start and finish work (almost whenever they want) so long as they work (say) 40 hours a week. You have been asked to give management a brief summary of the pros and cons.

twenty-one
human factors

Many considerations must be taken into account when one is determining how to employ the human mind and body in the production process. The study of such problems has given rise to the development of human factor models that are concerned with the way in which man fits into the working environment, the control he has over it, the design of the tools that he uses, and the design of the products and services that he requires.[1] Such studies are called by a number of different names. We have used the label "human factors," but we could have called this subject "human engineering," "biomechanics," or a British term, "ergonomics."

Part 2 of the text, on the life cycle management of goods and services, should be reexamined by the reader within the context of this chapter.

Design of the Job and the Workplace

The productivity of a motivated worker can be very poor if the assigned job is badly designed. Part of the design of the job is the layout of the work

---

[1]It should be noted that human factors pertain to workers or consumers with equal applicability. The worker is a consumer of facilities and equipment at the work place.

place. It is a managerial responsibility to recognize this interaction and to provide the worker with a safe and efficient task and environment.[2] This responsibility is harder to fulfill for the job shop than the flow shop, because new jobs are being assigned regularly to it. If the worker does not feel safe, one of the most basic human needs is not being satisfied. But the lack of safety does not always act as a disincentive. The worker, feeling compelled to earn as much money as possible, may disregard safety. Management has been known to "look the other way" when the pressure is great to deliver on time or to increase production output. After an accident, neither the worker nor management can find any way to rationalize the result.

The Knockaway Story

Circle Switch Corporation is not a giant organization, but it does have a full array of metal-working equipment to produce industrial switches. The market for these switches is highly competitive, and a crucial factor for obtaining business is to get an order and turn it out fast.

As a result of this pressure, the foreman looked the other way when several of the press shop workers disconnected their "knockaways." The "knockaway" is a safety arm that does just what it says it does, i.e., knocks away hands and arms that are near the heavy dies, which close with great force to press metal into switchboxes. The workers' motivation in doing this was that they were paid incentive wages using the piecework model with a guaranteed base. The knockaway slowed things up. They could operate the press faster without it. That is why the foreman looked the other way, until one of the workers lost an arm in the press.

It is unnecessary to dwell on the misery that this accident caused and on the time and money involved in litigation. (Although identities have been masked, it is a true story.)

Safety

Acceptable levels of safety are difficult to discuss and even harder to specify. We know that the ideal situation is "perfect" safety, but it is an unobtainable state. So-called "safety factors" are designed into bridges, ships, and planes. Sometimes, we speak about "fail-safe" systems. By this we mean that the system is immune to crucial accidents or disastrous, fortuitous events except where the probabilities of such occurrences are so small that they can

---

[2]For example, see E. R. Tichauer, "Biomechanics Sustains Occupational Safety and Health," *Industrial Engineering* (February, 1976), pp. 46–56.

be ignored.[3] To achieve this, high-level safety factors must be incorporated into the basic design of the system for all its vulnerabilities.

Safety poses a curious problem. We cannot really evaluate the value of an arm, or a leg, or a life. If faced with the question, we would state unequivocally that a life is of enormous value, but we do not act as though this were so, nor could we if we tried. It would mean that each and every swimmer have his own personal retinue of lifeguards; that after each flight, a plane would be completely overhauled, and new parts installed for all the old ones. The fact that we do not behave in this manner does not lessen our concern for safety. If anything, our concern increases as a direct result of the fact that we cannot act in accord with our moral values, but rather, in terms of an obscure compromise between moral and economic values.

Bypassing the complicated philosophical and ethical problems involved in this subject, we can all readily agree that safety is a major consideration. Although we cannot find a behavioral model to determine the value of life and limb, we can attempt to minimize accident rates subject to a reasonable set of system constraints.[4] Thus, machine designs must assure a reasonable level of safety to machine operators. Here, the differences between people play a part. A satisfactory machine design for a male worker may not prove to be equally safe or productive for a female operator.[5] (See the discussion, *design of equipment*, which follows on pp. 513–19).

In certain cases, humans are susceptible to damage where the source of trouble lies beyond the capabilities of their own sensory protection. This is true, for example, where odorless toxic gases find their way into the air supply. Another case is where workers are inadvertently exposed to radioactive materials that cause radiation poisoning before detection is possible. Positive steps must be taken to prevent these conditions from arising, correcting them immediately if they occur. Processes that produce toxic gases must be isolated so that they cannot contaminate the air supply. Nontoxic impurities can be kept out of the air by utilizing exhaust hoods close to the source of such impurities. For this vacuum cleaner-type action to be effective, the through-put rate of the air intake must be regulated according to the weight of the contaminent particles. Radioactive substances are being used with increasing frequency. They cannot be detected readily. For radiation hazards, proper shielding is a necessity. Where this is not possible, machines are substituted and controlled at safe distances from the radioactive materials. Geiger coun-

---

[3]According to Borel, these might be events associated with probabilities in the neighborhood of one in a million (0.000001).

Emile Borel, "Valeur Pratique et Philosophie des Probabilities," *Traité du Cacul des Probabilities et de ses Applications*, Tome IV, Fascicule 3, ed. by Emile Borel (Gautier-Villars, Paris, 1950).

[4]We maximize safety, but subject to economic constraints. In this way, we can soothe our consciences that all possible steps are being taken (although this is not so).

[5]During the Second World War, a famous movie actress started a fad for long hair that was worn partially over the face. Machine designers had not taken this possibility into account and a number of serious accidents occurred. Various government agencies requested the actress (Veronica Lake) to change her hair style, which she did. This improved the situation.

ters and other protective devices are used to provide warning if some dangerous malfunction occurs.

Many safety problems arise because of laziness or corner-cutting. In these
cases, the danger is apparent to all concerned, but somewhere along the line
adequate measures are not taken. It is not enough to supply goggles to
workers where, either because of intense light or flying particles, eye impair-
ment might result if they are not used. It is necessary to make *certain* that
they are used.

Problems of safety also involve a *proneness* to accidents which seems to
arise from psychological factors triggered by an initial chance occurrence.
The problem of accident proneness has been studied, but the search for an
antidote appears to require further research.

Safety problems for workers arise because of the complex equipment and
processes found in the production area. It is operations management's
obligation to insure worker safety. The model of man shows a hardy soul but
a vulnerable body. Fundamentally, the best way to ensure safety is to design
a total system of products, tools, facilities, and services that adequately considers the range of detrimental conditions that can occur. Safety models,
therefore, constitute an area of total interaction between individuals and
physical elements of the production system. Often, preventative measures
may be more effective than remedial ones.

The Man-machine Interface

The industrial revolution was based on the fact that for certain kinds of
operations a machine was superior to a man. Over a period of time there has
been an increasing level of sophistication with respect to the design of mechanisms. This has led to many instances where the replacement of man by
machine has been unequivocally warranted.

Initially, *repetitive physical jobs* were particularly susceptible to improvement by utilizing machines instead of workers. Now we find that mechanical
and electronic control systems can be substituted for many mental activities
formerly relegated exclusively to people. At the heart of this latter change is
the *computer*.

For most complex activities, neither man nor machine exclusively is ideal
for the job. Rather, some *combination* of man and machine, working as a
well-*coordinated* team is desirable. We speak of the way in which *man and
machine are intercoordinated as the man-machine interface*. For example,
man's eyesight is considerably augmented by both microscopes and tele-
scopes. Man's hearing is extended by audio-amplification. On the other hand,
no fully automatic recognition systems are available for either visual symbols
or for spoken phonemes. Where seeing and hearing are requirements, man
in the system is essential. The lever and the pulley served to enlarge the feats
of strength that man could perform. For pure muscle power, however, machines acting by themselves are capable of producing enormous forces. Man

in the system—where the objectives are brute power—will seldom provide meaningful assistance. Most often, he will cut down on the system's capabilities.

On the cerebral side of the ledger—just as is the case with the sensory system—a coordinated effort is usually rewarding. Books, films, tapes, and records provide mechanical storage or memory. But man's memory is of a basically different form. The two types of memory can be combined to produce a superior, coordinated memory. Memory is only one aspect of the thinking process. No one knows how man thinks, but we have learned a great deal about the nature of thinking as a result of the computer. For some jobs, man is ideally suited. For others, the computer has definite advantages. *The man-machine interface problem* is to find the optimal pattern and utilization for both kinds of systems components. This requires a knowledge of both behavioral models and machine models. Let us, therefore, make a brief comparison between man's abilities and the computer's abilities.

1. Human memory has approximately 10^{14} greater capacity than the largest available computing equipment. It will require a technological breakthrough in the design of computing equipment if this difference is to be reduced. On the other hand, an important characteristic of man's memory is that it is highly selective; it rejects repetitious data, and it forgets easily. Perhaps the most important liability of the human memory, aside from the forgetting characteristic, is the fact that it can so easily distort information *without realizing* that this transgression has taken place.

2. Perseverance is an area where man cannot compete with the computer. The brain fatigues rapidly when repetitive, routine operations are required. The computer, on the other hand, is indifferent to the number of repetitions that must be furnished. However, the computer is incapable of handling situations where no prior pattern has been discovered. Some people take this to mean that the computer cannot be creative. The conclusion does not appear to be valid. If anything, we must say that we do not yet know how to make the computer behave creatively. The failing lies with man—the model builder and computer programmer —not with the machine.

3. Man is able to devise intricate rules of logic and program these rules for use by the computer. He himself, however, is quite unable to consistently apply the logical rules that he has devised.

4. For speed of computation with routine operations the computer wins hands down. However, a substantial amount of time can be required to preplan the procedures and steps that will be followed by the computer system. Whenever automated systems are under consideration, the preplanning time must be included if a relevant man-machine interface analysis is to be made.

5. Variability is the last factor that we shall mention in this comparison. Man does not work at a constant rate. The distribution of times required

by a human operator has substantially greater variance (variability) than would apply to a machine or a computing mechanism. We can afford to sympathize with the fact that the human operator requires time off to refresh himself—be it a coffee break or a few moments of conversation with a fellow worker. Even if he tried to, man could not maintain the exact same rate of productivity. His time sense and motor controls would fail him.[6]

Analysis of the interface (or boundary) across which man and machine communicate reveals that the human senses are related to the monitoring function in control systems. In some cases, physical devices are clearly preferred; for example, for tracking temperature we use thermometers and thermostats. A particular advantage of mechanical sensing equipment is that it can be designed to handle cross-talk situations. *Cross-talk* occurs when several sensory perceptors are simultaneously called upon to receive input data. Human perception can be improved if the inputs to the different senses reinforce each other. For example, a message is shown on the TV screen and read aloud at the same time. However, when the inputs are not related to each other, then conflict can occur, causing an inability to treat either input. Because machines can be designed to operate efficiently with cross-talk, the design of the man-machine interface of a particular situation will depend upon the monitoring requirements for the system.

When control devices are too expensive if designed to handle continuous monitoring, *sample-data designs* can be substituted for continuous ones. The essence of the sample-data system is the fact that it will monitor each sensory channel at intervals. Where cross-talk exists, it can sample what is going on at various places in the system simultaneously. Man inherently acts as a sample-data system, being unable to continuously monitor the behavior of any system. Good systems design calls for proper scheduling of the sample periods, whether man or a device is used. Because the human monitor can be ineffective when subjected to cross-talk situations, it is necessary to permit him access to only one of these inputs at a time.

Many other interface characteristics must be explored if the manager is to properly assess the systems requirements. Under certain circumstances, man has an ability to blank-out background noise, for example, the ticking of a clock. Machines can also be designed to do this (for example, low-pass and high-pass frequency filters). It may be desirable to amplify some of the inputs. Man is subject to sensory illusions. Many examples can be found in psychological literature of physical relationships that are distorted by the human sensory mechanism. Machine sensing fallibility also occurs. Almost without exception, machines misinterpret different kinds of physical relations than do man's senses. Interface design takes advantage of this difference, using each where best applied.

---

[6]This discussion amplified points that were made when we discussed stochastic line balancing (see pp. 207–8).

Another topic of importance to job and work place design is the reliability of system components. For human machines, failures of physical and mental health are treated by the class of repairmen known as medical doctors and psychiatrists. Health is affected by various kinds of overloads. In addition, failings in one human component are frequently contagious. Thus, the common cold is readily communicable among a group of workers. Machine failures, on the other hand, are often independent of the condition of other mechanical units in the system. This is not always true, however. Figure 21-1 illustrates how the failure of one machine can result in the shutting down of other machines. The doctor in this case is the repairman. Interface design requires full consideration of such factors and must allow for the possibility of a speck of dust getting in the operator's eye, or a piece of grit getting into a gear train.

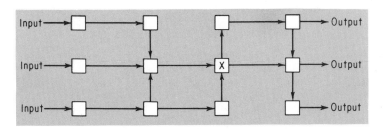

FIGURE 21-1. The failure of one mechanical component can produce the equivalence of failure in other mechanical components. There is only one mechanical unit in this diagram, which when broken down, will shut off the entire system.

Human Factors and the Information System

All activities are forms of information to be managed. *Every* operation has its counterpart in data form and is transformable into data. Plans are information maps; controls are information regulators. The job, as planned and produced, is fully described by information (see, for example, pp. 236–41). This realization has an important effect. It focuses attention on the necessity to manage information.

Both workers and machines require information to accomplish work. Each have characteristic ways of transmitting, receiving, channeling, and storing information. However, the use of mechanical storage systems is needed to augment the limited and fallible human memory system. Libraries, file drawers, microfilm records, and computer memories are important components of the total system, but the machine elements must be viewed in terms of their relationship to the human components of the system.

Information continually flows back and forth across the *man-machine interface*. People and machines can operate together only when there is adequate communication. Language translation must be taken into account. The syntax and grammar of the machine are far more precise, the vocabulary far smaller, than that of man.

Extensive mechanical storage of information creates serious problems, because significant costs must be incurred to maintain it as well as to search through it in order to obtain the required information. The cost of both storage and searching rises as the volume of information that is stored increases. The Dewey Decimal System of categorization developed for information retrieval from library storage has provided a model information storage system. However, the amount of information available for conducting business has increased at an exponential rate. Far more sophisticated schemes for retrieving information are now required.

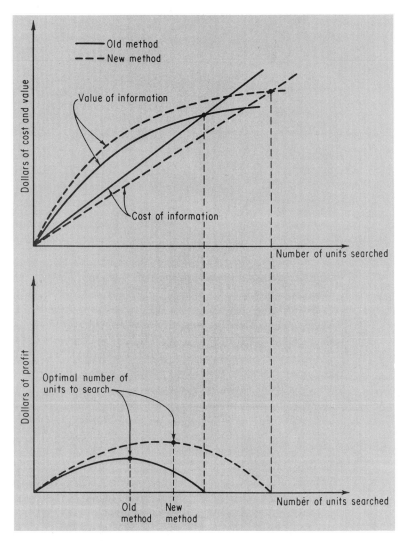

FIGURE 21-2. With improved information retrieval methods, it is possible to search more effectively, less expensively, and more rapidly. Consequently, the optimum number of units to search increases.

When the job and the work place (for a continuous stream of job shop operations) are being designed, duplication of efforts is not unusual. However, the time required to avoid duplicative efforts—by surveying all relevant data files to determine whether or not a similar job has previously been designed—may cost a greater amount than would be needed to recalculate or redevelop the same information. Thus, when the cost of searching equals or exceeds the cost of development, we choose to duplicate efforts. There is only one other potential course of action, that is, to reduce the cost of searching. This can be accomplished only if we design adequate systems for information retrieval.

We are in the midst of a technological revolution with respect to information handling and retrieval methods. Much research is being devoted to this subject. Advances in equipment and methods are being realized. As these new data systems are developed, the cost of searching through a given amount of information is being reduced; the value of the recovered information is increasing (in the sense that it is a purer grade of ore); and the probability of locating vital information quickly is being significantly improved. As a result, the optimum number of units of information to search through is being increased. The nature of the change is demonstrated by Fig. 21-2.

Another aspect of information searching is that it takes a given length of time to recover the information that is needed. The age of information can inflict severe penalties if it becomes excessive. For each situation the definition of what constitutes excessive age will differ.

Air Traffic Control at Logan International Airport

Job:	Control aircraft in the Boston sector
Workers:	Air traffic controllers
Work place:	Control center with radar surveillance and information about routes, destinations, speed, altitude, etc. of all aircraft in the controlled air space.
Specific situation:	Shown in Figure 21-3. (Planes are flying at 600 mph.)

At 9:01 AM, plane *A* reports 9:00 AM fix over Hartford Station. At 9:03, plane *B* reports 9:02 AM fix over Northfield Station. Both planes are flying at the same altitude. Without corrective action, there will be a collision at 9:10 AM.

There is little time to take evasive action. (Specifically, after two minutes the relevant information will have aged to the point that it is useless, because these jet aircraft are flying at speeds of 600 mph.) The controller must have time to determine what altitudes are free *and* how to move one of the aircraft to a clear altitude without interfering

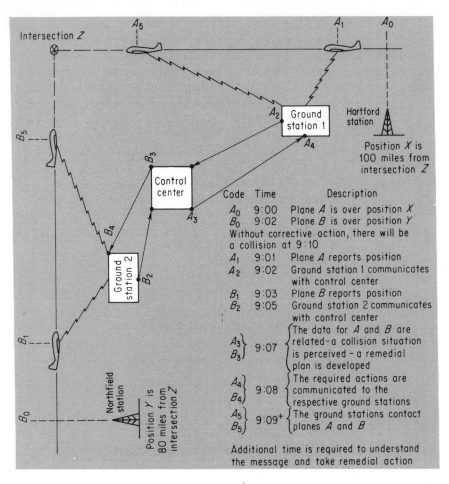

Intersection Z

Hartford station

Position X is 100 miles from intersection Z

Ground station 1

Control center

Ground station 2

Northfield station

Position Y is 80 miles from intersection Z

Code	Time	Description
A_0	9:00	Plane A is over position X
B_0	9:02	Plane B is over position Y

Without corrective action, there will be a collision at 9:10

A_1	9:01	Plane A reports position
A_2	9:02	Ground station 1 communicates with control center
B_1	9:03	Plane B reports position
B_2	9:05	Ground station 2 communicates with control center
A_3 B_3	9:07	The data for A and B are related–a collision situation is perceived – a remedial plan is developed
A_4 B_4	9:08	The required actions are communicated to the respective ground stations
A_5 B_5	9:09+	The ground stations contact planes A and B

Additional time is required to understand the message and take remedial action

FIGURE 21-3. Information will have aged excessively after spending two minutes at the control center without being acted upon.

with other aircraft. The job is full of stress; the work place is not as supportive as it could be.

This example is an accurate portrayal of reality. Production and operations management techniques sometimes deal with the value of profit; sometimes deal with the value of life. The problem just described did not (does not) have to happen. Methods exist for making such occurrences so rare that the air traffic control system could be designated "fail-safe" (see pp. 528–30).

Each situation dictates its own time scale for measuring the age of information. At some age either control is lost, an emergency has developed, or the information has become worthless. Relatively continuous control is an important factor when the system's performance is sensitive to the age of information. If the control system is not continuously fed information, then sample data intervals must be very small.

Another example of the detrimental effect of overly delayed or overaged information is in the inventory area. Here, the critical age of information is a function of various factors, such as the demand rate for items, the reserve stock policy (i.e., the extra units carried to meet unexpectedly high demand; see pp. 354–60), and the length of time required to get a replenishment order filled. Let us consider a perpetual inventory system.[7] Assume that the specified reorder level is reached for an item and that this information is not sent by the stock clerk to the purchasing department immediately. While the information that will trigger a purchase order is aging, further withdrawals can reduce the stock level and create a serious out-of-stock situation before a new order can even be placed, let alone filled.

Information recovery treats the problem of how to design the information transference characteristics of a system. It is concerned with directing various kinds of information to workers and machines at appropriate points in time. It is a critical determinant of control, safety, and other job factors of fundamental importance.

Design of Equipment

The design of facilities and the working environment is a form of industrial architecture. In many ways, it represents the same kind of approaches and the same set of human factors objectives as those of industrial designers. As a concrete example, look at the design for the foot pedal of an industrial lift truck (Fig. 21-4). The Henry Dreyfuss design group believed that the foot pedal should serve as an extension of the foot. Foot pressure studies were made, and the dimensions of workers' feet were taken into account. This is the kind of work place design that maximizes safety and productivity.

The human factors area treats both the physiological and psychological characteristics of people. It attempts to provide high levels of *safety* and comfort. It is concerned with "the appearances of things," and the way they affect efficiency. All the senses and the interrelationships of the senses to both motor and mental responses are part of the fabric of these factors, which describe the interactions of the worker, the work place, and the plant. Thus, not only sight, illumination, and color concern us, but also hearing, noise, taste, smell, the effects of temperature and temperature changes, body orientation, and all other factors that condition the performance and attitudes of the workers of a system.

The physical structure of human beings affects work place design in many ways. What is not immediately apparent is that the logic of an individual's using himself or herself as a physical model is not a sufficient design guide—

---

[7]See pp. 354–58.

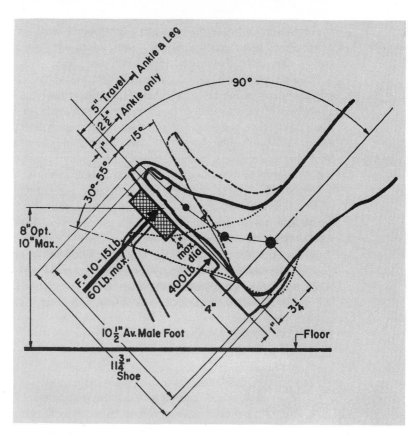

FIGURE 21-4. Detailed studies and drawings were made of the foot pedal to determine its final placement. The Henry Dreyfuss design group believes that the foot pedal should serve as an extension of the foot. Foot pressure studies were extremely important for the early development of Monotrol Control. [From William F. H. Purcell, A.S.I.D., *Designing for Heavy Duty*, Chilton Company, Automotive Industries, 1962.]

either for the consumer product design or employee work place considerations.[8] Instead, we should use the methodology of human engineering.

Because people come in different shapes and sizes, it is necessary to study their relevant statistical characteristics with respect to the objectives of the system's design. The analysis of physical differences between individuals has proven to be of great benefit in all areas where people operate on or interact with the physical environment. Our first example was the foot pedal in Fig. 21-4. Now consider how many jobs entail much telephone use. Yet all workers are not equally comfortable (nonfatigued and productive) with a given set

---

[8]This is a point of great importance. The design of the job, the work place, the product, and/or the service is frequently based on personal interpolations or extrapolations (see pp. 244–45) that are erroneously assumed to apply to a majority of other people. This section of the text recommends the use of statistical survey techniques to evaluate the needs and preferences of people rather than to assume that the designer's preferences are the best estimates of what satisfies or is satisfactory for the most people.

of design dimensions. These include the spacing between cap centers, angle of receiver cap, weight, etc. (see Fig. 21-5). Because of the differences that exist between people, we want to answer the question: comfortable for whom? It is operational, therefore, to select a design that satisfies a *statistical criterion* relative to the distribution of pertinent human characteristics.

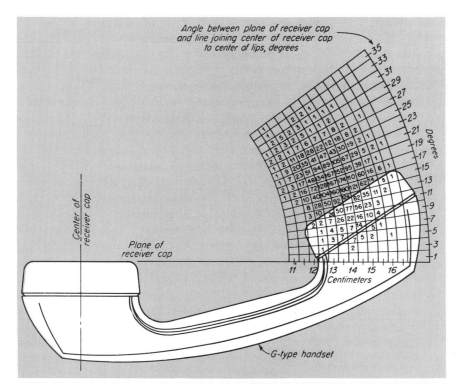

FIGURE 21-5. Summary of face dimensions used in design of telephone handset. The chart indicates the number of people for whom specific distances and orientations were found to be suitable. [From Ernest J. McCormick, *Human Engineering* (New York: McGraw-Hill, Inc., 1976); based on the work of W. C. Jones and A. H. Inglis, "Development of a Handset for Telephone Stations," *Bell System Technical Journal*, Vol. XI, 1932, p. 262. Reprinted with permission from *The Bell System Technical Journal*, Copyright 1932, The American Telephone and Telegraph Company.]

The requirements of a representative distribution of individuals can be determined. A design based on statistical knowledge regarding these dimensions would satisfy the minimum requirements for a majority of potential users. We know that an ideal handset for a small person could not, at the same time, be ideal for a large one. Design problems can be resolved only by determining the requirements of a representative cross section of potential users. The final design cannot provide equal satisfaction for all people, but it can be *sufficiently* satisfactory for an appropriate number of users.

Another example can be derived in terms of the search for comfortable shoes. Suppose that a department store, recognizing that its employees are on their feet all the time, decides to furnish them with a new line of shoes. The objective is to keep the same level of variety, but to alter the sizes and shapes of shoes with the intention of improving the resultant level of comfort. To achieve this objective it is necessary to obtain statistical distributions of foot measurements. These would describe the various foot characteristics of the *population of potential shoe users*. (In this case, department store personnel.)

The characteristics of feet chosen to be studied would be those that are relevant to the comfort of users. The appropriate set of dimensions have to be determined before an empirical study can be conducted. Then, with a sufficiently large sample of people properly measured for the appropriate dimensions, reasonable job and work place design decisions can be made.

Consider still another example. Presume that our objective is to design a chair that would be standard equipment in an office. Many different body forms, heights, and weights would have to be considered if we are to offer a reasonable level of comfort to the greatest number of potential users. Toward this end, we would measure a *representative sample of users* of these chairs. Again, first we must determine of what measurable dimensions is comfort a function. We note that the sample would be quite different if the office is to be staffed with men only, or women only, or a combination of men and women. (Chairs for a kindergarten would pose another problem.) Generally, the larger the diversity among users, the less the satisfaction that can be obtained for any one user. Although this is an argument for uniqueness among designs, it must be counterbalanced against the added costs of providing greater satisfaction to a smaller number of users.

As we consider the design of the work place, we are struck by the great number of factors that account for comfort and convenience. Shoes, telephones, typewriters, floors, chairs, etc., all contribute to the comfort and safety and convenience of workers doing their jobs.

Sensory Systems. Another aspect of human-factor models concerns the sensory abilities of humans. Again, differences between individuals must be taken into account. For example, a certain combination of colors may produce higher attention levels for one type of viewer than for another. Color relates to worker productivity. A practical problem is the determination of what colors to use to signal danger. Color-blind people will not sense red. How should we color the various parts of machines, the office, the company library, a plant cafeteria, etc.? Color affects the behavior of an individual in various ways, for example, the degree to which fatigue occurs, general alertness, mood, and attitude. The superiority of a certain color combination for a specific purpose must be predicated on the fact that differences exist among people. Design utility is statistically determined—just as it was in the case of the telephone handset (see Fig. 21-5).

Individual preferences vary with respect to the amount of light that is both comfortable and satisfactory for accomplishing a given job. The range can be quite large, as shown by the following distribution for the amount of light that is preferred for reading.[9]

FOOTCANDLES	0–50	50–100	100–150	150–200	200–250	250–300	300–350	350–400	400+
NUMBER OF PEOPLE	none	4	38	46	62	89	45	22	3

During the Second World War, many studies were undertaken to determine superior (if not optimal) designs for aircraft controls such as dials, gauges, tracking devices, gunsights, and the like. Since that time, a great deal more work has been done by various organizations and institutions. As a result, a large body of literature concerning the visual sensory system is now available. Certainly, much work remains to be done. The reader will find that the subject is treated under such headings as human factors, human engineering, and ergonomics.

The sense of hearing has been studied with equal fervor. Many production operations are quiet, but others produce extremely high noise levels, for example, a jet plane or a drop forge. Two questions arise with respect to this noise factor. First, how does it affect the workers' performance and second, to what extent can it damage hearing? The appropriate answers seem to be that within reasonable limits, noise does not decrease the performance of an individual; however, varying degrees of hearing loss are associated with exposure to a noisy environment.

Noise levels are measured in decibels. This is a logarithmic transformation of the ratio of a given sound level to a standard value.[10] Figure 21-6 presents a chart of some representative noise levels as they are generated by different sources. Because workers suffer a degree of hearing loss when repeatedly exposed to certain types of sound, it behooves management to provide adequate protection for all individuals exposed to such hazards. Appropriate materials and structures can be used to achieve noise control or abatement when it appears that the process is not susceptible to design changes that will decrease the noise levels.

Another issue concerns the nuisance effect of noise. If there is inherent, high-level noise associated with a particular production process, this fact should be taken into account when the plant is geographically located—for example, airport location, in the case of jet aircraft. Community goodwill can

---

[9]These results are reported by W. S. Fisher, General Electric Company, Large Lamp Department, Nela Park, Cleveland, Ohio, in November, 1963 in a private correspondence with Sylvester K. Guth, Manager, Radiant Energy Effects Laboratory, General Electric Company. The sample of 309 individuals were given the visual task of reading from the pages of a telephone book. See also: J. M. Ketch and W. S. Fisher, "Experience with High Level Office Lighting," *Illuminating Engineering*, Vol. 52, 1957, p. 529.
[10]The standard of just audible sound.

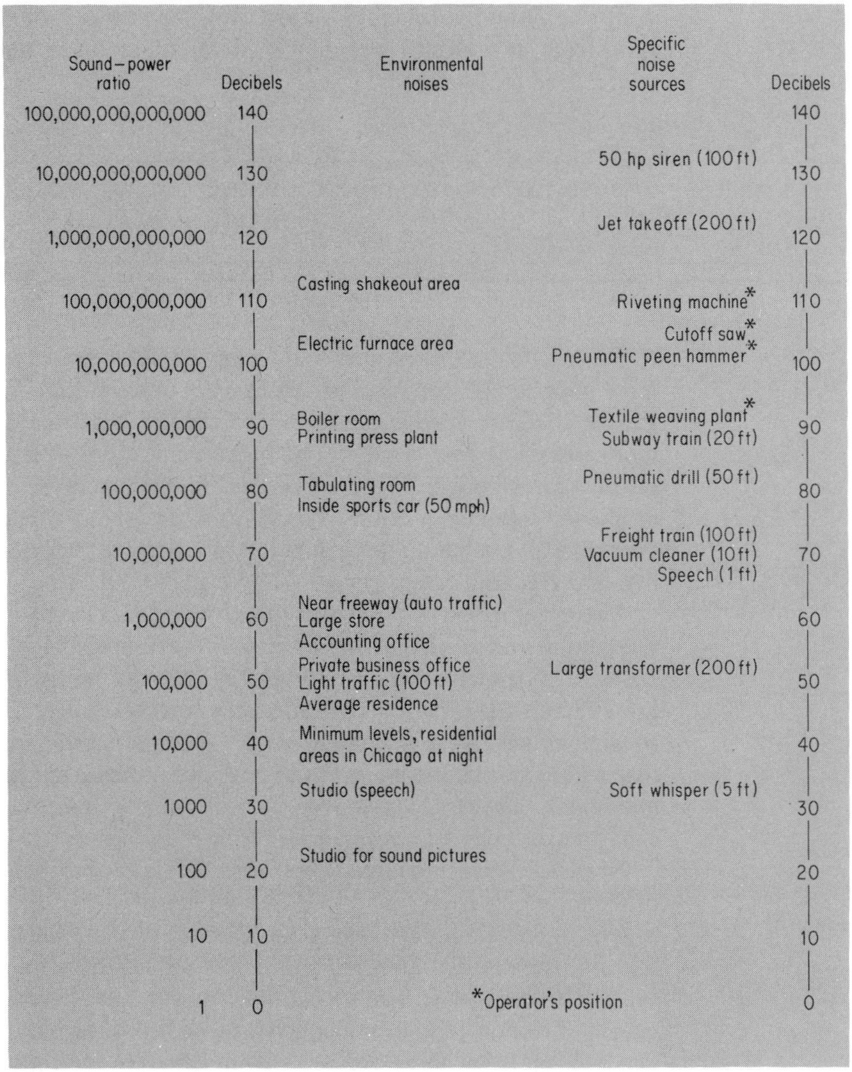

Sound–power ratio	Decibels	Environmental noises	Specific noise sources	Decibels
100,000,000,000,000	140			140
10,000,000,000,000	130		50 hp siren (100 ft)	130
1,000,000,000,000	120		Jet takeoff (200 ft)	120
100,000,000,000	110	Casting shakeout area	Riveting machine*	110
10,000,000,000	100	Electric furnace area	Cutoff saw* / Pneumatic peen hammer*	100
1,000,000,000	90	Boiler room / Printing press plant	Textile weaving plant* / Subway train (20 ft)	90
100,000,000	80	Tabulating room / Inside sports car (50 mph)	Pneumatic drill (50 ft)	80
10,000,000	70		Freight train (100 ft) / Vacuum cleaner (10 ft) / Speech (1 ft)	70
1,000,000	60	Near freeway (auto traffic) / Large store / Accounting office		60
100,000	50	Private business office / Light traffic (100 ft) / Average residence	Large transformer (200 ft)	50
10,000	40	Minimum levels, residential areas in Chicago at night		40
1000	30	Studio (speech)	Soft whisper (5 ft)	30
100	20	Studio for sound pictures		20
10	10			10
1	0	*Operator's position		0

FIGURE 21-6. Noise level of typical noises
This figure also shows the ratio of sound energies for various decibel levels. [From Ernest J. McCormick, *Human Engineering* (New York: McGraw-Hill Book Co., Inc., 1976).]

be rapidly alienated if this point is overlooked. Thus, the problem of noise has been a critical objection to SST aircraft.

Noise abatement can be achieved in a number of different ways. This is the job of the acoustical engineer, and we shall not attempt to delve into the technology relevant to noise control. On the other hand, it might be useful to specifically distinguish between three major ways of coping with noise:

1. Eliminate or reduce it by introducing technological (design) change.

2. Isolate it by moving the source to a remote or protected location.

3. Dampen or absorb it by using specially designed materials such as fiber-glass.

Human sensory systems have the ability to receive many other stimuli besides light and sound. Even as a beginning, we must include such sensations as smell, touch, taste; the perception of body orientation, temperature, humidity, vibration, and the sense of passing time. Pain is an additional factor produced by external conditions. Passing beyond the pain threshold can occur for each of the sense modalities. Human-factor models have been developed, and are being developed to measure such sensory characteristics not only for averages but also for differences between individuals. Thus, comfort and pain share the same dimensional continuum. What is comfort for one may be less comfort for another and perhaps painful for a third.

The key in all these considerations is the fact that most design, in the past, has proceeded on the basis of the designer's own personal set of sensory, anatomical, motor, and mental characteristics. Such egocentric design produces an amount of penalty that is proportional to the divergence between the designer's preferences and the statistical distribution of population preferences.

PROBLEMS

1. The British call the human factors area *ergonomics*. What is the derivation of this word? (*Hint:* you will find in the dictionary that ergon is the Greek word for work.)

2. What can be done to prevent accidents of the kind described in the knockaway story? (See p. 504.)

3. What is meant by a fail-safe system?

4. Certain workers have a history of numerous accidents, whereas most workers have few, if any, accidents. What can be done for those workers who exhibit accident-proneness?

5. What role does the computer play at the man-machine interface? Discuss the kinds of interactions that can take place.

6. In the text, it is stated, "Analysis of the interface (or boundary) across which man and machine communicate reveals that the human senses are related to the monitoring function in control systems." Explain this statement. Under what circumstances would you recommend a machine monitor rather than a human monitor?

7. For the air traffic control problem at Logan International Airport (described on pp. 511–12), substitute:
   a. Propeller aircraft flying at 350 mph; at 9:01 a.m. plane *A* reports

over Hartford Station, at 9:04 a.m. plane *B* reports over Northfield Station.

b. Concorde aircraft flying at 1200 mph; at 9:01 a.m. plane *A* reports over Hartford Station; at 9:02 a.m. plane *B* reports over Northfield Station.

What happens in each case? (*Hint:* convert the distances of positions *X* and *Y* from intersection *Z* into minutes of flying time.) Note in each case how much time there is for corrective action. Discuss.

8. What factors would ordinarily be considered when a proposed plan calls for replacing a worker with a machine? What criteria would apply to the decision?

Answer: The nature of the job that must be done is the basic determinant. Some jobs cannot be done by machines, except at an extremely high cost. As often, a variety of jobs cannot be performed by a human operator.

Aside from obvious physical constraints, we must consider the minimization of cost, given that both a man and a machine can suitably perform the required tasks. We could begin by comparing the costs of a list of human factors. Thus, the cost of memory should reflect the fact that machine memories are smaller but more reliable than those of man. The cost of dexterity—machines possess great advantages both in the speed and fineness of proscribed movements. Where movements cannot be specified exactly (e.g., the surgeon), then the machine costs rise rapidly, approaching infinity for the present state of machine technology. Learning ability costs can be included; machines have, at best, rudimentary abilities.

We must also characterize the statistical properties of the man and the machine in the system. Man contributes high variance to activities, while the performance of the machine insures low variance, approaching 0. By taking all such factors into account we are able to provide the appropriate man/machine configuration.

9. Prepare a human factors analysis, treating all variables that might be relevant with respect to the following situations:

a. The design and manufacture of a belt
b. The redesign of an automobile
c. The design of an electric circuit fuse
d. The design of a hearing aid
e. The arrangement of high noise-level equipment in a plant

Answer: In situations characterized by **a** through **e**, human factors analysis deals with questions such as the distributions of various anatomical proportions in the population. Thus, for example, we would consider waist sizes for the belt design, leg lengths for automobile seat design, hand sizes for installing and handling electric fuses, and ear shapes with respect to the design of the hearing aid. Other physiological factors also pertain, such as dexterity, reaction time, nature of the hearing loss, safety from electric shock, etc. Then, in addition, psychological considerations related to the feeling of safety, reliability, prestige, and embarrassment conveyed by the object are of the utmost importance, although they are usually harder to quantify and therefore more difficult to analyze in any objective fashion.

10. There is a visual phenomenon known as the Purkinje effect: The fact that a great decrease in the intensity of illumination darkens red, orange, and yellow much more than blue and green, so that the point of maximum brilliance in the spectrum is shifted from the yellow into the green. A suggested explanation is that the rods which give vision in faint light are tuned to shorter wave lengths than the cones that dominate vision in bright light. (*Webster's New International Dictionary* Second Edition, unabridged.)

    Under what circumstances might this human factor be of importance?
    Answer: This effect could have great significance with respect to the output of a factory where color matching is important and where reliance on external illumination is used. On a more individual level, the Purkinje effect is responsible for the difficulty in distinguishing whether a traffic light is red or green during twilight hours. It demonstrates the relevance of this "human factor" to the design of man-machine systems. (A well-designed red, green traffic signal could have different shapes in addition to different positions (i.e., red normally over green) to indicate positively —even to the color blind—a stop or go.)

11. How would you go about taking into consideration the percent and distributional characteristics of color blindness? When might this factor be significant?

12. Describe the characteristics of the man-machine interface with respect to the following:
    a. A pin-ball machine
    b. A dictionary
    c. A pencil
    d. A computer programmed to prepare invoices
    e. A continuous conveyor
    f. A television set
    g. A 35-mm camera
    Answer: This question is intended to encourage discussion concerning the relevant system of variables that is shared by the man in the system with the facilities that he uses, as well as the total environment that surrounds them both. Thus, for example, the dictionary is one form of memory. Access to it requires a corresponding memory for the appearance of the word on the part of the man. The individual who does not know the exact spelling can then undertake a search procedure to locate the sought-after word based on his memory of the sounds of the word and the various rules that he knows for translating sounds into spelling. Since conflicting rules exist in English, he must frequently use trial and error. Other rules would apply to different languages. This would be an environmental factor. The individual can use the dictionary to locate meaning if he knows the precise spelling. He can also obtain correct

pronunciation under these circumstances. Yet, frequently the dictionary is used for discovering or checking on the spelling of a word. The question of whether this is the best possible systems design resides in the nature of the man-machine interface and also leads to the consideration of the role of a thesaurus. Similar considerations can be given to each of the facilities listed for this question.

SUMMARY OF PART 8

Chapter 19

The management of human resources is a complex and demanding area. In Chapter 19, we examine the measurement of workers' performance. Time studies, used to measure output, are explained. An example is given for the Razormaker Corporation. The data derived from the time study are used to determine a productivity standard. Appendix 19-I presents (as optional material) the basis for determining the time study sample size. Since a worker's productivity will improve through learning as the job is repeated, Appendix 19-III explains (as optional material) the learning curve.

Next, work (or operations) sampling is introduced as a means of studying the way that workers spend their time when not engaged in the highly repetitive type of operations for which time studies are typically used. The manager of the State Court House decides to employ work sampling to help balance the budget, sharply reduced by the state legislature. The manager uses the results of the study to take some cost-saving, work-conserving actions. [Appendix 19-II presents (as optional material) the basis for determining the work sample size.]

Synthetic (or predetermined) time standards are explored. Two systems, MTM and Work Factor, are discussed. With synthetic time standards it is possible to obtain a productivity standard for jobs that have never been done, since actual observations do not have to be made.

The productivity problem for projects is involved with the question of how much labor to use. There is a time-cost trade-off which we had seen previously in Chapter 9 when discussing PERT. Now, this trade-off is explained in terms of the management of project groups. In particular, the tendency to overstaff projects is analyzed. Norden's model of the development function indicates that projects can be managed adequately only when the underlying project components have been identified.

Chapter 20

In this chapter, job improvement, job evaluation, and wage determination are discussed. To begin with, work simplification is described, including various charts that are used to study the job as it is presently being done. Then changes are proposed. Revised charts are drawn up to determine what improvement is achieved. In particular, man-machine systems are investigated for Foodpackers, Inc. (a job shop foodpacker). Using man-machine time charts, two figpacking plans undergo an economic analysis. The relationship of work simplification to methods study is described.

Human resources cannot be treated as another form of machine system. The question of job enrichment is explored, from which we move to examination of a "fair wage." Incentive wage plans are detailed after the point system for evaluating jobs and the key-job curve for pricing them have been developed. Foodpackers figpacking operation is used to study the effects of the different wage plan models.

Chapter 21

The design of the job and the work place constitutes the first major section of Chapter 21 on human factors. Safety first; productivity follows. Both can be obtained through careful job and work place design. The worker sometimes puts safety second in pursuit of higher earnings (see the knockaway story).

The man-machine interface refers to the combinations of people and machines that are brought together to physically interact (at their interface) in pursuit of organizational objectives. This aspect of the management of human resources leads to consideration of the way in which workers and machines communicate with each other, as well as process and retrieve information. An air traffic control problem at Logan International Airport is used as an example of the importance of information timeliness.

The human factors approach to designing equipment (and products) is discussed. This often involves a statistical criterion relative to the distribution of pertinent human characteristics. Sensory systems are explored as they relate to the design of a safe, comfortable, and efficient work place.

REFERENCES
PART 8

ATTNEAVE, F., *Applications of Information Theory to Psychology*. New York: Holt, Rinehart & Winston, Inc., 1959.

BARNES, R. N., *Motion and Time Study*, 6th ed. New York: John Wiley & Sons, Inc., 1968.

BELCHER, D. W., *Wage and Salary Administration*, 2nd ed. Englewood Cliffs, N.J.: Prentice-Hall, Inc., 1962.

S. W. Bither, *Personality as a Factor in Management Team Decision Making*. The Pennsylvania State University Press, 1971.

CHAPANIS, A., W. R. GARNER and C. T. MORGAN, *Applied Experimental Psychology*. New York: John Wiley & Sons, Inc., 1949.

CHAPANIS, ALPHONSE, *Man-Machine Engineering*. Belmont, Ca.: Wadsworth Publishing Co., 1965.

DALLA VALLE, J. M., *The Industrial Environment and Its Control*. New York: Pitman Publishing Corp., 1948.

FLETCHER, HARVEY, *Speech and Hearing*. Princeton, N.J.: D. Van Nostrand Co., Inc., 1950.

HANSEN, B. L., *Work Sampling: For Modern Management*. Englewood Cliffs, N.J.: Prentice-Hall, Inc., 1960.

KRICK, EDWARD V., *Methods Engineering*. New York: John Wiley & Sons, Inc., 1962.

LEHRER, R. N., *Work Simplification*. Englewood Cliffs, N.J.: Prentice-Hall, Inc., 1957.

LOUDEN, J. K. and J. W. DEEGAN, *Wage Incentives*. New York: John Wiley & Sons, 1959.

MCCORMICK, E. J., *Human Factors in Engineering and Design*. New York: McGraw-Hill Book Co., Inc., 4th ed., 1976.

MAYNARD, H. B., G. J. STEGEMERTEN, and J. L. SCHWAB, *Methods-Time Measurement* New York: McGraw-Hill, Inc., 1948.

MUNDEL, MARVIN E., *Motion and Time Study: Principles and Practice*. 4th ed. Englewood Cliffs, N. J.: Prentice-Hall, Inc., 1970.

NIEBEL, BENJAMIN W., *Motion and Time Study*, 5th ed. Homewood, Ill.: Richard D. Irwin, 1972.

QUICK, J. H., J. H. DUNCAN, and JAMES A. MALCOLM, *Work-Factor Time Standards*. New York: McGraw-Hill Book Co., Inc., 1962.

ROETHLISBERGER, F. J., and W. J. DICKSON, *Management and the Worker*. Cambridge. Mass.: Harvard University Press, 1939.

SAYLES, LEONARD R. and GEORGE STRAUSS, *Personnel: The Human Problems of Management*, 3rd ed. Englewood Cliffs, N.J.: Prentice-Hall, Inc., 1972.

SIMON, H. A., *Models of Man*. New York: John Wiley & Sons, Inc., 1957.

SPECIAL DEVICES CENTER, *Handbook of Human Engineering Data*, 2nd ed. Office of Naval Research, Technical Report SDC 199–1–2, NavExos P-643, Project Designation NR-783—001, 1951.

TEEVAN, RICHARD C. and ROBERT C. BIRNEY (eds.), *Color Vision*. Princeton, N.J.: D. Van Nostrand Co., Inc., 1961.

TICHAUER, E. R., "Biomechanics sustains occupational safety and health," *Industrial Engineering* (February, 1976), pp. 46–56.

VROOM, VICTOR, *Work and Motivation*. New York: John Wiley & Sons, 1964.

quality
management

Production and operations managers conceive of their job as requiring the *development* and *operation* of a process for *getting work done*. In their opinion, the organization has entrusted them with the responsibility of transforming *input* resources into a desired set of *outputs*. The transformation *process* is to be accomplished in a manner that is most compatible with the company's objectives. The operations manager interprets this to mean that the outputs should be of some *assured level of quality* produced at a *minimum cost*.

Quality has two interpretations. One is the consumers' view of value desired and value received. Such a view of quality is *marketing* oriented.

But in this part we shall be discussing the *production*-oriented *view of quality*. A close approximation to this use of the term quality is *consistency*. A set of standards is defined, and all units of production must consistently meet those standards. The consumer may consider such standards to be evidence of low or high quality depending upon what was expected. The consumer's concern is product service, performance, appearance, etc. The operations manager's quality concern, however, is that he meets specifications, *whatever* they may be.

To achieve specified output quality, two basic factors must be treated. The first is that the quality of *input* materials must be maintained at designed levels. This subject is a major concern of Chapter 22. Second, the *process* must be controlled to deliver the desired output quality. Chapter 23 addresses the problems of controlling output quality. Both aspects of quality can only be studied after we have described some of the important dimensions by which quality is often measured. This topic is treated in the first part of Chapter 22.

twenty-two
the quality control of inputs using acceptance sampling

Before undertaking the study of quality control, whether applied to process inputs (Chapter 22) or process outputs (Chapter 23), it is desirable to get a clear picture of what is meant by quality.

The Dimensions of Quality

To the consumer, quality and "high quality" are the same thing. The production and operations manager has a quandary here. As an individual, the manager wishes to produce an output that possesses "high quality." But the job calls for the delivery of an output of *specified* quality that is commensurate with the investment in the process and the budget for operating costs.

In this latter sense, quality is an agreed-upon set of standards and tolerance limits. These specifications are operational terms—not value judgments. But in order to consider quality in operational terms, it is an absolute necessity that dimensions of quality be expressed in measurable terms. Every manager would like to minimize costs and maximize "high quality." These objectives

527

cannot be achieved simultaneously. They are *conflicting*, multiple objectives. Therefore, it is necessary to specify the quality *constraints*. Then, subject to these, the cost is to be minimized.

Let us examine the attribute dimensions of output quality.

I. Functional Qualities

1. Utility of purpose
2. Reliability of function
   a. Accuracy in use over time
   b. Deterioration of function over time
   c. Failure characteristics and expected lifetime
   d. Cost of maintenance and repair
   e. Guarantees and warranties

3. Human factors
   a. Safety
   b. Comfort
   c. Convenience

II. Nonfunctional Qualities

1. Style and appearance
2. Self-image of user
   a. Price
   b. Prestige

3. Timeliness of design
4. Style and variety

Functional Qualities (I)

Purpose utility, in most but not all instances, is the most fundamental product quality. It is associated with a specific, functional class of use, e.g., soap to wash the hands and face or tires to keep the wheels rolling. The same applies to services. We know what the purpose of a credit card is, what range of services banks offer, why we pay our telephone and electric bills, and what purpose a college education is supposed to serve. It might not be easy, but we could devise measures of service quality for all these cases.

Generally, the purpose is relatively clear, but at other times it is intrinsically difficult to state. In either case, the measurement of how well a product or service performs its intended function is necessary if standards are to be set up. There are physical evaluations and consumer evaluations. Can we measure how good a food product tastes, how comfortable a chair is, or how convenient a hammer is to use? We can measure the sweetness of the food, the number of springs used in the chair, and the hardness of the steel head. There is always some kind of an assumption about the way in which the measurable, physical factors relate to the consumers' evaluation of the utility of function. The control of quality is directly related to specified standards of measurable physical factors.

Reliability is an important one of these. It concerns the ability of the output to perform according to *specifications* over a given period of time. This category of attribute raises some interesting problems. Production and opera-

529

*The Quality
Control of
Inputs Using
Acceptance
Sampling*

tions management is responsible for controlling the quality of a product during its manufacture. Thereafter, each output unit has a history of its own. Observations, measurements, and specifications of quality must include the variety of possible histories for each unit that is sold. It is on such a basis that warranties and guarantees are determined and set. We shall say more about this aspect of reliability shortly.

There are a number of different ways that we could go about describing reliability. Thus, when we discuss the reliability of a product, we are referring to the fact that the functional attributes will continue to perform within some set of limits over a given period of time. The width of the limits represents an important aspect of the definition of quality for the design. We expect that parts of the product will become worn with use, whereas other characteristics will age independently of use. Furthermore, chance events can occur that have a significant level of expectation that will affect the performance characteristics. Generally, the expected performance will exhibit increasing deviation from the initial design standard over a period of time, as shown in Fig. 22-1.

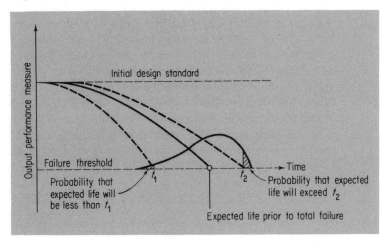

FIGURE 22-1. Expected performance over time exhibits increasing deviation from the initial design standard.

This phenomenon, which we call *drift*, is characteristic of a great many functional attributes of mechanical, chemical, and electrical products. Consider a simple electric light bulb. When it is first used it will generate some given number of lumens. Then as it ages and as a function of both hours of use and the number of times that it is turned on and off, the output of the bulb will vary. It will produce less and less light. At some point in time the light bulb will fail entirely.

Complete or total failure is easy to define. However, if we can no longer use our light source once its output falls below a certain threshold, then for all functional purposes the light bulb has failed and must be replaced. Our ordinary definition of failure for the light bulb specifies a 0 output threshold. A *more sophisticated definition* requires the specification of a given level of light below which the unit cannot be said to be performing satisfactorily. Thus, performance specification in terms of *operational limits* is equivalent to failure specification. When talking about quality, the manager must think in these more complex terms, because the output will be tested in terms of them.

A unit can have very erratic performance before it reaches the failure threshold; for example, the light bulb might get alternately brighter and dimmer. This constitutes still another measure of reliability, that is, the specification of allowable variability of performance. We see that reliability is not a simple dimension. Both reliability and failure can be described successfully only by using statistical terms because, at best, we can make a prediction of how long the unit can be expected to continue to function satisfactorily.

There are many reasons why failure and reliability, as definitions of quality, play an extremely important role. Some types of failure do not permit repair, whereas others do. The definition and specification of quality is concerned with *ease of maintenance* and the *cost of replacement parts*. These factors affect the consumer's judgment of quality. A multicomponent unit usually has different replacement characteristics for each of its parts. Generally, there are some parts which, when they fail, represent an irremedial breakdown. Should a unit be designed in this way, or should the development of replaceable parts be encouraged? The latter course of action requires that a service function be developed. How good must such a sales engineering service function be and how accessible to customers? Automobile manufacturers stress this aspect of their product's quality. Service organizations also stress reliability; e.g., airlines advertise that they are on time, and employment agencies that they have bonded personnel. Electrical and telephone failures create serious hardships. Voltage drops (drift) cause major inconveniences.

Management must know the reliability of its products or services to come up with the specification of *guarantee period*. How long should this period be; what terms are reasonable; how many different components should be covered? The essence of quality control and quality assurance is embodied in a realistic and complex evaluation of the way in which the product performs over its lifetime. It is only scratching the surface to measure the hardness of metals, to observe the number of rpm's of a motor, and so forth, without tying such measurements into the complete evaluation of product quality and performance.

In Chapter 21 we discussed the importance of *human factors*: safety, comfort, and convenience, as they apply to human resource management. The human factors area relates equally well to product and service management. We shall avoid duplication by not further developing these specialized topics here, but it is recommended that pp. 503–19 be reexamined at this time.

531

*The Quality
Control of
Inputs Using
Acceptance
Sampling*

Nonfunctional Qualities (II)

Nonfunctional qualities play an important part in the consumer's judgment of quality. They are extremely difficult to measure. Nevertheless, the role of these attributes is quite as important to the company's definition of quality as any that we found in the functional category.

Here, we are dealing with questions related to the appearance of the product or the style of the service. We are concerned with the way in which the consumer interprets the intangible qualities of the output. This involves us with sociological, psychological, and psychiatric implications of quality. To think in such terms requires a turn of mind that cannot easily be associated with the usual production department. This is why *industrial designers* have come to play an important role in the development of the nonfunctional attributes of a product.

The consumer's self-image concerning the use of a specific brand in a given product class raises many questions concerning this intangible aspect of quality specification. There has always been a belief in the marketing field that consumers are motivated, to some extent, by symbolic relationships of the product to their own personal life. One can find references to Freud, Adler, Jung, and related schools of symbol analysis in the literature of the motivational market researcher. In theory, at any rate, the designer is able to communicate with consumers on the different levels of their needs as consumers and, thereby, to produce a product or service that receives acceptance both in concept and in form.

For the complete specification of quality, still other attributes play a part. These include the package (which is constrained in form by the design of the unit), the label, and even the instructions given to the consumer for properly using the product. Another element is the variety of choice. We have discussed the product-mix aspect of variety and pointed to the marketing implications of modularity as a means of providing a broad selection base for the consumer.

All these factors taken together establish a frame of reference that is sufficiently psychoanalytic to make the average production man wonder how he can possibly specify standards of quality. Typical of these difficulties are questions concerning the visual appearance and *styling* of a design. Style changes are a function of time. What is in style today can be out of style tomorrow. The way in which one style replaces a previous style should follow some logical pattern—although not necessarily a predictable one with respect to time. In fact, various studies serve to confirm the fact that some form of stability does exist concerning changes in style. Consumer acceptance turns out to be not as erratic as one might suppose at first glance. In some cases, style cycles have been found, for example, in the clothing industry, in hair styles, and in millinery styles.[1]

Architects play a primary role in influencing the accepted styles of a par-

---

[1] See, for example: Agnes Brook Young, *Recurring Cycles of Fashion (1760–1937)* (New York: Harper & Row, Publishers, 1937).

ticular culture at any point in time. This relationship intrigued many designers and architects.[2] To the extent that *product design follows architecture*, reasonable predictions can be made about the evaluation of nonfunctional design characteristics of products. At the same time, we should not lose sight of the basic principles which, because they underlie all matters of shape and form, relate architecture, engineering, and industrial design.[3]

Each case of product design management demands its own analysis, but certain fundamentals appear to play a part whether we are talking about the ultimate consumer or an industrial consumer.[4]

1. There is a historical basis for the evolution of design forms. Thus, timeliness of a design can be critical. There are well-documented cases of designs that have been rejected because they appeared too soon.
2. There is need for complete specification of quality. It can be accomplished only if a coordinated effort is made by both operations and marketing management.
3. There is a technological basis which is predicated on available materials and process know-how.

With respect to the third point, some significant knowledge about technological change is available. It has no specific guidelines to offer product management, but it does have important conceptual ones.

Service systems evolve with predictable styles. Changes in social attitudes alter the nonfunctional dimensions of service quality far more rapidly than those of product quality. It is not easy to measure the success of a health care delivery system or of a change in postal procedures, but it is possible, and it must be done if quality control is to be established.

The Trade-offs of Cost and Quality

Cost and quality are critical trade-off dimensions. Not always, but almost always, to achieve better quality, one must increase costs. The interaction between specific cost and quality dimensions is complex. However, thinking

---

[2]See, for example: Henry Dreyfuss, *Designing for People* (New York: Simon and Schuster, Inc., 1955); Frederick J. Kiesler, "Architecture as a Biotechnique," *Architectural Record* (September, 1939); Le Corbusier, *Toward a New Architecture* (London: Architectural Press, 1948); Raymond Loewy, *Never Leave Well Enough Alone* (New York: Simon and Schuster, Inc., 1951); Eliel Sarrinen, *Search for Form* (New York: Reinhold Publishing Corp., 1948); Walter Dorwin Teague, *Design This Day* (New York: Harcourt, Brace & World, Inc., 1940).

[3]See, for example: George D. Birkhoff, *Aesthetic Measure* (Cambridge, Mass.: Harvard University Press, 1933); Samuel Coleman, *Nature's Harmonic Unity* (New York: The Knickerbocker Press, 1912); *Proportional Form* (New York: The Knickerbocker Press, 1920); Ozenfant, *Foundations of Modern Art*, trans. J. Rodker (New York: Dover Publications, Inc., 1952); J. Schillinger, *The Mathematical Basis of the Arts* (New York: Philosophical Library, 1948); D'Arcy W. Thompson, *On Growth and Form*, Vol. I and II, 2nd ed. (Cambridge, England: University Press, 1959 reprint); L. L. Whyte, ed., *Aspects of Form* (Bloomington, Ind.: Indiana University Press, 1961).

[4]It is uncertain to what extent an industrial consumer is concerned with the nonfunctional category of quality specification.

533

*The Quality
Control of
Inputs Using
Acceptance
Sampling*

generally, we can state:

$$\text{Service or product qualities} = f(\text{production costs})$$

$$\text{Price} = f(\text{production costs, sales promotion costs})$$

$$\text{Sales volume} = f(\text{price, quality, sales promotion costs})$$

$$\text{Dollar volume} = (\text{price})(\text{sales volume})$$

$$\text{Profit} = \text{dollar volume} - \text{total costs}$$

This formulation ignores the competitor, unless we consider our product qualities to be measured relative to competitive qualities (also, the relative consideration of sales promotion efforts). In any case, it is usually a safe bet that both dollar volume and total costs will increase with improved quality. The curve of dollar volume is a decelerating function because of market saturation. The curve of total costs is an accelerating function, because it gets increasingly difficult to improve quality (e.g., improving one's golf score).[5] Therefore, as shown in Fig. 22-2, there is a level of quality that will

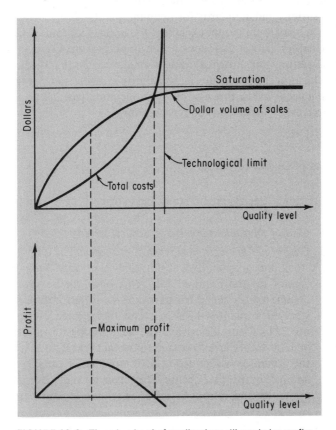

FIGURE 22-2. There is a level of quality that will maximize profits.

---

[5]There is an upper limit to the level of quality that can be achieved within a given technological framework.

maximize profits. To understand what is meant by quality level, we refer to the discussion of dimensional analysis, pp. 384–88. There, the quality (or value) of 1 option was measured relative to that of another by means of a ratio comparing the products of the factors raised to powers for each option. It will be recalled that the powers represented individual assessments of the importance of each (quality) attribute. Thus, the quality level is a multiattribute description of quality that requires managerial estimates of the relative importance of the different attributes that contribute to the judgment of overall quality level.

Input Quality and Acceptance Sampling

It is necessary, if we are to establish quality controls, to describe the dimensions of quality in such as way that they can be *measured*. In all discussions that follow, we shall assume that managerial agreement exists concerning the dimensions and standards for defining quality.

The first topic is input quality; the second, output quality, is the subject of Chapter 23. Let us focus on that important quality management function of inspecting incoming materials[6] to make certain that they conform to quality specifications. Input material standards must be stated explicitly, according to the needs of the process for workable materials and to *insure* that process outputs will satisfy market expectations.

Costs of Defective Inputs

Inferior materials create many kinds of costs. For example:

1. *Cost of unusable items* (generally refunded).
2. *Cost of not having a part when it is needed.* The item is thought to be in stock, but in actuality it is not. Only a *stock phantom* is on hand, which cannot do the required job. This cost can be severe. For example, assume that a generator part, known to fail occasionally, is carried in stock at a quantity level in excess of expected usage. (Specifically, see pp. 324–26 for discussion of the appropriate inventory model.) The high inventory level is geared to the fact that if no spare is on hand, then the generator is shut down. So a large buffer stock is maintained. Then a failure of this part occurs. The repair team discovers that all the spares are faulty and cannot be used. They should have been inspected when

---

[6]We use the generic term "materials" to include everything purchased from outside, or produced by another department of the same firm, including components, subassemblies, maintenance materials, and housekeeping supplies. Although service inputs are more difficult to evaluate, often they can be treated successfully by these same methods.

535

*The Quality
Control of
Inputs Using
Acceptance
Sampling*

they were received. In the same way, if a company manufactures a product that requires a raw material, or a subcontracted subassembly that is found to be unusable when it is needed, then production is stopped until a new and usable supply can be obtained.

3. *Cost of disgruntled customers.* In this case, we assume that the quality of the purchased items does not affect the production process but does affect the quality of the final unit. It is the consumer who perceives the difference in quality. It is the producer of the final unit who receives and deserves full blame—with consequent losses—for having passed the inferior material along to the consumer. The vendor of the inferior items enjoys relative anonymity. Inspection of the purchased item could have avoided this cost, but then, in turn, there is an *inspection cost*.

Proper management of the inspection function is based on the need to balance various costs. We spend as much on the inspection process as would be required to offset penalties of the types described above. A part of the total costs in Fig. 22-2 is the cost of inspection. If we could develop a model of the enterprise as a whole, then materials inspection costs would be part of this model, interacting with many items. As it is, the best that we can do is to isolate this inspection system and attempt to minimize its total costs.

One Hundred Percent Inspection

Total, or 100 percent inspection, has higher inspection costs than inspecting some portion (a sample) of all items. Such higher costs might be justified if increased accuracy is derived as a result of using 100 percent inspection and the penalty for being inaccurate is large. However, total inspection is *seldom the most accurate* method that can be followed. It has been found that 100 percent inspection tends to produce carelessness and error due to fatigue. The inspector's human debilities become apparent when there are many items to be totally inspected. Furthermore, 100 percent inspection is out of the question where *destructive testing* is required. A manufacturer of fire crackers, bullets, a food product, or soap flakes cannot destroy (eat, taste, make suds, etc.) a total shipment in order to find out if each item comes up to the standards. One hundred percent inspection, whether it be done by person or machine, is slow, costly, and frequently unreliable—even when it is possible. On the other hand, for a few truly critical items (where performance is a matter of life and death) 200 or 300 percent inspection might be insufficient. Especially, in the project shop (e.g., moon shots), repeated inspection with crosschecks is essential.

Acceptance Sampling Terminology

At Western Electric Company in the 1920s, a growing body of statistical theory was used to develop *sampling plans* that could be employed as substitutes for 100 percent inspection. These sampling inspection techniques were applied to purchased and subcontracted parts, raw materials, office supplies, and maintenance parts; they could also be used by producers to conduct sample tests of their own output.[7]

The only kinds of sampling procedures that had been used before this were *proportional sampling methods*, which are completely wrong (though apparently intuitively appealing to many). Before we can explain why this is so, let us develop the terms and symbols necessary for discussing sampling plans:

1. $N =$ *the lot size*

   This is usually the total number of items produced by the vendor within a single shipment. More generally, it can be the total production run of the producer for which the conditions of the system remained essentially unchanged. Thus, it is assumed that the *quality of items within a lot is homogeneous*. This means that the average number of defectives produced by the process does not change from the beginning to the end of the run.

   Every time there is a change of conditions, such as startup each day or one worker relieving another, it should be assumed that a new lot has begun. Where this information is not well-known, a reasonable number of shipping units should be termed a *lot*.

   The average fraction of defective parts (average percentage is also used) is called the *process average* and symbolized by $\bar{p}$. The fraction defective is called p.

2. $n =$ *the sample size*

   The items to be inspected should be a representative sample drawn at random from the lot. We do not just inspect material that happens to be at the top of the box. Housewives have always known this when they buy strawberries; managers have not always been so astute.

3. $c =$ *the sample criterion*

   This criterion is defined so that when n items are drawn from a lot size of N, and k items are found to be defective, then if $k > c$, we reject the entire lot. If $k \leq c$, we accept the lot. Therefore, c is called the *acceptance number* of the sampling plan.

   For example, if 5 items (n) are drawn from a lot size (N) of 20, and the acceptance number (c) is set at 2, then if 3 items are found to be defective ($k = 3$), we reject the entire lot because $k > c$. However, if 2

---

[7]At about the same time, the sequential test methods of statistical quality control were being developed. These are more frequently used by producers (having sufficient run sizes) to evaluate and control their own output. See pp. 561–79.

537

*The Quality
Control of
Inputs Using
Acceptance
Sampling*

or less items are found to be defective ($k \leq 2$), we accept the lot (minus the defectives we have found) because $k \leq c$. With the acceptance number $c = 0$, one defective item results in rejection of the lot.

Proportional Sampling at Farmers' Bank

The underlying assumption of proportional sampling is that if we had 2 lots, A and B, and A was twice as large as B, then we should draw twice as large a sample from A as from B.

Farmers' Bank is branching out. It engages a market research firm to find out how its present customers feel about the bank's services. The bank has 4 different kinds of accounts, including: no-interest checking accounts, day of deposit to day of withdrawal savings at 5 percent, 2-year 6 percent savings certificates, and 4-year 7 percent savings certificates. Also, it classifies its customers according to whether they are rural, suburban, or city dwellers. Thus, there are 12 categories of customers that will be sampled, and they are each of very different sizes.

The bank manager learns that the market research firm intends to mail the survey to 20 percent of the customers in each of the 12 categories. This procedure upsets the manager. Does it upset you?

Let us take a close look at proportional sampling. The percentage of a lot to be inspected is fixed at $n/N = K$; in this case, there are 12 lots and 20 percent of each is to be inspected. An unhappy customer will be classified as a defective item. If $c = 0$ is the acceptance number being used, then the total lot will be rejected if any defectives are found. The bank will interpret a rejected lot as an entire category of customers who are unhappy with the services it renders to that category.

Figure 22-3 illustrates 3 different 20 percent sampling plans. Once we explain how to read them, it will be evident why the bank manager has every reason to be concerned.

Operating characteristic curves (called *OC* curves), which are shown in Fig. 22-3, clearly demonstrate that the proportional sampling concept is fallacious. The horizontal axis is the *actual fraction defective* in the lot, called *p*. The OC curve shows how P_A, the probability of accepting the lot, changes with respect to *p* for a number of different sampling plans, all of which utilize the same sampling proportion of $n/N = 0.20$ and the same acceptance number, $c = 0$. Thus, these plans, all of which are based on the *policy* of proportional sampling, produce significantly different results. The probability of accepting a lot of 20 items is much higher than the probability of accepting a lot of 50 items, and both have higher P_A's than for 100 items—when proportional sampling is used. This is not an acceptable condition for inspection.

Assume that if 10 percent (or more) of the bank's customers in any category are markedly unhappy with the bank's practices, then the bank intends to change its present policies with respect to that category as it expands to new

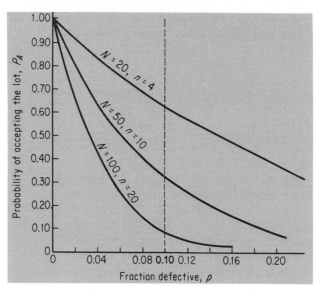

FIGURE 22-3. Operating characteristic (*OC*) curves for several proportional sampling plans

In all these cases $c = 0$ and the proportion sampled is 20 percent. Farmers' Bank will change its policy for any category of customer in which 10 percent or more of the customers are unhappy with the bank's practices.

locations. (*Note:* The bank's definition of a defective is an unhappy customer as measured by some explicit set of answers to the survey questionnaire. Since the acceptance number c is zero, if one or more defectives appear in the sample, the bank will reject the lot, i.e., change its policies.)

In one category, there are 20 accounts ($N = 20$). Four questionnaires will be sent ($n = 4$). If one or more replies is a defective (unhappy customer), then the policies for that category will be changed. The probability of accepting the lot (no change in policy) is more than 60 percent (P_A), given that the true degree of unhappiness is $p = 0.10$ (see Fig. 22-3).

In the second category, $N = 50$, $n = 10$, $c = 0$, and the probability of making no change is greater than 30 percent. In the third category, $N = 100$, $n = 20$, $c = 0$. Here, the probability of making no change is slightly under 10 percent, given that the actual degree of unhappiness is $p = 0.10$.

The bank manager has good reason to be distressed. Proportional sampling results in different and arbitrary criteria for determining what policies to follow. We have developed the example of Farmers' Bank in order to demonstrate several things. First, proportional sampling does not work. Second, the definition of acceptable quality and thereby of defectives does not have to conform to the usual manufacturing application of these terms. Now, however, let us return to the notion of a buyer's wanting to inspect the input shipments from a vendor.

539

*The Quality
Control of
Inputs Using
Acceptance
Sampling*

What sampling method should be used to manage input qualities? The answer is that by choosing appropriate values for *n* and *c*, we can develop an *OC* curve that should be acceptable to both the vendor and the buyer. The definition of what is acceptable cannot be the decision of the buyer alone. The situation calls for compromise and *negotiation* between the vendor and the purchaser. Reference to Fig. 22-4 shows what is involved.

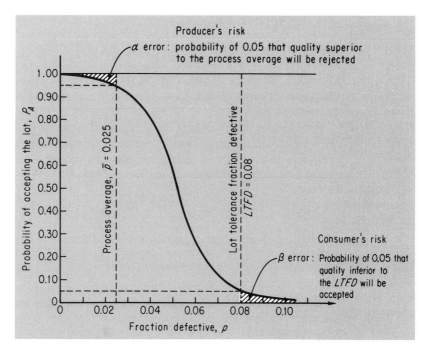

FIGURE 22-4. Consumer's and producer's risks, shown in this *OC* curve, are determined by negotiation.

Producer's and Consumer's Risks

The two shaded areas marked α and β in Fig. 22-4 are two different kinds of risk. The α area is called the *producer's risk*. It gives the probability that acceptable lots will be rejected. Specifically, it gives the probability that acceptable lots having a lower fraction of defectives than are normally produced by the process (i.e., the process average $\bar{p}$) will be rejected by the sampling plan that is shown.

On the other hand, the β area represents the probability that unacceptable levels of lot quality will be accepted by the sampling plan. Reasonably enough, this is called the *consumer's risk*. The limiting value, defined by the consumer, is called the *lot tolerance fraction defective, LTFD*.[8] It is the upper limit of

---

[8](If percentage defective is used instead of fraction defective, the limit is called *LTPD*).

fraction defectives that the consumer is willing to tolerate in each lot. Above this point, the buyer would like to reject all lots. But this is impossible if inspection by sampling methods is to be used. Therefore, the buyer compromises by saying that no more than β percent of the time will such quality be allowed to get through the *sampling procedure*.

The Cost of Inspection

Given a certain process average, $\bar{p}$, and the consumer's specification of *LTFD* and β, then a sampling plan can be found that *minimizes the cost of inspection*. In this cost, we include the expense of *detailing*, which is the operation of totally inspecting (100 percent) all *rejected lots* to remove the defective pieces.

Such a sampling plan imputes a dollar value to the probability of falsely rejecting lots of acceptable quality (i.e., α). If the producer wishes to decrease the α-type risk, he can do so by improving the process average $\bar{p}$. But an improvement of this kind may be costly. It is likely that the consumer would be forced to accept part of this increased cost in the form of higher prices. Whether it is the producer or the consumer who bears the cost of inspection —or if they share it—they must agree that the only rational procedure to be followed is to minimize inspection costs and negotiate about the values for *LTFD* and β. Under some circumstances, they might also consider improvements that can be made in $\bar{p}$.

It is important to observe that any sampling plan, of a specific c and n, completely specifies the α and β risks for given levels of $\bar{p}$ and *LTFD*. In turn, the sampling plan requires n inspections for every lot. If the process average $\bar{p}$, is the true state of affairs, then α percent of the time the remainder of the lot will be inspected. Thus, the average number of pieces inspected will be $n + (N - n)\alpha$.

As n gets large, all other factors remaining constant, then the plan becomes increasingly discriminating and α approaches one. The effect is illustrated in Fig. 22-5. This results in the average number of pieces to be inspected approximating N. We have $n + (N - n)1 = N$. On the other hand, we observe that as n gets small, approaching one, β increases rapidly and approaches one, while α tends to become zero. In this case, the average number of pieces that will be inspected will be negligible,[9] but the consumer's risk will be high. In between these extremes, there exist appropriate values of c and n that will minimize the average number of pieces to be inspected for some specified level of consumer protection. Thus, in Fig. 22-5, Plan A requires $[20 + 80(0.06)] = 24.8$ pieces to be inspected, on the average; Plan B requires $[10 + 90(0.21)] = 28.9$ pieces to be inspected (given $N = 100$). Both plans provide the same consumer risk.

---

[9] Close to one.

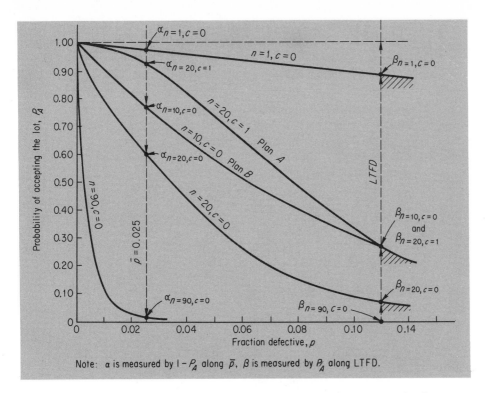

Note: α is measured by $1 - P_A$ along $\bar{p}$, β is measured by P_A along LTFD.

FIGURE 22-5. As the sample size increases, all other factors remaining constant, the plan becomes increasingly discriminating from the point of view of the consumer; that is, β approaches zero, but the cost of inspection increases rapidly as α approaches one. For a given level of β protection there is a sampling plan that minimizes the cost of inspection. Thus, for $LTFD = 0.12$ and β equals 0.26, Plan A has a lower cost of inspection than Plan B.

Constructing Acceptance Sampling Plans

How are the kinds of plans that we have been discussing constructed? One of the most direct approaches is to utilize tables that have been designed for this purpose.[10] On the other hand, OC curves can be derived directly from appropriate mathematical statements.

The hypergeometric distribution is used when the lot size N is small, so that the effect of successive sampling, which reduces the number of unsampled units remaining in the lot (i.e., N units, $N - 1$ units, $N - 2$ units, etc.), can be taken into account. When N is sufficiently large, the binomial distribution can be used. Neither the binomial nor the Poisson distributions require specification of N, since in both cases N is assumed to be infinitely large.

---

[10]Harold F. Dodge and Harry G. Romig, *Sampling Inspection Tables, Single and Double Sampling* (New York: John Wiley & Sons, Inc., 1951).

Figure 22-6 illustrates the fact that when N equals 1000, the assumption of an infinite N does not introduce great inaccuracy into the sampling plan. In fact, it is frequently quite reasonable to use mathematical methods based upon an infinite lot size when N is equal to much less than 1000.

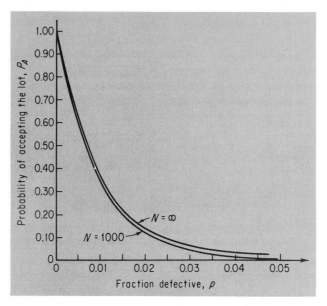

FIGURE 22-6. When the lot size N is reasonably large, say approximately 1000, the assumption of an infinite lot size does not introduce great inaccuracy into the sampling plan. The binomial and Poisson methods for deriving OC curves assume that $N = \infty$.

Consider the following simple hypergeometric formula for a sampling plan with acceptance number $c = 0$.

$$P_A = \frac{(N - x)!\,(N - n)!}{(N - x - n)!\,N!}$$

where $x = $ the *number* of defectives actually in the lot and x/N is, therefore, the actual fraction defective of the lot, p.

As we vary x from 0 to N, we determine the different values of P_A that are associated with each level of fraction defectives. Thus, in the case where $N = 4$, $n = 1$, and $c = 0$, the formula for P_A would be

$$P_A = \frac{(4 - x)!\,3!}{(3 - x)!\,4!} = \frac{(4 - x)!}{4(3 - x)!} = \frac{4 - x}{4}.$$

Then, for the different values of x we would get:

543

*The Quality
Control of
Inputs Using
Acceptance
Sampling*

TABLE 22-1

x	$x/N = p$	P_A
0	0.00	1.00
1	0.25	0.75
2	0.50	0.50
3	0.75	0.25
4	1.00	0.00

We can illustrate the binomial computation of the OC curve quite readily. For the situation where $c = 0$, the binomial formulation becomes

$$P_A = (1 - p)^n$$

As previously noted, there is no provision for specifying the lot size, N. Then, when $n = 1$, we obtain $P_A = (1 - p)$. In this case, the results are *identical* with those derived for the hypergeometric distribution above.

In Appendix 22-I (as optional material) the general form of the hypergeometric distribution is given (for cases where $c > 0$). Then, in Appendix 22-II (as optional material), the use of the binomial and Poisson distributions to derive OC curves is explained. It should be remembered that what counts here is the concept and the knowledge of how to employ OC charts. The capability to construct OC charts is of benefit, but it is not essential for the user who has handbooks of sampling plans available in the library.

Diamonte, Inc. Makes Industrial Diamonds.

The quality of the output is established by an expensive testing procedure that does not harm the product. One hundred percent inspection is considered too expensive, so hypergeometric sampling is used.

The company's OC curve is the one derived in Table 22-1. Four diamonds are made at a time, and one of them is selected for testing. If a defect is found, the remaining three diamonds are tested. The process average for defectives is $\bar{p} = 0.25$.

Question: What is the average number of pieces inspected?

Answer: Following the reasoning on pp. 540–41, if the process average, $\bar{p} = 0.25$, is the true state of affairs, then $P_A = 0.75$, whence $\alpha = 1 - P_A = 0.25$ or 25 percent of the time the remainder of the lot will be inspected. Thus, the average number of pieces inspected will be: $1 + (4 - 1)0.25 = 1.75$ diamonds.

Quality management is assisted by the idea of an *average outgoing quality* (AOQ). This is a measure of the average or expected *percentage* of defective items that the producer will ship to the consumer under different conditions of percent defectives.

First, every sampled lot is divided into n units to be inspected, and the remaining $(N - n)$ units. The probable number of defectives in the unsampled portion $(N - n)$ is $\bar{p}(N - n)$. Out of every 100 samples taken we expect that P_A will be the fraction of samples that is passed without any further examination. These are the only units that cannot be tagged as defectives and replaced (in the sense of detailing). Then, $P_A\bar{p}(N - n)$ is the *expected number of defectives* that will be passed without having been identified for every N units processed.

As another approach, the percentage $P_A p(N - n)/N$ is used. This percentage is called the AOQ (average outgoing quality), and it changes value as p does.

$$\text{AOQ} = P_A p(N - n)/N$$

Note that the value of P_A changes with p in accordance with the specifics of the sampling plan which are based on the values of n and c that are chosen. Thus, AOQ is a function of all of the elements of a sampling plan and can, therefore, be used as a means of evaluating a sampling plan. Specifically, for each value of p an AOQ measure is derived. It is the expected value of the percent defectives that would be passed without detection *if* the process were operating at the value p. The AOQ measure reaches a maximum value for some particular value of p. The maximum value is termed the average outgoing quality limit (AOQL).

For example, consider the following computations using our previous (hypergeometric and binomial) results (pp. 541–43):

p	P_A	$(N - n)/N$	AOQ
0	1	$\frac{3}{4}$	0
$\frac{1}{4}$	$\frac{3}{4}$	$\frac{3}{4}$	$\frac{9}{64}$
$\frac{1}{2}$	$\frac{1}{2}$	$\frac{3}{4}$	$\frac{12}{64}$ (AOQL)
$\frac{3}{4}$	$\frac{1}{4}$	$\frac{3}{4}$	$\frac{9}{64}$
1	0	$\frac{3}{4}$	0

Perhaps another example, based on a more refined hypergeometric OC curve would help. In this case $N = 50$, $n = 10$, and $c = 0$.[11]

---

[11]See Plan 1 in Appendix 22-I.

545

*The Quality
Control of
Inputs Using
Acceptance
Sampling*

p	P_A	(N − n)/N	AOQ
0	1.000	0.8	0.00000
0.04	0.637	0.8	0.02038
0.06	0.504	0.8	0.02419
0.08	0.397	0.8	0.02541 (AOQL)
0.10	0.311	0.8	0.02488
0.12	0.242	0.8	0.02130
.	.	.	.
.	.	.	.
.	.	.	.
0.20	0.083	0.8	0.01328
.	.	.	.
.	.	.	.
.	.	.	.

The maximum value of AOQ has been calculated as 0.02541. It is the AOQL also shown in Fig. 22-7.

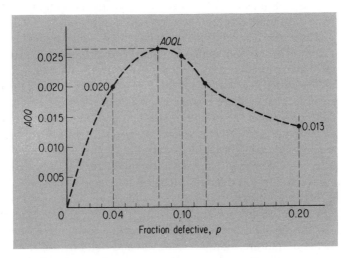

FIGURE 22-7. The average outgoing quality as a function of process defective rate *p* with the limit *AOQL* equal to 0.02541, occurring at *p* = 0.08

The average outgoing quality limit (AOQL) describes the worst case of percent defectives that can be shipped, if it is assumed that the defectives of rejected lots are replaced with acceptable products and that all lots are thoroughly mixed so that shipments have homogeneous quality.

Multiple Sampling

Other types of sampling plans are utilized when the amount of inspection required by the single sampling plan appears to be too great. By single-sampling plan, we mean that the acceptance decision must be made on the basis of the first sample drawn. If double sampling is used, a second sample can be drawn, if required. In general, with double sampling, inspection costs can be lowered.

The double-sampling plan requires two acceptance numbers c_1 and c_2 such that $c_2 > c_1$. Then, if the observed number of defectives in the first sample of size n_1 is k_1:

1. We accept the lot if $k_1 \leq c_1$.
2. We reject the lot if $k_1 > c_2$.
3. If $c_1 < k_1 \leq c_2$, then we draw an additional sample of size n_2. The total sample is now of size $n_1 + n_2$.

    If the observed number of defectives in the total sample is $k_1 + k_2$, then:

4. We accept the lot if $(k_1 + k_2) \leq c_2$.
5. We reject the lot if $(k_1 + k_2) > c_2$.

Figure 22-8 illustrates the way in which double sampling divides the graph space into unique acceptance and rejection regions.

There are also multiple sampling plans and sequential sampling plans. Tables exist[12] which enable a manager to choose an appropriate plan without having to engage in substantially onerous numerical calculations.

The cost criterion for choosing a plan has been implicit throughout our discussion. That is, there is some inspection cost per piece that can vary greatly, depending upon the nature of the item and the *definition of a defective*. The definition of a defective is unlikely to be a straightforward matter. Given such a definition, it might require days of testing to determine whether an item is acceptable. For example, a defective might be defined as a unit possessing any 3 flaws where 100 different kinds of flaws could occur.

It is both instructive and fascinating to see how so many different factors come together in a discussion of this kind. We observe that the process average, the quality expectations, the inspection cost, and the market's acceptance of the output are tightly interwoven and that any approach to management decision making that bypasses *synthesis* of these issues is bound to be absurd.

City Waste Disposal. A double sampling plan is used to inspect the quality of work of sanitation teams. The plan is straightforward. Out of 1000 streets, 36 are chosen randomly and inspected. If all 36 are satisfactory, then inspection is discontinued for that day. On the other hand, if more than 3 streets of the 36 are unsatisfactory, all streets are inspected, and the sanitation teams are required to return and clean up all unsatisfactory conditions.

If at least 1 and not more than 3 defective cleanups are found, then another 59 streets are chosen randomly and inspected. The number of unsatisfactory conditions found in the first sample are added to those found in the second

---

[12]For example, Dodge and Roming, *Sampling Inspection Tables*, op. cit.

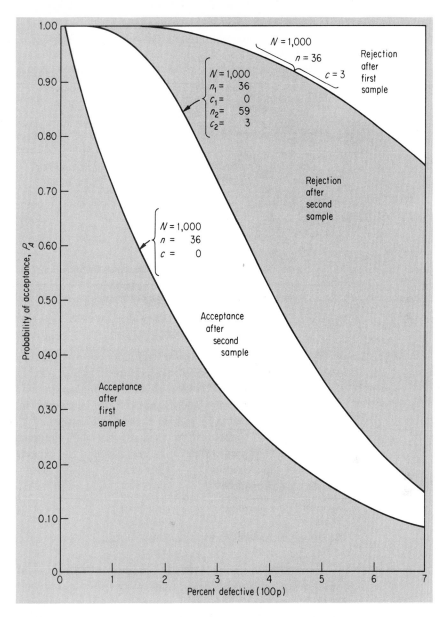

FIGURE 22-8. Characteristics of a double sampling plan [From Eugene L. Grant, *Statistical Quality Control,* 3rd ed. (New York: McGraw-Hill Book Company, Inc., 1972), p. 376.]

sample. If the total number of defective cleanups is 3 or less, then inspection is discontinued; otherwise, 100 percent inspection is required.

Let us assume that the average number of defective cleanups is 30 streets out of 1000. Using Fig. 22-8, note that for 3 percent defective:

The probability of discontinuing inspection after the first sample is about 34 percent (36 streets inspected). The probability of having to inspect 1000 − 36 = 964 streets is about 2 percent (1.00 − 0.98 on the chart). The probability of discontinuing inspection after the second sample is taken is approximately 70 − 34 = 36 percent (36 + 59 = 95 streets inspected). The probability of having to inspect 1000 − 36 − 59 = 905 streets is 0.98 − 0.70 = 0.28, or 28 percent. We can summarize these results as follows.

(1) Number of Streets Inspected	(2) Probability of Occurrence	Product (1) × (2)
36	0.34	12.24
964	0.02	19.28
95	0.36⎫ 0.64*	34.20
905	0.28⎭	253.40

The expected number of streets inspected = 319.12

*The probability of having to take a second sample is 1.00 − 0.34 − 0.02 = 0.64, or 64 percent.

This result is unsatisfactory to the manager of City Waste Disposal. Not only is the expected number of streets to be inspected too high, but the impossibility of inspecting 1000 streets at one time makes the plan unfeasible.

Instead, the manager suggests that the city be divided into 5 zones of 200 streets. Each day, a zone will be chosen randomly and a double sampling plan based on $N = 200$ will be used. In that way, the maximum number of streets to be inspected will never exceed 200, and the expected number will be well below the maximum.

The manager agrees.

Acceptance Sampling for Job Shop Output

Acceptance sampling is ideally suited to the management of the quality of process inputs. The statistical quality control methods that we will describe in the next chapter are ideally suited to the management of the quality of process outputs. However, there is another way of looking at the areas of application of acceptance sampling and statistical quality control.

In a job shop, where small batches of items are produced, there is insufficient output to use the statistical quality control method. Therefore, lot by lot sampling of small-batch production runs must be used to monitor quality. Statistical quality control can be used for large batch sizes, but it is ideally suited to continuous sampling of the serial production of flow shops and intermittent flow shops.

549

*The Quality
Control of
Inputs Using
Acceptance
Sampling*

APPENDIX 22-I

OC Curves Based on the Hypergeometric Distribution
(Optional Material)

For sampling without replacement, the *hypergeometric* distribution should be used. We cannot assume that each item drawn for the sample of size n is then replaced before the next unit is drawn. The lot size N is finite and small enough to allow such depletion to affect the results. If we replaced items, to keep N of constant size, we might by chance keep sampling exactly the same item over and over. Also, with destructive testing, we cannot replace sampled items that must be destroyed to ascertain their quality.

Assume that the number of defectives in the lot is specified as the variable x. Then, x/N is the *actual* fraction defective of the lot. When we draw the first unit for the sample, the probability of drawing a defective will be x/N. We do not replace this unit after recording its state, and, therefore, when the second unit of the sample is drawn—no matter what happened with the first sample drawn—the probabilities are a function of $(N - 1)$.

Thus, when the difference between N and $(N - 1)$ is significant, we use the combinatorial formulation:

$$P_j = C_{n-j}^{N-x} C_j^x / C_n^N = \frac{(N-x)!\, x!\, n!\, (N-n)!}{(n-j)!\, (N-x-n+j)!\, j!\, (x-j)!\, N!}$$

(All variables are described above except j, which equals the number of defectives in the sample.)

TABLE 22-2 EXAMPLE OF THE DETERMINATION* OF *OC* CURVES
FOR $c = 0$ AND $c = 1$; $N = 50$; $n = 10$

Abscissa Value	Plan 1 For c = 0 j = 0	j = 1	Plan 2 For c = 1 j = 0 + 1
$p = \dfrac{x}{N} = 0;\quad x = 0$	$P_{A,j=0} = \dfrac{50!\,10!\,40!}{10!\,40!\,50!}$ $= 1.000$	$P_{A,j=1} = 0.000$	$P_{A,j=0+1} = 1.000$
$p = \dfrac{x}{N} = 0.04;\; x = 2$	$P_{A,j=0} = \dfrac{48!\,2!\,10!\,40!}{10!\,38!\,2!\,50!}$ $= 0.637$	$P_{A,j=1} = \dfrac{48!\,2!\,10!\,40!}{9!\,39!\,50!}$ $= 0.326$	$P_{A,j=0+1} = 0.963$
$p = \dfrac{x}{N} = 0.10;\; x = 5$	$P_{A,j=0} = \dfrac{45!\,5!\,10!\,40!}{10!\,35!\,5!\,50!}$ $= 0.311$	$P_{A,j=1} = \dfrac{45!\,5!\,10!\,40!}{9!\,36!\,4!\,50!}$ $= 0.432$	$P_{A,j=0+1} = 0.743$
$p = \dfrac{x}{N} = 0.20;\; x = 10$	$P_{A,j=0} = \dfrac{40!\,10!\,10!\,40!}{10!\,30!\,10!\,50!}$ $= 0.083$	$P_{A,j=1} = \dfrac{40!\,10!\,10!\,40!}{9!\,31!\,9!\,50!}$ $= 0.268$	$P_{A,j=0+1} = 0.351$

*Note: These computations can be facilitated by using a log table of factorials, for example, E. L. Grant and R. S. Leavenworth, *Statistical Quality Control*, 4th ed. (New York: McGraw-Hill Book Company, Inc., 1974), pp. 655–659.

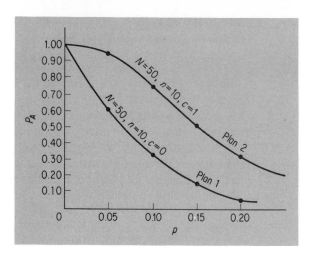

FIGURE 22-9.

The curves are drawn in Fig. 22-9, for both of the hypergeometric plans derived in Table 22-2. Note that the second column gives the probabilities for values of x when $j = 0$. This is equivalent to the $c = 0$ plan. However, the third column, which gives the probabilities for values of x when $j = 1$, must be added to the second column, resulting in the fourth column, which is the plan for $c = 1$. The reason is that the $c = 1$ plan must include both $j = 0$ and $j = 1$ events.

APPENDIX 22-II
OC Curves Based on the Binomial and Poisson Distributions
(Optional Material)

When the notion that N is finite and that the system is sensitive to lot size can be discarded, then either the binomial distribution or the Poisson distribution can be used. Both express the condition that the lot size is *infinite*, and, therefore, they require far less computation than the hypergeometric distribution. In the text, we stated that when N gets reasonably large (say 1000), the assumption of an infinite N does not introduce distortion. In many applications, even when N is as small as 100, the infinite assumption is satisfactory.

Binomial Distribution. Consequently, it is frequently sensible to use either the binomial distribution or the Poisson approximation to the binomial for such cases. Let us first consider the binomial distribution:

$$\text{Prob}\,(j; n, p) = \left[\frac{n!}{j!(n-j)!}\right]p^j q^{n-j}$$

where
$$p + q = 1.$$

When $j = 0$, the probabilities that are calculated represent the $c = 0$ plan.

To obtain the OC curve for $n = 100$, $c = 0$, we have[13]

$$P_A = \text{Prob}\,(0;\,100,\,p) = \left[\frac{100!}{0!\,(100-0)!}\right]p^0 q^{100} = q^{100} = (1-p)^{100}$$

Table 22-3 is derived by substituting values of p between 0 and 1 into the binomial formulation.

TABLE 22-3

Fraction Defective, p	1 − p	$(1-p)^{100} = P_A$
0.00	1.00	1.000
0.01	0.99	0.366
0.02	0.98	0.133
0.04	0.96	0.017
.	.	.
.	.	.
.	.	.
1.00	0.00	0.000

For the acceptance number $c = 1$, we require the same kind of addition as was the case for the hypergeometric. Thus, obtain the sum: P_A = Prob $(0;\,100,\,p)$ + Prob $(1;\,100,\,p)$ for values of p.

To derive the OC curve for $n = 100$, $c = 1$, using the binomial formulation, we compute

$$\text{Prob}\,(1;\,100,\,p) = \left[\frac{100!}{1!\,(100-1)!}\right]p^1 (1-p)^{100-1} = 100p(1-p)^{99}$$

Table 22-4 follows.

TABLE 22-4

Fraction Defective, p	1 − p	$100p(1-p)^{99}$
0.00	1.00	0.000
0.01	0.99	0.370
0.02	0.98	0.271
0.04	0.96	0.070
.	.	.
.	.	.
.	.	.
1.00	0.00	0.000

---

[13]$0! = 1! = 1$

By adding the third columns of Tables 22-3 and 22-4, we achieve the $c = 1$ plan, shown in the fourth column of Table 22-5.

TABLE 22-5

Fraction Defective, p	$j = 0$ $(1 - p)^{100}$ $P_A (c = 0)$	$j = 1$ $100p(1 - p)^{99}$	$P_A(c = 1)$
0.00	1.000	0.000	1.000
0.01	0.366	0.370	0.736
0.02	0.133	0.271	0.404
0.04	0.017	0.070	0.087
.	.	.	.
.	.	.	.
.	.	.	.
1.00	0.000	0.000	0.000

As expected, the OC curve for $c = 0$ is far more stringent than for $c = 1$.

Poisson Distribution. Even simpler to use is the Poisson distribution. It assumes sampling with replacement (i.e., N can be treated as infinite) and also the fact that p is small over the range that is of interest.

$$\text{Prob } (j; m) = \frac{m^j e^{-m}}{j!}$$

Let $j = 0$, which is equivalent to $c = 0$, and let $n = 100$; thus, since $m = np$ we have $m = 100p$.

TABLE 22-6
Prob $(0; 100p) = e^{-np} = e^{-100p}$

Fraction Defective, p	$100p = m$	Prob $(j; m) = P_A$
0.00	0	1.000
0.01	1	0.368
0.02	2	0.135
0.04	4	0.018
.	.	.
.	.	.
.	.	.
1.00	100	0.000

553

*The Quality
Control of
Inputs Using
Acceptance
Sampling*

We observe that this result is essentially the same as that obtained by using the binomial distribution. It should be remembered that a sampling plan where $c = 1$ requires computations of P_A for $j = 0$, which are then added to those of P_A for $j = 1$ to obtain the sampling plan for $c = 1$. Thus, we have Tables 22-7 and 22-8.

TABLE 22-7
Prob $(1; 100p) = (100p)e^{-100p}$

Fraction Defective, p	$100p = m$	Prob $(j; m)$
0.00	0	0.000
0.01	1	0.368
0.02	2	0.271
0.04	4	0.073
.	.	.
.	.	.
.	.	.
1.00	100	0.000

TABLE 22-8 COLUMN 3 SUMS OF TABLES 22-6 AND 22-7

Fraction Defective, p	$j = 0$	$j = 1$	P_A
0.00	1.000	0.000	1.000
0.01	0.368	0.368	0.736
0.02	0.135	0.271	0.406
0.04	0.018	0.073	0.091
.	.	.	.
.	.	.	.
.	.	.	.
1.00	0.000	0.000	0.000

The Poisson approximation of the binomial is good for small values of p. Comparing Table 22-8 and 22-5, through the range of $p = 0.00$ to 0.04, we see that the OC curves are sufficiently similar to use either approach.

Let us compare one larger value (for $c = 0$ and $p = 0.10$)

$$\text{Binomial } P_A = (1 - 0.10)^{100} = 0.000027$$

$$\text{Poisson } P_A = e^{-100(0.10)} = 0.000045$$

The Poisson approximation creates an error of 67 percent when $p = 0.10$, in this case. The fit will depend upon the specific numbers involved. It can be quickly checked for any situation.

1. "Quality" has two quite different interpretations (one is the consumer's; the other is the producer's). What are these interpretations, and why does the difference matter?

2. What inputs to the process require quality management?

3. Distinguish between functional and nonfunctional qualities. For example, are all of the functional attributes, and none of the nonfunctional attributes, measurable?

4. Describe the purpose utilities of food. Since there are multiple purposes, the question arises as to whether certain purposes consistently have greater utility than others. Also, do all foods follow the same pattern? Do patterns shift overtime? Discuss these specific questions and then draw generalizations about the concept of purpose utility.

5. Differentiate between services and products with respect to the dimensions of quality.

6. Explain what is meant by the "trade-offs of cost and quality." Why is there a level of quality that will maximize profits? Does this apply to both goods and services?

7. Can the quality of service inputs be managed by the methods of acceptance sampling? Explain your answer.

8. Why is 100 percent inspection unacceptable in most cases? When is it necessary, and what must be done then to make it feasible?

9. Are proportional sampling methods always wrong? Explain.

10. With reference to Fig. 22-2, p. 533, how is quality level defined?

11. In acceptance sampling, the lot size N must be known. What implications does this fact have for the job shop as compared to the flow shop?

12. *Quality is an operations management responsibility.* What is meant by this statement?

13. Discuss the concept of reliability as a measure of quality. What does it mean in the case of:
   a. A bar of soap?
   b. An automobile battery?
   c. Automobile tires?
   d. A die-casting machine?
   e. Steel girders?
   f. A sprinkler system for fire protection?
   g. The handle of a suitcase?
   h. Aspirin?

14. As a manufacturer of automobile batteries, you wish to offer the longest possible guarantee period. Your policy is predicated on the belief that a guarantee period that is substantially longer than your competitors' will increase your sales volume and provide a larger share of the market. For this reason, you have specified that the cost of replacements should entirely use up whatever additional profits you receive as a result of the increased sales volume.

555

*The Quality
Control of
Inputs Using
Acceptance
Sampling*

a. What information do you need?

b. How do you propose to handle this problem?

15. What role does the industrial designer play in the production manager's operations?

16. Creditcarter produces credit card blanks which are furnished to various organizations that offer credit to their customers in this manner. Petrogas buys the card blanks in lots of 20,000 and inspects each shipment with acceptance sampling. Through negotiations, it has been agreed to set the consumer's risk β at 0.06 and the producer's risk α at 0.08. Creditcarter's process average for defectives is 0.003. If $c = 0$; what sample size n should be used and what will be the value of the lot tolerance fraction defective?

Answer: First, we use the equation

$$P_A = (1 - p)^n$$

The value of P_A on the OC curve at the process average will be

$$(1 - \alpha) = 0.92 = (1 - \bar{p})^n = (1 - 0.003)^n$$

or

$$0.92 = (0.997)^n$$

In log form:

$$\log 0.92 = n \log 0.997$$

or

$$-0.0362122 = n(-0.0013048)$$

whence

$$n = 27.75, \text{ or } 28$$

Again, we use the binomial equation to determine the value of p_{LTFD}. Thus,

$$\beta = (1 - p_{LTFD})^n \quad \text{or} \quad 0.06 = (1 - p_{LTFD})^{27.75}$$

With logs, we have

$$\log 0.06 = 27.75 \log (1 - p_{LTFD})$$

or

$$\frac{-1.22184}{27.75} = -0.04403 = \log (1 - p_{LTFD})$$

whence

$$(1 - p_{LTFD}) = 0.90359$$

and

$$p_{LTFD} = 0.096$$

17. Omega Electronics uses flow shop methods to manufacture a vacuum tube that is highly resistant to vibration and heat. Only destructive testing

can be used to check the acceptability of a tube. Each tube is costly. The application of the tube is such that a failure endangers many lives. What inspection procedure would you use?

18. The Yukon Company requires a destructive test to determine the quality of the firecrackers that it manufactures. Assume that five giant firecrackers compose a lot. The company tests one and ships four, if the test is successful. If the test is not successful, the remaining four are sold as seconds.

   a. Specify the characteristics of this single sampling plan and derive the *OC* curve.

   b. What do you think of this plan?

   Answer: **a.** This is a sampling plan where $N = 5$, $n = 1$, and $c = 0$. If the process average, $\bar{p} = \frac{2}{5}$, then the probability of selecting a defective firecracker for the test is 0.40. This means that there is a $\frac{2}{5}$ chance of rejecting the lot, or a $1 - \frac{2}{5} = \frac{3}{5}$ chance of accepting it. Following this line of reasoning, the *OC* curve can be quickly derived. (See Fig. 22-10.)

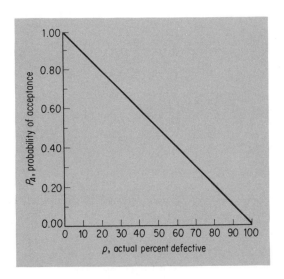

FIGURE 22-10.

   b. This plan does not give a very sensitive test (with $p = \frac{3}{5}$ there is still a $\frac{2}{5}$ chance of passing the lot), but the nature and cost of the product do not warrant too much fuss. There is a large producer's risk here (with $p = \frac{1}{5}$ there is a $\frac{4}{5}$ chance of rejecting the lot), but this fault is partially overcome by selling the remaining 4 as seconds, if a reasonable price can be charged for such items.

twenty-three
managing the quality of process outputs by using statistical quality control (SQC)

For both products and services, inputs and process are more or less invisible to the market. The impressions of an organization that the consumer forms are almost totally dependent on the outputs. Companies do arrange for consumers to visit their plants or research labs, so that they can be convinced of the efforts taken on their behalf. On the whole, however, the consumer's response is not a function of such impressions.

Only as the output is a reflection of sound design, planning, and control does the consumer respond to the image that the organization is trying to build for itself. Thus, the willingness of the consumer to pay a given price for an item, and willingness to repurchase the item, followed by word-of-mouth praise or criticism about a particular organization's product or service —all these result from what qualities are perceived in the output.

In other words, the life cycle timing is a reflection of the aggregation of opinions of people concerning their needs for certain functional and nonfunctional qualities and the degree of substitutability of one organization's output for the output of another. Output quality is the key.

What is visible in the output? What is the reason that consumers choose different brands? Quality in its infinite variety is difficult to measure, and may be defined incorrectly. Market research is essential to provide operational guidelines. We must include the obvious functionability, appearance, service offered by the company, the coverage and the period of guarantee, maintenance requirements, and the not-so-obvious many other factors (see pp. 527–32). The second consideration concerns how the output volume changes over a period of time and where this output is directed. Included are such *distribution* factors as delivery date, product availability, and the treatment of back orders. The production and operations manager is responsible for both quality control and schedule control.

The Output Quality Monitor

Walter Shewhart[1] helped develop a quality control model that completely altered the organization's ability to control the quality of its output. The primary component of this model is a *monitor*, which is able to determine whether or not a *stable system* exists. The model monitors a process to determine whether or not the system is regularly meeting expectations: delivering the specified outcome within the expected range of variation and achieving the manager's objectives while maintaining a stable process.

The monitor distinguishes between the many, small, random factors that perturb but cannot be removed from a system and the relatively large causal factors, which are called *assignable causes of variation*. Something can and must be done about assignable causes, since they are both unwanted and identifiable. The monitor, using the methodology of *statistical quality control* (SQC) can tell us that something seems to be changing; that the system no longer appears to be following an established (stable) pattern. This is very vital information. Figure 23-1 locates the SQC monitor within the information flows of the control system. *Feedback* is an essential function. The information that is fed back from the monitor to the control system identifies the possible existence of an assignable cause of variation, if one exists.

Assignable and Chance Causes of Variation

Assignable causes of variation are disturbances that can enter the system at any time. They can be there when the process is started, and can remain undetected until large penalties have to be paid for the poor quality of production. The SQC control monitor is designed to recognize that such assignable disturbances exist. Once spotted, assignable causes ordinarily can be removed.

[1]W. A. Shewhart, *Statistical Method from the Viewpoint of Quality Control*, W. E. Deming, ed. (Washington, D.C.: Department of Agriculture, 1939).

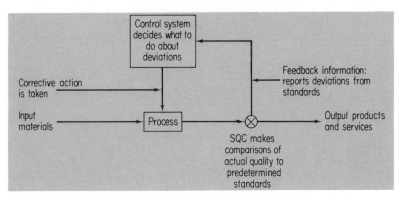

FIGURE 23-1. The general structure of a statistical quality control (SQC) system for an input/output process.

At the same time, other causes of variation can be found in all systems, and nothing can be done about them. They are called *chance causes of variation*. They can neither be identified nor removed. Chance causes arise from so many infinitesimal sources[2] that even if a few were found and something done about them, the overall effect would be negligible.

It is vital that the manager be able to *separate* the two types of causes of variation and not confuse or lump them together. The SQC model establishes a procedure for determining whether the variation that is observed is as small as it can be. That is, whether the observed variability is the result only of chance cause factors, or whether there is trouble in the system about which something can be done. This SQC monitor provides differentiation between types of disturbances. It is expected that the output of a machine will be stable, but various things can happen. A tool can shift position. The quality of material that is being worked on can change. The worker can make a mistake.

Shewhart proposed the notion that by measuring a *sequence* of outputs in terms of a specified characteristic, it would be possible to derive *control limits* that describe the range of process behaviors that *should* be expected *if* the process were stable (see Fig. 23-2). Observations are made of the output. As long as the observed values fall within the control limits and do so *without discernible patterns*, no disturbance to the system is believed to have occurred. Thus, as long as the measurements of outputs produced by the system fall between the limits and give evidence of purely random behavior, the process is called stable. When the observed results no longer appear to be random—one test of which is that they fall outside the limits—then the system is termed *out of control* and managerial action is called for. Process corrections are made.

---

[2]For example, variations in the temperature of every moving part of a machine, dust particles, and the positioning of work.

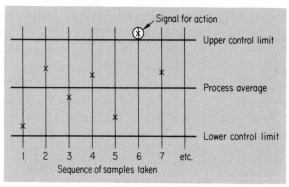

FIGURE 23-2. Prototype of a control chart

Inspection Standards

There is a *technology* of inspection that is no more appropriate to our present discussion than are the specific technologies of product and service processes. The operations manager is primarily involved with the *concept of specifications*, although in practice this will be translated into a large variety of detailed technical specifications such as hardness, tensile strength, color, and surface finish. To measure these characteristics the departments are provided with appropriate instruments such as gauges, micrometers, optical comparators, and devices for measuring hardness, tensile strength, and surface finish. These physical outputs are visible and can be measured. It is expected that they will conform to some set of specifications such as are communicated by a blueprint.

In some production areas, however, the specification of output quality is a far more elusive matter than can be dealt with by blueprints. Thus, the problem of providing exact and measurable quality specifications for the tastes of foods or the odors of perfumes is exceedingly difficult.[3] The derivation of a standard against which quality can be measured is the goal in every case, but only if standards can be found is it possible to measure quality. Thus, for example, the Food and Drug Administration (FDA) is required to develop and enforce standards that protect the consumer from hazards that could not otherwise be perceived. Setting such standards is not an easy matter, but once they are set, food and drug samples can then be tested to see whether they meet the selected standards. It is not unusual for these standards to be changed as additional laboratory or usage information is acquired. In a somewhat different sense, we have standard yards, standard meters, standard footcandles, and standard colors. Standard intervals between standardized maintenance procedures are specified by government fiat for aircraft.[4] Stan-

---

[3]For an interesting discussion with respect to these problems of taste and smell, see *Flavor Research and Food Acceptance*, sponsored by Arthur D. Little, Inc. (New York: Reinhold Publishing Corp., 1958).

[4]Rulings of the Federal Aviation Administration (FAA).

561

*Managing the
Quality of
Process Outputs
by Using
Statistical
Quality Control
(SQC)*

dards for on-time departure by airlines are also set and could be monitored as a dimension of quality by SQC.

Quality standards can exist only when design standards are met. The fact that more than one company subscribes to a set of design standards accounts for the fact that Company *C* can use a bolt manufactured by Company *A* and a nut manufactured by Company *B*. Standard designs for gauges have been generally accepted and are described as American Gauge Design Standards. Standard bulb sizes, screw threads, radio tubes, flashlight batteries, etc., are related to the interchangeability of parts between companies and across industries. The acceptance of such design standards has had an enormous effect on the growth of industry. (See the discussion on modular production and group technology, pp. 186–89.) Now, we must introduce the question: How should we monitor *and control* our own organization's repetitive output to assure consistent achievement of quality standards?

Sequenced Inspection

We must find out how the SQC model is used to control quality. We do not draw samples at random from a homogeneous lot, as we did for acceptance sampling. Instead, it is essential to monitor the *sequence* of the output. For acceptance sampling, the assumption of homogeneity of the vendor's output was assumed. For our own production process, we no longer make this assumption. On the contrary, we ask ourselves: Does our process exhibit homogeneity? If the answer is yes, we then ask: Is our product meeting quality standards? If, again, the answer is yes, then we query: How can we guarantee that it will continue to be homogeneous and of specified quality?

Quality control is an ongoing process inspection procedure. It is a *sequential sampling method* that is more powerful in many ways than 100 percent inspection. To insure control, the feedback link shown in Fig. 23-1 is required. The inspection operation costs money, and the gain to be derived from this expense at least must offset the costs incurred. Two basically different types of inspection exist. Each has different costs and abilities. Not unexpectedly, the more expensive procedures promise greater responsiveness and control. The added costs (as usual) occur because greater amounts of more refined information are required.

1. *Classification by attributes.* This is achieved by sorting the output by type. Thus, for example, we might divide our output into rejects and nonrejects, good and bad, "go" or "no go," or some other binary division. We followed this procedure with acceptance sampling. The definition used to define a defective unit of output may be very complex; nevertheless, the eventual label placed on each unit is *limited* to either accepted or defective.

2. Classification by variables. In this case, exact scaled measurements are made of particular variables such as length, hardness, weight, thermal

conductivity, thermal expansion, electrical resistivity, dielectrical strength, melting point, modulus of elasticity, impact strength, creep strength, pounds shipped, miles flown, food consumed, cases heard, and a variety of other physically measurable quantities for which some standard measures are available.

SQC Calculations—Buttonmakers Corporation

No matter how well-designed a system is, there will always be some variation from a standard level of performance. Consequently, it is only logical to set the standard as a range. That is why, on blueprints, one sees tolerance ranges stated for specific dimensions, for example, 2.41 $\pm$ 0.03. It is expected that the actual (and observed) quality of the item will fall within the specified range. Confusion frequently exists regarding the relationship of the engineer's specifications of tolerance and the characteristics of the production process that is used to produce the part. The engineer's *specifications cannot demand more than the process is able to deliver.*

To be reasonable, tolerance limits must be adjusted to the abilities of the facility. Every facility has a characteristic output variability that can be translated into a product quality range. Thus, if it is desired to cut a steel bar to a given length, *x,* then it is expected that variation evidenced as a distribution of observed values will occur between $x - a$ and $x + a$. An engineer can specify tolerances from now until doomsday. Unless there is a machine or facility capable of providing parts that fall within this tolerance range, the objective cannot be achieved. Only by means of a new technological development can such specifications be met.

SQC Fundamentals

Statistical quality control, or SQC, is able to differentiate between *chance cause factors,* which are fundamental to all processes, and *assignable cause factors,* which can be isolated and removed from the process. Thus, it is possible to determine when a facility is experiencing only the fundamental and inherent variations to which it is always susceptible.

A *control chart* such as the one in Fig. 23-2 is the monitor of the control system. The control chart can be used for several purposes: first, to determine the fundamental or inherent variation level of a process; and second, to determine whether the process is stable and continues to be so during the production process. Stability is defined as the condition of a process in which only inherent *chance cause factors* are at work.

Statistical control procedure is based on the fact that the observed variation within each of a set of samples of size *n* can be directly related to the variation between the means of each sample in the set.

Buttonmakers produces a variety of sizes, types, and colors of buttons, but the biggest seller is the fancy pearl shirtsleeve button, standard on men's shirts. A new, high-speed process has been activated, and the company, following its consultant's advice, has instituted a statistical quality control program. One of the key qualities to monitor is the outside diameter (OD) of the button. It is supposed to be 1.10 cm (approximately $\frac{7}{16}$ inch; we have converted to the metric system). The tolerance range for the button is generally stated as 1.10 ± 0.08 cm. If it is bigger than 1.18 cm, it passes with difficulty through the buttonhole; if it is smaller than 1.02, the shirt sleeve tends to slip open.

The data in Table 23-1 have been obtained during startup. The questions

TABLE 23-1 BUTTONMAKERS—SQC DATA SHEET FOR THE OD OF MENS FANCY PEARL SHIRTSLEEVE BUTTON

Subgroup Sample Number	Observation Number 1	2	3	4	Sample* Mean $\bar{x}$	Sample* Range R
1	1.14	1.12	1.13	1.12	1.1275	0.02
2	1.06	1.09	1.07	1.08	1.0750	0.03
3	1.09	1.10	1.11	1.09	1.0975	0.02
4	1.12	1.13	1.12	1.10	1.1175	0.03
5	1.10	1.14	1.10	1.09	1.1075	0.05
6	1.09	1.10	1.10	1.08	1.0925	0.02
7	1.10	1.12	1.13	1.11	1.1150	0.03
8	1.09	1.11	1.12	1.09	1.1025	0.03
9	1.10	1.10	1.10	1.15	1.1125	0.05
10	1.11	1.11	1.10	1.12	1.1100	0.02
.	.	.	.	.	.	.
.	.	.	.	.	.	.
.	.	.	.	.	.	.

*Sum of sample mean column = 11.0575; sum of sample range column = 0.30.

to answer are whether the process is adjusted satisfactorily and whether the output is stable by statistical quality control standards.

$$\text{Process average: } \bar{x} = \frac{11.058}{10} = 1.106$$

$$\text{Average range: } \bar{R} = \frac{0.30}{10} = 0.03$$

For each subgroup, using the associated observations, we calculate the sample average, or mean value $\bar{x}$. We can assume equally well that the observations are measurements of the length of a bar, the inside diameter of a pipe, the number of air bubbles in a piece of glass, or the temperature of a water-cooled, moving part. Then we add up all of our sample mean values and divide that total by the number of samples taken. This gives us the process average. For Buttonmakers, the sum of the sample means is 11.058, the number of subgroup samples is 10; therefore, we calculate the process average to be $\bar{x} = 1.106$ cm. (We will use 3 decimal places.)

Next, in addition to the *mean value*, we obtain for each subgroup the difference between the largest observation and the smallest observation. This is the measure of the *range*, called R. We add together all the sample range measures, R. We divide this total by the number of samples taken, and obtain the average range, $\bar{R}$. For Buttonmakers, the sum of the sample ranges is 0.30, the number of subgroup samples is 10; therefore, we calculate the average range to be $\bar{R} = 0.03$.

Thus, we have obtained the expected value for each subgroup as well as a convenient measure of the variation that appeared in the subgroup.

It is to be understood that these samples represent a *sequence* of observations, made over a period of time (see Fig. 23-3). Each sample is called a *subgroup*; each subgroup, composed of 4 observations, is obtained by securing 4 measures in successive order, without permitting intervening periods to occur.

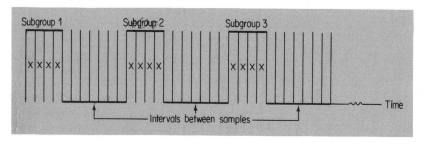

FIGURE 23-3. Subgroup size and the intervals between samples are critical determinants of control chart methodology.

Then an interval of time is allowed to elapse. The next subgroup sample is taken at a later point in time. It is vital that we preserve the order of these samples, though observations can be mixed within samples. Thus, observations taken for subgroup 2 must not be confused with observations taken for subgroup 3. The *preservation of order*, in this sense, is crucial to the use of statistical quality control.

Buttonmakers intends to take a sample of 4 consecutively made buttons once every 15 minutes. This will yield 32 subgroup samples per day. If a change occurs in the process, at most 15 minutes of production will be spoiled.

565

*Managing the
Quality of
Process Outputs
by Using
Statistical
Quality Control
(SQC)*

Sample Design

How is the subgroup size chosen? (Why did Buttonmakers choose $n = 4$ in the example above?) How does the interval between samples get set? This much we can say at the start: The interval between samples usually is fixed and unchanging—although methods do exist that decrease the between-sample interval when the value of a subgroup mean approaches one of the control limits. Similarly, if a *run* seems to be developing, the interval would decrease (see p. 571).

The point is that in the face of evidence that the system may be going out of control, the subgroup size should tend to increase and the interval between samples should definitely decrease until 100 percent inspection would be used during the emergency. Cost balance is involved, and so are specific system properties. Referring to cost, let us examine Fig. 23-4.[5] There is a point N_o

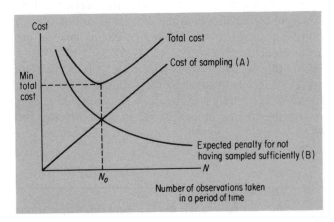

FIGURE 23-4. Determining the optimal number of observations N_o to be made in a given interval

at which minimum total cost occurs. In general, as more observations are taken (say in a day) there is an almost linearly increasing cost, line A. As fewer observations are taken, there is a greater chance that the system will go out of control and start producing defective items without its being noticed so that immediate remedial action can be taken. The expected penalty for defective output decreases as N gets larger, because the expected length of time that the system will be malfunctioning is decreased, curve B.

The question still remains, how to choose subgroup sizes and intervals between samples. Thus, if N_o is selected at $32 \times 4 = 128$ observations per day by Buttonmakers, should this be $n = 2$ repeated 64 times with appropriate intervals between, or $n = 4$ repeated 32 times, or $n = 64$ once in the morning and once in the afternoon?

---

[5]Note the similar inventory model on p. 341.

The fundamental criterion is that the successive observations within the subgroup should be close enough together to insure that they are relatively *homogeneous* and that no change is likely to have occurred in the process. We then space successive subgroups in such a way that any lack of homogeneity that might occur over time is likely to be picked up. In general practice, subgroup sizes of 4, 5, and 6 can be readily used. The spacing between subgroups will depend on the production rate and the inertial characteristics of the process, i.e., the speed with which change can take place.

Startup in the Flow Shop

A pertinent aspect of statistical quality control is the fact that *many* production systems, when they are first translated from design to practice and monitored by the SQC control model are revealed to be out of control. By making judicious changes in the process, it can be brought gradually under control. Thereafter, it can be monitored for new disturbances that might enter the system.

How many values are required before it is possible to set up a control chart? That is, how many subgroups should be collected? In Buttonmakers' example, we used only 10 subgroup samples. Ordinarily, this is far too few. It is desirable to have *at least* 25 subgroup observations before one attempts to draw up *and interpret* the control chart. Of course, 25 is simply a rule of thumb.

SQC Can Be Applied Only to Repetitive Operations

The SQC model is most applicable to the flow shop. Although we could invent examples of how it might be used for a project, the repetitive nature of work, to which SQC is addressed, is seldom found in projects. For sizable job shop orders, SQC might be used effectively, but, in this case, to justify the startup costs, the job shop would be employing intermittent flow shop methods.

SQC is a powerful model that provides economic leverage by relating consumer expectations with production capabilities. The fact that the flow shop is the major beneficiary, uniquely profiting from the application of SQC, is yet another economic advantage of the flow shop configuration.

Deriving Control Limits for the $\bar{x}$ Chart

The range R is a statistical measure of the observed variability within each sample subgroup. It is, in fact, directly related to the standard deviation σ

that could be derived for each sample group by statistical analysis.[6] $\bar{R}$ is the average range of the subgroups; i.e., it describes the average *within-group* variability.

To focus on *between-group* variability, we shall track the sequence of sample means $\bar{x}$ on the control chart. To construct the control chart, we must derive the control limits (see Fig. 23-2). The control limits must be based on the *distribution of the sample means*, since we will be plotting means $\bar{x}$ and not observations x. The control limits will be placed a distance from the process average, $\bar{\bar{x}}$, such that the area in the tails of the distribution describes the percentage of time that an observation $\bar{x}$ will fall above and below the control limits, even though nothing has happened to the process stability.

Figure 23-5 shows this relation for a spread of ± 3 standard deviations of the sample mean distribution (called s.d. of s.m.d.). With ± 3 s.d. of s.m.d.,

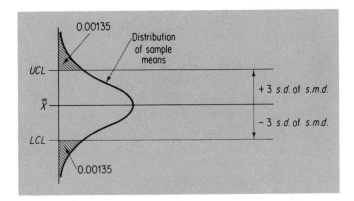

FIGURE 23-5. The construction of the control chart is based on control limits placed around the mean some given number of s.d. of s.m.d. In this case, three s.d. of s.m.d. are used. The unshaded area = 0.9973.

each tail has an area of 0.00135. For this setting of control limits, it is expected that 2.7 out of 1000-sample means will fall outside the limits, 1.35 above and 1.35 below.[7] If, instead, 1.96 s.d. of s.m.d. had been used, then 95 percent of all sample means would fall within the control limits (see p. 158 for additional data concerning tail areas).

Let us consider how to obtain the (s.d. of s.m.d.) standard deviations of the sample mean distributions. First, sample means must be distributed with less variation than the observed values of x. (See Fig. 23-6.) Averages necessarily will combine extreme values to produce in-between values.

It is known that as the sample size n gets larger, the sample mean distribution gets narrower. The *exact* relationship between the standard deviation of observations of x and the standard deviation of calculations of $\bar{x}$ is known

---

[6]Lowercase sigma σ is the Greek letter used to represent the standard deviation of a distribution.

[7]It may be easier to understand 27 out of 10,000 and for each tail 135 out of 100,000.

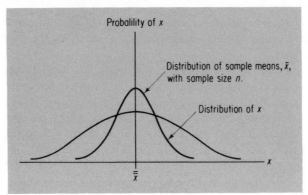

FIGURE 23-6. The distribution of sample means $\bar{x}$ has less variability than the distribution of observations x.

for all subgroup sizes used to calculate $\bar{x}$ (see the optional material in Appendix 23-I).

Accordingly, our derivation of control limits is as follows:

1. Obtain a set of range values R (measure of within-group variation).
2. Calculate the average $\bar{R}$ (average of within group variation).
3. $\bar{R}$ must be modified to describe the variability of sample means, where the sample size is n. Table 23-2 is based upon the known relationship between the range and the standard deviation. It provides a 3-sigma (s.d. of s.m.d.) protection level. Then, for the appropriate value of n, find the coefficient A_2, and multiply it by $\bar{R}$.
4. For the $\bar{x}$ chart: Upper control limit for $\bar{x} = \bar{\bar{x}} + A_2\bar{R}$
   Lower control limit for $\bar{x} = \bar{\bar{x}} - A_2\bar{R}$

Note that $\pm A_2\bar{R}$ represents ± 3 standard deviations of the sample mean distribution *as inferred from average within-group* variability. If the actual sample mean variability is the same as the inferred variability, then $\bar{x}$ values will fall outside the control limits with the expected frequency of 0.00270.

Using the $\bar{x}$ Chart for Variables

Figure 23-7 shows an $\bar{x}$ control chart on which we have marked the upper limit, the lower limit, and the process average $\bar{\bar{x}}$. We know that the distance between the process average and the 2 limits is a function of $\bar{R}$. The value $\bar{R}$, in turn, is the average range obtained for the subgroup samples of size n. Thus, the distance between the process average and the control limits is a function of the average variability associated with subgroups of size n.

On our control chart, in proper sequence, we enter the $\bar{x}$ values, which are the subgroup averages. Statistical theory tells us that if the process is stable, then the successive, observed values of the sample means will fall between the

569

*Managing the
Quality of
Process Outputs
by Using
Statistical
Quality Control
(SQC)*

**TABLE 23-2 COEFFICIENTS FOR DERIVING
3-SIGMA CONTROL LIMITS FOR $\bar{x}$ CHART
(COEFFICIENTS ARE BASED ON THE
NORMAL DISTRIBUTION)**

Number of Observations in Subgroup n	Factor for $\bar{x}$ Chart A_2
2	1.88
3	1.02
4	0.73
5	0.58
6	0.48
7	0.42
8	0.37
9	0.34
10	0.31
11	0.29
12	0.27
13	0.25
14	0.24
15	0.22
16	0.21
17	0.20
18	0.19
19	0.19
20	0.18

Texts on SQC present tables of coefficients for other than 3-sigma protection levels.

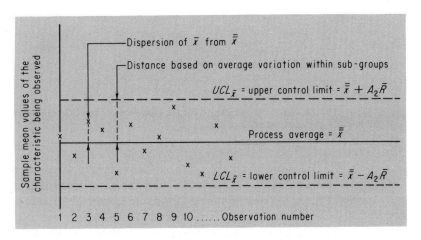

FIGURE 23-7. Control chart for variables—$\bar{x}$

control limits 99.73 percent of the time. This is true because 3-sigma limits were used. If we had utilized limits other than 3-sigma, we would have obtained different probabilities of exceeding the control limits.

Let us construct the $\bar{x}$ chart for Buttonmakers (pp. 562–64) using the data of Table 23-1, p. 563.

The process average $\bar{\bar{x}} = 1.106$ cm

The average range $\bar{R} = 0.03$

The sample size $n = 4$

The coefficient $A_2 = 0.73$ (see Table 23-2)

The upper control limit $UCL_{\bar{x}} = 1.106 + 0.73(0.03) = 1.128$

The lower control limit $LCL_{\bar{x}} = 1.106 - 0.73(0.03) = 1.084$

Figure 23-8 shows the $\bar{x}$ chart with all the subgroup mean values.

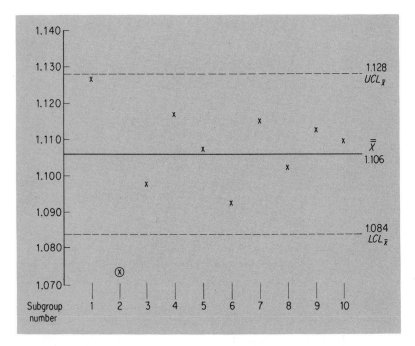

FIGURE 23-8. $\bar{x}$ control chart for the outside diameter (OD) of Buttonmakers' men's fancy pearl shirtsleeve button

One point is well below the LCL (subgroup sample number 2). Another reading is almost at the UCL (subgroup sample number 1). These two points occur at the very beginning of the startup period. Because of this, we will not worry about them. In fact, we should remove early out-of-control points (say any occurring within the first 25 observations). It is to be hoped that we can account for the causes of these outage signals, but if not, we can assume that

571

*Managing the
Quality of
Process Outputs
by Using
Statistical
Quality Control
(SQC)*

they are part of learning the job. (Problem 14 on p. 582 requests the recalculation of the control chart minus subgroup samples number 1 and 2.)

As things stand, Buttonmakers' stated objective of 1.10 cm is not being met (exactly) by the process average of 1.106 cm (which rounds off to 1.11). Yet, all of the values of x (in Table 23-1) fall within the tolerance range of 1.10 ± 0.08. On the basis of these too few subgroup samples, the buttonmaking process appears to be quite stable. We shall need more observations but, at least, as far as the $\bar{x}$ chart is concerned, we are off to a good start. Shortly, we shall consider the R chart for variables.

If the character of the process changes because assignable causes enter the system, then this should become apparent when some values of $\bar{x}$ fall outside the control limits. Another characteristic of an unstable system is that a *run* of values all above or all below the process average may occur. (The longest run in Buttonmakers' startup, Fig. 23-8, is of length two.) Runs are usually symptomatic that a process is *trending* in a particular direction.

For comparison purposes, let us examine the probabilities with which certain control emergency signals will appear when the process is stable. First, the probability of a point's falling outside the 3-sigma limits is approximately $\frac{1}{370}$.[8] Second, the probability that nine points in a row will lie on one side of the process average is $\frac{1}{256}$. The probability that ten points in a row will fall on a particular side of the process average is $\frac{1}{512}$.[9]

For most manufacturing processes it is assumed that the output dimensions conform to the normal distribution. Tables 23-2 and 23-3 are based on the normal distribution. An important question arises then as to what happens when the population is not, in fact, normally distributed. Ideally, we would like the control system to operate in much the same way. That is, as long as the distribution of the output quality measure remains stable, no matter what shape it has, we would like to be able to use the SQC criterion to tell us that no change has occurred in the process. It is a delightful gift of nature that distributions of sample means will tend to be normal even though the population from which the samples are drawn is not normally distributed. Shewhart had shown that even though samples are drawn from rectangular, triangular, and other types of distributions, the distributions of the sample means tend to be normal. It is sufficiently true so that, in general, we need not concern ourselves with this problem.

Using the R Chart for Variables

The $\bar{x}$ chart monitors the process average. When measurements of variables are used, it is also possible to construct a chart to monitor the *process dispersion*. This chart is called an R chart. It is based on the range measures that had to be derived for the $\bar{x}$ chart.

---

[8] $27/10,000 = 1/370$
[9] See Problem 13, p. 582, for these calculations.

The reasoning involved in the development of the upper- and lower-control limits for the R chart closely parallels our previous discussion for the $\bar{x}$ chart. The appropriate equations for 3-sigma limits are:

$$\text{The upper control limit for } R = \text{UCL}_R = D_4\bar{R}$$

$$\text{The lower control limit for } R = \text{LCL}_R = D_3\bar{R}$$

Table 23-3 presents the respective D_3 and D_4 values that must be used for the determination of 3-sigma R-chart control limits (just as A_2 was required for the $\bar{x}$ chart). Utilizing the appropriate D_3 and D_4 coefficients obtained from Table 23-3, we construct the R chart for our example.

**TABLE 23-3 COEFFICIENTS FOR DETERMINING FROM $\bar{R}$
THE 3-SIGMA CONTROL LIMITS FOR R CHARTS
(COEFFICIENTS ARE BASED ON THE NORMAL DISTRIBUTION)**

Number of Observations in Subgroup n	Factors for R Chart	
	Lower Control Limit D_3	Upper Control Limit D_4
2	0	3.27
3	0	2.57
4	0	2.28
5	0	2.11
6	0	2.00
7	0.08	1.92
8	0.14	1.86
9	0.18	1.82
10	0.22	1.78
11	0.26	1.74
12	0.28	1.72
13	0.31	1.69
14	0.33	1.67
15	0.35	1.65
16	0.36	1.64
17	0.38	1.62
18	0.39	1.61
19	0.40	1.60
20	0.41	1.59

Texts on SQC present tables of coefficients for other than 3-sigma protection levels.

The construction of the R chart is straightforward, as was that of the $\bar{x}$ chart. For Buttonmakers' data:

$$\text{UCL}_R = D_4\bar{R} = 2.28(0.03) = 0.0684$$

$$\text{LCL}_R = D_3\bar{R} = 0(0.03) = 0$$

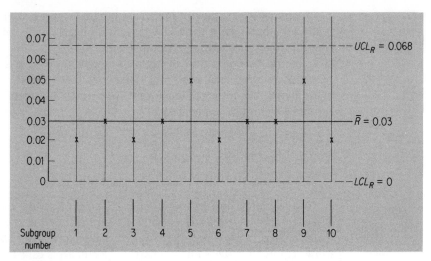

FIGURE 23-9. *R* control chart for the outside diameter (OD) of Buttonmakers' men's fancy pearl shirtsleeve button

Figure 23-9 presents the *R* chart for startup observations 1–10. The pattern is stable. There are no out-of-control subgroup observations, and no runs appear. *Diagnosing symptoms*, as read on the pair of $\bar{x}$ and *R* charts, we see that the process is stable, delivering the output quality that Buttonmakers desires, even though the process average (1.106 cm) does not exactly match the specifications (1.100 cm).

Symptoms and Diagnosis

The interpretation of the $\bar{x}$ and *R* charts is of crucial importance. If there is a shift in the process character, then it can be of the following types: (1) the process average may change; (2) the process dispersion may change; or (3) both of these changes may take place. If only the process average changes, this fact will probably be picked up by the $\bar{x}$ chart and not by the *R* chart. The situation might occur, for example, if a machine setting shifts permanently; that is, the change is of a *sustained* type. In certain cases, the process average will remain unchanged, but the dispersion of the process will shift. For example, an operator may be able to control output at the mean level, but he does this by working fast at certain times and slow at other times to compensate. Such performance should create a pattern of instability that is likely to be detected on the *R* chart and not on the $\bar{x}$ chart.

A variety of change combinations can occur when sporadic elements enter and leave the system in some unknown fashion. These sporadic assignable causes are more difficult to detect than the sustained types discussed above. Other kinds of changes can also occur, for example, a gradual shift in the mean. Tool wear could account for such *trend* shifts. Worker carelessness can produce *oscillatory* behavior in which both limits may be repeatedly violated. Runs will appear for a variety of reasons and can usually be associated with trend factors, such as tool or gauge wear.

It should be noted that the process is not always the guilty party. The inspectors and/or their tools might account for a signal of instability. To assist management, the entire relevant system must be identified so that useful process conclusions can be drawn.[10]

Using the *p*-Chart for Attributes—
Holiday Novelties, Inc.

We shall now consider a less elaborate control device, called the *p*-chart. The *p*-chart is less expensive to utilize than the $\bar{x}$ and R charts because only a *single* chart is used, and the required computations are less onerous than those required for the $\bar{x}$ and R charts. The *p*-chart is called the control chart for *fraction defectives*. It is based on sampling by attributes, which was previously described.

The key, as was the case for acceptance sampling, is the ability to define a defective. As might be suspected, the *p*-chart is less expensive to use than control charts for variables. However, it is not as sensitive as the combination of the $\bar{x}$ and the R chart. It is not as good a diagnostic tool, because it uses less information; even the $\bar{x}$ chart alone is a more powerful tool. However, the *p*-chart, with less sensitivity, will indicate the existence of assignable causes when they occur, and it does this at a lower cost than monitors based on variables.

If the measurement of quality as a variable is difficult, costly, or impossible, then the use of the attribute criterion for defectives is indicated. Consider, for example, the wine-tasting situation, where acceptable quality is based on judgment involving *multiple criteria* that are not even explicit.

The data must be collected in the same way as was previously explained for monitoring variables. That is to say, homogeneous subgroups are chosen, and a period of time is allowed to elapse between the subgroup observations. The same kind of reasoning applies to the determination of subgroup sizes and between sample intervals as was true for the $\bar{x}$ and R charts. The sequential character of the control chart is as much in evidence as it was before, and the preservation of the order of observation is as crucial. Let us consider an example of the use of a *p*-chart.

Holiday Novelties, Inc. has received an order to make 1800 sets of Christmas tree decorative lights. Management has decided to check the production

---

[10]One hundred percent inspection does not provide analytic assistance for the diagnosis of causes of change. The "zero-defects" programs, urged by many companies on their employees, should be interpreted in the light of control theory as being unobtainable goals set for psychological reasons rather than for strictly technological ones. Because the zero-defects goal is unobtainable, the eventual psychological effect may be worker frustration.

575

*Managing the
Quality of
Process Outputs
by Using
Statistical
Quality Control
(SQC)*

defect rate to see what the level is, and to determine if it is stable. A *p*-chart is to be used with 6 sample subgroups. The sizes of the subgroups can vary because of interference with other jobs which diverts or withholds required equipment and personnel. The SQC operator knows that one of the side benefits of the *p*-chart is the fact that sample size can vary without impairing the construction or use of the chart.

Thus, the data presented in Table 23-4 are collected.

TABLE 23-4 HOLIDAY NOVELTIES—CHRISTMAS TREE LIGHTS

Subgroup Sample	Number Inspected, n	Number Defective, d	Fraction Defective (d/n)
1	25	1	0.040
2	25	2	0.080
3	36	3	0.083
4	64	4	0.063
5	25	3	0.120
6	25	2	0.080
	200	15	

One hundred percent inspection of each subgroup is used for this test.

The number of observed defectives is recorded for each subgroup. The total number of inspected items is now divided *into* the total number of observed defectives. This gives the process average $\bar{p}$. For our example $\bar{p}$ is equal to 0.075.

$$\bar{p} = \tfrac{15}{200} = 0.075$$

To determine the control limits, we utilize the binomial description of the *standard error of the mean*; that is, to determine sigma (σ):

$$\sigma = \sqrt{\frac{\bar{p}(1-\bar{p})}{n}} = \sqrt{\frac{(0.075)(0.925)}{n}} = 0.263\sqrt{\frac{1}{n}}$$

This is a function of the subgroup sample size *n*. Because the upper- and lower-control limits are specified in terms of σ, the limits vary as a function of *n*:

For this example we have chosen 1σ limits, which means that 32 percent of the time a point can be expected to appear above or below the control limits, even though the process is stable. Because this out-of-control signal will occur often, in practice, the user might take one such event as a sign for alertness and two such events within a short interval as a signal that something is wrong.

TABLE 23-5 HOLIDAY NOVELTIES—CHRISTMAS TREE LIGHTS

| Subgroup Sample | Observations | | | Computations | | | Plot |
	Number Inspected, n	Number Defective	σ	UCL $\bar{p} + \sigma$	LCL $\bar{p} - \sigma$	Fraction Defective
1	25	1	0.053	0.128	0.022	0.040
2	25	2	0.053	0.128	0.022	0.080
3	36	3	0.044	0.119	0.031	0.083
4	64	4	0.033	0.108	0.042	0.063
5	25	3	0.053	0.128	0.022	0.120
6	25	2	0.053	0.128	0.022	0.080
	200	15				

The complete computations are shown in Table 23-5, and the results are plotted in Fig. 23-10. We note the variation in the spread between the control limits. When the subgroup size is constant, then the computations are even further simplified. Only 1 upper-and 1 lower-control limit need by drawn on the p-chart. The advantage of illustrating variable subgroup sizes is that, in practice, it is not always possible to draw samples of constant sizes.

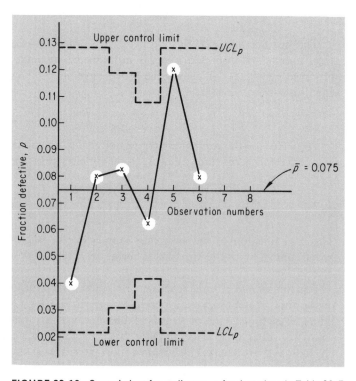

FIGURE 23-10. Control chart for attributes—p for data given in Table 23-5

Holiday Novelties appears to have a stable process. The fifth subgroup value approaches the upper limit, but the "alert" is called off when the sixth subgroup values approaches the mean. The defective rate of 7.5 in a hundred might be improved, and probably will be as the job is "learned."

It Is Economic to Use the p-Chart in Some Job Shops

The p-chart is not only less costly to use than the $\bar{x}$ and R charts; it is also constructed more rapidly. For these two reasons, it can be employed with smaller order sizes than the $\bar{x}$ and R charts. Still, it is not feasible to use the p-chart with the really small order sizes that characterize many job shops. Holiday Novelties' Christmas tree lights, with 1800 sets ordered, can check enough subgroups to make the effort worthwhile.

Design of Limits

Figure 23-11 illustrates a system in which a lack of control exists. We observe that a point has gone out of control. This usually is taken as a signal that something is awry and that corrective action should be taken. It is always possible, but improbable, that the "out" point occurred by chance. The run lends credence to the notion that a real change might be taking place and provides sufficient supporting evidence to the belief that our observation is not spurious.

For previous examples we chose 3σ and later 1σ limits.[11] *The choice of $k\sigma$*

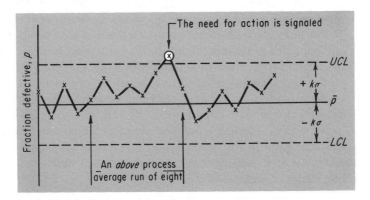

FIGURE 23-11. The control chart indicates that the system may be unstable.

---

[11]For Buttonmakers, 3-sigma limits; for Holiday Novelties, 1-sigma limits.

control limits, as to whether they are 1σ, 2σ, or 3σ, or some value in between, *is a management policy decision*. It is hard to defend a choice of one or another control limit, but the characteristics of the decision are such that *if the penalty is high* for not recognizing when the process is out of control, then it becomes more desirable to utilize *less than* 3σ limits. The distance between the limits decreases as the size of k decreases. This means that more events are likely to fall outside the control limits.

The choice of k is a matter of balancing costs. Pertinent costs include the expense that occurs when a signal is received upon which action will be taken. The system must be examined in an attempt to track down assignable causes, whether or not they exist in reality. An opposing cost is that of inaction when instability actually exists but is not recognized. Such a state of affairs can penalize the process heavily. With this guide in mind, the manager should choose those control-limit values that promise to balance the penalties.

Control-chart values must be regularly reviewed. This includes $\bar{x}$, $\bar{R}$, and $\bar{p}$ for the fraction defectives chart. Changes detected in averages can, in turn, affect the σ value that is computed and utilized. In all SQC methodology it is essential to *review* and *update* the system's parameters so that decisions can be based on "what is" and not on "what was." Particularly, after an assignable cause has been detected and removed from the system, it is necessary to readjust the control limits; sometimes another 25 subgroup observations are required before it is again possible to apply the control criterion.

Other Applications and Conclusions

Another control chart applicable for products and services is called the *c*-chart. This control chart can be applied to situations where it is desirable to record the frequency of occurrence of a *number of different types of defects* that are found for a particular item. For example, we can examine telescope lenses for different kinds of defects and flaws. Then, we might list the observed frequency of the different kinds of defects that occur in every inspected unit. When using the *c*-chart, it is most common to have a subgroup size of 1—although this is not a requirement. It *is* necessary, however, that the defects of different types occur at random with respect to each other. Otherwise the underlying assumptions of the *c*-chart will not be met.

New applications for SQC are being developed all of the time. It is even possible to employ variants of SQC with behavioral systems.[12] Worker productivity (including group performance) can be stabilized and monitored for stability with this methodology. We can readily appreciate why the *p*-chart has been used for monitoring observations obtained from work sampling methods; see pp. 462–66.

It is a requisite that basic processes should be demonstrated to be stable, and if not, made so, before full-scale production runs are undertaken. The

---

[12]See S. B. Littauer, "Technological Stability in Industrial Operations," *Transactions of the New York Academy of Sciences*, Series II, Vol. 13, No. 2, (Dec. 1950), pp. 67–72.

579

*Managing the
Quality of
Process Outputs
by Using
Statistical
Quality Control
(SQC)*

rate of output should be stabilized. Otherwise, the solutions to inventory formulations, line-balancing systems, and sequencing problems will be inapplicable. We must avoid applying solutions to a system that is shifting, and which no longer exists at the time of implementation.

The subject of statistical control is not one that can be taught in depth in a matter of minutes. It is essential that *experience* with the process and with the use of the charts be developed. Purely theoretical interpretations gloss over the kind of penetrating insights that an experienced practitioner can obtain from control charts.

SQC has been of enormous significance to the P/OM field, but its full potential has not yet been tapped. Reliability problems become increasingly important as equipment becomes more automated and the production system becomes more complex. Quality assurance for the consumer is the manager's obligation. The output, the process, and the inputs must be totally interlocked and matched. That is the objective toward which P/OM constantly strives.

APPENDIX 23-I
Statistical Quality Control Theory (Optional Material)

Standard Error of the Mean

The variance measure associated with each subgroup's sample size is represented by $\sigma_{\bar{x}_n}^2$, where n is the subgroup size. The standard deviation is simply the square root of this term, that is $\sigma_{\bar{x}_n}$. It is a well-known statistical relationship that

$$\sigma_{\bar{x}_n} = \frac{\sigma}{\sqrt{n}}$$

where σ is the standard deviation of the basic population from which the sample means are being drawn. The $\sigma_{\bar{x}_n}$'s are called the *standard error of the mean*. These standard deviations are measures of the variability of their respective subgroup distribution. That variability is directly affected by the particular sample size that is represented.

Figure 23-12 illustrates several distributions, each of which is based on a different sample subgroup size, and compares these *distributions of means* to the *population distribution*. The population distribution can be thought of as a distribution of sample means for which the subgroup size is one. In other words, if we set the subgroup size of n equal to 1, we obtain the relationship

$$\sigma_{\bar{x}_1} = \sigma$$

which is in accord with our definition.

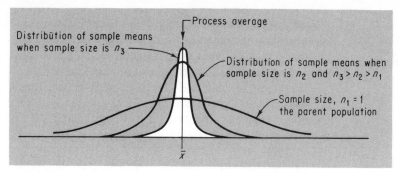

FIGURE 23-12. The standard deviation of sample means (measured from the process average) decreases in inverse proportion to the square root of the sample size.

The Range Measure

It is frequently more convenient to measure the *range* than to go through the calculation of the standard deviation. Tables have been prepared that give the relationship of the expected range to the population standard deviation for varying sample sizes assumed to be drawn from a normal universe.[13] This ratio factor is designated as d_2.

$$d_2 = \frac{\bar{R}}{\sigma}$$

Let us introduce this relationship into our previous equation for the standard error of the mean, and thereby derive

$$\sigma_{\bar{x}_n} = \frac{\bar{R}}{d_2\sqrt{n}}$$

It is usual to position control limits at some specified number of standard deviations away from the expected value of the process. We shall use 3σ control limits, which is the value most commonly selected for technological systems. Consequently, we can then write

$$3\sigma_{\bar{x}_n} = \frac{3\bar{R}}{d_2\sqrt{n}} = A_2\bar{R}$$

The A_2 factor is available in table form (see p. 569), where $A_2 = 3/d_2\sqrt{n}$. The upper-control limit and the lower-control limit, where the process average is $\bar{x}$, are given by

Upper-control limit for $\bar{x}$: $\mathrm{UCL}_{\bar{x}} = \bar{x} + A_2\bar{R}$
Lower-control limit for $\bar{x}$: $\mathrm{LCL}_{\bar{x}} = \bar{x} - A_2\bar{R}$

Thus,

$$A_2\bar{R} = \frac{3\bar{R}}{d_2\sqrt{n}} = \frac{3\bar{R}}{\dfrac{\bar{R}}{\sigma}\sqrt{n}} = \frac{3\sigma}{\sqrt{n}} = 3\sigma_{\bar{x}_n}.$$

---

[13]See the tables in Eugene L. Grant and Richard S. Leavenworth, *Statistical Quality Control*, 4th ed. (New York: McGraw-Hill Book Co., Inc., 1974), pp. 73 and 644.

Tolerance Limits and Control Limits

Figure 23-13 indicates the way in which output tolerance limits and statistical process control limits are related to each other. We have modified control limits so that they apply to the parent population. This modification was accomplished by means of the equation for the *standard error of the mean*. The tolerance limits do not require alteration, because they already apply to the parent population distribution.

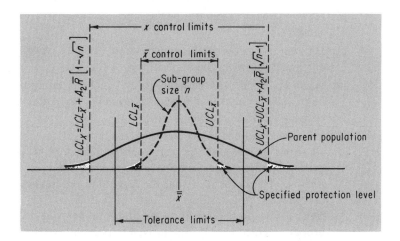

FIGURE 23-13. The relationship of tolerance limits and control limits. ($\bar{x}$ values can fall within tolerance limits, although x values will fall outside with greater frequency than the specified level of protection.) *Note:* tolerance limits are specified by engineers in line with product design; control limits characterize the particular production process that has been assigned to do the job. Management strives to achieve minimum costs in matching product requirements with process abilities.

PROBLEMS

1. A job shop that seldom produces in lot sizes greater than 20 units cannot employ the $\bar{x}$ and R charts of SQC. Why is this so? What can be done to enable it to use quality management?

2. A flow shop with a high-volume, serial production line makes cardboard boxes. An important quality is impact resistance, which requires destructive testing. Can SQC methods be used with destructive testing? What quality control method(s) do you recommend? Discuss.

3. How can the consumer tell that an organization employs statistical quality control? How can he or she tell if it does not?

4. What role does SQC play in life cycle management?

5. Differentiate between assignable and chance causes of variation. Give some examples of each kind of variation. How can you tell when an assignable cause of variation has arisen in a system?

6. What is a stable system? Why is the condition of stability so relevant to the activities of P/OM?

7. Why is the use of statistical quality control by drug and food manufacturers imperative? Would you recommend 2-sigma or 3-sigma control limits for food and drug applications of SQC?

8. How might SQC be used by the airlines to monitor on-time arrival and departure (service qualities highly valued by their customers)?

9. One of the major reasons that statistical quality control is such a powerful method is its use of sequenced inspection. Explain why this is so.

10. How should the subgroup size and the interval between samples be chosen?

11. Differentiate between the construction of the $\bar{x}$, R, and p-charts. Also distinguish between the applications of these charts.

12. What is meant by "between-group" and "within-group" variability? Explain how these two types of variability constitute the fundamental basis of statistical quality control.

13. It is sometimes possible to detect an unstable system when a *run* of values all above or below the process average occurs. What is the probability that a run of ten values, all above the process average, will occur?
Answer: The probability that the first value will be greater than the process average is $1/2$; that the first two values will be greater is $1/4$. In general, the probability that the first n values will be *greater* than the process average is $1/2^n$. Similarly, the probability that the first n values will be *less* than the process average is $1/2^n$. Consequently, the probability that the first n values will be *either* greater than or less than the process average is $1/2^n + 1/2^n = 2(1/2^n) = 1/2^{n-1}$. (See p. 571). The numerical answer to the above question is $1/2^{10} = 1/1024$.

14. Consultant's note to the quality control engineer: Request recalculation of the $\bar{x}$ chart for Buttonmakers's men's fancy pearl shirtsleeve button on p. 570. Remove subgroup sample data for points 1 and 2. Please furnish comments on results and further recommendations.

15. Can quality control exist without feedback? How about quantity control? Explain your answer.

16. A shampoo manufacturer specifies that the contents of a bottle of shampoo should weight 6 ± 0.10 ounces net. A statistical quality control operation is established and the following data are obtained:

Sample Number				
1	6.06	6.20	6.04	6.10
2	6.10	5.95	5.98	6.05
3	6.03	5.90	5.95	6.00
4	6.03	6.05	6.10	5.94
5	6.12	6.40	6.20	6.00

583

Managing the
Quality of
Process Outputs
by Using
Statistical
Quality Control
(SQC)

a. Construct an $\bar{x}$ chart based on these five samples.

b. Construct an R chart based on these five samples.

c. What points, if any, have gone out of control?

d. Comment on your results and briefly discuss the role of *SQC* in production and operations management. Include such factors as management's choice of tolerance limits, subgroup size, and sample size.

Answer: Utilizing the discussion of pp. 563–64, we first determine the sample means and ranges as follows:

Sample No.	Mean, $\bar{x}$	Range, R
1	6.10	0.16
2	6.02	0.15
3	5.97	0.13
4	6.03	0.16
5	6.18	0.40

$$\bar{x} = 6.06 \qquad \bar{R} = 0.20$$

a. The $\bar{x}$ chart is constructed from the equations

$$\text{UCL}_{\bar{x}} = \bar{x} + A_2\bar{R}$$

$$\text{LCL}_{\bar{x}} = \bar{x} - A_2\bar{R}$$

where for a sample subgroup size of 4, $A_2 = 0.73$ (Table 23-2, p. 569). Thus:

$$\text{UCL}_{\bar{x}} = 6.06 + (0.73)(0.20) = 6.206$$

$$\text{LCL}_{\bar{x}} = 6.06 - (0.73)(0.20) = 5.914$$

The appropriate control chart is shown in Fig. 23-14.

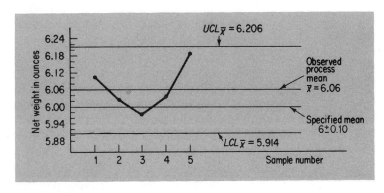

FIGURE 23-14.

b. For the R chart: $UCL_R = D_4 \bar{R}$ and $LCL_R = D_3 \bar{R}$, from Table 23-3, p. 572, for $n = 4$,

$$UCL_R = (2.28)(0.20) = 0.456$$
$$LCL_R = (0.0)(0.20) = 0.000$$

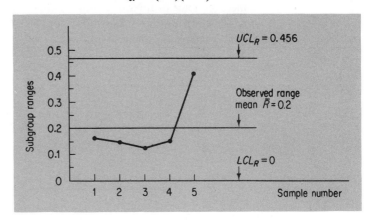

FIGURE 23-15.

c. No points have fallen outside of the control limits for either the $\bar{x}$ or R charts, so we can assume that the process is a stable one. (Of course, the sample is of absurdly small size.)

d. Statistical quality control is a vitally important mathematical tool capable of monitoring the output of a production process. It is able to provide the operations manager with reliable observations concerning the stability of the production process. In this way it performs a control function, because it keeps management aware of changes in the system's pattern.

In this example management has requested tolerance limits of ± 0.10 oz. These obviously cannot be satisfied even though the specified mean value of 6.00 is satisfactorily close to the observed process average of 6.06. Of the twenty individual values that are shown, none of them is less than the lower tolerance limit specification—but four, or 20 percent, are above the upper tolerance limit specification. We note that the process gives no sign of being out of control. It is not, however, able to deliver the goods with respect to tolerance limits. The stability of a system is a separate issue from its technological characteristics. In this case, the production system has not been (or cannot be) designed to meet engineering requirements.

The subgroup size of four may be unsatisfactory based on the fact that an unreasonable degree of variability is evident within each subgroup. The fact that there is variability between the averages of the subgroups would lead us to believe that adequate spacing has been provided between subgroups. We know, however, that, since

585

*Managing the
Quality of
Process Outputs
by Using
Statistical
Quality Control
(SQC)*

such variability exists, the sample size of five subgroups is far too small to base any real conclusions on it. Our objective has been to provide insight into issues such as those discussed above and to illuminate the importance of SQC as a fundamental operations management technique.

17. A food processor specified that the contents of a jar of jam should weigh 14 ± 0.10 ounces net. A statistical quality control operation is set up and the following data are obtained:

Sample Number				
1	14.02	14.04	14.08	14.06
2	14.10	14.24	14.00	14.90
3	14.80	14.75	14.70	14.51
4	14.59	14.90	14.01	14.02
5	14.96	14.26	14.81	14.17
6	14.40	14.83	14.68	14.93
7	14.86	14.32	14.90	14.04
8	14.56	14.96	14.69	14.63
9	14.85	14.71	14.05	14.91
10	14.75	14.19	14.05	14.09

a. Construct an $\bar{x}$ chart based on these 10 samples.
b. Construct an R chart based on these 10 samples.
c. What points, if any, have gone out of control?
d. What reasons could be given for the appearance of an assignable cause at some time in the future?
e. What can be surmised from the shapes of the curves on these charts?

SUMMARY OF PART 9

Chapters 22 and 23 treat the production-oriented view of quality as compared to the marketing-oriented view. In this context, a close approximation to the operations point of view is that quality is *consistency*.

Chapter 22

Quality dimensions must be explicitly defined and standards must be set, so that output qualities can be compared with expectations. Chapter 22 begins with a careful discussion of what we mean by quality, as a forerunner to our discussions about quality control.

The dimensions of quality, both of the functional and nonfunctional types, are described. The latter are particularly difficult to measure. Both kinds apply to product and service systems. The trade-offs of cost and quality are explored. It is shown that there is a level of quality that will maximize profits.

Chapter 22 treats the quality of inputs to the production process. (In Chapter 23, the quality of outputs from the production process is examined.) The costs of defective inputs are explained. Then the reason that 100 percent inspection is seldom used leads to an understanding of why acceptance sampling is superior. Sampling inspection terminology is introduced, including the lot size, the sample size, and the acceptance number. Proportional sampling is shown to be incorrect, an example of a market research survey contemplated by Farmers' Bank being used.

OC curves are explained in terms of the negotiation between the producer and the consumer to fix their respective levels of risk. The producer risks having output of an acceptable quality level rejected by the sampling plan. The consumer risks accepting output of an unacceptable quality level. The risk levels are determined by the design of a sampling plan (including detailing, which is 100 percent inspection of all rejected lots). A plan can be designed to minimize inspection costs.

Hypergeometric OC curves are constructed. These are used where the lot size is small. When the lot size is big enough, then it can be treated as though it were infinite and the binomial (or the Poisson approximation to the binomial) formulation can be used to derive OC curves. Appendix 22-I presents (as optional material) the full methodology for obtaining OC curves by using the hypergeometric distribution. Appendix 22-II (also optional material) does the same for the binomial and Poisson distributions.

The average outgoing quality limit (AOQL) is explained with numerical examples. Multiple sampling is examined, with an example of the way in which City Waste Disposal investigates the application of a double sampling plan.

Chapter 23

This chapter is concerned with output quality. The background for understanding statistical quality control (SQC) is developed. This requires a monitor of the output quality, an information feedback system, and a control system to take corrective action when necessary. Assignable causes of variation are distinguished from chance causes of variation. Only the former are fed back by the monitor for corrective control action.

The control chart is described and related to inspection standards. It is explained why sequenced inspection is the key to SQC. Then, using the problem of Buttonmakers Corporation, all necessary SQC calculations are demonstrated for the construction of the $\bar{x}$ (sample means) and R (range) charts. These are both control charts for *variables* (compared with the *p*-chart for *attributes*). We discuss how the sample is chosen. That is how many observations are taken at a time and what interval is allowed to elapse between samples.

587

*Managing the
Quality of
Process Outputs
by Using
Statistical
Quality Control
(SQC)*

It is pointed out that SQC is most applicable to the flow shop and not applicable to small orders processed by the job shop. Acceptance sampling can be used by job shops to control output quality, and in some cases, the *p*-chart can be applied. Startup of SQC in the flow shop is discussed. Diagnosis of symptoms found on SQC charts is offered. The *p*-chart for attributes (i.e., accepted or rejected) is constructed for Holiday Novelties. A discussion of how to set the limits on control charts follows. Then a range of possible applications of SQC is presented, completing the chapter. The theory behind SQC is offered as optional material in Appendix 23-I.

REFERENCES
PART 9

ARMSTRONG, W. H., *Mechanical Inspection.* New York: McGraw-Hill Book Co., Inc., 1953.

CROWDEN, D. J., *Statistical Methods in Quality Control.* Englewood Cliffs, N.J.: Prentice-Hall, Inc., 1957.

DODGE, HAROLD F. and HARRY G. ROMIG, *Sampling Inspection Tables*, 2nd ed. New York: John Wiley & Sons, Inc., 1944.

DUNCAN, A. J., *Quality Control and Industrial Statistics*, 3rd ed. Homewood, Ill.: Richard D. Irwin, Inc., 1965.

FEIGENBAUM, A. V., *Total Quality Control.* New York: McGraw-Hill Book Co. Inc., 1961.

FETTER, ROBERT B., *The Quality Control System.* Homewood, Ill.: Richard D. Irwin, 1967.

FREEMAN, H. O., M. FRIEDMAN, F. MOSTELLER, and W. ALLEN WALLIS (eds.), *Sampling Inspection.* New York: McGraw-Hill Book Co., Inc. 1948.

GRANT, E. L. and R. S. LEAVENWORTH, *Statistical Quality Control*, 4th ed. New York: McGraw-Hill Book Co., Inc., 1974.

HANSEN, B. L., *Quality Control: Theory & Applications.* Englewood Cliffs, N.J.: Prentice-Hall, Inc., 1963.

JURAN, JOSEPH M., *Quality Control Handbook*, 2nd ed. New York: McGraw-Hill Book Co., 1967.

KIRKPATRICK, ELWOOD G., *Quality Control for Managers and Engineers.* New York: John Wiley & Sons, Inc., 1970.

LANDERS, RICHARD R., *Reliability and Product Assurance.* Englewood Cliffs, N.J.: Prentice-Hall, Inc., 1963.

SHEWHART, WALTER A., *Economic Control of Quality of Manufactured Product.* Princeton, N.J.: D. Van Nostrand Co., Inc., 1931.

TOMPSON, JAMES E., *Inspection, Organization, and Methods.* New York: McGraw-Hill Book Co., Inc., 1950.

in conclusion

twenty-four
history and prospects of P/OM

In this chapter, we shall trace briefly:

The development of production technology
The development of P/OM
The prospects of P/OM

Development of Production Technology

Begin with the Renaissance period (fourteenth–sixteenth centuries), when a rebirth of vitality occurred in Europe that swept away the dark ages and fostered great accomplishments in the arts and sciences. Production activities centered around artisans, apprentices, and the craft guilds which were primarily organizations designed to protect and foster the interests of the artisans. By the seventeenth century, the effects of the European Renaissance were noticeably present in England.

The first signs of industrial *evolution* appeared in medieval Italy. It was hardly a revolution, but signs of industry began to appear. Industry can be said to exist when factories and plants are developed. The individual no longer owns the specific fruits of his labors. He is employed and receives a wage for his time or output.

The rudiments of industrial activity then spread northward to Augsburg, Lyons, Bruges, Antwerp, Amsterdam, and west to England during the sixteenth and seventeenth centuries. By the beginning of the nineteenth century, with the utilization of steam-driven machines, the *evolution* of industrialization in England became so rapid and dramatic that it could be described as an *industrial revolution*. Why did this occur in England? A complex of factors can help to explain why, including the presence of coal, a growing population with high unemployment, a limited agricultural output, the existence of investment capital, growth of trade with colonies, interest and belief in scientific methods, and the earlier acquisition of skilled refugees from the Inquisition.

Technological invention was the keystone. Hand labor in every field began to be replaced by machinery. The effects of this industrial revolution trickled to the North American continent as the years went by. But a variety of factors impeded the growth of American industry. These included a fundamental dependency on agriculture and English hostility toward the industrialization of its colony. In 1798, however, American industry received an enormous impetus. Eli Whitney developed and engineered the notion of interchangeable parts for the manufacture of guns. Within a short time, sewing machines, clocks, and other products were utilizing these same principles. There was no shortage of American inventiveness, and industry began to prosper. In the early 1900s, Henry Ford introduced the moving assembly line. Based on the high-level realization of Whitney's principle of *interchangeability*, Ford succeeded in achieving almost total *synchronization* of the production process flows.

By means of these two principles (interchangeability and synchronization) industrial empires emerged. Then, in the 1950s, electronic computing became available; by 1977 it had become highly cost effective for managing much of the information required to run the organization. Computers provided management with a third principle, namely, that of systems *controllability*. Further, the improvement of computers permitted the resolution of many problems by using methods that would otherwise have been untenable because of the computational burden involved.

Development of P/OM

To this point we have presented in capsule form the technological changes that brought the *production* field into being.[1] Now let us consider the growth

---

[1]See References, Part 10 (pp. 597–598), for a list of books that deal at length with the history of technology.

in understanding the *management* problems of production systems. Less than 100 years after Eli Whitney had obtained a United States government contract for "ten thousand stand of arms," Frederick Winslow Taylor[2] began a concerted attack on existent production management practices. He and his associates developed principles and practices that ultimately revolutionized the field of production and operations management. His work was essentially *analytic* and stressed the development of standards and improved efficiency.

Taylor's initial studies related to the cutting of metals. Many thousands of experiments were undertaken, and the results were recorded and analyzed. In order to carry out these experiments, Taylor and his group had to identify the *relevant variables* in the metal-cutting process. Thus, Taylor laid the groundwork for an era of operations-oriented analyses. (However, it was not until the 1950s that the term *operations management* appeared, and then it was in response to the need to find a name to describe the *application* of operations research to production problems.) In line with this thinking, operations that included an operator could be studied. The operator was thought of as an extension of the machine. Thus, Taylor found that the repetitive task of moving iron castings from one place to another could be achieved at a lower cost by improving the way in which the job was done and by giving the operator an incentive for increasing his output.

The time was ripe to be concerned about operations, operators, and their organization. In France, Henri Fayol was attempting to develop theories of management. In the United States, at about the same time, Henry Towne, Harrington Emerson, George Shepard, and others were similarly tussling with new concepts for managing. The emphasis was on the role and utilization of manpower in the enterprise. Taylor concentrated on the analysis of operations and operators. He labeled his efforts *scientific management*.

Henry L. Gantt[3] was an associate of Frederick Taylor. Gantt also was concerned with operators and operations in a basically analytic sense, but he added a new dimension. Gantt recognized the fact that a process was a combination of operations. He developed methods for sequencing operations which are still in use (the Gantt load chart and the Gantt layout chart).

A large group of operation specialists developed. Foremost among these was the team of Frank and Lillian Gilbreth. Working together, they categorized operations in a way that permitted these categories to be independent of the specific job. For example, *search*, *grasp*, *release*, and so on, were work components that could be put together in different ways to create different operations. In order to study each job and break it into its proper components, the Gilbreths began using motion picture records. They thereby advanced the cause of reliability and validity in the measurement of work. Later use of predetermined or synthetic time standards was based on these earlier efforts.

Lillian Gilbreth was a psychologist. Her training mitigated against a purely

---

[2] 1865–1915.
[3] 1861–1919.

mechanical view of the operator-machine team. In her work we find the seeds for the growing recognition of the importance of behavioral factors.

Eventually, operation specialists were called methods engineers—and more affectionately by the popular press—efficiency experts. The application of exclusively operation-oriented analysis continued unabated for many years, but gradually the emphasis shifted to the concept of a process that was composed of operations. Then, at both the operations and process levels of analysis, several new dimensions were added. First came the realization that risk and uncertainty exist and that they should play a part in production planning. It behooved engineers and production department managers to accept this change and to apply it to their own situations.[4]

Undoubtedly the greatest impact on P/OM resulted from Walter Shewhart's invention in the 1920s of statistical quality control (SQC). At last, the economic implications of Whitney's contribution for the interchangeability of parts was resolvable. Tolerances and specifications required technological capabilities that could be analyzed in cost and profit terms. More than this, Shewhart's work demanded application of the *system's principle*. It was not immediately recognized that *the operation in isolation* had been transcended. However, with the passing of time it became quite evident that product design, materials, equipment, labor skills, employee attitudes, work flow, and environmental factors interacted with consumer requirements of quality and price, and with financial considerations pertaining to the allocation of resources. Other statistical developments that affected P/OM included the use of sampling plans for inspecting materials, work sampling, and much later, queueing theory, inventory theory, and other operations research (OR) techniques.

Second, and also in the period of the 1920s and 1930s, psychological factors were understood to be a lot more complex than had been thought to be the case. F. J. Roethlisberger, reporting on the Hawthorne studies,[5] tells how the productivity of workers increased, whether desirable or undesirable changes were made in their working environment (in this case the illumination of the work area). The result of the study, it was hypothesized, could be traced to the fact that the morale of workers increases when attention is paid to them. As morale increases, so does productivity. The original corps of scientific management people believed that they could intuit the responses of workers without having to study these behaviors. The field of industrial relations has grown to be an accepted contradiction to this idea. The strength of the labor movement helped to convince management that it did not live in an egocentric world where the premise that "papa knows best" could be consistently applied. Therefore, not only were employees recognized to be as

---

[4]For an interesting discussion of this history, see H. F. Smiddy and L. Naum, Evaluation of a "Science of Managing" in America, *Management Science*, Vol. I, No. I, October, 1954, pp. 1–31.

[5]The studies were sponsored by Harvard University and began in 1924 at the Hawthorne Works of the Western Electric Company, in Chicago.

complex as employers, they were also recognized as being people. Much P/OM history and present-day effort is still involved with these developments.

We now speak about man-machine systems wherein the behaviors of people must be integrated with the attributes of machines in some "best possible" way. The recognition of the individual's psychological and physiological make-up is of paramount importance when mechanization and computer augmented systems are involved. Furthermore, the consumer is also recognized as a complex being to whom a product must be fitted in many different ways. The employee's relationship to equipment and work place environment is also vital. Therefore, the field of human factors analysis continues to receive much attention.

A third new force resulted from the growth in interest and knowledge of the field of economics. Governmental planning during the depression years triggered deep involvement with fundamental questions concerning the role of the government in welfare planning, and the responsibilities of the industrial community in this regard. Economic analysis formed the base for the planning function. An important achievement in economic analysis occurred in the 1930s when Walter Rautenstrauch,[6] an industrial engineer and professor at Columbia University, *invented* the planning device known as a break-even chart. It was one of the first tools for economic analysis that became available to production and operations managers. It permitted and, in fact, encouraged an integration or synthesis of the planning function.

Modifications of the break-even chart that introduce risk occurred as a result of interest in decision theory which underlay the development of operations research (OR) and management science (MS). Operations research was an offspring of the Second World War. Prior to 1940 the name OR did not exist.[7] The approach began in Britain, where it is still called operational research. Scientists from many fields were recruited by the United States and British governments to assist in the resolution of complex problems of logistics[8] and military strategy. These scientists were successful in spite of the fact that they had little training in military systems. The reason is that they were methodologists—willing and able to borrow knowledge and method from any and every field of scientific endeavor. Where no useful analogs existed, new ones were developed.

In the early 1950s, industrial interest in nonmilitary applications of OR led to the formation of The Institute of Management Sciences (TIMS). The field of management science, in turn, supported the development of P/OM, where the accent is not on research but squarely on the practical application

---

[6]W. Rautenstrauch and R. Villers, *The Economics of Industrial Management* (New York: Funk & Wagnalls Co., 1949).

[7]We can better understand the name "operations research" when we consider Operation Alpine Violets (the code name for the German plan to send reinforcements to Albania), or Operation Dynamo (the code name for the plan of the British Admiralty to evacuate Dunkirk).

[8]Problems concerned with transporting, sheltering, and supplying troops.

of decision-making techniques to the operational requirements of the production department.

Prospects of P/OM

At first, the production departments that employed the P/OM approaches were those of manufacturers, with standard (old-style textbook) types of problems. But this began to change as methods were modified and expanded. The modifications in methods enabled the production and operations managers to apply their models in new ways to many different kinds of problems (e.g., nonmanufacturing, service-oriented, public sector problems) leading to the need for this new-style textbook.

The prospects are good that P/OM methods will spread broadly to all kinds of work systems, as there is increased understanding that production activities are required and used by every organization, as the means by which it achieves its objectives. Thus, bankers are rapidly accepting the concept that banking is a production system, where the inputs and outputs are information. The P/OM methodology is totally applicable and is being rapidly absorbed by the banking community as the money society moves to credit cards and eventually to the checkless society. The fast food service industry has adopted P/OM techniques without which it could not exist. Transportation, communication, public health, agriculture, and many other socially productive endeavors have been giving up their traditional ways of doing "the job" and have hired people with P/OM skills, who can organize the work flows to be as efficient as present knowledge allows.

The prospects are good that production and operations managers will radically improve productivity worldwide. The capabilities of P/OM will be extended to developing countries whose productivities are exceptionally low. The basic principle is to adopt the flow shop configuration wherever possible. Developing countries, lacking managerial skills, can gain great advantages by specializing and thereby concentrating the use of their management talent. The flow shop has many decisions already built into it by predesign, further relieving the need for management skills. The sum effect of many poorly run jobs is low productivity. If the same level of investment funds were channeled into a few flow shops, productivity would be high, yielding the potential for successful world trade.

The prospects are good that P/OM methods will correct the poor productivity record of service systems. Increasingly, the flow shop configuration will be adopted. Where the job shop remains a necessity, it will be made an efficient job shop. Applying to the production of both goods and services, computer-controlled equipment often will be able to deliver job shop variety with flow shop economy.

The prospects are good that most public systems will be managed by P/OM methods, thereby improving the public sector's productivity and decreasing the waste of resources. Large amounts of the public's funds are expended on public works. Such projects will be better managed, P/OM techniques being used that focus on the achievement of satisfactory trade-offs between cost and time. Hospitals, schools, police and fire departments, waste disposal and water management systems, the post office, etc., all have inventories to manage, quality to control, work to schedule, output to deliver, facilities to lay out, workers to pay, and break-even points to determine.

The prospects are good that most industries will be managed by P/OM methods and that flow shop configurations will predominate because of their competitive advantage. Thus, the productivity of the private sector will increase, allowing marked reductions in the costs of goods and services to consumers.

REFERENCES
PART 10

ARNOLD, HORACE LUCIEN and FAY LEONE FAUROTE, *Ford Methods and the Ford Shops.* New York: The Engineering Magazine Company, 1915.

BARNARD, CHESTER I., *The Functions of the Executive.* Cambridge, Mass.: Harvard University Press, 1938.

BEARD, MIRIAM, *A History of Business.* Ann Arbor: The University of Michigan Press, Vol. 1, 1962, Vol. 11, 1963.

BURLINGAME, ROGER, *March of the Iron Men.* New York: Grosset & Dunlap, Inc., 1938.

CROMBIE, A. C., *Scientific Change.* New York: Basic Books, Inc., 1963.

DRUCKER, PETER F., *The Practice of Management.* New York: Harper & Row, Publishers, 1954.

———, *The Age of Discontinuity.* New York: Harper & Row, Publishers, 1969.

HERTZ, DAVID B., *New Power for Management.* New York: McGraw-Hill Book Co., Inc., 1969.

MUMFORD, LEWIS, *Technics and Civilization.* New York: Harcourt, Brace & World, Inc., 1934.

———, *The Myth of the Machine.* New York: Harcourt Brace Jovanovich, Inc., 1970.

NEWMAN, WILLIAM H: *Administrative Action.* Englewood Cliffs, N.J.: Prentice-Hall. Inc., 1950.

———, and CHARLES E. SUMMER, *The Process of Management.* Englewood Cliffs, N.J.: Prentice-Hall, Inc., 1961.

PARKINSON, C. NORTHCOTE, *Parkinson's Law.* Boston: Houghton Mifflin Company, 1957.

SARTON, GEORGE, *A History of Science.* Cambridge, Mass.: Harvard University Press, 1959.

SINGER, CHARLES, E. J. HOLMYARD, and A. R. HALL (eds.), *A History of Technology*, 5 Vols. London: Oxford University Press, 1954–58.

SIU, R. G. H., *The Tao of Science.* New York: John Wiley & Sons, Inc., 1957.

STARR, MARTIN K., *Management: A Modern Approach*, New York: Harcourt Brace Jovanovich, Inc., 1971 and Life Office Management Association, 1975.

———, "Productivity Is the USA's Problem," *California Management Review,* Vol. XVI, No. 2, Winter 1973, pp. 32–36.

STRASSMAN, W. PAUL, *Risk and Technological Innovation.* Ithaca, New York: Cornell University Press, 1959.

USHER, A. P., *A History of Mechanical Inventions.* Boston: Beacon Press, Inc., 1959.

WALKER, CHARLES R., *Modern Technology and Civilization.* New York: McGraw-Hill Book Co., Inc., 1962.

WHYTE, WILLIAM H., JR., *The Organization Man.* New York: Simon and Schuster, Inc., 1956.

WILSON, MITCHELL, *American Science and Invention.* New York: Bonanza Books, 1960.

WOLF, A., *A History of Science, Technology, and Philosophy in the 16th and 17th Centuries,* Vols. 1 and II. New York: Harper & Row, Publishers, 1951.

———, *A History of Science, Technology, and Philosophy in the 18th Century,* Vols. I and II. New York: Harper & Row, Publishers, 1961.

appendixes

APPENDIX A   TABLE OF THE NORMAL DISTRIBUTION

AREAS UNDER THE NORMAL CURVE FROM K_α TO ∞

$$\alpha = \int_{K_\alpha}^{\infty} \frac{1}{\sqrt{2\pi}} e^{-x^2/2} dx$$

Area = α

K_α

K_α	0.00	0.01	0.02	0.03	0.04	0.05	0.06	0.07	0.08	0.09
0.0	0.5000	0.4960	0.4920	0.4880	0.4840	0.4801	0.4761	0.4721	0.4681	0.4641
0.1	0.4602	0.4562	0.4522	0.4483	0.4443	0.4404	0.4364	0.4325	0.4286	0.4247
0.2	0.4207	0.4168	0.4129	0.4090	0.4052	0.4013	0.3974	0.3936	0.3897	0.3859
0.3	0.3821	0.3783	0.3745	0.3707	0.3669	0.3632	0.3594	0.3557	0.3520	0.3483
0.4	0.3446	0.3409	0.3372	0.3336	0.3300	0.3264	0.3228	0.3192	0.3156	0.3121
0.5	0.3085	0.3050	0.3015	0.2981	0.2946	0.2912	0.2877	0.2843	0.2810	0.2776
0.6	0.2743	0.2709	0.2676	0.2643	0.2611	0.2578	0.2546	0.2514	0.2483	0.2451
0.7	0.2420	0.2389	0.2358	0.2327	0.2296	0.2266	0.2236	0.2206	0.2177	0.2148
0.8	0.2119	0.2090	0.2061	0.2033	0.2005	0.1977	0.1949	0.1922	0.1894	0.1867
0.9	0.1841	0.1814	0.1788	0.1762	0.1736	0.1711	0.1685	0.1660	0.1635	0.1611
1.0	0.1587	0.1562	0.1539	0.1515	0.1492	0.1469	0.1446	0.1423	0.1401	0.1379
1.1	0.1357	0.1335	0.1314	0.1292	0.1271	0.1251	0.1230	0.1210	0.1190	0.1170
1.2	0.1151	0.1131	0.1112	0.1093	0.1075	0.1056	0.1038	0.1020	0.1003	0.0985
1.3	0.0968	0.0951	0.0934	0.0918	0.0901	0.0885	0.0869	0.0853	0.0838	0.0823
1.4	0.0808	0.0793	0.0778	0.0764	0.0749	0.0735	0.0721	0.0708	0.0694	0.0681
1.5	0.0668	0.0655	0.0643	0.0630	0.0618	0.0606	0.0594	0.0582	0.0571	0.0559
1.6	0.0548	0.0537	0.0526	0.0516	0.0505	0.0495	0.0485	0.0475	0.0465	0.0455
1.7	0.0446	0.0436	0.0427	0.0418	0.0409	0.0401	0.0392	0.0384	0.0375	0.0367
1.8	0.0359	0.0351	0.0344	0.0336	0.0329	0.0322	0.0314	0.0307	0.0301	0.0294
1.9	0.0287	0.0281	0.0274	0.0268	0.0262	0.0256	0.0250	0.0244	0.0239	0.0233
2.0	0.0228	0.0222	0.0217	0.0212	0.0207	0.0202	0.0197	0.0192	0.0188	0.0183
2.1	0.0179	0.0174	0.0170	0.0166	0.0162	0.0158	0.0154	0.0150	0.0146	0.0143
2.2	0.0139	0.0136	0.0132	0.0129	0.0125	0.0122	0.0119	0.0116	0.0113	0.0110
2.3	0.0107	0.0104	0.0102	0.00990	0.00964	0.00939	0.00914	0.00889	0.00866	0.00842
2.4	0.00820	0.00798	0.00776	0.00755	0.00734	0.00714	0.00695	0.00676	0.00657	0.00639
2.5	0.00621	0.00604	0.00587	0.00570	0.00554	0.00539	0.00523	0.00508	0.00494	0.00480
2.6	0.00466	0.00453	0.00440	0.00427	0.00415	0.00402	0.00391	0.00379	0.00368	0.00357
2.7	0.00347	0.00336	0.00326	0.00317	0.00307	0.00298	0.00289	0.00280	0.00272	0.00264
2.8	0.00256	0.00248	0.00240	0.00233	0.00226	0.00219	0.00212	0.00205	0.00199	0.00193
2.9	0.00187	0.00181	0.00175	0.00169	0.00164	0.00159	0.00154	0.00149	0.00144	0.00139

K_α	0.0	0.1	0.2	0.3	0.4	0.5	0.6	0.7	0.8	0.9
3	0.00135	0.0^3968	0.0^3687	0.0^3483	0.0^3337	0.0^3233	0.0^3159	0.0^3108	0.0^4723	0.0^4481
4	0.0^4317	0.0^4207	0.0^4133	0.0^5854	0.0^5541	0.0^5340	0.0^5211	0.0^5130	0.0^6793	0.0^6479
5	0.0^6287	0.0^6170	0.0^7996	0.0^7579	0.0^7333	0.0^7190	0.0^7107	0.0^8599	0.0^8332	0.0^8182
6	0.0^9987	0.0^9530	0.0^9282	0.0_9149	$0.0^{10}777$	$0.0^{10}402$	$0.0^{10}206$	$0.0^{10}104$	$0.0^{11}523$	$0.0^{11}260$

N	0	1	2	3	4	5	6	7	8	9
10	0000	0043	0086	0128	0170	0212	0253	0294	0334	0374
11	0414	0453	0492	0531	0569	0607	0645	0682	0719	0755
12	0792	0828	0864	0899	0934	0969	1004	1038	1072	1106
13	1139	1173	1206	1239	1271	1303	1335	1367	1399	1430
14	1461	1492	1523	1553	1584	1614	1644	1673	1703	1732
15	1761	1790	1818	1847	1875	1903	1931	1959	1987	2014
16	2041	2068	2095	2122	2148	2175	2201	2227	2253	2279
17	2304	2330	2355	2380	2405	2430	2455	2480	2504	2529
18	2553	2577	2601	2625	2648	2672	2695	2718	2742	2765
19	2788	2810	2833	2856	2878	2900	2923	2945	2967	2989
20	3010	3032	3054	3075	3096	3118	3139	3160	3181	3201
21	3222	3243	3263	3284	3304	3324	3345	3365	3385	3404
22	3424	3444	3464	3483	3502	3522	3541	3560	3579	3598
23	3617	3636	3655	3674	3692	3711	3729	3747	3766	3784
24	3802	3820	3838	3856	3874	3892	3909	3927	3945	3962
25	3979	3997	4014	4031	4048	4065	4082	4099	4116	4133
26	4150	4166	4183	4200	4216	4232	4249	4265	4281	4298
27	4314	4330	4346	4362	4378	4393	4409	4425	4440	4456
28	4472	4487	4502	4518	4533	4548	4564	4579	4594	4609
29	4624	4639	4654	4669	4683	4698	4713	4728	4742	4757
30	4771	4786	4800	4814	4829	4843	4857	4871	4886	4900
31	4914	4928	4942	4955	4969	4983	4997	5011	5024	5038
32	5051	5065	5079	5092	5105	5119	5132	5145	5159	5172
33	5185	5198	5211	5224	5237	5250	5263	5276	5289	5302
34	5315	5328	5340	5353	5366	5378	5391	5403	5416	5428
35	5441	5453	5465	5478	5490	5502	5514	5527	5539	5551
36	5563	5575	5587	5599	5611	5623	5635	5647	5658	5670
37	5682	5694	5705	5717	5729	5740	5752	5763	5775	5786
38	5798	5809	5821	5832	5843	5855	5866	5877	5888	5899
39	5911	5922	5933	5944	5955	5966	5977	5988	5999	6010
40	6021	6031	6042	6053	6064	6075	6085	6096	6107	6117
41	6128	6138	6149	6160	6170	6180	6191	6201	6212	6222
42	6232	6243	6253	6263	6274	6284	6294	6304	6314	6325
43	6335	6345	6355	6365	6375	6385	6395	6405	6415	6425
44	6435	6444	6454	6464	6474	6484	6493	6503	6513	6522
45	6532	6542	6551	6561	6571	6580	6590	6599	6609	6618
46	6628	6637	6646	6656	6665	6675	6684	6693	6702	6712
47	6721	6730	6739	6749	6758	6767	6776	6785	6794	6803
48	6812	6821	6830	6839	6848	6857	6866	6875	6884	6893
49	6902	6911	6920	6928	6937	6946	6955	6964	6972	6981
50	6990	6998	7007	7016	7024	7033	7042	7050	7059	7067
51	7076	7084	7093	7101	7110	7118	7126	7135	7143	7152
52	7160	7168	7177	7185	7193	7202	7210	7218	7226	7235
53	7243	7251	7259	7267	7275	7284	7292	7300	7308	7316
54	7324	7332	7340	7348	7356	7364	7372	7380	7388	7396

N	0	1	2	3	4	5	6	7	8	9
55	7404	7412	7419	7427	7435	7443	7451	7459	7466	7474
56	7482	7490	7497	7505	7513	7520	7528	7536	7543	7551
57	7559	7566	7574	7582	7589	7597	7604	7612	7619	7627
58	7634	7642	7649	7657	7664	7672	7679	7686	7694	7701
59	7709	7716	7723	7731	7738	7745	7752	7760	7767	7774
60	7782	7789	7796	7803	7810	7818	7825	7832	7839	7846
61	7853	7860	7868	7875	7882	7889	7896	7903	7910	7917
62	7924	7931	7938	7945	7952	7959	7966	7973	7980	7987
63	7993	8000	8007	8014	8021	8028	8035	8041	8048	8055
64	8062	8069	8075	8082	8089	8096	8102	8109	8116	8122
65	8129	8136	8142	8149	8156	8162	8169	8176	8182	8189
66	8195	8202	8209	8215	8222	8228	8235	8241	8248	8254
67	8261	8267	8274	8280	8287	8293	8299	8306	8312	8319
68	8325	8331	8338	8344	8351	8357	8363	8370	8376	8382
69	8388	8395	8401	8407	8414	8420	8426	8432	8439	8445
70	8451	8457	8463	8470	8476	8482	8488	8494	8500	8506
71	8513	8519	8525	8531	8537	8543	8549	8555	8561	8567
72	8573	8579	8585	8591	8597	8603	8609	8615	8621	8627
73	8633	8639	8645	8651	8657	8663	8669	8675	8681	8686
74	8692	8698	8704	8710	8716	8722	8727	8733	8739	8745
75	8751	8756	8762	8768	8774	8779	8785	8791	8797	8802
76	8808	8814	8820	8825	8831	8837	8842	8848	8854	8859
77	8865	8871	8876	8882	8887	8893	8899	8904	8910	8915
78	8921	8927	8932	8938	8943	8949	8954	8960	8965	8971
79	8976	8982	8987	8993	8998	9004	9009	9015	9020	9025
80	9031	9036	9042	9047	9053	9058	9063	9069	9074	9079
81	9085	9090	9096	9101	9106	9112	9117	9122	9128	9133
82	9138	9143	9149	9154	9159	9165	9170	9175	9180	9186
83	9191	9196	9201	9206	9212	9217	9222	9227	9232	9238
84	9243	9248	9253	9258	9263	9269	9274	9279	9284	9289
85	9294	9299	9304	9309	9315	9320	9325	9330	9335	9340
86	9345	9350	9355	9360	9365	9370	9375	9380	9385	9390
87	9395	9400	9405	9410	9415	9420	9425	9430	9435	9440
88	9445	9450	9455	9460	9465	9469	9474	9479	9484	9489
89	9494	9499	9504	9509	9513	9518	9523	9528	9533	9538
90	9542	9547	9552	9557	9562	9566	9571	9576	9581	9586
91	9590	9595	9600	9605	9609	9614	9619	9624	9628	9633
92	9638	9643	9647	9652	9657	9661	9666	9671	9675	9680
93	9685	9689	9694	9699	9703	9708	9713	9717	9722	9727
94	9731	9736	9741	9745	9750	9754	9759	9763	9768	9773
95	9777	9782	9786	9791	9795	9800	9805	9809	9814	9818
96	9823	9827	9832	9836	9841	9845	9850	9854	9859	9863
97	9868	9872	9877	9881	9886	9890	9894	9899	9903	9908
98	9912	9917	9921	9926	9930	9934	9939	9943	9948	9952
99	9956	9961	9965	9969	9974	9978	9983	9987	9991	9996

index